AF335397

ART FOR COEXISTENCE

ART FOR COEXISTENCE

UNLEARNING THE WAY WE SEE MIGRATION

CHRISTINE ROSS

THE MIT PRESS
CAMBRIDGE, MASSACHUSETTS
LONDON, ENGLAND

The MIT Press would like to thank the anonymous peer reviewers who provided comments on drafts of this book. The generous work of academic experts is essential for establishing the authority and quality of our publications. We acknowledge with gratitude the contributions of these otherwise uncredited readers.

This book was set in Arnhem Pro and Frank New by New Best-set Typesetters Ltd. Printed and bound in the United States of America.

Library of Congress Cataloging-in-Publication Data

Names: Ross, Christine, 1958- author.
Title: Art for coexistence : unlearning the way we see migration / Christine Ross.
Description: Cambridge, Massachusetts : The MIT Press, [2022] | Includes bibliographical references and index.
Identifiers: LCCN 2021047585 | ISBN 9780262047395 (hardcover)
Subjects: LCSH: Emigration and immigration in art. | Humanity in art. | Art and society—History—21st century. | Art, Modern—21st century—Philosophy.
Classification: LCC N8217.E52 R67 2022 | DDC 700/.45—dc23/eng/20220216
LC record available at https://lccn.loc.gov/2021047585

10   9   8   7   6   5   4   3   2   1

CONTENTS

PREFACE

I started writing my manuscript just after March 11, 2020, when the World Health Organization declared the COVID-19 outbreak a pandemic. The coronavirus crisis became the persistent background of my evolving research. Although not addressed in this book, it troublingly disclosed several realities that likewise define twenty-first-century migration. Here, I briefly discuss four of them, all of which are investigated further in the book's chapters.

First: *the vulnerability of the art world in moments of planetary crises.* During the pandemic, the sphere of art and culture was significantly impoverished: galleries and museums were temporarily closed in most European and North American countries at one time or another, leading to significant staff cuts and a substantial decline in public attendance; art exhibitions were suspended, sometimes transformed into virtual art shows; art projects became invisible or were simply canceled and left unpaid. This impoverishment was a significant outcome of the coronavirus crisis. However, as the artist and cultural organizer Ramaya Tegegne explained in a statement published in *Texte zur Kunst* in the spring of 2020, the pandemic weakened a milieu that was already fragile, especially for artists: "What I would like to share with you today is an account of litigation that is resonating with what artists and art workers are going through right now, and that too many of us had actually been going through even before this crisis."[1] The closing of art institutions was a sanitary decision. But it was also a governmental, political, and administrative decision to uniformize the management of sanitary measures in public buildings: museums, in particular, *did not have to be closed down* since they had already been transformed into some of the safest indoor spaces available to large publics. That decision intensified the economic instability of artists and art workers; it also devalued art's capacity to respond to the major predicaments of the historical present. Among this book's main motivations is the wish to counter this depreciation, to sustain art's critical capacity to respond and to declare it as an "essential service."

Second: *the persistent evolution of migration (as a constellation of migration, immigration, asylum, and border crises) during the pandemic.* The media coverage of migrating people leaving parts of Africa, Asia, and Central America for Europe or the United States (the book's main focus) significantly diminished during the pandemic, but when news started to reemerge, the continual deterioration of the conditions surrounding the migration process—what I later call the necropolitics of twenty-first-century migration—became outright manifest. Here are some pivotal moments, which I summarize using media "migrant" terminology to better transmit the journalistic and statistical dimensions of these findings. Between January and mid-September 2020, 8,581 people were intercepted as they attempted to reach Europe by sea from the Tunisian coastal zone;[2] since the beginning of 2020, the violation of nonrefoulement—the principle that states should not send back refugees and asylum seekers to unsafe countries—became common practice in Greece during the COVID-19 crisis;[3] the agreement between the European Union (EU) and Turkey continued to be effective, which means that Turkey acted "as border cop on Europe's behalf," preventing migrants from crossing to Greece or admitting them when deported from Greece before they apply for asylum "in return for financial aid and other diplomatic concessions";[4] the United Nations High Commissioner for Refugees (UNHCR) and the International Organization for Migration stated that at least 45 refugees died at the end of August "in the worst shipwreck reported so far this year off Libya's coast";[5] in September 2020, the UNHCR stated that the coronavirus pandemic had left countries (notably Tunisia) facing severe economic difficulties and unemployment and others (in particular Libya) trapped in civil war, so sea arrivals in 2020 in the EU (mainly Italy and Malt) significantly increased—Italy, for example, recorded 16,942 sea arrivals in 2020 up to September, compared to 11,471 in 2019;[6] the overcrowded Moria Refugee Camp in Lesbos was completely destroyed by fire in September 2020, temporarily leaving 13,000 refugees without a shelter—the camp was definitively closed down;[7] the International Organization for Migration reported on September 25 that three migrants had died and 13 were feared to have drowned after a boat transporting refugees capsized off Libya's coast—the survivors (from Egypt, Bangladesh, Ethiopia, Niger, Somalia, Syria, and Ghana) "were rescued by fishing vessels in coordination with the Libyan coastguard and later transferred to the Zliten detention centre";[8] on September 29, 2020, the French refugee camp in Calais, housing residents predominantly from Sudan, Iran, Erythrina, and Ethiopia, was redismantled—this was the second largest dismantling of the camp after the evacuation of the "Jungle" in 2016—but immediately following the demolition of the Calais infrastructure, refugees and asylum seekers came back to start new camps;[9] in October 2020, the US Department of State reduced to 15,000 the number of admissible refugees in the country, the lowest quota in recent American history;[10]

the new quota was introduced while 3,000 migrants from Honduras initiated a collective walk to reach the American border;[11] in early October, Guatemala sent back approximatively 3,500 Hondurans from the caravan heading to the United States "over concerns they might spread COVID-19";[12] another caravan of at least 9,000 Hondurans was substantially blocked in Guatemala in January 2021;[13] on October 11, 2020, a refugee boat sank off the Tunisian coast, leaving at least 21 people (from Tunisia and various sub-Saharan African countries) dead;[14] on November 12, 2020, more than 74 migrants drowned in a shipwreck yet again off Libya's coast—120 people were on board, 47 were rescued by fishermen and the Libyan coastguard;[15] on January 21 and 22, 2021, more than 370 migrants from sub-Saharan Africa were rescued by the *Ocean Viking* (operated by SOS Méditerranée), one of the last remaining nongovernmental organization (NGO) rescue boats operational in the Mediterranean Sea;[16] in March 2021, a few hours after having landed on the Greek island of Lesbos, Mustafa, his wife, and two young children were driven to the coast, beaten by masked men, brought out to sea, and abandoned there on a raft ("We were all forced on to the boat. If we looked up they shouted at us and hit us in the head. Then they stopped at a place in the sea where there were no other boats, they left us");[17] in late April 2021, the *Ocean Viking* attempted to reach a rubber boat in distress in the midst of a storm near Libya, only to find an "open cemetery" of at least 130 lifeless bodies floating on the waters (there were no survivors), adding to the 17,664 people who have lost their lives crossing the central Mediterranean since 2014;[18] 178,000 migrants, a record high since 2006, were concurrently arrested at the Mexico-US border, 82 percent of them from the "Northern Triangle" of Central America (Guatemala, Honduras, and El Salvador) as well as Mexico;[19] during the same period, 17 people from sub-Saharan Africa were found dead on a boat off the Canary Islands;[20] on May 8 and 9, 2021, more than 1,400 migrants reached the Italian island of Lampedusa;[21] a few days later, on May 17, 2021, more than 8,000 people (a record high: a mass crossing that involved unaccompanied minors, young men, and families) swam from Morocco to enter the Spanish enclave of Ceuta, using swimming rings and rubber dinghies—Spanish authorities replied by adding 200 border patrol agents to control the influx and by activating the agreement recently reached between Spain and Morocco that allowed the deportation of Moroccans swimming their way into Ceuta;[22] in the fall of 2021, attempts to cross the English Channel from the northern coast of France to the southern coast of England had doubled, even tripled, since 2020—between January and November 2021, 31,500 people attempted the crossing: 7,800 were rescued and more than 22,000 succeeded; on

November 24, an estimated number of 27 passengers—including 16 Iraqi Kurds, one Iranian Kurd, three Ethiopians, four Afghans, one Somalian, and one Egyptian—were reported dead as their boat (an inflatable dinghy) capsized off Calais, in what was the deadliest incident in the Channel since the beginning of the migration crisis in the area;[23] in November and December 2021, several thousand migrants—predominantly from Iraq, Afghanistan, and Syria—were stranded along the border between Poland and Belarus, lured to Minsk by Belarus authorities with the false promise of straightforward entry to the EU;[24] the lifeless bodies of more than 100 migrants, 62 migrants (the next day), and 28 migrants (a few days later) mainly from sub-Saharan Africa were found off Libya's coast on December 17, December 18, and December 25, respectively, following the sinking of their boat: these new deaths brought the count to over 1,500 migrants drowned in the central Mediterranean route in 2021.[25]

Third: *Black Lives Matter and Indigenous Lives Matter*. Though this reality is not directly related to the COVID-19 crisis, the pandemic coincided with the intensification of the Black Lives Matter movement and the flow of protests against police brutality not only in the United States but also in Europe and Canada—where the movement was further strengthened by Indigenous environmental protests and a series of demonstrations denouncing the systemic racism endured by Indigenous people. These events led to the dismissal, indictment, and/or conviction of some of the main perpetrators of brutality. They were triggered by (at least) two deaths in the United States: the killing of Breonna Taylor on March 13, 2020, a 26-year-old Black emergency medical technician, riddled with eight bullets inside her home by the police in Louisville, Kentucky—the trial of police officer Brett Hankison, charged with three accounts of first-degree wanton endangerment, was scheduled to take place in February 1, 2022;[26] and the killing of George Floyd, a 46-year-old African American, by a police officer in Minneapolis on May 25, 2020: witness and security camera videos showed Floyd lying face down on the ground and the police officer Derek Chauvin kneeling on his neck for several minutes, ignoring Floyd's complaints about his difficulty to breathe and his fear of dying—Chauvin was sentenced on June 25, 2021, to 22.5 years for the murder of George Floyd.[27] In Quebec, Canada, Joyce Echaquan, a 37-year-old Atikamekw woman, died at the Centre hospitalier de Lanaudière on September 28, 2020, after video-recording herself live on Facebook crying out for help—stating that she was being overmedicated, while racist comments by health-care workers could be heard in the background; a nurse and a beneficiary attendant were dismissed; these dismissals were followed by an inquest (led by coroner Géhane Kamel in May–June 2021) examining systemic racism in Quebec's health-care system.[28] That brutality—what the Cameroonian philosopher and political theorist Achille Mbembe has come to call the "brutalism" of necropolitics[29]—similarly sustains migration management in Europe and North America. As this book will show, these brutalities are historically connected, and justice must be made to end such brutalism.

Fourth: *interdependence*. In an interview published in *Le Monde* on March 24, 2020, the philosopher Claire Marin expressed in the following terms how the coronavirus crisis has raised public awareness of the interdependence of living organisms: "It is as though we are rediscovering that, as living beings, we are interdependent. By dint of considering ourselves as autonomous, separated individuals, distinct from one another, we have come to forget the extent to which we are caught in flows we do not merely coinhabit: we are bound to one another. We transmit to each other joy, fears but also viruses."[30] In this passage, Marin defines interdependence not only as a biological reality but also as an affective reality that inexorably connects humans; her definition dismisses any notion of human beings as fully discrete entities. This heightened awareness of interdependence, she insists later on in the interview, underscores the requirement to care for each other. On the same day, *Le Monde* published another interview with another philosopher: Giorgio Agamben. Invited to analyze the ethical and political consequences of the security measures taken to counter the spread of COVID-19, Agamben argued that their application reinforced a permanent state of urgency. The "other," he contended, is increasingly perceived as a threat; they become a possibility of contamination more than a possibility of mutually shared coexistence. As such, the management of health measures must be seen as an extension of the state of emergency implemented in response to the attacks on September 11, 2001: "The deceptive logic is always the same: facing terrorism, [state authorities] affirmed that freedom had to be suppressed to be preserved; similarly, we are told that life must be suspended to be protected. What the pandemic clearly shows is that the state of exception, to which governments have familiarized us for a long time, has become the normal condition. . . . Modern politics is from top to bottom a biopolitics, whose ultimate stake is biological life as such."[31] These two philosophical responses may appear contradictory—Marin defends our renewed awareness of the interdependence of living beings on the grounds that it might teach us to take better care of one another, whereas Agamben maintains that the pandemic confirms societies as states of exception in which interdependence is in fact repudiated. Humanitarian care on the one hand and biopolitics on the other. But these two positions are in fact complementary: together they posit coexistence—the deep interdependence of beings—as an indubitable yet mostly denied reality. Agamben's perspective reminds us that coexistence is not de facto a mutually beneficial relation for parties involved. To this dark coexistence, Marin opposes a more reciprocal model of coexistence. The two facets of coexistence sustain, as I contend in this book, the evolution of twenty-first-century migration. The book also addresses what the two philosophers leave unaddressed: the importance of daily gestures (in this case, social distancing, wearing a mask) that help overcome crises; the responsibility each one of us has to counter the deterioration of a situation.

On April 30, 2020, the American philosopher Judith Butler was also invited to delineate her own understanding of coexistence. Explaining how the pandemic "exposes a global vulnerability" and how, in so doing, it "names the porous and interdependent character of our bodily and social lives," she moved away from Marin's and Agamben's more universal premises by maintaining that some human groups were more vulnerable than others:

The vulnerable include Black and Brown communities deprived of adequate health care throughout their lifetimes and the history of this nation. The vulnerable also include poor people, migrants, incarcerated people, people with disabilities, trans and queer people who struggle to achieve rights to health care, and all those with prior illnesses and enduring medical conditions. The pandemic exposes the heightened vulnerability to the illness of all those for whom health care is neither accessible nor affordable. Perhaps there are at least two lessons about vulnerability that follow: it describes a shared condition of social life, of interdependence, exposure and porosity; it names the greater likelihood of dying, understood as the fatal consequence of a pervasive social inequality.[32]

In short, coexistence never simply gets rid of inequalities. As the anthropologist Didier Fassin stated when interviewed in *Le Monde* on May 24, 2020, the eagerness to protect lives during the pandemic did not include the lives of prisoners, undocumented migrants, and asylum seekers, even though the risk of contagion was higher in overpopulated prisons and camps.[33] Coexistence, then, is a relationality that recurrently reinforces disparities between so-called migrants and so-called citizens. The disclosure of this state of affairs and the possibility to counter it progressively became the book's main argument. That twofoldness constitutes contemporary art's unlearning of migration.

INTRODUCTION

Living with daily deaths. I think of the catastrophe of what living in a refugee camp must be, or being drowned at sea trying to make a better life somewhere else, or having your children taken from you and caged in the bosom of the heartland of democracy and wonder if we will have more compassion for those strangers who are now our kith and kin in catastrophe—and yet ours is still a far gentler catastrophe—to date, at least. There is toilet paper, after all. And running water. And health systems, albeit over-taxed.

The tears have now dried on my face, the paper lies open on the table before me: I think of the Covid-19 virus, invisible to the naked eye, which has wreaked such havoc in such an achingly short time and see the parallel with another virus, albeit metaphorical—the virus of greed that spawned that earlier global disruption and destruction of nations, peoples, cultures. Indeed, it uprooted the world as it was then. We can call it colonialism, imperialism, or whatever we care to, but like Covid it penetrated our lives and the lives of our ancestors and left in its wake a plethora of ills such as racism, sexism and classism, xenophobia—the bedrock of our catastrophic lives today.

—M. NourbeSe Philip, "Covidian Catastrophes: Resonances of Suffering"[1]

Might art afford new things to know and new ways to feel about matters that are so dismaying and depressing that they hobble the brain and lock down the heart? And might it do so without sacrificing the aesthetic and spiritual cultivation that is art's reason for being?

—Peter Schjeldahl, "The Art of War in 'Theatre of Operations'"[2]

In December 2015, Banksy, an anonymous British street artist known for his anti-authoritarian urban interventions, visited the Jungle Refugee Camp in the locality of Calais, France. The camp was built in January 2015 on a former landfill site and dismantled in October 2016, a period coinciding with the peak of the so-called European refugee crisis. The Jungle's population reached an estimated 8,143 just before its demolition. Primarily from Eritrea, Somalia, Syria, Afghanistan, Darfur, and Iraq, most of the residents were trying to reach Great Britain via the Port of Calais or the Channel Tunnel. The artist painted a series of graffiti in Calais: a mural portraying the late Apple cofounder Steve Jobs carrying a bag of his belongings over his shoulder and an early Macintosh computer in his right hand; another mural by the beach representing a child, with a suitcase and a telescope holding up a vulture, looking toward the English coast; and a third mural on the wall of a building in Calais's downtown district, a stenciled and subtly altered version of Théodore Géricault's legendary painting *The Raft of the Medusa* from 1818–1819. Though all of the murals were referring to a same theme (contemporary migration), their temporalization of the theme was significantly and complementarily distinct: the Jobs graffiti portrayed one of the most famous successes of migration (the near past—about the work Banksy stated: "We're often led to believe migration is a drain on the country's resources but Steve Jobs was the son of a Syrian migrant. Apple . . . only exists because they allowed in a young man from Homs"[3]); the telescope graffiti depicted the combination of hope and looming danger currently shaping the lives of migrating children (the near future); while the Géricault remake alluded to the inauspicious present of migration (figure 0.1).

Banksy's adaptation of Géricault's painting is particularly insightful. The original *Raft of the Medusa* represents a group of survivors and corpses on a raft following the wreck of the French naval frigate *Méduse* off the coast of today's Mauritania on July 2, 1816; it shows the survivors hailing the *Argus*—the ship that ultimately rescued them. Banksy's black stencil, in contrast, features an imperiled group of people on a sinking raft, hailing an indifferent luxury yacht or ferryboat just on the horizon. The nineteenth-century painting's central figure is that of an African crew member, Jean Charles, agitatedly waving his shirt to draw the ship's attention. Géricault's decision to place him at the highpoint of the composition has been interpreted as expressing his abolitionist sympathies.[4] By appropriating the work, Banksy can be said to have historicized present-day migration within the deeper history of the antislavery movement initiated in the eighteenth century as a counterpart to the transatlantic slave trade and its increase with European colonial

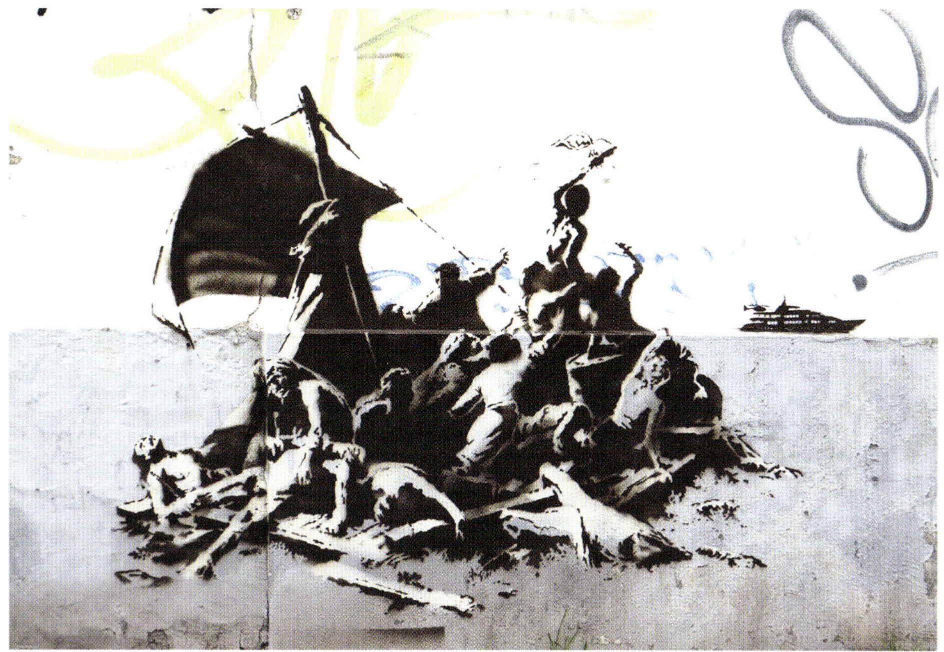

expansion—the forced displacement of enslaved Africans to Europe since the fifteenth century and then mainly to the Caribbean and the Americas between the
sixteenth and nineteenth centuries; the work ends up disclosing the persistence of
European colonialism despite abolitionism. Notwithstanding its aesthetic and historical breadth, however, the mural was painted over by the owner of the building
in September 2017 on the grounds that the wall needed to be renovated. The loss of
the work ironically reveals a similitude between the vulnerable bodies of migrating
beings and the vulnerability of street artworks—confirming the appropriateness of
the latter to represent the former. They share the likelihood of negligence, eradication, and disappearance.

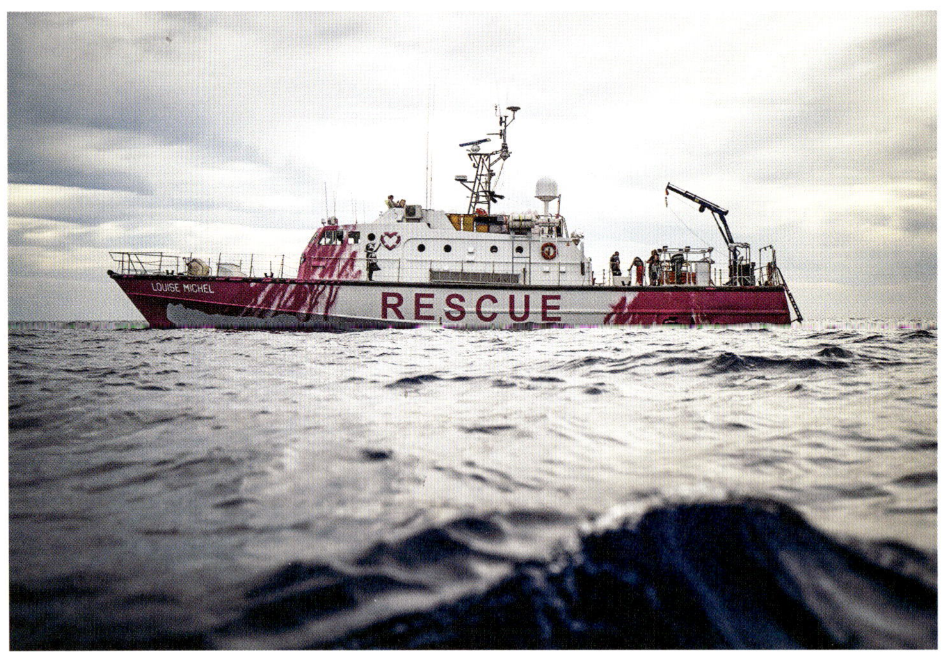

In August 2020, Banksy reconfirmed his sensitivity to the predicament of migration by exploring an unusual medium: a search-and-rescue boat—a former French patrol boat renamed *Louise Michel* after the nineteenth-century French feminist anarchist—acquired with proceeds from the sale of his work on the "migrant crisis."[5] The boat was partly spray-painted in bright pink, including the word *RESCUE* on its hull, and a stenciled image (a girl in a life vest holding a heart-shaped safety buoy) was painted on one of the boat's sides (figure 0.2). The boat is sponsored by Banksy but captained by the German biologist Pia Kemp and crewed by a team of activist rescuers: its main mission is to assist migrating travelers in distress who try

FIGURE 0.2

M. V. *Louise Michel*, 2020–. Rescue boat
funded by Banksy. Operated by Captain Pia
Klemp. Courtesy of Louise Michel Team.
© M. V. Louise Michel. © Pest Control.

to reach Europe by crossing the Mediterranean Sea. Reporting on the *Louise Michel*'s first undertaking, the journalists Lorenzo Tondo and Maurice Stierl stated that the rescue boat "set off in secrecy on 18 August from the Spanish seaport of Burriana, near Valencia, and is now in the central Mediterranean[,] where on Thursday it rescued 89 people in distress, including 14 women and four children. It is now looking for a safe seaport to disembark the passengers or to transfer them to a European coastguard vessel."[6] Bringing the passengers to safety took several days; it required a series of distress messages sent by the captain to EU border patrol, reporting the deterioration of the situation in the overcrowded boat. As I write in July 2021, the boat is ongoingly financed by Banksy, but—like the majority of rescue boats in the Mediterranean area, which are currently blocked in various European ports due to administrative forfeitures and criminal proceedings—it is prevented from leaving port "due to EU restrictions."[7]

The *Louise Michel* is unheard of: it stretches the definition of art by transforming it into a search-and-rescue endeavor, factually ending the famous saying that art cannot save the world. As the philosopher Santiago Zabala maintains, it might well be that "*only* art can save us."[8] Of course, it rarely does, at least in the literal sense of the word. Asked "What is art for?," the Moroccan French artist Bouchra Khalili, whose work is examined in chapter 8, states that "if [art] doesn't change the world, at least it can help us to think about how we can make it better."[9] As this book maintains, art responding to the contemporary conditions of migration is a *call* for change. Banksy's version of *The Raft of the Medusa* is such a call. It is a call for historicization and responsibility. The mural displays the dark coexistence between the raft and the yacht, which secures the blooming of the latter by the neglect and vulnerabilization of the former; it awaits the interdependence between its image and the wall on which it was initially painted, anticipating the likelihood of its disappearance in a historical context marked by migrating bodies correspondingly disappearing at sea. In contrast, Banksy's *Louise Michel* is a materialization of hope: the hope for a more reciprocal form of coexistence. That materialization, however, is a fragile one. In 2019, Italian state authorities had already accused Captain Pia Kemp of what is now informally termed the "crime of solidarity."[10] But solidarity, increasingly criminalized when it involves a person or a vessel assisting or rescuing illegalized migrants as the *Louise Michel* is devised to do, might well be the coexistence required to end the brutalism sustaining twenty-first-century migration.

When we speak about a crisis, it is crucial to ask the following two questions: Whose crisis are we talking about? And why has a specific turmoil been designated as a "crisis"? This is especially true of the alleged refugee or migrant crisis. In the strictest sense, the term refers to the European refugee or migrant crisis—a state of emergency (2004–) describing Europe's new and unanticipated challenge to manage and host the influx of people arriving in the EU overseas from across the Mediterranean Sea or overland through Southeast Europe. At the peak of the crisis in 2015, the UNHCR observed that the top three nationalities among the more than one million refugees arriving from the Mediterranean Sea were Syrian (46.7 percent), Afghan (20.9 percent), and Iraqi (9.4 percent). They also came and ongoingly come from other countries of mainland, West, Northeast, and East Africa (including Eritrea, Nigeria, Somalia, Sudan, Gambia, Burundi, and Mali), and South Asia (especially Pakistan), as well as from Myanmar and the western Balkans (Kosovo, Albania, Serbia).[11] Incoming people fled and continue to flee to escape war, structural violence, persecution (on the basis of religion, ethnicity, racialization, gender, sexual orientation, or political opinion), forced labor, natural disaster, and chronic poverty; in 2015, many were escaping the Syrian Civil War, the Iraq War, and the war in Afghanistan. The notion of "crisis," however, does not refer primarily to the high number of beings seeking protection in Europe, which is in fact considerably low in comparison to the numbers experienced by other host countries in Africa and Asia. Rather, as observed by the anthropologist-geographer Nicholas De Genova, the European refugee crisis is fundamentally a "crisis of *control*—a crisis of the sovereign power of the European border regime" seeking to restabilize its migration and border regime to contain the increased flow of displaced people.[12] It names the Eurocentric sense of being invaded by "others" (perceived as such though they come mostly from former colonies), a "clash of civilizations" to which the EU member states progressively replied by remilitarizing their borders; corridoring the movement of migrating travelers; decreasing the category of acceptable "refugees"; campicizing; prolonging detention; intensifying pushbacks, deportation, and risky repatriation—thus forcing people to take more dangerous routes to reach Europe and dying in that very process, even though most of them (85 percent at the end of 2018; 73 percent at the end of 2019) were and still are predominantly migrating not to Europe but to countries bordering their own.[13]

Put differently according to contemporary art's unique insight, the so-called refugee or migrant crisis has been from the start a problem of coexistence—the EU's attempt to contain and, more deeply, to deny the deep civilizational, social, economic, and cultural interdependences of countries of origin and countries of destination; the EU's noncompliance with international laws that forbid states from returning people to countries where they risk facing human rights violations. The refugee or migrant crisis must therefore be extended to include the American immigration, asylum, and US-Mexico border crises, which also partake in a denial of coexistence and result from a combination of anti-(im)migrant measures and policies targeted mainly against Mexican and Central American citizens and including the restriction of legal means of immigration (despite the demand for migrant labor and despite the increase of undocumented migrant workers in the United States); the presence of overflowing communities next to the US-Mexico border, populated by people expelled from the United States and waiting for the processing of their asylum claims; the separation of families requesting asylum in the United States; the unstable management of unaccompanied minors arriving at the border; the increased detention of illegalized migrants; and the blocking of large Central American caravans coming from Guatemala, Honduras, and El Salvador. These procedures ignore a past of high American military, political, and economic interventionism in these countries.[14] The so-called migrant crisis must likewise be extended to include the internal displacement of Indigenous people in North America, especially in Canada. Many other extensions could be considered here, but the book focuses mainly on Europe and North America.

The migrant crisis is thus best understood as migration tout court to avoid misconceptions about it being a crisis caused by the sudden and unexpected invasion of European territory by migrants from Africa and Asia or of the United States by migrants from Latin America. The term also has the merit of bringing to the fore the legacy of the internal displacement of Indigenous people. Twenty-first-century migration is more fundamentally an interdependence between movement and reception, between citizens-on-the-move escaping untenable life conditions (or compelled to leave tenable life conditions, as has been the case with Indigenous communities) in search for safety in Europe or North America and the latter's deployment of a series of measures to control that influx. To these counterforces should be added a variety of real yet largely unacknowledged crises experienced by migrating beings who make decisions as they move or are being moved, as they flee conflict, violence, persecution, and poverty, only to reach borders unexpectedly closing as well as the likelihood of detention and deportation, extortion, kidnapping, physical and sexual assault and human trafficking, crises of abandonment in refugee camps or settlements, injury and death.[15] Such is, persistently, the autonomy of migration: the decision to move despite being forced to move, a crucial component of twenty-first-century migration as well. In short, migration today is a combination of misnamed and undervalued crises, whose European and North American modus operandi is the ever-escalating refusal to provide asylum to citizens-on-the-move who are escaping threatening life conditions in their country or are internally required to leave their land of origin behind. Migration, art claims, is a cluster of dark coexistences.

Art for Coexistence: Unlearning the Way We See Migration is a study of contemporary art's response to that specific escalation, considered as the ongoing interaction between two counterforces: the influx of displaced people and the increased refusal to host these displaced people in Europe and North America. The book asks: What is European and North American art's original contribution to the understanding of migration, and why is this contribution critical to the development of the twenty-first century? The answer to these two questions can be encapsulated in a single yet multilayered term: *coexistence*—the nondiscreteness of beings; the state, awareness, and practice of existing interdependently.

This book is a claim for coexistence; it is a claim for artistic practices whose main response to migration is to reveal, contest, rethink, "delink,"[16] and relink more reciprocally the dark and potentially more luminous interdependences shaping migration today—the interdependences between citizens-on-the-move of some of the poorest, most colonially damaged, and most politically unstable countries worldwide (parts of Africa, Asia, and Latin America) and citizens of some of the wealthiest economies and democracies worldwide (Europe and North America), between these migrating beings seeking asylum and Europe's and North America's intensified unwillingness to grant them asylum. Art depicts the mechanisms of that refusal: the reinforcement of borders, campization, settlement, deterrence, detention, illegal pushbacks, and deportation—mechanisms that press deadly routes (e.g., the Mediterranean Sea, the Aegean Sea, the English Channel, the Sonoran Desert, the Białowieża Forest) on travelers to reach their destinations. These practices explore coexistence not as a living-together or a cohabitation but as a predominantly dark and forever-messy yet changeable relation, what the intellectual historian Mira Siegelberg designates as a "political organization of humanity,"[17] which turns exodus into a process of exclusion, marginalization, and latent elimination of one percent of humanity (1 in every 97 people worldwide).[18] Challenging that relation, art invents a set of interconnected calls for more mutual forms of coexistence: calls to historicize, to become responsible, to empathize, to story-tell.

In these calls, viewers (primarily though not exclusively or uniformly from Europe and North America), including myself as a French-speaking white Québécoise art historian, are interpellated as participating in the repressive forces of antimigration while being invited to question and counter these forces—to comake with citizens-on-the-move more just and equitable practices of migration.

These artistic practices include installations, performances, living rooms, video and virtual-reality works, webcasts, digital platforms, alarm phones, countermonuments, sculptures, graffiti, photographs and paintings, rescue boats, and forensic investigations. However diverse, they share the making of calls. Migration, they claim, is not about "citizens" over here and "migrants" over there but about coexisting citizens with and without rights. Migration in *not* a problem "from elsewhere," one that landed unexpectedly in Europe or North America. As the journalist Daniel Trilling points out, the latter continents have "played a key role, historically, in the shaping of a world where power and wealth are unequally distributed," and they "continue to pursue military and arms trading policies that have caused or contributed to the conflicts and instability from which people flee."[19] The artistic calls ask viewers to reconsider migration as a coexistence in urgent need of repair and reimagining, one that must be fundamentally rethought in its relation to citizenship—or what the legal scholar Dimitry Kochenov designates as "citizenship's inherent racism, its deep and chronic exclusion of women, and its upholding and reinforcing of class divisions between the haves and haves-not."[20] Contemporary art, in short, is inviting us—again, citizens mainly but not exclusively or uniformly from Europe and North America—to unlearn our preconceptions and assumptions about the refugee or migrant "crisis." Unlearning is about learning to see the crisis more critically and more disobediently as transformable. This is certainly the experience I had while writing this book.

These calls are performed in the most compelling artworks responding to migration today, including works by Banksy, Lyne Lapointe, Laura Waddington, Isaac Julien, John Akomfrah, Binta Diaw, Richard Mosse, Florian Schneider, Forensic Oceanography, Teresa Margolles, Guillermo Galindo, Kader Attia, Candice Breitz, Ai Weiwei, Alejandro González Iñárritu, Tania Bruguera, Bouchra Khalili, Angela Melitopoulos, Rafael Lozano-Hemmer, Tuan Andrew Nguyen, Isuma, Olu Oguibe, Stan Douglas, Decolonizing Architecture Art Research, and Kent Monkman. The artists considered here work mainly in Europe and North America, the continents where their artworks predominantly circulate, but most of them are either former refugee(s), immigrants, or children of immigrants—some living between countries or binationally, some in Mexico, Cuba, Vietnam, or South Africa while also in the United States or in Europe, some having left China but now living in exile in Europe, basically of Europe and North America but having established long-standing relationships with migrating beings—or Indigenous artists born in Canada and Black artists born in North America or in Europe, whose larger history has been significantly conditioned by the forced displacement of people structuring various colonial systems. Long-term encounters, interculturality, internationality, and (im)migration as well as deep history have made these artists particularly responsive to the prevalence of migratory injustices.

A FEW EXAMPLES BEFORE WE START: MIGRANTS—ART CLAIMS—ARE NOT SIMPLY A CATEGORY

Let us look briefly at a few works to introduce the book more concretely. Consider Laura Waddington's *Border* (2004)—a low-tech video showing Afghan and Iraqi men just outside the Sangatte Red Cross Camp (1999–2002), a refugee camp located in the Pas-de-Calais department on the northern coast of France, as they attempt to cross the channel tunnel to England at night, narrated and filmed by the artist with the camera's shutter wide open to compensate for the lack of light, creating images on the edge of dissolution that materialize the precariousness yet autonomy of migration (figure 0.3); Bouchra Khalili's *The Mapping Project Journey* (2008–2011), a series of suspended screens projecting video images of standard geographical maps whose cartography is redrawn by migrating travelers, their faces remaining off-screen as they trace and relate their hazardous journeys throughout the Mediterranean Basin—stories perceptually interrelated by viewers as they circulate between the screens (figure 8.1); Forensic Oceanography's *Liquid Traces—the Left-to-Die Boat Case* (2014), a repurposing of border-surveillance technologies to reconstitute the event of European nonassistance in which 63 people died after having been left to drift on a rubber boat for 14 days in the North Atlantic Treaty Organization (NATO) Mediterranean maritime surveillance area (figure 4.1); Ai Weiwei's documentary film *Human Flow* (2017), showing the artist witnessing the global movement and blocking-of-movement of men, women, and families alongside the proliferation of borders (figure 7.3); Alejandro González Iñárritu's *CARNE y ARENA* (2017), a virtual-reality work inviting viewers into a desertic environment where virtual nonactors from Latin America risk their lives as they struggle but fail to cross the Mexico-US

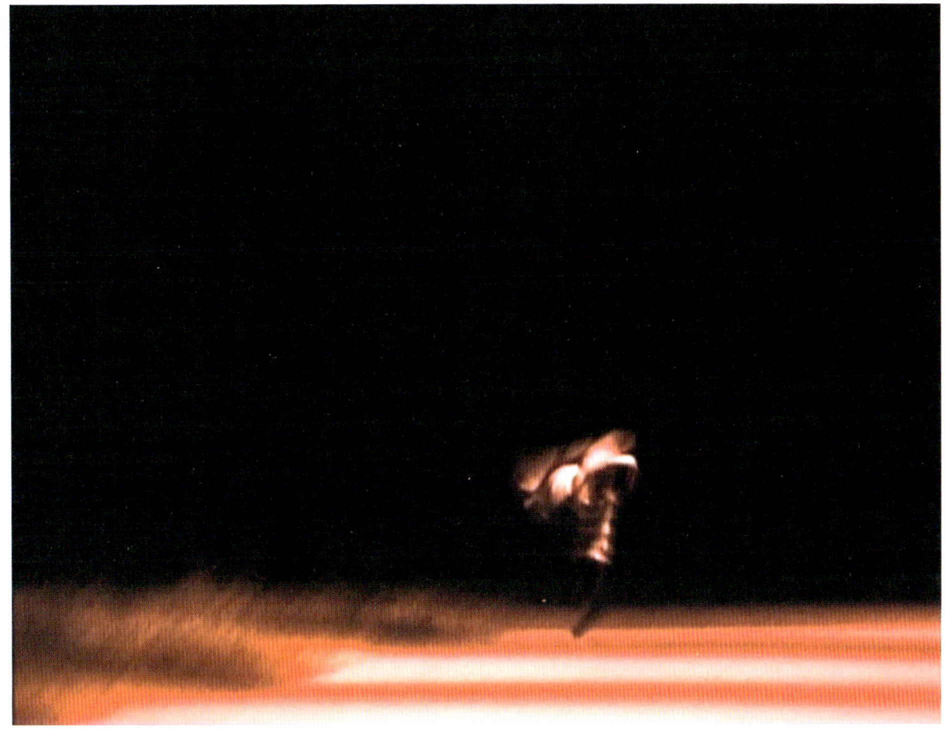

FIGURE 0.3

Laura Waddington, *Border*, 2004 (still).
Single-channel video, Digibeta PAL, color,
stereo, 27 minutes. Courtesy of the artist.

border (figure 7.8); Isuma's Venice Biennale video-and-webcasts, public-sphere intervention (2019) bridging two major predicaments of the twentieth and twenty-first
centuries—the internal displacement of Inuit communities and the environmental
degradation of the Arctic (figure 9.1); and Lyne Lapointe's multiple ink drawings
of lifejackets on old paper and maps (2019)—gear recalling Joseph Beuys's famous
vest but whose central zippers are transformed into spines and whose openings
make room for nonhuman animals, all endangered species and materials in need
of protection (figure 0.4).

However varied in their representation of twenty-first-century migration, these
artworks complicate our understanding of the very notion of the "migrant." That
notion, when used in the context of the so-named migrant crisis, belongs to the
category of what the social and political theorist W. B. Gallie has called "essentially
contested concepts."[21] That contestation is especially felt in works that uncover
the vulnerability of the beings they ambition to represent. The disputed use of
the term reinforces the treatment of refugees as "undesirables": To be legitimate,
protected, and have rights, should migrants include solely "refugees" strictly defined by the UN Refugee Convention of 1951, the document that defines refugees
as persons who are unable to return to their country "owing to a well-founded fear
of being persecuted" on the basis of race, religion, nationality, sexual orientation,
or political opinion, or should it not include economic migrants as well?[22] As the
anthropologist Michel Agier maintains, "Europe's 2015 crisis . . . has made manifest the uncertainty of the institutional classifications used for the description and
management of migratory flows. . . . Refugees, migrants, asylum-seekers, but also
war refugees, economic migrants, clandestine migrants, are as many apparently
descriptive terms, which nevertheless involve a whole epistemology and politics of
institutional, media, popular or specialized classification."[23] In the literature about
them, "migrants" include a variety of beings moving in a variety of border areas.
The "migrant" itself is an umbrella notion, not defined under international law,
that refers to a person who has been forced to move away or has moved away from
their home to find better living conditions. I use the term *migrant* throughout this
book as including refugees, asylum seekers, economic migrants, deported people,
undocumented migrants, and so-called illegal or irregular migrants, while privileging, when possible, the use of the terms *migrating beings*, *citizens-on-the-move*
(in contrast to *affirmed citizens*), and *citizens without rights* to remove them in part
from a categorization that works to exclude them from renewed citizenship.[24] The
term *migrant* is less reifying and less homogenizing than its sister terms because

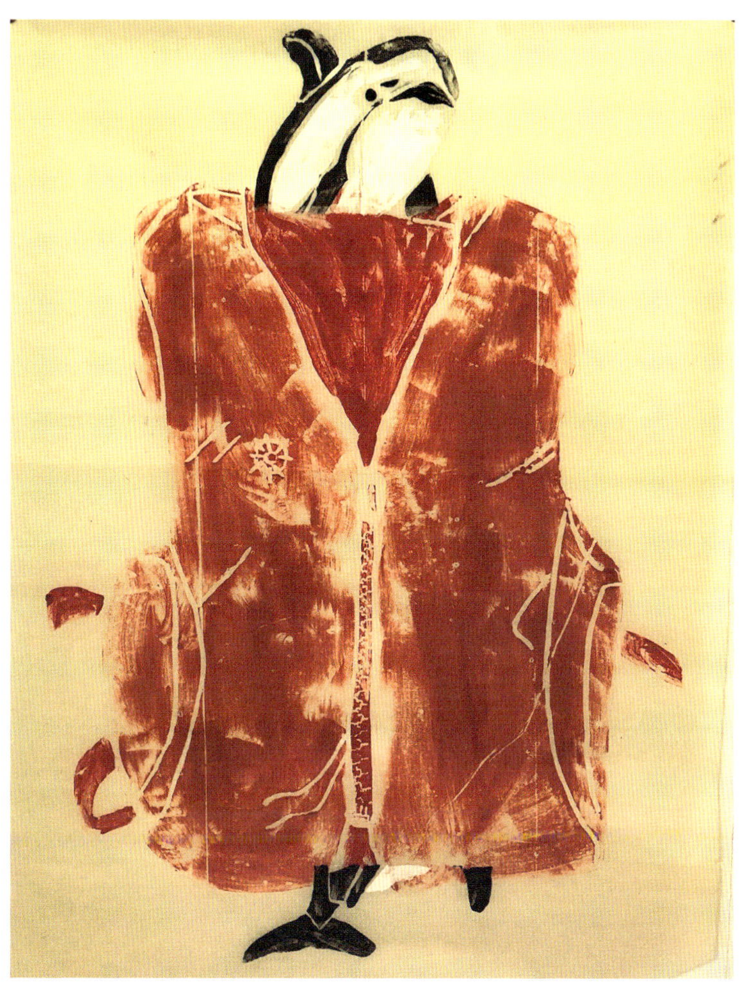

FIGURE 0.4

Lyne Lapointe, *Veste de sauvetage pour dauphin* (Life vest for a dolphin), 2019. Ink on paper. 32¾ × 23½ in. (83 × 60 cm). Courtesy of the artist.

it is not a legal concept and because it names some of the fundamental rights of the living: the right to move and to build a new home. Though the term, as Trilling has keenly observed, "implies an endless present" ("they are migrants, they move, it's what they do") and as such fails to suggest that the people so designated have a history and a future, contemporary art, as some of the works mentioned earlier suggest, insists on the imperative to historicize migration—this is one of its most fundamental calls.[25]

Migrant comes from the Latin *migrantem* (nominative *migrans*), which is the present participle of *migrare*, "to remove, depart, to move from one place to another." The notion of the migrant is tied to movement, and this is how migrating beings are depicted in the works. Coming from Africa, Asia, Central America, and the Arctic, they move or have moved from one country to the next, sometimes inside the same country, by sea, by land, or by ice, inside/outside camps, attempting to reach Europe, the United States, or their own land of origin. Movement is an action: though predominantly forced, it is a decision that migrating beings have in common, a decision that partakes of what the poet and cultural theorist Fred Moten terms "fugitivity," "a desire for and a spirit of escape and transgression of the proper and the proposed, . . . a desire for the outside."[26] There lies the autonomy of migration, what De Genova has called the autonomy of "the 'incorrigible' subject of virtually all contemporary border regimes," mobilized by "their own aspirations, needs, and desires, which necessarily exceed any regime of immigration and citizenship, . . . [and performing] mobility projects [that] enact an elementary freedom of movement to which borders are intrinsically a response."[27] The artworks never lose sight of that autonomy, of that subjectivity: migrating beings are telling stories, they struggle to reach a safer place to live, they mobilize their environmental concerns, they never simply make themselves fully visible. And yet in dissolving the fantasy of global mobility—the idea of an unconstrained circulation of goods, money, ideas, and people around the planet through the suspension of national barriers—the works disclose what another anthropologist, Anna Lowenhaupt Tsing, has designated the "frictions" of global encounters.[28] They deploy the freedom of movement gone wrong and bound to go wrong. Movement has been initiated to escape persecution, violence, poverty, and death. Movement has nevertheless been, is, or will be compromised. Some beings have been detained or have drowned in their attempt to move; others wait in borderzones or barely survive in camps; they have been displaced from their deep Arctic land and moved to settlements by government officials. To be more precise, then, the artworks are not so concerned about showing citizens-on-the-move as about making perceivable the management of their movement, their overdetermined vulnerability and yet their resilient decision to move; they make visible what affirmed citizens of countries of destination are made not to see or prefer not to really see.

Let us push this overview a bit further. These works elaborate calls. They address viewers who more likely belong to the richest economies in the world, inviting them to engage perceptually, sensorially, sensibly, cognitively, corporeally with the distressful conditions of migration that they are suggested to be a part of. They are a call for historicization: they situate the forced displacements as a prolongation of colonialism. They are a call for responsibility: they seek migratory justice, wanting us to become aware of our role in the repressiveness of migration and wanting us to put an end to its violence (for example, Forensic Oceanography's reconstitution approach, elaborated to make the EU accountable for the nonassistance of people in distress at sea). They are a call for empathy: the artists are voicing or depicting their own empathy (Waddington, Lapointe, Ai, and Iñárritu in particular); they want us to feel empathically the suffering of citizens-on-the-move. They are a call for storytelling: viewers are invited to participate in the unfolding stories by listening to the migrants' voices and performances. In short, the works mentioned here—like every single work examined in this book—express the challenge to better understand the destructive and potentially more life-enhancing interdependences between citizens dispossessed of mobility rights and citizens with mobility rights.

THE BOOK: ITS ARGUMENT AND STRUCTURE

With these works and comments in mind, we can now specify this book's overall claim, project, and structure. For the sake of clarity, I summarize them in four points.

First, the main argument of the book is threefold: contemporary art from Europe and North America is critically responding to migration (it exercises what Forensic Oceanography calls a "disobedient gaze"[29] on the deceptive yet standardized representation of migration as illegal or as a problem "from elsewhere" that landed advertently in Europe and North America); its main response is to disclose migration as a dark coexistence between citizens-on-the move leaving the untenable living conditions of some of the poorest and most politically unstable countries worldwide *and* affirmed citizens of some of the wealthiest yet increasingly unhosting countries worldwide; and it sets into play a variety of calls inviting viewers to reorient dark interdependence into a more mutually beneficial one. In short, we (the viewers) are invited to unlearn the way we see migration.

Second, this threefold argument supports art as a possible *re*distribution of the sensible, what the philosopher Jacques Rancière has designated the aesthetic *rear*rangement of a given society's "set of perception[s] between what is visible, thinkable, and understandable, and what is not."[30] The political potential of art lies in its capacity to assemble these relationships anew. If indeed a migratory aesthetics does exist, as the cultural theorist Mieke Bal has convincingly contended,[31] the connection between migration and aesthetics should be understood as political. Migratory aesthetics is articulated not so much in the messages artworks convey about migration than in the works' devising of a sensorium that makes ways of coexisting perceptible and changeable. The artistic practices considered in this book—here I borrow and widen the Cuban artist Tania Bruguera's clear-cut terminology—are politically time-specific. They are of the now, but they simultaneously make art "for the *not yet* and the *yet to come* . . . when politics and policies are taking shape," with the potential of "*generat[ing]* political situations."[32] Bluntly, they acknowledge present-day migration yet also aspire to change it by elaborating a series of calls.

Third, as the main argument suggests, the book maintains that a redistribution of the sensible requires a set of calls. What is a call? I see it as a vital and vibrant interpellation asking the viewer to meditate and rethink their assumptions, to perceive and transform coexistences. To paraphrase Paolo Baratta's introduction to the Biennale Architettura of 2021, an artwork, an exhibition, or architecture is "a call to become . . . attentive visitors, to become direct witnesses, . . . to be willing to broaden their gaze." "It's not enough to propagate knowledge," writes Baratta, "we must contribute to fostering awareness; it's not enough to reveal problems, we must nourish a desire for [art] through examples of proposals, projects, and achievements."[33] This book has identified four partly overlapping calls and so is structured in four parts, each part focusing on an interpellation that strives to transform—as much as it can—unequal coexistences into more equal relations: historicization, responsibility, empathy, and storytelling. These interpellations articulate a fundamental redefinition of what it means to historicize, to become responsible, to empathize, and to story-tell. Without these redefinitions, there is no *re*distribution of the sensible. *Historicization* becomes, for example, a nonlinear and "conversational" practice of montage combining archival images and new footage that define contemporary migration as an extension of the interrelated histories of modernity, colonialism, transatlantic slavery, environmental deterioration, and capitalism. *Responsibility* becomes a meditation on accountability in matters of migration; in some artworks, it is rethought as a forward-looking practice of social connection and de-idealized care for the sake of migratory justice. *Empathy*, the artist's or viewer's capacity to feel and understand the mental states and emotions of beings in situations of migratory distress, unfolds as a necessary yet insufficient condition of possibility for prosociality. And *storytelling* becomes storytell/ing: it is explored disruptively to make migrant voices heard by viewers who are invited to listen more profoundly; its disrupting strategies include the right to opacity, ventriloquial speech acts, chaosmosis, deep listening, and weird looping. The book, therefore, should not be considered a survey of contemporary art that addresses present-day migration. Rather, it is a study of some of contemporary art's most vibrant calls to disclose and improve coexistence. Art reinvents itself in these calls.

Fourth and last, this book must be seen as a critical response to the legacy of imperialist museology, which tends to dissocialize, dehistoricize, and depoliticize art. Most museums in Europe and North America—the main institutions where spectators experience artworks addressing contemporary migration—fail to convey the richness of the exhibited works precisely because of the residual imperialism that tenaciously sustains these institutions. Particularly relevant to the present study, the political and visual culture theorist Ariella Aïsha Azoulay situates compulsory migration at the center of the history of European and North American museology. The museum, she maintains, is the very institution that continues, even today, to disconnect the forced migration of people and the forced migration of artifacts—artifacts that become collectible objects in that very process. It disconnects them despite their inseparability. This operation is produced by the "camera shutter" effect of Western museums: similar to the photographic device that quickly opens and closes to let light reach the film and then blocks it off to produce an image, extracting that image from the ongoing world it belonged to, the museum—whose imperial and colonial evolution is historically tied to photography—isolates its objects from the world they were a part of.[34] This separation is manifest mostly in the looting of artifacts from the colonies, the imperialist gesture par excellence, but is still predominantly upheld in contemporary museology. Azoulay's insight is worded in the following paragraph:

It is no secret that millions of objects, never destined in museal white walls, have been looted from all over the world by different imperial agents. It is no secret that many of them have been carefully handled, preserved, and displayed to this day in Western museums as precious art objects. At the same time, it is no secret that millions of people, stripped bare of most of their material world, including tools, ornaments, and other artifacts, continue to seek a place where they can be at home again and rebuild a habitable world. These two seemingly unrelated movements of forced migration of people and artifacts, as well as their separation, are as old as the invention of the "new world." . . . In truth, however, neither the movements nor their separation are unrelated.[35]

Azoulay's central point is that the museum's tenacious imperialist view of the world decides what needs to be bracketed out, disregarded, repressed, and excluded from perception: it gets rid of coexistence—the interdependence of people and objects that together create worlds and worldliness. And yet this coexistence is exactly what must be shown to spectators. Twenty-first-century artworks whose main striving is to divulge and generate such interdependences—basically, the artworks examined in this book—can therefore be understood as requiring that museums "unlearn imperialism." Museums, however, are lagging behind in meeting this requirement: the restitution of artifacts to countries of origin is still significantly limited and slow; and the exhibition of contemporary artworks that question camera-shutter operations are desocialized, dehistoricized, and depoliticized—re-shuttered as it were.

The desocialization, dehistoricization, and depolitization of artworks tackling the afflicting conditions of migration have been manifested in the main museum exhibitions that have shown these works, in particular the following American shows: *Home Is a Foreign Place* (2019), proposed by the Met Breuer; *The Warmth of Other Suns: Stories of Global Displacement* (2019), presented at the Phillips Collection in Washington, DC; *Crossing Lines, Constructing Home* (2019–2020), organized by Harvard Art Museums; and *When Home Won't Let You Stay: Migration through Contemporary Art* (2019–2021), shown, among other venues, at the Institute of Contemporary Art (Boston). As some of these titles indicate, most of the exhibitions had "home" as their main subtext: the museum was turned into a provisional, unproblematized home or host for the wandering, dispossessed, and displaced beings represented in the artworks. As the art historian Greg Afinogenov has argued about the shows held at the Phillips, the Institute of Contemporary Art, and the Special Exhibitions Gallery (Harvard Art Museums), the political message conveyed by these institutions was far from being "the one the contemporary situation demands."[36] The odd regrouping of artworks representing the traumatic experiences of migration from political perspectives *opposed* to those perpetuated by museums;

the use of wall texts that leave unaddressed the geopolitical diversity of migration; the blending of diversity into the happy American melting-pot story "of who we are and how we got here over time"; the dismissal of questions to do with responsibility (even though these questions are raised in a significant number of artworks): all of these museological decisions denied the historical present to which the works were in fact responding.[37] In so doing, these exhibitions consolidated a recent variation of the imperialist museum: its "participatory turn," which discourages dissensus for the sake of consensus mainly by promoting a humanistic mission, which is to recognize the suffering others as human beings and to care for them in that capacity but only inasmuch as they remain "other," thus allowing spectators to leave the museum with the feeling of having a good conscience. They failed to discuss the relations between migration, imperialism, and colonialism—relations nevertheless established in some of the most powerful exhibited works, including John Akomfrah's video installations examined in chapter 2 and Kader Attia's *La Mer Morte* (The Dead Sea) discussed in chapter 5.

The desocialization, depolitization, dehistorization, and deworldliness of artworks operated by the tenaciously imperialist museum shrink the viewer's and listener's perceptual, sensorial, and cognitive experience. My conviction is that art's and art history's unlearning of imperialism and colonialism can contribute to undoing this shrinking. To do so, this book maintains, art history must engage with the fields of political philosophy; postcolonial, decolonial, Black, and Indigenous studies; and, more importantly, critical refugee and migrant studies. There is no understanding of European and North American art's unlearning of migration without these fields, without a dialogue between art and these fields. One important note, however, before we begin: This unlearning does not include the artistic response to the forced displacement of Ukrainians following the Russian invasion of their country, which began as the book was in production. But it provides aesthetic and analytical tools to better understand that displacement, as well as the planetary climate migration already underway.

HISTORY MATTERS

What is European and North American art's original contribution to the understanding of migration (as a cluster of misidentified and underacknowledged crises), and why is this contribution—implicitly, what makes migration itself—critical to the development of the twenty-first century? Part I raises these questions to show that historical consciousness is imperative to art's unlearning of the way we see migration. Its two-chapter structure is fully dedicated to a crucial call: the call to historicize. Chapter 1 provides a short history of contemporary migration as an extension and renewed reiteration of colonialism and necropolitics (the politics of injury and death). It is written from a political philosophy viewpoint mixed with a critical refugee and migrant studies perspective. Two artworks, Undocumented Migration Project's *Hostile Terrain 94* (2019–) and Isaac Julien's *Western Union: small boats* (2007), are examined to give a better sense of art's contribution to that specific perspective. Chapter 2 focuses on the work of John Akomfrah—which de facto becomes the book's first in-depth case study. Akomfrah's artistic practice is a rich reminder of how history matters in issues of migration: his video installations disclose these issues as a prolongation of the intertwined histories of colonialism, transatlantic slavery, capitalism (including the vast appropriation of land, exploitation of labor, and production of commodities enabling the accumulation of wealth), and environmental degradation. More importantly, they reinvent history making to narrate that intertwinement. A montage practice fashions the reinvention by putting a variety of human and nonhuman actors and agents in conversation and affective proximities. These coexistences steadily expose the brutalism of European modernity, which twenty-first-century migration is ultimately a part of; they also make room for restorative possibilities. In the two chapters, the call to historicize and to be historically inventive is explored to make us, viewers, aware of migration as a major crystallization of the tenaciousness of colonial presence in the present. The call for history is surely the interpellation that reveals the darkest coexistences structuring forced migration today. But that disclosure is also the affirmation of historical consciousness by which forcibly displaced persons or subjects living in the wake of past displacement as well as viewers have searched, are searching, and are invited to search for more equal forms of coexistence.

1

THE ENDANGERING, HAMPERING, AND CRIMINALIZATION OF MIGRATION

In its annual report for 2019, the UNHCR stated that the number of forcibly displaced people worldwide (terminology that refers to refugees, internally displaced people, and asylum seekers displaced "as a result of persecution, conflict, generalized violence or human rights violations") was the highest recorded since World War II. This population reached 70.8 million in 2018, up from about 43 million a decade earlier. The number of new displacements was equivalent to an average of 37,000 people forced to flee their homes every day.[1] They were and are still coming from a variety of countries, including Ethiopia, Syria, Afghanistan, South Sudan, Myanmar, Somalia, Iraq, Gaza, Haiti, as well as a dozen or so nations in sub-Saharan and North Africa, Central America, and Venezuela. Responding to these alarming figures and going beyond their mere acknowledgment, David Miliband, president of the humanitarian group International Rescue Committee, lucidly specified in 2019: "As the numbers of displaced grow, we are seeing a tragic retreat from diplomacy that should be addressing the root causes of conflict and displacement, whether in Libya or Yemen, Venezuela or Syria. . . . Instead of pursuing accountability for war crimes and investing in peace-building, we are trapped in an age of impunity that is placing civilians, as well as humanitarians, in the crossfire, and driving thousands from their homes every day."[2] Miliband's statement was remarkably unequivocal. It basically asserted that instead of analyzing the factors of forced displacement and identifying solutions to decrease it based on these findings, countries directly or indirectly involved in displacement sustain their impunity—an impunity that can only accelerate the proliferation of inflicted migration.

Forced displacement also means continual injury and death, nearly solely the deaths of non-European, non–North American, nonwhite migrants.[3] That violence is exacerbated by a variety of management procedures and policies implemented by countries of destination, including the reinforcement and militarization of borders, campization, deterrence, lengthy detention, deportation, and illegal pushbacks to countries of origin even if these countries remain a major threat of persecution and human rights violation for the deportees. To these measures must be added the generalized refusal to examine asylum applications when submitted abroad and the inability for most citizens of Africa, parts of Asia, and various Latin American countries to acquire a traveling visa to the EU or North America—policies that in effect turn migrating beings into "unauthorized," "irregular," and "illegal" asylum seekers when they arrive in Europe or in the United States without the proper papers, despite Article 14 of the Universal Declaration of Human Rights, which states that the right to asylum is a human right.[4] In 2016, the International Organization for migration's Missing Migrants Project documented the death of approximately 7,500 migrants, "more than 5,000 of whom perished in the Mediterranean"; in the first few months of 2021, it estimated that at least 1,146 died at sea, in contrast to 513 during the same period in 2020.[5] These figures represent only a minimum estimate insofar as it is presumed that the majority of migration-related deaths and disappearances are unrecorded. Since 2014, "more than 4,000 fatalities have been recorded annually on migratory routes worldwide"; between January 1, 2014, and October 22, 2019, the estimated cumulative total of deaths and disappearances was 33,686.[6]

In the Mediterranean region, these high numbers of migration-related deaths have been chronicled as one of the major consequences of the cessation of the Italian search-and-rescue Operation Mare Nostrum (2013–2014), which had succeeded in rescuing at sea at least 150,000 migrating travelers, mainly from Africa and western and central Asia. This operation was replaced by Triton (2014–2018), a border-security operation ultimately conducted by Frontex (2004–), the European Border and Coast Guard Agency, whose security equipment includes surveillance aircrafts, ships, and staff teams specialized in the gathering of intelligence and screening or identification processing. The agency's growth is tightly related to Europe's self-professed refugee crisis (its budget has increased from approximately €100 million in 2014 to €280 million in 2017 and €400 million in 2020; its staff grew to 6,500 in 2021).[7] In 2014 alone, this shift from a rescue operation to an operation whose main mission is to strengthen the EU's external borders cost at least 2,500 lives.[8]

Between January and early December 2015—the year considered to be the height of the "refugee crisis"—more than 911,000 people "irregularly" entered Europe, and some 3,550 individuals died during their journeys.[9] According to the UNHCR, the top three nationalities arriving in Greece, Italy, and Spain were Syrian, Afghan, and Iraqi.[10] The main route shifted in part from the dangerous Mediterranean crossing from Libya to Italy to what would prove to be an even deadlier crossing from Turkey to the Greek islands. Frontex is now in charge of the new European Travel Information and Authorisation System, which defines itself as "an immigration control tool used to address the potential threats of ineligible individuals before they can cross the borders of the EU": it screens EU visa-exempt travelers to assess their admissibility or nonadmissibility to the Schengen zone.[11] Frontex also runs the European Border Surveillance System, whose main mission is to collect and reconcile data from ships, drones, social media, and EU's Copernicus Earth-observation satellites to identify migrant flows, and is currently being investigated for misconduct, including illegal deportation (pushback) of travelers.[12] Even as immigrant and nonimmigrant visas were and are still increasingly denied to most citizens of Africa and parts of Asia, the influx persisted and continues to persist, making journeys "more dangerous and precarious, forcing people to cross the sea on ever more unseaworthy and overcrowded vessels."[13]

Besides in the Mediterranean, most migration-related deaths and disappearances "have been recorded along routes from countries in eastern and western Africa to and through Libya, from Bangladesh and Myanmar across the Bay of Bengal and Andaman Sea to Thailand and Malaysia, and from Central and South America north through Mexico to the US."[14] In his recent publication on the global proliferation, reinforcement, and militarization of borders as a riposte to the influx of refugees and asylum seekers, the geographer Reece Jones concludes that the ever-increasing militarization and securitization of borders are more about the production of violence than about protection against violence.[15] One of his key examples is the US government's "prevention through deterrence" (PTD) policies that redirect the routes of the migrants coming from Mexico, Central America, and South America into the Sonoran Desert to discourage them from crossing the US-Mexico border—a strategy that has not so much deterred "irregular" crossing than forced migrants to take more perilous pathways to enter the United States. This conclusion is shared by the anthropologist and director of the Undocumented Migration Project, Jason De León, whose research has documented the transformation of the Sonoran Desert in Arizona into a "killing machine."[16] Materializing that documentation, the Undocumented Migration Project devised the exhibition *Hostile Terrain 94* in 2019. The project was delayed by the COVID-19 pandemic but was still ongoing in late 2021. A global and evolving participatory art undertaking, *Hostile Terrain 94* is designed to assemble approximately 3,200 handwritten toe tags left blank or filled with the names and details of undocumented men and women who have died attempting to cross the Sonoran Desert between the mid-1990s and 2019. The geolocated tags are filled in by participants hosting the project and installed on a wall map of the desert to show the locations of their remains (figure 1.1).[17] *Hostile Terrain 94*'s call to historicize migration is an incitement to become aware of recent history: the dark interdependence between migrating beings from Latin America dying in the desertic borderzone environment on their way to the United States and the imperiling measures implemented by American state authorities to contain Latin American migration. It invites us to acknowledge that recent history, that growing evolution—and therein lies its uniqueness and richness.

THE NECROPOLITICAL UNFOLDING OF TWENTY-FIRST-CENTURY MIGRATION

This very brief statistical and policy overview gives us a snapshot of the necropolitics that sustains twenty-first-century migration.[18] *Necropolitics*, the Cameroonian philosopher Achille Mbembe's term to designate "subjugation of life to the power of death," structures today's wars, colonial occupations, and migration processes; as a politics of death, it creates "*death-worlds*" in which the "other" is biopolitically produced as an enemy to justify their injuring, dehumanization, and destruction.[19] Mbembe formulated the concept of necropolitics by revising Michel Foucault's concept of biopower as a central marker of modernity in reference to the state's management and administration of life, developed in his lectures at the Collège de France in the mid-1970s. Fundamental to Foucault's notion of biopower is its distinctiveness from the premodern sovereign's right to "'make die/let live,' which evolved into the modern 'make live/let die'"—an imperative to support life through a "series of interventions and regulatory controls: a biopolitics of the population."[20] The Mbembean claim is that biopower fails to account for modern and contemporary forms of subjugation in which injury, death, and murder are being authorized. Relating the Foucauldian notion of biopower with the Agambenian notion of the state exception as a process by which specific categories of beings are made "bare" by the loss of their political status, necropolitics perdures when these beings are

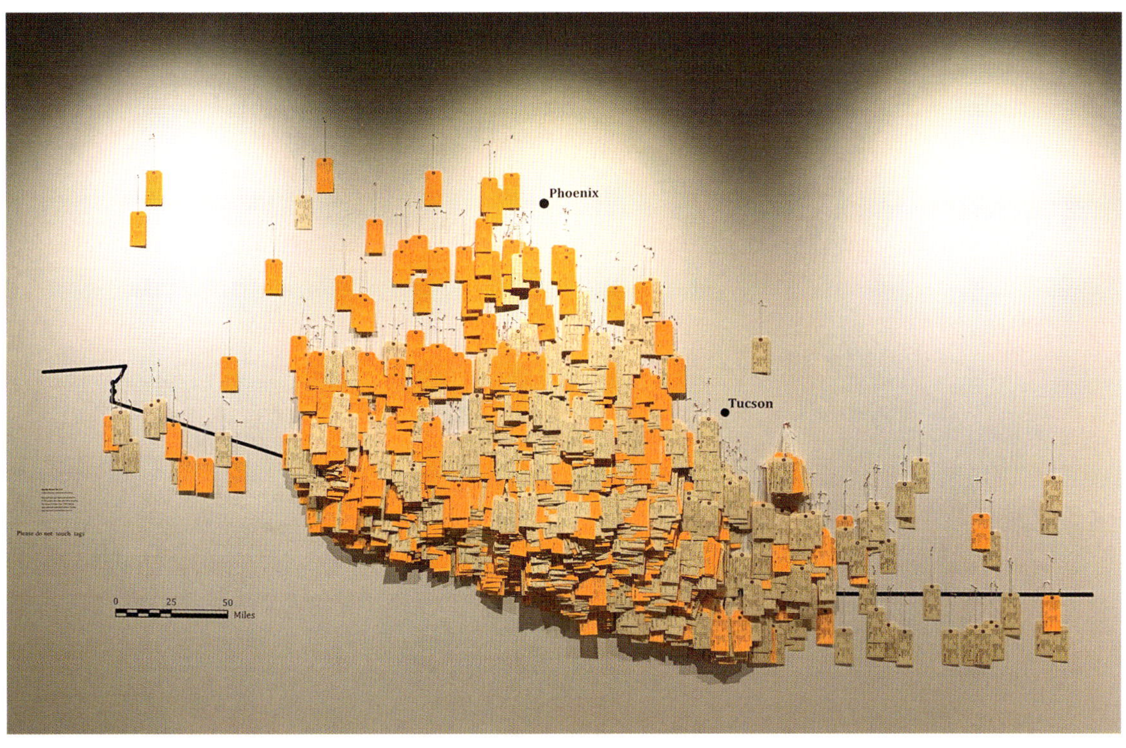

FIGURE 1.1

Undocumented Migration Project, *Hostile Terrain 94*, 2019–. Map of the Arizona-Mexico border filled with identification tags. Photo: Michael Wells (Undocumented Migration Project). Courtesy of the Undocumented Migration Project and Jason De León.

forced to live a permanent condition of "being in pain"—continuously and excessively aggressed, they are divested of their political rights, but they have also lost their homes and bodily rights:

To live under late modern occupation is to experience a permanent condition of "being in pain": fortified structures, military posts, and roadblocks everywhere; buildings that bring back painful memories of humiliation, interrogations, and beatings; curfews that imprison hundreds of thousands in their cramped homes every night from dusk to daybreak; soldiers patrolling the unlit streets, frightened by their own shadows; children blinded by rubber bullets; parents shamed and beaten in front of their families; soldiers urinating on fences, shooting at the rooftop water tanks just for fun, chanting loud offensive slogans, pounding on fragile tin doors to frighten the children, confiscating papers, or dumping garbage in the middle of a residential neighborhood; border guards kicking over a vegetable stand or closing borders at whim; bones broken; shootings and fatalities—a certain kind of madness.[21]

As the work of the social scientist Thomas Lemke has similarly argued, biopolitics needs to be defined more critically and limitedly as the use of power to protect, regulate, and manage the life of the *legitimate* population—a process that de facto excludes a category of not-so-legitimate beings whose death is justified not because they have confronted the sovereign but on the premise that their death is beneficial to the life of the rightful population.[22] For Mbembe, necropolitics was perfected on the plantation (the colony, in general), where "race" became the primary marker of the "other" as a fictionalized enemy whose life was systematically endangered to maintain the life of the deserving population—a fictionalization that persists in the contemporary management of migration.[23] He further specifies that necropolitics is a biopolitics where "others," enslaved people in particular but also more contemporary examples (including migrants), don't have to die—they can be "kept alive but in a state of injury, in a phantomlike world of horrors and intense cruelty and profanity," transformed into the living dead.[24] Mbembean scholars have shown that the politics of keeping the other alive, though only as permanently wounded, sustains states' inactions in their treatment of displaced people in refugee camps, where residents are subjected to major spatial compressions, lack of suitable accommodation, and inadequate public-health conditions—(non)measures that irreversibly lead to the deterioration of the residents' well-being.[25] Necropolitics, however, is not specific to refugee camps: it also sustains migratory journeys from beginning to end; it has likewise structured the internal displacement of Indigenous people in the United States and Canada, which materialized into a cultural genocide.

Why and how has migrancy evolved necropolitically? That question is central to art's call to historicize migration, in which the necropolitics of migration is revealed as a recursion of colonialism in the historical present—a colonial present and the tenaciousness of colonial presence, a prolongation of racist colonialism, which is populated in part by migratory beings most likely to become what the writer Christina Sharpe describes as "those already dead, those dying, and those living lives consigned to the possibility of always-imminent death, life lived in the presence of death."[26] As we will see, migration is also conditioned by the evolution of neoliberalism and the legacy of the War on Terror. This chapter is a serious albeit succinct attempt to elucidate these features, the ultimate goal being to historicize contemporary migration with the help of political philosophy and critical refugee and migrant studies—disciplinary fields that have brought necropolitics to the fore as the primary qualifier of current migration. It prefigures but also densifies the artworks' historical call addressed in the next chapter; in turn, that call will be progressively enriched by every single artwork in the book. A sense of that enrichment is provided in the chapter's final section, which examines one of the first substantial aesthetic disclosures of the necropolitics of migration unfolding in Europe in the mid-2000s: Isaac Julien's video installation *Western Union: small boats* (2007). The installation will allow us to return to the fields of political philosophy and critical refugee and migrant studies, notably the work of Hannah Arendt, Giorgio Agamben, and Didier Fassin, and to further posit that the historical call also entails the recognition of the migrant (in the most rewarding sense of the term as referring to beings who are attempting to fully own their freedom of movement) as the political subject par excellence of the twenty-first century precisely because of their resilient capacity to expose, tackle with, and sometimes transform necropolitics. Put differently, this chapter argues that if the call to historicize is an interpellation inviting viewers to become sensitive to the colonial roots of contemporary migration, it also finds innovative ways to acknowledge displaced people as subjects and political subjects involved in the making of history, and it invents aesthetic strategies to affirm the autonomy of migration. Historical consciousness is about the past and the now; it is about the possible as well.

Although there is no single explanation of migration's necropolitical evolution, some explanations have been persuasively formulated in the field of critical geography, policy, Black, refugee, and migrant studies. These studies converge in their highlighting of the post–Cold War period as a significant moment of change in migration management and policy making. Since the end of the Cold War—a period in which people escaping communist regimes were usually granted citizenship in the West to the detriment of those attempting to flee other problematic regimes—well into the War on Terror and the New Wars, Europe and North America have been ever progressively impeding migrancy from Africa as well as from parts of Asia and Latin America in the name of national security.[27] But the plea for national security has imperialist and colonialist undertones; it extends the histories of colonialism.

Necropolitical migration is one of the main outcomes of the conflict between cultural and religious identities unleashed by the end of the Cold War—as a device for "civilizational protection" against the alleged threatening "other," announced as early as 1996 by the political scientist Samuel P. Huntington in his famous book *The Clash of Civilizations*. Ongoing deployments—the fact that the majority of displaced people attempting to reach the EU come from former European colonies; the fact that the majority of people attempting to reach North America come from economically, politically, and criminally damaged Latin American countries in which the United States has repeatedly intervened; and the fact that Indigenous peoples struggling to survive in Canada and the United States have already been forcibly displaced from their land and culture—have only prolonged the long history of colonialism and its production of race "as a sociopolitical category of distinction and discrimination" to consolidate what the geographer Derek Gregory calls the global colonial present, of which migration is a significant part.[28] In other words, the hampering, deterring, and endangering of migration must be understood—and this is the first main point, out of two, I want to make about historical consciousness—as anchored in the histories of imperialism and colonialism, to which must be associated some of their central components: the violent history of transatlantic slavery, the genocide of Indigenous peoples, capitalism (as a vast project of land appropriation and exploitation of labor), and environmental degradation.

In the field of critical refugee and migrant studies, it is surprisingly only since the mid-2010s that the understanding of contemporary migration as an extension of European colonial history and American interventionism has been explicitly formulated, even though asylum seekers, refugees, so-called undocumented migrants, and internally displaced Indigenous communities have been increasingly voicing these connections at least since the 1990s.[29] To better account for these key studies, it is useful to provide a few definitions. First, the notion of modernity. I define European modernity as a worldview rather than as merely a geographical and temporal phenomenon. I also adopt a decolonial perspective informed by the work of the Jamaican writer and cultural theorist Sylvia Wynter, which is to suggest that European modernity has unfolded through the invention of the universal category of "man" (be it Man1 or Man2) by relying on a set of exclusions of humans declared unworthy of that categorization.[30] When referring to colonialism in recent centuries, I rely substantially on the definition formulated by the German historian Jürgen Osterhammel, despite its few shortcomings (its emphasis is on the power of the colonizers to the detriment of the agency—as restricted as it may be—of the colonized). He characterizes it as a system of power structured by at least four principles: (1) the domination of one people by another (which often takes the form of the paradox of an Indigenous majority being ruled by a minority of foreign invaders); (2) the disabling of the possibility of the former's autonomous development—altered as it is to fit the colonial rulers' interests; (3) the colonizers' refusal to establish cultural rapprochements with or concessions to the dominated societies (the colonized are expected to acculturate to the colonizers' values); and (4) an ethos of superiority among colonizers that supports European/American expansion as the accomplishment of a universal mission of salvation and civilization of beings considered not-quite-human "primitives" or "savages." Osterhammel's definition reads as follows: "*Colonialism* is a relationship of domination between an indigenous (or forcibly imported) majority and a minority of foreign invaders. The fundamental decisions affecting the lives of the colonized people are made and implemented by the colonial rulers in pursuit of interests that are often defined in a distant metropolis. Rejecting cultural compromises with the colonized population, the colonizers are convinced of their own superiority and their ordained mandate to rule."[31] Most early modern and modern colonies have been colonial empires: colonialism and imperialism are historically related but must be distinguished insofar as they have also existed independently from one another. Differentiating the two terms, the political theorist Margaret Kohn from the University of Toronto writes:

One of the difficulties in defining colonialism is that it is hard to distinguish it from imperialism. Frequently the two concepts are treated as synonyms. Like colonialism, imperialism also involves political and economic control over a dependent territory. The etymology of the two terms, however, provides some clues about how they differ. The term colony comes from the Latin word *colonus*, meaning farmer. This root reminds us that the practice of colonialism usually involved the transfer of population to a new territory, where the arrivals lived as permanent settlers while maintaining political allegiance to their country of origin. Imperialism, on the other hand, comes from the Latin term *imperium*, meaning to command. Thus, the term imperialism draws attention to the way that one country exercises power over another, whether through settlement, sovereignty, or indirect mechanisms of control.[32]

Colonialism is thus in many ways a "special manifestation" of imperialism, but insofar as the latter is devised as a worldwide spreading of an empire's interests and a capitalist infiltration of large economic areas, it applies mostly to modern (but not early modern) colonial empires.[33] Recent scholarship has also argued that colonialism and settler colonialism should be understood as overlapping yet structurally and analytically distinct—a distinction I go back to in chapters 9 and 10. In contrast to metropole colonialism or neo-colonialism, settler colonialism is a type of colonialism that operates through the ongoing substitution of Indigenous populations with a settler society (settlers are different from colonial sojourners—governors, administrators, militaries, missionaries, and traders—insofar as they come to the "new land" to stay) that progressively develops into a specific identity and sovereignty. But insofar as "colonialism with settlers and settler colonialism intertwine, interact, and overlap" (let us follow Lorenzo Veracini here, one of the key historians whose work has promoted that distinction),[34] it is crucial to keep settlement as an important necropolitical component of colonialism while being attentive to colonialism's variations, especially in relation to the internal displacement of Indigenous people. Modern colonialism's specific practice of domination involves the substantial expansion of the colonizing society as it incorporates adjacent territory and as it secures the settlement of the colonizers on that conquered territory. As maintained by the Māori scholar of education Linda Tuhiwai Smith, colonialism "became imperialism's outpost, the fort and the port of imperial outreach," subjugating Indigenous peoples to secure its domination while also seeking to control European colony-residents to maintain its image of what Western civilization stood for: "In this image lie images of the Other, stark contrasts and subtle nuances, of the ways in which the indigenous communities were perceived and dealt with, which make the stories of colonialism part of a grander narrative and yet part also of a very local, very specific experience."[35] Though not only a modern phenomenon (colonies existed in ancient Greece and the Ottoman Empire, for instance) colonialism significantly changed when technological developments in navigation enabled European connections with more distant parts of the world—fast sailing ships enabling both the transportation of large numbers of people (including settlers and slaves) across the ocean and the consolidation of the ties between the center and the "peripherical" colonies, a process that secured political sovereignty despite geographical distances, as well as the plantation exploitation of slaves for profit.

This decisive shift allows us to specify colonialism even further as (I rely here on Margaret Kohn) "the process of European settlement and political control over the rest of the world, including the Americas, Australia, and parts of Africa and Asia."[36] That process involves violence—a crucial component, as compellingly shown by the Black studies scholar Tiffany Lethabo King, that is frequently de-emphasized in critical colonial studies but underscored in recent Black and Indigenous studies—more specifically, the violence of conquest (the slave trade and white-settler colonialism, environmental destruction) in European imperial regimes. "This form of conquistador humanism and its view of the Native and Black Other—as a space of death—produced and sustained a genocidal violence and brutal system of enslavement that relegated Niggers and Indios to the bottom ranks of the human order," writes King; it established a hierarchy that still defines Indigenous and Black people "at its bottom rungs."[37] As this book will show, the majority of artistic practices responding to necropolitical migration understood as embedded in colonial histories insist on disclosing the inadmissible neocolonial violence to which migrating beings are subjected. While beings migrate to flee violence—persecution, the likelihood of injury and death, extreme poverty, natural disasters—they will reiteratedly be subjected to violence throughout their journeys; that violence is substantially sustained and practiced by the state authorities of the countries of destination, countries that have in the past colonized or militarily, politically, and economically intervened in the migrants' countries of origin. Kohn's definition insists on the ongoing action of colonialism (i.e., *colonialism* as a verb, as a process, as in "to colonize")—what Gregory has referred to as "the constellations of power, knowledge, and geography that . . . continue to colonize lives all over the world."[38] Most studies converge on that point. Today's migration cannot be defined as an unexpected and historically unrooted "crisis," widely used terminology that conveys the idea of a sudden massive influx of underprivileged people threatening to surpass critical thresholds for European or North American reception capacities—the perception of a threat to national security based on what Daniel Trilling calls "the impression of a hitherto unsullied [Europe and North America], visited by hordes of foreigners it has little to do with."[39] That impression is fundamentally racist (it reinforces the unstated in the use of any category referring to migratory beings, which is that they are predominantly Black, Brown, or Indigenous, "nonwhite"); it is also oblivious of the past; and it fundamentally denies coexistence.[40]

As mentioned earlier, colonialism (its history and its extension in the present) is not the sole player of the necropolitical growth of migration. The colonial present is inseparable from the neoliberalist phase of capitalism—notably, from the antimigrant sentiment of "displaced anger" expressed against the social effects of neoliberalism. As the Marxist economic geographer David Harvey characterizes it, neoliberalism is a "class project" that has resulted in the increase of the class power of economic elites to the detriment of the majority poor.[41] Its policies of economic liberalization—including the reinforcement of competition by the deregulation of social welfare, health, labor, and environmental laws; privatization; the reduction of state influence in the economy; free trade; the lowering of trade barriers; and the implementation of austerity measures—have fostered inequality between the ill-named Global South and Global North (inaccurate, misleading, and homogenizing terms used in the neoliberalist language of globalization). The economist Thomas Piketty has echoed Harvey's assessment but maintains that this inequality might well be principally ideological and political more than simply economy driven.[42] That inequality has contributed to the election of right-wing populist governments, whose economic orientation is not necessarily anti-neoliberalist but systematically anti-immigrant and nationalist.[43]

Studies have moreover demonstrated the impact of the War on Terror—the international military campaign launched by the US government after the attacks of September 11, 2001—on the necropolitical development of migration. The campaign has cultivated the perception that migration is inseparable from potential terrorism and that it must consequently be controlled, monitored, and contained by a series of intensified security measures.[44] This impact applies not only to the United States but also to Europe. On the European side, securitization has likewise rapidly increased in the 2000s, 2010s, and 2020s to manage and contain forced displacement from Africa and Asia toward the EU. Securitization has been consolidated by the reinforcement, militarization, and technobureaucratization of borders as well as by a series of dissuading operations. These European and North American operations include the refusal to grant traveling, immigrant, and nonimmigrant visas to most applicants from Africa and from parts of Asia (for the EU) and Latin America (for the US); the widespread refusal to consider asylum claims lodged abroad; the externalization of borders (the transfer of border controls to foreign countries); deportation; unjustified yet indefinite detention; the creation of hostile environments where migrating beings live "in desperate limbo" in dangerous borderzones; campization (the multiplication and transformation of migrant accommodation into outsized, camplike structures with reduced living standards and enclosed configurations); and the nonrespect of the principle of nonrefoulement (the principle that, as defined by the UNHCR, "prohibits States from transferring or removing individuals from their jurisdiction or effective control when there are substantial grounds for believing that the person would be at risk of irreparable harm upon return, including persecution, torture, ill-treatment or other serious human rights violations"[45]). As I write this chapter (it is now the end of December 2020), a 1,500-page "black book," the *Black Book of Pushbacks*, edited by the watchdog organization Border Violence Monitoring Network, has just been released. The book documents hundreds of illegal pushbacks by EU authorities against migrating populations. Simon Campbell, field coordinator for the network, summarized the study and its necropolitical findings in these terms: "This book—which brings together four years of work—points to a gaping hole in accountability for perpetrating authorities, including member states and EU agencies, like Frontex. . . . The testimonies, committed here to paper, represent a definitive archive of evidence, detailing systematic violations against people on the move, such as breaches of international law on asylum and returns, as well as the prohibition of torture."[46] A key recent example of illegal pushbacks is the Libyan coastguard's systematic interception and forced return of citizens-on-the-move attempting to flee Libya's overcrowded detention centers—breeding grounds for torture, sexual assault, extortion, and arbitrary detention, according to Suki Nagra, director of the Human Rights, Transitional Justice, and Rule of Law Service with the UN Mission in Libya—all done with the implicit support of the EU, which has delegated migrant management to Libya. A total of 15,200 migrating travelers were intercepted in the first six months of 2021, in contrast to approximately 11,000 in 2020 and 8,800 in 2019.[47]

Research on post–Cold War migration has come to the conclusion that the amplification of anti-(im)migration measures has finally instituted the criminalization of migrants as well the criminalization of the NGOs that attempt to assist them. The lawyer Idil Atak and the public-policy scholar James C. Simeon have described this criminalization as a process that involves the increasing use of criminal law in immigration matters, the criminalizing of public discourse, and other policies and practices that stigmatize migrants and refugees, and/or diminish their rights" in Canada and abroad. In fact, over the past decades, countries in the Global North have resorted to criminal law measures to deter and to punish migrants in irregular situations. Criminal penalties have been imposed on forced migrants, including refugees, for entering or staying in a country in an irregular manner, or using false documents, or for unauthorized employment. Detention has not only become increasingly common but pervasive. Transport companies, employers, and other persons who come into contact with or try to help irregular migrants, such as health professionals, humanitarian workers, landlords, family members, and friends, have also become the targets of criminal sanctions. Asylum systems have become stricter, especially for refugee claimants arriving in destination countries with the help of smugglers.[48]

These conclusions can be pushed slightly further. In her latest book on global migrancy, the geographer Alison Mountz has shown that this generalized illegalization, in particular the constant and repeated hampering of movement it entails as well as the quasi-inability to be granted refugee status in Europe and North America today (already by 2013, only 15 percent of asylum seekers were granted refugee status by EU member states), has resulted in the death of asylum itself, both as a concept and as an uninfringeable place of refuge and protection.[49] Two recent examples are telling in this regard. Canada rejected 5,000 humanitarian requests for permanent residency in 2020, a 20 percent increase compared to 2015; this evolution occurred during the COVID-19 pandemic even though government policies remained officially unchanged.[50] In the United Kingdom, the Nationality and Borders Bill (Bill 141) of 2021–2022 is currently proposing to include anti-migrant measures such as the following: asylum seekers considered to have reached the United Kingdom illegally and whose claim is successful will be given temporary refugee status and "face the prospect of being indefinitely liable for removal"; and asylum seekers may be removed from the United Kingdom as their claim or appeal is pending, "which opens the door to offshore asylum processing."[51] In both Canada and the United Kingdom, this means that even in the case of humanitarian requests or successful asylum claims, access to a permanent home and to citizenship in the host country is substantially reduced.

And yet, despite this history—despite the violations, torture, and quasi-insurmountable obstacles they face—migrating beings are still substantially on the move. A report compiled by the UNHCR in 2020, for example, shows "that more than 3,200 refugees from Syria are currently registered with the UNHCR in Malaysia, and only 122 have been resettled to any country since 2017." Citizens-on-the-move nevertheless *need* and *want* to be resettled. Raghda (a pseudonym used to protect this person's safety), who fled civil war in Syria in 2014 but is still waiting to be resettled in a safe country with their family, maintains: "I want to have the chance to send my son to school. . . . I dream about having a normal life like everybody else . . . that one day I will be a citizen in a country where I will feel at home."[52] In other words—and this is the second main point, out of two, I want to make about historical consciousness—historicizing migration as an extension of colonialism must also be (can also be) about proposing solutions to the distressful conditions of migration. There are no ultimate solutions to these conditions, mainly because migration will never end: people will always need to escape wars, persecution, poverty, and, increasingly, the devastating effects of climate change; and others will continue to be internally displaced.[53] Some historically informed solutions have been proposed, however. They could be implemented to make migration conditions not only less deadly but also more just, including the three durable solutions proposed by the UNHRC (voluntary repatriation, local integration, and the resettlement of refugees in a third country) and the more detailed, complex, and more inspired solutions suggested by specialized journalists, researchers, NGOs, activists, and citizens-on-the-move: the enforcement of international conventions to secure the basic rights and protection of refugees; hospitality rights for asylum seekers and refugees; the abolishment of detention centers and settlements; working rights for asylum seekers and refugees (rights that prevent them from simply being "passive recipients of humanitarian aid"); the establishment of more generous immigration policies through legal means; a more transparent and consistent processing of asylum claims; the ending of wars; support for economic development worldwide (countering the myth that "economic migrants" are attempting to play the immigration system); and, the most radical solution, the opening of borders to all.[54]

The question "Why and how can history help us understand the necropolitical evolution of migration?" brings us therefore to a second query: How does one, how can one, challenge such an evolution? The answer to that question, as one reads Raghda's statement, cannot simply be to expose the colonial history of migration; solutions to end or at least to deintensify the necropolitical evolution of migration must also be examined and explored based on that historical knowledge. Historical consciousness as an emphasizer of dark *and* more luminous coexistences, the remaining of this chapter argues, is precisely what art's call for historicization is about. Historical consciousness is not just knowledge—the knowledge of the history of migration as replaying what Mbembe has termed "some of the repressed topographies of cruelty" of the plantation and the colony by a variety of measures devised to exclude (injure or simply eliminate) the "other" arriving from former colonies.[55] Historical consciousness is also, as importantly, an acknowledgment—the acknowledgment of the migrating being as a political subject capable of changing that history.

COEXISTENCE IN ART: THE MIGRATING BEING AS A POLITICAL SUBJECT CENTRAL TO THE EVOLUTION OF THE TWENTY-FIRST CENTURY

That double comprehension of historical consciousness is formulated in *Western Union: small boats* (2007), a three-screen film transferred to high-definition by the British artist Isaac Julien (b. 1960, London). In this work, the call for history is both a call to become aware of the colonial history of present-day migration and to sustain the autonomy (the possible political subjectivity) of migrating beings as well as the autonomy of beings living in the wake of forcibly displaced people.

Western Union: small boats begins with a sequence of a gated archway opening onto the Mediterranean and the Black performer Vanessa Myrie walking toward the gateway (figure 1.2). As insightfully posited by the cultural studies scholar Jennifer A. González in her analysis of the work, this first scene generates a series of associations, "from the Atlantic Middle Passage to the proliferating incarcerations of the present."[56] It contextualizes the twenty-first-century sea journeys of African exiles to southern Italy—more specially Sicily, as the subsequent images specify—within the history of the transatlantic slave trade (from the sixteenth to the nineteenth century), in which 10 to 12 million Africans were forcibly displaced and transported as slaves to the supposed New World. It also brings to the fore the conditions of migrancy in 2007, whose media coverage in part inspired the work. Europe was a pivotal destination for migrating Africans, especially European countries bordering the Mediterranean Sea.[57] In 2004, the Libyan and Italian governments had reached an undisclosed agreement stipulating that Libya would accept African deportees from Italian territories—an agreement that led to the mass deportation of displaced people from Italy to Libya. At least 500 individuals per year have been estimated to have died attempting to reach Italy by sea during that period; a boat cemetery was eventually identified in the Sicilian town of Agrigento, where the shipwrecked boats

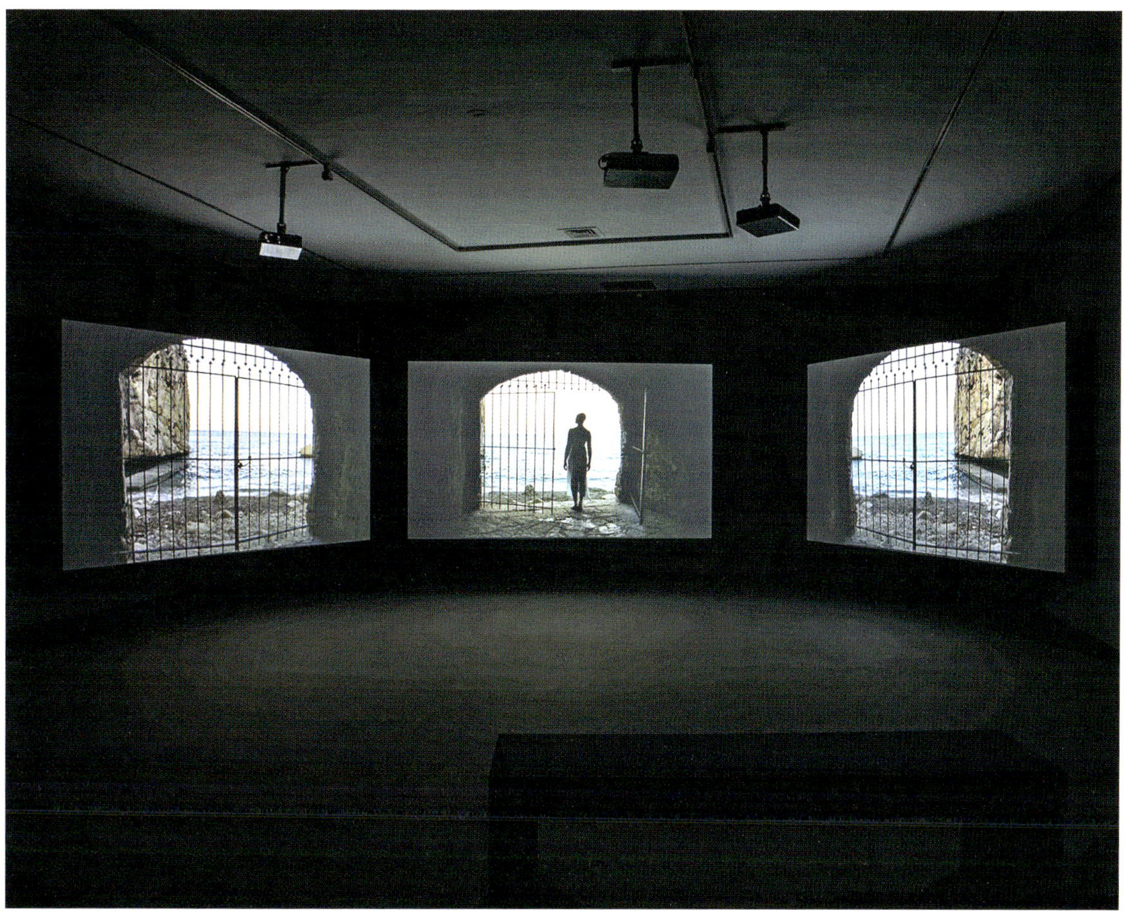

FIGURE 1.2

Isaac Julien, *Western Union: small boats*, 2007 (still). Three-screen installation, 35 mm film transferred to high definition, color, 5.1 surround sound, 18 minutes, 22 seconds. Edition of 5 plus 1 artist's proofs (IJS 109). Photo: Joaquin Cortes. Courtesy of the artist and Galería Helga de Alvear, Madrid, 2008.

were kept awaiting investigation—some of them appearing in Julien's video installation.[58] These events did not end in 2007 when *Western Union: small boats* was released. In October 2013, two back-to-back shipwrecks in Lampedusa resulted in the deaths of more than 400 people due to the tightening of restrictive border controls; before and after that tragedy, shipwrecks have been a constant in the area.[59] *Western Union: small boats*'s opening sequence, however, shows Vanessa Myrie moving and standing beyond the gate, suggesting the possibility of resilience within that very historical context.

Making full use of its three-screen structure, the installation, running 18 minutes and 22 seconds, juxtaposes documentary images of Italian fishermen on their boats, a cemetery of small boats painted with Arabic scripts and containing objects left behind, the inside of the Palazzo Gangi in Palermo (the palace that was the setting for Luchino Visconti's *The Leopard* [1963], a film that depicts the fall of the aristocracy concomitant to the rise of the bourgeoisie in the second half of the nineteenth century), with images of African men asleep in small vessels, possibly dreaming, as well as images of Black and white dancers performing on the Turkish Steps at Agrigento, in the Palazzo Gangi, and in the water. The soundscape combines a cappella music (the singing voice of Oumou Sangaré), electronic music, and quasi-indecipherable radio-frequency bits of information on migrants in distress.[60] The work creates a constant tension between the inside and the outside, the documentary and the theatrical, death and life, history and freedom, reality and dream, between what the art historian Kobena Mercer has called the "dream-like quality of the image" and the "critical reverie" typical of Julien's video works.[61] Halfway to the end of the projection, the installation juxtaposes, on different screens, images of white tourists swimming in the sea and five Black dead bodies wrapped in silver Mylar lying on the beach (figure 1.3). These two- to three-screen juxtapositions end with the juxtaposition, within a single image projected in one screen, of bathers in the background and corpses in the foreground. This image will soon lead to underwater images of drowning bodies struggling to stay alive, enacted by different dancers. Commenting on that whole section, González rightly concludes that it confirms the installation as a "critique of contemporary global economic relations": based on Iain Chambers's postcolonial reading of Julien's work, her argument is that the installation exposes migration as resulting from the colonialist unequal distribution of wealth between rich and poor countries—an inequality that forces African citizens to flee toward Europe and be criminalized in that very process.[62]

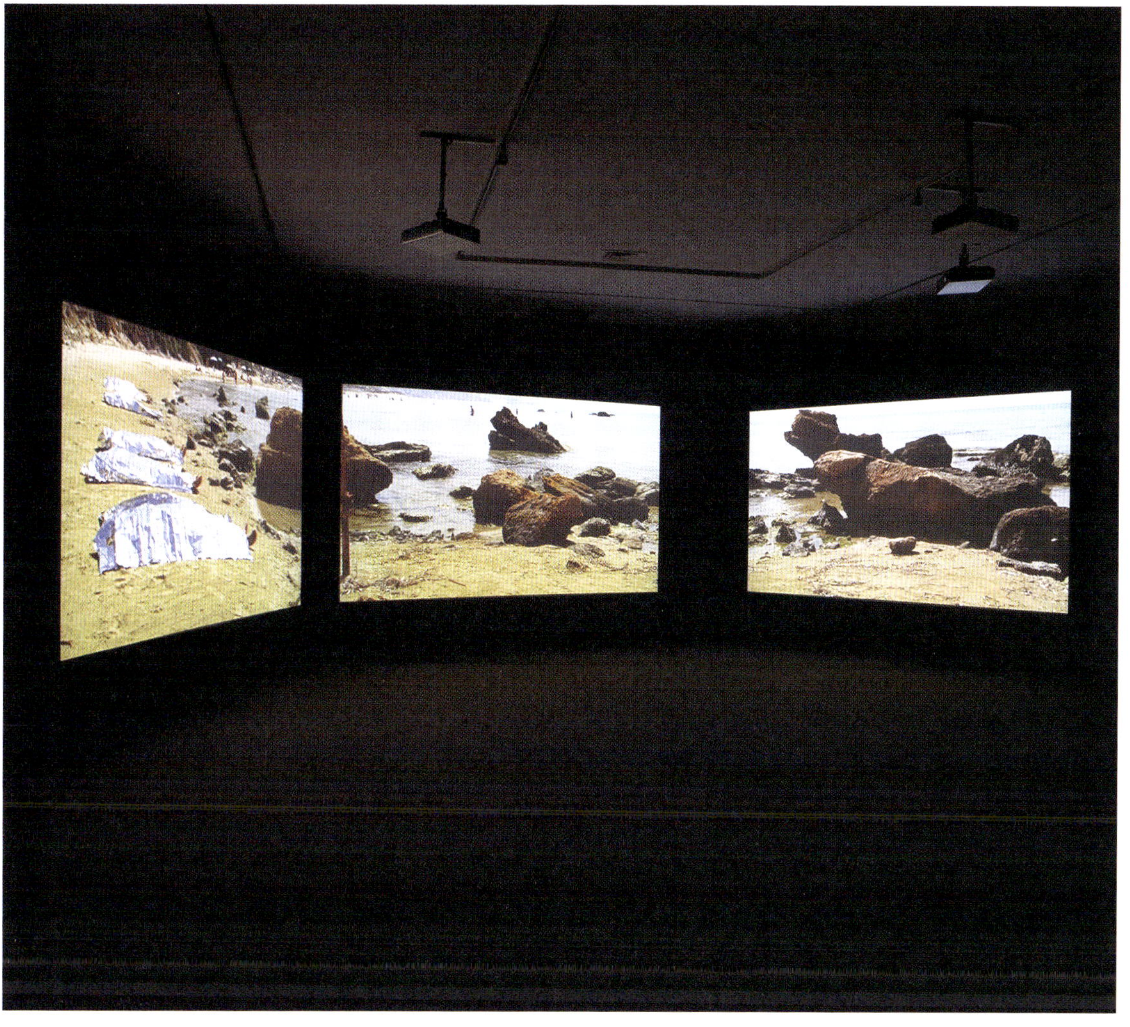

Isaac Julien, *Western Union: small boats*, 2007 (still). Three-screen installation, 35 mm film transferred to high definition, color, 5.1 surround sound, 18 minutes, 22 seconds. Edition of 5 plus 1 artist's proofs (IJS 109). Photo: Joaquin Cortes. Courtesy of the artist and Galería Helga de Alvear, Madrid, 2008.

González's analysis succeeds in illustrating how the work is especially enthralling in its historicity: most of the elements composing the history of migration—its necropolitics, its inscription in the histories of colonialism, transatlantic slavery, and capitalism—are exposed by Julien's unique approach to narrativity, one that intermixes dream and performance images through montage, documentary, fiction. Historical consciousness sustains the narrative from beginning to end. But I want to emphasize two other features to further appreciate Julien's complex call for historical consciousness. First, the work's deployment of necropolitical migration as a coexistence becomes particularly manifest in the juxtaposition (both the screen-to-screen juxtapositions and the single juxtaposition within one single image) of the tourists and the dead bodies lying nearby on the shore. Coexistence—the interdependence of European vacationers and African corpses—is visually rendered in these juxtapositions. *Western Union: small boats* does not identify what that coexistence *specifically* entails, although González's description of the work as highlighting the alarming increase of global income inequality is made manifest by the contrasting fates of the two groups. The bathers and the corpses, the privileged and the unprivileged, mobility and immobility, life and death: these categories of beings are shown to be interdependent, but the work never fully defines their interdependence. I see this as a strength, for it is what allows the work to become a call addressed to the viewer not only in 2007 but also today. It invites viewers to think about what that coexistence is, their role in such a dark coexistence and what it could possibly become, how it could possibly be unlearned and undone. It encourages spectators to think historically. Moreover, and this brings us to the second feature that works to complexify the notion and practice of historical consciousness, the performers, including the statuesque Vanessa Myrie, keep mobilizing the space in which they circulate as much as they are mobilized by it. The Black performers act in the landscape, in the Palazzo, in and on the water. I see them as political subjects—as much as the rising class described in Visconti's film—who move in space as manifestations of life, strength, dignity, and historical transformation; there is a sense that they are already the future of history.

What does it imply to say that the performers in Julien's installation are political subjects? It mainly implies that the artistic call to historicize—as this study demonstrates—is a call not only to meditate on the colonial roots of today's migration but also to acknowledge the displaced people's own historical consciousness as well as the historical consciousness of beings living "in the wake" of these displacements in the still unfolding recursions of coloniality (the state of wakefulness as a form of consciousness, richly posited by Christina Sharpe).[63] Philosophical studies by Hannah Arendt and Giorgio Agamben are particularly insightful in their argumentation of that claim, connecting as they do historical consciousness, political subjectivity, and refugeehood. Let us briefly consider these foundational texts to better specify what such an acknowledgment entails.

In an essay entitled "We Refugees" published in 1943 in the Jewish periodical the *Menorah Journal*, Hannah Arendt claimed that the refugee was central to the history of the twentieth century. She questioned the assimilation strategy by which Jewish people, who had escaped Nazi Germany only to be eventually expelled from some of the European countries they had fled to, refused to name themselves "refugees."[64] They proceeded to forget their identity—their culture and language, even their experience of concentration and internment camps—to better integrate into the host countries as "ordinary immigrants." This assimilative approach could only fail, she insisted, insofar as Jewish people, being "nothing but human beings," remained unprotected by laws and political treaties—a privation of rights that could only make them more vulnerable to social distinction, discrimination, and eradication. In contrast to assimilationism, Arendt speaks of a minor tradition of "conscious pariahs" who persisted in disclosing and examining their identity as refugees. These outsiders, she famously claimed, are "the vanguard of their peoples" insofar as they gained historical consciousness in that very nonassimilation process.[65] Explaining what that historical consciousness consisted in, she wrote: "Those few refugees who insist upon telling the truth, even to the point of 'indecency,' get in exchange for their unpopularity one priceless advantage: history is no longer a closed book to them, and politics is no longer a privilege of gentiles. They know that the outlawing of the Jewish people in Europe has been followed closely by the outlawing of most European nations. . . . For the first time Jewish history is not separate but tied up with that of all other nations. The committee of European peoples went to pieces, when, and because, it allowed its weakest member to be excluded and persecuted."[66] European history is (partly and yet substantially) Jewish history.

In his essay also entitled "We Refugees" (1995), Giorgio Agamben summarized and reinforced Arendt's arguments, maintaining that the deprived-of-rights condition of Jewish refugees—in the historical context of the World War II extermination of some 6 million Jewish persons across German-occupied Europe, Nazi Germany, and its collaborators—was overturned by those who refused assimilation. The conscious pariahs' lucid observation of their condition introduced a new historical cognizance: the awareness that the persecution of "its weakest member," Jewish populations, led to the fall of a significant part of Europe during World War II. This is why, argues Agamben, "the refugee is conceivably the only imaginable figure of our day." Historical consciousness has an ongoing relevance insofar as the proliferation of displaced beings as a global mass phenomenon persisted not only throughout the twentieth century (when the two essays were written) but beyond as well. The refugee is *the* political subject of our times or, said differently, the "category in which it is possible today to perceive the forms and limits of a political community to come," insofar as the very figure "that should have incarnated the rights of man par excellence, the refugee, constitutes instead the radical crisis of this concept."[67] Agamben's perceptiveness is fundamental. It designates the refugee as the central figure of our contemporaneity: refugees are profoundly political because their exposure to death discloses how political rights in the twentieth and twenty-first centuries rely on nation-states' attribution of citizenship from which the refugee is excluded: "in the nation-state system, the so-called sacred and inalienable rights of man prove to be completely unprotected at the very moment it is no longer possible to characterize them as rights of the citizens of a state."[68] This is a forceful answer to this book's question: What makes art's unlearning of the way we see migration—implicitly, what makes migration itself—critical to the development of the twenty-first century? Though or, indeed, because migrating beings are more and more marginalized, endangered, criminalized, and eliminated in democracies, they are decisive beings: their position enables them to sense that their "outlawing," to paraphrase Arendt, will be "followed closely by the outlawing" of democratic nations and by a generalized weakening of citizenship tout court (as Dimitry Kochenov's recent study affirms and as Stan Douglas's installation discussed in chapter 10 will troublingly disclose). Such is coexistence. Responding to necropolitical migration, art can be said to announce the current unfolding as well as the future of hazarded citizenship.

I come back to Agamben's formulation of bare life as an outcome of states of exception in part II. Suffice it to say for now that his (and Arendt's) insight is as powerful as it is . . . problematic. Why? Mainly because it relies on refugees being reduced to victims, though historically conscious victims turned into modern heroes as they help European nations look at their democracies, which are declining because these democracies have authorized the segregation of refugees. Such a process ends up articulating a divide between *bad* and *good* refugees, as though attempting to assimilate was de facto an immoral choice (assimilation is sometimes the only pragmatic temporary option available); it also ends up shrinking their political subjectivity to sacrificing their lives to the disclosure of failed democracies that reject them.[69]

Jacques Rancière has strongly contested the paradox of political beings who remain victims even when they become heroes. He maintains that a political subject "is a capacity for staging . . . scenes of dissensus" (*litige*, "dispute") about who is included (or not) in a specific collectivity.[70] Writing about history's silencing of the past, the anthropologist Michel-Rolph Trouillot speaks about how history "as social process" encompasses peoples in three different capacities: "1) as *agents*, or occupants of structural positions; 2) as *actors* in constant interface with a context; and 3) as *subjects*, that is, as voices aware of their vocality," specifying that peoples are subjects of history "the way workers are subjects of a strike": they delineate the very terms under which certain situations can be designated.[71] Such is dissensus: it redistributes the sensible—reconfigures the boundaries separating the haves and have-nots, beings who are allowed in and beings who must be kept out—as the *laissés-pour-compte* (social rejects) manifest their disagreement with a specific social order. Rancière's and Trouillot's perspectives show dissensus, dissension based on historical consciousness, to be the political action par excellence. In contrast to Agamben's assessment, their perspectives are attentive to the unfolding of political agency, to all of the minute dissensus actions that make that agency possible—a multiplicity of disputing and redistributing gestures that remain unaddressed by Agamben even when designating refugees as political subjects and that are just about inconceivable in Agamben's formulation of societies as states of exception. The Agambenean understanding of refugees as political subjects must be kept but substantially complicated.

Can it not indeed be argued that historical consciousness grounds political subjectivity—a subjectivity that materializes in a variety of microdissensus actions? This complication is what Julien's *Western Union: small boats* articulates as it puts into play the ongoing tension between the transatlantic slave trade and twenty-first-century migration, colonialism and decolonization, documentary and fiction, necropolitics and life. The dancing performers are part of the geohistory of the Atlantic Middle Passage, but their choreographies of stroll, observation, enactment, and struggle overturn that history. These dissensus beings live in the aftermath of but also concurrently with the corpses lying on the shore. The same must be said of migrating beings: they are dissensus beings insofar as leaving home is to be historically conscious of why one is leaving and of what is to be gained and lost when leaving; although their migration is forced, it is still an act of disagreement with a problematic social order or disorder. As the anthropologist-sociologist Didier Fassin maintains, one must never lose sight of the autonomy of citizens-on-the-move: their decision-making process, movement, fugitivity, storytelling (the story of the destructive forces that have played against them and the inadequacy of our political institutions to counter these forces[72]), and potential capacity to resist: "That the attitude of many states toward refugees seems to reduce their existence to its most basic expression does not imply that these refugees let themselves be reduced to it."[73] The call to historicize, then—as I hope to show throughout this book—is a call to meditate *both* on the colonial historicity of contemporary migration and on the political subjectivities of migration's damaged yet historically conscious and acting beings. Coexistence is dark, but it can be rethought more luminously.

AFFECTIVE PROXIMITIES: AS OPPOSITES HAVE CONVERSATIONS

When you put two images together, something else comes out, a third meaning. This is very, very true. But montage is also a way of understanding how opposites in general—not just in the cinema—can be persuaded to have a conversation. . . . As opposites have conversations, or as they are persuaded to at least potentially sit at the table in preparation for conversation, something miraculous happens[.] . . . Life itself happens.
—John Akomfrah, quoted in "John Akomfrah's Video Art Lures the Senses"[1]

In an interview held in 2019, the London-based artist John Akomfrah (b. 1957, Accra, Republic of Ghana) affirmed that artists' primary responsibility is to address the defining issues of their time. Referring expressly to *Purple* (2017), a six-channel video installation on climate change, he specified:

Just accepting the rather obvious fact that we're living it, is a step. . . . I live and work on a planet where people still deny that this is going on. Just being able to accept that, seems to me to be a step forward. The thing is that artists have both an ethical and an aesthetic responsibility to try and suggest a way of looking at, living with, and overcoming this, in their work. We have to act responsibly, not to necessarily lecture to people or preach to them about what it is, but show how to navigate it, emotionally, intellectually.[2]

Responsibility is described here as the artistic imperative to address the predicaments of the twenty-first century. The point, however, is not to impose a definite viewpoint or solution (Akomfrah says elsewhere that art is "about proposing, not imposing"[3]) but to suggest ways of looking at and "navigating" through these predicaments. These principles actively define the multiscreen video installations examined in this chapter, each part of a single trilogy: *Vertigo Sea* (2015), *Purple* (2017), and *Four Nocturnes* (2019). Key to this navigation is Akomfrah's unique—affective, associative, vital-materialist—exploration of montage as a practice of coexistence. Montage, the technique of editing and combining images and sounds from different sources in a single composition, is transformed into a dialogic technique. To be more precise: montage is explored to generate a multiscreen conversation between images of human and nonhuman actors, actants and agents, victims and perpetrators, whose interdependence partakes mostly of the dark side of modernity. It works speculatively by inviting a set of unconsidered, injured, destroyed, but also destroying actors and agents on the stage of history, asking, "Who should be on that stage acting and being—who populates this stage?"[4] The call for the historicization of contemporary migration rests essentially on four montage procedures, which I briefly delineate before outlining the chapter's leading question and claim.

First, montage is investigated as a process of connection between moving images—archival films and new footage—within each screen and between the screens; implicitly, it is a process of connection between what appears in these screens: human and nonhuman actors and agents. Second, as viewers, we are continuously made aware of these connections qua connections (what Akomfrah interchangeably calls "affective proximities," "associations," "vital materialism") because of their overabundance and because of their nonevident, unexpected, and troubling affiliation—this is to say that the act of connection is as important as what is being connected. Third, the actors and agents are brought together as historically related but following a nonlinear and noncausal conceptualization of history; this means that the connections are left sufficiently open to allow viewers to meditate on these associations. Akomfrah uses archival footage of past and present-day events and combines it with original documentary footage, historical reconstitutions, as well as literary and philosophical texts. This combination is not about explaining— chronologically and causally—the dark evolution of modernity. Rather, it is about bringing into close proximity images of events that do not obviously relate when considered individually but do relate as interdependent destructive forces within the long history of modernity, covering large historical time spans from the sixteenth to the twenty-first century or from the twentieth to the twenty-first century. These interdependent events include forced migration, the transatlantic slave trade, colonialism, resource capitalism, the mass killing of animals enabled by industrialization and the commodification of wilderness, the invention of technologies of mass destruction, wars, genocides, and environmental degradation. Within that history, present-day migration is shown as a prolongation and a reactivation of European modernity understood as a necropolitical project. Akomfrah himself emigrated from Ghana—a former British colony that gained its independence from Britain in 1957—to the United Kingdom with his family following the 1966 coup against the civilian government led by Kwame Nkrumah.[5] Montage is thus a motor for historical consciousness: it makes things from the past and present coexist, even anachronistically, to help us better understand the present. Fourth, montage creates environments composed of actors who draw from their milieu the resources necessary for their survival—most actors have been damaged in that very process, but some have survived; they have also been brought back to life by the safeguarding of their images, and life persists despite necropolitics.

How is Akomfrah's montage practice an original contribution to the unlearning of migration? Focusing on that question, my claim is that his multichannel installations—specifically the trilogy *Vertigo Sea*, *Purple*, and *Four Nocturnes*—explore montage as an aesthetic strategy of coexistence between humans and nonhumans in which certain beings exist through the cancellation of other beings, wherein that coexistence exposes the destructive forces of colonial modernity that underlie and have come to structure contemporary migration. It is a strategy that allows historical consciousness to unfold. To unpack my claim, I start with a description of the three works, *Vertigo Sea*, *Purple*, and *Four Nocturnes*, and follow it by an investigation of their montage procedures, of what montage does to produce coexistence, and of how coexistence becomes a historicizing call. I then analyze the specificities of that call and its implicit subcall for life by establishing a dialogue with the work of Christina Sharpe and Binta Diaw. That dialogue shows how historical consciousness is not only about understanding how the past informs and persists in the present but also about acknowledging the possibility of historical change. With these specifications in mind, this chapter also allows us to begin to understand why montage in multichannel installations—Akomfrah's trilogy as well as Richard Mosse's three-screen installation *Incoming* (2014–2017), examined in chapter 3; Angela Melitopoulos's four-screen installation *Crossings* (2017), discussed in chapter 8; and Stan Douglas's double-screen installation *Doppelgänger* (2019), studied in chapter 10—cannot be defined simply as an editing technique. Rather, montage is a philosophy, a world-making device, a praxis, a spatialization, a historicizing method, and a craft constitutive of coexistences; it is a call that invites viewers to become aware of their participation in these dark and sometimes more mutual forms of coexistence.

Vertigo Sea (2015), a three-channel color video installation running 48 minutes and 30 seconds, was initially presented at the 56th International Art Exhibition of la Biennale di Venezia in 2015 as part of Okwui Enwezor's *All the World's Futures* show. It brings together a multitude of images, such as material sourced from the BBC's Natural History Unit—including David Attenborough's sea-life documentary *The Blue Planet* (2001)—as well as new footage of the Isle of Skye, the Faroe Islands, Greenland, and northern Norway. The montage's soundtrack mixes journalistic reportage, whale sounds, the sound of rolling ocean waves, the more traumatic sounds of gunshots and explosions, music for string orchestra, as well as readings of literature in which the sea plays a salient role—such as Herman Melville's *Moby-Dick* (1851), Virginia Woolf's *To the Lighthouse* (1927), and Heathcote Williams's book-length poem *Whale Nation* (1988)—and of philosophical accounts, namely Friedrich Nietzsche's *Thus Spoke Zarathustra* (1883–1885) and John Newton's *Thoughts upon the African Slave Trade* (1788).[6] The best description of *Vertigo Sea* comes from the *Guardian*'s art critic Adrian Searle not only because of his reference to the installation's most impactful images but also because of his acute account of the feeling of excess experienced by the viewer attempting to absorb the multiple images interacting between the three screens:

Breaching whales, vast flocks of white birds moving over tidal lagoons and clouds of Monarch butterflies, gathering before their long migrations, segue into reports of migrants drowned at sea, shootings in the street, the plight of the refugee, the daily terrors of the news cycle. Readings from Melville's Moby-Dick, Heathcote Williams' epic 1988 poem Whale Nation and Virginia Woolf provide a murmuring undertow. There is too much to take in, at first or even second viewing.

Seabirds sheer into shoals of fish, killer whales plough into seals, crocodiles strike at the herd crossing the river in wide-eyed animal panic. Slaves are thrown overboard, mothers flung naked from airplanes into the ocean by the Chilean junta; blood coils in the water and frenetic starfish and eels feast on flesh. It's the procession of images that sticks in the mind: ice on the rigging, mist in the trees, the astonished round eye of a harpooned whale whose body is unpeeled and eviscerated, the deck awash with blood.

Flayed blubber slithers into the hold. Jerky old footage of the crew dancing, a harpoonist with his gun and the rope uncoiling across the water meets industrial slaughter on a modern whaler in a cold northern sea. The explosion of the 1946 atomic bomb in the Bikini Atoll weapons test—footage used so brilliantly by Bruce Connor in his 1976 film Crossroads—reminds us that the oceans are as much victim as protagonist. This is excess on a grand scale.

In several enigmatic scenes, the visual orchestration slows. Clocks litter a beach in a Dali-like image, as if washed up in geological time. A modern bicycle and an ancient pram stand up to their axles in the tide and people loiter on the foreshore, like actors waiting for their script to arrive, or for the world to end, or something. Who knows. They stand among a flotsam of upturned chairs and an abandoned bed-frame. There's a golliwog doll, with a knitted grin.[7]

As Searle maintains, "There is too much to take in, at first or even second viewing." For sure, it is impossible to acknowledge and precisely identify, even after multiple viewings, the numerous and sometimes highly heterogenous images assembled in *Vertigo Sea*. It is also the case that no single viewer can or will recognize all of the references at play here and that the viewer's memory (including Searle's and surely mine) of what they have perceived will never match what actually unfolds. But that's not the point. To look at and listen to this multichannel installation is precisely to allow oneself to take in what one can take in and, mostly, to be attentive to the evolving coexistence of images, their becoming-interdependent. The work will never provide a definitive historical narrative: not only is it impossible to perceive all of the digital images, but the montaged connections are also nonlinear and do not establish cause-and-effect associations between events. This means that the viewer's own mental images keep reopening the narrative following a logic that may recall the notion of the "open work" (*opera aperta*) developed by the Italian novelist and semiotician Umberto Eco in 1962—suggestive and unfinished works that make room for the performer's or addressee's own conclusions, works that are internally dynamic and unfold as *fields* of meaning rather than as *strings* of meaning.[8]

Beyond the diversity of the images, however, a recurrence unfolds throughout *Vertigo Sea*: most of the montaged images picture the sea or the ocean as a deathscape; as such, the installation resonates with Isaac Julien's *Western Union: small boats* (2007) but also with Forensic Oceanography's *Liquid Traces—the Left-to-Die*

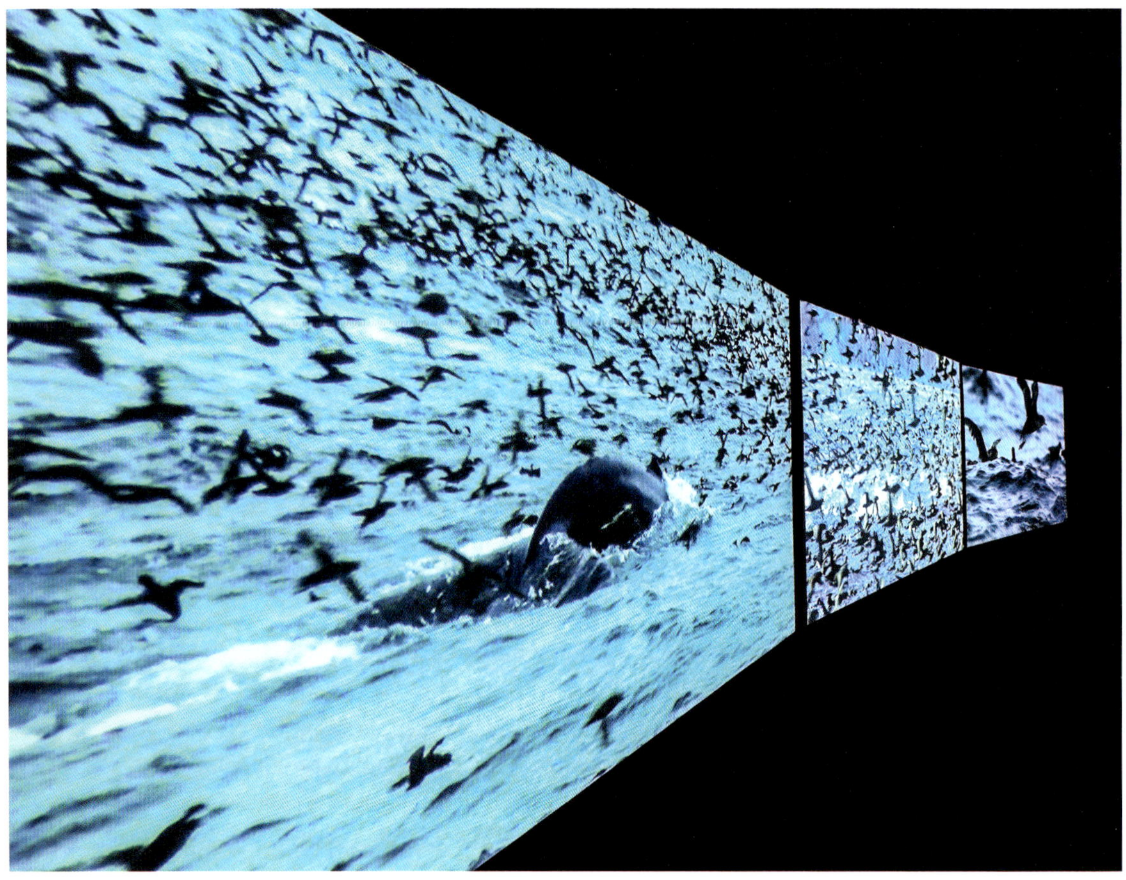

John Akomfrah, *Vertigo Sea*, 2015. Three-channel HD color video installation, 7.1 sound, 48 minutes, 30 seconds. © Smoking Dogs Films. All rights reserved, DACS/ Artimage 2021. Courtesy of Smoking Dogs Films and Lisson Gallery.

Boat Case (2014) examined in chapter 4 and Kader Attia's *La Mer Morte* (2015) discussed in chapter 5. And whereas these images of injury and death at sea unfold as a nonlinear narrative, it is crucial to emphasize that the installation starts with a journalistic coverage of the purported European refugee crisis, which was at its peak when Akomfrah made the work. We hear the journalist's spoken account, but the images of the deadly crossings of the Mediterranean Sea are not shown and, therefore, not spectacularized; we also hear a young Nigerian telling the story of his survival. Put differently, *Vertigo Sea* begins with the present and from there on discloses the historical layers informing that present.

Within this framework, the installation includes historical footage of industrial whale fishing off the shores of Newfoundland as well as polar bear hunting in the Arctic (figure 2.1); images of shackled Black men in a ship—a filmic reenactment of the Zong massacre of 1781, an insurance scheme in which some 150 enslaved Africans were deliberately forced overboard and drowned by the crew of the British slave ship (figure 2.2); images of their dead bodies lying on the shore (when reshown later isolated from the Zong story, they become specters haunting contemporary migration); spoken accounts and testimonies of the 1976–1983 Argentina military dictatorship describing how dissidents were put on planes, flown out over the Atlantic, and dropped into the ocean; TV coverage of a half-sinking boat of Vietnamese refugees in the 1970s (Vietnamese boat people fled Vietnam by sea following the end of the Vietnam War in 1975, a mass exodus of which an estimated number of 800,000 survived but between 200,000 and 400,000 died at sea) (figure 2.3); footage of a nuclear underwater explosion. Twenty-first-century migration is therefore historicized in a special way: it is connected to past events beyond the "literalism of historical causality"[9] and within the larger history of sea-enabled imperialism, colonialism, slave trade, assassinations, and the industrialization of whale fishing. History is an environmental dilapidation; it is likewise the turning of environments (the sea or the ocean) into destructive forces.

Pivotal to this historical call is the constant mobilization of images of the sea and the ocean from below, from surface level, and from above as the wellspring of colonial modernity, including some of its major components (the transatlantic slave trade, the mass killing of whales, the testing of nuclear weapons, climate change, and today's necropolitical migration) disclosed in their interdependence. The vertigo sea is shown as an energy harnessed for the injuring and destruction of certain categories of beings but also as a response to that harnessing, and in that sense it recalls William Turner's *The Deluge* (c. 1805), a work that Akomfrah

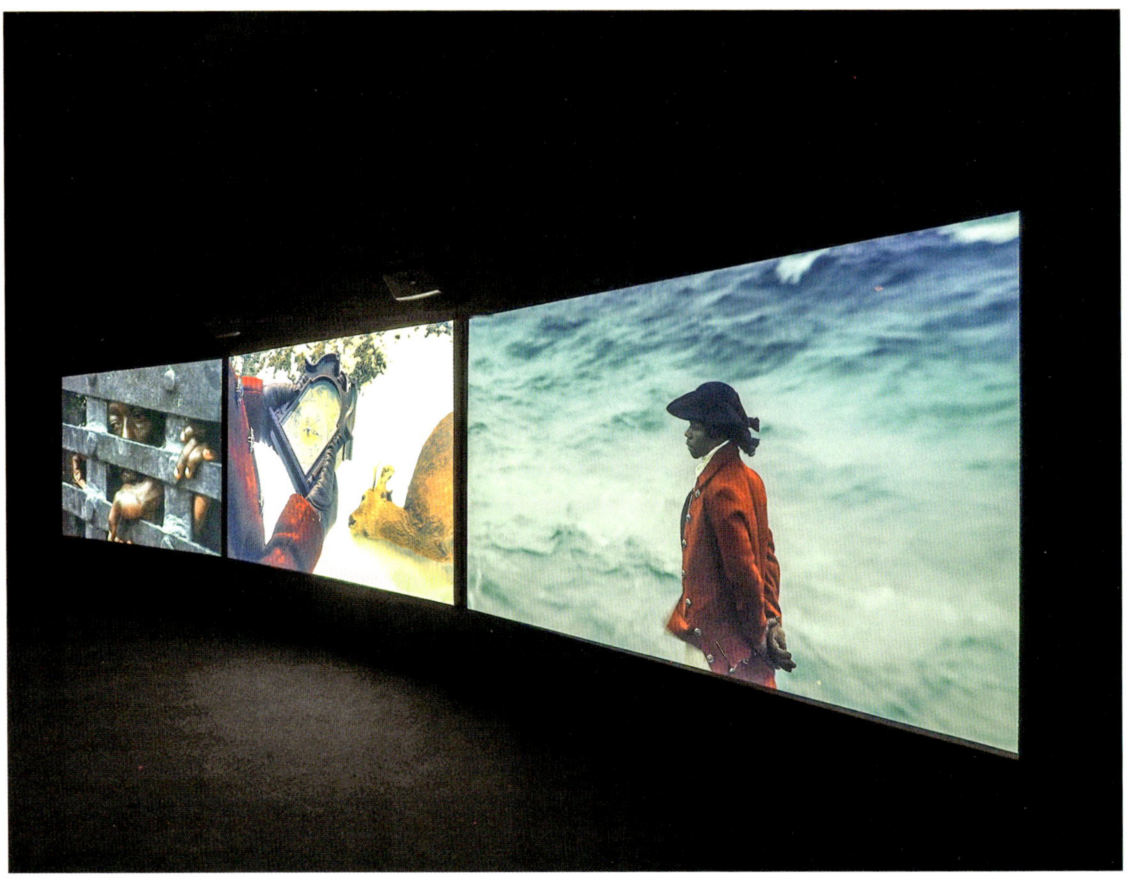

FIGURE 2.2

John Akomfrah, *Vertigo Sea*, 2015. Three-channel HD color video installation, 7.1 sound, 48 minutes, 30 seconds. © Smoking Dogs Films. All rights reserved, DACS/Artimage 2021. Courtesy of Smoking Dogs Films and Lisson Gallery.

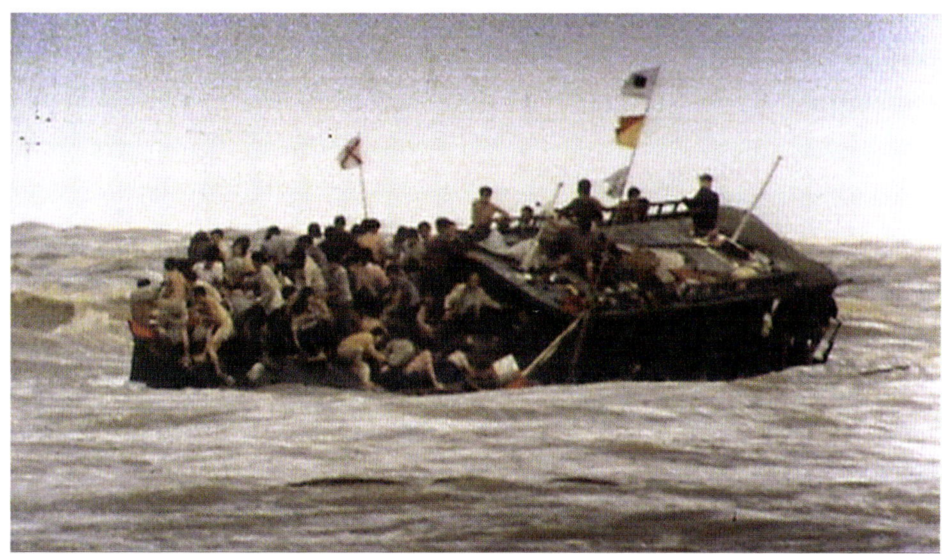

especially admires for its cinematic approach to painting.[10] The installation was informed in part by Paul Gilroy's book *The Black Atlantic: Modernity and Double Consciousness* (1993)—in particular Gilroy's discussion of the Middle Passage, the journey made by slave-trading ships across the Atlantic from the west coast of Africa toward the Americas—a passage constitutive of a combined African, American, Caribbean, and British Black Atlantic. But Melville's *Moby-Dick* (1851) was the main catalyst for the work. "It's sold to you as a novel, and of course it is a novel," says Akomfrah. "But it's also this vast, philosophical speculation about aquatic space, and the way in which that space [poses] questions of mortality, of becoming, of relativity, the demarcations of human and nonhuman. And, of course, the coming of *multicultures* and how they are formed. All of these are the speculative shape of

FIGURE 2.3

John Akomfrah, *Vertigo Sea*, 2015 (still). Three-channel HD color video installation, 7.1 sound, 48 minutes, 30 seconds. © Smoking Dogs Films. All rights reserved, DACS/Artimage 2021. Courtesy of Smoking Dogs Films and Lisson Gallery.

Moby-Dick."[11] This speculative approach, as we will see, is fully embraced in each of the installations composing Akomfrah's trilogy. In the work, one actor recurrently appears showing resistance to that deadly aquatic space in his capacity to look: the personification of Olaudah Equiano (c. 1745–1797, born in the Eboe region of the Kingdom of Benin, today's southern Nigeria), a slave who became a freedman and a prominent figure of the British abolitionist anti-slave-trade movement. We see him as a lonely figure looking at the sea and wearing a historic uniform in a composition that evokes Caspar David Friedrich's painting *Wanderer above the Sea of Fog* (c. 1818). The composition of the figure contemplating the sea allows the viewer to gain insight into Equiano's experience of the sublime in which beauty mixes with terror. It is in this practice of observation and meditation that historical change becomes thinkable (figure 2.2).

The second work of the trilogy, *Purple* (2017)—a six-channel color video installation—focuses on the environmental issues raised in *Vertigo Sea*, associating images pertaining to the impact of global warming on the environment, human communities, and biodiversity (figure 2.4). Its main theme is the environment. It combines archival footage with new video images shot in ten countries—including Alaska, Greenland, and the volcanic Marquesas Islands, where ecosystems are particularly sensitive to climate change—as well as words and music. Its timespan extends from the Industrial Revolution to the digital, biotech, and artificial-intelligence present, while images of solitary observers recurringly appear gazing silently at landscapes threatened or already devastated by human intervention.[12] The installation fully reactivates *Vertigo Sea*'s associative aesthetics of montage, the requirement to understand the present by connecting it to the past, as well as the belief in the human capacity to look at and meditate on the forces of destruction of modernity. Although more directly concerned with climate change, that predicament, as the two other installations of the trilogy make manifest, is inseparable from migration: they have coevolved within and have shaped the same dark deployment of colonial modernity.

Four Nocturnes (2019), also called *The Elephant in the Room—Four Nocturnes*, the last work of the trilogy, brings back the environmental concerns of *Vertigo Sea* and *Purple*, while rearticulating the connection of those concerns with the migration concerns explored in *Vertigo Sea*.[13] A three-channel color video installation, *Four Nocturnes* probes the relationship between the sixth mass extinction—actualized in Africa's decreasing elephant populations, much as it was actualized in the declining whale populations represented in *Vertigo Sea*—and contemporary migration. The

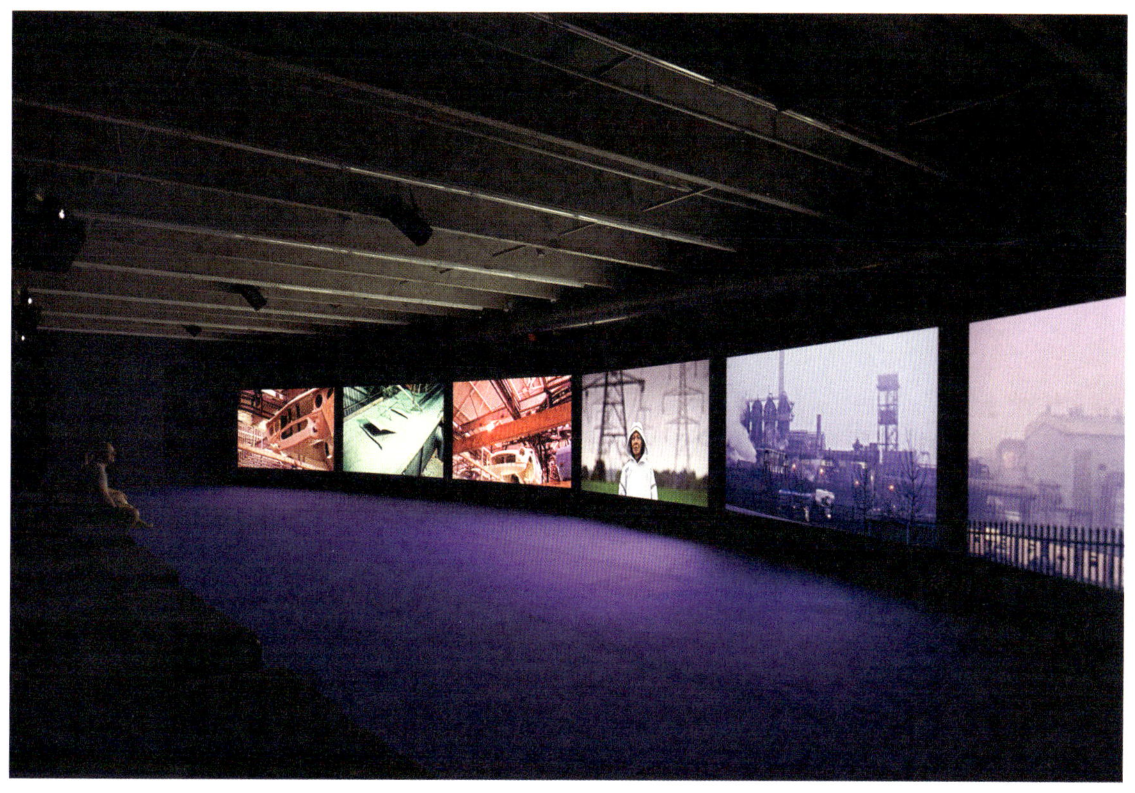

John Akomfrah, *Purple*, 2017. Six-channel HD color video installation, 15.1 surround sound, 62 minutes. © Smoking Dogs Films. All rights reserved, DACS/Artimage 2021. Courtesy of Smoking Dogs Films and Lisson Gallery.

work was commissioned for the inaugural Ghana pavilion at the Biennale di Venezia in 2019 as part of the pavilion's show entitled *Ghana Freedom*, designed by Sir David Adjaye and curated by Nana Oforiatta Ayim.

The installation associates archival footage of Africa's recent past from a variety of institutions (including the Namibia National Archives, the National Library of Senegal, the British Film Institute, the BBC, the Nobel Foundation, and Greenpeace) and fictional footage of migrating African men and women wandering in the desert, shot on location in Sharjah in the United Arab Emirates.[14] It juxtaposes various episodes of violence in West Africa: the slaughtering of elephants; Ghana's mid-twentieth-century political history (images of Kwame Nkrumah, independent Ghana's first prime minister and president, and of the military brutalizing the Ghana people; and the massacre of the Herero people (1904–1908, considered to be the first genocide of the twentieth century, conducted by the German Empire against the Ovaherero, the Nama, and the San in German South West Africa). Pivotal here is the reiterated association of the wanderers and the endangered elephants, strongly crystalized in the images of men and women wearing head masks representing elephant heads. African elephants are shown either being hunted and butchered or walking across unfertile land in search of food and shelter (figure 2.5). Their declining population (between 2007 and 2014, their estimated number was 352,000 in contrast to 12 million in the early twentieth century, 1 million in the 1970s, and 415,000 in 2016) is due largely to the illegal killing of elephants for the ivory trade, massive poaching and hunting of them, the human destruction of their natural habitat for agriculture and forest exploitation, and now climate change as a major factor contributing to the collapse of fruit availability for fruit-dependent forest elephants.[15] These images are often shown simultaneously with images of the men and women carrying bags as they seek refuge across the desert (figures 2.6 and 2.7). These citizens-on-the-move walk in and around an abandoned building, they run, they sit and meditate, they observe their environment but also look directly at the viewer; they mostly drift. The actors perform migrating beings as *wanderers*—a term that the philosopher Étienne Balibar prefers to *migrants* when referring to today's *errance migratoire* or *migrance*[16]—though these wanderers are performed here as political subjects. Their agency is apparently limited: they are individuals literally turning in circles, trapped somewhere they can't simply get out of. And yet their masks express and communicate a shared fate of extreme vulnerabilization (submitted to similar forces of destruction, they show themselves as vulnerable as the

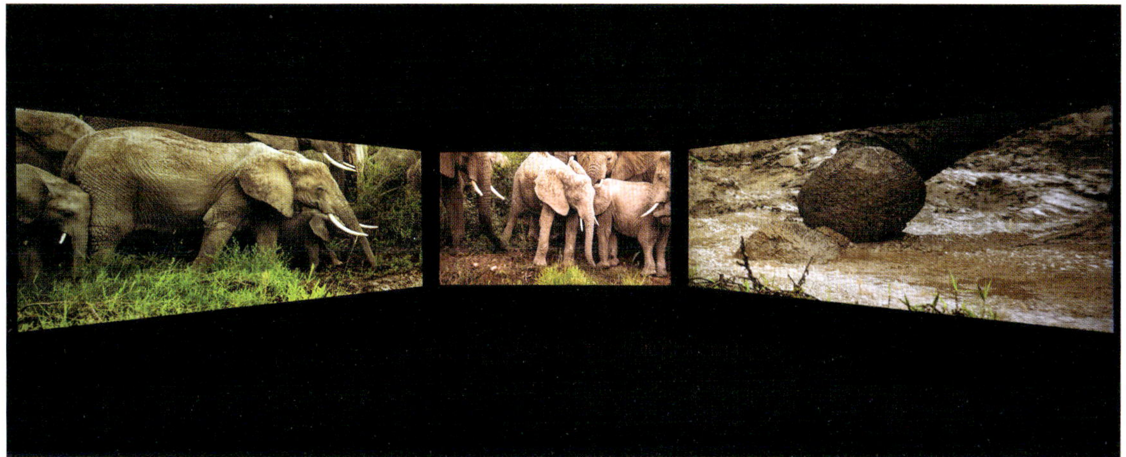

elephants), solidarity (both with each other—as a group—and with the mammals), and the right to opacity (Édouard Glissant's claim for uncategorizable alterity).[17]

MONTAGE AS A PRACTICE OF COEXISTENCE

Let us now be attentive to how montage is turned into a practice of coexistence in the trilogy's installations and how it mobilizes a call for historicization. A founding member of the Black Audio Film Collective (1982–1998), Akomfrah established from early on in his career and within that collective the centrality of montage to film production. The integration of archival footage was seen as an editing technique that could critically historicize the "figuration of identity."[10] The collective's and,

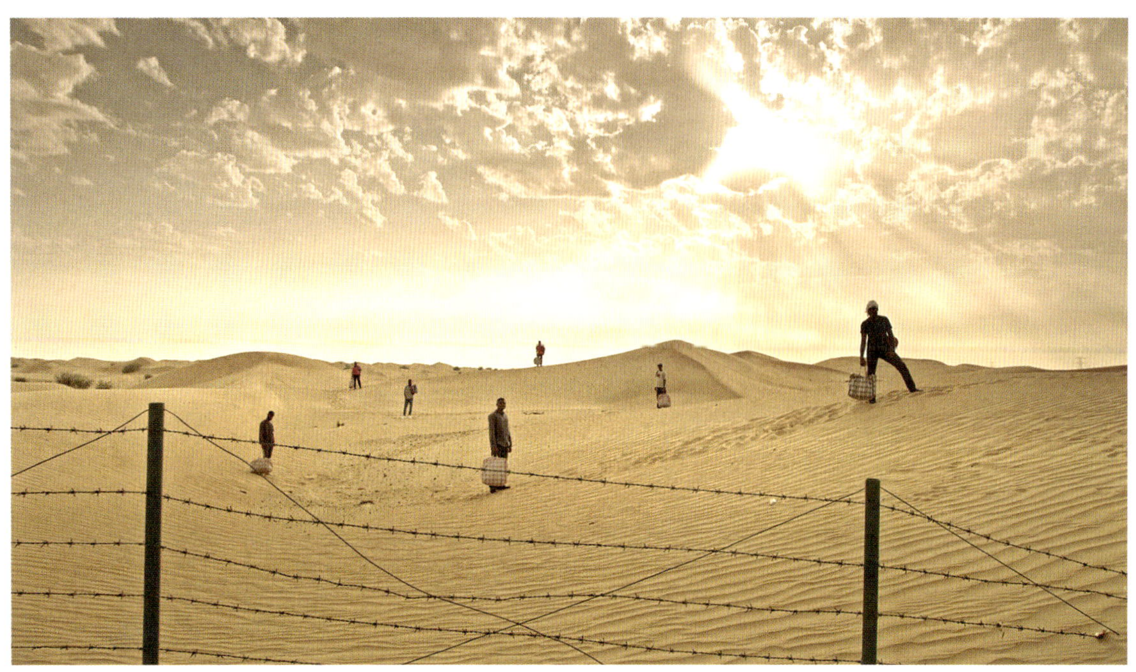

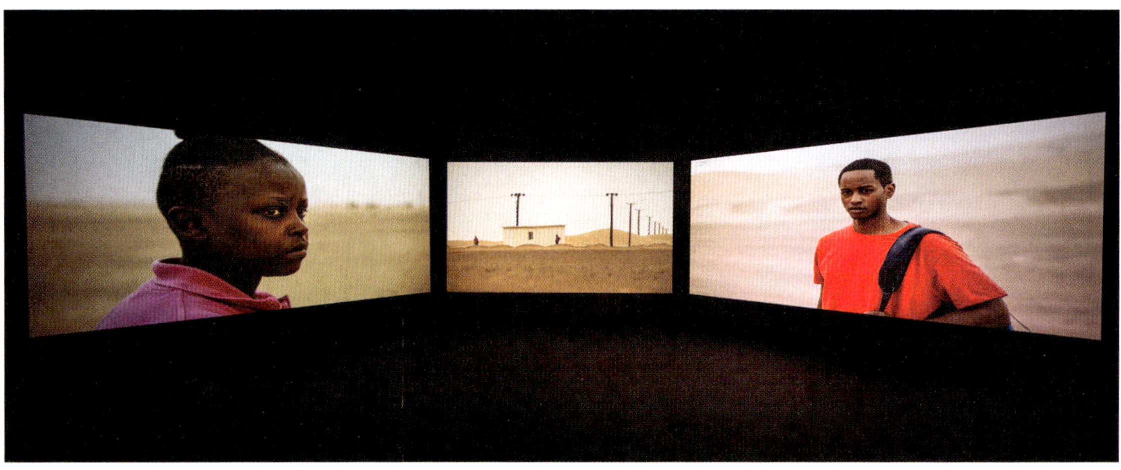

FIGURE 2.6

John Akomfrah, *Four Nocturnes*, 2019.
Three-channel HD color video installation,
7.1 sound, 50 minutes. © Smoking Dogs
Films. All rights reserved, DACS/Artimage
2021. Courtesy of Smoking Dogs Films and
Lisson Gallery.

FIGURE 2.7

John Akomfrah, *Four Nocturnes*, 2019.
Three-channel HD color video installation,
7.1 sound, 50 minutes. © Smoking Dogs
Films. All rights reserved, DACS/Artimage
2021. Courtesy of Smoking Dogs Films and
Lisson Gallery.

after 1998, the artist's own exploration of montage has unfailingly resisted straightforward narratives as well as historical cause-and-effect chronology even though the "historical" is an entrenched dimension of these experimentations. Paul Gilroy, whose publication *The Black Atlantic* was crucial to the development of the collective's postcolonial perspective, saw in montage a groundbreaking technique, identifiable in W. E. B. Du Bois's sociological methodology as well as in rap, in which "formerly separated" elements acquire new meaning once combined:

The non-linear approach which European cultural criticism refers to as montage is a useful principle of composition in trying to analyse all this. Indeed it is tempting to endorse the Brechtian suggestion that some version of "montage" corresponds to an unprecedented type of realism, appropriate to the extreme historical conditions which form it. But these dense, implosive combinations of diverse and dissimilar sounds amount to more than the technique they employ in their joyously artificial reconstruction of the instability of lived, profane racial identity. An aesthetic stress is laid upon the sheer social and cultural distance which formerly separated the diverse elements now dislocated into novel meanings by their provocative aural juxtaposition.[19]

Gilroy's defense of montage as an "aesthetic stress" applied to separate elements so that they may mean anew through their rapprochement is tightly related to his conception of the Black Atlantic. Similarly, Akomfrah—explaining how "unspeakable moments" emerged in his three-channel installation *The Unfinished Conversation* (2012), a work that combined images of the post–World War II (im)migration of approximately 500,000 million Caribbean people to the United Kingdom and images of the personal life of the cultural theorist Stuart Hall—stated that in his portrait of Hall, montage had the potential to trigger "unconscious relations between the subject and historical forces," "uncanny" proximities beyond the "literalism of historical causality," as much as it could convey Hall's conception of identity as a "matter of becoming," an "ever unfinished conversation."[20] Montage was thus articulated from the start as a renewed technique of historicization.

Since then, Akomfrah has used different terms to describe his use of montage in multichannel installations, but these early notions of "historical forces," "becoming," and ongoing "conversation" are always explicitly or implicitly at play. In a Tate interview about *Vertigo Sea* in 2015, he speaks about his dedication to documentary film as a dialectical assemblage of images—a philosophical understanding of filmic montage that underscores its capacity to create a "third meaning."[21] He doesn't elaborate on that notion, but one can think of Roland Barthes's essay "The Third Meaning: Research Notes on Some Eisenstein Stills" (1970), where Barthes examines the three orders of meaning in a film shot: the informational, the symbolic, and the obtuse. Barthes defines the latter as occurring beyond the language system, but it is at that level that the filmic arises as a signifier without a signified: "It is at the level of the third meaning, and at that level alone," he writes, "that the 'filmic' finally emerges. The filmic is that in the film which cannot be described, the representation which cannot be represented. The filmic begins only where language and metalanguage end."[22] What is pivotal in this account is the third meaning's reliance on the viewer, explained by Barthes's own experience of an Eisenstein film: "Is that all? No, for I am still held by the image. I read, I receive (and probably even first and foremost) a third meaning—evident, erratic, obstinate. I do not know what its signified is, at least I am unable to give it a name, but I can see clearly the traits, the signifying accidents of which this—consequently incomplete—sign is composed."[23] The filmic image is not the transmission of a specific message to the viewer but the viewer's reception of the image's material, affective, and nonrepresentational dimension, which will ultimately be unique to each viewer—involving a freer response from the addressee. The third meaning invites the viewer in as a producer of meaning; it confirms film as an open work (*opera aperta*).

In 2015, Akomfrah gave a name to the productivity of that third meaning: *reflection*. He uses that term specifically in relation to contemporary migration. In an interview about his upcoming work *Auto da fé* (2016)—a two-channel video installation that investigates migration through the lens of religious persecution—he declares that the work is "much more about living with precarity"; it is much more about his attempt to develop a "forensic approach" to the precarity of refugeeship and the conditions that "underpin it."[24] He explains: people who leave their country are subjected to "forces of destruction" that incite them to flee as a means of survival; but those wanting to reach Europe must travel by sea and risk their lives in that very attempt: "They have to navigate death. They have to navigate the corridor of uncertainty. In that corridor is really death. . . . Why should that be?" Mobilized by that question—the central question of why citizens-on-the-move must be exposed to death as they try to escape death, a question grounded in the consideration, as João Costa Vargas and Joy James argue elsewhere, "that the very notion of justice . . . produces *or* requires black exclusion and death as normative"[25]—Akomfrah states that he needs montage to address it. To be successful, however, montage must be approached as a practice of "association" rather than "counterpoint," for it is the associative logic of montage that invites viewers to reflect on beings exposed to death as they attempt to escape death.[26] Montage is affirmed as a historical *call* addressed to viewers, for the fundamental challenge of his multichannel association of images is to incite them to reflect upon necropolitical migration.

But what does that associative activity consist in exactly? In a later discussion—an interview on *Purple* published in *Mousse Magazine* in January 2018—Akomfrah defines montage as a strategy of "affective proximity," in which different affects are "brought into some kind of proximity to each other."[27] This associative view is also central to his discussion on vital materialism with the visual culture scholar Anthony Downey in October 2017. Montage is specified here as an occasion to decenter the human (the vital-materialist gesture par excellence)—that is, to defeat the alleged exceptionalism of human beings based on their capacity for rational thought. Akomfrah goes on to stipulate that *Vertigo Sea* and *Purple* are part of the "on-going post-war debate about the stage of being, and who should be on that stage acting and being—who populates this stage?"[28] In these works, different human and nonhuman actors and agents are invited on the stage of acting and being, which I understand as being the stage of history. The invitation takes the form of a sequestration of images (a term Akomfrah borrows from his friend Bonaventure Ndikung), so that the actors and agents may be introduced on that stage and allowed to converse. He also speaks about how the elements ("the wind, the rain, the snow, the air we breathe") act as mediators between the actors. These passages are worth quoting in full:

It is about inviting in all the actors and then mediating between them through the elemental, vital components that you see in the film—the wind, the rain, the snow, the air we breathe—and those very things that animate the stage of being. To do that you have to clear the stage and then invite each actor back onto it. . . . And in doing so, the idea was to then speak to them each individually by inviting them to come on to the cleared stage, to take up a screen. At some point, you are not in control of this process. I am not even the conductor of this at a certain point. I am just one of the players in this drama of becoming. But what I am able to do is to try to tease out each layer of the film by forcing it to just engage with the other, you know, and slowly something called *Purple* emerges.

. . . [O]ne of the things that I knew we were trying to do . . . was to sequestrate or appropriate layers—both of time and space—so in the film I am commandeering people and ideas—literally, in a legal sense—to come to the "court" of a narrative. And those are either chapters in the post-war unfolding of industrialisation, chapters to do with accidents, independencies of different kinds . . . , individual chapters . . . ; all of which remain unique, they are all separate, they are all individual and are usually quite reluctant to come together on a single-screen, or even in a three-screen film. And the more you multiply the screens the more reluctant they are to talk, especially to you or to each other. So you literally have to sequestrate them, you have to slap a writ at their door saying, you know you are wanted; you are needed here! And they come reluctantly. So there's no logical dialogue between storms and people shopping, for example, but there can be one, if you force them. And that's what I mean by the sequestrations: you have to force them to engage with each other; and literally in this space of montage where things are being forced to clash with each other, something starts to merge. Now I don't know in advance of that what will emerge, but once I smell it, we're off. So the works start in effect at that moment of sequestration and convergence, when these screens are forced to have this dialogue with and amongst themselves. . . . As I sequestrate these images to orchestrate this new fugue, this film called *Purple*, I want them to bear the trace of what they once were and their innate autonomy. The idea of the multi-screen is precisely that: that you would allow these multiple agents to have agency and have it in a way that suggests that things can make sense.[29]

Montage materializes the new-materialist premise that humans and nonhumans are interdependent, that they both are sources of action, and that humans and nonhumans are "actants" who have enough coherence to change "the course of events."[30] Interdependence or relationality, as the new-materialist philosopher Rebekah Sheldon claims, "begins from the assumption that ideas and things do not occupy separate ontological orders but instead are co-constituents in the production of the real. . . . Matter draws together what appears separate and makes the totality subject to mutation and emergence."[31] The installations' new materialism is best comprehended in light of the work of the political theorist Jane Bennett, especially her consideration of vitality as intrinsic to matter—that is, as the capacity of nonhuman things or beings (storms, nonhuman animals, artifacts, commodities) to act as agents or quasi-agents, to hinder, complicate, or reorient human thought-out designs.[32] More importantly for our argument here is Bennett's view that the relationality of human and nonhuman actants is a "safety net" for humans who are unaccounted for or socially excluded. Relationality requires that we treat them "more carefully, more strategically, more ecologically" insofar as actants never act alone.[33] Montage can therefore be explored, as it is in Akomfrah's work, as a technique that will enable and disclose the association of humans (damaged beings: slaves, displaced people, the Herero people, politicians, and observers; as well as damaging beings: hunters and fishermen involved in industrial fishing and hunting, politicians gone wrong, murderers, the military brutalizing the people) and nonhumans (the sea, the desert, elephants and whales, slave ships, fishing ships and migrant boats, electric pylons, and the nuclear bomb) coacting, coshaping, and coexisting within the stage of history. This coexistence is about complexifying historical consciousness; it is about inviting the viewer to risk historical consciousness, dismantling history in that very process—history as "the discourse through which the West has asserted its hegemony over the rest of the world."[34]

One might want to distinguish between actors and agents, as Katherine Hayles proposes in her study on what she calls the "cognitive nonconscious," keeping the term *actors* for "cognizers" because of their capacity to choose, interpret, and decide and reserving the term *agents* "for material forces and objects . . . that may be harnessed to perform cognitive tasks when suitable constraints are introduced."[35] Be they actors or agents, they are equally invited onto the stage of acting and being. Also note how the actors are mostly beings that have been injured, brutalized, or destroyed, but the artist's invitations are bringing the perpetrators in as well. Let us not forget, finally, that although the installations are associating images of actors, the images themselves are agents. The montaged archival footage that refers to beings who have disappeared or are about to disappear is what provides "immortality" to these beings.[36] "This act of using the images," explains Akomfrah, "is part of an act of exhumation for people who will never be exhumed practically, literally again. They are gone. . . . Something has gone, and I want to have now a language of mourning and elegy, which is not just a poetic language but has a certain political efficacy and part of that political efficacy is to say to power, 'You thought they disappeared, well think again, 'cause they're back.'"[37] Montage as coexistence, following new materialism's search for life and the living, is ultimately "a politics of the living . . . beyond humanism," to paraphrase Mbembe, that serves as a counterforce to necropolitics.[38]

MONTAGE'S NONLINEAR DISCLOSURE OF COLONIAL PRESENCE

The conception of montage as a practice of coexistence of actors and agents is first and foremost a historical endeavor. The multichannel installations situate present-day migration and environmental degradation within the longer history of modernity, which has been shaped by the damaging impulses of imperialism, colonialism, the transatlantic slave trade, industrialization, resource capitalism, and technological development. In a discussion with the curator Rudolf Frieling, Akomfrah insists on the need to confront amnesia, which is fundamentally a license to forget the past and misunderstand contemporary migration: "I was compelled to make *Vertigo Sea* because you are sitting there listening to someone refer to migrants as cockroaches. And you think, what is going on here? How do people migrate from being humans to cockroaches? What do you have to forget? What is the process of amnesia that allows the kinds of forgetting that builds into hierarchies in which there are beings and nonbeings?"[39] Elsewhere he has stated: "We act as though the current refugee crisis is an isolated incident, . . . but actually flight and migration [have] defined modernity since the 14th century."[40]

Montage, then, brings the migrating undervalued beings of the twenty-first century onto the historical stage of being and acting. In so doing, it breaks with history as the grand narrative through which European modernity and conquest of the Americas are totalized as the accurate account of all humanity; it makes the unaccounted beings coexist with other actors and agents on the destructive stage of modernity—a stage that also makes room for the beauty of nature and mediates historically conscious humans, showing them to be interdependent. Akomfrah's historical accounts look back in time to reveal, address, and confront today's injustices, but they are more conclusively forward-looking. In looking both backward and forward, what does montage become if not a means of disclosure of the colonial present, what Derek Gregory has described as "the constellations of power, knowledge, and geography that . . . continue to colonize lives all over the world."[41] But what does this persistence of the "colonial" consist of? As a reminder, when referring to colonialism, I essentially rely on Margaret Kohn's broad definition of it as "a practice of domination, which involves the subjugation of one people to another" and her more precise definition of it as "the process of European settlement and political control over the rest of the world, including the Americas, Australia, and parts of Africa and Asia."[42] As emphasized in Akomfrah's work, such a process involves and is sustained by a variety of genocidal practices and ruthless procedures of enslavement and environmental devastation; it depends on what Tiffany Lethabo King designates as "the most violent forms of Black and Indigenous death,"[43] to which must be added nonhuman wild-animal death.

The historian-anthropologist Ann Laura Stoler has further refined that terminology by speaking of the *colonial histories of the present* and *colonial presence*, in which colonial histories of the past persist, "despite having been so concertedly effaced," as they yield new damages and disparities; in this historical present, "the vestiges of colonial constructions" are nevertheless difficult to perceive, identify, and verify insofar as colonial structures and forms evolve, change, and become obscure as they are transformed.[44] Montage, as an invitation, a sequestration, and a conversational modality, is ultimately best understood as a method that enables that perception. Stoler insists on the "tenacious presence" of the colonial subjugation of one people over another as never consisting simply in a reemergence of earlier forms of colonialism. This is to say that the historical present is a *re*fashioning of the old, an oblique and "strange" reworking of colonial histories. Colonial pasts "are sometimes so ineffably threaded through the fabric of contemporary life forms they seem indiscernible as distinct effects, as if everywhere and nowhere at all," and yet they remain not merely as haunting traces but as durable fissures, renewed and easily unperceived.[45] Stoler explores the analytical concept of "duress" to capture the tenacity of colonial effects, their prolonged temporalities, the durability of their constraints and confinements, as well as their capacity to last and damage in this endurance.[46] Her call "to train our senses beyond the more easily identifiable forms"[47] of resilient colonialities can be understood—and this is how I understand it—as a call for art in which aesthetics becomes political in its *re*distribution of the sensible. For, if we are to extrapolate on Stoler's claim, it is our (the viewers' living in ill-declared hosting countries) very inability to perceive subjugation, our very incapacity or unwillingness to comprehend it as authorizing the death and injury of migrating beings, that consolidates the renewal of colonialism.

WHY AND HOW DOES ART MATTER?

Akomfrah's historical call relies on montage's capacity to make images and things coexist. It unlearns the alleged European refugee crisis by revealing it as a prolongation of the intertwined necropolitical forces of modernity and by imagining its possible reversal. Put differently: art matters! At three levels, at least.

First, as mentioned earlier, Stoler's plea that we "train our senses beyond the more easily identifiable forms" of resilient colonialities can be assumed as a plea for art in which aesthetics becomes particularly political in its *re*distribution of the sensible. Akomfrah's montaged coexistences are a training of our senses that is not about imposing but about proposing and suggesting. Coexistence goes as follows: the artist invites a set of unconsidered, injured, destroyed, but also destroying actors and agents on the stage of history and asks, "Who should be on that stage acting and being—who populates this stage?"[48] If, indeed, colonial presence, as Stoler convincingly claims, is not what and where we expect it to be, vital-materialist speculation must be part of the artist-as-historian's activity. In Akomfrah's trilogy, it involves linking a flow of images pertaining to the dark side of modernity: images of the mass killing of whales and elephants; endangered migrating beings; the disappearing Herero people; slave ships, slave murderers, and the enslaved Africans of the transatlantic trade; the sea and the desert transformed into hostile environments; nuclear testing; politicians and the military gone wrong. In *Vertigo Sea* and *Four Nocturnes*, in particular, migration is shown as mobilized by these destructions and destructive forces—a legacy that is largely underacknowledged in the historical present and whose underacknowledgment contributes to its recursion in the current conditions of migration. But the montages always include more luminous coexistences: accounts by writers and philosophers as well as a series of silent observers (including Olaudah Equiano in *Vertigo Sea* and the wanderers in *Four Nocturnes*). An invitation is always a question addressed to viewers. It asks: How is our comprehension of the historical present enriched by the integration of specific undervalued actors and agents of modernity? The stage of history can always be reopened by other actors and agents, whose disclosed coexistence might complexify anew our perspective of colonial presence. Imperative here are the associations and proximities enabling us, viewers, to perceive—to navigate, to make our way through—the predicaments of the twenty-first century, predicaments that are not easily perceivable or that we too easily dismiss as though we have nothing to do with their unfolding, namely migration as one of the main necropolitical practices of our time.

Second, Akomfrah's trilogy highlights a constant in artistic practices unlearning present-day migration: not one single artwork does not include necropolitics—governance through death- and injury-sustaining colonialist presence—as a central dimension of that predicament. In Akomfrah's multiscreen installations, death and the dying are everywhere, as are beings kept alive in a state of injury. Yet his works never abandon the possibility of life beyond or in the cracks of necropolitics. The chapter's epigraph is telling in that regard: "As opposites have conversations," says Akomfrah, "or as they are persuaded to at least potentially sit at the table in preparation for conversation, something miraculous happens, . . . [l]ife itself happens."[49] Life "happens" in the revival of archives that have memorialized disappeared and disappearing beings. Life also "happens" in the renewal of actors and agents coexisting on the stage of being and acting, in the renewed understanding of what the colonial present consists in. Life "happens" in all of the observing beings (including Olaudah Equiano, the *Four Nocturnes*' wanderers, the viewers of the installations) looking at, thinking about, becoming historically conscious of, and making time to meditate on the devastations of their worlds. To give a better sense of what this entails, let us briefly consider here three works that are particularly insightful in their capacity to make life "happen" despite and within necropolitics: Christina Sharpe's breathtaking book *In the Wake* and two compelling artworks by Binta Diaw.

In her publication *In the Wake: On Blackness and Being* (2016), Christina Sharpe, scholar of English literature and Black studies, situates twenty-first-century migration as an extension of the histories of modern colonialism and Atlantic chattel slavery, but her writing project is ultimately a call for survival, for slavery's afterlives, and for the possibility of finding new ways of living "in the wake of slavery":

Living in the wake on a global level means living the disastrous time and effects of continued marked migrations, Mediterranean and Caribbean disasters, trans-American and -African migration, structural adjustment imposed by the International Monetary Fund that continues imperialisms/colonialisms, and more. . . . [T]hose Black people transmigrating the African continent toward the Mediterranean and then to Europe . . . are imagined as insects, swarms, vectors of disease. . . .

[W]e join the wake with work in order that we might make the wake and *wake work* our analytic, we might continue to imagine new ways to live in the wake of slavery, in slavery's afterlives, to survive (and more) the afterlife of property. In short, I mean wake work to be a mode of inhabiting *and* rupturing this episteme with our known lived and un/imaginable lives. With that analytic we might imagine otherwise from what we know *now* in the wake of slavery.[50]

Sharpe's call is specifically a belief in the possibility of life in a historical present still significantly conditioned by the history of the slave trade, which persists while being transformed by twentieth-century migration. Mobilized by historical consciousness, the belief in life and afterlife is easily perturbed by the persistence of necropolitics, but it stands despite that persistence; it unlearns it. Two works by the Milan-based Senegalese Italian artist Binta Diaw (b. 1995) share a similar historical call. Diaw's *Chorus of Soil* (2019), an installation made of soil and melon seeds installed directly on the gallery floor, is a large-scale reproduction of an eighteenth-century slave ship plan. It both recalls Atlantic chattel slavery and resonates with contemporary boat migration, providing an image of colonial presence (figure 2.8). Particularly relevant to our discussion, the installation enables the emergence of life: new buds grow from the soil inside the slave ship (figure 2.9). Diaw's *Chorus of Zong* (2020) similarly discloses the possibility of life despite, within, and in response to migration—this renewed occurrence of colonial presence. The audio work consists in a polyphonic choir of young African Italians, whose interconnecting voices evolve amid the sound of water. The chorus recites verses written by the poet M. NourbeSe Philip compiled in her poetry collection *Zong!* (2008), in which she gives voice to the slaves thrown into the Atlantic Ocean during the Zong massacre of 1781. More specifically, *Zong! #14* states:

the truth was

the ship sailed

the rains came

the loss arose

the truth is

the ship sailed

the rains came

the loss arose

the negroes is

the truth was.[51]

As in *Chorus of Soil*, the historical past is recalled (the Zong massacre is also referred to in Akomfrah's *Vertigo Sea* and Sharpe's publication), but recollection becomes the means by which young African Italians establish a dialogue—a coexistence—with the voices of their ancestors to find their own identity.[52] Brought together as companions, Afomkrah's, Sharpe's, and Diaw's works show how art and literature respond to migration by aesthetically inventing calls to historicize: coexistence becomes an aesthetic strategy that endeavors to disclose the imprint of the historical past on the historical present *and* to acknowledge the autonomy of migration; it also articulates the possibility of historical change.

Third and last, Akomfrah's installations ecologize and environmentalize history. His montage practice unravels colonial presence as an intertwinement between necropolitical migration and environmental degradation (climate change, the loss of biodiversity, and the earth's sixth mass extinction). Beyond the more

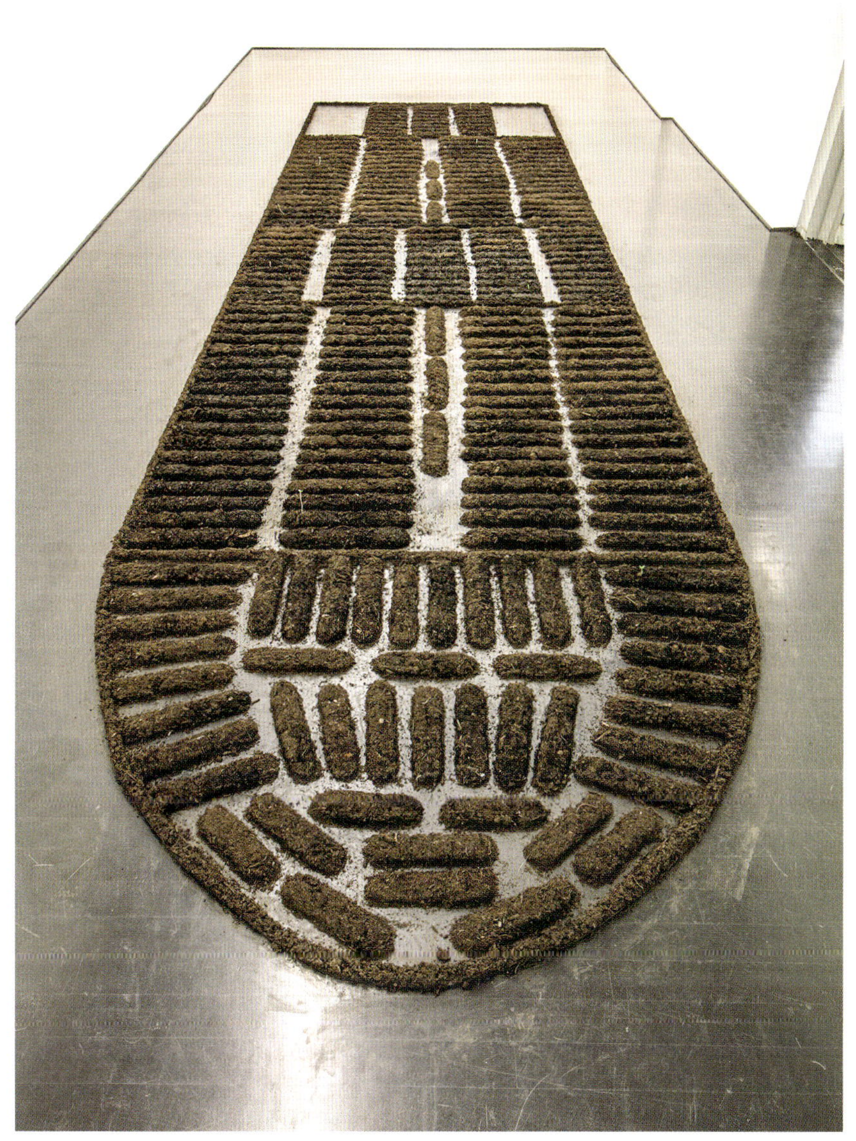

FIGURE 2.8

Binta Diaw, *Chorus of Soil*, 2019. Installation, soil, melon seeds. 27½ × 1 × 94½ in. (700 × 2.5 × 240 cm). Installation view: Galleria Giampaolo Abbondio, Milan, Italy. Photo: Antonio Maniscalco. Courtesy of the artist.

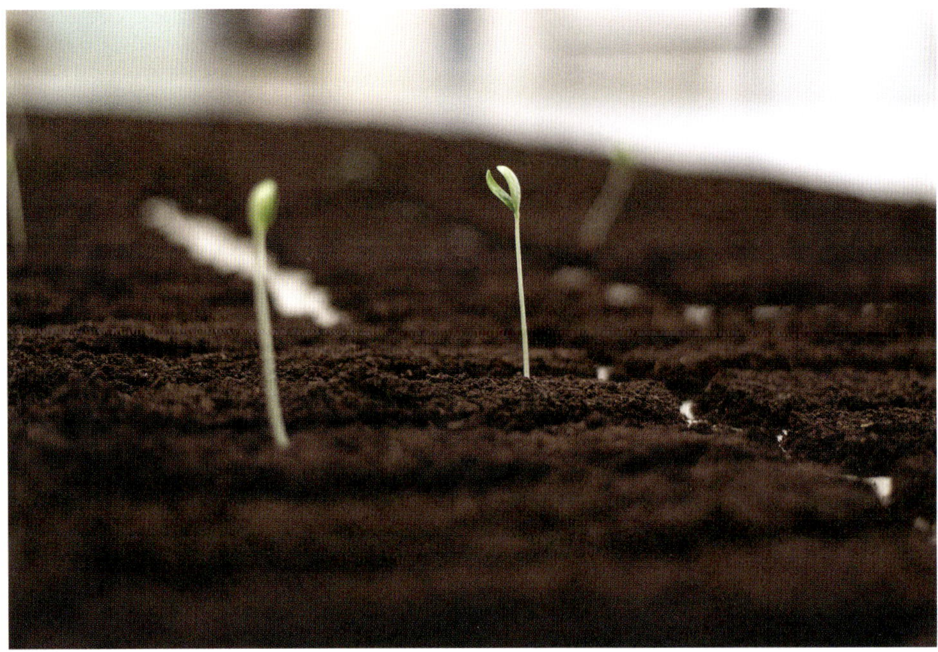

obvious comprehension of that intertwinement—the twenty-first-century prolifer-ation of climate migrants—his trilogy is more about disclosing the common thread connecting the two predicaments: mainly, their turning of milieus into "space[s] of death" as well as the possibilities of life within these spaces.[53]

Let us push this conclusion a bit further. In an interview about racism in 2020, the artist explains his environmental view of racism in the following terms: "Rac-ism isn't some self-contained gesture; it impacts and explodes and takes all kinds of forms and shapes *in environments. And it creates environments*. So, the idea that

FIGURE 2.9

Binta Diaw. *Chorus of Soil*, 2019, close-up of the melon plant emerging from the soil. Installation, soil, melon seeds. 27½ × 1 × 94½ in. (700 × 2.5 × 240 cm). Shown at SAVVY Contemporary, Berlin. Photo: Raisa Galofre. Courtesy of the artist.

environmentalist discourse should be alien to Black people is like, well, sorry: you haven't been listening. Slavery took place on plantations. They weren't just businesses, they were environments, agricultural spaces. . . . You need the optics of space and environment and climate to fully grasp its totality."[54] What constitutes an "environment"? In its etymological progression, the term *environment* has come to designate "contour," "what is around," and "what surrounds" but also "the state of being environed" and "the action of surrounding," suggesting that while the environment is mostly "what surrounds us," it is also a movement and an action.[55] To these attributes must be added responsiveness—an attribute that recent social sciences and environmental humanities have identified as pertaining both to living organisms who draw from their milieu the resources necessary for their survival, not by simply adapting to them but by creating their own environment, and to milieus transformed by these actions.[56] The notion of the environment finds its full potential once it is recognized that it is a *living* milieu and that, although the possibilities of an organism's adaptation to its milieu are not infinite, the milieu does not impose solutions: rather, organisms propose diverse solutions "to a same problem raised by a milieu."[57] In light of that definition, it is now possible to understand Akomfrah's montage practice as environmental as much as it is historical. The two notions are inseparable in his work. Montage invites actors (the enslaved, migrating beings, whales, elephants) within damaging environments (the sea, ice, the desert, fire, the slave ship, the migrating boat, the whale ship, the whaling industry, wars, genocides, mass hunting of nonhuman animals), as victims but also as political subjects capable of dissensus. It is also the case that the trilogy turns natural environments—the sea in *Vertigo Sea*, the different landscapes in *Purple*, the desert in *Four Nocturnes*—into large multiscreen environments that include viewers. A multichannel installation that works as an environment from within and from without is one that is conceived as a milieu seeking coexistence. As insightfully formulated by the philosopher John Durham Peters, human-made technologies are media, but the elements are media as well: they are "containers of possibility that anchor our existence and make what we are doing possible[,] . . . invit[ing] us to think of media as environmental, as part of the habitat, and not just as semiotic inputs."[58] Such is the becoming-environment of art as it calls for the historicization of contemporary migration.

RESPONSIBILITY

Part II focuses on three artworks: Richard Mosse's *Incoming* (2014–2017), Forensic Oceanography's *Liquid Traces—the Left-to-Die Boat Case* (2014), and Teresa Margolles's *La promesa* (2012). These works share a similar concern for the endangering of migrant lives in borderzones—not only areas that include borderlines but also the expanses immediately adjacent to those lines. Border zones extend farther inside and farther outside the borders of given countries on either side of their international lines. The delimitation of borderlands enables state authorities to enhance their security operations beyond but also deeper into their territory; it also allows them to externalize these operations into nearby countries or states.[1] Borderlands encompass waiting zones and camps as well as border cities. In the EU, the creation of border-zone agreements between states intensified particularly following the Schengen Agreement of 1985—a treaty that officialized the abolishment of most national borders within Europe (including almost all EU member states as well as all of the European Free Trade Association member states and European microstates)—to compensate for that dissolution. More and more since the mid-2000s, these areas have become the most hazardous spaces for citizens-on-the-move insofar as extortion, kidnapping, physical and sexual assault, human trafficking, detention, deportation, refoulement, and dying are always a likely possibility. As the sociologist Özgün E. Topak maintains in his study of the Frontex-facilitated control of the Greece–Turkey border (the main border of "irregular" entry into the EU), "While borders are diffusing beyond and inside state territories, their practices and effects are concentrated at the edges of state territories—i.e., borderzones":

these zones are highly surveilled biopolitical expanses in which "migrants suffer the direct threat of injury and death," in firm violation of the Universal Declaration of Human Rights of 1948 and the UN Refugee Convention of 1951.[2] Yet studies (including Topak's) show that despite these necropolitical conditions people continue to attempt to cross the borderzones of Europe and North America, including environmentally hostile terrains (the Mediterranean Sea, the Sonoran Desert), risking their lives in that very process. Cities grow within and close to these zones, endangering the lives of urban residents as well.

The works analyzed in part II have already been reviewed elsewhere, although the literature is far from abundant, except for the material on Mosse's installation, which is extensive and controversial. These reviews have focused mainly on the works' representation of migration; they predominantly fail to historicize what is actually being represented and fall short of examining how art reinvents itself as it strives to represent the dangerous territories of migration. This part's objective is to investigate the artworks' call for responsibility as a response to borderzones. Responsibility is not only a call for accountability and liability against impunity but also a call addressed to the viewers asking that they act connectively and collectively against migratory injustices. As European and North American citizens, they are interpellated as participating in these injustices even if they haven't directly caused them. The call for responsibility is a practice of coexistence: it establishes that necropolitics is an interdependence between some of the poorest and some of the wealthiest nations in the world; it is also based on the premise that migrating beings cannot be held solely responsible for their necropolitical exclusion and elimination.

What types of responsibility are these works invoking? What, when, and why is responsibility? Whose responsibility is being called for? How is art refashioning itself in light of the imperative to become responsible? Are aesthetics and responsibility compatible? Addressing these questions, part II's main claim is that artistic practices unlearning migration bring the question of responsibility to the fore not only in the making but also in the reception of art; they are a call for responsibility addressed mainly (yet, again, not exclusively) to viewers and state authorities of rich democracies where they are predominantly being exhibited; they formulate responsibility as a coexistence—as a blaming or an imperative to become aware of Europe's and North America's role in the unfolding of migration as well as an imperative to act collectively in making migration more just. There lies their inventiveness: these practices materialize aesthetic strategies to responsibilize spectators qua citizens, including thermovision, forensics, and care. Such a call, as we will see, has its failures, semi-failures, and successes; and responsibilization is certainly a difficult task; one never knows if the viewer will indeed assume responsibility or not. But suffice it to say that these outcomes do not prevent the works from formulating calls for responsibility.

The conception of art as a responsible practice has been unambiguously affirmed by John Akomfrah in a statement briefly considered at the beginning of chapter 2. His statement specifies that artists must attempt to respond to the main predicaments of their time. The essayist, novelist, playwright, poet, and activist James Baldwin designated responsibility—in the context of the civil rights movement and the gay liberation movement of the 1960s and 1970s as well as in the context of his own engagement against racist oppression—as a practice that makes us "recognize that there is nothing under heaven—no creed, and no flag, and no cause, more important, than a single human life."[3] Following these generous definitions, this book's assumption is that most artistic practices responding to the necropolitics of migration are responsible, and this is already a significant achievement. But the artworks included in part II are also investigating responsibility as a call addressed to the viewer; they are changing aesthetics in that very call. This critical reorientation of art needs to be cautiously investigated. The work of the political and feminist theorist Iris Marion Young on the backward-looking and forward-looking models of responsibility are central to this investigation, especially her forward-looking social connection model of responsibility, which posits that all beings participating in structures of injustice share the political responsibility to jointly struggle against them. As a variant of the social connection model, the field of care studies will progressively make its way into our inquiry, especially in the analysis of Margolles's sculptural works, which associate responsibility with collective care and raise the fundamental question: How to care?

SEARCHING FOR RESPONSIBILITY

This chapter ponders *Incoming* (2014–2017), a three-channel documentary video installation by the Irish artist Richard Mosse (b. 1980, Kilkenny, Ireland). The installation is fully dedicated to the exposure of borderzones as they evolved during the so-called European refugee crisis in the mid-2010s. It captures them along two major routes, from Africa and from western and central Asia to Europe (Turkey, Greece, and France), disclosing them as sites of convergence of humanitarian rescue, migrant management, surveillance, and securitization. Grippingly, it observes these processes using a thermal camera—a surveillance technology used for the tracking of migrants but remodeled here to uncover the hidden world of border areas. In contrast to Forensic Oceanography, discussed in the next chapter, whose work *Liquid Traces—the Left-to-Die Boat Case* (2014) also repurposes surveillance technologies but refuses to make "clandestine migrants" visible, *Incoming* makes them visible but uses a surveillance technology that doesn't make them recognizable. In both works, the repurposing procedure invites the viewer—let us follow once more James Baldwin's speech on the responsibility of the artist—to "see reality *again*"[1] by showing the invisible operations of migration while opacifying the visibility of the surveilled. But in *Incoming* the aesthetic strategy is explored mainly to invite viewers to consider their own responsibility as citizens in the perpetuation of the alienating conditions of migration. Mosse has been rather explicit about that ambition. This is how he voiced his plea for *accountability* and *responsibility* (terms he uses interchangeably, together with *complicity*) in an interview held in the context of the National Gallery of Victoria Triennial (Melbourne, Australia), where his work was shown in 2017–2018:

The targeting and killing of the world's most vulnerable people, refugees, particularly when crossing international boundaries, is an outrageous criminal violation of international human rights law. Yet we turn the blind eye. . . . A central point of tension in this body of work is complicity: my own complicity, as a citizen of a European nation, and by extension that of a Western viewer of the work. Without knowing you, reader of this book and the viewer of the work, it's quite probable that you, like me, are a citizen of a relatively affluent nation that has ratified the 1948 Universal Declaration of Human Rights and the 1951 Refugee Convention. . . . If so, then both of us, as citizens, are responsible for the societies in which we live and for the governments that we elect and are accountable for the ways in which our nations fail the people who flee violence and seek safety in our prosperous homelands. As a documentary photographer, I have chosen to try to convey these narratives of human displacement, and the ways in which governments fail these people, but to do so in a way that discloses our complicity, that doesn't let us off the hook, which I hope will allow us to apprehend our own complicity in the suffering of these people who we have failed.[2]

The statement clarifies Mosse's call for responsibility. That call is first and foremost a disclosure: the work reveals the vulnerability of people as they attempt to cross borders in search of shelter and safety. But disclosure here is not simply a matter of representing fragilized beings; it is, more importantly, a matter of holding governments and, more significantly, viewers supporting these governments accountable for that vulnerabilization—an endangerment perpetuated in strict violation of the Universal Declaration of Human Rights of 1948 and the UN Refugee Convention of 1951. *Incoming* wants to show that the fates of both citizens fleeing Africa or Asia to reach Europe and citizens of the EU (in fact, any citizen belonging to the wealthiest countries that are migrant destinations in the world) are deeply interdependent; that they exist in relation to one another—the latter ensuring its existence as it negates the former; and that such a dark coexistence could be progressively undone if viewers became aware of their responsibility in the comaking of borderzones. The statement allows us to raise a series of questions pertaining to coexistence. How is Mosse's concern for the responsibility of citizens of countries of destination palpable in *Incoming*? How does the work responsibilize viewers or invite them to become responsible? What is gained and lost in the process of responsibilization? What is responsibility?

This chapter's main postulate is that *Incoming*'s call for responsibility is activated by a unique (historically accurate) disclosure of the necropolitical management of migration. It relies substantively on the thermal rendering of images to articulate that call, yet the use of the thermographic camera makes the call deliberately ambivalent: repurposed, the camera captures images of migration management but it also participates in that management—it persists in tracking, silencing, and visually distorting the bodies it captures. In so doing, it activates a tightrope between denouncing and perpetuating borderzones so as to invite the viewers' questioning of their own role in the evolution of necropolitical migration. The thermographic disclosure is, to paraphrase a notion central to Bernard Stiegler's philosophical study of technology, a *pharmakon*-disclosure: it works both as remedy and poison. Explaining how technologies and techniques are *pharmaka*, Stiegler writes: "Any technique is a *pharmakon*, that is any technique can be used either to build, elaborate, heighten the world or to destroy it. . . . The knife, more precisely a carved flintstone, is the first human-made technical object: it serves to kill as well as to build."[3] To favor the positive (therapeutical and pharmacological) side of the pharmakon, he proposes care as a political responsibility—caring for the other, self-care, caring for the planet, healing (*panser*) as partaking of thinking and meditating (*penser*).

This specification helps us refine the chapter's claim: although *Incoming* certainly succeeds in making the viewer cognizant of the role of some of the wealthiest economies and democracies worldwide in the proliferation of borderzones, it thermographs what it seeks to rescue, preserving the surveillance management of migration in that very process so that cognition be transformed into responsibility: as viewers, we can't simply detach ourselves from the apparatus that makes us see what and how we see; we are part of the dark coexistence being denounced. Concomitantly, however, the victims are revictimized to substantiate that denunciation. Such is *Incoming*'s pharmakon: it is both remedy (it reveals migratory injustice) *and* poison (it prolongs migratory injustice). The revictimizing of victims is a problem that remains unresolved. It must therefore be addressed. But let us push this claim a bit further. I want to argue that *Incoming* wants to make this ambivalence less unavoidable; it wants to start repairing the ambivalence: it uses thermovision as a presence detector and not an identification detector. In so doing, it protects the identity of the beings under surveillance; moreover, the images that the thermovision produces have been slowed down so that we are invited to meditate on what it lets us see. Put differently, the technology partakes of a Stieglerian ethics and politics of care: that endeavor is rather inventive but still falls short of solving the problem of revictimizing victims for the sake of calling for responsibility. I want to stay as close as possible to that knot. Why? Because the work brilliantly reveals the challenges intrinsic to the call for responsibility—its potential and its limits. It also qualifies us to start thinking about responsibility as care.

To elucidate *Incoming*'s call for responsibility, the chapter first situates it within the context of the humanitarian–securitization shift that occurred in EU border-zones at the peak of the "European refugee crisis." It then proceeds to examine the installation as well as the thermal technology explored by Mosse to expose that shift. These different steps will lead us to the assessment of the work's paradoxical pharmakon-disclosure of borderzones. This investigation will take the form of a dialogue among the installation, political philosophy (notably the work of Sabine Hess, Bernd Kasparek, Jacques Rancière, Hannah Arendt, and Giorgio Agamben), responsibility studies (Roger Silverstone, Gayatri Chakravorty Spivak, and Iris Marion Young), as well as other relevant migratory artworks by other artists (Ursula Biemann, Chantal Akerman, Laura Waddington, and Florian Schneider). These studies and artworks will help clarify the notion and practice of responsibility and responsible care, teasing out the requirement to acknowledge the autonomy of migration, even in borderzones where that autonomy has been substantially incapacitated.

THE TWENTY-FIRST-CENTURY EUROPEAN MIGRATION AND BORDER REGIME

In two pivotal articles published in 2017 and 2019, the anthropologists Sabine Hess and Bernd Kasparek established that 2015—the year corresponding to what has from thereon been called the height of the "refugee crisis" or the "European refugee crisis"—was a determining moment in the evolution of the EU's migration and border regime: that regime was destabilized by the increase in a quantitatively and qualitatively new type of migration; it literally collapsed but was quickly albeit temporarily restabilized and redefined.[4] The EU border regime had already been defied by the events of the Arab Spring of 2011: the downfall of the dictatorships in Tunisia and Libya had de facto abolished the central Mediterranean border regime based on the delegation of the EU practices of migration containment to these countries. However, the regime's destabilization and restabilization in 2015–2016 was far more complex and enduring. Hess and Kasparek's fieldwork in Turkey, Greece,

Macedonia, Serbia, and Hungary in 2016 reveals unforeseen methods of governing and managing migration, "aimed at reasserting control, and introducing new infrastructural materialities, administrative processes, institutional cooperations, legal innovations, reconfigurations of sovereignty and spatial practices that we could then trace from our field sites into the emerging policy proposals on the level of the various institutions of the EU."[5] This new system of governance and administration includes several procedures, four of which are particularly salient: the externalization and multiplication of borders, the transformation of routes of migration into corridors, campization, and the development of a hybrid humanitarian-military approach to migration. It is crucial to keep in mind, however, that these procedures were and will always be unstable, open as they are to new migration movements.

The externalization and multiplication of borders. This process was already active before 2015 but to a lesser degree; its main goal has been to (re)locate border controls not only at the border but also away from the border, farther inside and outside member states. Étienne Balibar described this proliferation, heterogeneity, and growing ubiquity in his famous article "What Is a Border?" (2002) in the following terms: "the tendency of borders, political, cultural and socioeconomic, to coincide—something which was more or less well achieved by nation-states, or, rather, by some of them—is tending today to fall apart. The result of this is that *some borders are no longer situated at the borders at all*, in the geographico-politico administrative sense of the term. They are in fact elsewhere. Wherever selective controls are to be found, such as, for example, *health* or *security* checks (health checks being part of what Michel Foucault termed bio-power)."[6] The EU increasingly applied this extension of the border beyond the borderline after 2015 to reinforce its migration and border regime.

The creation of corridors. Migration routes previously outlined by the movement of migrating beings were transformed into corridors whose main modus operandi is to control that movement. This transformation was a critical answer to the Schengen Agreements of 1985 and 1990, which had abolished internal border controls in the EU while still maintaining the protection of international borders through police cooperation.[7] The corridor—an example of "the proposed declaration of specific parts of Europe's external borders as 'hotspots' and the shift of sovereignty toward centralised European institutions legitimated through these denominations"—was conceived as a highly organized infrastructure of transit to orient the movement of migrants. Its primary architectural features were and remain not only walls and fences but also the transit camp (i.e., hot spots) "geared towards processing migrants as fast as possible, as well as [engaging] the connecting lines of transport."[8] The confined corridor, an infrastructure that *Incoming* incessantly exposes in all of its different materializations, is fundamentally a channeling of movement that paradoxically enables the movement of migrating populations by restricting and managing them:

[T]he corridor turned the active movement of people, which had constituted the route in the first place, back into a passive mechanism of being transferred. Migrants didn't travel the route anymore; they were hurriedly channeled along, no longer having the power to either determine their own movement or their own speed. One thoroughly consistent testimony from migrants is heard in many places along this corridor. Asked why they do not leave the corridor and pursue an alternative path, the answer is that if you leave the flow, you are lost. Outside the corridor, you are subject to the regime of asylum, detention, and deportation. Only inside the corridor, you are allowed to move.[9]

This is to say that the corridor is itself a pharmakon: a paradoxical mechanism of control *and* protection.

Campization. The transformation of the movement of migrating beings into a passive procedure of "being transferred" from one place to another was reinforced by the building of camplike infrastructures, which expanded and continue to expand throughout the EU, in order to facilitate the control and immobilization of citizens-on-the-move.[10] The urban researcher René Kreichauf coined the term *campization* to describe these new accommodation infrastructures, which I discuss further in my examination of Mosse's work in this chapter. Suffice it to say for now that the camp is a site of management, whose main effect is to temporarily halt the movement of refugees and delineate a space that separates them from the outside world.

The emergence of the humanitarian-military complex. Since 2015, corridor-like and camplike infrastructures have been orchestrated by a humanitarian-military management approach "where military forces are deployed under a humanitarian rationale" to protect migrating individuals while policing them and reinforcing the securitization of borderzones.[11]

All of these procedures are indicative of the new governance and management methods that have come to characterize the European migration and border regime since 2015, methods that nevertheless always require renewal and reinforcement in response to the movements of migration that persistently contest them.

But they are likewise indicative of the tenaciousness of colonialism: they refashion colonial presence. Colonial practices have persistently involved restricting the mobility of the colonized while facilitating the mobility of the colonizers. The reinforcement of borders, campization, and the corridorization of the movement of non-European racially marked "others" partake of that divide by selecting who has and who does not have access to the purported universal mobility of twentieth- and twenty-first-century globalization. These procedures establish a special interdependence: citizens of some of the richest economies in the world have significantly gained greater mobility not only to the detriment of citizens of some of the less privileged parts of Africa, Asia, and Latin America but mainly because of their capacity to restrict the latter's movement.[12] The restabilization of the European migration and border regime, subject as it is to new forms of destabilization and restabilization as a response to the continual movements of migration, is the world documented in *Incoming*. It is therefore in light of that historical shift that the work must be—and has surprisingly not been—examined. I get back to Hess and Kasparek's findings later to discuss their theoretical and methodological implications. That discussion will provide analytical tools to refine our analysis of *Incoming*'s call for responsibility. But now let us take a moment to look at the work.

INCOMING: THE WORK

Mosse's *Incoming*, made in collaboration with the cinematographer Trevor Tweeten and the electronic composer Ben Frost, consists in a grayscale (black, white, and gray) three-channel HD video installation with 7.1 surround sound, running 52 minutes (figure 3.1). It was initially shown in the Barbican's Curve Gallery in London in 2017 and has been circulating in Europe, Australia, and the United States ever since. The images were captured by a military-grade thermal surveillance camera used mainly for long-range border enforcement; they could be taken more than 30 kilometers away from their subjects. The thermal camera measures the vitality of human bodies as heat, which translates as dark in the installation: it is a presence detector rather than an identity detector—which means that we can't recognize the beings being captured, who exist more as evolving bodies than as specific individuals. The image speed has been slowed down from 60 frames to 24 frames per second to facilitate a meditative observation of the bodies.

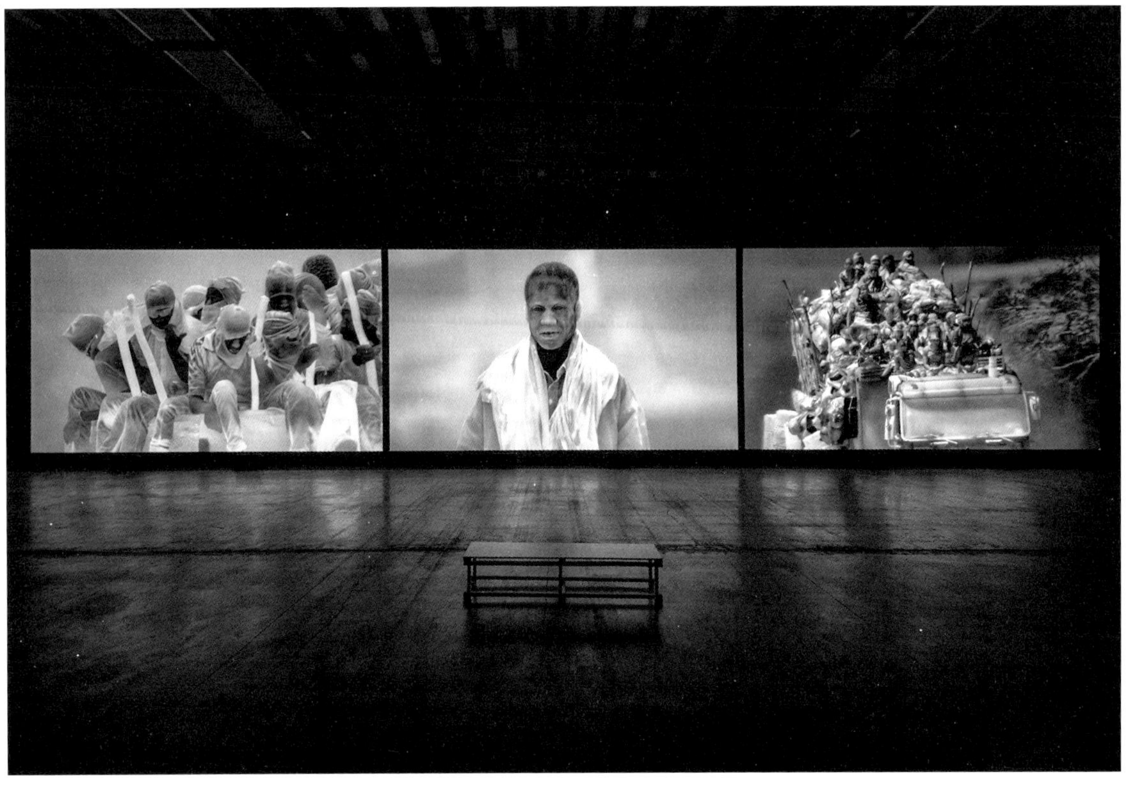

Richard Mosse, in collaboration with Trevor Tweeten and Ben Frost, *Incoming*, 2014–2017 (still). Three-channel HD video, 7.1 surround sound, 52 minutes, 10 seconds. Installation view: Le lieu unique, Nantes, France, June 27–September 1, 2019. Photo: David Gallard. Courtesy of the artist and Jack Shainman Gallery, New York. © Richard Mosse.

The images unfold simultaneously on the three 3-meter-wide screens but sometimes appear only on the central screen. More importantly, they are never juxtaposed to create a unified representation unfolding over the three screens: the projection is a divided one, and although a narrative does unfold—this is migration at its most intense, involving migrating travelers across the Turkish–Syrian border as well as from Africa (the journeys include travelers from Syria, Iraq, and Afghanistan as well as from Somalia and Senegal) to the EU—that narrative is nonlinear and rather abstract. This double quality comes from a series of aesthetic decisions: the three-screen structure persistently fragments the overall composition (the screens present close-up views as well as traveling shots, but even when the images on the different screens relate to the same scene or object, they remain disjointed); there is no narrator or voice-over; there is no contextualization (the installation never explicitly identifies, visually or aurally, the locations in which the footage was shot); the installation doesn't have any explicit beginning or end and is shown in a loop. In short, the narrative of traumatic events is shown and experienced as never fully seeable and unifiable. The documentation of the locations is provided by the exhibition catalog as well as by the large-scale print series *Heat Maps* and a series of framed video stills taken from *Incoming*. The European locations include the Mediterranean Sea, the island of Lesbos, the Idomeni Camp on the Greek coast, the Jungle Refugee Camp in Calais, and Berlin's Templehof Airport.[13] Mosse documented the migrant journeys along two routes leading into Europe: the route from the Persian Gulf and the Syrian border to Berlin's former Tempelhof Airport building and the route used mostly by Africans from Senegal to Somalia in the East, crossing the Sahara Desert of northern Niger and heading north for Libya.[14] The soundtrack suggests a random but harsh clashing of metals, the sound of machinery, ambient reverberations and drones, sometimes silence. The seating area is installed close to the screens—a proximity that, together with the large screens and the surround sound, favors an immersive experience of the work. The whole is fluid and liquid, remote and unresolved.

What do we perceive here? In my description, I follow the chronology of the installation's unfolding of images. That is, I follow it as much as possible. To reiterate the comment I made earlier: the unfolding is a fragmented one; it remains impossible to see the whole as an unfluctuating whole, and so many images escape our observation. We see migrating beings transferred with the help of rescuers from a big ship to a small rubber boat and then from a rubber boat to another ship in the Mediterranean off the coast of Libya (figure 3.2)—a rescue involving a Croatian navy vessel alongside Italian navy and Guardia di Finanza ships. While the left screen shows a close-up of young men sitting behind a wired barrier, and the right screen shows a close-up of the ship's surveillance equipment. Humans are thermographically visible as three-dimensional X-rays—their clothing usually seems white, their masklike faces are typically dark but appear sometimes with white spots, and their eyes materialize as white or dark sockets. We see military staff on an American aircraft carrier (the USS *Theodore Roosevelt* CVN-71) inspecting the deck, loading up weapons, and guiding the launching of a F-18 fighter jet through take-off; images of water fragmented between screens; the moon; a volunteer from Team Humanity off the coast of the island of Lesbos looking out through binoculars for boats in distress. Water again. We see a dinghy on the horizon, its passengers being saved from a shipwreck (an estimated 100 out of 300 died in the wreck) and moving toward the shore of Lesbos (figure 3.3). On the left screen, rescuers warm up the bodies of the survivors in a state of hypothermia—a procedure that leaves black fingerprint traces on the blankets protecting the bodies. We are then exposed to a long close-up of a Syrian female survivor on the shore; rescued, she looks around, lost and exhausted. On the left screen, the wringing out of a wet cloth expels water that thermographically appears like blood. Other bodies are covered with a mylar thermal blanket to reduce the heat loss—the blankets shiver in the wind. Soon, on the left screen we see an aerial view of a fire; a helicopter; long lines of men sitting on the ground, waiting at the port of Mytilini on Lesbos (with a few tents remaining) (figure 3.4); women with children; a multitude of trucks and a large ferry boat on which they all will board; the migrants boarding; ferries navigating their way to Athens. Then we see a pathology laboratory where Greek pathologists conduct an autopsy on a young woman drowned off the island of Leros—they unwrap the body and remove a section of a bone for DNA identification. This is followed by a few scenes unfolding at the former Tempelhof Airport in Berlin, transformed into an emergency refugee shelter, where adults wait, while children and teenagers play and fight or stare at their iPhones. The sky; kites flying. Fire again, but it is now intense and its image captured with a close-up view; firemen struggle to contain the fire: we are in the Jungle Camp in Calais—someone is filming the scene; camp residents (but also riot police) watch the fire consuming the camp, said to have been set by refugees protesting against their expulsion and the dismantling of the camp by the French Compagnies républicaines de sécurité; we see debris and a site of worship— the gate of a temporary Eritrean church inside the Jungle; the religious paintings from the church are being rescued, recalling the rescuing of boat passengers seen

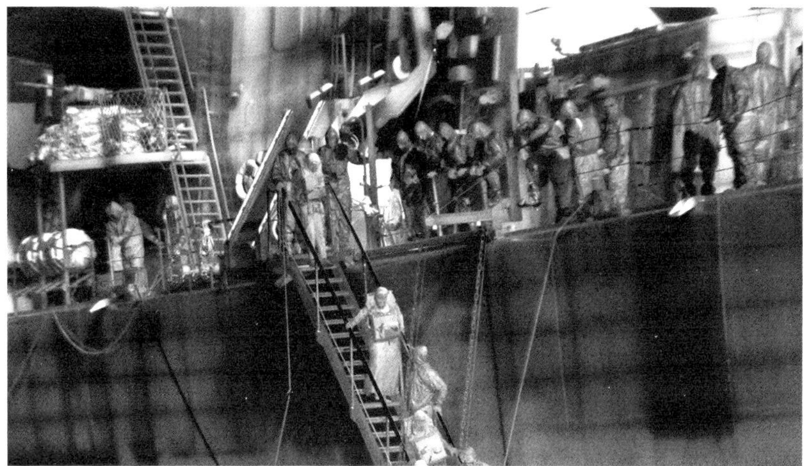

earlier. A Muslim from sub-Saharan Africa is now shown in the middle of a truck stop in the Sahara Desert in northern Niger: he kneels to pray after washing his face with water, which looks again like spurting blood (figure 3.1). Meanwhile, the right screen shows a truck overloaded with men and women, suitcases and bags, and the left screen shows a close-up view of the group being transported through the desert to the Libyan border. The night sky again; the moon; jets in the sky sending missiles.

What makes this work vital for the understanding of contemporary art's unlearning of the "European refugee crisis" is its depiction of the becoming bare life of migrating beings (their exposure to injury and death)—a becoming bare life that

FIGURE 3.2

Richard Mosse, in collaboration with Trevor Tweeten and Ben Frost, *Incoming*, 2014–2017 (still). Three-channel HD video with 7.1 surround sound, 52 minutes, 10 seconds. Co-commissioned by National Gallery of Victoria, Melbourne, and Barbican Art Gallery, London. Courtesy of the artist and Jack Shainman Gallery, New York. © Richard Mosse.

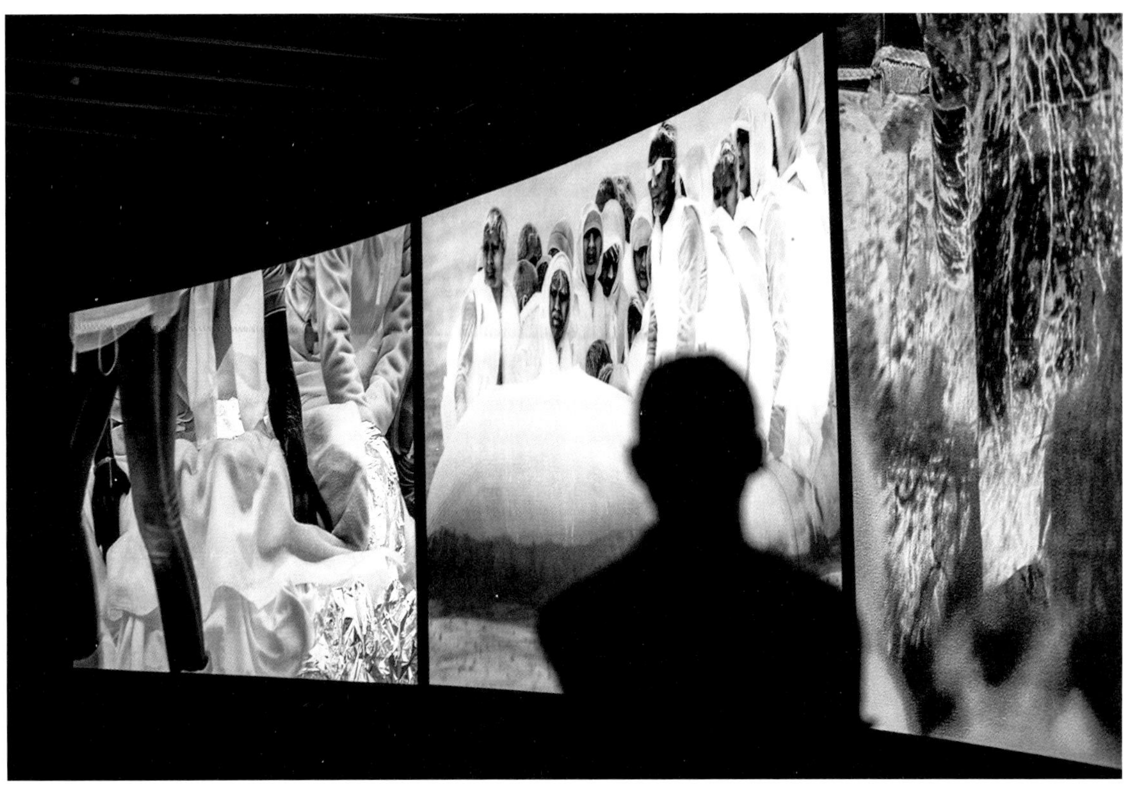

Richard Mosse, in collaboration with Trevor Tweeten and Ben Frost, *Incoming*, 2014–2017 (still). Three-channel HD video, 7.1 surround sound, 52 minutes, 10 seconds. Installation view: The Curve, Barbican Centre, London, February 15–April 23, 2017. Photo: Tristan Fewings/Getty images. Courtesy of the artist and Jack Shainman Gallery, New York. © Richard Mosse.

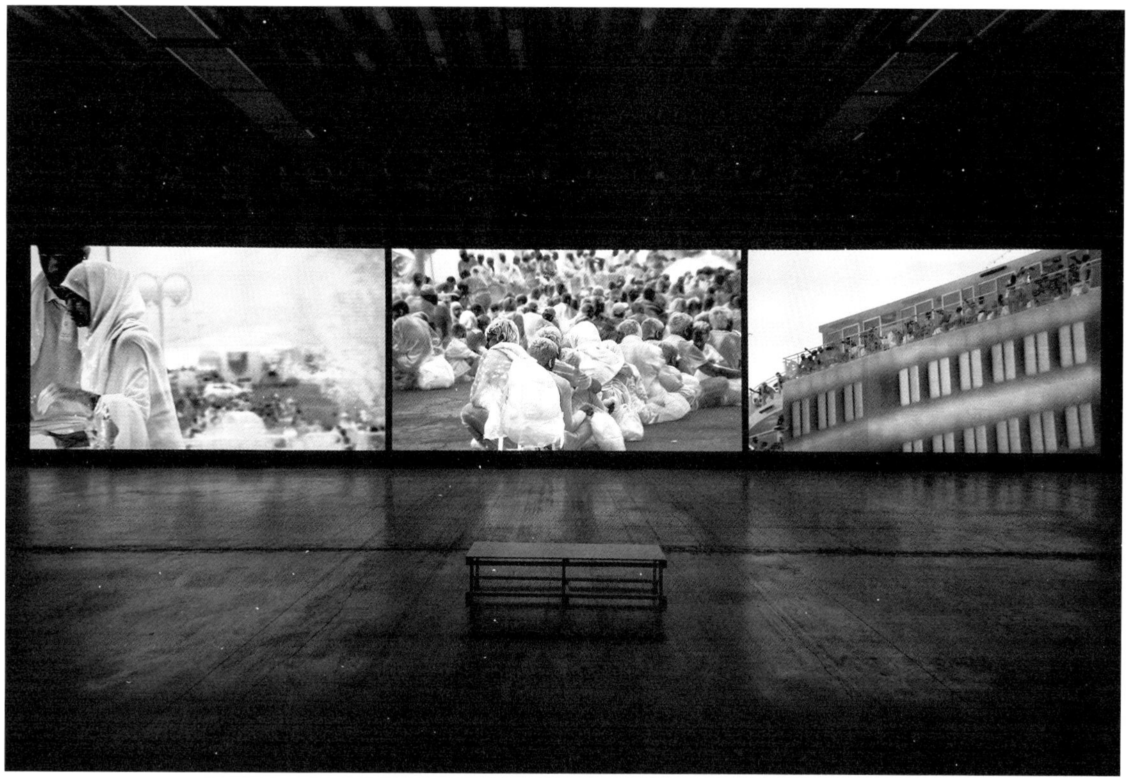

Richard Mosse, in collaboration with Trevor Tweeten and Ben Frost, *Incoming*, 2014–2017 (still). Three-channel HD video, 7.1 surround sound, 52 minutes, 10 seconds. Installation view: Le lieu unique, Nantes, France, June 27–September 1, 2019. Photo: David Gallard. Courtesy of the artist and Jack Shainman Gallery, New York. © Richard Mosse.

reached a highpoint in 2016, when more than 5,000 people died while attempting to cross the Mediterranean.[15] I define the Agambenian notion of "bare life" more explicitly later, but suffice it to say for now that bare life is "life exposed to death," an exposure particularly effective in camps and waiting zones where living beings are subject to the rule of law (camps and waiting zones are exceptionally established by decree by governments to respond to situations of emergency) but can never actively appeal to the rule of law (camps and waiting zones are exceptions to the rule of law—a temporary suspension of that rule). As Agamben states, bare life is life "included in politics in the form of the exception, that is, as something that is included solely through an exclusion."[16] The installation exposes three key components of that becoming bare life.

First, it shows the freedom of movement reversed into migrating populations being moved (or being transferred, to paraphrase Hess and Kasparek) from one place to another without any sense of clear destination. That transfer is managed by a humanitarian-military complex of rescuers and border patrol agents. The people being transferred are totally incapacitated. Throughout, from one screen to the next, they massify; they are surveilled, transported, never shown to transport themselves; they wait in delimited spaces separated from the outside world.

Second, the work exposes the containment of migrating beings in waiting zones—hot spots and camps. Campization is secured by a variety of overlapping measures of differentiation, as delineated in Kreichauf's analysis of that specific management procedure: demarcation (the separation of "migrants" from the local population); containment (a camp's main objective is to enclose its residents—an enclosure that makes them visible as strangers and possible criminals—in which processes of racialization, segregation, and "territorial stigmatization" are amplified); legal exceptionality (camps are governed following legal frameworks that are different from those applied to citizens); temporality (a camp is a place of permanent temporariness—whereas a camp is not made to remain, a resident's length of stay is always unknown and can last for years); and problematized protection (camp inhabitants steadily state how accommodations give them a sense of being protected but how that protection decreases their autonomy).[17]

Third and last, *Incoming* discloses and thermographically performs the biologization of the bodies detected by the camera: individuals and groups appear as traces of heat; their existence is reduced mainly to being vulnerable bodies whose lives must be managed by the humanitarian-military migration complex in order to survive. Not only is thermovision used to capture the hidden borderzones as they evolved during the 2015–2016 destabilization and restabilization of the European migration and border regime, but it is also the biologizing technology through which we, the viewers, perceive migrating populations. Although thermography is absolutely essential to *Incoming*—it is a technology of disclosure of hidden border-zones—it paradoxically reinstates the becoming bare life of citizens-on-the-move. That reinstatement is part of the work's call for responsibility; it wants viewers to perceptually and affectively experience their complicity in that becoming. For, indeed, the necropolitical management of migrating beings, which we stubbornly fail to perceive or acknowledge or choose to dismiss, has established a new category of colonial rulers, to paraphrase Jürgen Osterhammel's famous definition of colonialism, "in pursuit" of their own interests, "convinced of their own superiority and their ordained mandate to rule."[18] This is what Mosse means when he states that he does not want to cancel the distorting effects of thermovision. This use raises a fundamental question that I address in the following section: Although thermovision's benefits certainly lie in the dark coexistence it reveals, to what extent do these benefits elaborate or require the revictimization of victims?

THERMOGRAPHY

A thermographic camera is a device that forms heat-zone images using infrared radiation. A weaponized surveillance technology, it is intended for the detection of human presence: it senses thermal radiation, especially bodily heat, at vast distances. Used for "situational awareness," the technology captures a larger percentage of the electromagnetic spectrum, in which visible light takes up only a small area. It doesn't produce an image using visible light as is the case with common cameras. Rather, it detects radiation in the long-infrared range of the electromagnetic spectrum (from about 9,000 to about 14,000 nanometers), which is invisible to the human eye; it detects the infrared emitted from the surface of objects and converts the distribution of surface radiation into visible images. Since infrared radiation is emitted by any object with a temperature higher than absolute zero according to the black-body radiation law, thermography or thermal imaging makes warm objects stand out against cooler backgrounds; humans and other warm-blooded animals become easily visible against the environment, day or night. The technology was slightly modified for Mosse's usage to facilitate transportation and fieldwork.[19] The artist has explored four thermographic features in particular.

Thermovision is first and foremost a nonhuman vision technology insofar as its telephoto capabilities allow it to "see far beyond the human eye."[20] Its capacity to detect human bodies from some 30.3 kilometers has given visual access to otherwise inaccessible borderzones. Second, it is more specifically a technology that combines surveillance and weaponization. As specified by Mosse, "The camera is produced by a multinational defence and security corporation that manufactures cruise missiles, drones, and other technologies. Primarily designed for surveillance, it can also be connected to weapon systems to track and target the enemy. . . . The camera is sanctioned as a weapon under international law, and falls under International Traffic in Arms Regulations (ITAR). . . . [T]he camera belongs to the biological technologies of discipline and regulation."[21] This feature represented a major challenge for the artist when crossing international borders and led to the hiring of an export lawyer to obtain permission from different consulates to cross borders with the camera.[22] Third, thermography is a surveillance technology, but for the artist's project its surveillance capacity was limited to visually capturing borderzones. When the images were shot, the EU had already implemented a new surveillance network called the European Border Surveillance System (Frontex's EUROSUR) to systematize migration and refine the tracking of so-called illegal migrants. Instigated in 2013, the system uses a variety of surveillance technologies—including drones, satellite remote sensing, reconnaissance aircraft, and thermal camera systems—to secure its external borders. As the curator Louise Wolthers reports, EUROSUR was devised to facilitate the distribution of information between member states, each of them becoming "responsible for compiling all relevant data, analysing and interpreting it, deciding what to share and with whom, and creating a coherent 'national situational picture.'"[23] By isolating thermography from computational surveillance and the computational processing of data, *Incoming* restricted its usage as a detector of human presence to capturing biological traces of heat, sweat, saliva, and moisture. This restriction allowed Mosse both to protect the identity of the travelers and to emphasize the technology's biological processes. Fourth and finally, Mosse has stated that thermography is a technology that dehumanizes migrating beings: it "portray[s] people in zombie form as monstrous," "strip[ping] the individual from the body" and depicting them "as mere biological trace" (figure 3.5). The whole point of his project was not "to rescue this apparatus from its sinister purpose" but "to work the technology against itself, to brush it against the grain."[24]

What do all of these thermographic features and decisions amount to? For sure, *Incoming* presents migrating beings as biological traces of heat, and these

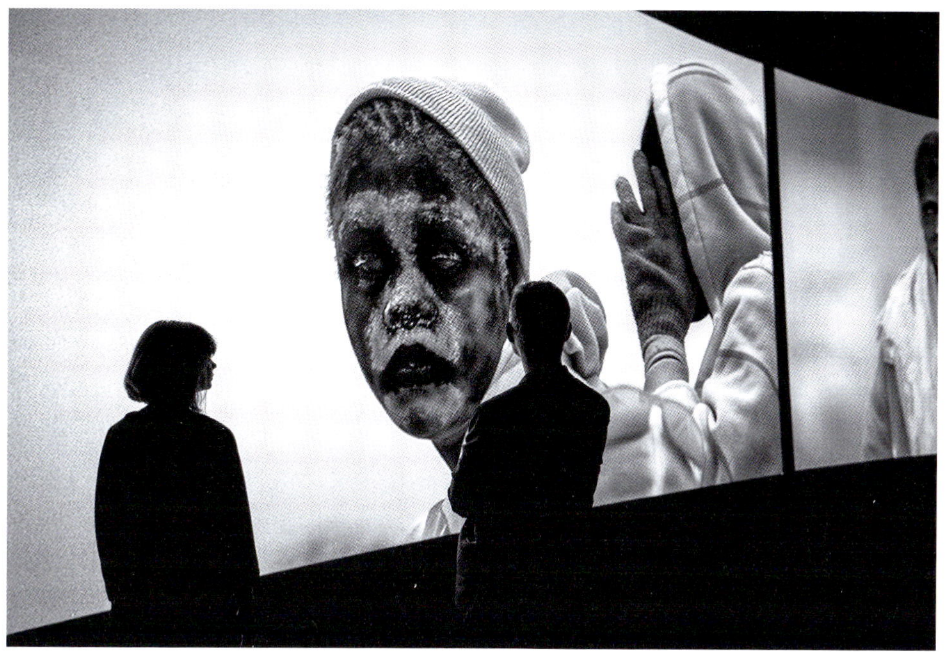

figures are often grotesquelike. Paradoxically—such is the parergon remedy–poison functioning of that specific technology—Mosse's use of thermovision reinforces the designation of these beings as a danger to be contained and alleviated. This is what thermal surveillance cameras are made to do. As the anthropologist Karen Fog Olwig and her team from the University of Copenhagen specify, presence-detection technologies of surveillance "are place-oriented and can detect signs of life and other forms of presences, substances, heat emissions and sounds, and they can

FIGURE 3.5

Richard Mosse, in collaboration with Trevor Tweeten and Ben Frost, *Incoming*, 2014–2017 (still). Three-channel HD video, 7.1 surround sound, 52 minutes, 10 seconds. Installation view: The Curve, Barbican Centre, London, February 15–April 23, 2017. Photo: Tristan Fewings/Getty images. Courtesy of the artist and Jack Shainman Gallery, New York. © Richard Mosse.

also to some extent qualify that presence. . . . The links they establish are generally between a body and a place, and it is that link, that presence, that can define the body as a threat, an intrusion—a body in the wrong place."[25] Explored as such by Mosse, thermovision can only but reinforce the presence of "others" as unspecified danger, biologized enemy, intruder. Technologies of vision are never simply recording machines: they also make what they film. *Incoming* wants us to experience that performativity. The media scholars Lilie Chouliaraki and Tijana Stolic have further specified that one of the main media regimes of visibility of migrating populations today is the visual regime of biological life. Media images pertaining to that regime "depict a 'mass of unfortunates' on fragile dinghies or in refugee camps," following "a field of representation that reduces their life to corporeal existence and the needs of the body. This biological subjectivity entails a thin definition of humanity as an 'anthropological minimum'—a humanity fully reliant on Western emergency aid or rescue operations to survive and so inevitably dispossessed of will and voice."[26] The visual regime of biological life represented in and produced by *Incoming* is what makes the installation work as a call for responsibility. If the "generalized pity" for victims, as postulated by the sociologist Luc Boltanski, is typically made possible by witnessing the suffering of others "from the standpoint of distance" in situations where sufferers are not there in person,[27] *Incoming* seeks to reduce that media distance as much as possible in order to turn pity into responsibility. That closeness is reinforced by the immersiveness of the installation—the large screens, the surround sound, and the proximity of the viewers in relation to the screens.

As posited by the writer Ben Eastham in his review of *Incoming*, "The danger of these estranging techniques is that they dehumanise the subjects they depict in much the same way as the bureaucracy of statehood reduces them to statistics"; these techniques risk "reinforcing the attitudes that this unquestionably compelling work seeks ostensibly to critique."[28] Such is *Incoming*'s remedy-and-poison ambivalence. *Incoming* has been both supported and denounced by critics specifically because of its ambivalence, even though ambivalence is crucial to its aesthetics and even though Europe's answer to the movements of migration coming from Africa and Asia is itself fundamentally ambivalent (both defending democracy and failing to comply with the 1951 Refugee Convention). It has been criticized for its sublime rendering of the necropolitics of migration and its demonization of refugees as well as for speaking *for* (instead of *with*) them, despite Mosse's positioning of himself—a position shared by most viewers—as "a citizen of a relatively affluent nation" searching for accountability.[29] The writer Daniel Blight goes as far as to argue that the installation maintains a perspective of "social salvation" that reinscribes what the philosopher Linda Martín Alcoff has called the "hierarchy of civilizations" between a "well-meaning" First World and an underprivileged Third World.[30] In his review of the work at the Barbican's Curve Gallery, Sean O'Hagan asks "the inevitable question": "Does an artwork that sets out to challenge documentary tropes end up aestheticising human suffering by rendering it mere spectacle?"[31] My answer to this insightful question is: not necessarily.

SEARCHING FOR COEXISTENCE

Incoming's pharmakon-disclosure is not a problem but a strength: it challenges the idea that migrating beings can be represented straightforwardly; it is a search for responsibility. *Incoming* has also taken the risk of representing citizens-on-the-move engaged in borderzones, as has Ai Weiwei in *Human Flow* (2017), discussed in chapter 7—a feature-length film that follows their journeys during the purported "European refugee crisis," showing men, women, and families searching for asylum but predominantly finding closed borders, routes transformed into corridors, overcrowded camps, and destroyed homes. I say *Incoming* has "taken the risk" because disclosing hidden borderzones is crucial to understanding the ongoing necropolitics of migration even though it necessarily entails the filming of beings without their consent. *Incoming* counterbalances that absence of consent by sustaining thermovision's veiling of identities and by slowing down the images to allow viewers to meditate on what they are seeing. A responsible caring practice is at play here. To succeed in its disclosure, however, *Incoming* must revictimize the victims. It leaves us with that problem: it suspends the imperative to acknowledge the autonomy of migration. It is this imperative that I want to address in the final section of this chapter. Its justification can be summarized in four points.

Borderzones are conditioned and shaped not only by securitization operations but also by the movement of migration. Let us follow Hess and Kasparek on this point. Although the field of border studies has been key to the assessment of borders as overdetermined, polysemic, and heterogeneous, it tends to "conceptualize migrants as structurally powerless and as 'victims'"; like *Incoming*, it reproduces borderzone exclusions by epistemologically excluding the agency of migrating beings.[32] Wanting to challenge that field, the two anthropologists insist on the need to understand borders and borderzones as conflictual—that is, as sites in which securitization and migration are understood as "coconstituting the border":

This approach allows [us] to look at the border regime as a space of conflict and contestation between the various actors trying to govern the border and the movements of migration—without minimizing the border regime's brutality. These conceptualizations represent a methodological and theoretical attempt not only to think about the relationship between migration movements and control regimes in a different way than in the classical sociological way of object–structure, but also to conceive of migration differently than has previously been the dominant practice in the cultural and social sciences—namely, not thinking about it in the sense of a "deviation" from the paradigm of the sedentary way of life in the modern nation state, or as a functionalist variable of economic processes and rationalities. Instead, this theoretical and methodological approach represents an attempt to conceptualize migration both historically and also structurally as an act of "flight" and as "imperceptible" forms of resistance, in the sense of withdrawal and escape from miserable, exploitative conditions of existence. . . . Yann Moulier-Boutang (2006) described this aspect as the "autonomy of migration." This draws attention to migration as a co-constitutive factor of the border, with the forces of the movements of migration challenging and reshaping the border every single day.[33]

To maintain that social sciences and the humanities must find ways to examine how opposing forces of securitization and migration co-constitute borders is to argue for the autonomy of migration. These findings show the limits of the Agambenian perspective. Agamben maintains that bare life—"life exposed to death"—finds its main materialization in camps or any *zones d'attente* in which residents are subject to the rule of law but can never appeal to the rule of law because these spaces result from the implementation of a state of exception.[34] Invoked by governments as a necessity in emergency situations and times of crisis, the state of exception—the necessary use of exceptional measures—is legitimized by the government's power to legislate by decree the suspension of the rule of law for the public good, for the reestablishment of a lost social order.[35] To say that the camp is the paradigmatic space of the state of exception is to reveal it as a space in which exception is indistinguishable from law and *zoë* (natural life) is indistinguishable from *bios* (qualified life in the polis). Confirming Agamben's logic of exception, campization in *Incoming* is shown as a biopolitics of migration management involving the surveillance, channeled transportation, immobilization, isolation, and bioanalysis of incoming populations—a series of operations that reduces them to bodies and exposes them to injury and death in that very process. Yet in this depiction both the philosopher and the artist lose sight of the autonomy of displaced people—their decision-making process, their capacity to act and sometimes resist; the unfolding of power relations within and despite states of exception; the fact that the reinforcement of securitization is a reaction to the movements of migration. To get out of the historico-ontological trap of defining corridors and camps as fully deterministic, it is useful to bring back Jacques Rancière and Didier Fassin's understanding of the political subject referred to in chapter 1. Contesting Agamben's notion of bare life, Rancière defines humans as political subjects who have the "capacity for staging . . . scenes of dissensus" (*litige*, "dispute") about who is included (or not) in a specific social order.[36] Fassin has likewise maintained that the state's reduction of migrant existence "to its most basic expression" never simply implies that displaced people "let themselves be reduced to it."[37] Similarly, *Incoming* reaches the limits of its otherwise rich ambivalence strategy when it ignores what it must ignore—the autonomy of migration—in order to responsibilize the viewer. Although it remains crucial to expose the becoming bare life of migrating beings, it is as equally crucial to investigate how borderzones are space–times where "political subjectivities and practices" are not only possible but in fact necessarily played out; borderzones are more convincingly envisaged not as instruments of "totalizing exclusion" but as spaces mobilized by different mobilities and subject positions.[38]

Dialogues can be established between artists and citizens-on-the-move. The strong borderworks made in the late 1990s and early 2000s, namely Ursula Biemann's single-video *Performing the Border* (1999) and Chantal Akerman's film and multiscreen video installation *From the Other Side* (*De l'autre côté*) (2002), captured the lives of individuals living along and across the US-Mexico border so as to convey the embodied experience of Mexicans attempting to pass to the North. Shot on location and consisting mainly of interviews and testimonies, the works were haunted by the injuring and death of those who didn't make it as well as by the endangerment of women in these specific borderzones. They elaborated innovative aesthetic strategies—the video essay in Biemann's *Performing the Border* (figure 3.6) and the tight rows of monitors in Akerman's *From the Other Side* (figure 3.7)—to preclude a unified view of the whole. The contact the artists established with their subjects, their subjects' families, border patrol agents, and legal representatives had the advantage of documenting conversations and voices of contestation, embodying Gloria Anzaldúa's poetic vision of border cultures as mixing voices from the inside and the outside.[39] As Bertha Jottar—the first protagonist in Biemann's video—declares in the opening shot, "There is nothing natural about the border; it's a highly constructed place that gets reproduced through the crossing of people, because without the crossing there is no border, right? It's just an imaginary line, a river or it's just a wall": borders are performed by people who have a story to tell about the difficulties of such performances. Let us also recall *Border* (2004) by Laura Waddington—a low-tech video evanescently showing Afghan and Iraqi refugees next to the Sangatte Red Cross Camp as they endeavor to cross the channel tunnel to England at night (figure 0.3). The work results from Waddington's close connection with some of these refugees during the early stages of the European migrant crisis—she was next to them in the fields as they attempted to flee in 2002 and when they protested against the camp's dismantlement that same year; she films them nocturnally from that perspective, producing unstable low-resolution images that capture in their very materiality the precarious albeit resilient autonomy of migration. Art historian Georges Didi-Huberman speaks insightfully of "*firefly-images*: images on the brink of disappearance, always altered by the urgency of [the migrants'] flight, always close to those who, to fulfill their plans, hide in the night and attempt the impossible, risking their lives."[40] Waddington narrates their journeys off-screen. Her voice ascertains her not as an expert or an authority but as a witness whose main responsibility is to recount as much as one can the refugees' struggle for movement, freedom, equality, and dance/joy (Didi-Huberman: "Gratuitous and unexpected beauty, as when a Kurdish refugee dances in the night, in the wind, with only his blanket for covering: this vestment for his dignity, and, somehow, for his fundamental joy, his joy in spite of all"[41]), without losing that sense of connection. *Border* emerges from that reciprocity, that embodied ephemeral yet tangible coexistence.

Although such connections are not always possible, and even though borderzones have in some regions become too dangerous for such encounters, the process of creating these works opened the path for dialogue, especially dialogue between artists and citizens-on-the-move. We, the viewers, were invited to hear, feel, and witness that dialogue. As we will see in my brief examination of Gayatri Chakravorty Spivak's definition of responsibility later in this chapter, dialogue can take different forms, but it steadily relies on the acknowledgment of the autonomy of migration.

Technologies of vision—including the thermographic technology used by Mosse—can be and could have been repurposed to *affirm* the autonomy of migration.

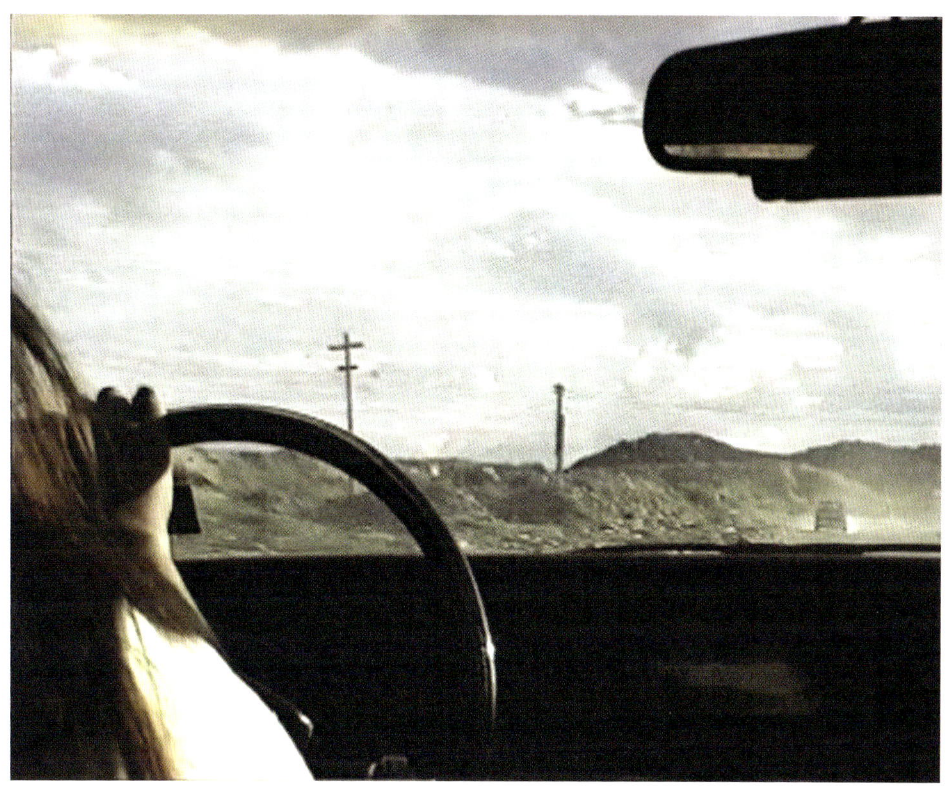

Ursula Biemann, *Performing the Border*, 1999 (still). Video essay, H-8 video, color, 43 minutes. Courtesy of the artist.

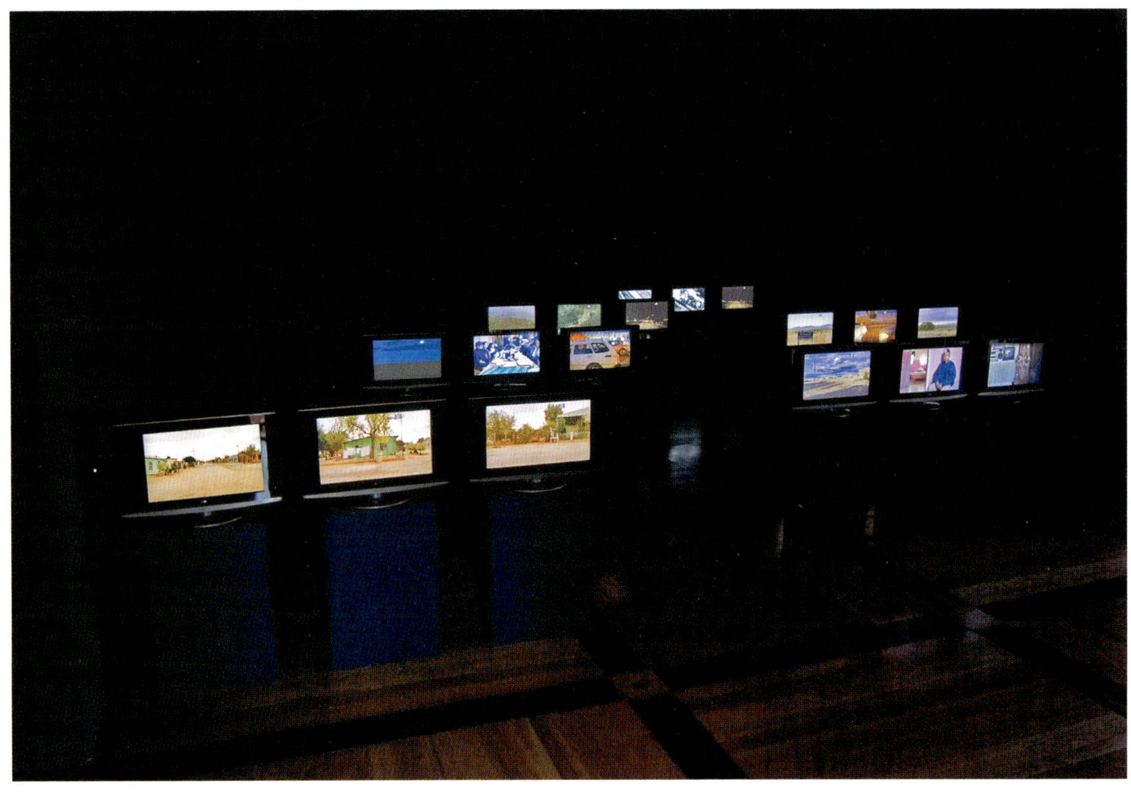

Chantal Akerman, *From the Other Side*, 2002 (still). Video installation in three parts (1 monitor + 18 monitors + 1 projection), color, sound. Made out of the film *De l'autre côté* (2002). Running time: 10 minutes, 29 seconds—in loop. Projection time: 52 minutes—in loop. Direction: Chantal Akerman. Image and sound editing and spatialization: Claire Atherton. Courtesy of Chantal Akerman Foundation and Marian Goodman Gallery.

An early video work responding to the "European refugee crisis"—a single-channel video entitled *Ceuta* (2006) by the German filmmaker Florian Schneider (b. 1967, Munich, Germany)—shows how artists also explore the repurposing of surveillance technologies to reassert the autonomy of migration and thus to avoid oblique revictimization. Ceuta is an autonomous Spanish city located in northern Morocco at the level of the Strait of Gibraltar: as a Spanish enclave, it belongs to the territory of the EU; bordered by Morocco, it is one of nine populated Spanish zones in Africa; more importantly for migrant journeys, it is one of the only two routes (together with Mellila) leading to the EU directly from Africa without passing over the Mediterranean Sea. As an enclave, it is surrounded and protected by a barrier that is now approximatively 16 meters high. On the night of September 29, 2005, an estimated 250 men and women (the Moroccan police's estimation was more than 500) climbed across the fence that separates the Spanish enclave of Ceuta from Moroccan territory.[42] News reporting the September event described it as migrants massively storming Europe, a claim that overshadowed the fact that it was a deliberate collective decision made by a group of citizens-on-the-move from sub-Saharan and western Africa who had been hiding for months in the mountain forests of north Morocco—a fact corroborated by Moussa K., one of the survivors, interviewed by Schneider.[43] They used ladders made from branches and string in their attempt to scale the fence, while the Spanish police used rubber bullets against them as they climbed (most of them were wounded, five fatally). After a few days, the news agency Reuters published video footage provided by the Spanish authorities, filmed by the CCTV surveillance cameras of the Guardia Civil (the Spanish gendarmerie force), showing an anonymous mass of bodies crawling over the fence. The footage was shown on the German TV station ZDF.

As explained by Schneider, the 11-second sequence shown on TV was a condensed version of the entire surveillance video—the compression and acceleration of an event that lasted hours. Condensed, the event looks like a violent attack by "a swarming mass . . . [of] insects bereft of all human agency," suggesting illegal migration.[44] Responding to that sequence, Schneider's video unlearns the technological manipulation of the material: the artist reversed the editing process that speeded up the footage so as to restore what in fact might have been lived during the original timespan of the event (figure 3.8). In that deceleration, "the specters supposedly overrunning Fortress Europe seem to stand still."[45] In *Ceuta*, abrupt jump cuts occur between the single frames, drawing attention to the off-screen

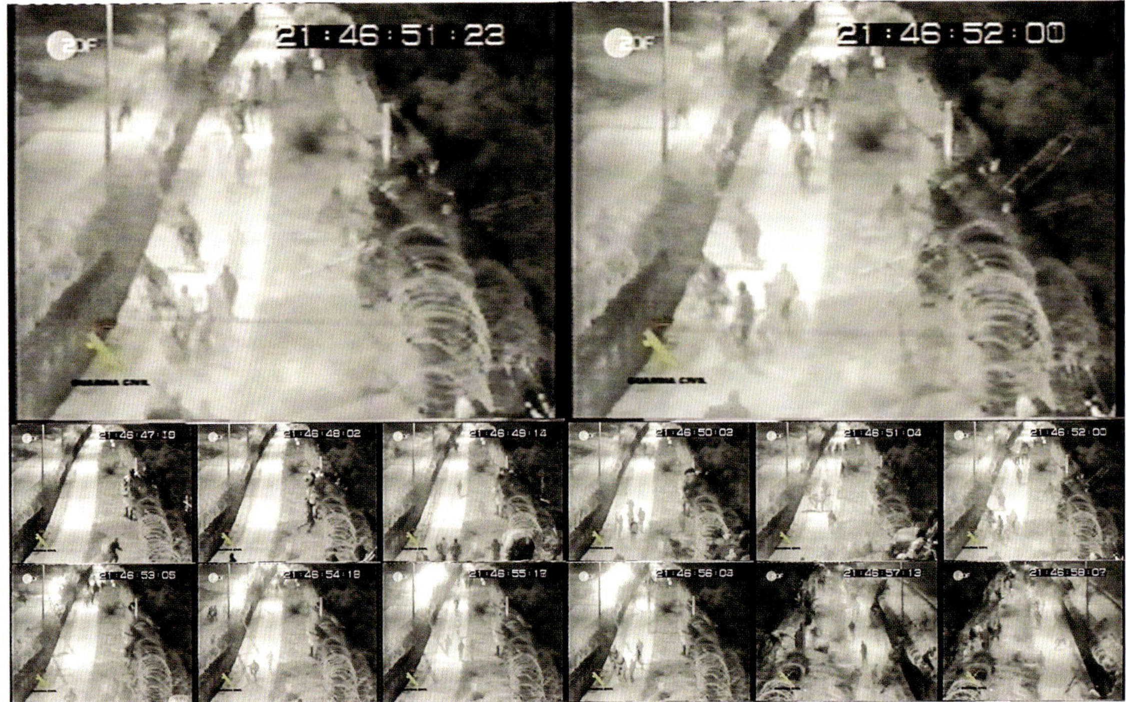

Florian Schneider, *Ceuta*, 2006 (stills). Single-channel video. Border crossing, recompilation of screenshots from the video installation *The Museum of the Stealing of Souls*, Manifesta 7 (Trento, Italy, 2008), by Florian Schneider. Eleven seconds of footage from CCTV cameras of the Spanish border police Guardia Civil, spread by the news agency Reuters across the globe in early October 2005, captured in the undercranked version broadcast by the German news, but rendered back into real time by the artist. Courtesy of the artist. © Florian Schneider.

space that lies outside the static frames of the slowed-down version, inviting the viewer to reflect on the actual event. As Schneider explains,

In this respect, the events of the 29th of September serve as an exquisite example of what activists and theorists of the "noborder network" have, since the early 1990s, called the "autonomy of migration." This expression seeks to understand migration as a much more complex process than its usual reduction to misery and calamity. The patterns of victimization are as omnipresent as the ubiquitous control system. Both advocates and adversaries of the contemporary border regime seem to understand migration as a logical result of the movements of capital—as its unsavory aftereffect or appendix. The "autonomy of migration" claims that both research and activism should refrain from indulging in recurrent tropes of charity and compassion. Instead, it recognizes the manifold social and political processes needed to practically cross a border. These processes are, politically, constituting migrant subjectivities.[46]

The point I want to make here is not that surveillance technologies *must* necessarily be repurposed but that they *can* be repurposed to acknowledge the autonomy of migration. Interestingly, *Ceuta* shows how repurposing is never in or of itself a critical or disobedient endeavor: it can be practiced to make the autonomy of migration either invisible (as the Spanish authorities and Reuters did) or visible anew (as Schneider did). The video was exhibited at Manifesta 7 (European Biennial of Contemporary Art, 2008) in Trento, Italy, as a component of Schneider's video installation *The Museum of the Stealing of Souls*. This is to say that Mosse's rich (ambivalent) exploration of the pharmakon—his use of thermovision as a means to disclose *and* reproduce the necropolitical management of migrants to elaborate a call for responsibility—does not require the mere revictimization of migrating beings.

RESPONSIBILITY

The recognition of the autonomy of migration has another benefit: a more robust definition of responsibility is achieved. When Mosse refers to the viewer's responsibility (even to the viewer's complicity), he explains that it comes from our support of governments that sustain the necropolitical evolution of migration.[47] But are we really accomplices? What does it entail to be held accountable for migration? I want to discuss briefly here three contemporary thinkers of responsibility—Roger

Silverstone, Gayatri Chakravorty Spivak, and Iris Marion Young—whose work is particularly helpful for clarifying that dense notion as a call, especially when responsibility is about establishing a relation of equality between persons involved. These studies are further mobilized in the book's following chapters.

The media theorist Roger Silverstone speaks in his famous essay "Complicity and Collusion in the Mediation of Everyday Life" (2002) about the producer's, director's, and audience's responsibility for improving media representations when they fail to reflect on how these representations may well betray the world they depict. His main argument is that "insofar as the persisting representational characteristics of contemporary media, above all in our media's representation of the other, remain unchallenged—as for the most part they are—then those who receive and accept them are neither mere prisoners of a dominant ideology nor innocents in a world of false consciousness; rather they are willing participants, that is, complicit, or even actively engaged, that is, collusive, in a mediated culture that fails to deliver its promises of communication and connection, with enduring, powerful and largely negative consequences for our status as human beings."[48] Silverstone defines complicity as our participation in the media representation of the other as "other": if the other is represented as another, media representations necessarily fail insofar as they bluntly reproduce the dominant ideology. They must therefore be contested, but they rarely are. Our moral obligation is to challenge such representations. This contestation is exemplified in chapter 7. Suffice it to say for now that complicity—one of the terms Mosse uses when explaining *Incoming*'s call—is not the same as responsibility. Silverstone's essay has the merit of distinguishing them: to be an accomplice is to be part of a wrongdoing; responsibility is about challenging that complicity. But the question remains: Can responsibility be more than a moral obligation?

In the essay "Imperative to Re-imagine the Planet" (2009), the postcolonial thinker Gayatri Chakravorty Spivak raises the question of responsibility in light of what she calls the planetary subject. The essay's pertinency to the study of contemporary European and North American art's attempt to bridge responsibility and aesthetics in matters of migration cannot be overstated. Spivak thinks the responsibility toward the "subaltern" political subject to be a shared unlearning of imperialism, colonialism, and even migration. She is searching for a definition that could deepen Mikhaïl Bakhtin's notion of answerability as a dialogic practice (a speaker–listener relationship that makes discursive room for the other), asking us to imagine the other outside of the Master–Slave dialectic. She writes:

In order to think the migrant as well as the recipient of foreign aid, we must think the other. To think the other, as everyone knows, is one meaning of being human. To be human is to be intended toward the other. . . . If we imagine ourselves as planetary accidents rather than global agents, planetary creatures rather than global entities, alterity remains underived from us, it is not our dialectical negation, . . . [and] we must persistently educate ourselves into this peculiar mind-set. . . . It is only then that we will be able to think the migrant as well as the recipient of foreign aid in the species of alterity, not simply as the white person's burden. . . . Let me then modify my title: I speak of an imperative to re-imagine the subject as planetary accident.[49]

In the imperative "*to re-imagine the subject as planetary accident*," the other ceases to be attributed to a specific category of being—notably "the migrant" in need of care or foreign aid. The whole point of her intervention is to dislodge the other from the imperialism and colonialism sustaining capitalist globalization by insisting on the interdependence of beings while removing that interdependence from the Master–Slave dialectic. When subjects are considered planetary creatures outside of that dialectic, they are ontologically "accidental": every subject is both self and other in relation to one another. The imperative to reimagine migrating beings as planetary accidents is the grounds on which she reconsiders responsibility as an *obligation* to claim it instead as a *right*. That new understanding of responsibility "requires earning a right to win responses from both sides"; it displaces answerability into a reimagining of "yourself and them—as both receivers and givers—not in a Master–Slave dialectic, but in a dialogic of accountability."[50] Spivak's insightful planetary rethinking of the subject helps to tease out the challenges intrinsic to any artistic practice addressing migration in terms of coexistence: the challenge is to speak not for but with the speaking other as well as to understand any planetary being as made of selfhood *and* otherness so that responsibility may become a matter of right. Presupposing such a definition is the belief that subjects are both interdependent and autonomous. Without that postulate, responsibility cannot be a far-reaching dialogical encounter—a reciprocal deployment of coexistence. The definition is also a caution against the slippery use of "care," for care (even Stiegler's defense of care as a relation that supports the positive pharmacological side of pharmakon technologies and *Incoming*'s creative rapprochement of care and responsibility) standardly sustains the wealthiest economies' *obligation* toward the poorest economies worldwide. Spivak's main point is that we need to question that standard and rethink care more reciprocally.

Finally, the feminist social scientist and philosopher Iris Marion Young has formulated a social connection model of responsibility in relation to social injustices that posits that we (the privileged not directly harmed by social injustices) all participate in "the same structures of privilege and disadvantage, constraint and enablement," as those who are harmed by these structures.[51] It proposes a non-blame, forward-looking view of responsibility as a set of political actions, small as they may be, to solve social injustices. The view is forward-looking because the point of that model is not to blame ourselves for our participation in social injustices but to act against injustice when we become aware of our participation in such unjust structures. What is needed, she maintains, is a model of responsibility closer to Hannah Arendt's distinction between guilt and political responsibility: "To the extent that we participate in the ongoing operations of a society in which injustice occurs, we ought to be held responsible. This does not, however, make us guilty or blameworthy or directly liable."[52] Young puts coexistence at the center of her description: "Our responsibility," she writes, "derives from belonging together with others in a system of interdependent processes of cooperation and competition through which we seek benefits and aim to realize projects. All who dwell within the structures must take responsibility for remedying injustices they cause, though none is specifically liable for the harm in a legal sense."[53] Put differently, as much as we are part of and participate in structures of injustice, even minimally so, and as long as we are not the cause of someone's injury (as is the case in matters of accountability and liability), we likewise must participate in the structures of justice.

I explore Young's model in my discussion of Forensic Oceanography's and Teresa Margolles's work in chapters 4 and 5. For now, it helps to specify that *Incoming*'s thermographic pharmakon-disclosure of the European migration and border regime—a disclosure that is both remedy (it exposes the regime's necropolitics) and poison (it likewise participates in the regime's necropolitics by rebiologizing the surveilled beings)—is better understood as a call for a forward-looking model of responsibility. As the book's case studies show, the forward-looking model is more accurate when the call for responsibility is addressed to the viewer who in all likelihood has not caused but nevertheless participates, as a citizen, in necropolitical migration as a significant component of colonial presence, whereas the backward-looking model of responsibility is more effective in works tackling liability.

FORENSICS

Forensic Oceanography (FO) is both an artist collective and a collaborative research project between the architect Lorenzo Pezzani (b. 1982, Trento, Italy, based in London) and the American Swiss filmmaker Charles Heller (b. 1981). Initiated in the aftermath of the Arab uprisings in 2011, the project emerged from and remains based in Eyal Weizman's Forensic Architecture research agency at Goldsmiths (University of London)—a cluster of architects, filmmakers, coders, and journalists using technical and analytical tools from architecture, archaeology, media studies, and other disciplines to elaborate counterinquiries on crimes and violent actions that would engage the responsibility of states. *Report on the "Left-to-Die Boat"* (2012)—made in collaboration with SITU Research and considered here—was FO's first investigation. It was followed by *Blaming the Rescuers: Criminalising Solidarity, (Re)enforcing Deterrence* (2017), *The Seizure of the Iuventa* (2018), *Sea Watch vs the Libyan Coastguard* (2018), and *Privatised Push-Back of the Nivin* (2019). FO is also the conceptualizer of the WatchTheMed platform (2012–), an online participatory platform that maps, monitors, and documents the deaths of migrating travelers and the violation of their rights in the Mediterranean Sea.

FO's main area of investigation is the EU migration and border regime in the Mediterranean: the project mobilizes a range of forensic techniques and methodologies to reconstruct events of nonassistance to citizens-on-the-move in distress or who have died at sea as they attempted to reach Europe. These techniques and methodologies include remote sensing, geolocation, fluid dynamics; the repurposing of surveillance technologies, satellite images, and Automatic Identification Systems

(AIS) used for vessel tracking; as well as interviews with survivors, witnesses, and state officials. The investigations have taken the form of reports presented in the context of legal proceedings against state authorities on the grounds of nonassistance at sea as well as of reports on EU policy making. Following Weizman's "counterforensic" terminology, however, these investigations do not consist in a straightforward forensic development of art. Whereas forensics refers to the scientific collecting, preservation, and analysis of physical evidence elaborated in the context of a criminal investigation as well as the testifying of forensic scientists as expert witnesses in civil and criminal court cases, Forensic Architecture's reports have been conceived as an effort to remove forensic science from the hands of the state; they are also meant to circulate in the public sphere in a variety of forums, including courts, truth commissions, the media, the web, as well as human rights and art venues.[1] FO's own investigations are made in collaboration with specialists in architecture, oceanography, geographic information systems, EU policy, international law and migration studies, as well as NGOs specializing in the defense of human and migrants' rights. Published in written reports and videos, FO's findings are available online at forensic-architecture.org.

Key to this chapter's examination of the call for responsibility is FO's redefinition of art as a counterforensic practice. The project's call for responsibility is first and foremost an activity of inquiry and disclosure: disclosure unfolds as a gathering of evidence on the necropolitics of migration in the Mediterranean basin; its main objective is to demonstrate the responsibility of EU member states for the endangering of migrants in that specific borderzone. This approach is not completely new. As early as 2002, Multiplicity—a multidisciplinary network of artists, architects, researchers, and geographers founded in Milan in 2000—made a multiscreen video installation entitled *Solid Sea 01: The Ghost Ship* for documenta 11 on the basis of an investigative report by the journalist Giovanni Maria Bellu for the Italian newspaper *La Repubblica*. The report divulged an overlooked Mediterranean shipwreck—the sinking of the *Yiohan* in the Canale di Sicilia in 1996, which led to the death of 283 Tamil, Pakistani, and Indian migrants during a storm as passengers were being transshipped from one boat to another. The installation included two opposing projections in one room—video footage of the underwater remains (filmed by Bellu with an underwater video camera) and the meteorological image of the day of the tragedy taken from weather websites—as well as interviews with fishermen recounting the event in a second room.[2]

FO's novelty lies in both its investigation techniques and its unique take on responsibility—an approach that combines liability and social connection models of responsibility. The project's backward-looking model (making states accountable for their inactions as a cause of injury or death) blends with a forward-looking model (acting politically with others for social change). My central claim is that this combination is an original aesthetic response to migration. This claim raises a series of questions that the chapter seeks to address: How does this hybrid call for responsibility unfold in FO's work? How is FO's call an endorsement—or not—of the autonomy of migration? When and how does coexistence emerge? For the sake of clarity and argumentation, my analysis focuses primarily on the Left-to-Die Boat investigation, which is the first of FO's cases. The collective's subsequent cases are mostly variations of that initial work (not in terms of content but in terms of investigation techniques and methodology) and motivated by a similar purpose: to demonstrate EU's "war on migrants."[3] The Left-to-Die Boat is the most documented of all FO's inquiries and the one that has been the most circulated up until now; it fully embraces the liability model of responsibility but already partakes of a more forward-looking perspective. The chapter progressively considers later investigations and projects that make manifest FO's growing determination to extend the liability into a social connection model of political responsibility. *Blaming the Rescuers: Criminalising Solidarity, (Re)enforcing Deterrence*, for example, was conceived primarily as a report for circulation outside the courtroom, within the larger public sphere, to illustrate how state policies themselves have become "a threat to migrants' lives."[4] FO's concomitant creation of the WatchTheMed online platform and contribution to the WatchTheMed Alarm Phone—devices that allow nongovernmental actors to assist migrating beings in distress at sea—profusely confirm its engagement in the social connection model of responsibility. It is this unique combination of responsibility models that this chapter aims to ascertain.

THE LEFT-TO-DIE BOAT INVESTIGATION

Let us start, then, with a close look at *Liquid Traces—the Left-to-Die Boat Case* (2014), a 17-minute video made after the publication of the initial 90-page *Report on the "Left-to-Die Boat"* (2012), cowritten by Heller, Pezzani, and the architecture firm SITU Research. The video displays a digital map of the Mediterranean Sea (figure 4.1). But

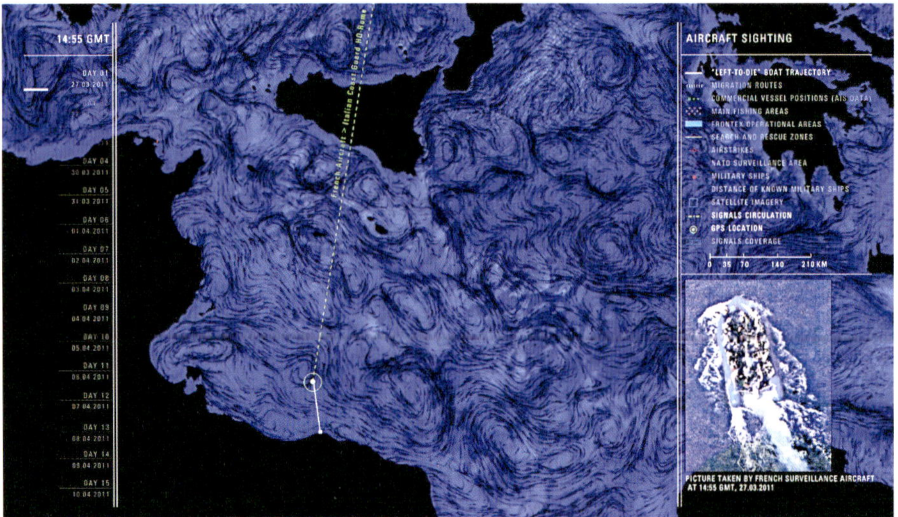

it is closer to an operational dashboard than a straightforward map—an evolving map of the Mediterranean shows progressively added information relative to the event of the Left-to-Die Boat in 2011, in which 72 passengers of a small rubber boat, after leaving the Libyan coast to reach the island of Lampedusa, were left to drift for two weeks in the Mediterranean. The video proposes a reconstruction of the event: narrated by Heller, the account is made visible by the gradual insertion of the names of relevant cities, pixels of light signaling the presence of ships, as well as lines representing the movement (mostly the drifting) of the boat. Simultaneously, a vertically outlined section on the right side of the screen gives written, photo, graphic, sound, and video information on the event, including television footage

FIGURE 4.1

Forensic Oceanography (Charles Heller, Lorenzo Pezzani, Richard Limeburner, Samaneh Moafi, Rossana Padeletti), *Liquid Traces—the Left-to-Die Boat Case*, 2014 (still). Video, 17 minutes. Produced within the frame of Forensic Architecture with the support of the House of World Cultures (HKW). © Forensic Oceanography.

of the Tunisian Spring revolution that set off the movement of migrants in the area, interviews with two survivors—Abu Kurke Kebato and Dan Haile Gebre—and research sources. This section works as a reconstruction glossary, guiding the viewer through the tragedy's chronology. The visual mapping is dramatized throughout by the sound of water waves—whose apparent quietness is troubled by cavernous sounds, some of them suggesting an undersea environment (as though introducing a perspective from below, from the very site of those who drowned in the Mediterranean)—a mixture of extracts from "Music for Loom" by James Wyness, and sound samples from the "Listen to the Deep Ocean Environment (LIDO)" Project of the Laboratory of Applied Bioacoustics at Barcelonatech (Universitat Politècnica de Catalunya).

The video begins with a map of the Mediterranean Sea in dark blue, surrounded by black, supported by the soundtrack. Heller's voice-over seems to emerge from the deep ocean environment—clear, dramatic, and affirmative: "Modulations of the sea's ever-moving surface immediately fold back into its immense liquid mass. What traces might death at and through the sea leave? How to reconstruct violations when the murder weapon is the water itself? What are the conditions that transform the sea into a deadly liquid?" The questions gradually lead to the reestablishment of the event, narrated by Heller and made visible by the various dots, lines, and diagrams appearing on the map: "In the early hours of the twenty-seventh of March 72 people embarked on a 10-meter-long rubber boat" equipped with a GPS and a satellite phone, leaving Tripoli in direction of Lampedusa, Italy. Forced to flee Libya because of the civil war as well as out of fear of persecution, the boat's passengers came from Ghana, Sudan, Ethiopia, Eritrea, and Nigeria (a configuration not mentioned in the video but specified in the report). Although the passengers called for help, using the satellite phone when their boat was starting to run out of fuel; although one of the messages of distress was relayed to the Italian Coast Guard; although the Italian Coast Guard, after identifying the position of the boat as outside of its jurisdiction, sent an alert to relevant agencies and then a signal (emitted every four hours for the next 10 days) to nearby vessels informing them about the boat's "distress and position"; and although a French patrol aircraft, an unidentified military helicopter, and commercial and fishing vessels came into direct or indirect contact with the passengers or circulated in the area, the boat—drifting for 14 days on the Mediterranean Sea—was left to die. After a few days of drifting, passengers—left without food or water—started to die every day. The boat's drifting ended when it re-reached the Libyan coast, landing in Zlitan on April 10, 2011. Out of a total of

72 passengers, only nine survived the failed crossing. The video, together with the report, builds a case of nonassistance. The main claim supporting the case is the following: the nonrescuing response was overdetermined but far from accidental. The boat was positioned outside of Italy's and Malta's search-and-rescue zones (within which they are responsible to coordinate rescue) following a fragmentation of jurisdictions that can easily allow a state to evade rescue operations; the boat was located within NATO's maritime surveillance area, but its surveillance operations were minimal so as to leave the rescuing to the country whose zone was occupied at that point in time; and fishing vessels were then, as they are now, discouraged to rescue—they are often accused of facilitating migration by attempting to save displaced people.

The video and the report, however, do not simply tell a story. This aspect is crucial to the counterforensic approach: they detail the methodology elaborated to reconstitute the event. In the video, as Heller reconstructs the Left-to-Die Boat incident, he raises questions about *how* to find the evidence of nonassistance—that is, how to retrace the traces of death "at and through the sea" and how to uncover "violations when the murder weapon" is the sea itself. Although part of the evidence relies on the testimonies of some of the survivors, the methodology consisted mainly in turning the data produced by NATO's high surveillance of the area in the aftermath of the Arab Spring and the civil war in Libya into evidence of nonassistance. Early in the video, the voice-over explains how the sea itself has increasingly become media. FO's main methodology is based on that very understanding: the acknowledgment of the mediality of the Mediterranean that derives from the sea's own liquid sensitive materiality but that has also been conditioned considerably by the proliferation of surveillance and sensing technologies in the region. The methodology involves repurposing surveillance technologies and reusing the data generated by these technologies, in particular AIS data from vessel-tracking systems on large commercial vessels as well as Synthetic Aperture Radar (SAR) satellite imagery (imagery regularly collected over the Mediterranean Sea for different purposes, one of which is to monitor illegalized migration), as "evidence of guilt." FO also relied on the passengers' initial calls for help via the satellite phone and wind- and sea-current data to demonstrate its claim. As John Durham Peters has shown in his study of elemental media, although media are often understood as environments, it is pivotal to start to understand environments themselves as media.[5] The Mediterranean Sea is a media environment not only because of its increased technological medialization but also because its elemental composition itself is a sensor: water has "prehended" (following the mathematician-philosopher Alfred North Whitehead's definition of *prehension* as a mode of absorption[6]) the shipwreck and the bodies that have been left to die. That sensing is inseparable from the sea's medialization by surveillance, sensing, and communication technologies as well as by FO's refashioning of these technologies. As Weizman claims about Forensic Architecture's methodology, the sea, to be read as a sensor, must be captured by other (analog or digital) sensors that translate the sensorial findings of the sea into data to make sense of these elemental findings.[7] The evolving pulsating digital map should thus be seen as a translator, a mode of visualization par excellence of the sensing sea, by which the crime of nonassistance is reconstructed.

But let us be more attentive to FO's methodology: How does the Left-to-Die Boat investigation actually repurpose technology to establish a case of nonassistance? Describing the mediality of the sea in *Liquid Traces—the Left-to-Die Boat Case*, Heller's voice-over explains: "In addition to its war ships and maritime controlled aircraft, NATO relied on a complex assemblage of remote sensing technologies so as to detect threats hidden within maritime traffic. These included . . . vessel tracking systems which emit the signal to coastal radar systems with information as to the identity, speed and position of large commercial vessels. . . . NATO also relied on . . . radar imagery which emits radar signals from satellites snapping the surface of the earth according to their orbit." Although several of these remote-sensing technologies as well as the data they generate are exclusively controlled by EU member states and agencies, some are available to the larger public.[8] The reconstruction of the Left-to-Die Boat event through the repurposing of technologies of surveillance includes using some of these accessible systems, more precisely SAR satellite imagery to confirm the presence of a significant number of vessels in the vicinity of the drifting boat, as well as the analysis of AIS-generated signals (AIS is a ship-borne navigational system that automatically provides live information about the position of large commercial ships to other ships and coastal authorities; it is not required, however, for warships) to "negatively" identify the military vessels in close proximity to the boat, thus establishing which ships were not accounted for in the AIS data (figure 4.2). FO georeferenced the position of the passengers' distress satellite phone calls. It also relied on the work of the oceanographer Richard Limeburner from the Woods Hole Oceanographic Institute, who modelized the fourteen-day trajectory of the drifting boat by analyzing data on winds and currents collected by buoys in the Sicily Channel—a collaboration that allowed FO to determine that, except for a very brief wandering in the Maltese rescue zone, the boat remained for

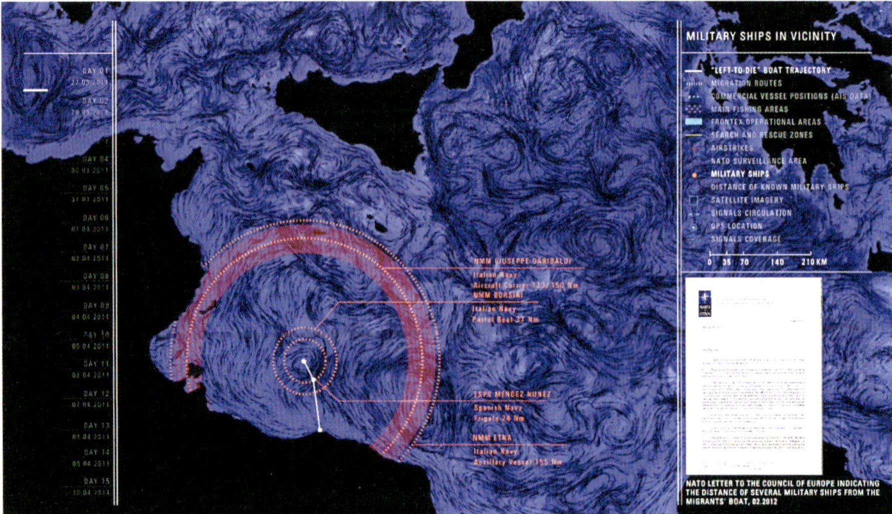

most of its trajectory within the NATO maritime surveillance area.[9] Finally, after collecting official statements by military officers specifying the technical potential of the means of surveillance deployed in the Mediterranean, the research team analyzed the range of the ships' technologies to demonstrate that the ships had the means to sense the drifting boat.[10] FO, in short, turned the data produced by a variety of surveillance and sensing technologies into evidence of responsibility.

FO's participation in the liability model of responsibility is summarized in the following statement: "While the fragmentation of juridical regimes at sea so often allows for the evasion of responsibility, in this case it was mobilized strategically toward the multiplication of potentially liable actors and of forums where

FIGURE 4.2

Forensic Oceanography (Charles Heller, Lorenzo Pezzani, Richard Limeburner, Samaneh Moafi, Rossana Padeletti), *Liquid Traces—the Left-to-Die Boat Case*, 2014 (still). Video, 17 minutes. Produced within the frame of Forensic Architecture with the support of the House of World Cultures (HKW). © Forensic Oceanography.

they could be judged and debated."[11] It is on the basis of this understanding that FO's report was presented as a support document in legal proceedings concerning nonassistance at sea undertaken by a coalition of European human rights groups and NGOs, including the Aire Centre, Agenzia Habeshia, Associazione Ricreativa e Culturale Italiana, Associazione per gli Studi Giuridici sull'Immigrazione, Boats-4People, Canadian Centre for International Justice, Groupe d'information et de soutien des immigrés, Migreurop, Coordination et initiatives pour réfugiés et étrangers, Fédération internationale des ligues des droits de l'homme, Ligue belge des droits de l'homme, Ligue française des droits de l'homme, Progress Lawyers Network, Réseau euro-méditerranéen des droits de l'homme; Unione Forense per la Tutela dei Diritti Umani; and Human Rights Watch. The legal cases were filed against the countries claimed to be responsible for nonassistance in the Left-to-Die Boat tragedy: Italy, France, Spain, and Belgium. Although the legal proceedings were successful in forcing member states to release further data about the event and the evidence reported by FO has not been contested, the coalition has not yet been successful in establishing legal responsibility for the deaths of the migrating passengers.

IRIS MARION YOUNG'S MODELS OF RESPONSIBILITY

Liquid Traces's evolving digital map represents and reconstructs the EU's nonassistance to people endangered at sea; as a whole, the Left-to-Die Boat case is a counter-forensic endeavor whose main outcome has been the filing of a legal case against the countries involved. It is a liability claim, but it is not *solely* a liability claim. Its call for responsibility is more complex insofar as it already blends with the social connection model of political responsibility—one that has progressively become central to FO's investigations. I focus on that evolving hybridity for the remainder of this chapter. To help us circumscribe that unique amalgamation, it is useful to go back to Iris Marion Young's comparative study of the main models of responsibility: the liable, moral, and socially connected (political) models. Even though Young never addresses migratory injustice, her triad is particularly promising as an analytical tool to appreciate the originality of FO's call.[12]

I briefly discussed Young's social connection model of responsibility in the preceding chapter. Bringing coexistence to the fore, the model claims that those of us who are not (yet) experiencing a specific social injustice nevertheless participate in "the same structures of privilege and disadvantage, constraint and enablement" as those who are harmed by these structures.[13] Once we become conscious of that participation, each one of us must act to undo that injustice. The model applies to actors who have not caused prejudice (it is not a backward-looking attribution of responsibility), and it mainly applies to problems of social injustice. It proposes a nonblame, forward-looking view of responsibility as something shared between individuals who become cognizant of their involvement in specific structures of injustice and who decide to act against them. Their actions, as minor as they may be, will be effective—Young explains—when motivated by the intention to mobilize others and "act together to transform the institutions to promote better ends."[14] The model is first and foremost a political responsibility whose temporality is "always now, in relation to current events and in relation to their future consequences."[15]

I find this social connection model particularly compelling for the understanding of Europe's and North America's responsibility in the evolution of migration. In Richard Mosse's *Incoming* and FO's *Liquid Traces*, responsibility is thought out as a detrimental coexistence between citizens of poorer countries of origin and wealthier countries of destination in which the latter confirm their sovereignty by excluding the former from their territory. The social connection model provides a description of a collective struggle against that type of injustice: it proposes a more luminous form of coexistence. Whereas some actors can and should be found liable for the endangering of the lives of migrating beings (the demonstration of liability remains pivotal to FO), most citizens are not responsible in that way. They are not necessarily guilty. Most citizens cannot be said to *cause* necropolitics. Rather, they reproduce the neocolonial norms and structures by which migratory injustice is consolidated; they support governments that implement these norms and structures. This is why the social connection model is a forward-looking form of responsibility: it does not involve blame because the point of the model is not to focus on the identity of those who are imputed for a specific harm. In matters of social injustice, responsibility never simply concerns one individual who is uniquely accountable for structural injustice. The model is forward-looking because it politically reorients toward actions of justice the nonintentional actions that are part of the structures of social injustice. The collective and interdependent qualification of responsibility is a response to the reality of injustice, which is likewise collective and interdependent. As specified by Young, "The social connection model finds that all those who contribute by their actions to structural processes with some unjust outcomes share responsibility for the injustice. This responsibility is not primarily backward-looking, as the attribution of guilt or fault is, but rather primarily forward-looking. Being responsible in relation to structural injustice means that one has the right to join with others who share that responsibility in order to transform the structural processes to make their outcomes less unjust."[16] Responsibility for social injustice is therefore a double effort: it implies connecting with individuals who participate in the same injustice and acting with them to reverse that injustice.

Young defines the struggle for social justice in contrast to the assignment of legal and moral responsibilities, which rely on notions of "blame" or "fault" for their articulation. FO's initial forensic deployment of responsibility, as I suggested earlier, was mostly legal, so the distinction is useful. As formulated by Young, "Within standard frameworks of moral and legal responsibility, it is necessary to connect a person's deeds linearly to the harm for which we seek to assign responsibility."[17] The liability model—the most common model of responsibility—stems from legal reasoning, which attributes guilt for the harm inflicted. In that model, "one assigns responsibility to particular agents whose actions can be shown to be causally connected to the circumstances for which responsibility is sought."[18] The actions causally connected to the event must be exposed as voluntary, and evidence must be collected and related to demonstrate the causal connection between an actor and an impairment. More importantly for our discussion of FO's model of responsibility, Young maintains that the liability model is unsuitable for assigning responsibility in relation to ongoing structural injustices. As specified by the political theorist Maeve Catherine McKeown, "The liability model is *isolating* and *backward-looking*"; it seeks to attribute blame or liability to particular actors for harm that has *already* happened.[19] These features suggest that FO's call for responsibility is somewhat more complex than a straightforward liability model.

FO'S HYBRID MODEL OF RESPONSIBILITY

In light of Young's specifications, could it not be argued that FO's inventiveness lies in its capacity to bridge the liability and social connection models of responsibility? Of course FO's counterforensics articulates a liability claim—its oceanography in the Left-to-Die Boat case involved the making of a report that was used to legally establish the responsibility of EU member states on the basis of their wrongful actions of nonrescue. And yet hasn't FO simultaneously elaborated a political deployment of responsibility involving a variety of citizens? Might it not be the case that the backward-looking liable model and the forward-looking connection model reinforce one another in the collective's investigative endeavors? This hybridity becomes especially manifest when we consider the following three orientations of FO's evolution: (1) The Left-to-Die Boat video and report posit that the death of most of the boat's passengers was inflicted by state authorities, but FO's contribution to the legal cases is inseparable from the investigation's impressive socially connected authorship and from its circulation in various public forums (a wise decision considering that the legal cases remain unresolved to this day and that they will in all likelihood either last for years or end unsuccessfully)—a collectivity that is inherent to what I designate as FO's counteraesthetics. (2) FO's subsequent investigations of lethal EU policies have only rarely taken the route of courts; although backward-looking in their effort to blame governmental policy making for the increase of migrant distress at sea, these reports have circulated in a variety of forums, and that wide circulation has likewise become a prompt for collective political responsibility. (3) FO's more recent involvement in the WatchTheMed online platform and Alarm Phone initiative has significantly increased the level of participation of citizens-on-the-move and citizens tout court in the forward-looking defense of migratory rights. Let us consider closely these three developments.

1.   In his discussion of the aesthetic component of counterforensics, Weizman insists on the need to align aesthetics and knowledge production. Aesthetics, he claims, has "the capacity to sense and detect," and that capacity makes it amenable to the forensic search for evidence. As a "mode and means for narration, performance, and staging," it contributes to any project that seeks to make evidence *public*. A variety of institutions—museums, legal forums, universities, activist organizations, and NGOs—can act as complementary forums to enlarge that public sphere.[20] Could it not be contended that FO has complicated Weizman's definition of aesthetics by elaborating a counteraesthetics—a practice specifically invented by FO "to put into practice a *disobedient gaze*" in relation to EU's aesthetic regime?[21] In an interview for *Text zur Kunst*, Heller expands on that notion of disobedience: "We conceived of this gaze as aiming *not* to disclose what the regime of migration management attempts to unveil—clandestine migration—but to unveil that which it attempts to hide: the political violence it is founded on and the human rights violations that are its structural outcome."[22] The decision to exercise a defiant gaze against EU's migration and border regime—an aesthetic regime that rests on the denegation of the European injuring and elimination of migrating beings as they

attempt to flee the threats of injury and elimination unfolding in their countries of origin—is not without recalling the "right to look" defined by visual studies scholar Nicholas Mirzoeff as a countervisuality critical of dominant visualities—a disobedient look that makes visible what visuality conceals, depreciates, and marginalizes.[23] The productivity of that terminology lies in its capacity to emphasize how much FO's inquiries, as is the case with *counter*forensics, remove aesthetics from the sole hands of the artist and the sole venue of art institutions to include a cluster of human actors, nonhuman actors, and agents (technological and elemental media) as well as a multiplicity of forums (the media, courts, truth commissions, human rights venues, museums, and galleries) in the struggle for migratory justice.[24] FO's *Left-to-Die Boat* video and report are a collaborative work that brought together survivors, human rights and migration activists, NGOs, and scientists; that bridges art, critical refugee and migrant studies, media studies, geography, international development, law and criminalistics; and that has been largely disseminated in the international press. The case was presented in court but also to different activist and academic audiences across Europe and North America; the video has been screened on television as well as in festivals and was shown in close to 30 exhibitions in Europe and the United States. In short, while partaking of a liability model of responsibility, FO's Left-to-Die Boat investigation has been mixing that model (from the start) with a social connection model of political responsibility. Both models remain active and complementary, creating a new hybrid, liable-political form of responsibility. That hybridity has been especially productive in light of the pending legal proceedings that might well never find any resolution because the dispute involves too many SAR zones and jurisdictions.[25]

2. Particularly relevant to the process of collectivizing responsibility, FO opened up a whole new sphere of counteraesthetic investigations after the Left-to-Die Boat inquiry: although still backward-looking and sometimes supporting legal cases, the inquiries focus on establishing the role of state policies in the endangerment of migratory journeys. The analysis of "the structural, long-term, and largescale outcome of the EU's exclusionary border regime"[26] aims to outline the responsibility of states especially since 2014—when the Italian rescue-oriented Operation Mare Nostrum was ended and Frontex's budget increased to hold the new security-oriented Operation Triton. The naval and air Operation Mare Nostrum was launched after the migrant shipwreck off the Italian island of Lampedusa on October 3, 2013—specified at the time as one of the worst shipwrecks (in terms of lost lives—a reported 366 out of 500 passengers) in the recent history of the

Mediterranean; it was ended a year later on the unproven basis that it constituted a "pull factor" for migration. The Triton shift was devised to strengthen the security approach to migration—a decision based on the deceptively humanitarian premise that such an approach would help save lives. As the study by the international relations and EU studies expert Eugenio Cusumano illustrates, the security policies ended up increasing the number of migrating beings dying at sea: in 2015, "over one million migrants crossed the Mediterranean sea to reach Europe . . . amounting to 3771 estimated casualties," and 2016 was "the deadliest year in the recent history of migration movements to Europe."[27]

The study of the effects of that shift in policy sustains FO's video *The EU's Lethal Policies of Non-assistance* (2016) summarizing the report *Blaming the Rescuers: Criminalising Solidarity, (Re)enforcing Deterrence* (2017) (figure 4.3). The report and video initiated what Heller and Pezzani have called a "forensics of policies"—the making visible of what remains invisible in policy making: "the causal relation between policies of closure and migrant deaths" as well as the masquerading of the dehumanitarianization of the border as a humanitarian operation.[28] As was the case with The Left-to-Die Boat video and report, for *Blaming the Rescuers* FO held wide-ranging interviews with state officials, displaced people, and survivors; it used the methodologies of remote sensing and geolocation as well as the creation of an evolving digital map of the Mediterranean Sea to reconstitute a death event (here, a double event). *Blaming the Rescuers* reconstructs two shipwrecks that occurred in the central Mediterranean on April 12 and 18, 2015, and resulted in more than 1,200 deaths in a single week—deaths that ensued from the very attempt to rescue them. Commercial vessels approached the overcrowded migrant boats in an effort to rescue the passengers, but the boats were overturned by their approach. The main claim of *Blaming the Rescuers* is that the two boat incidents resulted largely from a significant change in EU policies, "particularly the retreat of state rescue operations and a resulting onus on commercial vessels to fill the 'rescue gap,'" as well as from the illegalization of NGOs (mainly Sea-Eye) wanting to fulfill their rescue mission.[29] Key here is the difficulty in making EU agencies and policy makers legally accountable for policies of nonassistance—hence, Heller's and Pezzani's decision not to privilege the legal route, even though their investigation still relied on a backward-looking model of responsibility, which seeks to blame policy making for the shipwrecks.[30] Their policy videos have circulated in several art exhibitions, chiefly in Europe. Each new art and cultural forum becomes an occasion to involve citizens in the resolution of migratory injustice. But the complementary liability

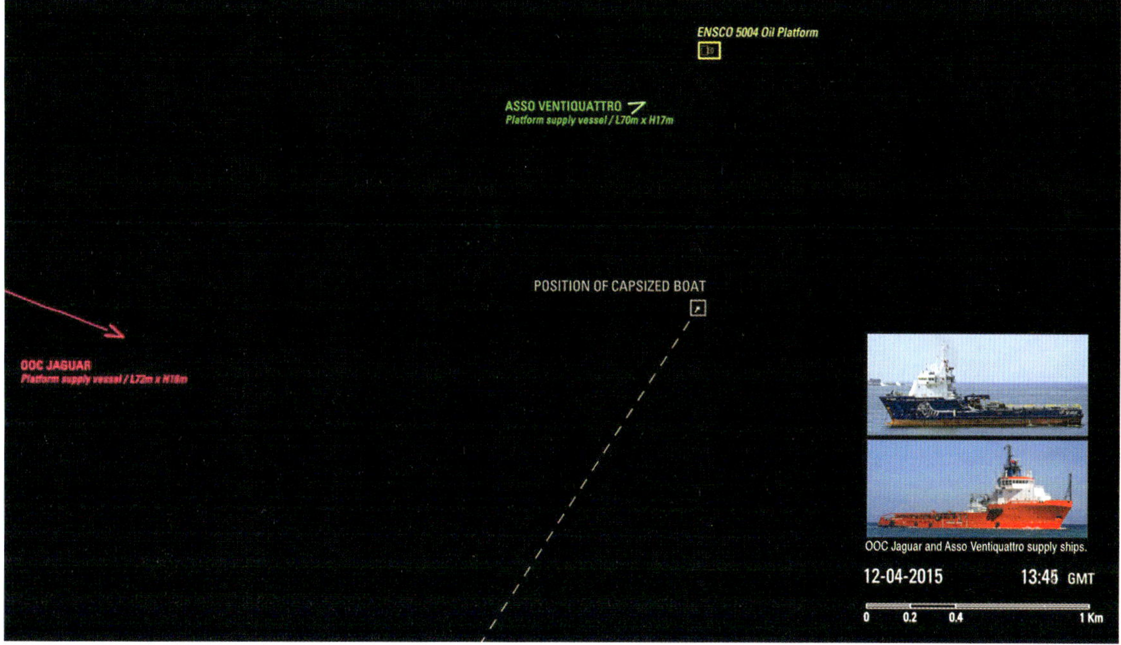

model never simply vanishes: the FO sent its report *Sea Watch vs the Libyan Coastguard* (2018), for example, to the European Court of Human Rights.

3.　Finally, in line with the understanding of counteraesthetics as a hybrid call for responsibility, FO conceptualized and launched the WatchTheMed online mapping platform (watchthemed.net) in 2012 (figure 4.4). The platform was

FIGURE 4.3

Forensic Oceanography (Charles Heller, Lorenzo Pezzani, Richard Limeburner, Sabine Llewellyn, Samaneh Moafi, Rossana Padeletti, Laure Vermeersch), *The EU's Lethal Policies of Non-assistance*, 2016 (still). Video, 14 minutes. Produced within the ESRC-funded Precarious Trajectories research project with the support of the Economic and Social Research Council (ESRC). © Forensic Oceanography.

introduced as part of the Boats4People (B4P) campaign in the central Mediterranean—a three-week campaign undertaken by a coalition of organizations navigating on B4P's boat the *Oloferne* to demand the reopening of the EU's maritime borders.[31] It then went on to involve a network of NGOs, activists, researchers, migrants' rights organizations, displaced people, and seafarers "active in, around and beyond the Mediterranean" to monitor and document the deaths and violations of people at sea and inform survivors of their rights.[32] It was devised as a counterpart to backward-looking postevent analysis.[33] FO's participatory platform led to the creation of the WatchTheMed Alarm Phone in 2014 by activists and civil society actors in Europe and North Africa who were already active in migratory justice networks, such as Welcome to Europe, Afrique Europe Interact, Borderline Europe, Noborder Morocco, and Watch The Med. The Alarm Phone is a 24/7-operating nongovernmental emergency phoneline designed to help endangered boatpeople in real-time interventions—the help is provided by the passengers themselves as well as by journalists, activists, survivors of shipwrecks, and relatives of exiles who disappeared when traveling to Europe (figure 4.5).[34] Understood as a crucial step in the "collectivization of . . . activist and militant practices," its main aim has been to "offer travelers alternative ways to make their distress heard and pressure states into complying with their obligations."[35] Since its creation, the Alarm Phone initiative is said to have supported more than 2,000 endangered boats not through direct rescue but through the rerouting of the distress calls to a large number of volunteers located in different European countries, whose role is to ensure that the calls are heard and acted upon but also to exercise pressure on patrol guards in real time as the violation of migrant rights at sea is unfolding.[36]

The WatchTheMed mapping platform and WatchTheMed Alarm Phone confirm FO's increased consolidation of the forward-looking social connection model of political responsibility. Interestingly, the more the model is embraced, the more migrating beings and the more non-European activists from countries of origin have a say in the unfolding of migratory justice. The Left-to-Die Boat investigation included interviews with two survivors, but the WatchTheMed Alarm Phone operations are live; they unfold in real time, before deadly outcomes: they involve an ongoing communication with the passengers initiating the distress calls and a collective of carers from Europe and Africa. As a preventive measure, they promote the acknowledgment of the autonomy of migration. The forward-looking model of responsibility is better equipped to connect citizens-on-the-move, artists, activists,

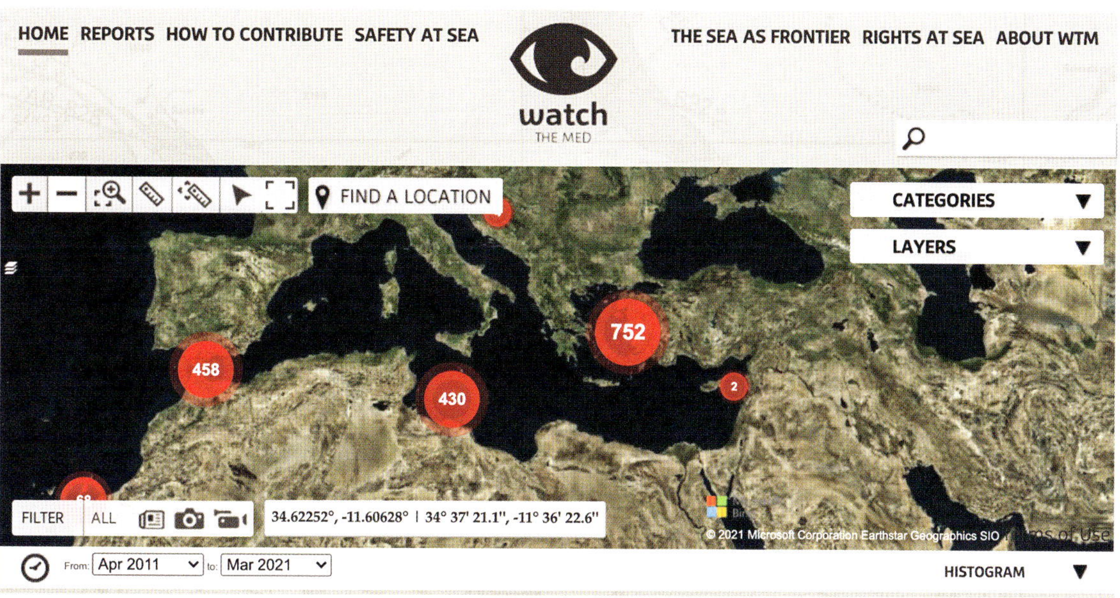

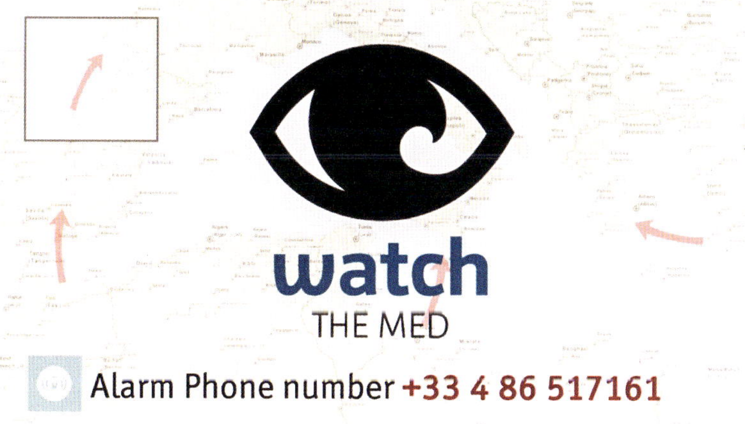

FIGURE 4.4

Screenshot of the Watch the Mediterranean Sea homepage. At https://watchthemed.net (accessed October 6, 2021). © WatchTheMed Alarm Phone. Map data: © 2021 Microsoft Corporation Earthstar Geographics SIO.

FIGURE 4.5

WatchTheMed logo and Alarm Phone number. At https://alarmphone.org/ (accessed January 7, 2021). © WatchTheMed Alarm Phone.

and organizations in the fight against migratory injustice. As Weizman maintains, collaborative modes of investigation, evidence making, and verification rely upon:

the creation of a community of practice in which the production of an investigation is socialized; a relation between people who experience violence, activists who take their side, a diffused network of open-source investigators, scientists and other experts who explore what happened. The presentation of evidence must also be socialised with lawyers, journalists, and sometimes, in our case, cultural institutions that help fund, produce, and present the work. As such, the open process of the investigation establishes a social contract that includes all the participants in the uncanny assemblage of production and dissemination.[37]

Persisting in that socializing and collaborative call, WatchTheMed has more recently formulated the idea of a humanitarian ferry that would reach Libya, evacuate the migrating men, women, and children currently held in overcrowded detention centers (documented as breeding grounds for extreme violence against the inmates[38]), "and bring them to Europe[,] where they should receive unconditional protection," thus reaffirming, as it were, their freedom of movement.[39] Banksy's search-and-rescue boat the *Louise Michel*, discussed in the introduction, is a partial materialization of that vision, but the ferry has larger aspirations: its objectives would include both rescue and evacuation. FO's Lorenzo Pezzani is now also assisting another socially connected political deployment of responsibility: the Pirate Care Project—an international research-and-creation project supported by a network of activists, scholars, and practitioners "who stand against the criminalization of solidarity & for a common care infrastructure."[40] For Pezzani, pirate care is a political action that specifically contests the defunding, discouragement, and illegalization of care "understood as a political and collective capacity of society."[41] As discussed in the next chapter as well as in chapters 7, 8, 9, and 10, care is finding its place within the development of the forward-looking and collaborative model of responsibility. One of the primary reasons for its emergence in artistic practices is the increased outlawing of migratory care and so the imperative to question that banning. On June 14, 2019—a key moment in that criminalization—the Italian government presented a security decree illegalizing sea-rescue NGO ships entering Italian waters without permission; sanctions include "up to 50,000 euros fines, the arrest of crew members, and the requisition of vessels."[42] The decree was approved and passed into law by the Chamber of Deputies and the Senate respectively on July 24 and August 5, 2019.

CARE

The U.S.-Mexican border es una herida abierta [is an open wound] where the Third World grates against the first and bleeds. And before a scab forms it hemorrhages again, the lifeblood of two worlds merging to form a third country—a border culture.
—Gloria Anzaldúa, *Borderlands/La Frontera*[1]

La promesa (2012), a long, compact, voluminous rectangular block by Mexican artist Teresa Margolles (b. 1963, Culiacán, Mexico), is installed directly on the museum floor. Troubling its title and reversely suggesting a promise gone wrong, its materiality evokes a salvaged wall fragment extracted from an archaeological site, a collapsed monument, a fallen column waiting to be lifted back into its vertical position. Its heaviness, however, grounds it to the floor. In the version shown at the Musée d'art contemporain de Montréal, where I experienced it in 2017, it was made of 15 tons of rubble from an abandoned social welfare house located on Puerto de Palos Street in Ciudad Juárez's Praderas de Oriente neighborhood (figure 5.1).

The origins of the assembled debris—Ciudad Juárez, a border city part of the Mexican state of Chihuahua just south of El Paso, Texas—establish the work as a dramatic response to migration, especially when migration is understood as a constellation of undervalued (im)migration crises. Together with the neighboring areas, these two cities make up the second-biggest binational metropolitan area on the Mexico-US border (following San Diego–Tijuana): El Paso–Juárez. A city within a borderzone, inseparable from what the poet and cultural theorist Gloria Anzaldúa calls in the chapter's epigraph a "border culture"—a culture that separates

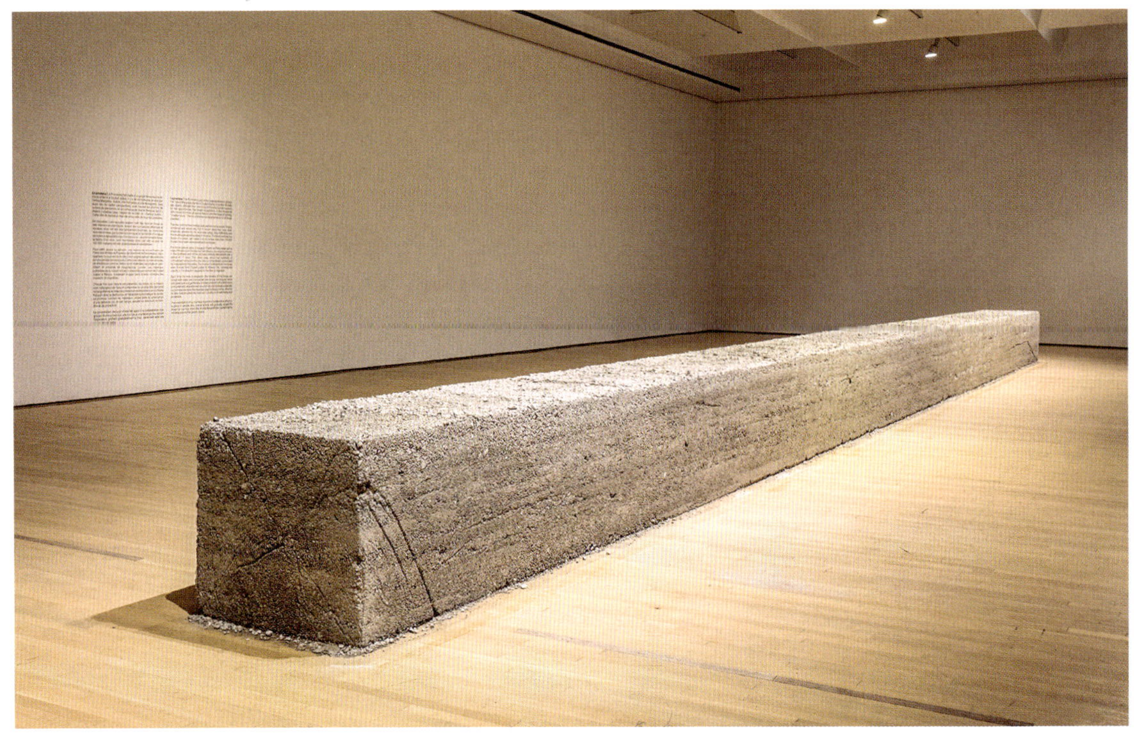

Teresa Margolles, *La promesa*, 2012.
Sculptural block made from the pulverized
rubble of a demolished house in Ciudad
Juárez, Mexico. 15 tons, 55 × 80 × 1,600
cm. Installation view: *Teresa Margolles:
Mundos*, Musée d'art contemporain de
Montréal, Montréal, Canada, February 16,
2017–May 14, 2017. Collection of the
Museo Universitario Arte Contemporáneo
(MUAC), Universidad Nacional Autónoma
de México (UNAM), Mexico City. Installation
commissioned by the MUAC, UNAM, with
the support of the Ford Foundation Latin
America in commemoration of its fiftieth
anniversary. Photo: Richard-Max Tremblay.
Courtesy of Musée d'art contemporain de
Montréal. © Teresa Margolles.

but also combines elements inside and outside different types of (geographical, sexual, and social) crossings—Ciudad Juárez is the poor counterpart of the rich city of El Paso. Its border culture has been fundamentally reshaped by the North American Free Trade Agreement (NAFTA) of 1994 between the United States, Mexico, and Canada, which led to a substantial influx of people migrating to Juárez from Mexico City, rural regions of Mexico, as well as Central America in search of jobs in manufacturing and engineering in assembly plants called "maquiladoras." This influx, however, was followed by a significant exodus of people due to the city's increased violence—a high rate of homicides and feminicides, most of them perpetrated with impunity—resulting from dense narcotics trafficking, high military and police presence, rising economic inequality, as well as a corrupt public administration. In 2010, the *Wall Street Journal* estimated more than 116,000 deserted homes, the equivalent of approximatively 400,000 people leaving the city, and the *Guardian* stated that approximately "10,670 businesses—40% of the total—ha[d] shut down," resulting in the abandonment of 116,000 houses and the departure of 230,000 people.[2] Violence and unemployment, added to the tensions between security cultures attempting to contain the violence and the continuous flow of incoming and exiting people due to work opportunities and cutbacks, have sustained the progression of large slum-housing communities called "colonias," from which the rubble for *La promesa* was extracted.

The house that constitutes the rubble was an injury resulting from migration: abandoned, it originally sheltered a family forced to leave Ciudad Juárez. The block was conceived from the start as an investigation of that abandonment. In the early stages of *La promesa*, Margolles asked herself the following questions: "In Juárez, there are more than 115,000 or 120,000 abandoned houses. Why does one abandon one's house? . . . Why abandon a house when the house is the family's patrimony? Why did the people abandon their houses in Juárez? . . . [O]n what basis can one say to one's family, to one's children, to believe in their country by abandoning the foundation, their house; to be productive, to believe in the future, while abandoning one's house because of terror?"[3] In other words, why would one leave behind their most intimate infrastructure of everyday life, whose function is to provide shelter, permanency, and sociability to a family? More generally, why was the family induced to forced displacement? The answer to these questions can be found in Margolles's deliberation: terror. The artist purchased the house after its residents had left the city, deserting their home following the murder of their daughter.[4] The house was meticulously dismantled by her crew in June 2012 over a period of 11 days;

the rubble was produced by crushing the house's building materials as well as its remaining objects. Disassembled, the house became unrecognizable yet transportable.[5] The ultimate reply to Margolles's query took the form of sacks for transport and a wooden formwork so that a rectangular block of rubble may be built by any art institution interested in re-creating the installation anew in different sizes.

This is *La promesa*, an ongoing work of art—which exists in its ongoingness. Its rubble is made of the fragmented elements of the house (except for human-body components and toxic residues, which have been discarded), including walls, floors, countertops, buttons, threads, strings, books, paper, pieces of pottery, and so on. The complete version is composed of 45.76 tons of debris. It is part of the collection of the Museo Universitario Arte Contemporáneo at the Universidad Nacional Autónoma de México, Mexico City, and was first exhibited there in its fullest version in 2012. The work was subsequently presented in a reduced version at the Staatliche Kunsthalle Baden-Baden in 2013 and then at the Centro de Arte Dos de Mayo in Madrid in 2014 and the Musée d'art contemporain de Montréal, where it stood as the largest of the reduced versions shown outside Mexico—its dimensions for the Canadian show were 55 × 80 × 1,600 centimeters, and its weight more than 15 tons. Each time it is exhibited, several tons of rubble are sent to the gallery or the museum, which is responsible for assembling the wooden formwork and adding water to the rubble to give a rectangular shape to the mixture. After each exhibition, the wreckage that the block eventually becomes again is shipped in construction sacks either to the Museo Universitario Arte Contemporáneo or to the next institution showing the work. Once the block is installed, volunteers from the city in which it is shown will transform it further—one hour per day and one person at a time—by scraping it with care and in silence as they meditate on their own experiences of broken promises (figure 5.8). These are Margolles's instructions. The block is thus progressively undone, but its matter is preserved and eventually sent away to be remixed, reinstalled, redone, and re-undone.

La promesa offers an unparalleled perspective on contemporary migration. It discloses violence- and poverty-inflicted displacement as it evolves in daily borderland life, within and just beyond the border-crossing zones between the United States and Mexico. I encourage readers to establish their own conversation between the sculpture and the other artworks examined in this book that likewise pertain to the US-Mexico border, all of which have violence as one of their major concerns: Undocumented Migration Project's *Hostile Terrain 94* (chapter 1), Ursula Biemann's *Performing the Border* (1999) and Chantal Akerman's *From the Other Side* (*De l'autre côté*, 2002) (chapter 3), Alejandro González Iñárritu's *CARNE y ARENA* (2017) (chapter 7), and Rafael Lozano-Hemmer's *Border Tuner* (2019) (chapter 8). A significant part of a larger corpus of works made by Margolles in relation to Ciudad Juárez, *La promesa* emphasizes the border city's recurring feminicides—showing how gender and sexuality are key components of imperiled migrancy. It discloses that reality, but its main aesthetic procedures lie elsewhere—in memorialization, grieving, and healing. The work is rooted in but also renews the memorial tradition developed by survivors and activists from Juárez to account for feminicides, murdered and disappeared victims; Margolles has stated that it was made "in memory of a family, of the 60,000 people assassinated in the country."[6] The work introduces the possibility of grieving what the philosopher Judith Butler has called an "ungrievable life"—a life "that cannot be mourned," at least in the public sphere, "because it has never lived, that is, it has never counted as a life at all"[7]—while also inviting viewers and volunteers to come to terms with failed or unkept promises of a better life. I want to propose, and this will be my central postulate in this chapter, that *La promesa* is more decisively a call for a shared forward-looking responsibility that takes the form of a fully assumed nonidealized practice of care.

The installation offers a unique opportunity to deepen and conclude our study on the call for responsibility. Of all the works studied in part II, *La promesa* goes the furthest in associating responsibility and care. The dismantling and reassembling of matter, memorialization, grieving, and healing are some of the pivotal tasks of responsible care. To circumscribe the singularity of that call, the chapter first contextualizes the work both within Ciudad Juárez and in relation to Margolles's overall production—a production that is fully dedicated to a forensic contact with unaccounted-for corpses. Building my argument from that specific geopolitics of migration as well as from the artist's forensic work, I then examine the value and challenge of care as a response to contemporary migration. Drawing from care studies, I show care to be an innovative deployment of mutual coexistence.

CIUDAD JUÁREZ

Ciudad Juárez is Mexico's fifth-largest city, with an urban-area population of approximately 1.5 million. It is separated from its twin city El Paso by the Río Bravo/ Rio Grande, which demarcates the natural border between Mexico and the United States, even while being connected to that US city by four international bridges (figure 5.2). This binational metropolitan area is decidedly contrasted: from an urbanistic perspective, the Mexican side is characterized by "the dense and sprawling cityscape of Ciudad Juárez, which is dominated by its miles of shanty dwellings (*colonias*)," while El Paso is known for its recent revitalization of various districts, including the downtown area.[8] Security-wise, although El Paso stands out as one of the five safest cities in the United States, Juárez is considered one of the most dangerous cities in the world, excluding war zones.[9] Especially between 2007 and 2012, the city became the site of violent killings resulting in 10,000 deaths (many of them feminicides) as well as of other violent crimes, including extortion, carjacking, torture, and disappearances. As specified by the international relations scholar Mary Martin, although "most of this violence was linked to competition among drug cartels," its sources were "in the 'subsoil' of corrupt and dysfunctional public administration and rule of law in Mexico. The killing spree itself was exacerbated by the Mexican army troops and federal police who were deployed to halt the narco-traffic turf battles."[10] After this wave and in all likelihood as a result of adjustments within the drug-trafficking network, violent crimes slightly declined in the early 2010s: as of January 2013, for example, Ciudad Juárez's homicide rate was "placed #37 of the highest reported in the world, at 38 murders per 100,000 inhabitants," a trend that continued in 2015, with 300 reported murders.[11] These figures show both a decrease *and* a persistence of violence. I briefly discuss here the three main factors that have been identified as contributing to Juárez's violence-oriented evolution: the city's unequal border position in relation to El Paso, NAFTA, and the proliferation of conflictual security cultures. The aim of this discussion is to show how Juárez's ubiquitous terror, predominantly conditioned by the worldwide unequal distribution of global wealth, has significantly contributed to its migratory distress.

1.   *Ciudad Juárez as an Unequalized Border City.* Juárez's sociogeography as a border city—it strategically sits midway along the 2,000-kilometer-long national border—has been crucial to its development since 1848, when the Mexico-US border was established by splitting the city of El Paso del Norte into two economically unequal parts: El Paso, Texas, and Paso del Norte, Chihuahua (renamed "Ciudad Juárez" in 1888). Corrie Boudreaux, a border studies scholar specializing in the study of inter-American borders, specifies that Juárez's "structural exploitation and homicidal gang- and cartel-related activities" stem from "the economic logic of production and exportation across an international boundary between disparate countries."[12] Even though armies, traders, and citizens have been crossing the international border since its implementation, the founding inequality between El Paso

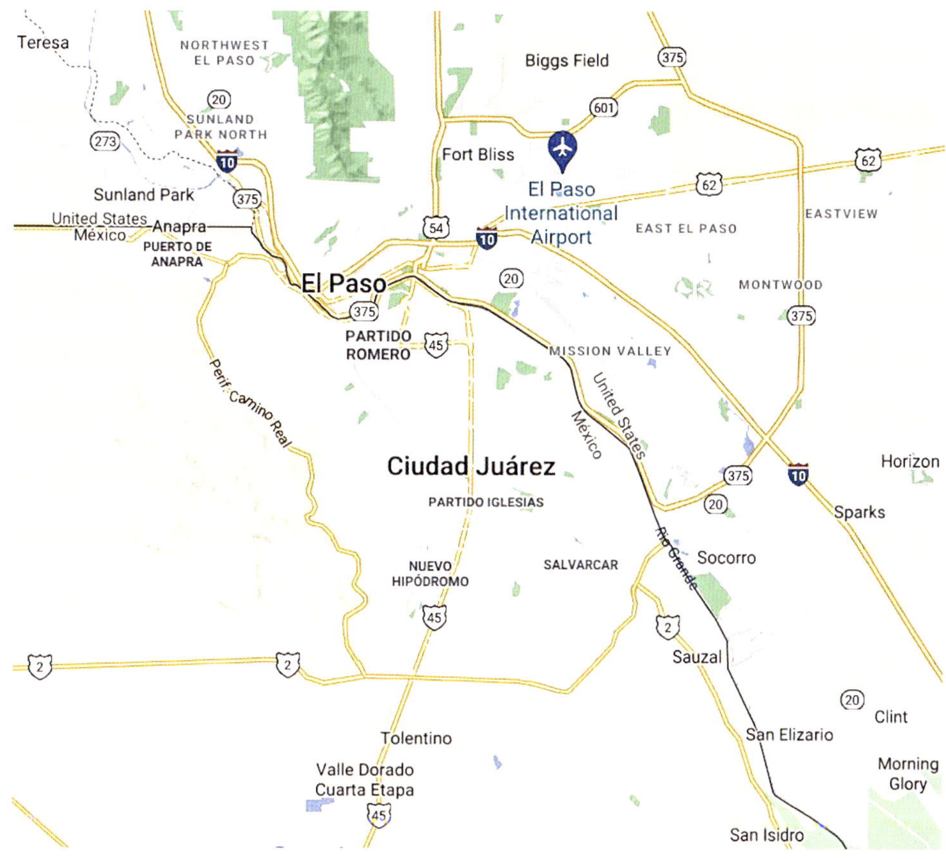

Teresa
NORTHWEST EL PASO
Biggs Field
375
20
601
273
SUNLAND PARK NORTH
Fort Bliss
10
El Paso International Airport
62
Sunland Park
375
62
EASTVIEW
United States
México
Anapra
EAST EL PASO
PUERTO DE ANAPRA
54
10
MONTWOOD
El Paso
20
375
375
PARTIDO ROMERO
45
MISSION VALLEY
Ciudad Juárez
Perif. Camino Real
United States
México
Horizon
PARTIDO IGLESIAS
375
10
20
Sparks
NUEVO HIPÓDROMO
SALVARCAR
Rio Grande
Socorro
45
2
Sauzal
2
2
20
Clint
Tolentino
San Elizario
Valle Dorado Cuarta Etapa
Morning Glory
45
San Isidro

FIGURE 5.2

Ciudad Juárez, Chihuahua, Mexico. Map
Data: Google. © INEGI.

and Ciudad Juárez became especially detrimental from the 1960s on. The expiration of the Bracero bilateral agreement of 1942–1964 between the United States and Mexico instigated the return to Mexico, via Juárez, of temporary Mexican workers who had been employed in the United States, and the maquiladora industry—a duty-free import-export industry of foreign-owned assembly plants operated on Mexican soil—was actively supported by the Mexican government: these two transformations facilitated the elaboration of an economic model providing cheap labor to assemble products that would later be exported to and sold in the United States or other foreign countries for larger profit.[13] Boudreaux emphasizes how this pre-NAFTA growth established Ciudad Juárez as a migration epicenter whose fate was the impoverishment and vulnerabilization of Mexican workers: Juárez "became the collection point for deportees, for migrants hoping to enter the US, and for migrants attracted by work in the *maquiladoras*. Private interests controlled the planning, or lack thereof, of urban growth, and the migrants and workers generally settled in *colonias* around the outskirts of the city. . . . The *colonias* are characterized by cheap housing, lack of infrastructure, placement in undesirable locations at considerable distance from city center, and proximity to the *maquiladoras*."[14] Juárez's pivotal position as a border municipality, whose economy, urbanism, and demography have been shaped by a growing correlation between migration, violence, and poverty, still defines its contemporary development.

2. *NAFTA*. The North American Free Trade Agreement of 1994 has intensified economic disparities in its establishment of tariff-free zones among the United States, Canada, and Mexico—an intensification that progressively led to a peak of violence in Juárez between 2008 and 2013. Studies show that Mexico's maquiladora-related economic growth only really began with the inauguration of NAFTA in 1994.[15] Sayak Valencia's study of NAFTA's impact on Juárez's border culture of violence and economic inequality is unequivocal in that assessment: NAFTA's launch in 1994 led to Mexico's "descent into capitalism gore—the embodiment of hegemonic and economic processes in specific (geographical) border spaces, where death is visibly the source of surplus value."[16] As the political scientist Elva Fabiola Orozco explains, this growing inequality became manifest urbanistically—an outcome that is crucial to understanding *La promesa*, whose rubble was extracted from the Praderas de Oriente colonia:

Compared to southern cities in Mexico, Juárez began to look modern, urban, dynamic, skilled, and even affluent. However, economic prosperity became highly concentrated around industrial parks and the city center. . . . In contrast, the majority of the maquiladora workforce live in slums located in the city's outskirts. Slums feature poorly finished brick houses and dwelling spaces built out of discarded and shoddy materials. Neighborhoods lack paved roads and basic services, including clean water, electricity, sewage, garbage collection, and efficient public transportation. The point about the stark contrast between industrial parks and slums is not merely that one is rich and the other poor, but rather that the city's spatial arrangements are designed to make industrial parks thrive while the material environments available for workers and average people imperils [*sic*] their subsistence. Public space around maquiladora industrial parks is ordered, clean, protected, and provided with first-class services, while slums subsist in the midst of environmental degradation, wrenching violence, and decaying infrastructure.[17]

NAFTA amplified violence during this period—the very period when Margolles visited Juárez and created *La promesa* from the slum area just described by Orozco, together with other works related to Juárez's feminicides—mainly because of its reinforcement of the uneven development of Mexico in relation to the United States and Canada. This development precluded local Mexican factories from competing; it also confirmed the maquiladora as the main working place for Mexican workers. More than 300 maquiladoras were built in and nearby Juárez following the signing of the agreement; they were operated by international companies, including Sony and IBM.[18] This growing globalization-induced inequality intensified the migration of Mexican and Central American peasants to but also eventually out of Juárez. It created an underclass of manufacturing labor composed of (im)migrant workers for the production of global products. As the cultural studies researcher Denisa Krásná and the international lawyer Sagar Deva state, NAFTA has been a central factor in forced, poverty-inflicted displacement:

The figure of a displaced farmer became the new Mexican stereotype as whole families were forced to leave their traditional lands. In response to these dynamics, NAFTA promised prosperity and improvement of living standards and offered a seemingly ideal solution to the crisis (that it inflicted) by creating thousands of new jobs in newly built foreign factories—the maquiladoras. . . . Since NAFTA made it hard for southern peasants who had lost their land to self-sustain themselves, their immigration to the north of Mexico occurred as a means of survival. Nonetheless, not all of the displaced workers found the promised employment in the transformed industrial north as their numbers far exceeded the numbers of available positions. . . . The most suitable candidates for labor positions in maquiladoras

The forced displacement of workers—about 1.3 million Mexican agricultural jobs were lost after the signing of NAFTA, a loss that compelled farmworkers and families to migrate to Juárez, whose urban-area population increased from approximately 959,000 in 1994 to today's 1,540,000[20]—was supported by the drug-trafficking industry, which also relied on Juárez's proximity to international shipping and its supply of cheap, disposable labor.[21] Krásná and Deva's study emphasizes how displaced women workers have been particularly vulnerabilized by NAFTA-supported employers looking for "'docile, undemanding, nimble-fingered, nonunion' workers . . . [characteristics] stereotypically attributed to women": dehumanizing working conditions were established "in which women are frequently subjects of violence, . . . and indeed in many cases their disappearances and deaths."[22] The movement of workers toward the peripheral colonias—themselves zones of "poverty, marginalization and criminalization,"[23] factors that eventually pushed inhabitants out—and their employment in maquiladoras combined to produce an underclass of ungrievable lives not "worthy of protection."[24] In a study on Juárez feminicides published in 2005, the political scientist Verónica Zebadúa-Yañez defines these undervalued, abandoned, and exposed-to-death lives, especially the lives of the young working-class women, as bare lives, following Agamben's theorization of *homo sacer* as a life that may be taken but not sacrificed; life exposed to death.[25] Homicides and feminicides resulting from Juárez's civil warfare are left mainly unpunished—inherent as they are to a state whose authorities maintain impunity by derailing the investigation of killings on the premise that the victims—especially prostitutes, dark-skinned women who migrated to Juárez from the South to work in maquiladoras, and drug dealers—are fully responsible for their own deaths.[26]

3.   *The Proliferation of Conflicting Security Cultures.* Martin's study, published in an edited volume eloquently titled *Cities at War*, proposes a compelling reading of the violence-oriented evolution of Ciudad Juárez as a coevolution of three competing security cultures—border, public or citizen, and neoliberal—between 2006 and 2013,[27] a period that corresponds to Margolles's fieldwork in the area. A *security culture*, following the global governance expert Mary Kaldor's definition of the term, is a "style or a pattern of doing security" that involves a specific combination "of ideas, narratives, rules, people, tools, practices and infrastructure" to grapple

with large-scale violence.[28] Juárez's security cultures in the period 2006–2013 were composed of distinct cultures defending their own comprehension of the city's insecurity, protection needs, and solutions to violence. In 2005, US president George W. Bush initiated the construction of the first fixed border fence between El Paso and Juárez. The fence was reinforced as a "smart border"; stations and checkpoints multiplied in the area, and patrol agents were heavily militarized. This renewed border security culture was a key component of President Bush's call for a global war on terrorism following the terrorist attacks of September 11, 2001. The border security culture was further reinforced by the Trump administration on the basis that the border had become a main entry point for the ill-named "illegal migrants" from Latin America into the United States—a migration perceived as a threat to American culture, identity, and safety.[29] Conflicting with this border security culture, the public or citizen security culture of 2006–2013 underscored the necessity to protect and empower citizens not only against drug-related violence but also against Mexican president Felipe Calderón's instigation of a war on drugs and his deployment of military troops and federal police across Mexico—a war on drugs that ended up worsening the border city's cultivation of violence (swelling the number of murder-related deaths from 316 in 2007 to 1,607 in 2008 and 2,643 in January 2009).[30] The public security culture's main goal was and still is to include citizens in the urban rehabilitation plans designed to improve security. Despite the proliferation of restoration schemes, however, groups such as citizens-on-the-move, women, and young people continue to be marginalized and excluded from the planification process.[31] Finally, the neoliberal security culture was basically designed to protect the deployment of the free market: in Ciudad Juárez, "this means securing and enabling the unfettered operation and growth of manufacturing. The key space surrounds the industrial plants, known as maquiladoras."[32] The factories not only have been gated but have benefited from a "permissive attitude" by government authorities that has increasingly desecuritized the border for international companies to support a more fluid exportation of goods—a desecuritization that does not easily coexist with the rehabilitation programs promoted by the citizen security culture.

What did this coexistence of security cultures in 2006–2013 amount to? How does it persist today? Martin's conclusion is that the coexistence is fundamentally conflictual and that the persistence of these frictions can only sustain the city's violence: "Insecurity in Ciudad Juárez can be seen in terms of a failure to reconcile the tensions among security cultures, to harmonize the use of public spaces and align policies, and to develop a consensus attitude toward the frontier that both unites and divides Ciudad Juárez from El Paso."[33] The American antimigration security policy has intensified; and though the ubiquity of terror has decreased in the past few years, it is now on the rise again, leaving unresolved the necropolitics of borderzones and the internal displacement of residents it entails. When using the notion of internally displaced persons (IDPs), I follow the UNCHR's definition: IDPs are "persons or groups of persons who have been forced or obliged to flee or to leave their homes or places of habitual residence, in particular as a result of or in order to avoid the effects of armed conflict, situations of generalized violence, violations of human rights or natural or human-made disasters, and who have not crossed an internationally recognized State border."[34] To this list of factors causing internal displacement must be added the burden of poverty. To use Anzaldúa's terminology, the US-Mexico border is "*una herida abierta* [an open wound] where the Third World grates against the first and bleeds."[35] Terror does not come about from or within a vacuum. World inequalities remain a major factor in its deployment.

FORENSICS AGAIN, OR LIVING IN THE AFTERLIFE OF UNDERVALUED LIVES

Margolles made several visits to Ciudad Juárez before and after *La promesa*, starting in 2010. Her fieldwork and community work resulted in a series of installations, photographic series, and videos on victims of violence, including *Muro Ciudad Juárez* (Wall of Ciudad Juarez, 2010)—a wall of concrete blocks from a public school that bear bullet holes left by the execution of four youths involved in organized crime (figure 5.3); *Pesquisas* (Inquiries, 2016)—a series of photographs of damaged street posters of missing women covering the walls of the city between the 1990s and 2016; *Pista de baile* (Dance floor, 2016)—a photographic series portraying transgender sex workers resiliently standing on the remains of what were once dance floors of now-destroyed nightclubs; *Karla, Hilario Reyes Gallegos* (2016)—a photograph of a transsexual sex worker beaten to death at the age of 64 on December 22, 2015; *La Gran América* (The great America, 2017), a rectangular assemblage of 1,000 cobblestones installed on the gallery wall dedicated to Mexicans who died while attempting to cross the Mexico-US border—its cooked and burnished tiles made by the artisan Israel Gómez following a traditional technique from Paquimé, Chihuaha, using mud extracted from the bed of the Rio Grande/Río Bravo (figure 5.4); and *Sillón*

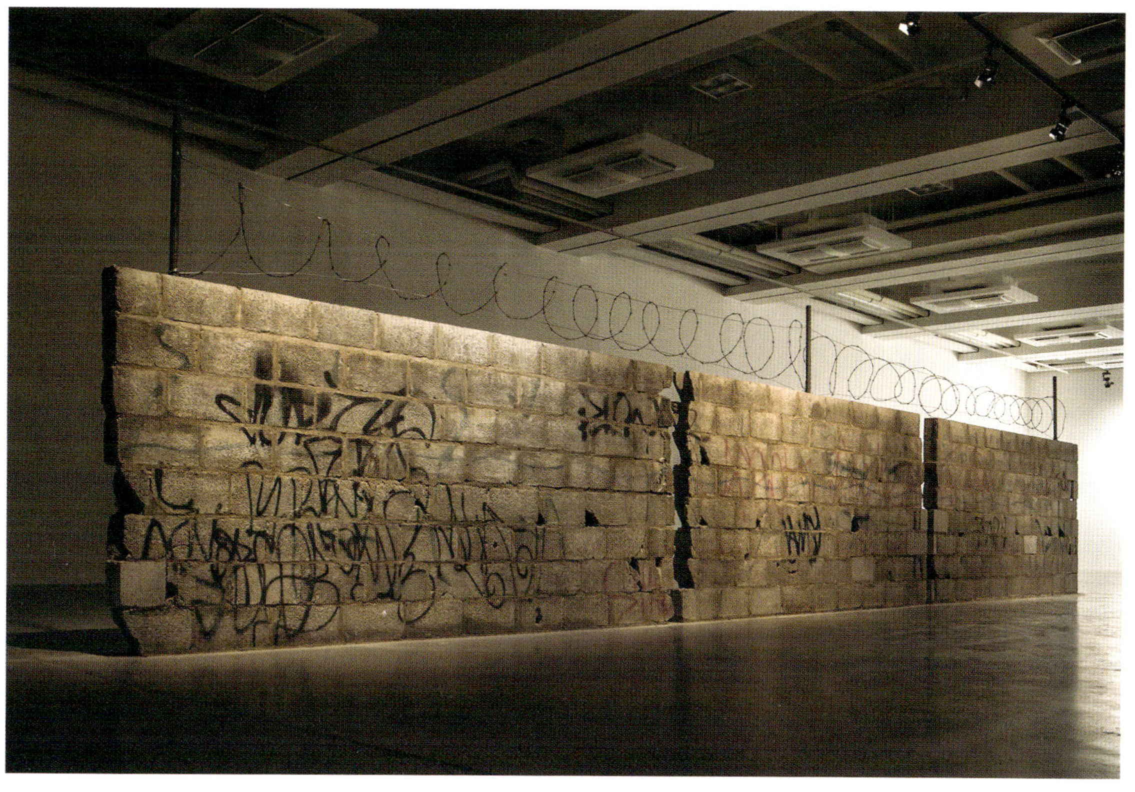

Teresa Margolles, *Muro Ciudad Juárez*, 2010. Wall of concrete blocks from a public school where a reckoning with four people involved in organized crime took place in Ciudad Juárez, Mexico. 69¼ × 496⅛ × 5⅞ in. (176 × 1,260 × 15 cm). Installation/performance view: *Frontera*, Kunsthalle Fridericianum, Kassel, Germany, May 27–August 21, 2011. Photo: Nils Klinger. Courtesy of the artist and James Cohan, New York. © Teresa Margolles.

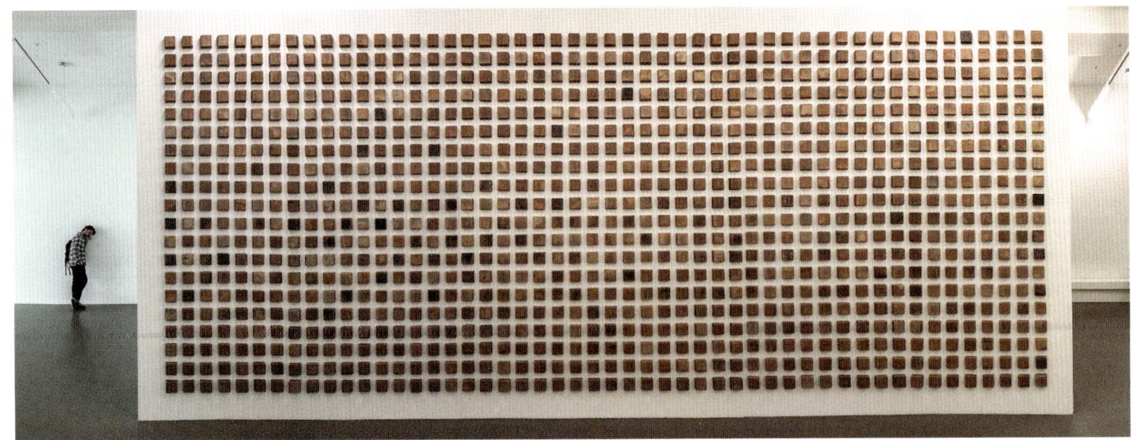

tapizado frente a línea fronteriza (Upholstered armchair facing a borderline, 2019)—an armchair recuperated from the ruins of the Hotel Rex in the city's historic center, covered with fabric impregnated with fluids from a violent event in the area.

Though specific to the terror context of Ciudad Juárez, this body of works, including *La promesa*, is fully rooted in Margolles's overall production and continuous concern for the life of corpses and remains. Originally trained as a forensic pathologist (she holds a diploma in forensic medicine from the Universidad Nacional Autónoma de México) and employed as a mortician in Mexico City in the early 1990s, Margolles was one of the founding members of the Servicio Médico Forense Organization (SEMEFO) in 1990, which collected unclaimed corpses and delivered

FIGURE 5.4

Teresa Margolles, *La Gran América*, 2017. One thousand handmade cobblestones made from dirt and clay from both sides of the Rio Grande. Dimensions variable. Each brick: 3½ × 3½ × 1⅝ in. (9 × 9 × 4 cm). Installation view: *Sutura*, Daadgalerie, Berlin, 2018. Photo: Jens Ziehe. Courtesy of the artist and James Cohan, New York. © Teresa Margolles.

them to the morgue. Her artworks during that time were based on her access to unidentified, unclaimed, and mostly drug-trafficking-related victims. SEMEFO's main philosophy has continued to permeate her work. That philosophy sustains the imperative to produce artworks that reflect upon—let us follow the art historian Julia Banwell here—"the post mortem disintegration of the physical body, a phenomenon termed 'la vida del cadáver,' the life of the corpse,"[36] connecting art, forensics, violence, and death in a society where drug-, mafia- and police-related crimes persist with impunity. Seeking to maintain the life of the corpse, her work typically incorporates and makes perceivable, visually, tactically, and olfactorily, the physical remnants of violent conflicts—postmortem matter such as a tong, body fat from victims of violence, blood, water used to clean corpses in morgues or medical labs, threads used after autopsy to sew up the bodies of victims of a violent death, bullet-ridden walls, and the remains of an abandoned house. The selected matter is always indexically related to the victims' bodies—an indexicality anchored in the Peircean formulation of the index as a sign bearing "a spatio-temporal contiguity to the occurrence of the entity signaled."[37]

Hence, while FO's counterforensic aesthetics is an investigating practice that aims to establish the accountability of state actors in their nonassistance to migrating beings endangered at sea, Margolles explores her forensic accessibility to ungrievable victims (a notion I get back to later) not only to account for the murdering or injuring of these unaccounted beings but also to save the victims' bodily remains. She receives unclaimed victims of violence—beings whose death was violently inflicted—or objects carrying signs of violent deaths; she also keeps traces of their bodies to expose them, transformed, in the public realm. Forensics gives an afterlife to the cadaver and makes that formerly unaccounted-for life matter posthumously as its traces are perceptually and sensorially experienced by the viewer. In some cases, this means experiencing the work through touch and smell. In *Vaporización* (2001–2018), for example, viewers are invited to circulate in a space filled with vaporized water from a morgue—water used to wash the bodies of murdered victims (figure 5.5); in *En el aire* (2003–), another key example, bubbles made of used water float down from the ceiling and break up when they touch the spectator's skin; in *La promesa*, volunteers are invited to slowly remove the rubble from the block. As Banwell specifies, "Margolles does not want to distance her art from the spectator, and uses various tactics to bring the two in intimate contact, setting out to erase the supposed distance between art and reality."[38]

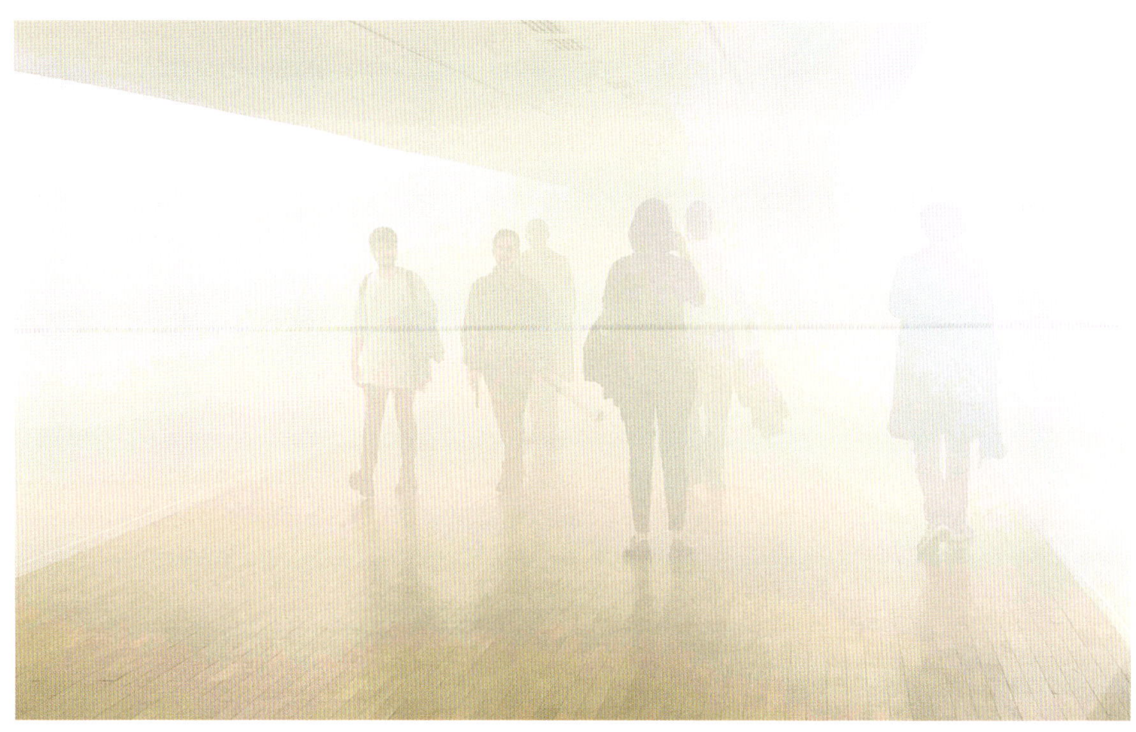

FIGURE 5.5

Teresa Margolles, *Vaporización*, 2001–2018.
Vaporized water from the morgue that
was used to wash the bodies of murder
victims after autopsy, one or two fog
machines. Installation view: *Ya basta hijos
de puta*, Padigliogne d'Arte Contemporaneo,
Milan, 2018. Photo: Rafael Burillo. Courtesy
of the artist and James Cohan, New York.
© Teresa Margolles.

There is no understanding of Margolles's response to the migration conditions of Ciudad Juárez without acknowledging the specifics of her forensic investment in the life of the corpse. The investment's call for responsibility is inseparable from care, from the difficulty to care for dead or injured bodies. Forensic Oceanography's call for responsible care became particularly manifest in its elaboration of the WatchTheMed mapping platform and one of its main outcomes, the WatchTheMed Alarm Phone, a 24/7-operating nongovernmental emergency phoneline designed to assist migrant boats in distress in a period when assistance is more and more criminalized. FO participant Lorenzo Pezzani's involvement in the Pirate Care Project has confirmed this inclination for responsible care. Margolles's work involves the artist's caring for the corpse: its reception, acknowledgment, documentation, sheltering, readying, transformation, and relaying to the public. Her work wants the museum staff, viewers, and participants to care as well. Resonating with FO's initiatives, it requires a collective care: this is where FO's and Margolles's calls for responsibility meet; this is where responsibility as a more mutual practice of coexistence becomes palpable. This is especially true of *La promesa*.

The block's rubble comes from a colonia house that was abandoned by residents forcibly displaced due to Juárez's overdetermined terror, which led to a daughter's death; the rectangular block is itself made of displaced rubble. The installation brings forced displacement to the fore. Its call for responsibility is a call addressed to a variety of actors invited to make, unmake, perceive, and ponder. Without these complementary gestures, there is no work. This is how Margolles describes *La promesa*—a collective caring effort that unfolds as a social connection model of responsibility:

Promises unkept, promises made to youth like "study and you will become someone," transform themselves in fragments of unkept promises, betrayed promises. . . . Once it is installed here, the sculpture activates itself with the participants. People are invited to move it, to displace it, to dismember it, to make this compact memory visible, to make visible what was hidden. . . . This, I cannot do by myself, alone. The complexity of what is happening in the country . . . there cannot be a single response. There must be a collective response. This collective response constitutes itself through the participants. Through these dismemberments. Through that hour they each offer, while they mobilize this idea, the piece starts to become everyone's piece. I disappear, *that is* the author disappears, and the work becomes collective.[39]

Note first how Margolles begins her statement by defining the deserted house as the materialization of broken promises. Let us recall Orozco's description of the slums from which the abandoned house was extracted: "Slums feature poorly finished brick houses and dwelling spaces built out of discarded and shoddy materials. Neighborhoods lack paved roads and basic services, including clean water, electricity, sewage, garbage collection, and efficient public transportation. . . . Public space around maquiladora industrial parks is ordered, clean, protected, and provided with first-class services, while slums subsist in the midst of environmental degradation, wrenching violence, and decaying infrastructure."[40] The colonia is the infrastructure where violence, poverty, death, migration, and displacement converge. Margolles then insists on the collectiveness of the work as a response to that convergence—a collective endeavor without which the work would simply not exist or coexist. Let us recall that joint effort: for each version of *La promesa*, the gallery or the museum is responsible for building a formwork, filling it with the rubble, and adding water to shape the rectangular block; at the end of each exhibition, when the block has once again become rubble, the rubble is shipped to the Museo Universitario Arte Contemporáneo or to the next institution showing the work. When the block is installed, volunteers are invited to further transform it—one hour per day and one person at a time—by scraping it with care and in silence as they meditate on their own experiences of shattered promises. At the Musée d'art contemporain, volunteers included people who had experienced exile, unrooting, and abandonment.[41] The block was thus partly scraped away, but its matter was saved, scattered on the floor yet kept close to the fading block and eventually sent away to be redone and re-undone (figure 5.6).

The collective work reinvents the tradition of minimalism by adopting an anthropological approach to the rectangular beam. It *worries* Robert Morris's untitled plywood or stainless-steel beams from the 1960s by allowing troubling matter—the recycled remains of an abandoned house from Ciudad Juárez—to fill the beam. The block progressively becomes a disintegrated mass: its matter spreads into the space. This is a disquieting aesthetics.[42] Could it not be hypothesized that the work's cultivation of care is an aesthetic opening to reciprocal coexistence? What does the block cultivate if not care as a practice in which a series of relaying actors become aware of their responsibility to address necropolitical migration? In fact,

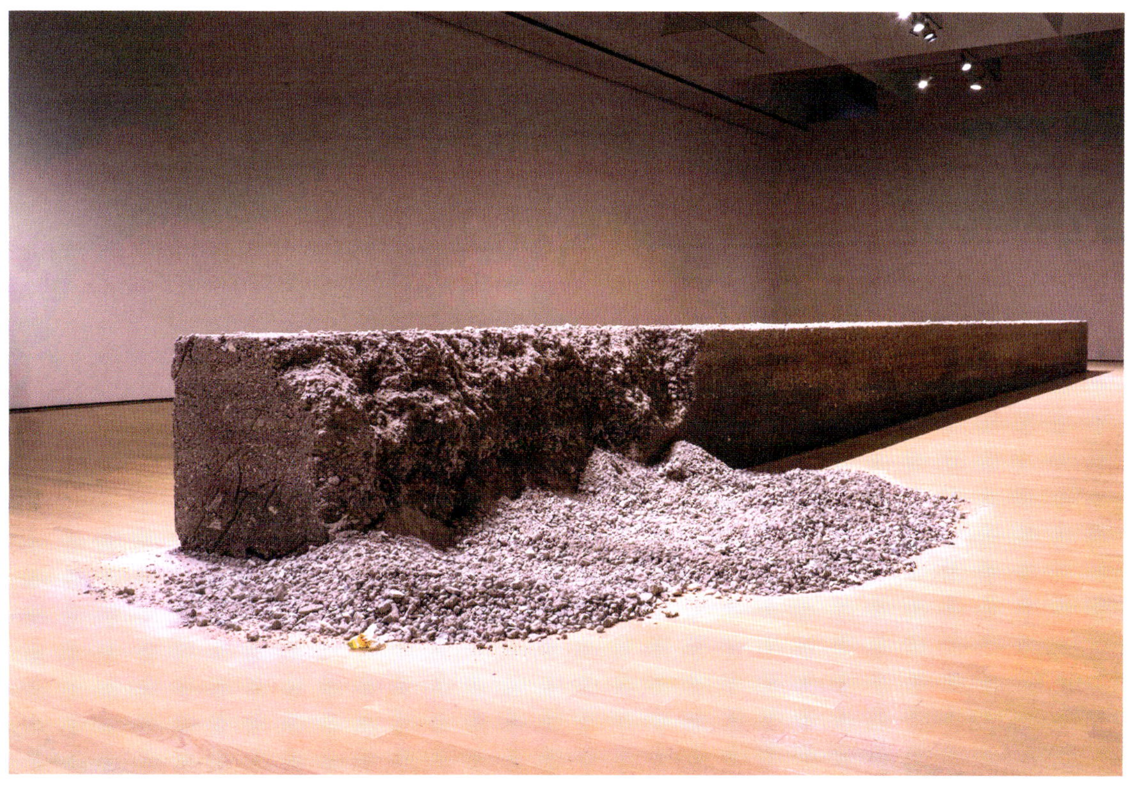

FIGURE 5.6

Teresa Margolles, *La promesa*, 2012.
Sculptural block made from the pulverized
rubble of a demolished house in Ciudad
Juárez, Mexico. 15 tons, 55 × 80 × 1,600
cm. Installation view: *Teresa Margolles:
Mundos*, Musée d'art contemporain de
Montréal, Montréal, Canada, February 16,
2017–May 14, 2017. Collection of the
Museo Universitario Arte Contemporáneo
(MUAC), Universidad Nacional Autónoma
de México (UNAM), Mexico City. Installation
commissioned by the MUAC, UNAM, with
the support of the Ford Foundation Latin
America in commemoration of its fiftieth
anniversary. Photo: Rafael Burillo. Courtesy
of the artist and James Cohan, New York.
© Teresa Margolles.

from the start it's been asking this of a diversity of relaying actors: the displaced survivors, the artist and her crew, museum and gallery institutions, spectators, and volunteers. Caring involves breaking apart, packing, sending, circulating, mixing, forming, installing, perceiving, meditating, remembering, grieving, scraping, scattering, repacking, resending, and re-undoing. The block is a performative piece. To follow the thread of my argument, it is helpful to recall the chapter's main claim: *La promesa* is a call for a shared forward-looking responsibility that takes the form of a fully assumed nonidealized practice of care. But is this care? What, how, and when is care?

CARE

Care studies uphold the ethical, social, political, and cultural significance of interpersonal relationships and dependencies in human life. One of the key originators of this field, the feminist ethicist and psychologist Carol Gilligan—whose work challenged traditional moral theories as downplaying values and virtues culturally associated with women—suggests that "the ethics of care starts from the premise that as humans we are inherently relational, responsive beings and the human condition is one of connectedness or interdependence."[43] Care studies' central postulation is the interdependence of beings, but its main challenge is to complicate the understanding of that not-so-straightforward relationality. The field doesn't provide a definite answer to that challenge: its interdisciplinarity prevents it from securing a definite definition of care, and the notion of interdependence keeps gaining in complexity. But the field does provide analytical tools and philosophical findings that help circumscribe the potentiality of care for artistic practices responding to present-day migration.[44]

As recently emphasized by the medical anthropologist Carlo Caduff, the call for care and the "call to care about care with care" have been articulated predominantly as a "reparative response" to the precarious conditions resulting from neoliberalism. "The promise of care," he explains, "is that it will allow people to survive a time of austerity, of systematic institutional withdrawal, by providing a form of support not organized by the state."[45] This orientation is fundamentally paradoxical insofar as the establishment of care as an informal and alternative structure for the elementary support of life ends up sustaining the neoliberalism it seeks to compensate for; it does not oppose neoliberalism. As the field of care studies attempts to resolve its main paradox, he concludes, it wants a lot from care: it wants care to be institution-alized and more robustly—perhaps more normatively—defined; it wants to protect life *à tout prix* and efficiently attend to (let us paraphrase Susan Sontag's famous book here) the pain of others; it wants care to crystalize into a practice of solidarity with others in need, to ground and improve our moral world, to be about loving and being loved. And yet care is not necessarily all those things. Fundamentally, "care is often difficult for those who require it, those who receive it, and those who provide it."[46] This is not to posit, however, that care should be disposed of. On the contrary, care is simply part of life and gains to be acknowledged in its complexity, strenuousness, and exigencies.

The philosopher María Puig de la Bellacasa's study of care, *Matters of Care: Specu-lative Ethics in More Than Human Worlds* (2017), has been vital to the reassessment of care studies and its call to care about care with care. It bridges the field's most influential studies to formulate an imperative: the necessity to de-idealize care—an imperative that Caduff reaffirms in his essay published two years later. Puig de la Bellacasa adopts but then proceeds to complicate Joan Tronto's generic definition of care as "a species activity that includes everything that we do to maintain, continue, and repair our 'world' so that we can live in it as well as possible. That world includes our bodies, our selves, and our environment, all of which we seek to interweave in a complex, life-sustaining web."[47] Tronto's definition takes its robustness from its insistence on open-endedness (care is "everything that we do"), maintenance and repair (caregiving and care receiving are work), ethics (caring *for* another's well-being might not be enough if it doesn't entail caring *about* that other's well-being), and the world being cared for (the objects of care are human and nonhuman; they include bodies, selves, and ecosystems). The strength of that model also comes from its valorization of interconnected and interdependent relationality in a world that predominantly depreciates dependency and overappreciates individual agency.[48] But Puig de la Bellacasa wants to complicate that definition: she seeks to de-idealize care. Her de-idealization doesn't so much discredit care as emphasize its pharma-kon deployment as both remedy and poison. This view challenges Bernard Stiegler's suggestion, discussed in chapter 3, that care alleviates the ambivalence of pharmaka by reinforcing their therapeutic side. Care itself is a pharmakon!

De-idealizing care is especially vital to caring practices that can never simply transcend the unequal distribution of wealth, power, and health that structures the labor, affects, ethics, and politics of caregiving and care receiving—an inequality that is particularly relevant to present-day migration. Care is inherently ambivalent:

that ambivalence will never disappear, but its inequalities and contradictions can be questioned and significantly attenuated.

Puig de la Bellacasa proposes that caregivers and care-receivers integrate the question "How to care?" in practices of care—that is, they must "pay attention to moments where the question of 'how to care?' is insistent but not easily answerable."[49] To care *for* someone, for example, doesn't necessarily imply caring *about* someone; care is not an unmediated labor of love accomplished by perfect carers, nor is care achieved in relationships that sustain care-receivers as victims without autonomy. Rather, care needs to be reclaimed as we ask ourselves how it can make a difference in the lives of people who suffer; it means "acknowledging our own involvements in perpetuating dominant values rather than retreating to the sheltered position of an enlightened outsider who knows better."[50] This is what Caduff calls "the life of care"—the pragmatics of care in which normalized and normative ideals necessarily clash with the practice and conditions of caring. Care is never simply a model "for safe social interaction."[51] Integrating the question "How to care?" into our care means accepting that care is a complicated relation that includes a caregiver and a receiver as well as a third party (let us think of *La promesa*'s viewers) who as an observer, a witness, or an assessor looks at the unfolding of care. It also means de-idealizing touch as the privileged sense of care on the too easily accepted premise that touch solves the abstractions and detachments associated with vision. Puig de la Bellacasa's study warns us against the idealization of knowing–touching in these terms: "To touch or to be touched physically doesn't automatically mean being in touch with oneself or the other. . . . Unwanted touch, abusive touch, can induce a rejection of sensation, a self-induced numbness in the touched. So maybe we have to ask what kind of touching is produced when we are unaware of the needs and desires of that what/whom we are reaching for[.]"[52]

The imperative to demystify care ultimately suggests that alterity is steadily at the center of care and that the awareness of that alterity matters; caring requires that caregivers and care-receivers ongoingly address the fundamental ambivalences and inequalities inherent to the persistence of alterity in any caring endeavor, without reifying it. Raising the question "How to care?" means decentralizing the human to include not only humans but also nonhumans and other-than-human agents and actors in the practice of care, "such as things, objects, other animals, living beings, organisms, physical forces, spiritual entities"—a colonia house for example—with which humans are inevitably intertwined.[53] As Caduff compellingly observes, in care situations "the most intimate people put on a mask to hide how strange they are to each other. What care reveals, here, is a dimension of alterity at the heart of intimacy. . . . To care is to endure the noise of the other. It's a response to and a symptom of the difficulty of being in relation."[54] Such is the de-idealization of care: an interdependence in which the receiver is not taken for granted, assumed, or known in advance. That de-idealization must be galvanized if care is to have any value at all.

LA PROMESA'S RESPONSIBLE CALL FOR CARE

With these findings in mind, we can ask, How does Margolles's *La promesa* care? A carer "is someone who is responsible for looking after another person, for example, a person who has a disability, or is ill," and the verb "to care" etymologically refers to *carian, cearian* (Old English), to "be anxious or solicitous; grieve; feel concern or interest," and *karo* (Proto Germanic), to "'lament,' hence 'grief, care.'"[55] *La promesa* mobilizes these definitions from the start; it is a call for responsibility that is tied to grief, concern, and attentiveness. But care is significantly de-idealized, and this is what, I believe, makes this work an inventive and insightful unlearning of migration—enabling as it does a more reciprocal deployment of coexistence. Caring unfolds, but it is sustained by a question—"How to care?"—that makes it revisable. De-idealization is central to its caring operations at several levels. I outline six of these levels.

First, caring is exposed as labor. The museum staff's labor can be said to reenact and reorient Mierle Laderman Ukeles's Maintenance Art performance series of the early 1970s. While Ukeles's *Washing/Tracks/Maintenance: Outside and Inside, July 22, 1973* performance focused on the cleaning of the museum's entrance staircase and inside floors to make visible the unrecognized yet essential care work of low-paid custodial workers (figure 5.7), *La promesa* involves a series of maintenance activities (dismantling, packing, shipping, framing, shaping, installing, scraping, cleaning, repacking) to produce it. Let us also be attentive to Ukeles's bodily position: she kneels down to wash the outside staircase; she kneels on the inside floor to wash it. This is the position adopted by the volunteers as they scrape the block (figure 5.8). It privileges a Bataillean base materialism—the depreciation of the vertical position of the standing human body and the concomitant reappreciation of devalued body parts (the feet and the knees rather than the head) interacting with the floor's filth. Care as maintenance: this is already a form of de-idealization of art and care.

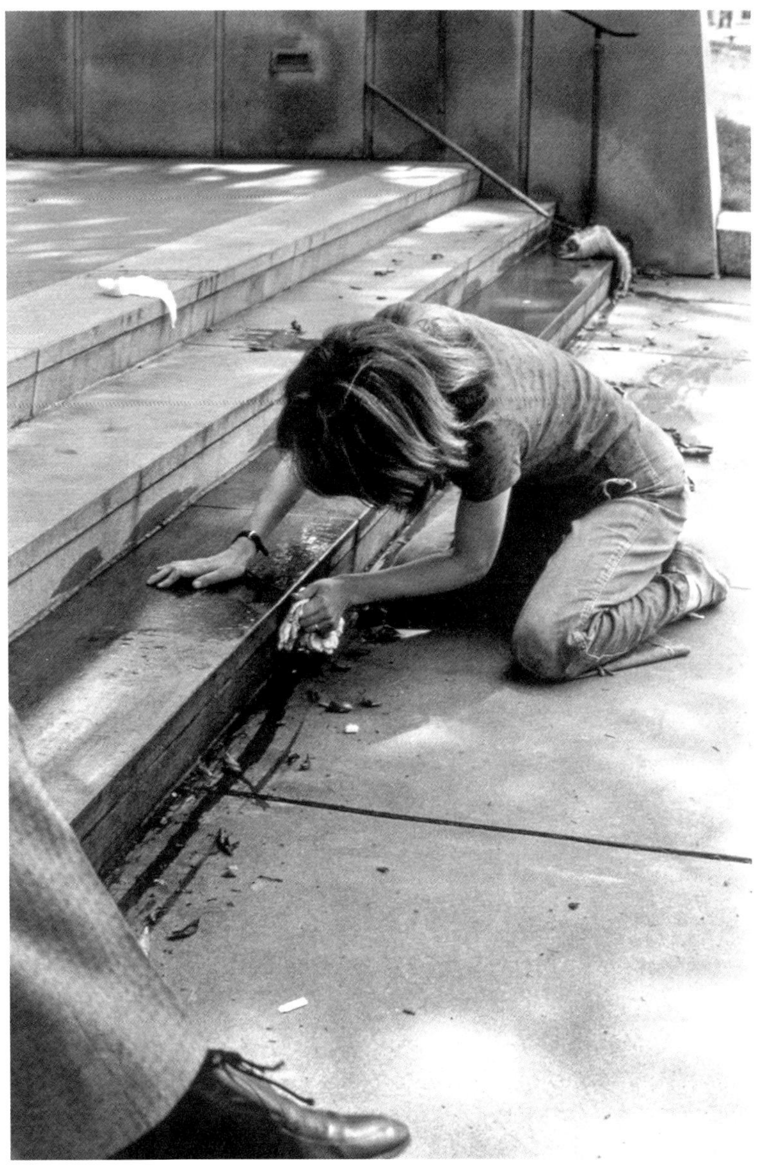

FIGURE 5.7

Mierle Laderman Ukeles, *Washing/
Tracks/Maintenance: Outside and Inside,
July 22, 1973*. Part of the Maintenance
Art performance series, 1973–1974.
Performance at Wadsworth Atheneum,
Hartford, CT. © Mierle Laderman Ukeles.
Courtesy of the artist and Ronald Feldman
Gallery, New York.

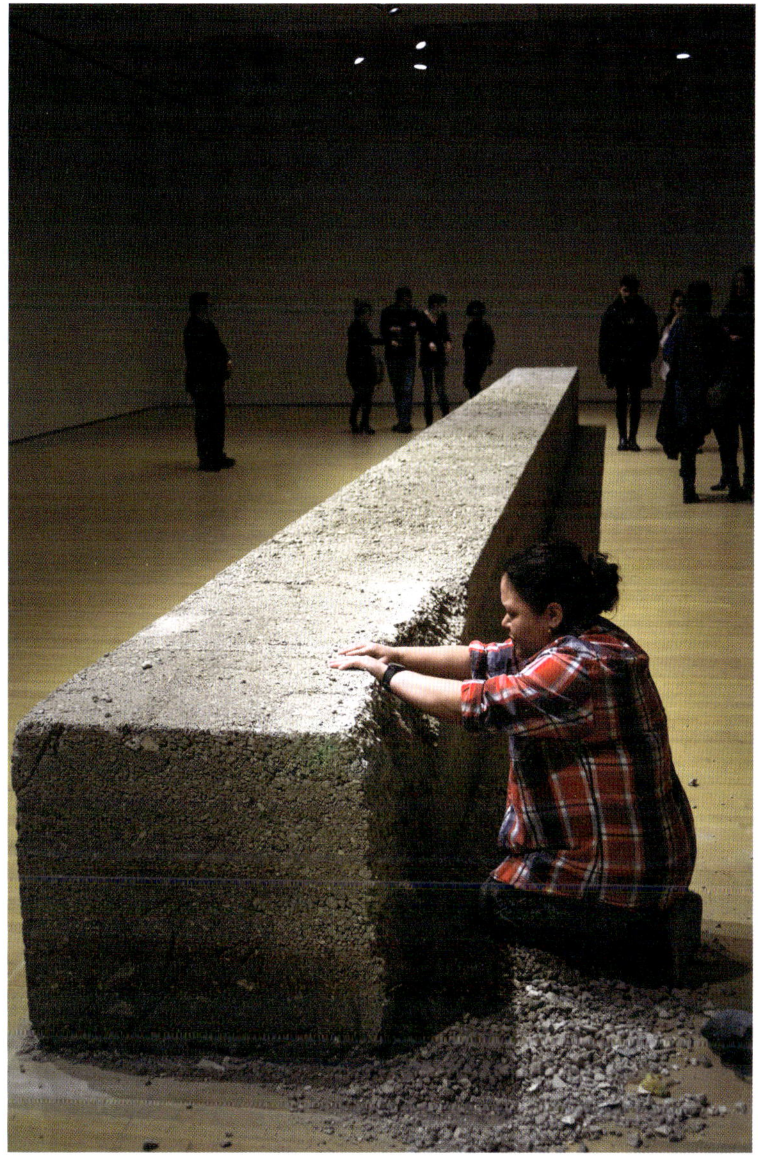

FIGURE 5.8

Teresa Margolles, *La promesa*, 2012. Sculptural block made from the pulverized rubble of a demolished house in Ciudad Juárez, Mexico. 15 tons, 55 × 80 × 1,600 cm. Installation view: *Teresa Margolles: Mundos*, Musée d'art contemporain de Montréal, Montreal, February 16, 2017–May 14, 2017. Collection of the Museo Universitario Arte Contemporáneo (MUAC), Universidad Nacional Autónoma de México (UNAM), Mexico City. Installation commissioned by the MUAC, UNAM, with the support of the Ford Foundation Latin America in commemoration of its fiftieth anniversary. Photo: Rafael Burillo. Courtesy of the artist and James Cohan, New York. © Teresa Margolles.

Second, the not-so-human house's materiality is intrinsic to the caring activity—its noise is made manifest; it is not mute. Margolles insists on that point when she speaks of the block as a body and when she stipulates that "the sculpture activates itself with the participants."[56] As a substitute for a cluster of damaged bodies (an abandoned house, a displaced family, a dead daughter-victim of Ciudad Juárez's prevailing violence, a borderzone), *La promesa* materializes care through the rubble as its unique component. The rubble both resists and is amenable to the scraping; these complementary properties are perceivable during the volunteers' performances. The rubble also shows its ultimate uncontainability as it spreads out on the floor with the scraping; its alterity cannot be simply contained (figure 5.6). Caring is a human–nonhuman unfolding.

Third, the victims are never directly made present. The rectangular block is persistently opaque and protective: it doesn't allow us (the museum staff, the viewers, the volunteers) to see the beings who were forcibly displaced; they remain strangers, despite our proximity to the block. Hence, no one is asked here—as the queer studies thinker Sara Ahmed convincingly argues in her own understanding of care—to feel the pain of the other or to make the wound stand in for the identity of the victim as though the wound weren't historical (made and changeable).[57] To be responsible is to care for beings who are only obliquely perceivable and are, in fact, always elusive; such is their right to opacity, à la Édouard Glissant.

Fourth, however, the victims are brought to the fore via the materiality of the rubble within the gallery space in which viewers and volunteers establish contact with the debris. This is how they are acknowledged as having existed, as existing and coexisting. *La promesa* partakes of Ciudad Juárez's memorial tradition established by survivors, mothers, and activists to account for the lives of unaccounted-for beings—a tradition that has taken the form of black and pink crosses painted on electric poles and walls around the city center; anonymous graffiti in downtown Juárez; murals; embroidery and antifeminicide protests (street protests, caravans, rallies, sit-ins, and the occupation of public buildings by mothers of victims showing pictures and sharing personal testimonies).[58] Judith Butler's notion of the ungrievable is useful for the understanding of that specific deployment of de-idealized care. When discussing the precariousness of living beings and the value of lives in war contexts, Butler explains that value is mobilized by a "presupposition for the life that matters," a life that is understood as having been lived and therefore grievable when lost. But lives are not always acknowledged as such. Especially in times of war, any being on the planet can learn about how they coexist with others by asking whose lives are considered valuable, whose lives are mourned, and whose lives are considered ungrievable. We might think of war as dividing populations into those who are grievable and those who are not. An ungrievable life is one that cannot be mourned because it has never lived, that is, it has never counted as a life at all. We can see the division of the globe into grievable and ungrievable lives from the perspective of those who wage war in order to defend the lives of certain communities, and to defend them against the lives of others—even if it means taking those latter lives.[59]

As stipulated earlier, Margolles has consistently explored aesthetic strategies to account for ungrievable beings. The ungrievable is the unaccounted-for being, the being whose life is considered as having no value and who cannot therefore be grieved. Bringing the materiality of the rubble within the gallery space and asking that we care for the deserted house are the very processes by which the endless yet necessary act of grieving the ungrievable is set into play. This is why *La promesa* cannot take the form of a resolved, definitive object.

Fifth, volunteers are instructed to think about their own experiences of broken promises and abandonment as they scrape the rectangular block. This instruction brings in the possibility of healing as a significant dimension of caring. That healing process highly resonates with the performative component of Richard Misrach's and Guillermo Galindo's *Border cantos* series (2004–). For the Mexican composer Guillermo Galindo (b. 1960, Mexico City), in particular, responsibility entails transforming artifacts of migration found in the borderzones between the United States and Mexico—fragments of border walls, border patrol "drag tires," ladders, water bottles, discarded clothes, children's toys, and backpacks—into musical instruments (he calls them sonic objects) and to perform them as "healing rituals" that make migration wounds "audible" (figure 5.9).[60] That healing process never loses sight of the damage: the artifacts remain, as much as *La promesa*'s injury is never healed once and for all—the rubble remains; the block is never definitively undone. This approach also recalls *La Mer Morte* (The Dead Sea, 2015) by the French artist Kader Attia (b. 1970, Seine-Saint-Denis, France)—an installation made of second-hand blue garments scattered on the gallery floor (figure 5.10). Attia's installation evokes migrating bodies lost in the Mediterranean Sea, but the repair it activates—the creation of a memento mori—is a responsible act because the injury stays visible as it calls for care. Most of the garments have been grouped into a pile to suggest bodies looking after one another and not simply left to die alone. The garments are nevertheless dispersed on the floor: that traumatic dispersion shows the repair to

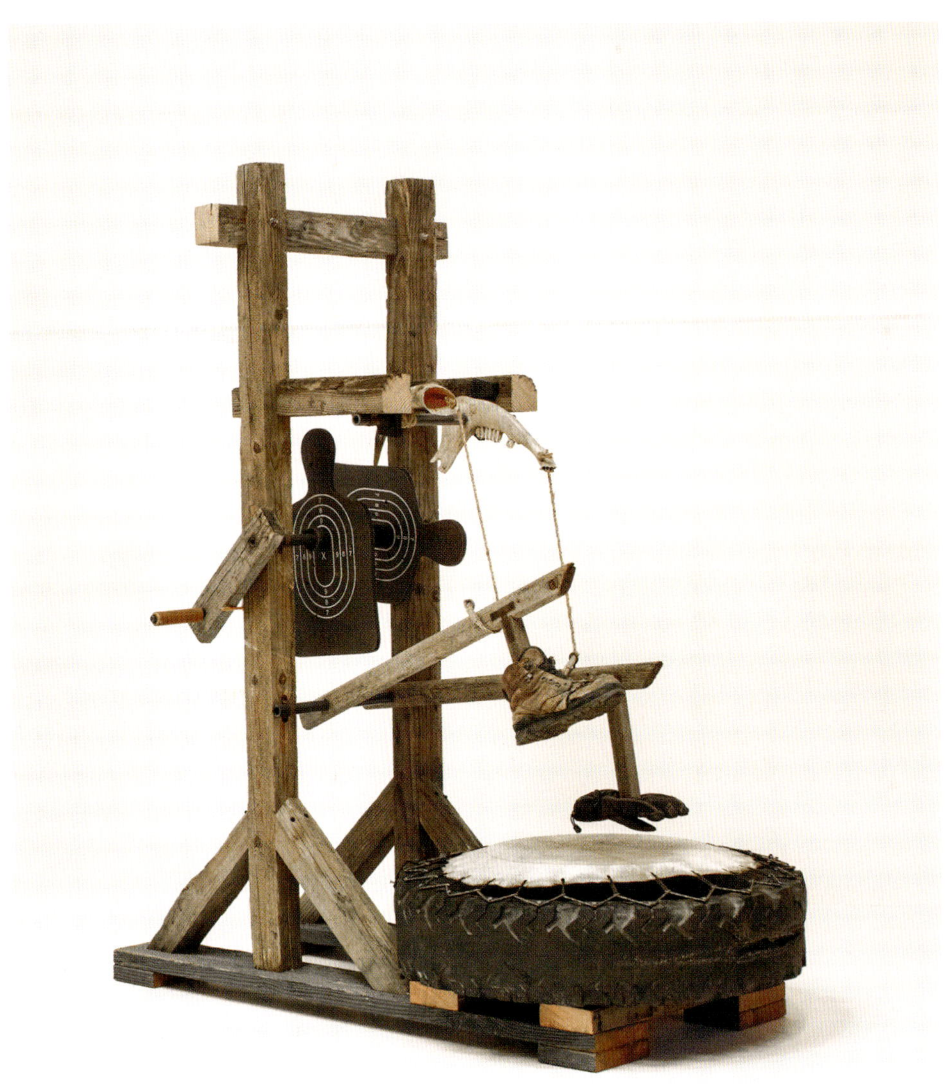

FIGURE 5.9

Guillermo Galindo, *Zapatello*, 2015. Found tire, found leather shoe, found nylon glove, found border patrol targets, rawhide, bull horn, horn, and wood, 70 × 30 × 76 in. (177.8 × 76.2 × 193 cm). Photo: © Richard Misrach. Courtesy of Fraenkel Gallery, San Francisco, and the artist.

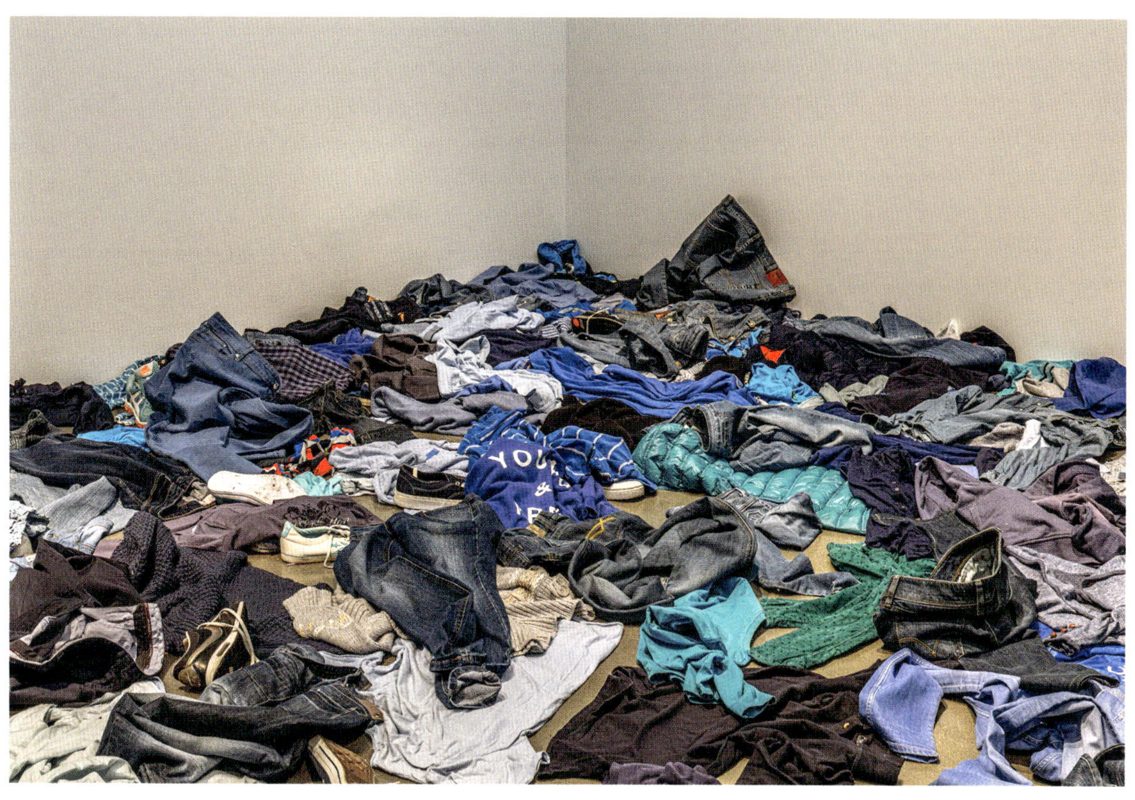

FIGURE 5.10

Kader Attia, *La Mer Morte*, 2015. Installation with blue secondhand clothes. Dimensions variable. Installation view: Regen Projects, Los Angeles, 2020. Photo: Evan Bedford. Courtesy of the artist, Regen Projects, and Lehmann Maupin, New York, Hong Kong, Seoul, and London.

be incomplete for those who have survived as well as for the beings whose bodies were never found and whose deaths are still unreported.[61] Margolles's block of remains cannot—will not—be a *resolved* monument. It keeps the traces of the dead and the injured in our world, ensuring a perennity that invites viewers to reflect on the larger legal, political, and social structures of violence and exclusion that have enabled these injuries. The block is an indexical trace, a witness that requests migratory justice.

Sixth and last, *La promesa* is fundamentally a collective deployment of care, performing the main features of Iris Marion Young's social connection model of responsibility. And this is where coexistence becomes fully manifest. The installation proposes a nonblame view of responsibility as something shared by the artist, her team, the museum staff, the volunteers, and the spectators—relaying subjects who are part of the structural injustices of migration but who now act for migratory justice. Our political responsibility derives from "belonging together with others in a system of interdependent processes of cooperation and competition through which we seek benefits and aim to realize projects."[62] In all likelihood, the actors invited to care have not caused the necropolitical harming of the displaced beings who lived in *La promesa*'s house: but all of them can take up the responsibility to reverse that injustice once it is acknowledged. This is a collective endeavor: to take political responsibility is to speak out against social injustices "with the intention of mobilizing others to oppose them, and to act together to transform the institutions to promote better ends."[63] De-idealization comes from the imperative to acknowledge care as a flow of complications, worries, strangeness, resistances, amenabilities, contradictions, irresolutions, inequalities, and collectivities. These are the conditions of possibility for a more mutual deployment of coexistence—a practice of coexistence that admits while attempting to work through the dark coexistences that structure the migration conditions described in this chapter. They essentially derive from art's renewed interest in materiality.

EMPATHY?

Empathy—in essence, "the action of understanding, being aware of, being sensitive to, and . . . experiencing the feelings, thoughts, and experience of another . . . without having the feelings, thoughts, and experience fully communicated in an objectively explicit manner"[1]—is a coexistence in which a being feels and understands the distress lived by another being but without living that distress (not "as if" experiencing that distress, however, as is the case with sympathy). Increasingly investigated in the fields of psychology, philosophy, and neuroscience, empathy has also made its way as one of the main affective calls in recent media and visual culture. This evolution is supported by the belief that empathy entails prosociality— the attempt, if not the desire, to help suffering beings whose pain we feel and comprehend. In line with that definition, it is safe to say that contemporary art's account of the fraught conditions surrounding migration processes can't really exist without empathy. Empathy is likewise the main affective relation that supports humanitarianism. That being said, *empathy* is nevertheless a contested term: definitions abound conflictingly, and recent literature is more and more attentive to the dark sides of empathy—deployments that trouble the notion of empathy as a prosocial orientation (i.e., acting to help others in pain[2]) essential to the caring of others. Media covering victims of crises and traumatic events do not hesitate to explore empathy but only to spectacularize it, *emptying* it out, as it were (I follow here E. Ann Kaplan's terminology discussed in chapter 7) through that spectacularization.

What is one to do with empathy, especially in light of the work of artists who explicitly explore empathy as a necessary component of more just migratory conditions?

Part III sets out to examine three major artworks that have responded empathically to the migratory predicament: Ai Weiwei's *Human Flow* (2017), Alejandro González Iñárritu's *CARNE y ARENA (Virtually Present, Physically Invisible)* (2017), and Tania Bruguera's *10,142,926* (2018). Covering 23 countries in western, eastern, and central Europe; central, southern and western Asia; northern and eastern Africa; and North America, Ai's *Human Flow* evokes the planetary scale of mass migration as it unfolded during and in the aftermath of 2015—at the height of the assumed European refugee crisis. Focusing on the movement of people as they attempted to reach Europe by land and by sea when EU borders were starting to close down as well as on their daily life in refugee camps, the 140-minute-long documentary films Ai caring for, assisting, and wanting to counter the dehumanization of migrating beings in distress. Iñárritu's *CARNE y ARENA* consists in a virtual-reality (VR) environment that invites viewers into the Sonoran Desert where a digitally captured group of men, women, and children attempt to cross the Mexico-US border. Exploring VR as the empathic machine par excellence, Iñárritu has stated and restated that his intention was to produce a work that could trigger an empathic response from the viewers; he wants them to feel the fear and vulnerability of Mexican and Latin American citizens as they walk through the hostile terrains of American borderzones. Bruguera's *10,142,926*—a series of interventions in and around Tate Modern addressing twenty-first-century migration—included a gallery where an organic compound made visitors cry (irritating the viewers' eyes and throat and making breathing difficult). Seeking to activate "forced empathy," the work sustains Bruguera's understanding of empathy as a necessary yet waning human capacity.

These works explore empathy as an aesthetic strategy of awareness of the dehumanizing conditions of contemporary migration, the unacceptability of these conditions, and the requirement to counter them. They explore empathy as a prosocial endeavor. But the critical reception of these works shows how much empathy has become an attractive–repulsive venture: whereas it might well succeed in making us (the viewers of the artworks at least) feel the pain of others, the empathic experience seems self-defeating because it tends to revictimize displaced people and to desubjectivize them in that very process; it becomes more about the empathizer than about the sufferer; for the viewer, it can insidiously transform itself into good consciousness or a sense of powerlessness.

But these are major works made by major artists that bring to the fore the unacceptability of present-day migration. They must be taken seriously. Why are they bothering with empathy? Why does empathy matter to them? How and when is empathy effective in these works? What are the possibilities and limits of empathy as a prosocial strategy? I believe it is crucial to address these questions if we are to have a better comprehension of contemporary European and North American art's challenges when it seeks to find ways to respond to the necropolitical evolution of migration and if we are also to continue to address the book's main twofold inquiry: What is art's original contribution to the understanding of contemporary migration, and why is this contribution important to the development of the twenty-first century? As suggested earlier, it is hard to imagine how art can do without empathy in matters of aesthetics and politics, especially if we are attentive to the history of the philosophical conceptualization of empathy. *Empathy* emerged as a term and concept in the field of aesthetics—it was first defined as an aesthetic feeling (*Einfühlung*) to describe the viewer's mode of access to the meaning of the artwork. But where does its effectiveness lie?

Stretched over part III's two chapters, my claim is that the effectiveness of empathy—the affective and cognitive capacity to act prosocially for more mutual forms of coexistence between viewers and citizens-on-the-move—lies in empathy's materialization as a necessary but ambivalent and insufficient condition of possibility for prosociality. I propose that artistic practices concerned with migratory justice—*Human Flow*, *CARNE y ARENA*, and *10,142,926* in particular—are especially inventive in their tensed exploration of empathy, whose ambivalence can never simply be erased or mastered: ambivalence unfolds, but the works concomitantly elaborate other calls—notably, the historicization and acknowledgment of the autonomy of migration—to counterbalance the call for empathy. I argue my claim in two steps: first, I assess the current literature on empathy to tease out its conflicting definitions and briefly conclude on their relevance to the understanding of our three case studies (chapter 6); second, I conduct an investigation of—a thinking-with—the three artworks in light of that literature (chapter 7). Together, these two chapters seek to show art's contribution to the fields of empathy studies and critical migrant studies. Art's originality lies in its exploration of empathy as a pharmakon, but an unavoidable and worthwhile pharmakon in which the therapeutic side of empathy sometimes manages to partly overcome its poisonous side.

6

THE FUNDAMENTAL AMBIVALENCE OF EMPATHY

DEFINITIONS AND APPROACHES

Amy Coplan and Peter Goldie's study of the history of empathy in philosophy, psychology, and neuroscience traces its beginnings back to David Hume's and Adam Smith's work on sympathy. The term *empathy* was coined in 1858 by the German philosopher Rudolf Lotze as a translation of the ancient Greek word ἐμπάθεια (*empatheia*, "passion, state of emotion") into *Einfühlung* (from *ein*, "in," and *Fühlung*, "feeling"). Throughout its history, empathy has steadily been defined as a cognitive and affective capacity central to intersubjective relations. Its importance has been perceived as twofold: "First, it has been seen as important in relation to our capacity to gain a grasp of the content of other people's minds, and to predict and explain what they will think, feel, and do. And secondly, it has been seen as important in relation to our capacity to respond to others ethically—enabling us not only to gain a grasp of the other's suffering, but also to respond in an ethically appropriate way."[1] Empathy, put differently, is a confirmation of our capacity to feel and understand, beyond communication, the mental states and feelings of others, especially when others are in a situation of distress.

Despite this consistent claim, however, definitions, explanations, and assessments of empathy vary rather substantially and sometimes conflictingly from one discipline to another (including philosophy, psychology, anthropology, and neuroscience as well as the subdisciplines philosophy of mind, aesthetics, ethics, and phenomenology). More problematically, these differences are often misunderstood or simply ignored. As the neuroscientists Jean Decety and Jason M. Cowell emphasize, "The concept of empathy has become an umbrella term and, therefore, is a source of confusion to too many of our colleagues."[2] By and large, empathy has been divided into two main yet not so independent types: (1) affective or emotional empathy—the capacity to feel or understand another's emotions; and (2) cognitive empathy—the capacity to understand another's perspective or mental state. A variety of nuances, approaches, and explanations abound to explain the unfolding of these capacities. It is impossible here to account for all of them; it is also impossible to provide a full account of the contemporary development of empathy studies. But generally speaking and differences notwithstanding, affective empathy has found some of its major and most convincing definitions in the work of the neuroscientists Jean Decety, Jason M. Cowell, Tania Singer, Olga M. Klimecki, Frédérique de Vignemont, and Claus Lamm. It names our capacity to feel the feelings of others when "perceiving the (real or imagined) emotional state of someone (or perhaps something) else."[3] As we will see later in this chapter, the literature on affective empathy is rather resolute in its assertion that empathy involves—more accurately, that it *must* involve—a self–other differentiation. This differentiation is seen and promoted as securing healthy empathic relations. Singer and Lamm's phenomenological and neuroscientific definitions sustain that requirement: "At a basic phenomenological level, empathy denotes an affective response to the directly perceived, imagined, or inferred feeling state of another being. . . . In our own understanding, empathy occurs when an observer perceives or imagines someone else's (i.e., the target's) affect and this triggers a response such that the observer partially feels what the target is feeling."[4] We empathize with others, add de Vignemont and Singer, "when we have (1) an affective state (2) which is isomorphic to another person's affective state, (3) which was elicited by observing or imagining another person's affective state, and (4) *when we know that the other person's affective state is the source of our own affective state*."[5] The self–other differentiation sustaining affective empathy is particularly emphasized in the literary scholar Fritz Breithaupt's postulate that empathy is based on "the idea that observing another's emotions activates in the observer the neural mechanisms responsible for the production of a similar emotion, with an awareness of the difference between self and other."[6]

The division between affective and cognitive empathy, however, remains a challenging one to sustain insofar as affective empathy necessarily entails cognitive

activities. As the philosopher Heidi L. Maibom observes, most researchers maintain that affective empathy involves high-level cognitive abilities:

First of all, one must be able to ascribe the emotional state in question to the other person.
Second, one must be aware that one is feeling what one is feeling because the other person
is feeling what he is feeling or because of the situation he is in. This involves some comprehension that one's own feeling is not a merited response to the situation one is in oneself,
but is a response better suited to the other person's situation (or possibly state of mind). At
the same time, one must understand that one's emotional response is not simply irrational
or inappropriate. It is appropriate as related to the other. This is pretty complicated stuff, as
I'm sure you can see, and so to maintain that affective empathy does not involve a heavy
dose of cognitive activity would be foolish. And so it is better to say that cognitive empathy
does not have to involve affect and that affective empathy typically involves a mix of cognitive and affective processes than to suppose that affective empathy somehow only involves
affective processes.[7]

Maibom's account describes empathy as multidimensional and fundamentally
mixed (combining emotional and cognitive articulations). This view has now become predominant in neuroscience, especially in the work of Decety (with Cowell
and with Philip L. Jackson), which proposes a hybrid conceptualization of empathy
as requiring "both the ability to share the emotional experience of the other person (affective component) and an understanding of the other person's experience
(cognitive component)."[8] Decety and Cowell insist on the importance of joining
affective and cognitive components when defining empathy; they especially highlight *affective empathic concern*—the caring-for-the-other dimension—and cognitive
perspective taking as essential to the empathic relation because these two factors
help sustain the demarcation between the empathizer and the empathized: "The
emotional component of empathy reflects the capacity to share or become affectively aroused by others' emotions (in at least in valence, tone, and relatively inten-
sity). The motivational component of empathy (empathic concern) corresponds to
the urge of caring for another's welfare. Finally, cognitive empathy is similar to the
construct of perspective taking"—the ability "to consciously put oneself into
the mind of another individual and imagine what that person is thinking or
feeling."[9] I will come back to perspective taking later as a pivotal constituent of
empathy, a promising counterpart to what we will come to understand as the
"empathy bias."

This very brief overview gives us a sense of the field's insistence on the self–other differentiation. This emphasis is overdetermined: the self-other differentiation secures empathy as something different from emotional contagion (although the latter is said to derive from the former) and as a prosocial endeavor. For it is empathy's prosociality and occasionally its morality that make empathy unique and progressive. The remainder of my discussion focuses on these two related constituents: self–other differentiation and prosociality. Not only are these constituents among the most debated conditions of possibility of empathy, but they are also key to understanding empathy's ambivalence and potentiality in artistic practices motivated by the empathic desire to prosocially respond to the injustices, inequalities, exclusions, and distress sustaining twenty-first-century migration.

Especially relevant to this discussion is the emergence of the term *Einfühlung*, "feeling into," in aesthetics and psychology in the mid-nineteenth and early twentieth centuries. First explored in aesthetics by Robert Vischer in his doctoral thesis "On the Optical Sense of Form: A Contribution to Aesthetics" (1873), *Einfühlung* was taken up and substantially studied by Theodor Lipps in *Ästhetik: Psychologie des Schönen und der Kunst: Grundlegung der Ästhetik, Erster Teil* (1903) and *Einfühlung, innere Nachahmung, und Organempfindungen* (1903). Lipps's exploration of *Einfühlung* evolved into describing the experience of aesthetic objects as well as the human capacity to know another's mental states: both were defined as inner imitations or inner resonances, involving empathizers who imitate the movements and expressions they perceive in physical and social objects. As Coplan and Goldie explain, to experience *Einfühlung*, in Lipps's view, was to "experience the other's feelings as our own because we project our own feelings onto the other. In a similar way, we experience the properties of aesthetic objects as our own because, according to Lipps, aesthetic objects elicit the same responses in us that are elicited by expressions and movements of the body, and we project these inner subjective qualities onto them."[10] Although Lipps's concept of empathy is frequently criticized because of its projective dimension (the projection of one's own feelings onto the other), it was particularly influential in the fields of psychology and philosophy. At the beginning of the twentieth century, it was coupled with the concept of *Verstehen* (understanding) in phenomenological and hermeneutic studies—especially in the work of Edmund Husserl and Edith Stein. These two philosophers defined empathy as "a unique mode of consciousness through which we directly experience others' thoughts, emotions, and desires," enabling us "to experience others as 'minded.'"[11] Lipps's influence on Husserl's and Stein's analyses of empathy (even though the two philosophers proceeded to revise the notion) shows that art and aesthetics matter a great deal in the deployment of empathy. Although the term *Einfühlung* became more and more marginal in the twentieth century, recent attempts to revitalize it suggest that empathy—and here I briefly refer to the philosophical work of Dominic McIver Lopes—is experienced by viewers when perceiving pictures especially designed to evoke empathy—be they paintings, photographs, or videos. Experiences of such pictures "can help build up a person's capacity for empathic response"; in other words, pictures can be seen as contributing "to a skill" that persists in daily life beyond the experience of the pictures that have initiated it.[12] The film and media studies scholar Jane Stadler has also emphasized the empathic experience of watching films: her examination of the viewer's affective engagement with cinematic characters is based on Dan Zahavi's phenomenological claim that empathy provides some form of knowledge by acquaintance with the inner lives of others.[13] Decety and Cowell likewise refer to different studies showing "that reading, language, the arts, and the media provide rich cultural input that triggers internal simulation processes and that leads to the experience of emotions influencing both concern and caring for others."[14] Whereas the "carry-over" in daily life of one's skill to perceive empathically through art is certainly difficult to demonstrate, *Einfühlung* suggests the centrality of empathy in the making and reception of artworks and images as well as in the attempt to explore artworks and images as what cultural studies scholar E. Ann Kaplan, in her study of empathy as a possible form of witnessing (discussed in chapter 7), has described as involving "feeling so shocked by suffering that one is moved to act. . . . [O]ne is motivated to see that justice is done."[15]

The phenomenological reorientation of Lipps's account was a way to secure empathy as an intersubjective phenomenon that would more clearly ensure the empathizer–empathized distinction instead of articulating their merger. Although too hasty in their conclusion that Lipps's concept implied such a merger (as the philosopher Rudolf Makkreel has postulated, *Einfühlung* is, after all, a "feeling into" and not a "feeling-one with"[16]) but attentive to how it formulated a problematic projection of the empathizer's inner qualities onto an other's movements and expressions—something close to emotional contagion—Husserl's and Stein's inquiries became central to the twentieth- and twenty-first-century field of empathy studies and its determination to secure some form of differentiation between self and other.[17] As Singer and Klimecki contend, "Importantly, in empathy one feels with someone, but one does not confuse oneself with the other; that is, one still knows that the emotion one resonates *with* is the emotion *of* another. If this self–other distinction is not present, we speak of emotion contagion."[18] This attempt to separate empathy from emotional contagion has become a constant in the field, implicitly showing how much that distinction is easily muddled in empathic experiences.

The self–other differentiation is crucial to the development of studies on empathy that define it as prosocial—a prosociality that is jeopardized when the differentiation is blurred. We will see this cautioning at play in Kaplan's promotion of prosocial empathy in chapter 7: its prosocial outcome, she argues, involves empathizers' capacity *not* to identify with and their ability to distance themselves from the other's suffering overrepresented in the media. Some of the most significant studies on empathy have concentrated on its role as a mediator for prosocial behavior, defining empathy as an altruistically, morally, or ethically competent behavior—empathic actions that are beneficial to others.[19] This correlation, however, is difficult to demonstrate empirically because of the lack of consensus on what empathy actually consists in and the misuse of the same term to refer to different processes—a "lack of uniformity in terminological usage and measurement [that] has made it difficult to interpret and synthesize the empirical findings."[20] The neuropsychologist Douglas Watt has sturdily underlined that epistemological weakness: "One cluster of literature emphasizes empathy as dependent on perception of affective states, theory of mind, conscious imitation, perspective taking, and the like; the other group emphasizes the centrality of affective activation in the empathizing subject. These differential concepts of empathy often lead to disparate methodologies and confusing empirical results."[21] Nevertheless, at least at the conceptual level there is strong support—especially in the work of Nancy Eisenberg, Bill Underwood and Bert Moore, Martin L. Hoffman, C. Daniel Batson, Nel Noddings, and Jean Decety—for the claim that empathy is key to intersubjectivity as an enabler of prosocial behavior, what Watt calls "one of our most critical social abilities and essential to the mitigation of human suffering."[22]

Studies by the social psychologist C. Daniel Batson, the care theorist Nel Noddings, and the neuroscientists Decety and his colleagues have been particularly central to the debate concerning the moral, prosocial implication of empathy. Batson claims that empathy is an altruism—"a motivational state with the ultimate goal of increasing another's welfare"—that amounts to an individual's ability to perceive the other as being in need and an individual's desire to reduce that need with the ultimate goal of improving the other's welfare.[23] Noddings has emphasized empathy as an essential component of the ethical understanding of others, especially in situations of care, which require a "feeling-with" the other—an attempt to help the other from one's own perspective.[24] Decety and Jackson published an influential paper in 2004 whose main argument is that "self–other awareness and self-regulation of emotions are vital components of human empathy."[25] Empathy is both an affective response to another person's emotional state and a cognitive capacity to understand the perspective of the other person, but it also involves "some regulatory mechanisms that keep track of the origins of self and other-feelings."[26] In other words, although empathy suggests a shared-representation mechanism and although human consciousness is "inherently intersubjective," the "self and other are similar but separate, and we usually do not confuse first-person knowledge from third-person knowledge"—something that Decety and Jackson proceed to prove through an assessment of neuroimaging studies and neuroscience research, indicating that at the neural level certain areas of the brain "may be critical in distinguishing the self from the other and therefore navigating shared representations."[27]

WHEN EMPATHY GOES WRONG

In the same article where Decety and Jackson describe the prosocial benefits of empathy, they observe that it can nevertheless easily distort intersubjective relations:

Even though empathy provides obvious benefits at both the individual and societal level by allowing people to coordinate their behavior and care for the other, it also has its cost in terms of maintaining an expanded self—that is, a self that is linked to others. . . . One example of such cost is the tendency to assume that others will feel the same way the self does, which is referred to as the false consensus effects. . . . Another example is the anxiety that can result from watching an unpleasant situation happening to another person. It has also been argued that some aspects of psychopathology may be in part regarded as the evolutionary cost of humankind for the development of our advanced capacity to empathize. . . . How this cost–benefit equation is solved within each individual depends on regulatory mechanisms as well as several personality and situational characteristics.[28]

This warning—the empathizer may well assume that others feel the same way the empathizer feels or would feel in a similar situation, or the empathizer may well experience distress as a reaction to the other's distress—has become typical in empathy studies since the 1990s, especially in neuroscience and its investigation of the role of mirror neurons in empathy. Mirror neurons are said to "mediate understanding of actions done by others" according to the following mechanism: "Each time an individual sees an action done by another individual, neurons that represent that action are activated in the observer's premotor cortex. This automatically induced, motor representation of the observed action corresponds to that which is spontaneously generated during active action and whose outcome is known to the acting individual. Thus, the mirror system transforms visual information into knowledge."[29] Neuroscientists have found that people with a high level of empathy have significantly active mirror neuron systems in their brains.[30] But one cause for concern is the very fact that this prosocial response implies an automatic activation of the observer's premotor cortex neurons' capacity to represent another's action: Isn't this prosocial response confusing the self and the other?

The field of neuroscience has increasingly maintained that empathy is not a systematically prosocial behavior elaborated for the benefit of the other in need. As Singer and Lamm summarize this view, there are "real-life examples of how empathy can 'go awry' (from a prosocial point of view). . . . For example, a torturer may use empathy in order to sense how to increase his victim's suffering; . . . and experiencing too much empathy can lead to an aversive distress response and selfish instead of other-oriented behavior."[31] In other words, empathically understanding the mental state of a person in distress can be used instrumentally as an occasion to amplify the other's suffering, or can be egotistically motivated—as is most often the case when the empathizer becomes personally distressed while observing the other's suffering and ends up withdrawing from the situation altogether for their own welfare, to alleviate their own suffering or to protect themselves from the contagion of suffering.[32] Such is the challenge facing individuals working in helping professions (doctors, nurses, therapists, for example) where they are continuously exposed to the pain of others. Studies suggest that in these situations empathy tends to become inoperative. Singer and Klimecki, for instance, recommend training to help professionals respond to another person's suffering with compassion instead of empathy insofar as compassion "is feeling for and not feeling with the other": more stably prosocial than empathy in its motivation to help the other in need, compassion is "characterized by feelings of warmth, concern and care for the other, as well as a strong motivation to improve the other's wellbeing."[33] Singer and Klimecki as well as Decety, Paul Bloom, and Jesse Prinz propose not only compassion but also sympathy and empathic concern as viable alternatives to empathy. These capacities are perceived as more apt for the appreciation of the lives of others *as* others insofar as they do not require that we share the feeling of others in distress.[34]

This scientific anxiety over more adversarial, distressed, or egoistic forms of empathy has led to a stronger insistence on empathy as a self–other differentiation—a definition that brings us back to Husserl and Stein. Successful empathy, in short, is distinct from emotional contagion. Singer and Lamm, relying on Decety's work with Jackson and Lamm, affirm that discrete neural substates are activated in empathy and sister emotional states: the prosocial success of empathy therefore "crucially depends upon self-awareness and self/other distinction; in other words, on our ability to distinguish between whether the source of our affective experience lies within ourselves or was triggered by the other. . . . Without this ability, witnessing someone else's emotions could, for example, result, purely, in personal distress and a self-centered response in the observer."[35] As C. Daryl Cameron and his colleagues maintain in a statement that strongly resonates with the medical anthropologist Carlo Caduff's main argument about care discussed in chapter 5, empathy is hard work: it is cognitively taxing and costly. Their empirical findings show that when given a choice, potential empathizers tend to avoid empathic situations: "We found a robust preference to avoid empathy, which was associated with perceptions of empathy as more effortful and aversive and less efficacious. Experimentally increasing empathy efficacy eliminated empathy avoidance, suggesting that cognitive costs directly cause empathy choice. When given the choice to share others' feelings, people act as if it is not worth the effort."[36] This is not the only situation where empathy is acknowledged as going "awry." Empathy has now been proven to be fundamentally biased. As Amy Coplan summarizes, "Empathy is subject to biases based on one's familiarity and identification with a target individual; we are more likely to empathize with those we know well and whom we judge to be like ourselves in some important respect. Not surprisingly, we're also more likely to succeed in our attempts to adopt their perspectives."[37] Put differently, in situations that require us to represent the experiences of others we know less or others who are socially and culturally different from us, we will most often fail to feel or understand their situated affective, mental, and psychological states.

In 2016, the psychologist Paul Bloom published his provocative book *Against Empathy: The Case for Rational Compassion*, where he condemns empathy as a "poor moral guide" to our relationships with others. Bloom does not deny the prosocial dimension of empathy, but he maintains that its obstinate biasedness as well as its capacity to stimulate violence and destroy personal relationships prevent it from being a genuine concern for the well-being of others.[38] Focusing on affective empathy ("the act of feeling what you believe other people feel—experiencing what they experience") while also reproving cognitive empathy ("the act of understanding other people, . . . figuring out what they are thinking") as "overrated," his claim is based on studies that show empathy to appeal mainly to our narrow prejudices and to be short-spanned.[39] "Empathy," he states, "is a spotlight focusing on certain people in the here and now. This makes us care more about them, but it leaves us insensitive to the long-term consequences of our acts and blind as well to the suffering of those we cannot empathize with. Empathy is biased, pushing us in the direction of parochialism and racism."[40] His condemnation is based in part on the work of the philosophers Jesse Prinz and Peter Singer as well as on the work of scientists and philosophers (including Decety, David DeSteno, Martha Nussbaum, and Steve Pinker) that discloses the limits of empathy as a justice-oriented faculty. Bloom essentially agrees with Prinz's compilation and confirmation of studies showing that empathy is biased toward members of one's group: empathy fails to expand beyond those who are socially, culturally, and politically most like the empathizer—a failure that affirms the limited range of empathy as well as its limited moral stance.[41] He and Prinz also denounce empathy as being chiefly individualistic (Bloom: empathy "is shortsighted. . . . It is innumerate, favoring the one over the many"[42]), leaving empathizers unconcerned about larger social patterns of distress and inequality. In light of these distorting effects and as the title of his publication underscores, Bloom insists on the need to replace emotional empathy with "rational compassion." I briefly come back to this recommendation later. Suffice it to say here that empathy studies do predominantly agree on the prejudicial dimension of empathy—a conclusion firmly enunciated in the work of Xiaojing Xu, Xiangyu Zuo, Xiaoying Wang, and Shihui Han (2009); Yawei Cheng, Chenyi Chen, Ching-Po Lin, Kun-Hsien Chou, and Decety (2010); and Decety and Cowell (2014).[43]

Especially since the mid-2010s, the humanities and social sciences have been likewise consistently skeptical not about the value of empathy but about its doability and reliability as a prosocial action. Although empathy is still considered to be the capacity to feel the emotions and mental states of others in distress, it is increasingly perceived as *causing* distress. The anthropologists Nils Bubandt and Rane Willerslev, for example, maintain that there is a "dark side" to "tactile empathy"—a form of empathic identification that legitimizes empathizers' ambition to "destroy the other" and their actual harming of the other. "Crucially," they argue, "this oscillation entails an inescapable ambivalence: empathy strives toward identification, yet does so while (re-)producing radical alterity."[44] Also seeking to uncover empathy's dark side, Fritz Breithaupt—a specialist in cultural studies and cognitive science, author of "The Bad Things We Do Because of Empathy" (2018) and *The Dark Sides of Empathy* (2019)—doesn't deny the prosocial potentialities of empathy but insists on the need "to disconnect empathy from morality."[45] Breithaupt's book was initially published in German the same year as Bloom's, but its main aim is not to make a case *against* empathy or to replace empathy with more suitable prosocial relational practices. His study relies mostly on an analysis of philosophical texts (from Burke to Nietzsche to Lipps's formulation of *Einfühlung* and Sartre) and contemporary political events (notably, Chancellor Angela Merkel's plea to open the borders of Germany to Syrian refugees in 2015). Its objective is more complex than Bloom's and so more interesting: Breithaupt maintains that we must try to understand the bad things we do because of empathy precisely because empathy is not something we can simply get rid of—humans are "homo empathicus," beings coexisting in a social world in which they continuously affect one another.[46] In that social world, interdependent coexistence is shaped by empathic relations, which are potentially both luminous and dark:

We observe others, we are affected by the experiences of others, we resonate with them and participate in the world to a degree via others. The suffering of others is our suffering; their happiness can be ours as well. Conversely, our emotions and moods affect others, too. Perhaps seeking such resonance in others is the core structure of being prosocial. . . . Empathy can save lives, whether by connecting emotionally with a suicidal teenager, for example, or by motivating humanitarian aid workers, donors, peacekeeping soldiers, and those who work for organizations like Doctors Without Borders. . . . How can one object to empathy? To present the counterargument, we need to start with a more sober assumption: Like most other human abilities, empathy probably serves the empathizer first and foremost and not the target of empathy. This assumption is certainly no great insight but it inoculates one from the idea that "more empathy" alone is the best guard against egocentrism, narcissism, and self-interest. By coexperiencing, the empathetic person enriches first of all his or her own experiences and knowledge before possibly also helping the other person.[47]

Defining empathy as "the coexperience of another's situation," Breithaupt's primary postulate is that the self–other differentiation in empathic relations is not strong enough to prevent self-interest and acts of absorption of the other.[48] Taking seriously Alexander Gottlieb Baumgarten's eighteenth-century notion of aesthetics as the ability to judge sensorially (an ability enabled by what was assumed to be the clarity of sensual perception), Breithaupt maintains that the empathizer's position is the same as the one described by Jean-Paul Sartre in *Being and Nothingness* (1943), when Sartre suddenly realizes that the relations in the park (notably, the bench between the trees) that he experienced earlier as fully available to him were disintegrated by the arrival of another person in the park, whose own relation with the bench will remain unknowable to him: that relation is nevertheless presented to him as knowable—the looker ends up reducing the situation of the other "to a few major features," perceiving not what the other sees but what the other should see. In short, as Breithaupt explains, "the empathetic observer has an *aesthetic* advantage" over the observed other.[49] From that Sartrean protodefinition of the empathizer's perception, Breithaupt identifies a variety of empathic reductions that harm the other instead of contributing to the other's well-being. These adverse harms include polarization, driven by the combination of side taking and empathy (the tendency "to quickly take sides in conflicts and use empathy to glorify their chosen side while condemning and demonizing the other side"); false empathy; filtered empathy ("using identification with a third person as a medium to have empathy with another"); and selfish empathy ("such as sadistic empathy, vampirism, and helicopter parenting").[50] Empathy is shown to cause insensitivity, false pity, exploitation, vampirism, sadism, and even terrorism, all of which are committed "not out of a failure of empathy but rather as a direct consequence of successful, even overly successful, empathy. . . . In many cases, empathy not only fails to stop such negative acts but in fact motivates and promotes them. In short, these malicious acts happen *not in spite of* empathy, but *because* of it."[51] In empathetic sadism, for example, empathizers experience enjoyment from observing tragedies and from witnessing harmful microevents such as embarrassment and domination: they may go as far as desiring the pain of others "in order to empathize with them."[52] In empathic vampirism, the other is reduced to being a mere medium for the empathizer's own experience—an experience intensified "by over-identifying with another person's experiences"; in these occurrences, the empathizer has only the empathizer's own interests in mind.[53]

Breithaupt's as well as Bubandt and Willerslev's findings, considered together with recent studies in neuroscience, philosophy of mind, and psychology, compel us to raise the following question: Can empathy defeat empathy?

WHAT TO DO WITH EMPATHY?

Fundamentally biased; individualistic and restrictive; sometimes so distressing as a response to the other's distress that its outcome can only be to egotistically look after one's own well-being; a labor that is so demanding that one's response might well be to simply retreat from it; dark to the point of reducing the other to a medium of one's own experience of the world or of enjoying the other's suffering; a source of insensitivity, false pity, and exploitation; a vehicle for the destruction of the other: empathy is far from being the straightforward and emancipatory ability to feel, understand, and experience the emotions and mental states of others, compelling us to prosocially help those in distress. Empathy studies are advising us to be vigilant in our empathic relations when we react to suffering others. This warning is especially relevant to unlearning the way we see migration. Necropolitical migration, as the artworks investigated in the book thus far have shown, is a dark coexistence between the displaced beings fleeing damaged regions of Africa, Asia, and Central America *and* the hosting beings of some of the wealthiest countries worldwide (in Europe and North America), which are nevertheless putting an end to asylum. It is difficult to imagine how the elaboration of more reciprocal forms of coexistence can come about without a substantial injection of empathy, but it is likewise difficult to imagine how empathy can in and of itself counter the dark coexistences of our times. This darkness can only but nourish the ambivalences of empathy. Embracing empathy is clearly not enough.

Note how scholars critical of empathy still acknowledge its beneficial potential. As the visual culture writer and curator Jill Bennett maintains, whereas research in the fields of psychology and neuroscience has established the empathy bias—a conclusion that insists on the fact that empathy "may serve to reinforce social boundaries and thereby stigma and discrimination"—its intersubjective and prosocial value must be preserved. To secure that value, Bennett suggests, it is imperative *to find ways* to enrich, extend, and uphold empathy as "the capacity to receive, hear, understand and support such communicated distress."[54] Breithaupt concurs: empathy must be "learned and practiced"; its blooming requires experimenting with different models of practicing empathy.[55] The replacement of empathy with compassion might not be the way to go. As the philosopher Stephen Morris succinctly observes, "It is difficult to see how one could experience the kind of genuine concern or compassion for others that could move us to assist them without us empathizing with their plights to some extent. After all, doesn't any genuine recognition of another's misery require that one puts oneself in another's shoes by imagining (and feeling) what such misery is like?"[56] That is, compassion itself requires a certain dose of empathy! The straightforward promotion of compassion, especially as elaborated by Bloom, is even more problematic when it ends up reaffirming the cartesian valorization of reason over passion. It denies and seeks to control the affective dimension of living beings (including their empathic capacities) for the sake of rationality. The return of the reason/emotion divide (Bloom: "We are emotional creatures, then, but we are also rational beings, with the capacity for rational decision-making. We can override, deflect, and overrule our passions, and we often should do so"[57]) appears fully anachronistic in light of the neurobiologist Antonio Damasio's work, which has established how there is no thinking without feeling.[58] Finally, as argued in the analysis of care in chapter 5, critics arguing against empathy tend to focus on the empathizer, as though that position were the only component of the empathic relation. As best summarized by the pluralistic counsellor Philemon Eva in his critique of Bloom, "There is little or no discussion of empathy as a social, dialogic *practice* of communication: the attempt to listen and respond, to understand and to feel, but also to check the accuracy of understanding and clarify feeling; to actively acknowledge, and attempt to bridge, difference; to reach for a shared understanding while recognizing the limitations of this."[59] Let us insist on that point: empathized persons are active in their response, in their autonomy. Bringing the empathized back into the empathic picture is a way to improve the prosocial outcome.

In light of this rich set of debates, I want to posit the following claim as a guideline that will accompany us when examining the strategically empathic artworks in the next chapter: empathy is a necessary but ambivalent and insufficient condition of possibility for prosociality and more reciprocal forms of coexistence. Empathy cannot simply be erased in all of its luminosity and darkness. This is how artistic practices addressing present-day migration explore empathy as an aesthetic strategy: they uphold its ambivalences without presuming to resolve them but struggling to have them or allowing them to unfold prosocially. They want empathy but are implicitly or openly searching for aesthetic strategies that can counterbalance its problematic effects. Instead of suppressing the empathic impulse or attempting to replace it with compassion, sympathy, empathic concern, or reason as though that suppression or substitution were fully controllable, achievable, or beneficial, the three case studies composing the next chapter (Ai Weiwei's *Human Flow*, Alejandro González Iñárritu's *CARNE y ARENA*, and Tania Bruguera's *10,142,926*) find it more useful to explore perspective sharing and historicization to offset the ambivalences of the empathic drive. Perspective sharing or perspective taking has been shown in neuroscientific studies "to reduce prejudice and intergroup bias."[60] As Breithaupt himself has contended, the prosociality of empathy can be productively enhanced when it involves the ability to consider the other's perspective: we complicate our perception and awareness of social situations "when we consider and share the various cognitive and emotional perspectives of others."[61] The case studies in chapter 7 also historicize migration (though some less actively than others) to better guide the empathizer's response: this historicization permeates the works we are about to consider; never simply disavowing the inevitable ambivalences of empathy, it evolves as a loop circulating between these ambivalences to alleviate them.

THE PHARMAKON AESTHETICS OF EMPATHY

Questions such as: Can the Other, in light of all that is happening, still be regarded as my fellow creature? When the extremes are broached, as is the case for us here and now, precisely what does my and the other's humanity consist in? The Other's burden having become too overwhelming, would it not be better for my life to stop being linked to its presence, as much as its to mine? Why must I, despite all opposition, nonetheless look after the other, stand as close as possible to his life if, in return, his only aim is my ruin?

If, ultimately, humanity exists only through being in and of the world, can we found a relation with others based on the reciprocal recognition of our common vulnerability and finitude?

—Achille Mbembe, *Necropolitics*[1]

Let us recall the three works that will serve as case studies here: Ai Weiwei's *Human Flow* (2017); Alejandro González Iñárritu's *CARNE y ARENA (Virtually Present, Physically Invisible)* (2017); and Tania Bruguera's *10,142,926* (2018). These artworks—a feature-length documentary film, a VR environment, and a multicomponent installation—have this is common: they explore empathy as a central aesthetic strategy of interpellation; they are a call for empathy. *Human Flow* explores that call as a counterpoint to exclusion, indignity, and indifference—one that is exemplified by Ai's caring relationship with the migrating beings he encounters in border areas and camps. Iñárritu's *CARNE y ARENA* sustains the view of VR as a generator of empathy: the work facilitates the meeting of real/physical viewers with digital protagonists located in a simulated borderzone so that the former may sense the vulnerability of the latter as they attempt to cross the Mexico-US border. In Bruguera's *10,142,926*, empathy is induced by an organic compound that makes viewers cry. These works have been highly successful in making necropolitical migration visible. Their mixed critical reception, however, shows how much empathy is a tricky strategy. As exemplified later in this chapter, most reviews stipulate that whereas empathy is a legitimate affect, the works do not necessarily succeed in doing what they are set up to do, which is to make viewers feel the suffering of others. Other reviews insist on empathy's insufficiency and distortions as well as its implicit reinforcement of world inequalities—most specifically, its consolidation of a hierarchical and distancing relationship (despite empathy's promise of proximity) between concerned citizens of some of the wealthiest economies worldwide and migrating beings from some of the poorest countries worldwide. These reviews resonate with the empathy studies discussed in chapter 6, which have proceeded to identify empathy's numerous dark sides, especially its bias, its questionable prosociality, as well as its vampirism of others' emotions or mental states.

This chapter seeks to examine the three works precisely because of their mixed success. It asks: Why and how does empathy matter in artistic practices addressing present-day migration? Why do artistic practices persist with calls for empathy despite findings that suggest that the prosociality of empathy should be mistrusted or, at least, facilitated by other means? And how and when is empathy effective? Let me restate the claim I formulated in the previous chapter: in each of these artworks, empathy is a necessary albeit ambivalent and insufficient condition of possibility for prosociality and more reciprocal forms of coexistence. This is to say that although *Human Flow*, *CARNE y ARENA*, and *10,142,926* sustain empathy as a relational capacity essential to the resolution of the devastations of migration, they always end up exploring it ambivalently; they cannot simply be presumed to be blocking out its insurmountable ambivalences. That pharmakon paradox, I want to argue, is a strength, however: the works' inventiveness lies in their exploration of empathy as a coexistence essential to migratory justice while allowing its ambivalence to evolve. Ambivalence is never simply expunged or controlled, and the prosociality of empathy, if it is to emerge, emerges from within that very ambivalence. Empathy, however, remains insufficient: the call for empathy cannot be prosocially effective without a certain level of perspective sharing, nor is it effective without a certain level of historical contextualization that is detailed enough to disclose the structures of inequality, injustice, and violence inherent to contemporary migration. Perspective sharing and historical contextualization are unevenly articulated in the works—unexpectedly generated in *Human Flow*, it schematically structures *CARNE y ARENA*'s and *10,142,926*'s environments. None of these works provides a deep historicization of migrancy (that's not their ambition), but they all provide enough perspective sharing and historicization to potentialize empathy. Prosociality becomes conceivable within that very blend.

To argue my claim, I start with a discussion of E. Ann Kaplan's compelling article "Empathy and Trauma Culture: Imaging Catastrophe" (2011), which identifies what is at stake in visual culture's empathic representation of conflicts and disasters. With these findings in mind, I then examine each artwork individually but also comparatively in light of the contemporary literature on empathy. Discussion of the three case studies is followed by a compilation and discussion of recent research on humanitarianism in the field of critical refugee and migrant studies—focusing on the work of Mariam Ticktin, Didier Fassin, Forensic Oceanography, Lilie Chouliaraki, and Pierluigi Musarò to suggest that the works' call for empathy is ultimately a humanitarian call. Humanitarianism has been strongly criticized in that field as much as empathy has been in the fields of philosophy, psychology, neuroscience, and cultural studies. This critique allows us to better understand the paradoxes inherent to the call for empathy, while making room for current developments in the field of migratory justice, which indicate that, despite the problematic ambivalences of empathy and humanitarianism, their sheer suspension is not an option in a period when assistance to displaced people in distress is steadily being defunded and criminalized.

RESPONSIBLE EMPATHY

In her study of early twenty-first-century media images of catastrophes—notably, images of the Iraq War (2003–2011) and Hurricane Katrina (2005)—and their participation in what she calls a "culture of trauma," the cultural studies scholar E. Ann Kaplan considers three possible types of empathic responses to such images: secondary or vicarious trauma, empty empathy, and witnessing. Although Kaplan doesn't examine artistic representations or media images of migration, her typology helps circumscribe the challenges of exploring empathy as an aesthetic strategy of awareness of traumatic events. Images of twenty-first-century migration are, after all, images of a necropolitical disaster; they contribute to the development of a visual culture in which representations of distressed victims not only predominate but also make viewers "vulnerable to traumatization through the media—second-hand, as it were."[2] Kaplan's analysis asserts empathy's limits and downfalls. Media images of suffering people are shown as predominantly impoverishing the viewer's capacity to prosocially feel and understand the victims' emotions or mental states. Viewers are left with two unsatisfying empathic responses: *secondary or vicarious trauma*, "a response in which the viewer is shocked to the extent of being emotionally over-aroused; that is, the empathic response to an image of a catastrophe may be so strong and personally painful that the individual turns away, or thinks distracting thoughts, unable to endure the feelings aroused"; and *empty empathy* "because of the transitory, fleeting nature of the empathic emotions that viewers often experience; that is, what starts as an empathic response gets transformed into numbing by the succession of catastrophes displayed before the viewer, as in TV newscasts or reading a newspaper."[3] In these two types of responses, empathy goes wrong: viewers are either so shocked that they are compelled to cancel out the unbearable images, or their empathic emotion is simply numbed away by the continual flow of catastrophic images, which tends to banalize the tragedies it incessantly represents.

Despite these empathic failures, Kaplan does not want to discard empathy, which she defines as "a complex pro-social emotion, with limitations."[4] Prosociality is crucial here; it sustains the third empathic response—*witnessing*—which she finds particularly promising from an ethical perspective. As Kaplan suggests, "'Witnessing' requires much more than empathizing with suffering of a person one sees in front of [one] (whether an image or a live event). It involves feeling so shocked by suffering that one is moved to act. . . . [O]ne is motivated to see that justice is done."[5] Such an empathic call—a call that compels the viewer to act for social justice—is possible when empathy ceases to be an individual-to-individual relationship and becomes a "collective response-ability for national or international policies."[6] Her claim is that prosocial possibilities are heightened when sufferers are situated within their historical context, when media images capture the politics of that suffering, and when viewers are invited to elucidate the raison d'être of suffering. In other words, as the literature on empathy has also shown, observing, representing, or feeling the pain of others is not in and of itself prosocial; it doesn't de facto lead to a prosocial alleviation of the other's suffering or to a political participation in the struggle for social justice. Observing is not in and of itself witnessing. The call for empathy must be consolidated by a critical unraveling of the historical present.

Kaplan's account emphasizes how the media use, overuse, and abuse empathy. As the media studies scholar Roger Silverstone has maintained in his own research on media and morality, it is not only the maker's and the producer's but perhaps even more so the viewer's responsibility to challenge the problematic media representations of the suffering other. As noted in my short discussion of Silverstone's work at the end of chapter 3, *not* to challenge these representations is to be in a relation of complicity or collusion with the media; it is to deny that audiences are indeed "actively engaged, that is, collusive, in a mediated culture that fails to deliver its promises of communication and connection, with enduring, powerful and largely negative consequences for our status as human beings. . . . Without challenge, without interrogation, and above all without our willingness to take responsibility for them [our media], they both fail us and, crucially, we them."[7] Silverstone's is but a noteworthy reminder that participants in media culture (which is in fact just about everyone) are complicit insofar as they most often not only assume that media are indispensable for our comprehension of the world and our ability to value the other but also accept these media framings and representations as *sufficient*—"which they cannot be": media are "sanctuaries" for everyday life and, as such, mostly fail to "invite us to engage with the other" or to "accept the challenge of the other."[8] In 2019, a study by the Displaced in Media strategic partnership—a group of journalists, activists, and migrant filmmakers invited by the European Cultural Foundation to reclaim media accounts of migration in Europe—implicitly confirms Silverstone's insight in its conclusion that European media "have systematically failed" in their coverage of the "European refugee crisis": most often reduced to statistics, migrating beings are reported binarily as either victims or threatening strangers; they are turned into "silent actors"; or their testimonies are not really heard but merely summarized and barely contextualized.[9]

The uses and abuses of empathy in media are a constant. Though these uses and abuses are never simply controllable, Kaplan suggests that empathy could be explored more inventively (as a form of witnessing, for example) to activate its prosocial potential.

Love Story (2016), a seven-channel video installation by the Berlin-based South African artist Candice Breitz (b. 1972, Johannesburg, South Africa), is a rich example of this kind of exploration. The work incisively materializes Kaplan's critical analysis of media-induced empathy and Silverstone's moral questioning of media's representation of the other as it replies to the intense unfolding of the purported

European refugee crisis in the mid-2010s. Divided in two rooms, the installation consists of a first section featuring a large video screen presenting successively the American actors Alec Baldwin and Julianne Moore sitting against a broadcast-quality green screen, movingly narrating migrant stories in the first person, and a second section composed of six smaller screens portraying men and women narrating the same stories, which can be heard individually through headphones (figures 7.1 and 7.2). Each monitor installed in that second room features a displaced person who has left their country to escape war or persecution: Sarah Ezzat Mardini, a competitive swimmer from war torn Syria; José Maria João, a former child soldier from Angola; Mamy Maloba Langa, a survivor from the Democratic Republic of Congo; Shabeena Francis Saveri, a transgender activist from India; Luis Ernesto Nava Molero, a political dissident from Venezuela; and Farah Abdi Mohamed, an atheist from Somalia.[10]

The installation's two-room structure is key to the evolution of empathy within the work: the second room discloses the stories *retrospectively* as empathically appropriated, *re*performed, and staged by Baldwin and Moore in the first room. This retroawareness shows how effective the actors were as we first encountered them; it shows the efficiency of the Hollywoodian empathy machine: as media consumers, we become sensitive to the distress of others when their stories are told by celebrities, even if that mode of telling entails silencing the others' voices. *Love Story* allows the ambivalence of empathy to unfold. Indeed, as we enter the second room and are invited to listen to the singular stories of every migrating being assembled there, the initial empathy is never simply swift away: it brought us into that second room and eventually sustains our listening capacity. As each viewer individually listens to a story, sitting on a bench with headphones on, that person is positioned face-to-face with the storyteller in an equal (or, at least, more equal) relationship. As viewers silently and meditatively listen, as they gain personal knowledge of the narrated journeys, they become witnesses (let us follow Kaplan here) of contemporary migration and might thereon be compelled to act prosocially for migratory justice. That transformation, however, will occur only if the viewers attend to each storyteller's perspective and hear the historicization of migration materialized in the narration of the storyteller's journey.

Kaplan's analysis, understood in light of Silverstone's notion of responsibility and Breitz's *Love Story*, sets the table for the consideration of empathic artworks. The chapter's questions gain in clarity: Why and how does empathy matter in artistic practices addressing the contemporary crises of migration? Why do artistic

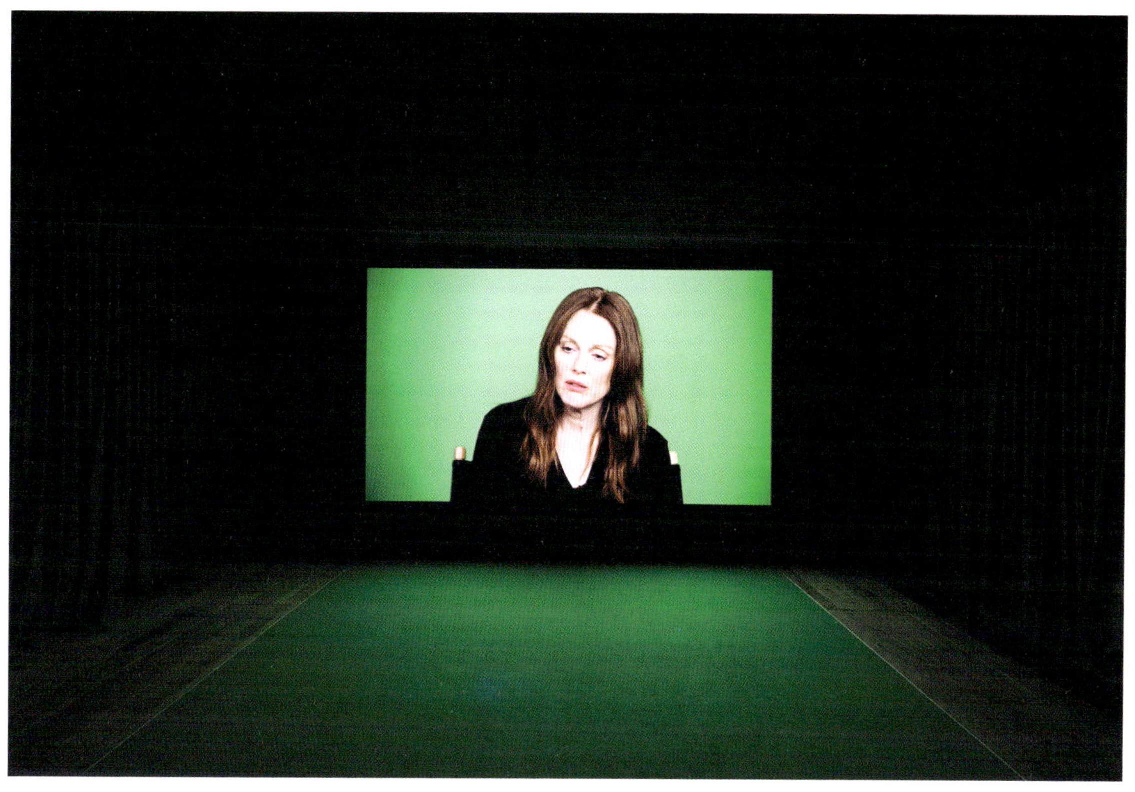

FIGURE 7.1

Candice Breitz, *Love Story*, 2016 (still).
Seven-channel video installation, 73
minutes, 42 seconds, loop. Featuring Alec
Baldwin and Julianne Moore. Commissioned
by the National Gallery of Victoria, Outset
Germany + Medienboard Berlin-Brandenburg.
Installation view: South African Pavilion,
Venice Biennale, 2017. Photo: Andrea
Rossetti. Courtesy of the artist.

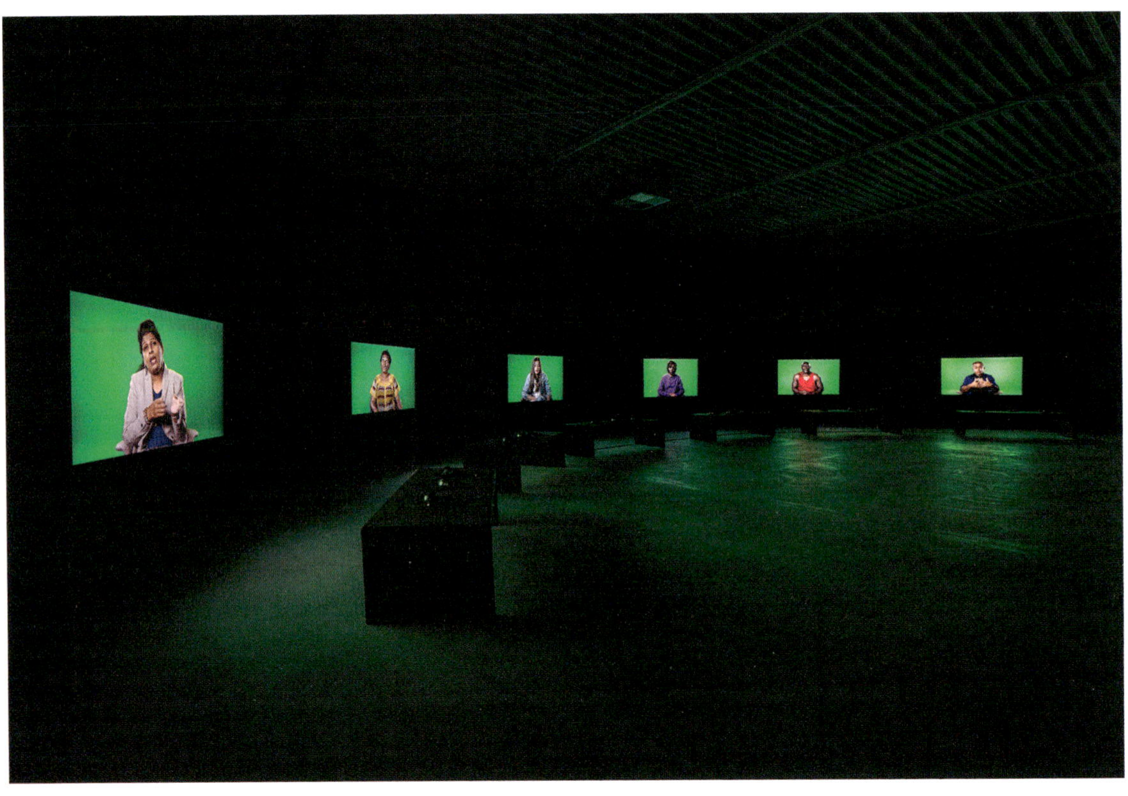

FIGURE 7.2

Candice Breitz, *Love Story*, 2016 (still). Seven-channel video installation, 73 minutes, 42 seconds, loop. Featuring Alec Baldwin and Julianne Moore. *Left to right*: Shabeena Francis Saveri (03:38:51), Mamy Maloba Langa (04:15:36), Sarah Ezzat Mardini (02:47:51), Farah Abdi Mohamed (03:31:36), José Maria João (03:27:58), and Luis Ernesto Nava Molero (03:49:53). Commissioned by the National Gallery of Victoria, Outset Germany + Medienboard Berlin-Brandenburg. Installation view: Arken Museum of Modern Art, Ishøj, 2018. Photo: Anders Sune Berg. Courtesy of the artist.

practices persist with empathic calls despite findings that suggest that the prosociality of empathy must be mistrusted or, at least, facilitated by other means? How and when is empathy effective? The inventiveness of such artistic works, I want to contend, lies in their ability to keep the tensions of the pharmakon (remedy + poison) alive while allowing counterbalancing calls to ease its ambivalences.

AI WEIWEI'S *HUMAN FLOW*

The 140-minute-long high-definition film *Human Flow* (2017) by the Chinese artist Ai Weiwei (b. 1957, Beijing, People's Republic of China, based in Europe since 2015, first in Berlin, then in Cambridge, UK, and now in Montemor-o-Novo, Portugal) was made in collaboration with the following three writers: Chin-Chin Yap, Tim Finch, and Boris Cheshirkov. A documentary film, it depicts the planetary dimension of migration as it unfolded during and in the aftermath of 2015, the year when more than a million people crossed into Europe (more than one million arriving by sea and about 35,000 by land), at the acme of what was called the "European refugee crisis."[11] As stipulated in chapter 3, in this period the European migration and border regime was considerably destabilized by the influx of a new quantitative and qualitative level of migration but then substantially restabilized once the EU was able to assert its control over the influx.[12] *Human Flow* captures the same historical moment as Richard Mosse's *Incoming* (2014–2017). To restabilize the border regime, member states started to close down their borders to citizens-on-the-move mostly coming from Syria, Afghanistan, and Iraq, forcing them to adopt more dangerous ways (e.g., the Mediterranean Sea, the Aegean Sea) of reaching Europe; they transformed migrant routes into corridors to manage the migrants' movement; and they intensified campization (figures 7.3 and 7.4). The film's main focus is the EU's imperiled reception of displaced people, but the work seeks a larger terrestrial view. It covers 23 countries or regions, including Turkey, Syria, Iraq, Lebanon, Jordan, Gaza, Libya, Kenya, Afghanistan, Bangladesh, Pakistan, EU countries (Greece, Italy, France, Germany, and the Hungary/Croatia border), and the US-Mexico border area. Shot over two years using various technologies, including iPhones and drones equipped with high-definition cameras, it also covers 40 refugee camps. In contrast to *Incoming's* continual nonhuman (quasi-inhuman) thermal recording of borderzones, *Human Flow*'s large drone shots from above are interspersed with more intimate iPhone shots as well as with interviews and quotes from state representatives,

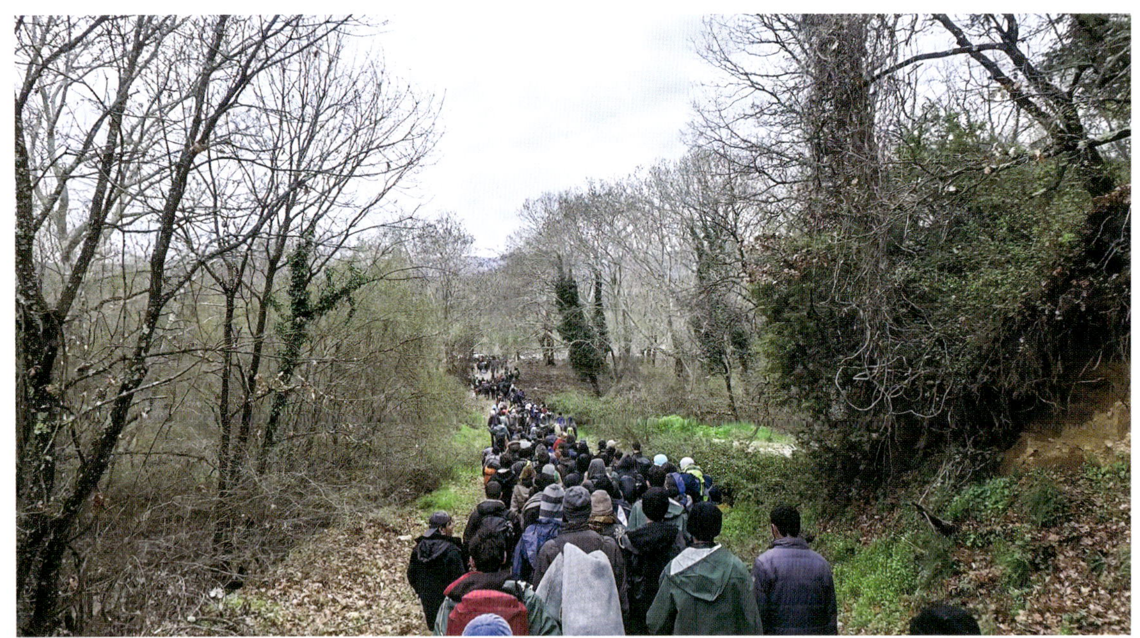

FIGURE 7.3

Ai Weiwei, *Human Flow*, 2017 (still). HD film, color, 140 minutes. © Ai Weiwei Studio.

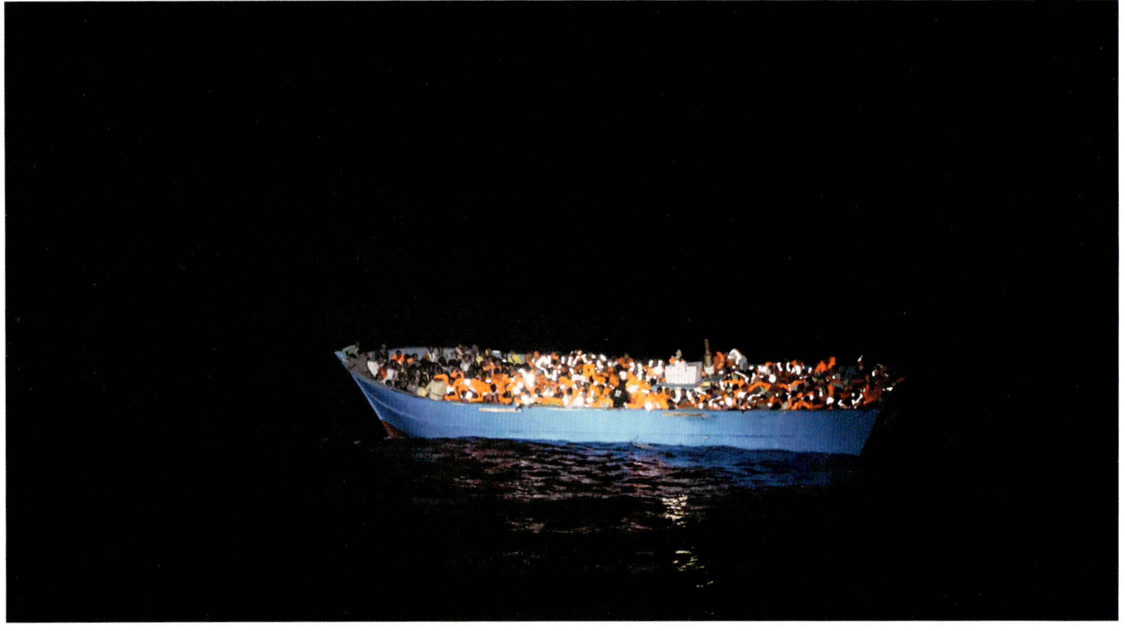

FIGURE 7.4

Ai Weiwei, *Human Flow*, 2017 (still). HD film, color, 140 minutes. © Ai Weiwei Studio.

humanitarians, and experts on migration as well as with sequences showing Ai accompanying migrating groups in their journeys—listening to their stories, assisting rescuers, caring for the men and women who have just been rescued (figure 7.5), and participating in the daily life of refugee camps. The whole is held together by a humanistic and rescue-oriented humanitarian approach, materialized in Ai's empathic relation with the migrating individuals captured by the camera and in a variety of written and spoken statements affirming the imperative to humanize displaced people—to become aware that, as a man from the Rohingya Muslim people summarizes it, "we have feelings too, we are humans too."

Though *Human Flow* was generally well received, its critical reception was mixed mainly because of the film's empathic drive. And yet the work is absolutely unique and breathtaking in its coverage of the planetary scale of twenty-first-century migration, in its inclusion of the artist-filmmaker in the images so that his perspective isn't hidden behind the camera, and in its elaboration of personal sequences where travelers and camp residents tell their stories of forced displacement.

Ai Weiwei's other migration-related installations made during that period were also calls for empathy. The one-room *Laundromat* (2016) presented at Deitch Projects in New York relied on Ai's photographic presence—most of the walls were covered with photographs of migrating travelers and the Idomeni Refugee Camp in Greece taken by Ai as well as with numerous selfies of Ai standing next to the residents. But the installation also displayed garments collected by the artist and his team from the refugee camp, regrouped according to clothing categories (figure 7.6). *Soleil Levant* (2017), made specifically for Kunsthal Charlottenborg in Copenhagen, consisted in more than 3,500 orange life jackets—salvaged from the Greek island of Lesbos, where they were abandoned after the passengers' arrival—packed in the museum's facade windows and seen from the vantage point of the street. In the two installations, the garments were cleaned up and reordered in their display (figure 7.7). They nevertheless functioned as indexical traces of bodies, even more so as rescued bodies, signaling the underacknowledged crises experienced by displaced people—namely, dispossession, displacement, endangerment, disappearance, and death. Empathy, as the relational capacity to feel the other's distress, was enabled by these indexicalities. In these works—including *Law of the Journey* (2017) shown at the National Gallery in Prague, a suspended 230-foot-long inflatable boat containing similar yet faceless human figures on which viewers could mentally project their own faces—empathy is explored as the most powerful affective state to reach humanistic awareness—the awareness that these beings are humans, just like "us."

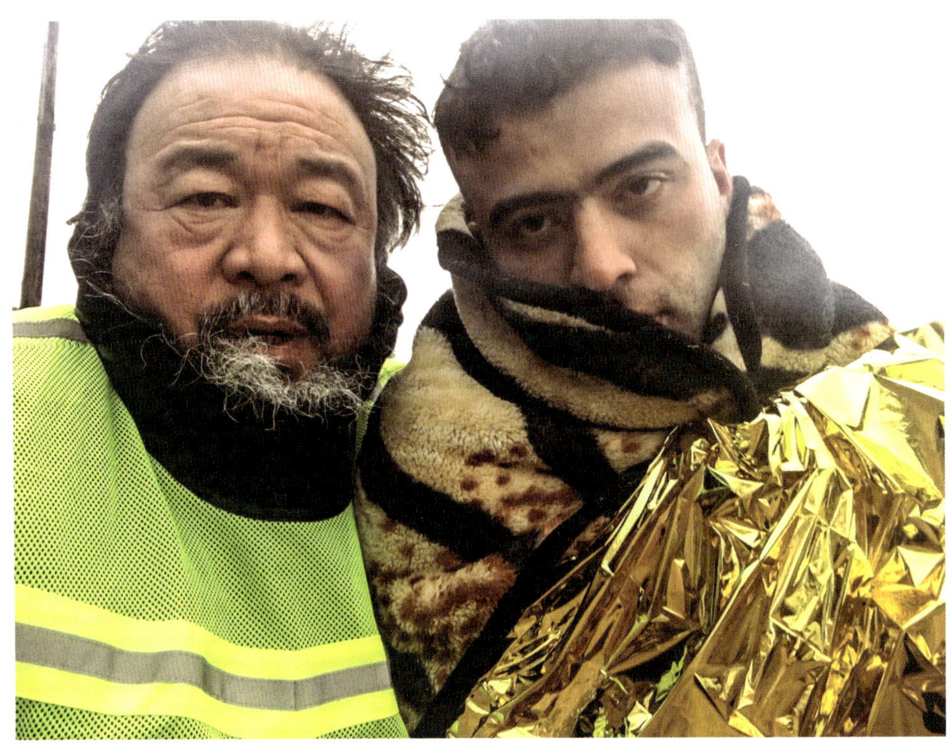

FIGURE 7.5

Ai Weiwei, *Human Flow*, 2017 (still). HD film,
color, 140 minutes. © Ai Weiwei Studio.

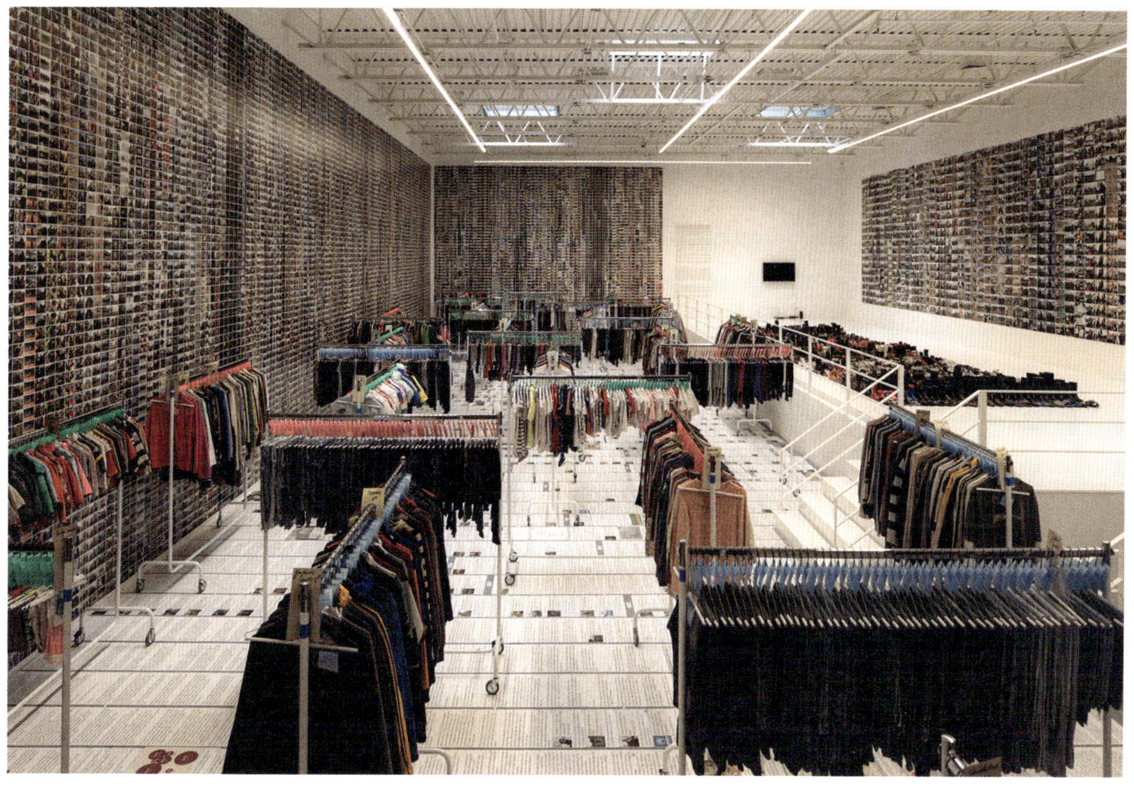

Ai Weiwei, *Laundromat*, 2016–. Installation, 2,000 items of clothing, shoes, and blankets collected from the Idomeni Refugee Camp in Greece. Installation view: Jeffrey Deitch Projects, New York, November 5–December 23, 2016. © Ai Weiwei Studio.

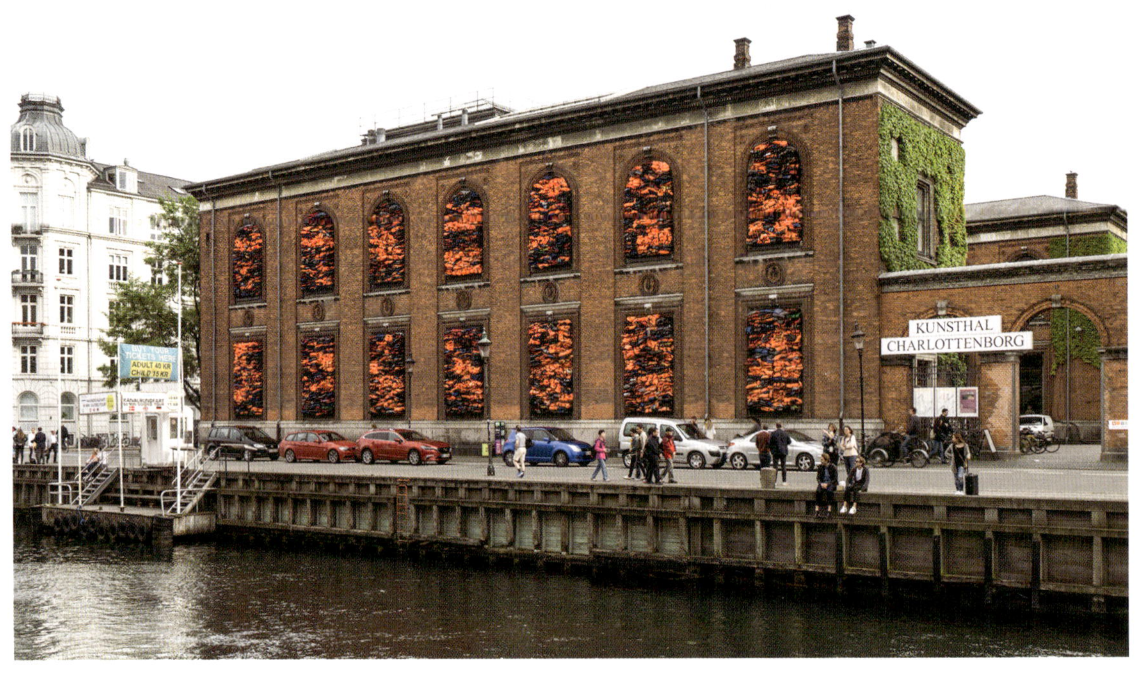

FIGURE 7.7

Ai Weiwei, *Soleil Levant*, 2017. Installation, more than 3,500 salvaged orange life jackets collected from refugees arriving at the Greek Island of Lesbos. Installation view, Kunsthal Charlottenborg, Copenhagen, June 20–October 20, 2017. © Ai Weiwei Studio.

Here I follow the artist's own claim: "The refugee crisis is not about refugees, rather, it is about us": not only is it a human crisis, argues Ai, but it is also primarily caused by "[our] prioritisation of financial gain over people's struggle for the necessities of life. . . . The west has all but abandoned its belief in humanity and support for the precious ideals contained in declarations on universal human rights. It has sacrificed these ideals for short-sighted cowardice and greed."[13] Humanism—the imperative of humanism in the aftermath of its loss in economically privileged societies—is what the migration works are ultimately set out to assert, and the mobilization of the viewer's empathy is the vehicle to restore that humanism.

I have briefly referred to these other installations to show how Ai is not an occasional humanistic thinker or activist of migratory justice. On the contrary. The son of a Mao dissident poet, he has been and remains highly and publicly critical of the Chinese government's standpoint on human rights; while living in China, he made a series of artworks denouncing the Sichuan schools corruption scandal in 2008.[14] He was imprisoned for 81 days in 2011 on the grounds of "economic crimes." He left China in 2015 when his passport was returned to him and is now living in exile in Europe. As Ai contends, "My experience clarifies why I identify so deeply with all these unfortunate people who are pushed into extreme conditions by outside forces they are powerless to resist."[15] The works addressing contemporary migration that he made around 2017 result from that deep identification; they are empathically made and are made to be empathically experienced by the viewer. The artist's empathy (his capacity to feel migrant distress) is represented in the artworks by the garments and life vests he has not only collected but also taken care of, as well as by his own statements in *Human Flow*, where he continuously affirms the value of the migrating beings he meets in camps and borderzones. His empathy is what potentially draws us—the viewers—into the artworks. But the installations, photographs, and film also show that whereas the call for empathy is a constant in Ai's artistic exploration of the dehumanization of migration, it tends to be ambivalent precisely because of its identificatory dimension. That dimension became manifest as early as 2016 when Ai responded to the highly mediatized death of the three-year-old Syrian Kurdish refugee Alan Kurdi, whose tragic fate was captured in Nilüfer Demir's photograph showing his body lying face down on a beach in Turkey on September 2, 2015. The inflatable and overcrowded boat that Alan and his family had boarded capsized a few minutes after leaving Bodrum in Turkey in an attempt to reach the Greek island of Kos. The photograph is certainly one of the most pivotal images of awareness of the "European refugee crisis" to have circulated on the internet and mainstream media during that period. Ai re-created the event in 2016 in an image taken by the *India Today* photographer Rohit Chawla: he staged himself lying face down on a beach in Lesbos—an enactment that might have been propelled by Ai's own empathic reaction to Kurdi's death but that also problematically appropriated Kurdi's fate by literally canceling out the young boy's body, vampiristically absorbing it, as it were, while asking the viewer to empathize with it via Ai's own body. The ambivalence of Ai's empathic drive is not a problem in itself. On the contrary, I believe that the photographic image is richer when it does not attempt to repress that inevitability. Yet the inevitability is left to itself, unproblematized, untransformed. In her unambiguous support of the image, the curator Luísa Santos has stated: "Ai's image confronts us—his face is turned towards us—in what seems to be, on the one hand, a call to action and, on the other, a message telling us that anyone, despite their social, economic, professional status, could be in the position of a refugee."[16] Yet it is hard to see *how* the photograph works prosocially as a call to action insofar as it only stages Ai's identification with Alan; moreover, its humanism (the sense that *anyone* could be Alan) blurs the world inequalities that secure the likelihood that not *anyone* can or will *be* Alan.

Though *Human Flow*'s press release emphasized how viewing the documentary was a unique opportunity to "witness" the "refugee crisis" as a global mass-migration phenomenon, that witnessing—the empathic response that represents for Kaplan the only promising form of empathy because of its ethical ability to "change the viewer in a positive pro-social manner"[17]—was far from being straightforwardly productive. *Human Flow*'s critical reception was unanimous in claiming that its humanistic empathic drive was one of its main raisons d'être, but critics also noted that Ai was overly present in the film and that his empathic approach prevented him from addressing the politics, causes, and configurations of the necropolitics of migration. I will be brief here and focus on four reviews (the most substantial ones)—summarizing them but eventually asking if their assessments could not be somewhat complicated.

The journalist Peter Bradshaw of the *Guardian* stated: "Clearly, *Human Flow* is vulnerable to the charge of fetishising or aestheticising the migrants as spectacle." This charge is nevertheless countered by Bradshaw's claim that Ai's perspective is not political but empathic: the work "make[s] the leap of empathy, to understand what being a migrant is like in human terms."[18] The empathic drive is seen here as antithetic to politics yet celebrated because of its humanistic dimension. I come back to the notion of humanism later, but suffice it to say for now that in this

chapter I want to suggest that the plea for humanism is not as inclusive and reparative as it appears to be. I furthermore want to suggest that empathy and politics
are not necessarily incompatible and that this merger does powerfully make its
way into *Human Flow*, even if only obliquely. In his review of *Human Flow*, the art
historian T. J. Demos also emphasized the limits of empathy, but he more critically
(and, I would add, more convincingly) explained its limitations by deploring the
absence of any investigation of the factors that structure the increased worldwide
forced displacement of beings: "*Human Flow* is a cinema of liberalism: to manifest
empathy for the wretched of the earth in an effort to humanize the dispossessed
and disenfranchised. It leaves viewers with a nagging feeling of undefined guilt, but
also with reassuring visions of redemption, manifested in images of encompassing
filmic splendor and Ai caring for the less fortunate. *Empathy is a position few of us
would oppose. But some would want to take matters deeper in terms of interrogating
the causes of the oppressive conditions that make life miserable for multitudes and that
propel displacement.*"[19] The art critic Hanna Schenkel was harsher in her account
of the work precisely because of what she considered to be the artist's narcissism:

Between genuinely heartfelt moments showing refugees interviewed in camps all over the
world, there are shots of Weiwei awkwardly posing for selfies and self-consciously looking
at the frame of his mobile camera as he films himself accompanying a freezing, exhausted
man who came off a boat moments prior to find tea and a warming fire. . . . [S]elfie sticks and
the extreme close-ups of faces that result when turning a mobile camera on yourself can't
help but evoke a certain air of narcissism, which feels out of place at best and deeply offensive at worst—potentially calling into question Weiwei's motivation for being in the camps.[20]

Finally, Georges Didi-Huberman echoed most of these reviews, observing Ai's *staging* of himself looking compassionately at the displaced people. The problem with
that staging, posited Didi-Huberman, lies in its disabling of the look as an encounter between beings, mainly between the artist and the subjects he films; looking is
prevented from unfolding as a form of exchange with the other; it lacks criticality;
it "ends up producing *visual clichés*—as opposed to truthful images—of our world,
like the glossy pages of certain so-called geographical magazines which are, in truth,
more touristic than anything else."[21] In contrast, the engagement of a critical eye
would entail listening to the migrating being's demand for equality and civic status;
it would entail moving away from "philanthropy . . . to attribute blame, to dig deep,
to publicly pinpoint this wound of history."[22]

What these reviews share is a common denunciation not so much of empathy as of its insufficiencies as well as of its ambivalences when empathy is not counterbalanced by a historicization of twenty-first-century migration (Demos) and by a recognition of the autonomy of migration (Didi-Huberman). Their arguments are forceful. Ai's overpresence can indeed be said to transform empathy into what Fritz Breithaupt calls a selfish or vampiristic endeavor: empathy as the capacity to feel and understand the feelings and mental states of suffering others ends up reducing the other to a mere medium of the empathizer's own experience—an experience expanded "by over-identifying with another person's experiences."[23] It is useful here to note Kaja Silverman's Lacanian-based psychoanalytical distinction between *idiopathic identification* and *heteropathic identification* to grasp what such an empathic distortion entails. Whereas idiopathic identification corresponds to the cannibalistic propensity to absorb the other within the self, heteropathic identification unfolds when the subject identifies with the other as another.[24] Ai's overpresence keeps suggesting idiopathic identification. My claim is not that he is actually overidentifying (my intention here is certainly not to psychoanalyze him) but that his reiterated representation of himself being moved by the pain of migrating beings produces overidentification for the viewer. That visuality depreciates the self–other differentiation of empathy; it doesn't leave much room for the viewers' own empathic or nonempathic relation with the documented beings. Allowed to unfold beyond any obvious attempt to historicize migration, the artist's empathy reinstates Saidiya V. Hartman's conclusion regarding the epistolary account by the abolitionist John Rankin (1793–1886) of the suffering of the enslaved through identification. Although his letters attempted to establish the "common humanity of all men on the basis of this extended suffering," they relied on an empathic relation that was fundamentally "double-edged": in making the other's suffering his own, Rankin not only obliterated the other's suffering but also ended up denying the other's capacity for sentience.[25]

I want to reaffirm, however, that identification is not at issue here and that ambivalences of empathy are unavoidable—this is certainly what the fields of philosophy, psychology, neuroscience, and cultural studies maintain. What becomes important, then, is to see how empathy can be made less distorting, less obliterating, and less limiting—how it can be effective *because of* and not simply *notwithstanding* its ambivalences. Let us therefore be attentive to *Human Flow*'s most singular moment, when empathy is exposed as a reversible ambivalence, when the "poisonous" side of the pharmakon is overtaken by its "therapeutic" side. This is the moment (at 52:36 into the film) when Abdullah Mahmoud, a man fleeing Syria, and Ai exchange passports. In this sequence filmed in the improvised camp in Idomeni, Ai talks about them being the same—that is, humans—and starts to suggest the possibility of swapping homes: a tent in exchange for the artist's Berlin studio. The artist then embarrassingly takes his passport back. In that moment, a sequence that Ai decided not to remove from the film (to his credit), the artist's own belief that "establishing the understanding that we all belong to one humanity is the most essential step for how we might continue to coexist on this sphere we call Earth" is perturbed by an intersubjective exchange that shows that we in fact *do not* belong to *one* humanity. Such is necropolitical migration: a hierarchized dualism embedded in Europe's and North America's structural categorization of valued and undervalued lives.[26] The limits of *Human Flow* do not pertain to its call for empathy or its deployment of the ambivalences of empathy. Rather, they pertain to its humanism—a humanism that the empathic drive ultimately questions as it teases out, in that very exchange between Abdullah Mahmoud and Ai Weiwei, the inequities structuring migratory injustice. There is no universalism or sameness here. Recalling that sequence with the *Guardian* journalist Xan Brooks, Ai stated: "Yeah, that was the worst feeling. That really got me. Because [if] you're passionate, you think you mean what you say. You tell these people that you're the same as them. But you are lying because you are not the same. Your situation is different; you must leave them. And that's going to haunt me for the rest of my life."[27] His statement is about recognizing that inequality, that nonsameness.

The effectiveness of that sequence cannot be overestimated, for it is how and when the historical present and the autonomy of migration—schematic as they may well be—make their way into the film: the disparities of migration are not demonstrated but lived and exposed within the empathic drive. These few minutes establish a self–other differentiation as Ai's empathy unfolds. They are troubling and inventive. They produce what Didi-Huberman calls for: an encounter. Ai Wei wei listens to Abdullah Mahmoud as Abdullah Mahmoud listens to Ai Weiwei and responds. Such is perspective sharing at its best—one that psychology and neuro-science have shown "to reduce prejudice and intergroup bias" when they unfold in empathic relations.[28] Mahmoud emerges as a political subject as his encounter breaks humanism apart: the whole point of necropolitical migration is that it is *not* universally human. In such an interchange, each subject becomes both self and other in a radicalized dialogical relation à la Gayatri Chakravorty Spivak. Empathy, even in its vampiristic or idiopathic unfolding, was necessary to the dialogical encounter! Historicization also unexpectedly emerges from within empathy and not as a supplement despite empathy. In the dialogue, colonial presence starts to be disclosed. It is only then that empathy becomes a potential condition of possibility for prosociality and a more reciprocal form of coexistence.

ALEJANDRO GONZÁLEZ IÑÁRRITU'S *CARNE Y ARENA*

Why and how does empathy matter in artistic practices addressing necropolitical migration? Why do artworks persist with their empathic calls, despite findings that suggest that the prosociality of empathy must be mistrusted or, at least, more complexly defined? And how and when is empathy effective in these works? These questions are likewise crucial for understanding *CARNE y ARENA (Virtually Present, Physically Invisible)* (2017), a VR work by the Mexican, Los Angeles–based filmmaker Alejandro González Iñárritu (b. 1963, Mexico City). Here, viewers are invited to be part of a digital 3D desert environment where a small caravan of migrating beings attempts to cross the Mexico-US border (figure 7.8). Iñárritu has explicitly stated that he wanted to raise awareness of the dangerous conditions experienced by people from Mexico and Central America when crossing borderzones as they seek asylum in the United States. Exploring what has repeatedly been called the "ultimate empathy machine,"[29] he has also explicitly stated that he wanted to reach that objective by creating a VR work that the viewer could empathically and compassionately experience.[30] Empathy is therefore understood as an experience of awareness that is affectively lived; it is understood as the affective state most likely to make viewers cognizant of the imperiling American reception of migrating beings from Latin America as they are compelled to cross the hostile terrain of the Sonoran Desert. Before expanding on this specific call for empathy, it is useful to describe the work first.

Iñárritu made *CARNE y ARENA* (Flesh and sand) in collaboration with the cinematographer Emmanuel Lubezki and the immersive-entertainment studio ILMx-LAB as well as with the support of Legendary Entertainment, the Fondazione Prada, and Emerson Collective (a social justice organization). The work premiered in 2017 at the Cannes Film Festival and was the first VR project to be featured at the festival. It was later shown at the Prada Foundation in Milan, the Tlatelolco University Cultural Center in Mexico City, the Los Angeles County Museum of Art (where I experienced it for the first time), the Atlas Performing Arts Center in Washington, DC,

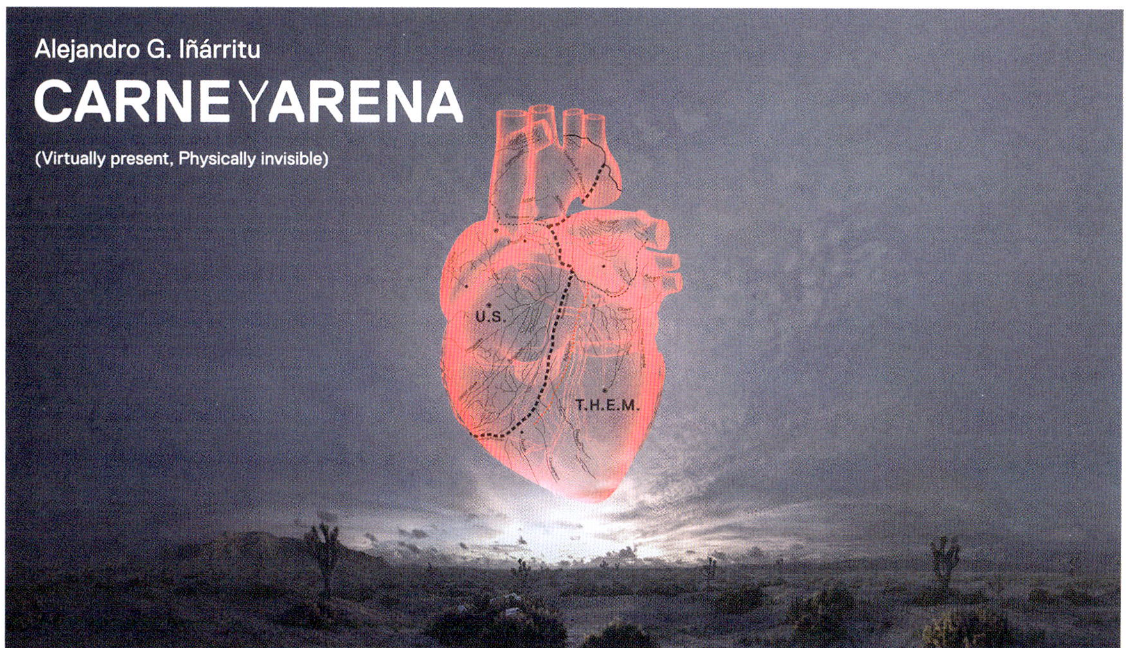

and since then many other venues. The VR places the viewer in a simulated desert among a group of people led by a coyote (paid guide or human trafficker) across the Mexican borderline into the United States until they are stopped by border patrol agents. The story is based on interviews Iñárritu held with Mexican and Central American refugees—men and women who have crossed borderzones in precarious conditions, some of whom were hired as nonactors in the making of *CARNE y ARENA*. Their faces were 3D scanned and their bodies' motion captured for the purposes of a virtual reenactment; they were asked to reperform "their own story"

FIGURE 7.8

Alejandro González Iñárritu, *CARNE y ARENA (Virtually Present, Physically Invisible)*, 2017. Virtual reality, 6.5 minutes. Promo "heart + desert" image. Graphic design: Neil Kellerhouse. © Legendary.

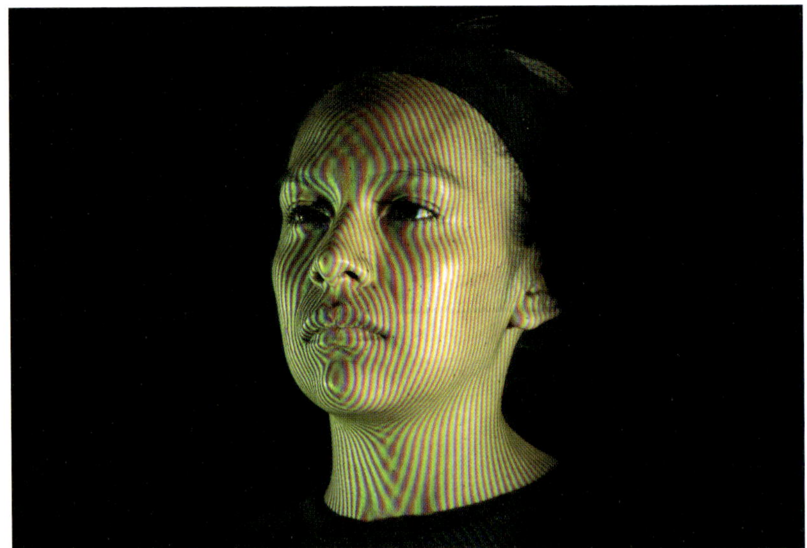

(figures 7.9 and 7.10).[31] The work therefore rests on the acknowledgment of the autonomy of migration; it does not speak *for* but *with* the nonactors. And although it discloses the necropolitics of migration, it does not simply revictimize the migrants: they were heard; they were invited to narrate their stories environmentally.

The viewer's empathic experience, if it occurs, will unfold in that already schematically historicized and migrant-informed environment. The work relies on VR's immersive capacity to bring viewers closer to the imperiled protagonists. How does this proximity unfold in *CARNE y ARENA*? Mainly by introducing viewers to an environment where they coexist with the digital protagonists. They can move around, look in front or behind the protagonists, observe them while standing in the middle of the scene or on the side, circulate with them, even attempt to touch their virtual

FIGURE 7.9

Alejandro González Iñárritu, *CARNE y ARENA
(Virtually Present, Physically Invisible)*, 2017.
Virtual reality, 6.5 minutes. Selena, a mother
from Guatemala, has her image digitally
re-created. Photo: Chachi Ramirez.
© Legendary.

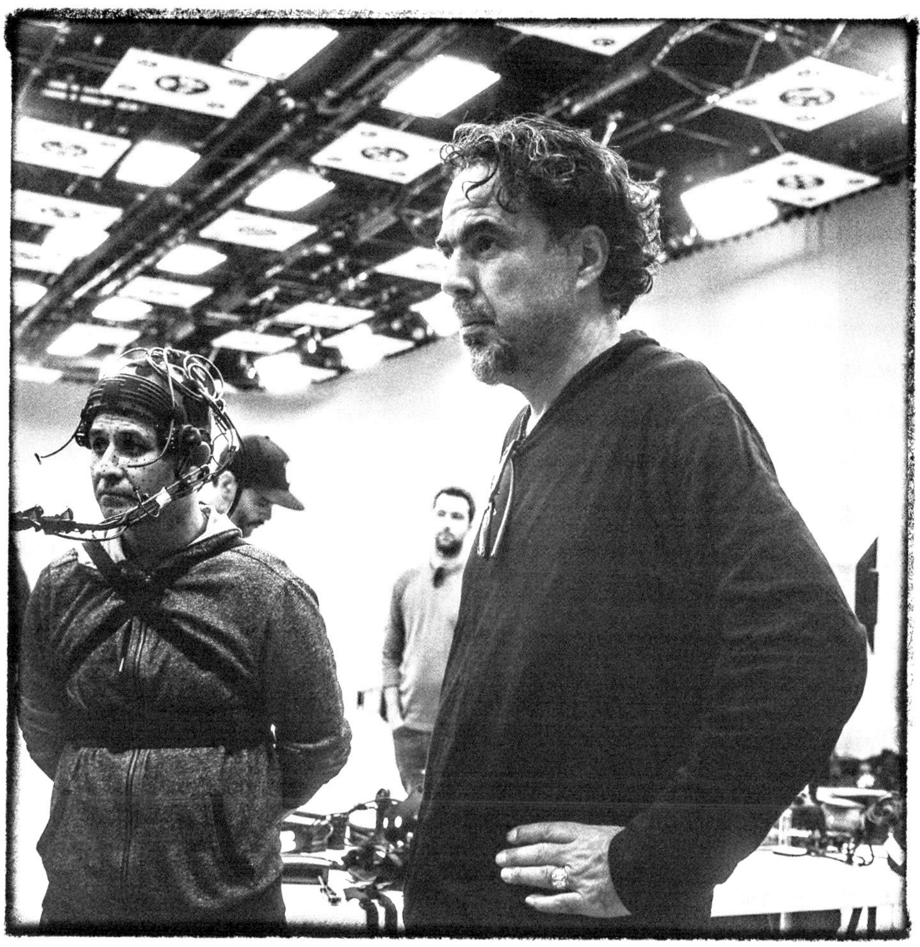

FIGURE 7.10

Alejandro González Iñárritu, *CARNE y ARENA*
(Virtually Present, Physically Invisible), 2017.
Virtual reality, 6.5 minutes. Iñárritu directing
during a motion-capture shoot. Photo:
Chachi Ramirez. © Legendary.

bodies to discover their nonphysical presence. But the viewer-as-user remains invisible to the protagonists. *Virtually Present, Physically Invisible*, the work's subtitle, describes rather well how the VR technology introduces viewers into a predefined environment that they nevertheless perceptually co-create as they move imperceptibly within that space—a double status (present and invisible) that is fundamental to the coexistence unfolding in the work. That coexistence is real albeit desynchronized, slightly off, staggered: it consists in a viewer–protagonist interdependence where the former is encouraged to empathically feel the latter's pre-enacted suffering but without any live reciprocity. That delayed reciprocity restricts the prosocial drive—the viewer cannot transform the event unfolding in the environment—but it never simply prevents prosociality as an outcome of the VR experience. On the contrary—and this is my main claim—prosociality is made possible by the combination of the empathic experience, the historical context provided by the installation, and the enablement of perspective sharing (which acknowledges the autonomy of migration).

Let us be more precise about *CARNE y ARENA* and the type of experience it sustains. It is important to highlight that the viewer enters the VR environment after experiencing a first room that reproduces the conditions—surveillance and cold temperature—of the cells where illegalized migrants are detained for hours, sometimes days, after their arrest. The viewer is instructed to remove shoes, socks, and bags. Shoes collected at the border have already been spread in the space. A light goes off, and an alarm calls the viewer into the main room: a darkened space with a sand-covered floor where an assistant helps with the adjustment of the backpack and VR gear—a head-mounted display device, including Oculus Rift VR goggles and headset (figure 7.11). The backpack contains the VR computer, which allows the user to circulate in the space without cables; it adds to the realism of the experience by giving a sense of the weight of objects men and women carry with them as they walk in the desert, but it is also used as a security measure: the museum assistant will pull the backpack's straps if and when the viewer is about to hit a wall. The sand's mixed texture—smooth and rocky—and the wind are the two nonsimulated elements of the desert that viewers experience as they walk in the space. The six-and-a-half-minute VR experience then begins, explained here as I lived it. I am now immersed into the Sonoran Desert at sunup, feeling the wind's breeze. A small group of people walks toward me across the desert plain. They are in transit. There are men, women, and children—among them, a pregnant woman with a child. An older woman is complaining of a broken ankle. I hear some of them

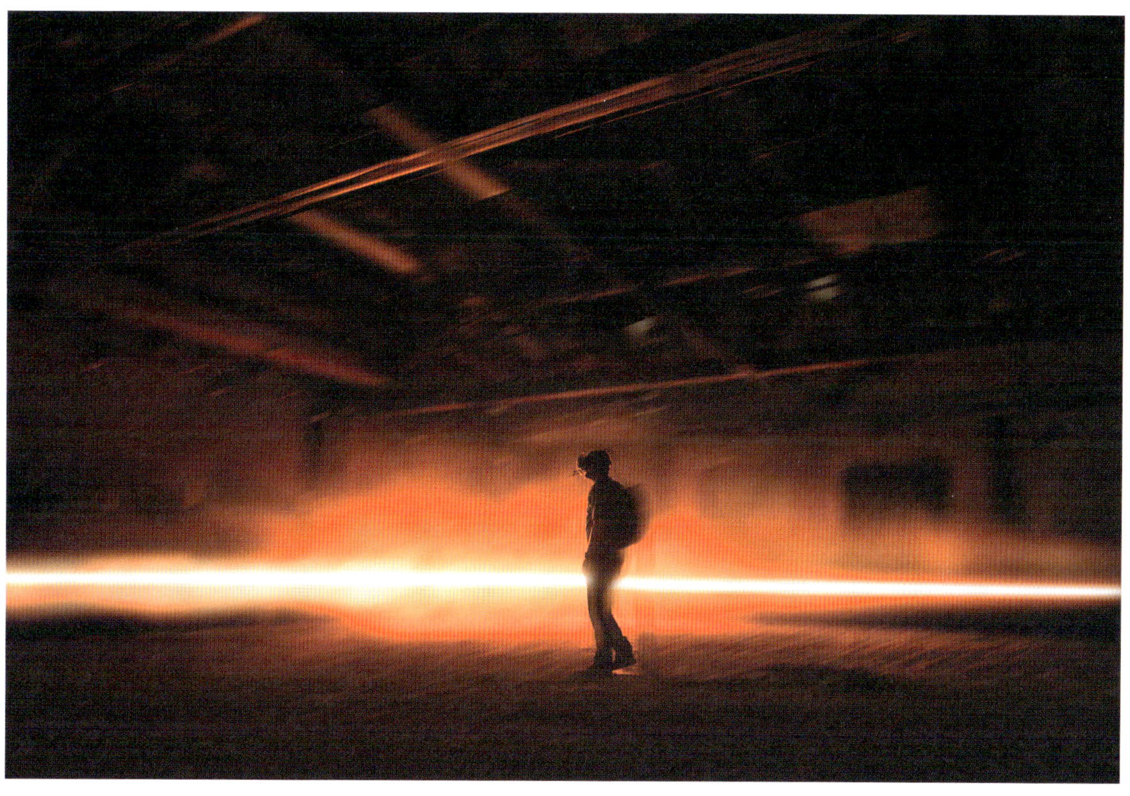

FIGURE 7.11

Alejandro González Iñárritu, *CARNE y ARENA*
(Virtually Present, Physically Invisible), 2017.
Virtual reality, 6.5 minutes. A user in the
experience. Photo: Emmanuel Lubezki.
© Legendary.

crying, whispering in Spanish to one another. The coyote is on his cell phone. Just as they are about to reach me, a helicopter with a searing, blinding spotlight bears down loudly on all of us, while two border patrol, immigration-enforcement SUVs show up. The police, equipped with guns, violently arrest the whole group. What follows is a chaotic encounter where men, women, and children are ordered onto their knees, thrown to the ground, threatened with guns and barking dogs. I both feel fear and observe their fear. The officers command them to take off their shoes. In a moment of magical realism, the older woman with a broken ankle hums at a long table upon which a boat floats and then capsizes, spilling its human cargo. I am then brought back to the live-action scene. Some of the men are interrogated, handcuffed, and searched. Everyone will eventually be taken away. This sequence ends with a last, concluding experience I lived only on my second VR immersion (busy as I was adapting to the virtual environment during my first immersion): a border patrol agent turns his semiautomatic toward me, threatening me, asking me to put my arms in the air; this makes me realize that I am not completely invisible after all and that the software has tracked my position in the environment.[32] The halo persists in the sky above; and, abruptly, the VR experience is over. Viewers are subsequently guided out of the virtual environment to an in-between space where they will get their personal belongings back. They then enter a third room, a corridor exhibition of 14 video portraits of some of the men and women (including one border patrol agent) whose stories inspired the VR work. They are recorded individually in close-up—we mostly see their faces, with their gaze directed toward us. In each portrait, a text unfolds on the screen describing the portrayed's journey. We learn that they are from Guatemala, El Salvador, Honduras, and Mexico; their stories of migration are written in the first person. These stories give a better sense of what Iñárritu means when he speaks of a "semi-fictionalized ethnography."[33]

In his main statement about *CARNE y ARENA*, Iñarritu is especially attentive to the precariousness of people in their attempt to cross the hostile terrain of Mexico-US borderzones and VR's capacity to make that reality tangible to its users:

During the past four years in which this project has been growing in my mind, I had the privilege of meeting and interviewing many Mexican and Central American refugees. Their life stories haunted me, so I invited some of them to collaborate with me in the project. . . . My intention was to experiment with VR technology to explore the human condition in an attempt to break the dictatorship of the frame, within which things are just observed, and claim the space to allow the visitor to go through a direct experience walking in the immigrants' feet, under their skin, and into their hearts.[34]

The belief here is that VR facilitates and may well generate an empathic response in the user: circulating in the simulated borderzone environment, the visitor is described as directly experiencing the refugees' affliction, as if the highly mediated VR experience—notably, the technological suspension of what Iñárritu calls the "dictatorship of the frame, within which things are just observed"—were unmediated or, at least, more "direct" than film. This sensation of nonmediation comes from what the immersive-media researcher Christian Stiegler calls the dissolution of "the frames of the mediation" and the ultimate merger "with our physical reality" characteristic of immersion.[35] As the computer scientist and musician Jaron Lanier rightly maintains, a VR environment in its most basic formulation consists in an interface between a user and a simulated environment, but the interface, in contrast to film, loses in rigidity what it gains in its responsiveness to users' bodily motion as they look around while immersed in the environment. That responsiveness is what makes a VR narrative a protonarrative. The enabling of the user's sensorimotor loop connecting the user with the VR world is crucial to achieve the simulation.[36] Put differently, the VR computer "must constantly and as instantly as possible calculate whatever graphic images [the viewer's eyes] should see were the virtual world real."[37] Enhanced by a few nonvirtual components (the sand, the wind, the backpack), *CARNE y ARENA*'s mixed VR environment is explored to sustain that responsiveness as an empathic relation.

VR is frequently promoted by a rhetoric or promise of empathy. The literature on VR as an empathic machine is much too extensive to address here. Suffice it to say that research in this area is inconclusive, despite claims to the contrary made by fervent defenders of VR. The media scholar Jeremy Bailenson's recent publication on VR dedicates a whole chapter to how VR environments enhance empathy because of the realism of virtual worlds and the first-person perspective from which users experience them.[38] That view is likewise central to another rather famous VR work (a VR film, however, rather than an environment), *Clouds over Sidra* (2014) by the American filmmakers Chris Milk and Gabo Arora, made in response to present-day migration before Iñárritu created *CARNE y ARENA*. The work—the story of Sidra, a 12-year-old Syrian girl living in the Zaatari Refugee Camp in Jordan (which opened in 2012 and has now become a permanent settlement)—was made using a 360-degree camera (figure 7.12).

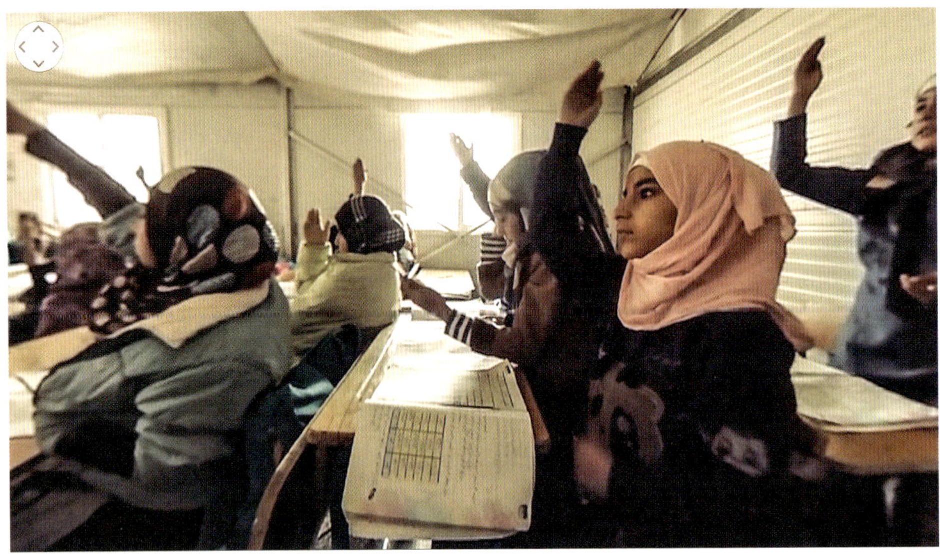

In their experience of *Clouds over Sidra*, spectators are invited to wear Oculus Rift goggles and observe the life of the camp's residents; they can adopt Sidra's daily-life perspective, from which most of the film was made. Originally created to support the United Nations secretary-general's Millennium Development Goals Advocacy Group's call for partnerships, the film was produced in collaboration with the UN Sustainable Development Goals Action Campaign, UNICEF Jordan, and VRSE (a VR production studio now rebranded as Within) with the intention of "using the medium to generate greater empathy and new perspectives on people living in conditions of great vulnerability. Its powerful capacity to allow anyone on a global scale [to] experience life within a refugee camp has the ability to inspire the message of hope among not only the millions displaced but also those motivated to act."[39] *Clouds over Sidra* was released on the VRSE application and iTunes and screened at different festivals, including the Sundance and Tribeca Film Festivals,

FIGURE 7.12

Chris Milk and Gabo Arora, *Clouds over Sidra*, 2014 (film still). Virtual reality. Courtesy of the artist.

as well as at several UN forums and conferences. As Milk put it in his TED Talk in 2015, VR is "the ultimate empathy machine": "It's a machine, but through this machine we become more compassionate. . . . We become more empathetic. We become more connected. And ultimately, we become more human."[40] Once again, the presumption—likewise Iñárritu's presumption—is that VR allows users to feel closer to the displaced beings, that proximity makes users realize that the protagonists are humans just like "us." Such a presumption, however, is historically inaccurate: it blurs the fundamental inequalities structuring contemporary migration; it also reinforces the ambivalences of empathy by depreciating the self–other differentiation. Paul Bloom, the author of *Against Empathy* discussed in chapter 6, has written about *Clouds over Sidra*. He maintains his primary claim—empathy doesn't work because it is fundamentally prejudiced. He also insists on how a short VR episode can never capture what it is to be a refugee, for it is the protracted duration of living in a refugee camp, what has been more generally called the "temporary permanence of camps," that makes refugeehood either a hellish experience or an environment that some residents eventually adapt to:

VR is far from the moral game changer that some make it out to be. In part, this is because it's so focused on creating empathy, and as I've argued elsewhere, empathy is a poor guide to charitable giving. . . . It's not hard to try out certain short-term experiences, such as dealing with a crying baby for a few minutes, sitting alone in a closet, or having strangers gawk at you on the street. But you can't extrapolate from these to learn what it's like to be a single parent, a prisoner in solitary confinement, or a famous movie star. You can't take an event of minutes and hours and generalize to months and years. Why not? One consideration is that some experiences are fine in the short-term, but wear you down over time. Solitary confinement is an obvious example here. Or consider subtle forms of sexual and racial discrimination—certain seemingly minor attacks on one's dignity are easy to shrug off in any single instance, but if they are repeated and relentless, they can lead to anxiety and depression. On the flip side, some experiences that are awful in the short term aren't so bad in the long run; we habituate and adapt.[41]

Bloom does not so much question VR's capacity to generate empathy as argue that the VR experience enhances empathy's dark sides: once immersed, the viewer might well experience empathy, but the short-term timeframe of the immersive experience can never convey the complexities and fluctuations of the migrant's distress over time. Steve Anderson, in his own study of VR, remains similarly unconvinced, but for other reasons: "Claims that 'VR' . . . inherently functions as an 'empathy machine' ring naïve and anachronistic."[42] His point is that empathy can be facilitated by any medium; more importantly, the supposed sense of empathy lived by VR viewers when experiencing disquieting environments related to war or migration remains "largely ineffective for informing them about historical contexts and structural inequality, which are necessary to pose an effective critique of power."[43] Anderson's point, which echoes Kaplan's argument, is that empathy is insufficient and inconsequential when the event's historical circumstances are not provided to the user. In other words, VR technology does not solve one of the main problems inherent to any artwork that draws on empathy to raise consciousness about distressing situations: when the work fails to historicize the situation, the viewer's (temporary) empathic experience remains suspended in midair between feeling and prosociality. Why? Mainly because to feel the other's misery in a prosocial way, one needs to understand that misery (affective and cognitive empathy are fundamentally inseparable): empathy's promising productivity—prosociality, the possibility to act socially or politically to help resolve the other's misery—requires historical cues to materialize.

In short, Iñarritu's desired empathy can never be simply guaranteed and is not necessarily what occurs when one experiences the work. In *CARNE y ARENA*, that experience varies from one viewer to the next, depending on each person's knowledge of how to operate VR, political sympathies, and, as we have seen in my assessment of the literature on empathy, biases. The empathic experience becomes one in which viewers might share the fear of the migrating beings—especially when threatened by the firearm in the concluding sequence—but they do so without any live reciprocity with these beings, and, in all likelihood, from the relatively safe position of the nonmigrant within the secure environment of a museum or gallery. The VR narrative is ultimately experienced alone. Isn't the viewer's experience sometimes akin to what an intruder might experience? After all, I am present but invisible to the simulated group. I observe them, and this looking activity might well become somewhat similar to what Fritz Breithaupt describes when he posits that false empathy, filtered empathy, or selfish empathy results from the empathizer's *aesthetic* advantage over the other: the other's situation can easily be reduced "to a few major features" when the empathizer presumes to be able to perceive what the other perceives or should perceive.[44] It is as though the experience—this is how it was described on the radio and in newspaper articles when the installation was shown in Montreal in 2021—were ultimately more about *me* the viewer-turned-user, about *my* emotional and embodied experience, than about the protagonists' ordeal. It is impossible to know the actual empathic ambivalences lived by the viewers, but the likelihood of such ambivalences, especially biases—as in any empathic state—is rather high. The solitary experience of the viewer-user, the delayed non-live coexistence with the protagonists, might well favor such ambivalences. Saidiya Hartman's historicization of empathy—her description of how nineteenth-century antislave abolitionists' empathic relation with the suffering of the enslaved as a humanistic claim to eradicate the slave trade in fact ended up occluding the suffering other—extends itself into the colonial present. How does *CARNE y ARENA* counterbalance these possible and potential ambivalences? Let us recall our main claim: empathy is a necessary but ambivalent and insufficient condition of possibility for prosociality and more reciprocal forms of coexistence. This is where Anderson's comments about the need to historicize the events staged in VR environments become especially insightful.

Immersed within the virtual environment of *CARNE y ARENA*, the user is occasionally encouraged to adopt an observational stance—a position that turns the user into a witness. That shift is particularly active in the magical-realist sequence that interrupts the realism of the VR environment: a long table appears in the desert, upon which floats the specter of a sinking boat. This scene displays the hostile terrain of the Mediterranean Sea as it unfolds simultaneously with the hostile terrain of the Sonoran Desert—two key instances of border patrol strategies of deterrence that continue to endanger displaced people. Referring to that sequence in his Phillips Collection interview, Iñarritu states: "These oceans are our deserts. . . . What we need now is more like planetary decisions, we share the seas and the atmosphere and the earth. . . . So, to try to put a wall . . . that's not right . . . it's not real. I wanted to expose the complexity of the situation and the lives of these people for everybody to understand."[45] My point is that, as in the sequence in Ai Weiwei's *Human Flow* where the artist participates in a passport exchange with Abdullah Mahmoud only to realize the ambivalence of his empathic relation and the inequalities that structure necropolitical migration, *CARNE y ARENA*'s magical-realism sequence enriches the empathic relation: it geopoliticizes that relation; it transforms the user into a witness of history-in-the-making. That experience is further enriched by the third exhibition room, where we are invited to look at the video portraits of some of the men and women who have inspired the work. In these videos, they look straight at the viewer, calling for and acknowledging coexistence; they tell the stories (with written words unfolding on the screen) of their journeys. We learn where they come from; their narratives of migration are written in the first person. These stories, a substantial component of Iñárritu's "semi-fictionalized ethnography" approach, help historicize the necropolitics of US anti-(im)migration measures and policies.

This historicization may be (yet again) too schematic to activate the rich empathy of witnessing so compellingly described by Kaplan: it is perhaps too minimal and surely not collective enough (in a VR environment, the invisible user is always a solitary observer) to prompt the viewer to act and "see that justice is done."[46] But I want to propose that there is enough historicization to potentially "carry over" the *Einfühlung* experience (as Dominic McIver Lopes would put it) into the social realm, and to begin to turn dark coexistence into a more luminous unfolding of coexistence.[47] Why? I have already highlighted how the magical-realism sequence articulates a consciousness of the planetary scale of deadly migration and how the third room deepens that historical understanding by providing video portraits of survivors—a display that also works as an acknowledgment of the autonomy of migration by enabling a perspective sharing that is already active in the survivors' participation in the writing and performance of the narrative. But it is also important to highlight that the narrative itself focuses on disclosing the vulnerabilization of Mexican and Central American citizens attempting to cross the Mexican-US borderzones.

What is the history that *CARNE y ARENA* invites us to meditate on? As stipulated by the political geographer Reece Jones, the enforcement of the US-Mexico border as a militarized security borderzone intensified after the attacks of September 11, 2001. The borderzone was reinforced by the construction of walls, the expanded use of security-surveillance infrastructure, the use of force, the extensive criminalization of migration, a surge in deportations, as well as the increased militarization of border patrol agents and deterrence measures.[48] The US-Mexico border has been further endangered on the Mexican side, where drug cartels work to tighten control over lucrative smuggling routes. Between 2007 and 2013, about 47,000 migrants died in Mexico before reaching the border—murdered by cartel-related gangs or succumbing to train or car accidents or to the elements.[49] The launching of the US Customs and Border Protection Agency's enforcement strategy of "prevention through deterrence" (PTD) has likewise been pivotal to the US buttressing of its border. PTD is a strategy "premised on instrumentalizing the difficult climate and terrain of the US-Mexico border by pushing migration routes away from traditional urban crossing areas and into increasingly rugged and remote desert areas."[50] The Border Protection Agency's rationale for the PTD policy is to gain "tactical advantage" over people attempting to cross the border "illegally": it is based on the deceptive claim that the hostile terrains and hard climate of deserts will dissuade them from actually undertaking the journey across these borderzones. As Geoffrey Alan Boyce, Samuel N. Chambers, and Sarah Launius state, however, the policy has not so much discouraged as encouraged them to take riskier routes—thus increasing mortality rates and the number of missing persons:

Even in the mid-1990s, it was anticipated that PTD would have deadly outcomes. By the turn of the century, as migration routes shifted away from Texas and California, the number of human remains of unauthorized border crossers recovered from the southern Arizona desert began to skyrocket. Between 1990 and 1999, this number averaged 12 per year. In 2000, it grew to 136. By 2005, the number peaked at 282, before declining to 205 the following year. Although there has been some fluctuation, the number of recovered human remains has stayed between 120 and 250 every year since 2007. The cause of death is primarily (although by no means exclusively) exposure to the harsh desert climate and mountainous terrain where the vast majority of unauthorized crossings occur. Meanwhile, the number of recovered human remains is certainly an undercount of the total number of fatalities. In 2015 alone, southern Arizona's Coalición de Derechos Humanos counted more than 1,200 missing persons cases, involving families who contacted the organization seeking help to locate a loved one.[51]

Looking at these figures, researchers have come to the conclusion that the Border Protection Agency has been using the hostile terrain of the Sonoran Desert as a weapon "intended to exhaust the bodies of unauthorized border crossers."[52] Jason De León further specifies that the hostile terrains evolving around the US-Mexico border are a relation of power and control: "The terrible things that this mass of migrating people experience en route are neither random nor senseless, but rather part of a strategic federal plan that has rarely been publicly illuminated and exposed for what it is: a killing machine that simultaneously uses and hides behind the viciousness of the Sonoran Desert."[53] As stipulated in this book's introduction, the alleged US immigration, asylum, and southern border crises partake of a denial of coexistence—they result from a combination of antimigrant measures largely targeted against Mexican and Central American citizens, including the restriction of legal means of immigration, the separation of families requesting asylum in the United States, the inadequate management of unaccompanied minors arriving at the border, the increased detention of illegalized migrants, and the blocking of large Central American caravans coming from countries (Guatemala, Honduras, and El Salvador) in which Americans have militarily, politically, and economically intervened in the past.

The empathic experience in Iñárritu's *CARNE y ARENA* is never guaranteed, and it can easily become ambivalent, but the installation as a whole does sustain the autonomy of migration and does provide historical cues to prosocially orient that experience. *CARNE y ARENA* persists as a call for empathy. Art is positing that empathy is a necessary condition of possibility for prosociality in matters of migratory justice. The analysis of the work given here does not refute that premise, but it shows empathy to be an insufficient condition of possibility for prosociality. The pharmakon requires a historicized environment at least to minimally secure the viewer's capacity to participate in that cause.

TANIA BRUGUERA'S *10,142,926*

The Cuban artist Tania Bruguera (b. 1968, Havana, Cuba; based in Havana and New York) has been exploring issues of migration and immigration at least since *Tribute to Ana Mendieta* (1985) but more explicitly since Immigrant Movement International (IMI) was initiated in 2010—a partly ongoing series of works addressing the rights of migrants and immigrants. IMI was and is composed of several short-term and long-term performances and projects, including Immigrant Movement International, Corona (2010–2015), which was made in partnership with Creative Time, the Corona neighborhood of Queens, and Queens Museum and consisted of a series of actions that took place mainly in a community resource center for immigrants that offers workshops, courses, and legal aid. One of the highpoints of the Corona project was the publication of a Migrant Manifesto on the rights of (im)migrants, which denounced the hostile categorizations they are subjected to ("Illegals. Aliens. Guest Workers. Border crossers. Undesirables. Exiles. Criminals. Non-citizens. Terrorists. Thieves. Foreigners. Invaders. Undocumented") and in which they proclaimed their autonomy ("We have the right to move and the right to not be forced to move").[54] IMI also included Partido del Pueblo Migrante (Migrant People's Party) (2010–2011), a political party for immigrants established in Mexico and active during the Mexican presidential election that year; *Surplus Value* (2012), an installation performed at Tate Modern wherein visitors were required to stand waiting in a queue, some randomly allowed to enter the inner gallery and others submitted to lie-detector tests questioning them on their travel history (figure 7.13); the Francis Effect (2014–ongoing), an international online and signature campaign to provide Vatican City citizenship for migrants worldwide; Referendum (2015–16), a voting campaign asking audiences to reply to the question "Borders kill; should we abolish our borders?"; and Party of Migrant People's Assembly (2017–ongoing), a series of conversations with immigrant rights organizations in art institutions on finding ways to create solidarity among immigrants and to support the citizenship rights of migrating beings.[55]

IMI was devised as a series of *arte útil* (useful art) interventions, a term coined by Bruguera to describe artworks that "do something with" art or nonart audiences rather than have them just "look at" artworks. Its main objective was to create "possibilities for exploited and unprotected beings" by imagining and implementing a parareality of doings to reach that goal.[56] It established Bruguera's reiterated concern about issues of migration and her exploration of aesthetic strategies that merge art and politics to include (im)migrants in the making and reception of art. *10,142,926* (2018)—the work I discuss here—is more representative of *arte de conducta* (behavior art) and its emphasis on social presence: its "material is the social field—attitudes and behaviors," and it asks, "How can we use and transform behavior?"[57] An assemblage of in situ interventions made in and around Tate Modern's Turbine Hall in London, *10,142,926* was shown between October 2, 2018, and February 24, 2019. The exhibition facilitated a string of migrancy-related actions that visitors were invited to carry out, including embodiment, social engagement, a commitment to communal and collective effort, and, significantly (for this chapter, at least), the cultivation of empathy. The necropolitics of migration was not so much represented as disclosed. It was disclosed as a situation that citizens have the potential to contest and change through behaviors mobilized by values of mutuality, equality, and solidarity.

The exhibition brought together four major interventions: (1) low-frequency sub-bass noise, felt physically by the viewer as a disquieting vibration; (2) a large heat-sensitive floor hiding the portrait of Yousef, a young immigrant who left Syria in 2011 and had been living in London since then—a portrait that visitors could reveal when they collectively pressed their bodies on the floor and generated enough body heat to allow its image to resurface (figure 7.14); (3) a closed gallery that released an organic compound that made visitors cry, "forcing" the release of empathy; and (4) the involvement of Tate Neighbours, a group of twenty-one participants living and working in the same SE1 postcode as the museum, selected to establish

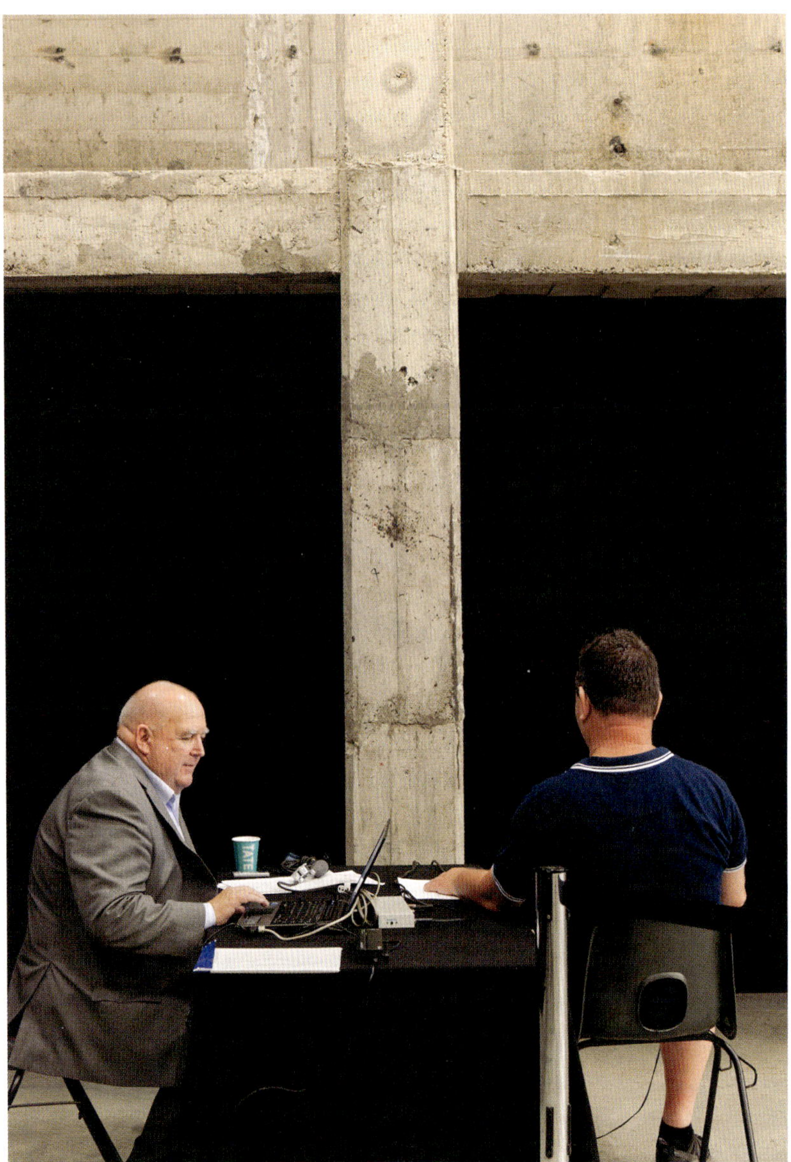

FIGURE 7.13

Tania Bruguera, *Surplus Value*, 2012.
Part of the project Immigrant Movement
International, 2010–2015. Performance. The
Tanks, Tate Modern. Visitors being submitted
to lie-detector tests that ask about their
travel history. Photo: © Tate Photography.
© Tania Bruguera/SOCAN (2021).

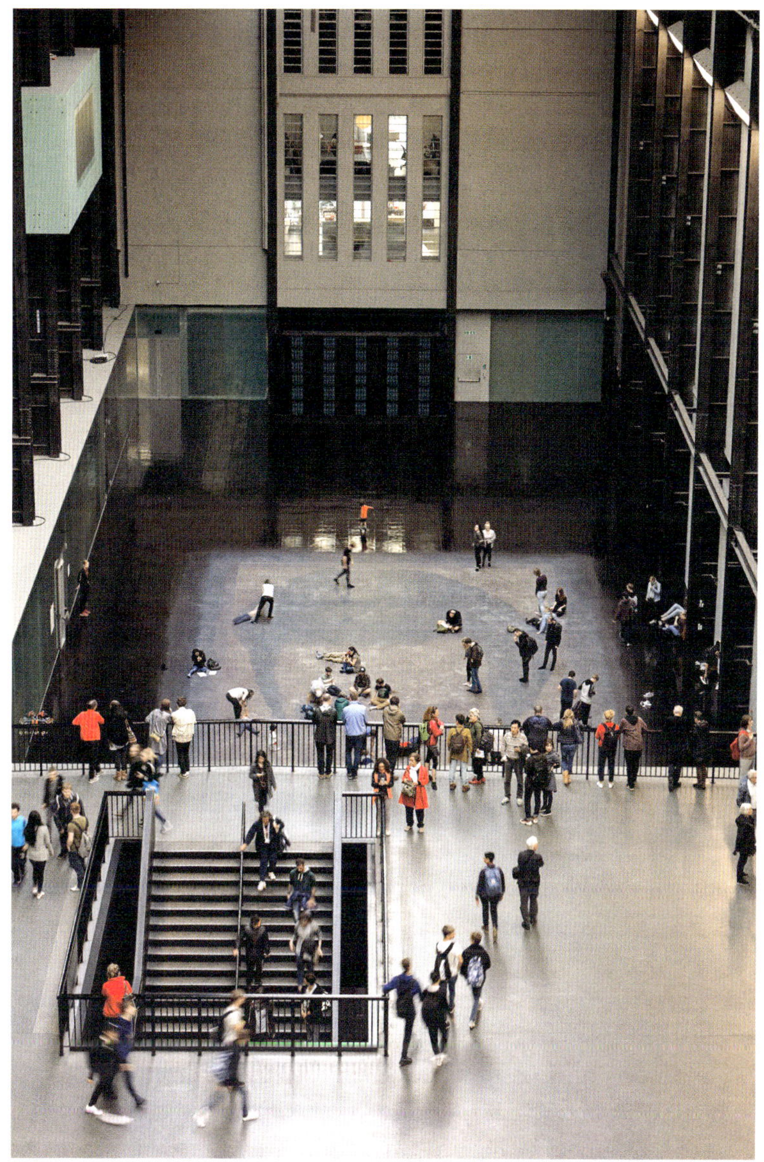

Tania Bruguera, *10,142,926*, 2018. Hyundai Commission. Tate Modern, Turbine Hall. Heat-sensitive floor. Photo: © Tate Photography. © Tania Bruguera/SOCAN (2021).

a connection between the institution and its local community. The connection led to at least two concrete yet barely visible outcomes: the one-year renaming of the Tate's Boiler House as the Natalie Bell Building in honor of a local activist who supported Yousef's immigration process (figure 7.15) as well as the writing of a manifesto, which automatically appeared on the visitors' cell phones when they signed into the Tate's Wi-Fi.[58] The exhibition's title referred to a fixed number, but the number increased throughout the duration of the exhibition to refer to the global number of displaced people who had migrated to another country the previous year (i.e., in 2017) plus the evolving number of migrant deaths recorded in 2018 and 2019—the end of the exhibition. These statistics were supplied by the International Organization for Migration's Missing Migrants Project. The changing figure was stamped in red ink on visitors' hands when they entered the crying room.

Coexistence was central to the exhibition: *10,142,926* invited visitors to participate in interventions that required more reciprocal forms of interdependence. The interventions materialized only when coelaborated and coexperienced. They unfolded as a way to collectivize and complicate the participants' unlearning of present-day migration. Of particular relevance to these productions of coexistence, collectivity was upheld as a necessity but repeatedly shown as a difficulty and a quasi-impossibility—often leading to the failure of the intended actions. This unsteadiness was manifest at several levels. Yousef's portrait could be revealed only by the concerted regrouping of an estimated 150 to 200 visitors[59] (an ideal in all likelihood never met) so that they are lying side by side and thus working together to activate the heat-sensitive floor. Bruguera spoke of the floor portrait as a "horizontal mural" that could be seen—with the correct perspective—only from the standpoint of the bridge above.[60] The exhibition explicitly promoted empathy as *the* necessary affect of mutuality-oriented coexistence, but empathy was forced upon visitors and, as such, experienced ambivalently (more on this later). Finally, Tate Neighbours' participation, although real, was just about unperceivable.

Considering this chapter's overall objective, I want to raise the following question: What is the value of empathy if it is organically forced upon the viewer and if its achievement is anticipated as just about unattainable? Its use is surely ironic. But Bruguera's aesthetic strategy is more complex insofar as it doesn't condemn empathy and seeks in fact to revitalize it. *10,142,926* wants empathy from us. Forced empathy—and this is my main claim—is the aesthetic strategy devised by Bruguera to save it as a necessary condition of possibility for migratory justice. In contrast to Ai's *Human Flow* and Iñárritu's *CARNE y ARENA*, Bruguera's *10,142,926*

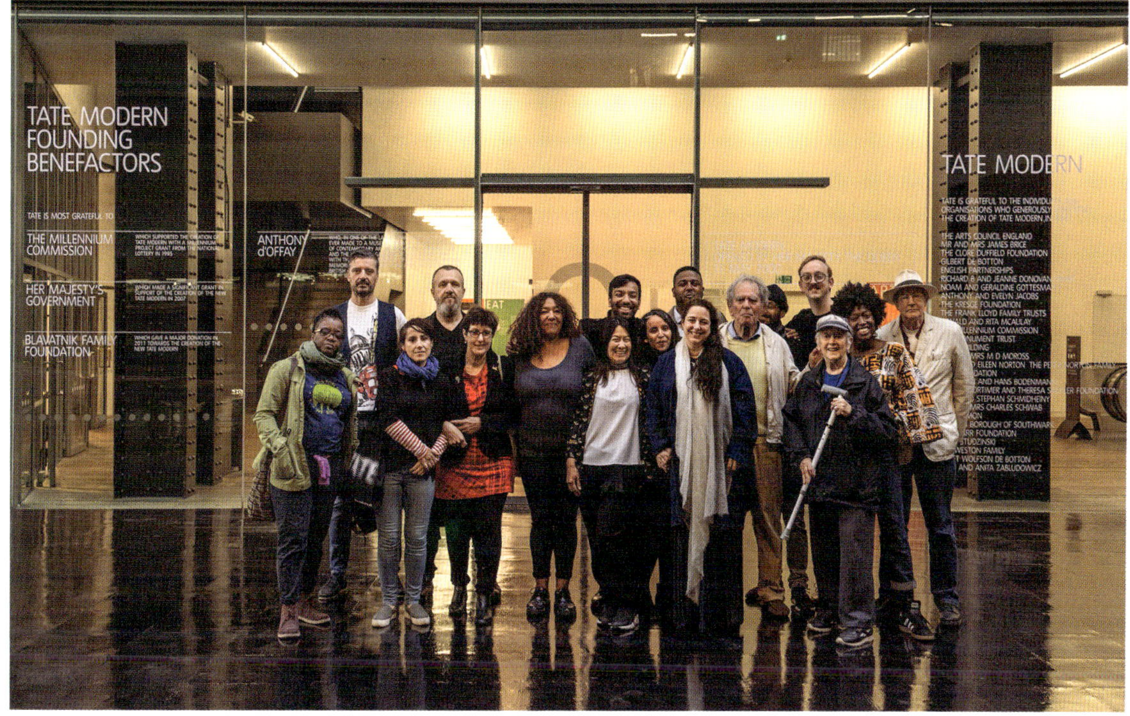

FIGURE 7.15

Tania Bruguera, *10,142,926*, 2018. Hyundai
Commission. Tate Modern, Turbine Hall.
Tania Bruguera with Tate Neighbours at the
inauguration of the Natalie Bell Building.
Photo: © Tate Photography. © Tania
Bruguera/SOCAN (2021).

fully assumes—anticipates and adopts—the ambivalence of empathy by inducing it. Empathy is a pharmakon (remedy + poison) that her work struggles to orient toward its therapeutic side (care), which itself is a pharmakon. Indispensable to the migrant cause, as I show later in this chapter, empathy requires other components to prosocially contribute to the struggle for migratory justice.

Let us, then, be attentive to the crying room's modus operandi and from that description look into this chapter's three leading questions: Why and how does empathy matter in artistic practices addressing migration? Why do artistic practices persist with empathic calls despite findings that suggest that the prosociality of empathy must be mistrusted or, at least, facilitated by other means? How and when is empathy effective in these works?

The crying room invited visitors to empathize with the suffering of migrating beings, whose tragedy was evoked by the number stamped on visitors' hands when they entered the space (the total number of recorded migrants in 2017 plus the number of migrant deaths recorded in 2018 and 2019). But the room significantly diminished the visitors' agency by imposing empathy on them (figure 7.16). A label at the entrance of the small brightly lit room located alongside the Turbine Hall (figure 7.17) stipulated that "this room contains an organic compound that makes you cry."[61] The art critic Yoli Terziyska provides a vivid summary of the visitor's experience—which was more about producing emotionless tears than about experiencing emotional empathy from within: "As each viewer entered, the intense smell immediately irritated their eyes and throat and breathing and seeing became difficult. Some participants' eyes teared. Some visitors exited quickly, while others stayed to test the limits of their endurance."[62] In her catalog essay, Catherine Wood, the exhibition's curator, corroborates that view: "Bruguera created this organic compound [with Sassel Tolaas from the Nasalo Lab in Berlin] to provoke an involuntary physical reaction that she describes as 'forced empathy.'"[63] How is this reaction about empathy at all, then? The curator and the artist have provided many explanations. Wood states that "crying together in public breaks down the usual social barriers and leads to a shared emotional response. . . . [T]heatricalization in a public space potentially prompts social interaction. The induced crying, in particular, while being a synthesized reaction, can nevertheless produce an after-effect of real emotion through the associated memories connected with the physical act."[64] The menthol-based compound was thus not meant to support a straightforward unfolding of empathy but to create situations that allowed participants to see each other crying and from that observation share an empathic response. This rationale

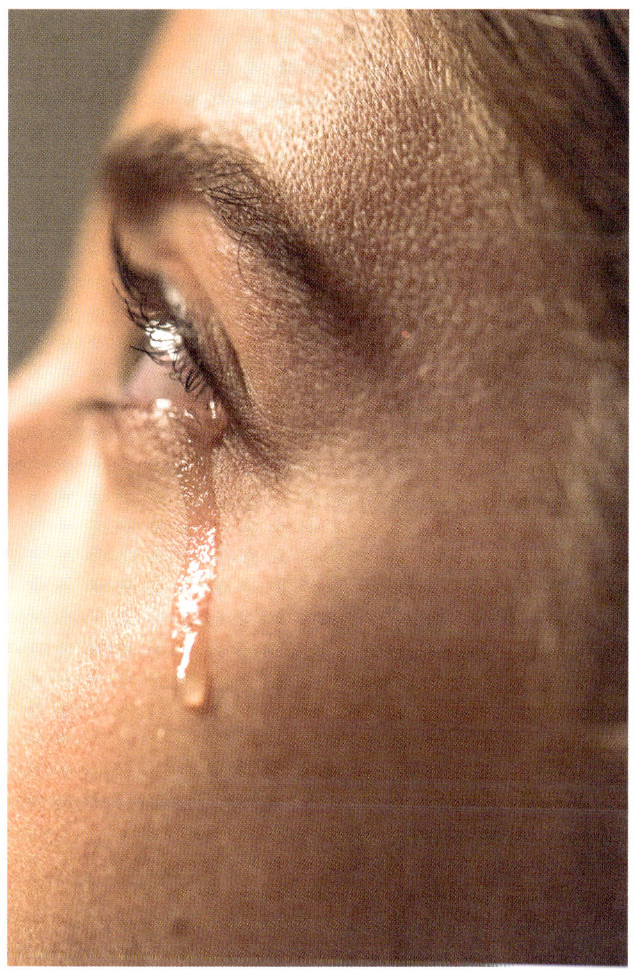

Tania Bruguera, *10,142,926*, 2018. Hyundai
Commission, Tate Modern, Turbine Hall.
Crying room. Photo © Tate Photography.
© Tania Bruguera/SOCAN (2021).

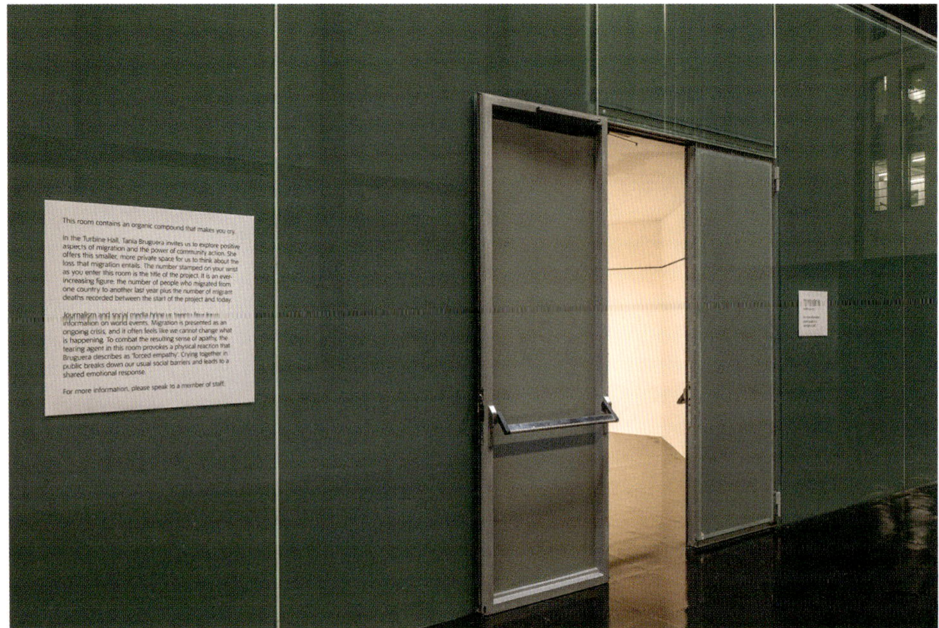

relied on the contagiousness of empathy—exploring it to generate a community of empathizers. The room was also meant to create situations that could trigger memories related to experiences of teargassing in social and migrant protest rallies. The two rationalizations embraced empathy in all its ambivalence, favoring affective contamination and the recall of antimanifestation aggressions.

This messiness was supported by accounts suggesting that visitors mainly experienced their own distress when responding to the distress of others—la bête noire of empathy studies, what is believed to impair the prosociality of empathy. Let us recall Tania Singer and Claus Lamm's reference to personal distress: there are

FIGURE 7.17

Tania Bruguera, *10,142,926*, 2018. Hyundai Commission. Tate Modern, Turbine Hall. Crying room. Photo: © Tate Photography. © Tania Bruguera/SOCAN (2021).

"real-life examples of how empathy can 'go awry' (from a prosocial point of view). . . . For example, . . . experiencing too much empathy can lead to an aversive distress response and selfish instead of other-oriented behavior."[65] As is often the case when the empathizer becomes distressed when observing the other's distress, empathy ends up being about attending to one's own anguish or simply withdrawing from the situation altogether.[66] Terziyska's description of the crying room emphasizes that distorted empathic response:

Each attendee left the room once their personal physical threshold was reached. Despite being reminded, when stamped at the crying room's door, of the large volume of people who suffer because of migration, the experience lacked emotional impact. Empathy—a strong, positive driving force that has transformative powers—was trumped by visitors' own sense of physical discomfort. It is possible that this outcome was, in itself, Bruguera's implicit statement: society forces people to mourn migrants' struggles, but this mourning typically lacks emotional substance and is frequently ineffective. The stamped number was forgotten. Forging connection with other participants was impossible while focusing on one's own inability to breathe. Collective empathy failed because each individual was preoccupied with their personal well-being.[67]

Terziyska's account is insightful: empathy was, after all, induced and, as such, was bound to be an ambivalent experience. Why *forced* empathy, then? How can such an ambivalence be productive? It is useful here to look at some of Bruguera's earlier works that share a similar imposed component. *10,142,926* strongly resonates with works where museumgoers were assaulted or forced to experience an oppression usually reserved for "others." Let us recall *Art in America (The Dream)*, performed at Gallery Two in Chicago in March 1997, where visitors were invited to relinquish their ID cards, enter a dark, cell-like space, and move apprehensively between "the soothing prophecies of two women reading our future in a deck of cards" and an unforgiving interrogation by women acting as Immigration and Naturalization Service officers. A flashlight was eventually oriented toward the visitor's face while the visitor was asked to quote the Bill of Rights and sing the national anthem.[68] Let us think as well of *Tatlin's Whisper #5*, performed at Tate Modern in January 2008, where two mounted police officers in uniform (genuine members of London's Metropolitan Police) arrived—unannounced—in the Turbine Hall bridge to patrol the space, guiding and controlling the public by using different crowd-control techniques and thus turning the "safe space" of the museum into the threatening public spaces where dissensus and protest are expressed, where one can easily be subjected to police control and induced to fear for one's life. The same can be said about *Surplus Value*, briefly discussed earlier (figure 7.13). In *10,142,926*, empathy likewise becomes a tool that forces the public to live an emotion oppressively. In *10,142,926*, this strategy of assault permeated not only the crying room but also Bruguera's decision to work with Kode9, author of *Sonic Warfare* (2009)—a book examining the US Army's use of sound and music to manipulate and torture prisoners. The artist wanted to explore sound as something "disturbing, instead of creating enjoyment," so that hearing the soundtrack as one walked around would amount to feeling "uncomfortable rather than relaxed."[69]

The art historian Christa Noel Robbins has convincingly shown that Bruguera's work doesn't fit neatly into relational aesthetics, participatory art, and social practice art as respectively theorized by Nicolas Bourriaud, Claire Bishop, and Nato Thompson, to which should be added Grant Kester's notion of collaborative art—practices diversely yet similarly committed "to enabling community formation through various means of participation," where the "participatory is described . . . as enabling interpersonal encounters" capable of opposing the impersonality of our highly technologized and neoliberalist lives.[70] Bruguera's performances and installations do not so much create situations for the coming-together of spectators or confirm communities but rather attend to their formation processes. "That is to say," writes Robbins, "it is not simply the group or community that is the focus . . . but the specific terms of its generation, the particular conditions of participation as such."[71] This approach is especially potent when the "we" hailed out in participatory art is a cruelly optimistic one, as Lauren Berlant might put it.[72] Robbins suggests that Bruguera's work mobilizes what Judith Butler has called "the structure of address itself"[73]—the moral demand around which a community forms itself with an expectation of consensus and through modalities that are in fact modalities of inclusion and exclusion, without any clear understanding of who is articulating this demand and to what end. In these works, Bruguera significantly troubles the formation of homogenous well-intentioned communities. As Robbins keenly observes, the artist "readily acknowledges the potentially manipulative role she assumes in relation to its participants. In these arguably coercive elements of the artist's work, there is, to borrow Berlant's language, a cruelty in what Bruguera does, which might be most marked when she anticipates our own optimistic attachments to participatory practice. . . . If Bruguera's work manages to articulate a kind of 'lateral agency' . . . it is to be located in its intervention into the optimistic structures of so-called participatory art itself."[74]

Robbins's point is compelling: it helps us understand the forcefulness of the empathy produced in *10,142,926*—the productivity of that coerciveness. Induced empathy destabilizes the viewer's optimistic relationship with art and "our" (spectators from Europe and North America, notably) belief in the empathic capacity to prosocially feel or understand—through art—the emotions or mental states of others in pain; it hurts; it complicates aesthetics as an *Einfühlung*; it easily becomes a personal distress that makes *me* more interested in *my* own ordeal than in the other's; and yet it is necessary. In an interview with the art writer Amandas Ong, Bruguera contends that empathy is indispensable precisely because of its devaluation and downgrading in the media. On the one hand, social media tend to overempathize; in so doing, they undervalue the distance through which we tend to empathize with migrating "others" and the closeness through which we tend to de-empathize with them. On the other hand, the flow of media news about migration crises tends to numb the audience (Kaplan is not far here). Bruguera: "Social media has skewed the way we empathize with other people. When we see images of starving children and victims of drug cartels in countries far away, we feel bad for them, because their realities don't intrude on ours. *But once they flee to somewhere safer and closer to us, and they become refugees or migrants, suddenly we're suspicious and hostile. . . .* [W]e watch the news and see people suffering to the point that we become totally *desensitised*. I want people to first respond physically, then hopefully that triggers an emotional reaction."[75]

What "forced empathy" affirms, then (and there lies its productivity), can be summarized in the following terms: it is precisely because empathy is a necessary yet increasingly unproductive condition for the possibility of prosociality in matters of migratory justice that it must be forced; that is, it must be experienced as essential yet strenuous *and* imperiled. It cannot but be forced in a historical moment in which citizens of Europe and North America have become numb to the suffering of citizens-on-the-move from Africa, Asia, Latin America, and elsewhere, even though the former coexist with the latter; in which empathy seems only possible from afar, at a distance; in which empathy is mass-media fabricated through the cult of celebrities (a reality grippingly described in Candice Breitz's *Love Story*). The aesthetic decision to impose empathy already implies a historical consideration of its rising disappearance as a prosocial relation. The crying room produces empathy as a cruel optimism. The hope is that forced empathy will trigger "real" emotions of empathy, but with the understanding that its ambivalence will never vanish and that it might make us realize its persistent difficulty, just like Teresa Margolles's *La promesa* made us realize the difficulty of care. What makes that outcome conceivable, however, is the Tate Neighbours project, more precisely the group's capacity to agree on the one-year renaming of the Boiler House as the Natalie Bell Building in honor of a local humanitarian activist who supported (through her own engagement with SE1 United) Yousef's immigration process—a success story insofar as Yousef became a student in biomedical science and was working for the National Health Service at the time of the Tate exhibition.[76] The Tate Neighbours initiatives recognized (im)migrants "as political subjects rather than economic bodies."[77] They shed light on the dark historical present (the necropolitics of migration management) disclosed by the ever-evolving number of dying migrants stamped on the visitors' hands when entering the crying room. As with Ai's *Human Flow* and Iñárritu's *CARNE y ARENA*, *10,142,926*'s call for empathy blends into the call to historicize—a combination that potentializes the prosocial outcome of empathy.

HUMANITARIANISM TAKE ONE

To conclude this chapter on art's call for empathy, I want to expand on the findings discussed so far to suggest that *Human Flow*'s, *CARNE y ARENA*'s, and *10,142,926*'s interpellation is ultimately a humanitarian call. This broadening becomes manifest when we consider one of the main responses to twenty-first-century migration: humanitarianism—an approach and a movement, some say a "political economy," a component of the humanitarian-military complex described by Sabine Hess and Bernd Kasparek when referring to the post-2015 unsteady yet effective restabilization of the European migration and border regime (detailed in chapter 3) as the EU devised new ways to contain the influx of displaced people in European territory. Humanitarianism is likewise committed to the alleviation of the pain of suffering beings and the protection of endangered lives.[78] Mobilized by an empathic thrust, humanitarianism has, however, been strongly contested in the field of critical refugee and migrant studies, as much as empathy has been questioned in the fields of psychology, philosophy, neuroscience, and cultural studies.

Humanitarianism's main moral concern is the suffering of subjugated others: the poor, the homeless, displaced people, as well as victims of war, conflicts, or famine. The artworks examined in this chapter were made in a period that consolidated humanitarianism as a practice of rescue of endangered, distressed, and injured "wanderers" (as Étienne Balibar puts it). The anthropologist Miriam Ticktin has established that actions in 2014 and 2015 were key to that consolidation: "The language of humanitarianism has played a central role in political and media debates about undocumented migrants/refugees crossing into Europe and North America. The unaccompanied minors entering the United States reached the designation of 'humanitarian crisis' in the summer of 2014, whereas the tipping point in the Mediterranean came in April 2015, when at least five boats sank and close to 1,200 people drowned en route to Europe."[79] The language of humanitarianism must also be understood as inseparable from the military reinforcement of European and American borders. As Hess and Kasparek's work has shown, Europe replied to the "refugee crisis" by securing a humanitarian-military complex "where military forces are deployed under a humanitarian rationale" to protect migrating beings while policing them and strengthening the securitization of borderzones.[80] These findings can be generalized to account for the evolution of most migration and border regimes in the wealthiest economies worldwide. The physician, medical anthropologist, and sociologist Didier Fassin has designated this turn as "humanitarian reason." His critique of humanitarianism denounces its inflated attention to suffering and its cultivation of compassion and empathy for the sufferers, which leaves unaddressed and unexamined the actions of the regimes that are responsible for the inequalities, violence, and policies that have created these suffering beings:

What, ultimately, is gained, and what lost, when we use the terms of suffering to speak of inequality, when we invoke trauma rather than recognizing violence, when we give residence rights to foreigners with health problems but restrict the conditions for political asylum, more generally when we mobilize compassion rather than justice? And what are the profits and losses incurred in opening listening centers to combat social exclusion, requiring the poor to recount their misfortunes, sending psychologists to war zones, representing war in the language of humanitarianism?[81]

These questions concerning the losses and the gains of humanitarianism are pivotal to the understanding of art practices that promote empathy as a response to the damaged beings of necropolitical migration. Fassin's answer is that the compassionate or empathic attention to the suffering other has problematically set into place a humanitarian governance of migrant sufferers. Following Michel Foucault's notion of governmentality as a series of "techniques and procedures designed to direct the behavior of men,"[82] Fassin defines the humanitarian government as the introduction of moral sentiments within contemporary governmentality whose main modus operandi is to establish a set of procedures "to manage, regulate, and support the existence of human beings." The humanitarian government of the living "includes but exceeds the intervention of the state, local administrations, international bodies, and political institutions more generally": as it manages and regulates suffering lives, it tends to biologize the misery of others—notably refugees—to demonstrate and administrate their misery.[83]

Richard Mosse's *Incoming* (2014–2017), as illustrated in chapter 3, has insightfully disclosed that biologization process. Humanitarianism has infiltrated the very measures taken by state officials to increase border control. As Forensic Oceanography's Charles Heller and Lorenzo Pezzani have observed, humanitarian governing has now become undetachable from securitization: "While rescue at sea has long been the humanitarian counterpart of the illegalization of migrants, over the last few years, border control operations themselves are frequently being framed as acts of saving, blurring the notions of rescue and interception. In this respect, the humanitarian border echoes the inextricable connection between violence and care that characterizes colonial power."[84] Such is the humanitarian-military complex: a migration and border regime that justifies "increasing measures of border control in the name of saving migrants' lives."[85] The sociologists Lilie Chouliaraki and Pierluigi Musarò have designated that complex as it unfolded in Greek and Italian border-zones in 2014 and 2015 as "a hybrid configuration of emotions and practices that exclude as they rescue and police as they care."[86] This is to say, in short, that critical refugee studies and migrant studies converge in their assessment of humanitarianism as detrimental to the resolution of the migration predicament: it has evolved into a practice of management of suffering beings; it ambivalently combines caring and policing, rescuing and securitizing. It carries the same twisted effects of empathy—which is one of its main clusters of emotions. Ticktin corroborates this view:

Humanitarianism is far from soft; indeed, it can often end up hurting those it intends to help. . . . That is, while humanitarianism is often understood as driven by emotions—compassion, empathy, benevolence, pity—in fact, it relies on a very narrow emotional constellation, and this in turn constrains our responses. Humanitarianism provides little room to feel and recognize the value of particular lives (versus life in general), or to mourn particular deaths (versus suffering in general); and little impetus to animate political change. If we want to change the situation at the borders of Europe and the United States, we need another form of political care, one that reaches beyond care as welfare in nation-states, and beyond the benevolence of humanitarianism. . . . Innocence structures our relationships to make some of us saviors and others victims. Indeed, the process of saving innocent victims often promises absolution to the saviors. It leaves little room to think that we might also be responsible for these migrants' plight. . . . Yet talking about any situation as a humanitarian emergency makes it seem as if it is an exception to an otherwise peaceful order. There is no space to understand causes or histories that might have led to or shaped this moment.[87]

This passage provides a good summary of Ticktin's argument against humanitarianism; it also has the merit of providing the clearest critique of humanitarianism. For the anthropologist, its problems are threefold. First, humanitarian compassion posits binary oppositions—either innocent victims or criminal smugglers—that overlook "those who are neither innocent nor guilty, neither victims nor heroes"; it also posits another problematic binary coupling—European or North American caretakers helping migrant care-receivers coming from some of the poorest economies worldwide—a divide that ends up diverting us from thinking about Europe's and North America's responsibility in the evolution and consolidation of the necropolitics of migration.[88] Second, humanitarianism is trapped in the presentism of crises and emergencies—what sociologist Craig Calhoun has designated "the emergency imaginary"[89]—which requires immediate action in response to human suffering while leaving unaddressed the history and predictability of the conflicts and catastrophes that have caused these alleged crises. Long-term solutions remain unexamined in order to make room for a managerial/governmental response that merely restores or buttresses the existing global order.[90] Finally, humanitarianism is more about empathy and compassion, generosity and pity, as moral sentiments than about rights: it fails to be, Ticktin insists, a political response.[91] Yet, let us be attentive to the fact that her point (and Fassin's point) is not to dismiss humanitarian care. What is needed is "political care" beyond welfare and benevolence. As with empathy studies, humanitarianism studies are critical but do not advocate for the mere abandonment of empathy and humanitarianism. The chapter's case studies materialize this complex approach.

In this chapter, I have argued that empathy is a fundamental—surely unescapable—dimension of artistic practices addressing today's migration. The three examined artworks, Ai's *Human Flow*, Iñárritu's *CARNE y ARENA (Virtually Present, Physically Invisible)*, and Bruguera's *10,142,926*, have turned that insight into a call for empathy. Mobilizing the scientific, cultural, and philosophical literature on empathy, I have also argued that empathy cannot but be ambivalent—because of its inherent biases and tendency to induce personal distress, absorption of the other, and idiopathic identification. That ambivalence permeates our three case studies. And yet the prosociality of empathy is potentialized when the works provide enough historical context and perspective sharing to channel that prosociality, even more so when the autonomy of migration is acknowledged.

The chapter's assumption is that this persistent enablement of empathy and humanitarianism must be taken seriously—especially when considered from the perspective of social and transcultural psychiatry, which has established that "being an asylum seeker, refugee, or forcibly displaced has a profound impact on mental health, with an increased risk of developing common psychiatric disorders, such as, depression, anxiety, post-traumatic stress disorder (PTSD), psychotic disorders as well as disabling symptoms of psychosocial stress."[92] Despite this acute vulnerability, mental-health-care systems for citizens-on-the-move remain underfunded and not readily accessible. The call for a humanitarian response must also be understood in relation to the increased criminalization of humanitarianism in Europe and the United States—a reality not particularly addressed in the work of Ticktin, Fassin, Chouliaraki and Musarò, and others whose research has been addressed here. More recent literature, including articles by Forensic Oceanography's Charles Heller and Lorenzo Pezzani, is now pressingly warning us *not* to abandon humanitarianism despite its shortcomings and failures. Since 2017, state actors have accused NGOs whose humanitarian mission is to rescue people in distress of constituting a "pull factor" that encourages "illegal" migration. To counter that supposed pull factor, state authorities have proceeded to illegalize rescue, a measure that has further endangered the working conditions of humanitarian actors.[93] Rescue is becoming as illegal as migration. As Heller and Pezzani have specified, "In a phase of marked *de-humanitarianization* of the border, in which the lives of migrants appear to have increasingly lost even their discursive value, the very act of rescue has been increasingly criminalized as NGOs have been accused of 'colluding' with smugglers."[94] In response to that increasing criminalization, No More Deaths and the Coalición de Derechos Humanos have produced a three-part report entitled *Disappeared: How U.S. Border Enforcement Agencies Are Fueling a Missing Persons Crisis* (2016–2021), where they recommend a series of policies to discontinue the US Border Protection Agency's interference in humanitarian aid—recommendations that could easily be applied throughout Europe as well. These policies include calls to "End the harassment of humanitarian-aid volunteers and the obstruction of humanitarian-aid stations by establishing federal policy guidelines prohibiting the destruction and confiscation of water and other humanitarian-aid supplies. Cease and desist from any and all operations placing humanitarian-aid stations under surveillance or concentrating enforcement efforts around humanitarian-aid stations."[95] In 2020, Tuan Andrew Nguyen directed a 71-minute-long video installation entitled *Crimes of Solidarity/Crimes de solidarité*, which explicitly seeks to undo France's criminalization of civilian acts of assistance to migrating beings (figure 7.18). I examine this work in chapter 8.

In short, it might well be that a rethinking of humanitarianism is what is needed instead of a pure and simple discrediting of humanitarianism, even more so when its rethinking succeeds in integrating and understanding its paradoxes and ambivalences. As already stipulated in chapter 4, Pezzani is now unequivocally endorsing the Pirate Care Project—an international research and creation project sustained by a network of activists, scholars, and practitioners "who stand against the criminalization of solidarity & for a common care infrastructure."[96] As Pezzani maintains, pirate care—what could also be called "pirate or critical humanitarianism," "pirate or critical empathy"—is a form of political care that "primarily considers the assumption that we live in a time in which care . . . is becoming increasingly defunded, discouraged and criminalised." In contrast and opposition to neoliberal policies that are reorganizing the elementary practices of democratic life—"healthcare, housing, access to knowledge, right to asylum, freedom of mobility, social benefits, etc."—into tools for surveillance and marginalization of the most vulnerable, pirate caring is imagining "technologically-enabled care & solidarity networks."[97] Throughout this chapter, we have been exposed to artworks that insist on the double requirement to keep and transform the empathic-humanitarian call. They extend yet renew art as an aesthetic feeling (*Einfühlung*). That insistence must be understood as an oblique critical response to the criminalization

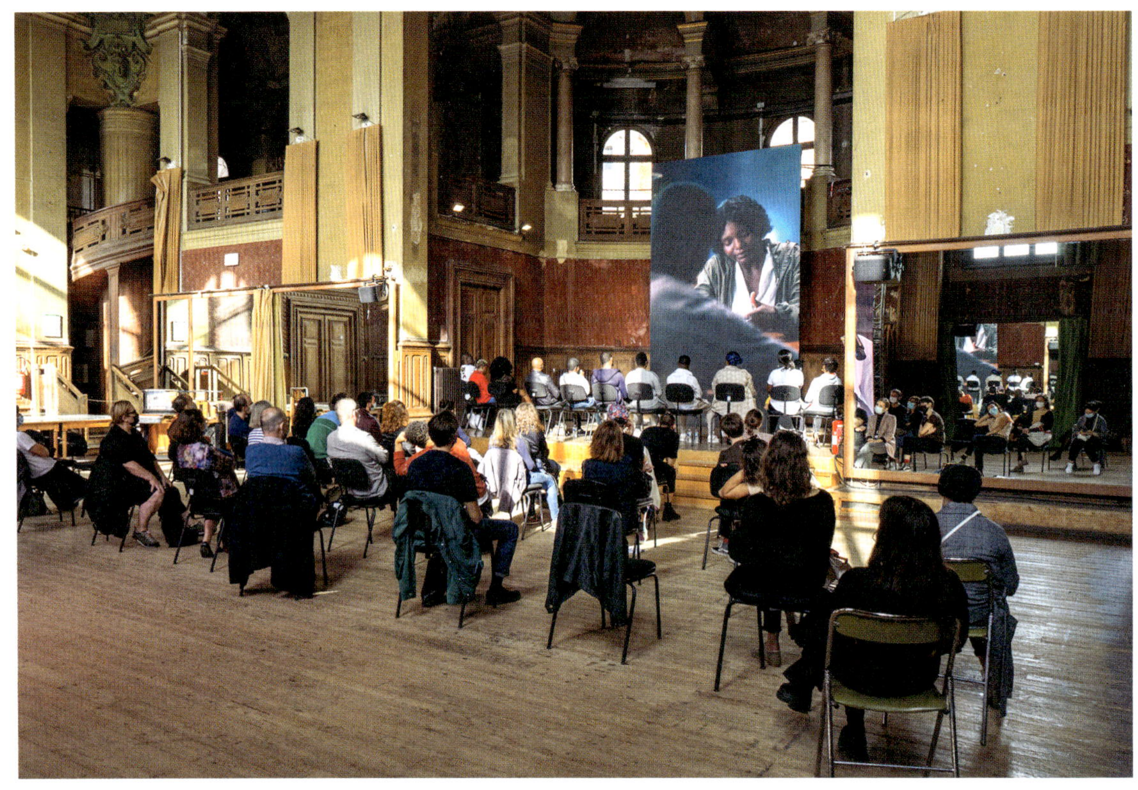

FIGURE 7.18

Tuan Andrew Nguyen, *Crimes of Solidarity/ Crimes de solidarité*, 2020. Two-channel video installation, 71 minutes. Performance at Salle Magaud at the Conservatoire for Manifesta 13, Marseille, France, October 9, 2020. Photo: Anaïs Baseilhac. Courtesy of the artist and James Cohan, New York.

of humanitarianism, itself a reinforcement of the criminalization of migration. In light of this paired illegalization, empathy cannot (for better *and* for worse) be relinquished: the call for empathy has the merit of affirming the affective state by which one can feel and acknowledge the distress of suffering others; it also has the merit of affirming prosocial empathy as a relation qualified to sustain more reciprocal forms of coexistence. Its ambivalences, however, must unfold and be accounted for. They must be complicated by the call to historicize, to share perspectives, and to recognize the autonomy of migration.

STORYTELL/ING

In 2019, the Displaced in Media strategic partnership—a group of journalists, activists, and migrant filmmakers commissioned by the European Cultural Foundation to investigate media accounts of contemporary migration—denounced EU's media coverage of migration events. Some of the identified shortcomings included the media's reduction of migrants to statistics and its oversimplified representation of migrating beings as either voiceless victims or threatening strangers or "virtuous" others (valued as honorable when confirming neoliberalist values). The group's edited volume, *Lost in Media: Migrant Perspectives and the Public Sphere* (2019), is an inspired and inspiring counterpart to that reductionism: the editors' selection of texts and artworks was mobilized by the question "Who gets to tell migrant stories?" Their answer was guided by the imperative to hear the *complex* stories of migrating beings as well as the imperative to hear *more* displaced voices.[1]

All of the works analyzed thus far have been telling us stories about displaced people. These stories—in the majority of cases—rely in part on testimonies and encounters with citizens-on-the-move, refugees, and survivors. They produce narratives that invite us to unlearn the way we see migration. In these works, however, who gets to tell the migrants' stories? The answer to that question is: mainly the artists, many of them (im)migrants or living transnationally. As stipulated in the book's introduction, these artists are either former refugees or immigrants or children of immigrants; they live between countries or are binationals; they are citizens of Mexico, Cuba, Vietnam, and South Africa but also live or have lived in the United States or in Europe; some have left China and are now living in exile in Europe; they are citizens of European or North American countries but have established long-standing relationships with people in a state of migration. Or they are Indigenous artists born in Canada and Black artists born in Europe or in Canada, whose larger history has been conditioned by the displacement of people imposed by colonial systems. Long-term encounters, interculturality, internationality involving people between countries of origin and countries of destination, immigration and migration, as well as deep history have made these artists particularly responsive to contemporary migration. In many of the works investigated so far, displaced beings and beings living in the afterlife of colonial displacement are telling the stories or are represented telling their stories, either orally or performatively—notably in works by Laura Waddington, Isaac Julien, John Akomfrah, Binta Diaw, Forensic Oceanography, Candice Breitz, Ai Weiwei, Alejandro González Iñárritu, Tania Bruguera, and Tuan Andrew Nguyen.

In the next five to ten years (Am I too optimistic?), when the lives of twenty-first-century migrating beings will cease to be primarily about *surviving* migration, their voices will be increasingly heard, and their artworks increasingly shown. The works examined in part IV are already partaking of that nearby future. Here, storytelling is explored to make displaced voices more compellingly heard even when they are not directly heard or are fictionally heard. As they are heard, the imperative remains to establish what Gayatri Chakravorty Spivak has called a radical form of dialogics—a responsive and responsible dialogue that confirms humans as "planetary accidents rather than global agents, planetary creatures rather than global entities," and in which alterity begins to stop being derived from "us": "it is only then that we will be able to think the migrant as well as the recipient of foreign aid in the species of alterity, not simply as the white person's burden."[2] In such a coexistence, each subject becomes both self and other in relation to one another. This is an ideal, an imperative, to imagine; the double imperative that the migrating being's voice be heard and that it be heard as part of a more reciprocal relation between tellers and viewers-listeners, with the acknowledgment that "representation has not withered away."[3] Storytelling is a coexistence of at least two beings, a number that grows with every new teller, viewer, and listener.

Part IV investigates artworks that explore a variety of aesthetic strategies—conversation, collective voice, the right to opacity, ambivalence, chaosmosis, movement, voice-induced pulsations of light beams intercrossing in the sky above the US-Mexico border, ventriloquial speech acts, deep listening, and weird looping—to enable storytelling as a practice of storytell/ing. In these works, storytelling unfolds disruptively [qua storytell/ing] for the sake of more mutual forms of coexistence involving migrating beings and beings whose larger history involves forced displacement, who are telling their stories, or whose stories are being told *to and with others*. Why? Mainly because to tell stories to and with others requires the disruption of the distribution of the sensible, which standardly excludes the voices of migrating beings, whose crises and autonomy are undervalued or underacknowledged. There is no mutuality without disturbance. Chapter 8 introduces that disruption by addressing four artworks that have been key to the development of storytell/ing as a collective endeavor: Bouchra Khalili's *The Mapping Journey Project* (2008–2011), Angela Melitopoulos's *Crossings* (2017), Rafael Lozano-Hemmer's *Border Tuner/Sintonizador fronterizo* (2019), and Tuan Andrew Nguyen's *Crimes of Solidarity/Crimes de solidarité* (2020). Chapter 9 follows Isuma's video-and-webcasts intervention made for the fifty-eighth edition of the Venice Biennale in 2019—a public-sphere intervention that upholds deep listening to uncover the twentieth-century internal displacement of Inuit communities and their nevertheless ongoing struggle to reverse the environmental degradation of the Arctic. The works examined in chapter 10 share a narrative looping strategy, devised to question, twist, and substantially rethink hospitality—its failures and renewed possibilities—in the context of twenty-first-century migration: Olu Oguibe's *Das Fremdlinge und Flüchtlinge Monument* (2017), Stan Douglas's *Doppelgänger* (2019), Decolonizing Architecture Art Research's *Al-Madhafah/The Living Room* (2016–2021), and Kent Monkman's *mistikôsiwak (Wooden Boat People)* (2019).

All of these case studies share the resourcefulness of a call (storytell/ing) that de facto tends to confirm and enable more luminous forms of coexistence because it enables migrants' voices to be heard. Whereas the call to historicize, as argued in part I, is certainly the interpellation that reveals the darkest coexistences structuring migration today, the call to story-tell is inviting viewers to listen to political subjects expressing their journeys. The book has articulated a spectrum of calls! But like the call for history that never loses sight of life and the possibility of historical change, storytell/ing never loses sight of necropolitics: it emerges from the acknowledgment of necropolitical migration and knows its tenaciousness.

WHY STORYTELL/ING?

This chapter introduces the call for storytell/ing by bringing together four installations that investigate migratory storytelling as a joint, collaborative activity between tellers and listeners: Bouchra Khalili's *The Mapping Journey Project* (2008–2011), Angela Melitopoulos's *Crossings* (2017), Rafael Lozano-Hemmer's *Border Tuner/Sintonizador fronterizo* (2019), and Tuan Andrew Nguyen's *Crimes of Solidarity/Crimes de solidarité* (2020). The "/" in "storytell/ing" suggests that a structure of mutual coexistence between tellers and listeners is made possible by a series of inventive disruptions: whereas migrating beings are repeatedly required to tell their stories to state officials when interrogated about the legitimacy of their claims, the artworks bring storytelling back to its fundamental role, which is—and here I follow Paul Ricoeur's hermeneutical understanding of the narrative—to reorganize past experience into meaningful patterns and to imagine future potentialities. The artworks sustain an alliance between tellers and listeners in the activity of storytelling, but these tellers and listeners are never made fully present to one another, and they never fully master their stories—an incompleteness that works both as a claim (even as a right) to impenetrability and as a manifestation of the memory failures that arise when stories of crises and distress are told. The works systematically involve third parties (the viewers or other participants), who are invited in turn to witness or listen to the stories while being physically decentered by the multiscreen, multirelational, or multiperformative structure of the installations. These disruptions never break the teller–listener pact, which is to make sure that stories are never told or listened to alone; they paradoxically enable more mutual relations of coexistence.

The Mapping Journey Project (2008–2011), an eight-channel video installation by the Moroccan French artist Bouchra Khalili (b. 1975, Casablanca, Morocco), has been widely exhibited and reviewed. My intention here is not to add to the reviews. Rather, I want to tease out Khalili's storytelling methodology, which has come to structure most of her artistic practice but was initially formulated in *The Mapping Journey Project* as a response to migration as it unfolded in the early 2000s.

The installation consists of a series of screens suspended from the ceiling. Each screen presents an image of a standard geographical map whose cartography will be redrawn by citizen-travelers with the use of a permanent marker as they orally narrate their illegalized trajectory throughout the Mediterranean Basin (figure 8.1). They tell their stories to Khalili, who remains off-screen and whose own voice is never heard; each traveler's body (except for that person's hands) also remains off-screen. The travelers tell their stories of migration through Africa; through central, western, northern, and southern Asia; and through European countries. We hear mostly about their back and forth movements between countries and their extended periods of waiting between borders. But the stories progressively become more specific: the voices talk about their labor conditions as migrant workers, their detention and negotiations with smugglers, the death of travel companions. Accounts vary from one screen to the next. Each screen describes a singular journey, including journeys from Algeria to Morocco, from Mogadishu and Somalia to Italy, from Bangladesh to India and Russia, from Tunisia and Libya to Italy and France, and from Afghanistan, Pakistan, Iran, and Turkey to Bulgaria, Hungary, Austria, Germany, Belgium, England, France, and Italy (*Mapping Journey #6*)—through land, the desert, seas, and checkpoints. For each journey, the overall hope is consistently to reach Europe. Each screen presents a fixed long-shot view of the printed color map being redrawn; the map is frontal. Some stories are narrated in Italian and English, others in a variety of Arabic languages with English subtitles. Viewers are invited to sit by themselves on a bench in front of each projection and listen to each story with a pair of headsets.

The Mapping Project Journey is a countergeography or what might be called a geography of resistance: the travelers' tracing of the lines and the accompanying spoken narration of their clandestine journeys subvert the colonial normativity of the maps. But let us be more precise. Four aesthetic strategies (at least) have been devised to prevent the stories from unfolding linearly, univocally, monosensorially,

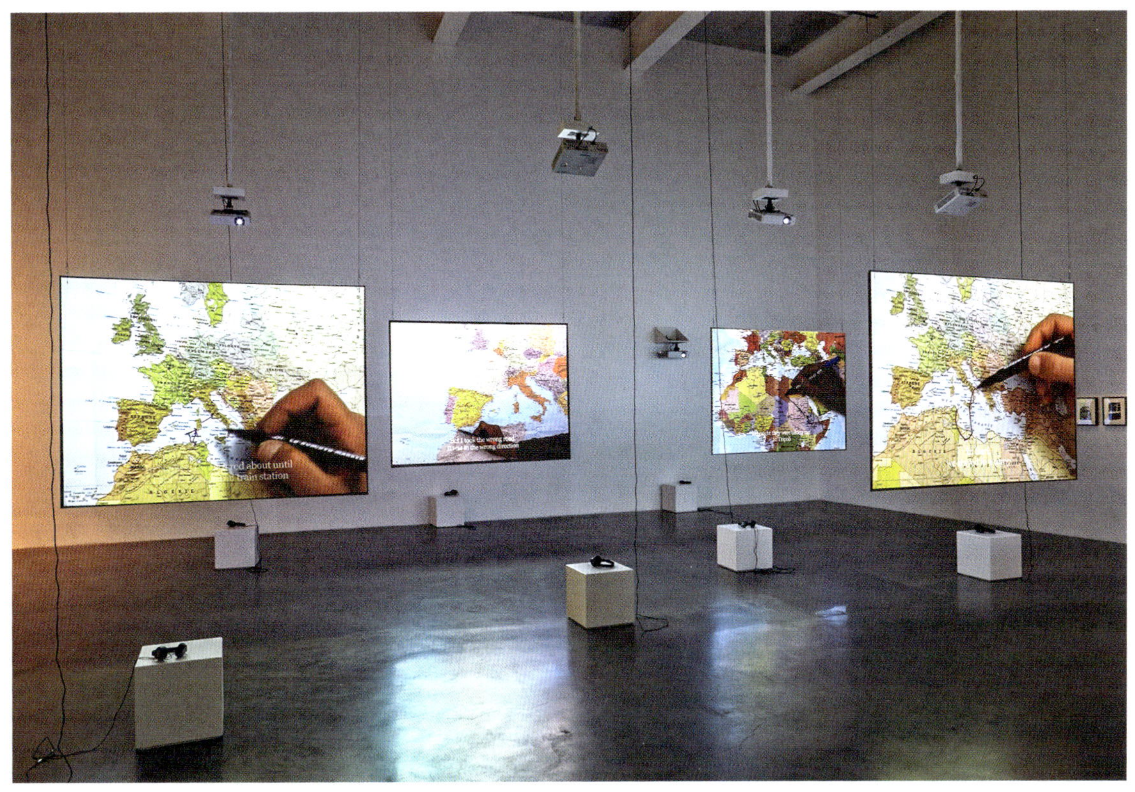

FIGURE 8.1

Bouchra Khalili, *The Mapping Journey Project*, 2008–2011. Eight-channel video, color, sound. Installation view: *Here and Elsewhere*, New Museum, New York, July 16–September 28, 2014. Photo: Benoit Pailley. Courtesy of the artist, Mor Charpentier, and New Museum.

and hierarchically. First, the stories are told by voices and tracing hands, but the tellers' faces remain off-screen. Occluding the faces is a countersurveillance strategy that not only protects the travelers' identities but also preserves their opaqueness—their "right to opacity"—defined by the Martinican poet and philosopher Édouard Glissant as the right *not* to completely reveal oneself to the listener ("the opaque . . . is that which cannot be reduced"[1]), concomitant to the requirement that the listener accept not fully understanding the teller.[2] Second, storytell/ing emphasizes the movement and autonomy of migration—that is, the travelers' decision to move despite illegalization so as to flee what they need to flee or because they are forced to flee. Storytell/ing itself is a movement: it relies on the fluctuation of the voice and the motion of the hands to narrate movement. Third, storytell/ing is a memorialization process insofar as the traces irreversibly mark the maps and have been recorded—archived—as such, and yet remembering the events is disclosed as a challenging endeavor. Finally, and most importantly, storytell/ing is a collaborative effort—a crucial deployment of coexistence that implies interdependent tellers and listeners; that emerges from the interdependence between the migrating narrators and the artist.

In a video interview from 2018, Khalili states that she considers herself mainly a storytelling performer: "I am maybe more of a storyteller than an artist. I am not the one who tells the stories, but there is sort of a community that is built up around the project that becomes a community of storytellers . . . , it's . . . about meeting people" rather than casting and writing a script.[3] She met her subjects—mostly unexpectedly insofar as she did not have a strict plan as to whom to meet and precisely where to find them—by traveling to and immersing herself in transit points in different cities across North Africa, western Asia, and Europe. Following an initial encounter and after a few conversations where Khalili and a migrant "learn[ed] how to speak to each other," she invited each traveler to narrate their journey.[4] In all of her works staging storytellers, she adopts the position of the listener when the story is being told to the camera, giving tellers "the time to speak freely" so that they may "take possession of their own voice, their own story and their own narrative."[5] Her methodology brings together two major storytelling practices. First, Pier Paolo Pasolini's idea of the civic poet and his formulation of the cinema of poetry as a "free indirect point-of-view" (speech or subjectivity)—a technique that merges the narrator's and characters' voices, reconciling a multiplicity of voices that equally share the speech act. Adopting the Pasolinian speech model, Khalili insists particularly on the voice no longer being "a voice alone, or a lonely voice"; each voice "articulates itself as a collective voice from the singular."[6] That model led her to a second tradition: al Halqa—a vanishing tradition of performing arts in Morocco involving a "public storyteller" who evolves within a "circle" (the English translation of the Arabic word *al-halqa*). In these public performances, storytelling unfolds as an encounter between the audience and the teller: "The performer within the Al Halqa tradition can be seen as a living archive," states Khalili, "mixing up popular tales delivered in dialect as well as sacred texts and ancient poems performed in classical Arabic. Somehow, my work approaches language similarly: literature, poetry, and oral history meet, the same way that various languages and dialects are brought together, creolised. From that perspective, I want to be more a storyteller than anything else, a storyteller whose stories are told by multiple voices. And that's maybe one role that art can play in vernacular culture: a space for creolisation and encounters."[7] Adapting the al Halqa ritual, Khalili becomes a living archive of stories narrated by citizens-on-the-move, who are themselves living archives of stories, within a space for creolization—whose main principle is the refusal to essentialize cultures or the imperative to mix them.[8] In that space, each storyteller voices their perspective autonomously but interdependently with the perspectives of others.

How does this collective voice—storytelling as a space for creolization and encounter—translate in *The Mapping Journey Project*? It is both expressed and made by the video installation. Expressed: the travelers tell their stories to Khalili off-screen; they are not interviewed by her, spoken about, or spoken for; and although each story is a monologue,[9] the monologues are addressed to a listener—to the artist adopting that very position. Made: the coexistence of the eight screens collectivizes and networks the different map markings, establishing a solidarity between the travelers; the frontal views make the maps appear as blackboards being scrutinized, examined, and annotated for the viewer sitting on the bench; the viewers become listeners as well, invited—as they are in Candice Breitz's *Love Story* (2016), discussed in the previous chapter—to meditate individually and silently as they listen. The preliminary steps (the conversations with the artist) leading to the monologues are not manifest in the work, but they are obliquely represented: they have shaped the monologues as a collective voice, a creolization. The subsequent steps (the reception of the installation) are not represented either, but the viewers may well become the new storytellers relaying and reinterpreting the stories. The "/" in "storytell/ing" signals the collectivity responsible for migratory stories, but it also affirms movement: the tracing of the trajectory is never linear and, as such, reproduces the nonlinearity of the journeys.

Crossings (2017), a four-channel high-definition video and sixteen-channel audio installation by the German artist Angela Melitopoulos (b. 1961, Munich, Germany), was made in collaboration with Angela Anderson and Maurizio Lazzarato for documenta 14, held in Kassel, Germany, that same year (figure 8.2). A meditation on the affectivity of migration in Greece following the "European refugee crisis" of 2015–2016, the installation relates migration, Greece's struggle with the debt crisis after the signing of the Memorandum of Understanding between the European Commission, the Hellenic Republic, and the Bank of Greece (2015), and gold mining in Skouries, northern Greece. Echoing Akomfrah's use of multichannel installations to associate images of diverse events coshaping modernity, *Crossings* narrows down that use to a specific historical present: Greece in the mid-2010s (the footage was shot in 2016). It depicts Greece at a junction of "different crisis poles" that overlay and interweave: migratory flows, neoliberalism, and resource extraction. The viewer is physically located somewhere between the four screens, immersed in the surround sound. Melitopoulos stipulates that the sound indicates to the viewers "where to look and which screen to focus on," and this is exactly how the soundscape unfolds—prompting viewers to change the direction of their gaze as a new sound emerges and allowing them to eventually look at what they have selected; it wants viewers to move while looking so as to compose a story "within the composition."[10] The installation itself is structured as a composition of 15 videos—one, two, or three videos running simultaneously in parallel. The sequences appear and disappear, inciting visitors to circulate in space and shift their perspective insofar as they can never be sure about when and where the next sequences will arise[11]—a chaosmic reception of a chaosmic historical condition. The devising of this mode of transmission and reception materializes notions that are key to Melitopoulos's work: Félix Guattari's notion of chaosmosis, to which I return later, as well Gilles Deleuze's and Guattari's idea of disclosing or creating deterritorialized situations—or situations that entail a drastic change of life, a chaos, a becoming-other, a crisis similar to those experienced by inhabitants of Greece in 2016.[12]

The installation depicts four different sites—one screen per location: the Moria Refugee Camp on the Island of Lesbos (figure 8.3); the self-governed camp of Kurdish migrants in Lavrion located in the southeastern part of Attica; Skouries; and an archaeological site in Athens. Emblematic of and faithful to its preoccupation with deterritorialization, *Crossings* is especially attentive to the people living their

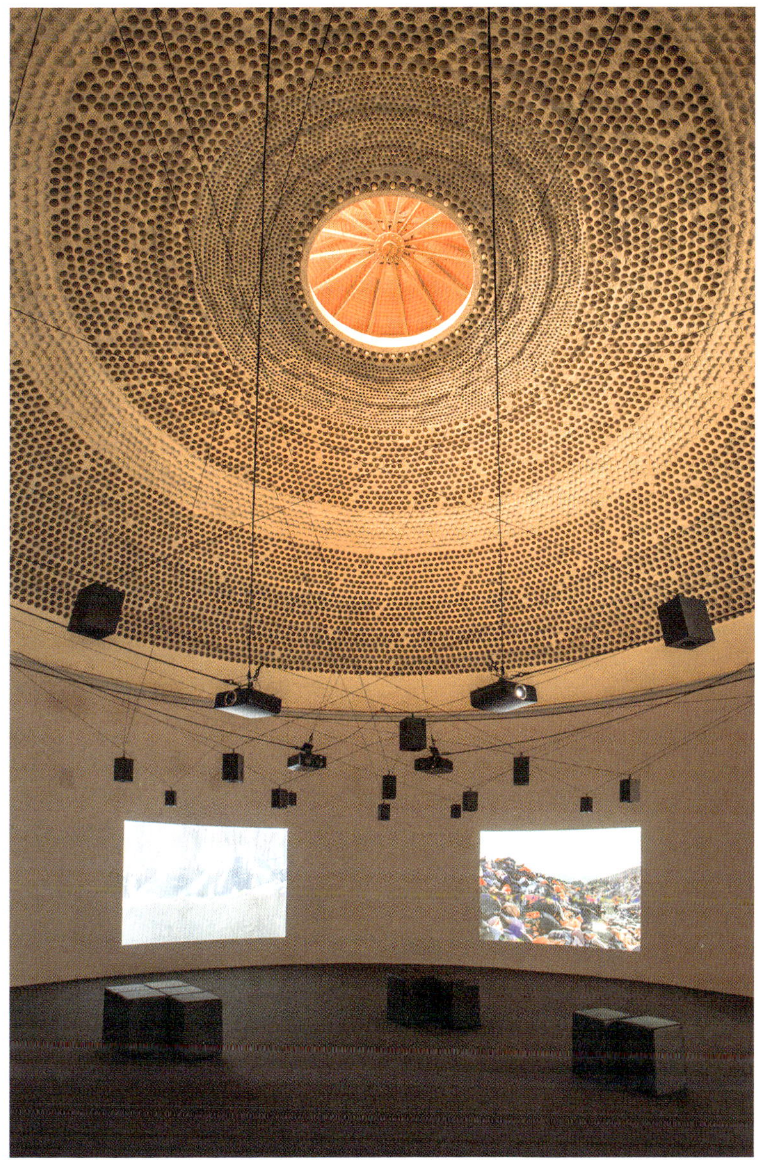

FIGURE 8.2

Angela Melitopoulos, *Crossings*, 2017.
Four-channel, high-definition, color video
and sixteen-channel audio installation.
Installation view: documenta 14, Kassel,
Germany. Photo: © Nils Klinger. Courtesy of
the artist and documenta archiv.

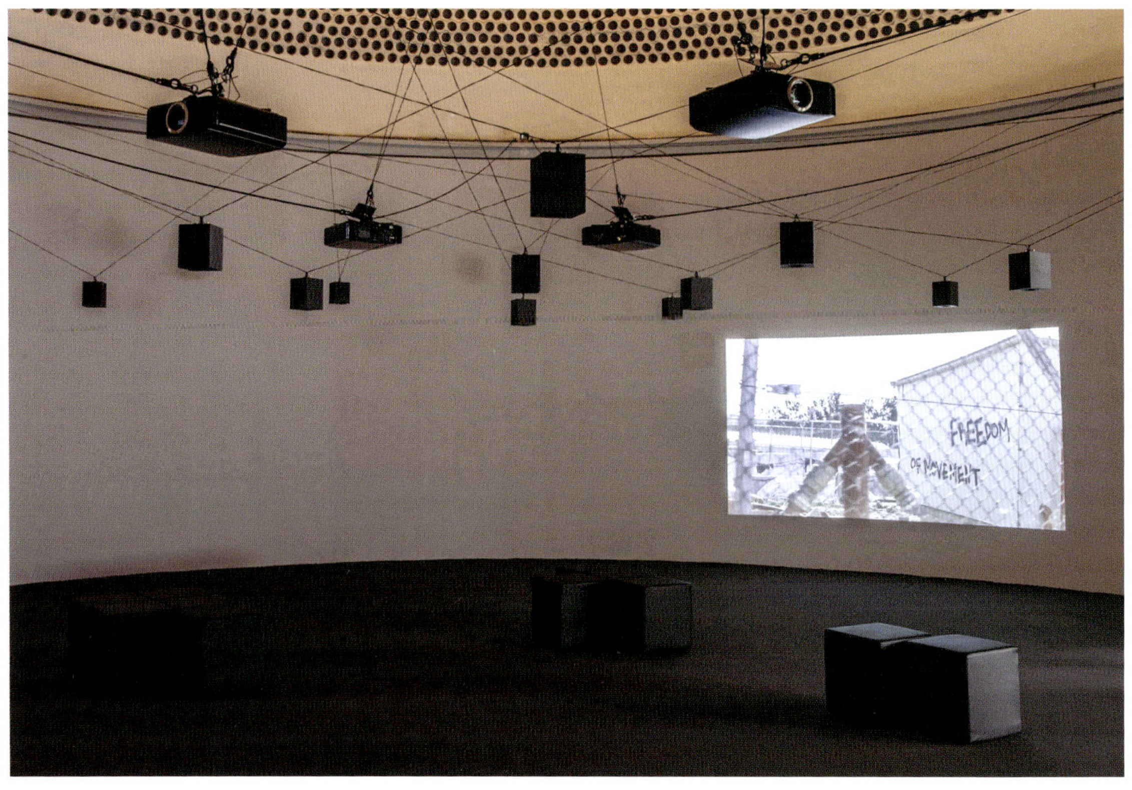

FIGURE 8.3

Angela Melitopoulos, *Crossings*, 2017.
Four-channel, high-definition, color video
and sixteen-channel audio installation.
Installation view: documenta 14, Kassel,
Germany. Photo: © Nils Klinger. Courtesy of
the artist and documenta archiv.

respective predicaments, especially the refugees who had recently arrived in Moria (coming mainly from Syria, Afghanistan, and Iraq) and the residents of Skouries concerned about the environmental deterioration of their region resulting from the open-pit goldmine activities of the Canadian mining company Eldorado Gold. The latter concern led to the formation of the "most acute protest movement in Greece in the last ten years, increasing in scope after 2015," when the debt crisis enabled EU-imposed so-called fast-track programs to accelerate the permission to proceed with the gold-mining project.[13] Melitopoulos describes her decision to look at the crises "from the position of the people forced to endure" their shattered environment and concomitantly to interconnect their stories of migration, capitalism, and extractivism. The passage is long but worth quoting in full:

We have been looking at Eldorado Gold, the mining company, but we were looking at it from the position of the people who are forced to endure this mining project. That means the inhabitants of the area who have been protesting against the mining project for a long time and who have created an incredible knowledge base that helps us understand how this mining industry is actually taking power within Greece. . . . In *Crossings* you have people talking about how they cannot go on living as they did. In Skouries you have people who are farmers and who have been living there all of their lives. They are now confronted with the crisis, with not having enough money to leave, and at the same time with the fact that they must leave the place once the gold mine is active because of pollution. Even now, the people face the fact that their parents are dying very early due to very high cancer rates. In a very near future, they know that they will become migrants themselves, so they are very interested in the migrants that come from Syria and other places. . . . While we have the people of Skouries, who may be forced to leave the country, we also have the migrants arriving from war zones outside of the EU. . . . I was in a Kurdish refugee camp in Lavrion—a camp that has existed since the 1990s—when the first big wave of Kurdish refugees came to Greece due to the destruction of Kurdish villages on the borders of Turkey, Iran and Iraq. The Lavrion camp is connected to another topic: the ancient silver mine of Lavrion. Lavrion is located 60 kilometres from Athens and was the slave port of ancient Athens, so in ancient Athens the triangle between extracting silver, slavery and war was already established. . . . [T]here's a part in the film about the silver mines: we see an archaeologist taking us through this incredible landscape from the mountains to the sea, a landscape full of ancient technology of mining. So the history of mining in Lavrion connects again to the archaeological history of Skouries, because the Eldorado Gold company not only want to establish a new open pit mine; they are also located in a place of ancient mining activity. Skouries is the birthplace of Aristoteles, so he was born in a mining area. This establishes a connection to Lesbos where we filmed the refugee camps; Aristoteles also lived shortly near Lesbos. And there's the theme connecting the camp in Lavrion with the camp in Lesbos. We made some specific workshops with migrants in Lesbos and a schizoanalyst called Paula Cobo Guevara. She developed a kind of workshop with the migrants, aimed at making a cartography of affects. You can be affected by landscape or by a lot of other things. This was a very elaborate way of trying to approach people in such difficult circumstances and allow them to speak about their own experiences in different ways. . . . So we have people coming towards Greece who are actually carriers of . . . contemporary conditions of war, coming into a county where wars are carried out by other means, through debt crises or extractionism.[14]

Note how the artist associates the different events defining Greece in 2016: acting as a listener and an observer, involved in the making of a workshop with the residents of the Moria Refugee Camp and the schizoanalyst Paula Cobo Guevara, Melitopoulos films the testimonies as well as the protest movements; she also explores the multichannel structure of the installation to tightly interconnect the crisis poles. They intersect with one another and become explainable in relation to each other, complexifying the geopolitics of Greece as it unfolded during that period; they coexist and are shown to be interdependent. She never wants to lose sight of the human and nonhuman actors living, subjected to, but also acting to resolve these crises. This is exactly what is shown on the different screens. Residents in Skouries are engaged—individually and collectively—in their environmental fight against the mining company; they are already thinking about migration as they contemplate escaping the heavily polluted environment. Residents in the Moria Refugee Camp express the intense affects that have come to define them in the already overcrowded and increasingly violent camp, where they are in fact trapped—the EU struck an agreement with Ankara in 2016 to reduce migrant flows to Greece from Turkey, stipulating that asylum seekers could not leave the Greek island camps until their claims were assessed.[15] The camp's inhabitants voice their hopes, their curiosity, but also their anger, fear, and need for care.

Underlying these testimonies and protests is the Guattarian belief in the human subject's ability to reappropriate life[16] and to gain in complexity, multiplicity, and heterogeneity when doing so—the belief in the citizen's and citizen-on-the-move's capacity to act as political subjects, affectively but also out of historical consciousness, a capacity for dissensus. In *Chaosmosis* (originally published in French in 1992), Guattari specifically states the imperative to connect the three ecologies so powerfully depicted in Melitopoulos's *Crossings*: *"Our survival on this planet is not only threatened by environmental damage but by the degeneration of the fabric of social solidarity and in the modes of psychical life, which must literally be re-invented. The re-formulation of politics will have to pass through the aesthetic and analytical dimensions implied in the three ecologies—the environment, the socius and the psyche."*[17] Guattari's plea for an aesthetic redefinition of politics—a politics that could counter the three damaged ecologies of our times (the environment, the socius, and the psyche)—is a plea for art, for the affective and the sensorial. In *Crossings*, this redefinition takes the form of storytell/ing. How? By conveying the testimonies and claims of subjects whose lives have been and are being fundamentally perturbed. These testimonies and claims are affectively expressed (and here I follow Lauren Berlant's notion of the affect as "the body's active presence to the intensities of the present"[18]) as the residents try to make sense of the historical present. The "/" marks that uncontrollable charge as it disrupts the linearity of the narrated stories. It marks the transformation of that charge into historical consciousness when dissidents meet to protest and unsettle the public sphere.

The above analysis of Khalili's work helps us identify two other features of *Crossings*'s storytell/ing deployment. First, its inherent collectivity. The collective voice is manifest not only in each individual projection (the stories being voiced are referring to collective realities; they are often uttered by groups) but also across the projections (the stories are ecologically intermixed in the Guatarrian sense). Second, storytell/ing is a movement. The soundscape and multiscreen layout of *Crossings* compel the listening viewer to move within the exhibition space. "When the body moves in a space," Melitopoulos suggests,

it creates thought and thinking. In modern culture, we tend to think the opposite is true: that we think of something and then we move. But through my studies and my work I claim that the physical movement comes first, and then there is thinking. That we sense the environment and that sensing makes us reflect. That is also why I am so interested in the topic of migration. Not just as a theoretical topic of people who come into our land to get citizenship. But as people who experience a certain world in a specific way that I think is relevant for us. . . . [I]f you're living in an unstable, disrupted reality—like the people of Skouries or the refugees in Lesbos—you have a different kind of knowledge. And that is a knowledge that can help build a future.[19]

Insofar as movement enables thought, and insofar as *Crossings* incites viewers to move as they look and listen, storytell/ing can be said to propel one of the key features of the autonomy of migration—the migrating being's desire and decision to move—in the exhibition space. In so doing, the multichannel structure of the installation affirms the political potential of movement. The image of the Moria Refugee Camp reproduced in figure 8.3 is highly suggestive in that regard; it shows graffiti painted on the wall of a shed behind the camp's wired fence, reading "Freedom of Movement."

BORDER TUNER/SINTONIZADOR FRONTERIZO

Border Tuner/Sintonizador fronterizo, Relational Architecture 23 by the Mexican Canadian, Montreal-based artist Rafael Lozano-Hemmer (b. 1967, Mexico City) consisted in a large-scale installation that connected communities in El Paso, Texas, and Ciudad Juárez, Chihuahua, Mexico, between November 13 and November 24, 2019. Interactive stations—each composed of a dial, a microphone, and a speaker—were installed on both sides of the US-Mexico border: three at Bowie High School, El Paso; three in Chamizal Federal Park, Ciudad Juárez. The two locations were by then separated by layers of transport and security infrastructure, including the Cesar Chavez Border Highway/Avenue Rafael Pérez Serna, a few mesh fences, and the very recent border wall constructed under President Donald Trump's administration. At night, participants on each side could turn a dial to activate and orient the light created by a robotic searchlight. The intersection of light beams in the sky would automatically open a live computer-generated bidirectional sound channel for communication between the participants across the border or within one of the two cities (figure 8.4). As they spoke to one another as tellers and listeners, the brightness of the light beams would modulate in sync.

An estimated 12,000 people visited the *Border Tuner* sites, exchanging on a variety of subjects—personal, cultural, social, and political.[20] Each evening would begin with a curated 30-minute "activation," featuring *fronterizo* artists, activists, poets, musicians, historians, and Indigenous leaders on both sides of the border, invited to establish cross-border performances around issues of migration, LGBTQ+, and Indigeneity (figure 8.5).[21] These activations included one by Puro Borde, a group of urban muralists from El Paso and Ciudad Juárez, as well as one directed by Las Platicadoras, an activist and academic feminist and decolonial collective working

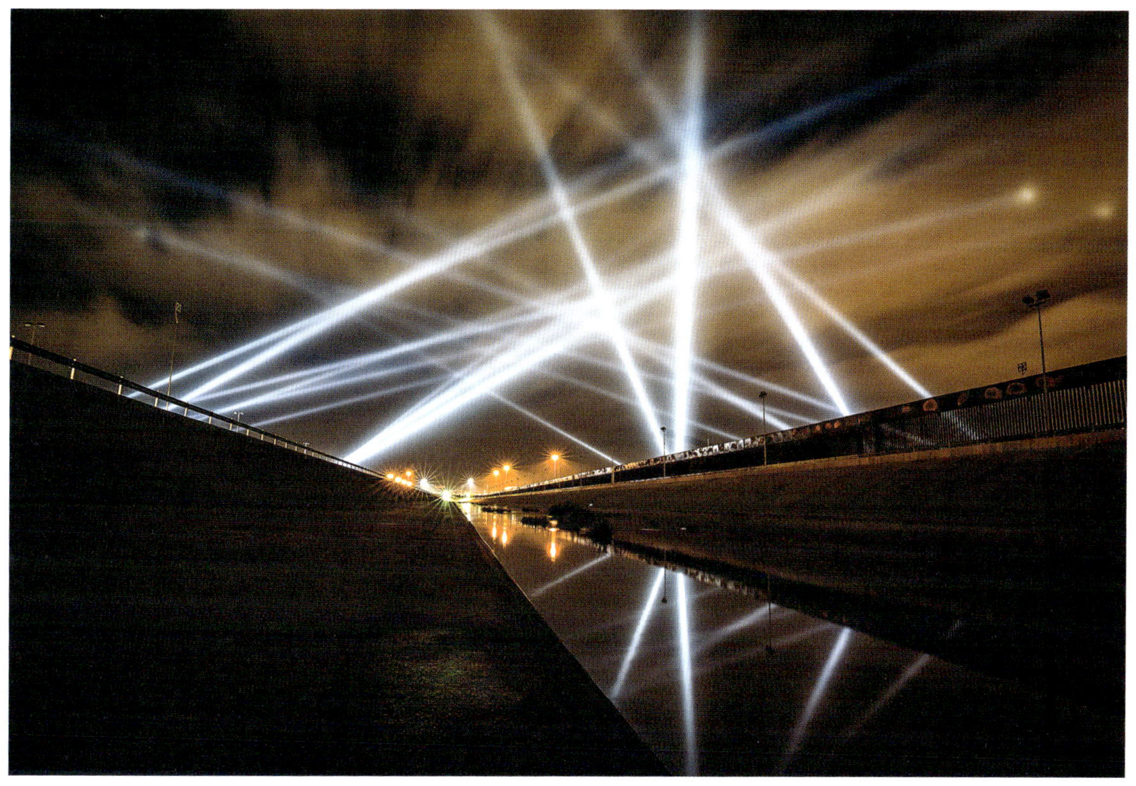

FIGURE 8.4

Rafael Lozano-Hemmer, *Border Tuner/ Sintonizador fronterizo, Relational Architecture 23*, 2019. Xenon 7kW robotic searchlights, dials with digital encoders, webcams, GPS, speakers, microphones, custom software. Interactive area 300 × 300 yd. (275 × 275 m). Bowie High School/ Parque Chamizal, El Paso/Ciudad Juárez, Texas/Chihuahua, United States/México. Photo: Monica Lozano. Courtesy of the artist, Lozano-Hemmer Studio, and Antimodular Research. © Rafael Lozano-Hemmer, "Border Tuner/Sintonizador fronterizo, Relational Architecture 23," 2019.

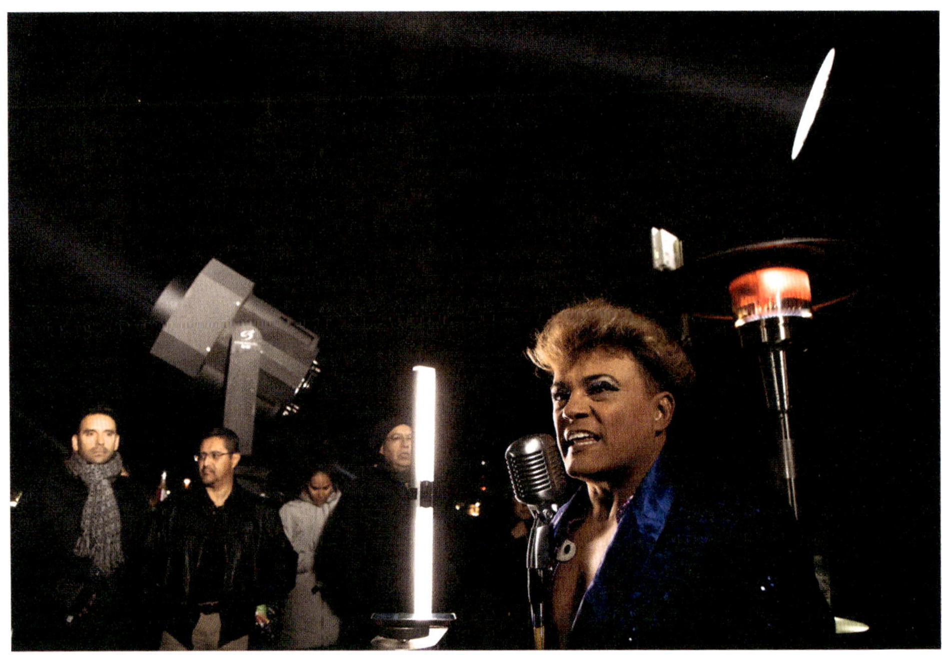

Rafael Lozano-Hemmer, *Border Tuner/
Sintonizador fronterizo, Relational
Architecture 23*, 2019. Xenon 7kW robotic
searchlights, dials with digital encoders,
webcams, GPS, speakers, microphones,
custom software. Interactive area 300 ×
300 yd. (275 × 275 m). Bowie High School/
Parque Chamizal, El Paso/Ciudad Juárez,
Texas/Chihuahua, United States/México.
Photo: Mariana Yañez. Courtesy of the artist,
Lozano-Hemmer Studio, and Antimodular
Research. © Rafael Lozano-Hemmer, "Border
Tuner/Sintonizador fronterizo, Relational
Architecture 23," 2019.

on migrant narratives and testimonies surfacing at the US-Mexico border. The latter took the form of a 30-minute-dialogue in Spanish and English between two migration advocates in Juárez and three in the United States. The conversation focused on explaining how migrating citizens are required to wait for their court hearings in tent settlements and shelters in Mexico after filing their asylum application in the US. Especially relevant to the question of coexistence, the dialogue was also about solidarity—that is, about declaring "that migrants need radical love and radical friendship, and that the migrants at the Parque Chamizal in Ciudad Juárez are not alone."[22] After the performances, participants could activate the dial and eventually communicate with someone else—strangers connecting with each other for the first time or, in many cases, individuals who already knew each other, whose relationality or relationship was made perceptible by the modulation of the light bridge's brightness.

This was Lozano-Hemmer's main finding: expecting a more divided El Paso–Ciudad Juárez community, he was exposed to coexisting communities with deep historical ties that they have maintained over time. Consolidating his project as a "civilian platform," he progressively confirmed the installation as a device completely operated by residents and visitors, allowing for what became a continuum of "bipolar" (in the figurative sense of the word, ranging from joy to sadness) conversations and statements.[23] Observers, people traveling near or toward the border, could contemplate the intersecting beams of light, which were visible ten miles away. *Border Tuner* highlighted El Paso's and Ciudad Juárez's coexistence as sister cities, together constituting the second-largest binational metropolitan area on the US-Mexico border. More importantly, resonating with Khalili's *The Mapping Journey Project* countergeography, *Border Tuner* worked as a counterbalance to the border-zone's violence and the Trump administration's adversarial rhetoric depicting the border as a porous boundary in need of securitization. As observed by the political philosopher Wendy Brown in her study on the twenty-first-century spread, bolstering, and theatricalization of border walls, the effectiveness of US-Mexico fences in deterring the flow of "irregular (im)migration" has been rather limited. They have in fact been more successful in rerouting the flow by forcing Mexicans and Central Americans to take more dangerous borderzones to reach the United States. The reinforcement of border walls has also intensified the blooming of criminal industries (including the drug-smuggling industry) that are never simply confined to borderzones but generate drug gang wars "deep inside both nations"; it has increased the violence of border areas as well as xenophobic nationalism.[24] President

Trump's 131-mile-long, 30-foot-high border wall in the El Paso sector of Texas and New Mexico was upgraded and built between 2018 and 2021. In his State of the Union speech in February 2019 (made nine months before *Border Tuner* was installed), the president stated that the border fence built in El Paso in 2008 had turned it from being one of the most unsafe into one of the safest cities in the United States; the statement was uttered to support his claim for further reinforcement, despite the fact that El Paso, as maintained by border patrol officials and government officials, "already had one of the lowest violent crime rates in the US" before the fence was erected in 2008, and experienced a rise of its violent crime rate "over the next four years, after the fencing went up."[25] The new wall's main effect has been one of deterrence—inciting people to cross the hostile Chihuahuan Desert, "where deaths from exposure have risen."[26]

Border Tuner's visualization and auralization of the binational coexistence of El Paso and Ciudad Juárez were key to the work's counterbalancing of the Trumpian rhetoric. *Border Tuner* worked only if there were at least two participants turning the dial to activate the light beams and generate the possibility of storytelling. Storytell/ing unfolded then less as a utopia of togetherness than as a meeting device for strangers or an amplification device for preexisting relationships—relationships typically concealed by the discursive and physical antimigrant reinforcement of the border wall. Light was used not to make material borders visible but to enable the reciprocal coexistences they deny or disable.

Lozano-Hemmer has more specifically stated that the installation could be explored by local people to "reclaim their narrative of the border" instead of having that story defined for them by others. I understand this to be the quintessence of Gloria Anzaldúa's notion of border culture as a possibility to mix cultures.[27] "[T]his platform," he added, "is one of communication and reconciliation."[28] But the poetics of most of Lozano-Hemmer's light works, including *Border Tuner*, lies in their unpredictability: they never fully predict the relational encounters in advance, nor can they fully control them. As in the work of Richard Mosse and Forensic Oceanography, the installation repurposed surveillance technology—here, large robotic searchlights used "to track any attempt on the fence"[29]—to generate the possibility of unscripted countervisualities and counternarratives. *Border Tuner*'s inventiveness came from the light beams' capacity to de- and reborder the two sides of the wall, much like Chico MacMurtrie's giant border-crossing robot (a work that Lozano-Hemmer particularly admires) that was designed to bend over border walls. Its inventiveness came from its materialization of storytelling (about migration, among other issues) in unique modulations of brightness and, ultimately, from the dramatic reversal of the light beams' orientation: instead of coming from above— let us recall Alejandro González Iñárritu's *CARNE y ARENA* (2017) and its simulation of a searchlight controlled by a border patrol helicopter—the beams were now initiated and controlled from the ground by civilians.[30] Teresa Margolles's *La promesa* (2012) discussed in chapter 5 (Lozano-Hemmer knows Margolles's work[31]) invites us to complicate even further the simplistic understanding of *Border Tuner/Sintonizador fronterizo* as a relational, participatory, and interactive work. As the installation activated the continual relaying of storytellers, some residents and visitors were in fact taking care of each other—both giving and receiving stories, as fragmented as they may well have been.[32] In short, the "/" in "storytell/ing" accounted for collectivity, interdependence, and movement (echoing Khalili's and Melitopoulos's installations), while adding the dimension of care, the challenge of care.

CRIMES OF SOLIDARITY/CRIMES DE SOLIDARITÉ

The Vietnamese American artist Tuan Andrew Nguyen (b. 1976, Saigon, Vietnam) made *Crimes of Solidarity/Crimes de solidarité*—a 71-minute-long two-channel video installation and performance—in the context of Manifesta 13, which took place in Marseille in the fall of 2020. Due to the COVID-19 pandemic, the work was produced remotely from Ho Chi Minh City (formerly Saigon) in southern Vietnam, where the artist works and lives. He worked in collaboration with refugees who lived in Marseille's Squat Saint-Just, a building that sheltered roughly 300 residents at any given time between 2018 and 2020. The occupants had received an eviction notice to leave the premises in February 2020. The initial plan had been to extend the life of the squat during the biennial by using it as a filming locale and exhibition place, but the squat burned down in June, forcing the evacuation of the residents. The resulting work took the form of an "incomplete" video. In an interview with *Artforum*, Nguyen described the production as a growing script made in conversation and in collaboration with the former squat tenants (most of them Nigerians), whom he invited to share what they were willing to share with him and eventually with a larger audience. The Skype discussions were recorded and turned into scripted scenes.[33] More than 70 percent of the script was made using the former tenants' words.[34] The work evolved into live performances held in a new venue, the Music Conservatory of Marseille. The video was played with muted dialogue on a large screen installed on the conservatory's stage, where the storyteller-actors were sitting—facing the screen, with their backs turned to the viewers—attempting to sync their voices with the movement of their lips on-screen while reading the displayed captions (figures 7.18 and 8.6). Nguyen explains some of the footage and performances as well as the questions he wanted to raise with the work in the following terms:

Sharon Omoreuyi reads a letter addressed to her son, Marvelous, in the year 2033, when he will be eighteen. Blessing Yacouhou, uncomfortable with speaking about her children for the video, sings a ballad instead at Cours Julien. Characters also ask each other about how the film is going, talk about IP contracts and event content. Sekou Fofana mentions how the director wants him to become a production manager. My hope is that this self-referentiality questions assumptions about who is telling whose stories, as well as emphasizes my own complicity, alongside that of the viewer, in circulating and consuming such stories within the context of the biennial. . . . It's about reclaiming voice and prioritizing the presence of the body from which the live voice speaks. But I'm also interested in the idea of being able to throw one's voice, how the slippages and synchronicity of ventriloquism can, if done right, become a kind of magic. You're at once embodied and disembodied, occupying multiple spaces, present, past, even future tense. . . . Storytelling can be a form of care, transmission, and memorialization, but it can also be a negotiation, or an audition.[35]

In his description of the work, Nguyen defends storytell/ing as a counterpart to mainstream media's representation of migrating beings as voiceless. More importantly, he obliquely endorses Khalili's, Melitopoulos's, and Lozano-Hemmer's aesthetic strategies by upholding storytelling as a fundamentally collective voice that disrupts the status quo of the voiceless migrants. The "/" of *Crimes of Solidarity*'s collective storytelling activity unfolded at many levels, including the making of a script that brought together the stories of migration narrated by the ex-squatters with the artist's participation, and the possibility of solidarity between the tellers as well as between the tellers and the listeners (the artist, the viewers) generated by such a process. But the originality of *Crimes of Solidarity*'s "/" lies in its attempt to problematize speech as the ultimate transmitter of the true story of the migrant. The video stories were separated from their initial voices and the voices were arduously reenacted by the performers when the videos were shown at the Music Conservatory. The difficulty of matching the live dialogues with the captions and of syncing the live voices with the movement of the lips on-screen could be interpreted

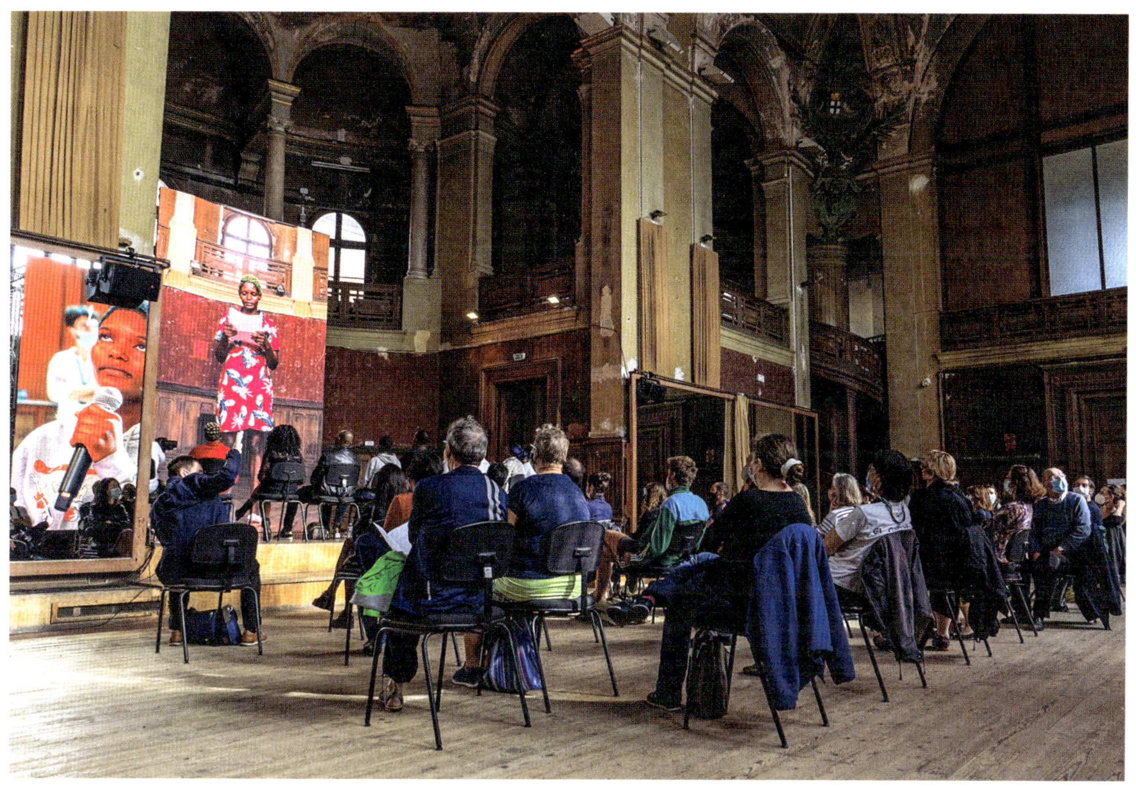

Tuan Andrew Nguyen, *Crimes of Solidarity/ Crimes de solidarité*, 2020. Two-channel video installation, 71 minutes. Performance at Salle Magaud at the Conservatoire for Manifesta 13, Marseille, France, October 9, 2020. Photo: Anaïs Baseilhac. Courtesy of the artist and James Cohan, New York.

not only as revealing the storytellers' migratory traumas that prevent their stories from being wholly remembered and told but also as a deliberate decision to exercise their right to opacity. That right is also manifest in the significant divergence of the video stories from those performed by citizens-on-the-move for state authorities to justify their asylum claim.[36] Nguyen, based in Ho Chi Minh City, was a refugee who immigrated with his family to the United States in 1979 (he grew up in California). His work has steadily dealt with migration-related experiences, exploring new forms of storytelling and community engagement to depict these experiences. The video installation in 2020 was unique in its reference to France's Délit de solidarité (Solidarity Offense), which criminalizes any NGO or private citizen who facilitates the "irregular" entry or stay of a foreigner in France. On July 6, 2018, the French Constitutional Council ruled the Offense partially unconstitutional when assistance is provided for humanitarian purposes, but arrests, trials, and court decisions continue to compromise "facilitation," terminology that remains vague and unclarified.[37] As such, the installation ultimately worked as a question addressed to the viewer: Can listening be a practice of solidarity against the criminalization of care, which is itself grounded in the criminalization of migration? The work replied in the affirmative, but it advocated for the requirement to keep the breakdowns of telling and listening alive to enable that solidarity so as to allow for the *re*distribution of the sensible.

DEEP LISTENING

THE WORLD I was born into has changed forever. . . .

In a sense, Inuit of my generation have lived in both the ice age and the space age. The modern world arrived slowly in some places in the world, and quickly in others. But in the Arctic, it appeared in a single generation. Like everyone I grew up with, I have seen ancient traditions give way to southern habits. I have seen communities broken apart or transformed dramatically by government policies. I have seen Inuit traditional wisdom supplanted by southern programs and institutions. And most shockingly, like all my fellow Inuit, I have seen what seemed permanent begin to melt away.

The Arctic ice and snow, the frozen terrain that Inuit life has depended on for millennia, is now diminishing in front of our eyes.
—Sheila Watt-Cloutier, *The Right to Be Cold*[1]

Of special relevance to this chapter, cyberbalkanization—the splintering of the internet community into subpublics with specific interests, whose division is typically reinforced along regional or national lines and whose modus operandi is the systematic avoidance of viewpoints that contradict each subpublic's belief system—weakens the possibility of a shared truth about migration.[2] If truth is shared, its sharedness has shrunk to reach and reconfirm the beliefs of isolated digital tribes, a ghettoization that weakens the possibility of recognizing other perspectives or establishing a common ground between publics around acknowledged facts. Belonging to such digital communities becomes even more problematic when balkanization is unknown to the users themselves, caught as they are in the information streams oriented by the new global media giants, including

Google, Facebook, and Twitter. What is art to do? What truth can it distribute in a historical present conditioned by postfactuality? One possible resisting route—a form of resistance I investigate here—is to expand the publicness of art, to support art and art institutions that not only connect different publics so that they may contest one another and expand their worldviews in light of other worldviews but also make manifest what postfactuality tends to deny: a worldview is always necessarily situated. A worldview's truth value is a perspective, never the ultimate truth: truth comes from the ongoing verification of perspectives on a planetary scale. In this chapter, I ask: Could a planetary-oriented public sphere be thought out in line with what Gayatri Chakravorty Spivak refers to as a radicalized dialogical practice—an exchange between coexisting publics, between citizens-on-the-move of some of the poorest economies worldwide *and* affirmed citizens of some of the richest economies worldwide, between Inuit and settlers, on "a two-way road" (outside the Master–Slave dialectic) following the "imperative to re-imagine the subject as planetary accident" rather than a "global agent" defined by the economic forces of neoliberalism?[3] But, then, how can publics and citizens be responsible? How can they respond to one another without one simply absorbing the other's perspective into one's own worldview?

With these two questions in mind, I examine here a work fundamentally driven by the challenge of public dialogue as a means of mutual coexistence: Igloolik Isuma Productions' video-and-webcasts intervention in the Canada Pavilion during the fifty-eighth edition of the Biennale di Venezia in 2019—a work that connects and asks us to deliberate on two related planetary predicaments: internal displacement (following the UNHCR definition of internally displaced persons as "persons or groups of persons who have been forced or obliged to flee or to leave their homes or places of habitual residence . . . and who have not crossed an internationally recognized State border"[4]) and environmental degradation (namely, biodiversity loss as part of the ongoing sixth mass extinction and global warming). John Akomfrah's pivotal concern for environmental degradation as well as Angela Melitopoulos's association of refugeehood and the environmental deterioration of Skouries, Greece, resulting from the open-pit goldmine activities of the Canadian mining company Eldorado Gold obliquely resurface in Isuma's intervention. To address these issues, Akomfrah's trilogy proposes conversations between underacknowledged actors and agents on the stage of history, while Melitopoulos's *Crossings* (2017) explores chaosmosis. The collective Isuma is more specifically searching for a transformed public sphere. Its dialogics mobilizes but significantly troubles, as I show later in this chapter, Jürgen Habermas's notion of the public sphere as a realm of social life where public opinion takes shape through deliberations between subjects who "come together as a public" around matters of common concern. The intervention's public sphere consists in a media encounter between an Inuit counterpublic and publics south of the Nunavut mainland, and its structure of deliberation follows a storytelling tradition of "oral delivery and aural reception" that privileges listening over mere voicing.[5] Some of storytell/ing's central features discussed in the previous chapter are also mobilized: the public sphere allows marginalized voices to be heard while maintaining their right to opacity; the public sphere is likewise a collective heterogeneous voice. But storytell/ing is fully anchored in Inuit culture and tradition: it is sustained, as an ideal, by Inuit Qaujimajatuqangit principles of mutual respect, commonality, collaboration, acquisition of knowledge, and care for humans and nonhumans (the land, animals, and the environment); it favors deep listening to meet these principles. There lies the uniqueness of the Biennale di Venezia intervention: Isuma's exploration of media and storytelling renews the public sphere to call attention to environmental degradation as one of the central preconditions or pitfalls of the forced migration of Inuit communities in the twentieth century; environmental degradation in the Arctic becomes a matter of discussion and collaborative struggle. Its public sphere is a countercyberbalkanization.

To unpack my claim, I have divided the chapter into five sections. The chapter first describes Isuma's video-and-webcasts intervention; it then contextualizes that intervention within the history of colonialism in Canada and historicizes the relation between internal displacement and environmental degradation. These three steps will allow us, fourth, to establish Isuma's reinvention of the public sphere together with the two main aesthetic strategies that sustain that reinvention: webcast mediality and deep listening. The fifth and last section is fully dedicated to the listening strategy as a unique storytell/ing process, enriched as it is by Inuit Qaujimajatuqangit principles and the requirement, compellingly formulated by the Stó:lō scholar Dylan Robinson, to keep the incommensurability of the Indigenous and the settler alive as the latter listens to the former.

ISUMA'S DOUBLE INTERVENTION AT THE 2019 VENICE BIENNALE

Isuma (Inuktitut syllabics: ᐃᓱᒪ) is an Inuit collective of creators based in Igloolik, Canada—the first to be invited to exhibit their work in the Canada Pavilion in Venice. Cofounded in 1990 by Zacharias Kunuk, Paul Apak Angilirq, Pauloosie Qulitalik, and Norman Cohn and devoted primarily to the production of independent video art, Isuma has also helped establish several Inuit media institutions, including NITV, an Igloolik-based Nunavut independent television network center offering video on demand and live video conferencing; Arnait Video Productions, a women's collective; Artciq, a youth media and circus group; SILA, an e-learning website about Inuit culture; IsumaTV, a website for Indigenous media art launched in 2008; and Digital Indigenous Democracy, an internet network initiated in 2012 whose main mission is to inform and consult with Inuit communities on the development of the Baffinland Iron Mines Corporation and other resource projects.[6] These media undertakings have digitally materialized Inuit storytelling as a practice of oral history transmitted by Elders to younger generations—a practice increasingly understood as a means of empowerment, whose effectiveness rests on its listening activity and multiperspectivism.[7] As best summarized by the Inuk artist, filmmaker, and curator asinnajaq, Isuma's projects "share stories of Inuit who have been disempowered, and who find power by being given the opportunity to speak up. There isn't one simple truth in the world, so understanding a subject requires listening to many perspectives. Isuma isn't the one and lonely voice for Inuit, but they do cover a vast array of topics, including relocations, climate change and international social politics. . . . In the process of producing historically accurate narrative films, the knowledge of Elders is being shared, heard and valued."[8] The collective's specialization is intergenerational media storytelling.

The Canada Pavilion introduced two new works by Isuma: a feature-length video in Inuktitut and English (with English and French subtitles) entitled *One Day in the Life of Noah Piugattuk* (ᓄᐊ ᐱᐅᒥᑦᑐᑉ ᐅᕐ ᔪᓂᒪᐅᖃᑕᙱ, 2019) and a series of four webcasts titled *Silakut Live from the Floe Edge* (ᓯᓚᒃᑯᑦ ᓴᖅᑭᔭᖅᑐᑦ ᓯᐊᓂ, 2019). Both the video and the livecasts were screened in the pavilion (figure 9.1) but could also be viewed online on IsumaTV as well as in different galleries in Canada. The *Silakut* livecasts were held on May 8, 9, 10, and 11, 2019. However, it is the joint presentation of the video and the livecasts that makes this intervention unique and crucial. Considered together, they show how the internal displacement of Inuit communities in the twentieth century has contributed to the environmental degradation of the Arctic by making their land available for colonial extractivism; they also show the resilience of the Igloolik community as it fights (despite its past displacement) to counter biodiversity loss and global warming—a rising environmental degradation identified in the webcasts as resulting in and from ice melt as well as from the Mary

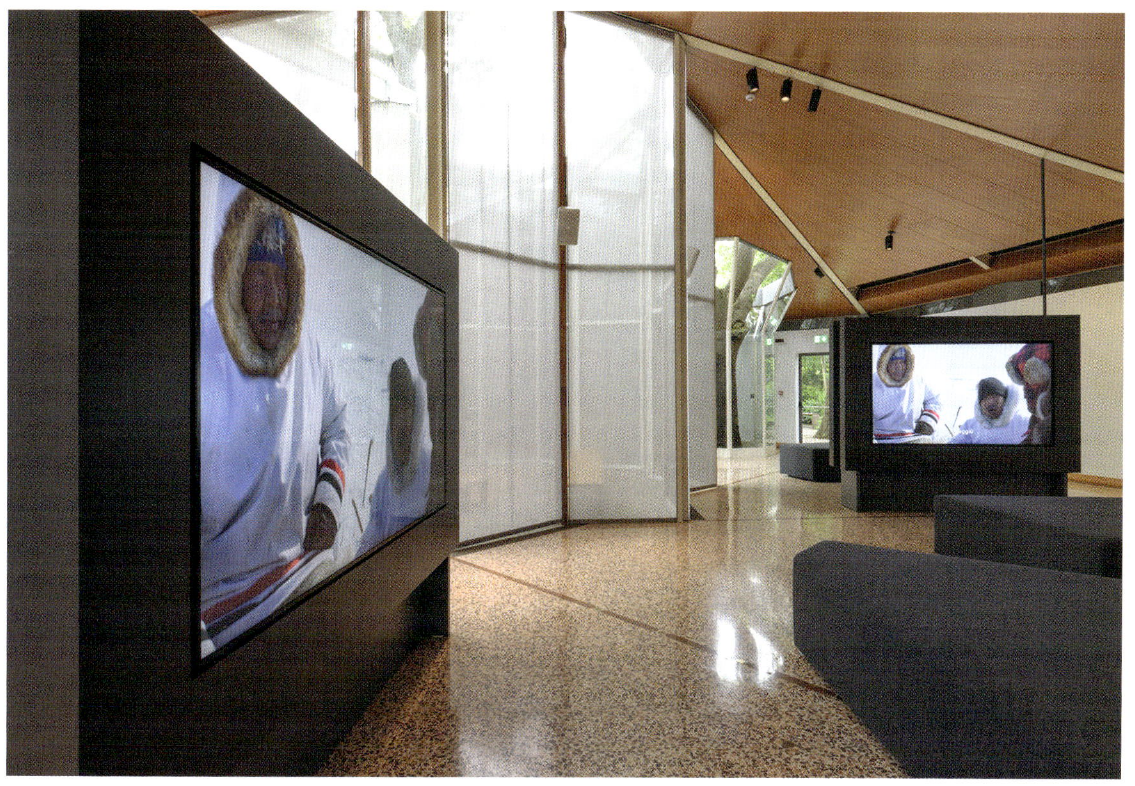

Isuma, *One Day in the Life of Noah Piugattuk*, 2019. 4K digital video installation, 112 minutes, Inuktitut-English. Installation view: Canada Pavilion, 58th International Art Exhibition—la Biennale di Venezia, May 2019. Photo: Francesco Barascutti. Courtesy of the National Gallery of Canada and Isuma Distribution International.

River Project. The latter is an open-pit iron mine operated by the Baffinland Iron Mines Corporation in the Mary River area of Baffin Island, Nunavut; the project's plans for a phase-two expansion were scheduled to be heard by the Nunavut Impact Review Board in Iqaluit in the summer and fall of 2019.[9] For the sake of clarity, I define environmental degradation as "any change or disturbance to the environment perceived to be deleterious or undesirable," especially through the deterioration or destruction of ecosystems, as in biodiversity loss ("a decrease in biodiversity within a species, an ecosystem, a given geographic area, or Earth as a whole") and global warming ("the phenomenon of increasing average air temperatures near the surface of Earth over the past one to two centuries").[10]

Both the video and the livecasts situate the public sphere at the center of Inuit life: in the 112-minute-long 4K digital docudrama *One Day in the Life of Noah Piugattuk*, Inuk hunter Noah Piugattuk, surrounded by his band, and a white man called the "boss"—an agent of the government assigned to get Piugattuk to move his band to a government-designated settlement—meet at Piugattuk's hunting camp. Among other reasons, the boss invokes the context of the "war" (i.e., the Cold War) to justify his request for displacement and relocation.[11] Staged in 1961 and shot on location in Kapuivik, northern Baffin Island, where Piugattuk and his band seminomadically lived and hunted, the docudrama is based on the life of Noah Piugattuk; it exposes the Canadian government's program of forced migration of Inuit families, from their hunting and fishing land into permanent settlements in the 1950s and 1960s. Most of the video—and this is important when speaking about the constitution of publics—centers on the conversation, translated by an Inuk interpreter, between Piugattuk and the government official. They talk; they hear one another; they deliberate; they are publics to each other, although in a dialogue that is far from being dialogical, ruled as it is by a colonizer–colonized relation. Their statements are translated yet often mistranslated or translated approximatively by the interpreter sitting between them. The deliberation ends when Piugattuk refuses to accept the boss's proposition. "I wanted to look at the moment that they [the Inuit] were told to move," says Isuma cofounder Zacharias Kunuk. "They were saying, 'We don't want to go anywhere. We don't want to move.' But they were told they had to. So that's what we're looking at."[12] Although Piugattuk said no to the move, his was a unique voice amid the Inuit people, whose destiny took mainly the form of imposed displacement (figures 9.1 and 9.2).

Filmed from within the Igloolik area, the four *Silakut Live from the Floe Edge* webcasts capture and transmit another public sphere in the making fifty-eight years

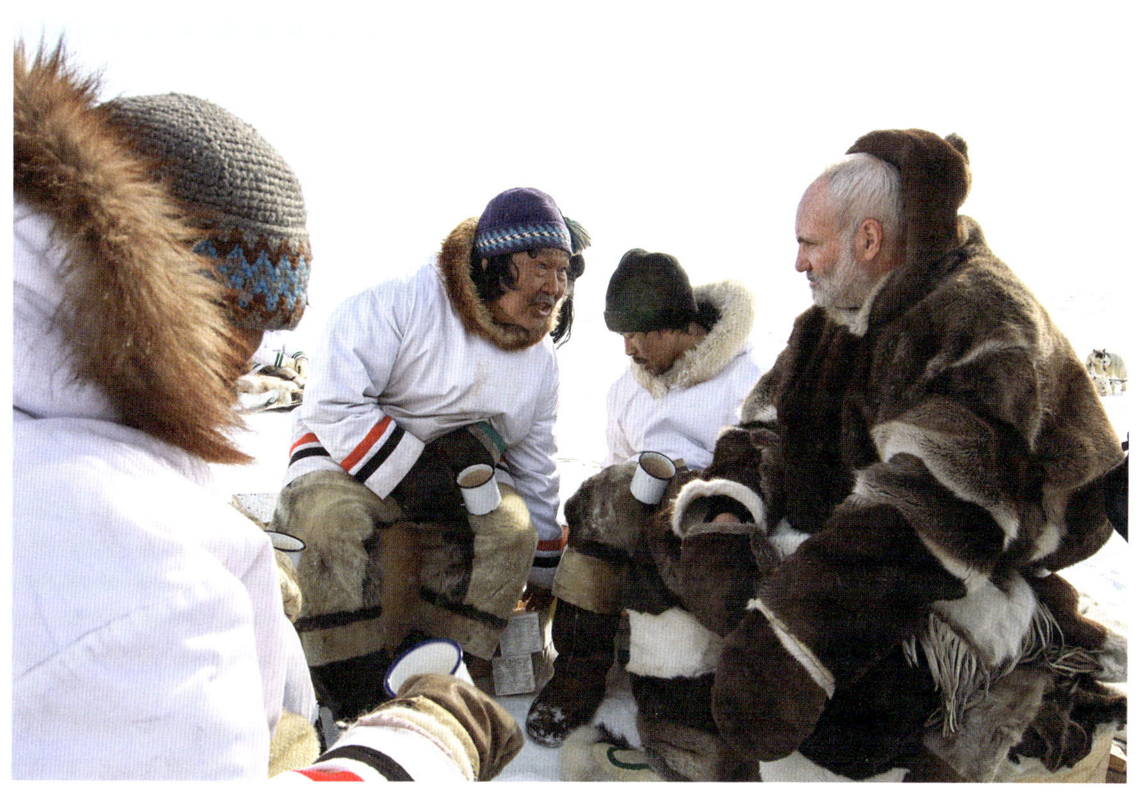

FIGURE 9.2

Isuma, *One Day in the Life of Noah Piugattuk*,
on location, 2018. Photo: Levi Uttak.
Courtesy of Isuma Distribution International.

after this imposed displacement. They show Kunuk sitting inside a cabin with Elders and a member of the younger generation of the Igloolik community. In this gathering, each member is invited to talk, one after the other, recounting memories of childhood, telling stories about human and shaman relationships, sharing their knowledge of different traditional cultural practices (including string games and drum dancing) (figure 9.3). Kunuk progressively asks them to talk about the development of the Mary River Project and its impact on the community (discussed in more detail later in this chapter). The webcasts also present archives on past Inuit life; they transmit live shots of the floe edge—the *sinaaq*, "where the open sea meets the frozen sea" attached to the shoreline, an especially dynamic place in the spring and summer, when arctic wildlife abounds[13]—as well as the film crew and hunters active on the land. In the webcasts of May 9 and 10, seal hunting was filmed live: at first abandoned because the melting ice was too thin to hunt on, the hunting resumed and was successful on the next day. Outlining *Silakut Live*, Kunuk stated that the webcasts were specifically designed to make the community's environmental concerns public, implicitly echoing the Inuk activist Sheila Watt-Cloutier's climate-change-informed call for "the right to be cold"[14]: "Silakut means 'through the air.' . . . We plan to film live at our floe edge, from the ice and the sea, where hunters hunt seals, and broadcast halfway around the world to Venice. . . . The land is melting, and we want to show that this summer."[15]

Key here is how media are understood by Kunuk as a means to make public the environmental consequences of extractivism—extractivism understood as a mode of accumulation, as the process of extracting large quantities of natural resources from the earth, mainly for export.[16] At the beginning of each webcast and after each pause, Kunuk explicitly welcomes the public (which is always necessarily a shifting public—the Venice Biennale public; the Inuit, non-Inuit, and settler publics listening live to the webcasts from anywhere in the world; and the public watching the archived webcasts on IsumaTV after the event) and invites it to listen. When asked about phase two of the Mary River Project, each member expresses, although some more forcibly than others, their distrust of the planned expansion. What is abundantly voiced is the project's depreciation of the interdependence between the Inuit and the nonhuman animals living in Baffinland as well as its endangerment of the animals (fish, walrus, narwhal, caribou) and what this represents for a community who has traditionally hunted for food. "They don't know nothing about what they will be doing . . . our land, our animals"; "Our land has much resources. . . . People, we eat from land and water . . . the metal will go into our bodies. The things we eat

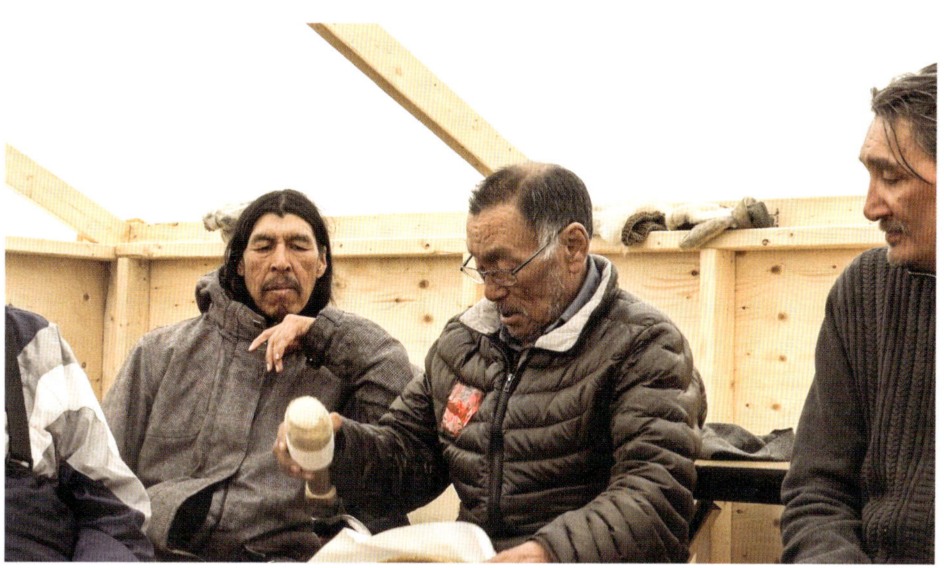

will have to be tested"; "If they continue, the animals won't be there anymore. That's all I have to say"; "I already know what's going on . . . the high area is much colder than the lower area, and if they combine . . . it's a bad sign." Recalling *One Day in the Life of Noah Piugattuk*'s deliberation structure, a translator—now off-screen and addressing the off-screen audience exclusively—translates from Inuktitut to English, yet only approximatively. But both the video and the livecasts value listening more than talking. Listening *enables* different tellings insofar as it provides the necessary silence for each individual to express themselves. The dialogue is thus never direct or straightforward and is not particularly conversational—the comments are answers to Kunuk's questions, but there is no back-and-forth discussion between the members of the group on-screen: each member gives their perspective after

FIGURE 9.3

Isuma, "Stories and Bannok," episode 4 of the Silakut documentary *Silakut Live from the Floe Edge*, webcast live on May 11, 2019 (still). Inuktitut-English. Courtesy of Isuma Distribution International.

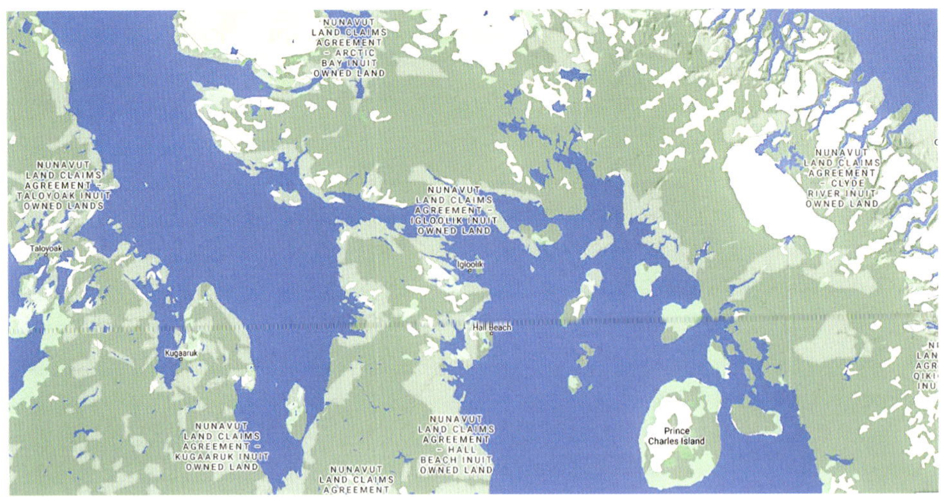

hearing out the other's perspective. We, the audience, are positioned as listeners in the same way: as guests, we are invited to hear out the different worldviews voiced from within the Igloolik community and eventually act accordingly—if we so desire.

A BRIEF HISTORY OF COLONIAL DISPOSSESSION: IGLOOLIK, NUNAVUT

Igloolik (Δᴸᗆᑕᵇ; also spelled "Iglulik" in Inuktitut) is a small island of the Foxe Basin located between the Canadian continental mainland and Baffin Island in the Qikiqtaaluk Region of Nunavut, 200 miles north of the Arctic Circle (figure 9.4). Nunavut (ᓄᓇᕗᑦ) is the largest and northernmost territory of Canada (the fifth-largest country subdivision in the world)—a semiautonomous territory that separated from the Northwest Territories on April 1, 1999, following the Nunavut Act and the Nunavut Land Claims Agreement Act signed in 1993. Nunavut's population—approximatively 36,000 (predominantly Inuit)—lives on a land area of about 1,877,787

FIGURE 9.4

Igloolik, Nunavut, Canada. Map data: Google,
© 2021 Google.

square kilometers; Igloolik's population (95 percent Inuit), estimated at 1,682 in 2016, lives on an area of 103 square kilometers.[17]

Igloolik's first contact with Europeans dates back to 1821–1822, when British navy ships under Captain William Edward Parry's authority stayed there for eight months. The first permanent institutions led by southerners there—a Roman Catholic mission, a Hudson's Bay Company trading post, and then the Northwest Mounted Police—were established in the 1930s. Studies show that Igloolik's (more generally, Nunavut's) *grand renversement* occurred mainly in the 1950s and 1960s. Particularly relevant to Isuma's video-and-webcasts intervention are the early 1940s and more forcibly the two decades following World War II, when the Inuit people and their land became a federal responsibility after most of them were moved off the land. The Canadian government, advocating the need to assist Inuit communities experiencing hardship (notably starvation) after the collapse of the fur trade, began to relocate them into settlements. Inuit were subjected to assimilation policies imposing the "Canadian way of life": pressured to abandon their traditions, they became increasingly dependent on the government for education, health care, police, housing, food, work, social welfare, and other services.[18] Inuit were traditionally hunter-gatherers who migrated regionally and seasonally on the land from camp to camp—large regional groupings divided into smaller seasonal groups in winter camps (called "bands") of approximatively 100 people and summer groupings of about a dozen.[19] The Inuit's seminomadic camp-dwelling existence was transformed—in most cases through internal displacement—into a sedentary lifestyle.[20] Research has shown how this period was devastating to their communities, leading to a profound overturning of Inuit life—which the final report of the recent Truth and Reconciliation Commission of Canada, *Honouring the Truth, Reconciling for the Future* (2015), designated a cultural genocide—"the destruction of those structures and practices that allow the group to continue as a group."[21] As subsistence hunters, they lived interdependently—they depended both on nature and on each other to survive in the harsh Arctic climate; yet that interdependence decreased as their dependency on Qallunaat (White People) increased.[22] Representatives of the Canadian federal government as well as private transport and energy companies progressively made their way into what is now known as Nunavut. A family-allowance program was initiated in 1947, soon to become the primary source of household income among the Inuit.[23] The anthropologist Robert Paine describes this historical moment of government inflow as an "invasion."[24] This was the 1950s and 1960s, the period in which Noah Piugattuk's story unfolds—telling of a subjugation administered by a Qallunaaq area administrator called the "boss," a representative of the Northern Administration Branch of the Canadian Department of Indian Affairs and Northern Development, who supervised most of the settlement operations.[25]

The settlements were both a settling and a welfare-state policy. They were specially one of the means by which Canadian sovereignty was reinforced against the threat of the Soviet Union in the context of the Cold War.[26] As postulated by the cultural psychologist and medical anthropologist Michael Kral, the settlements just about erased the human–nonhuman interdependence structuring Inuit kinship, social organization, and hunting tradition: "The most significant force of change in Inuit history was the creation of settlements in the 1950s and 1960s. . . . [T]he dynamics of change in kinship and social organization were far-reaching and beyond anything Inuit had ever experienced previously."[27] Children were removed from their families and sent to residential, boarding, or day schools—a displacement widely acknowledged today as "one of the most destructive tools fashioned by the federal government in its attempts to forcibly assimilate Aboriginal people"; the Inuit's wealth of geographical knowledge of the land became irrelevant; the distancing between humans and nonhuman animals expanded; ancestral ties to place that anchored Inuit stories, identity, and self-knowledge dissolved; and the Inuit social organization as a social network of cooperation fell apart.[28] Key here is the decline of hunting and fishing, which was central to Inuit communities for subsistence, social organization, and identity. The anthropologist Willem Rasing has specified settlement as one of the major causes of that decline: "Settlement life *enabled survival without hunting. . . .* Sedentary life ended the necessity to hunt for subsistence."[29] Of special relevance to this book's study of contemporary European and North American art's reply to necropolitical migration, sedentarization was made possible by the displacement of the Inuit population through forced internal migration and relocation. One of the most dramatic events of internal displacement is investigated by the writer Melanie McGraph in *The Long Exile: A Tale of Inuit Betrayal and Survival in the High Arctic* (2006),[30] the study of the resettlement of three dozen Inuit from Inukjuak to the Arctic Archipelago—Resolute (Cornwallis Island) and Grise Fiord (Ellesmere Island) in an area now part of Nunavut—in the 1950s. Seeking to affirm the area's strategic geopolitical position in the context of the Cold War, the Canadian federal government repositioned the families, basically abandoning them there in a hostile environment.

As stipulated in chapter 1, I follow here Margaret Kohn's definition of colonialism as "the process of European settlement and political control over the rest of the world, including the Americas, Australia, and parts of Africa and Asia," a process in which violence is inherent.[31] Canada is a settler-colonial state that aimed to replace Indigenous populations with a new society of settlers; the progressive establishment of the settlers' identity, sovereignty, and juridical control over land involved what the historian Patrick Wolfe has called a "logic of elimination" of Indigenous communities.[32] But the Inuit of Nunavut have their own history of colonialism, which is noticeably different from First Nations and Métis histories in Canada. As Kral emphasizes, it consists mainly in "a *colonialisme interne* or domestic colonialism conducted from within a nation, so to speak, even though it has been in the form of a powerful outsider taking over an insider culture. . . . Inuit signed no treaties and had no economically and politically restricting reservations, yet the government created aggregated and restricting settlements."[33] Internal colonialism, a notion developed by a variety of scholars in the 1970s and 1980s—including the political economist Mel Watkins (*Dene Nation: The Colony Within*, 1977), the anthropologist Hugh Brody (*The People's Land*, 1975), and the historians Kenneth Coates and Judith Powell (*The Modern North: People, Politics, and the Rejection of Colonialism*, 1989)—designates a post–World War II necropolitical management of Indigenous peoples and land from within Canada in which economic dependency plays a central role in the upholding of power relations between the colonial rulers and the Natives. Paine, in *The White Arctic: Anthropological Essays on Tutelage and Ethnicity* (1977), speaks more specifically of "welfare colonialism." Although these concepts have been complexified in recent scholarship, their usefulness comes from their insistence on colonialism as a forced disconnection of a people from its land, culture, and community that persists especially in the context of extractive economy. Despite the Nunavut Land Claims Agreement of 1993 (an agreement signed in Iqaluit by representatives of the Tunngavik Federation of Nunavut, the Government of Canada, and the Government of the Northwest Territories, giving the Inuit of the central and eastern Northwest Territories a separate territory called Nunavut) and the Nunavut Act of 1993 (establishing the territory to be known as Nunavut), which gave the Inuit of Nunavut the right to hunt and fish all through the settlement area as well as mineral rights, and allowed them to increase their share of extraction-based wealth, most wealth still advantages non-Inuit jurisdictions. The extractive economy remains a colonial economy because it continues to benefit external interests disproportionately and because it is premised on the dispossession of Indigenous land and resources.[34] As explained by the geographer Warren Bernauer, "According to this model, the core exerts political domination over the periphery, as the latter is wholly dependent on decisions made in the former. . . . The extractive economy develops the core at the expense of the periphery, as most of the wealth produced by extraction—corporate profits, government royalties and taxes, economic multipliers and the resources themselves—flows to the core. . . . The periphery is left with several negative consequences, including environmental degradation and vulnerability to boom bust economic cycles."[35]

As a forced disconnection from land, culture, and community, colonialism has also substantially manifested itself as a form of acculturation. The work of the anthropologist Hugh Brody (*The Other Side of Eden: Hunters, Farmers, and the Shaping of the World*, 2000) and the historian Colin G. Calloway (*One Vast Winter Count: The Native American West before Lewis and Clark*, 2003) shows that colonialism was an attempt to eliminate the interdependence-based kinship system, gift giving, cosmology, shamanism, hunting practices, and oral tradition (including storytelling, singing, and drum dancing) that were pivotal to Inuit survival in the Arctic environment.[36] These externally induced transformations of human–nonhuman interdependence relate to a depreciation of the interrelatedness promoted in Inuit culture—values of and beliefs in connectedness or belongingness that have been identified and now documented by Inuit Elders as intrinsic to Inuit Qaujimajatuqangit (IQ), a body of "beliefs, laws, principles, values, skills, knowledge and attitudes" passed from generation to generation, which serves today as an educational framework for curriculum in Nunavut educational institutions.[37] As stated by the Inuk storyteller and language educator Mark Kalluak, "Inuit Qaujimajatuqangit means knowing the land, names, locations and their history. It also means knowledge of the Arctic environment—of snow, ice, water, weather and the environment that we share. It encompasses being in harmony with people, land and living things—and respecting them."[38] That land-oriented body of knowledge outlines eight fundamental principles: *inuuqatigiitsiarniq* (showing respect and a caring attitude for others); *tunnganarniq* (being welcoming and hospitable to others, being open-hearted and inclusive when interacting with others); *pijitsirniq* (serving others in order to improve the common good); *aajiiqatigiinniq* (making decisions "through discussion and consensus"); *pilimmaksarniq* (developing skills "through observation, mentoring, practice, and effort"); *piliriqatigiinniq* (developing a collaborative relationship or "working together for a common purpose"); *qanuqtuurniq* (being resourceful when solving problems); and *avatimik kamattiarniq* (developing environmental stewardship; being aware of your surroundings and caring for the land, animals, and the environment).[39] These principles are highly relevant to Igloolik's and, more largely, Nunavut's environmental protest against the Mary River Project, centering on the Inuit's request that Baffinland Iron Mines Corporation recognize IQ principles in its development of the mine.[40] These principles ground a definition of coexistence between humans as well as between humans and nonhumans in mutual respect, hospitality, inclusion, commonality, collaboration, consensus-oriented discussion, skill development, the acquisition of knowledge, resourcefulness, and care for the land, animals, and the environment. This ideal is what was and remains depreciated and devalued in colonialism and extractivism; it is what Inuit are attempting to reclaim. Acculturation is not, therefore, a complete *renversement*.

THE HISTORICAL LINK BETWEEN INTERNAL DISPLACEMENT AND ENVIRONMENTAL DEGRADATION

The video and the webcasts were presented together in the same exhibition. They were thought out together and are in fact inseparable. That jointness establishes a historical link between forced migration and the deterioration of the environment. The Canadian government's settlement-oriented policy of internal displacement has significantly disconnected Inuit communities from their land, culture, and community; in so doing, it has opened the door to extractivism and the environmental degradation of the Arctic, whose immediate victims are the Arctic's inhabitants. Such is the tenaciousness of colonial presence, as compellingly described by Ann Laura Stoler in chapter 2. This is what the video and the webcasts work together to disclose. Inuit are not simply climate victims but also first and foremost victims of colonial displacement and dispossession. Despite their dispossession, Inuit have voiced and are voicing their concerns about the environmental deterioration of their land—they are political subjects updating, as it were, Piugattuk's dissensus. Studies show that Arctic Indigenous communities are especially vulnerable to climate change because of their remoteness, their dependency on local species and habitats, and their historical marginalization. They also show Indigenous resilience threatened by the acceleration of sociocultural changes in the communities as well as the "ongoing shifts in seasonal weather patterns," which "may make seasonally specific subsistence adaptations to landscape particularly vulnerable."[41] The video-and-webcasts project is therefore a media intervention of resilience pushed to its limits, a media reclamation and transmission of disappearing traditions and disappearing environments. It is primarily a media public sphere that allows publics to meet around the evolution of the extractive Mary River Project. It seeks to counter these disappearances.

What does that extractive project consist in? I follow here the cultural critic Macarena Gómez-Barris's definition of the extractive view as a perspective that makes not only territories but also peoples extractible, that "sees territories as commodities, rendering land as for the taking, while also devalorizing the hidden worlds that form the nexus of human and nonhuman multiplicity."[42] Extractivism or extractive capitalism, understood both as "the production of value through physically extractive processes (mining, oil extraction, certain kinds of agriculture, etc.)"[43] and as an ideology, reorganizes land, Indigenous populations, and nonhuman life as resources for profit and wealth accumulation. Historically, in northern Canada at least, the disconnection of Inuit from their land facilitated and continues to facilitate this extraction of resources from depopulated territories.

The Mary River Property—I will be brief here—is said to be "one of the most northern mines in the world." It consists in a complex of nine-plus high-grade iron ore deposits (the proportion of iron contained in the ore at the site). Baffinland Iron Mines Corporation acquired the original land claim over the sediments in 1986 to develop a mine on the property. This mine became the Mary River Project, which was expanded in 2012. Key to its ongoing development was the Inuit Impact and Benefits Agreement signed in 2013 with the Qikiqtani Inuit Association, which led to the federal approval of the project—an agreement that ensures benefits from the corporation's operation flow to nearby communities in North Baffin. The agreement allows Baffinland exploration and resource-development rights to 170 square kilometers of Inuit-owned land adjacent to the mine site. Baffinland Iron Mines is now in the process of seeking approval of its phase-two expansion to double and eventually triple iron ore production and export (from an estimated 4.2 to 6 million tons of iron ore to 12 million tons a year), including the construction of a 110-kilometer railway to carry the iron ore from the mine to Milne Inlet, near Pond Inlet, Nunavut, from where it will be shipped throughout the world.[44] The project has raised significant environmental concerns within the scientific community as well as within the Inuit community. In 2008, in an interview with the Canadian

Broadcasting Corporation, Igloolik resident Jaypetee Palluq and the former mayor of Igloolik, Paul Quassa, had already expressed their concern that the mine's operations would hinder the hunting of the walrus "because [the project's] proposed marine shipping route cuts through Foxe Basin, where generations of Inuit have hunted for walrus."[45] These concerns persist today, together with more precise concerns over the effect of freighters on the ice necessary for the survival of marine mammals (notably, the walrus and the narwhal—an arctic-dwelling whale that relies on sound to navigate, communicate, and find its prey but now found to be less vocal near the mine shipping routes); the railway's anticipated "major impact for the North Baffin caribou herd whose population is currently at a critically low level"; Baffinland's acknowledgment of fuel spills and water contamination claimed to have been "damage free"; the company's inability to demonstrate its capacity to reduce greenhouse-gas emissions—considered to be one of the main causes of human-induced climate change; and complaints from members of Inuit communities of a loud hum or buzz soundscape evolving within the Fury Strait and Hecla Strait and distressing the sea mammals that the communities rely on for food.[46] In November 2017, the Pond Inlet, Mary River Phase 2 Review Committee chaired by Enookie Inuarak submitted a report to the Nunavut Planning Commission, stipulating its position on phase two: "The Baffinland Phase 2 Review Committee of the Hamlet of Mittimitalik is opposed to the construction of a railway in this corridor. The Hunters and Trappers Organization, represented on the committee, passed a motion on September 29, 2017. The HTO rejects the Phase 2 Plan put forward by Baffinland. They, and the committee, do not support Baffinland's request to build a railway and plans for winter sealift shipping. The Committee is aware that plans for winter sealift shipping have since been withdrawn."[47]

The Nunavut Impact Review Board held its hearings on the expansion in Iqaluit in November 2019. The hearings were transmitted on IsumaTV by Digital Indigenous Democracy. Kunuk's initial plan had been to film the proceedings of the board hearings and to hold interviews with the intervenors.[48] The hearings were initiated but have been suspended. The conflict is still ongoing. As the Isuma video artist and filmmaker Norman Cohn explained, "One of the main reasons that Aluki Kotierk, President of Nunavut Tunngavik Inc. (and daughter of Apayata Kotierk, the actor of *Noah*), cited for asking that the hearings be postponed 9–12 months was her assertion that Baffinland had failed to acknowledge the importance of IQ in its development of the mine and its proposals."[49] More specifically, according to Cohn, the Nunavut Land Claims Agreement [NLCA] gave Inuit Title (ownership) to 17% of the land surface in the Nunavut Settlement Area and 5% of the sub-surface mineral rights under that 17% of surface ownership. While the Crown now legally "owns" the rest of the land and sub-surface rights, all of Nunavut is subject to the NLCA's constitutional "treaty" protection of Inuit rights in general. One of the general rights the NLCA protects is the consultative importance of Inuit Qaujimajatuqangit in all developments in the Nunavut Settlement Area that impact Inuit. . . . That's what is happening to Baffinland, and that's what's new in the past two years. NLCA treaty rights are amplified on Inuit-owned land[,] giving Inuit more political and legal leverage to require Baffinland to listen to IQ or risk more effective opposition.[50]

The Inuit opposition is also based on the United Nations Declaration on the Rights of Indigenous Peoples, passed in 2007 and endorsed by Canada in 2010, which states that member states must consult with Indigenous peoples on specific matters, such as "legislative or administrative measures that may affect them," to obtain their consent. It is likewise based on rights guaranteed under section 35 of the Canadian Constitution Act of 1982. These rights have been protected and reaffirmed in Canadian courts, which have established "the doctrine of the duty to consult and, where appropriate, accommodate Indigenous groups."[51] As the lawyer Isabelle Brideau specifies, the Supreme Court of Canada's guideline of the duty to consult "is to foster reconciliation."[52] In one of the most famous cases enouncing that doctrine, *Tsilhqot'in Nation v. British Columbia* (2014 SCC 44), the Supreme Court of Canada stated that Indigenous title over land derives from the sufficient, continual, and exclusive "occupation" of the land, an occupation that includes Indigenous culture, hunting, and fishing.[53] The Inuit communities of Nunavut are therefore engaged in a legal and political dispute with the Government of Canada and Baffinland Iron Mines on that very basis—a battle on the matter of use of and access to land, including control over the development of natural resources, extractivism, and environmental protection.[54]

Note, however, how the speakers in the webcasts never simply blame citizens living south of the Nunavut mainland—they question the activities of the multinational company sustaining the Mary River Project as well as the Canadian government. The point of the webcasts is to speak about the problem and make it as public as possible. The campaign's model of responsibility is forward looking. It seeks a public sphere understood as a practice of social connection. It seeks to resume the sphere of the 1960s represented in *One Day in the Life of Noah Piugattuk* but lost through displacement. Some members of the group mention—often as a statement—how the people from the south could help fund their cause, but the campaign is never about Inuit saying that environmental degradation is a condition lived in the same way by everyone on the planet; they insist mostly on the problem of the Mary River Project being an Inuit cause—they are the main actors and not simply the victims seeking pity or empathy from the rest of Canada or the rest of the world. This Nation-to-Nation approach is "consistent" with the aims of Indigenous self-determination.[55] It is their cause, and, strategically, their cause needs to be heard by the largest public possible, including Inuit and non-Inuit peoples. Hence, the value of the livecasts, which, while being firmly sited in the floe edge ("where the open sea meets the frozen sea"[56]), can potentially be heard from everywhere and by anyone on the planet to reestablish and reaffirm what colonialism works to disconnect: the connection between land, culture, environment, identity, and knowledge. Implied, of course, is the hope that the webcasts' publics realize that this cause is not only worthwhile, especially in light of the Canadian government's responsibility for the internal displacement of Inuit populations, but also beneficial to all as an ongoing cause in which they must get involved once they become aware of the environmental predicament they participate in. The voices from territories south of the Nunavut mainland were not heard in the webcasts; for now, it is too early to assess the scope of their responses. But they were certainly invited to become aware. That becoming-aware follows the logic of the webcasted counterpublic sphere encounter among members of the Igloolik community, where each member expresses dissent—as would the classical Habermassian public sphere—but only by listening, only *after* listening, to each other. They listen to the tellers' expertise. As the geographer Andrew Baldwin concludes from his investigation of the impact of climate change on Newtok, Alaska, residents, "Their invocation of human rights" is based mainly "on their historical knowledge of the land from which they have been forcibly displaced."[57]

THE REINVENTION OF THE PUBLIC SPHERE

What is Isuma's video-and-webcasts intervention of 2019 if not a public-sphere instantiation? Cohn has identified it as such,[58] although one that substantially redefines the Habermassian formulation. Let us recall Habermas's conceptualization of that particular form of critical publicity. In *The Structural Transformation of the Public Sphere* (first published in 1962 and translated into English in 1989), Habermas defined the modern public sphere as a realm of social life where public opinion takes shape. This realm forms itself around rational-critical deliberations between individuals who "come together as a public" as they debate on matters of general interest and common concern.[59] Its ideal type is the eighteenth-century bourgeois public sphere, whose efficiency lay in its capacity to act as a normative principle of democratic legitimacy, producing public opinion that influenced political action against the domination of the state. In subsequent revisions of his formulation, Habermas emphasized the role of deliberative language and communicative rationality in the consolidation of the public sphere, which he redefined as "a network for communicating information," where participants rationally express their points of view by adopting positions and assuming illocutionary obligations that support mutual speech acts.[60]

The Habermassian theorization of the public sphere has been contested from the start. Critics have questioned its alleged universalism as well as its rationalist structure. The critical theorist Nancy Fraser has shown that the bourgeois public sphere was constituted through a considerable number of exclusions—women and other social groups, who in fact constituted counterpublics where members could formulate oppositional understandings of their identities and interests.[61] The philosophers Oskar Negt and Alexander Kluge have demonstrated the interdependence between the bourgeois public sphere and the proletarian counterpublic sphere.[62] The political philosopher Chantal Mouffe has contested Habermas's rationalistic model of argumentation and has proposed instead an agonistic model where antagonism is *the* necessary passion of politics.[63] Media scholars have shown that the interpersonal relationships composing the public sphere were much more mediated than Habermas initially presumed and that the development of mass media does not necessarily lead to the decline of the public sphere.[64]

In light of these critiques, what remains of the public sphere today, and what can be rescued from it? How can it be reinvented to address forced migration, including that migration's colonial unfolding as well as its environmental causes and consequences? How can the public sphere be rethought as a coexistence based on Inuit Qaujimajatuqangit principles? Much more passionate and mediated than initially formulated, certainly much weaker in a postfactual society, Isuma's video-and-webcasts public sphere has three main features. First, it consists in an Inuit counterpublic sphere. Second, it explores the webcast technology to counter cyberbalkanization, attempting to reach any region in the world above, within, and below the Arctic Circle. The webcasts are from the Igloolik floe edge, but they seek the interdependence between Inuit communities and any other interested public—thus sustaining the view that while decolonization requires "the repatriation of land," as Eve Tuck and K. Wayne Yang have convincingly maintained, land is not promoted here as a thing or a commodity to be owned and controlled by a specific community but as a creation that all peoples should experience as a caring relationship, following the principle of mutual respect between nations as well as between humans and nonhumans.[65] Third, the video-and-webcasts public sphere includes storytell/ing: the deliberations between members of the Igloolik community reenact the "oral delivery and aural reception" of storytelling as a collective voice. This is not a united, homogeneous, and resolved voice, and listening plays a privileged role in this voicing. The webcasted statements from the Inuit members assembled together in their own counterpublic sphere, listening to each other yet also asking their publics to listen as well, redefine the public sphere as a foundational listening practice: "Do they hear what the Inuit want?" In their individual statements, they advocate for a connection between publics not only across difference but also through listening: "We would have to have meetings ourselves . . . our people. . . . We would have to expect something from us for ourselves and not people who want to land"; "People would have to start helping each other more and negotiate with each other for all that to stop"; "We are live right now all over. We are showing this in Venice. We want these people to know and we want you guys to watch when we are live. . . . We want to get help from the people instead of just saying this"; "I want people to know"; "Since they are looking for iron or in this area, we are trying to prevent this from happening and we will talk about it and you guys just listen."

Listening might well be the forgotten practice of our times. Could it not be envisaged as a way to weaken postfactuality—a mode of listening to the other's story that holds open, as suggested by the philosopher Jean-Luc Nancy, the threshold between sending and resending, sense and signification?[66] Isuma's reinvention of the public sphere is fundamentally based on the revalorization of listening; this is how storytell/ing unfolds to structure the public-sphere deliberations that bring to the fore the historical link between internal displacement and environmental degradation. This is crucial. What type of listening does this reinvention uphold?

The work of the Stó:lō scholar Dylan Robinson, who specializes in the study of Indigenous music, art, and culture, shows how listening in and of itself is not a solution to a problem; it doesn't necessarily sustain reciprocity. Listening is mobilized by positionalities—by "how we listen as Indigenous, settler, and variously positioned subjects."[67] Resonating with María Puig de la Bellacasa's invocation—that the question "How to care?" be raised in any assessment of care—Robinson's book *Hungry Listening: Resonant Theory for Indigenous Sound Studies* (2020) integrates the question "How to listen?" into the activity of listening. He especially draws our attention to a recursive positionality called "hungry listening," which persists even in inclusive and collaborative performing practices between Indigenous and non-Indigenous musicians as well as between Indigenous musicians and settler audiences. Hungry listening reproduces the colonial, colonialist, and neocolonial conditioning of perception that seeks to "civilize" and assimilate Indigenous voices and "that has been imposed on Indigenous people who grew up in residential school, boarding school, and day school systems; who were part of the sixties and seventies scoop; who have been disfranchised by the Indian Act and forced migration; who grew up on-rez and in urban centers."[68] Following the journalist and environmental activist Naomi Klein's insight into extractivism—as being not only a mining and drilling practice but more importantly a colonialist assimilative "mindset" in which not only land but also Indigenous people and knowledge are seen as resources "to be mined"—Robinson defines hungry listening as an extractivist activity.[69] Settlers (a term generically used to refer to non-Indigenous citizens living in a tenaciously colonialist country, such as Canada) absorb what is "digestible" to them in Indigenous music—sonorities, song content, and stories (from trauma to healing to reconciliation) that "fit" their sensibility—but without transforming their own positionality.[70] Seeking reciprocal performances where listening encounters between Indigenous and settler positionalities resist extractivism (a resistance designated "Indigenous+art music"), Robinson proposes the privileging of sound over recognizable (digestible) content and the hearing of the land as we listen to music and songs; he also asks that musicians and listeners "attend to being between . . . ontologies and sound worlds" so that the incommensurability of Indigenous and settler cultures can be preserved.[71] Sound is therefore understood "in its irreducible alterity": as María Puig de la Bellacasa's and Carlo Caduff's conceptualization of care (discussed in chapter 5) emphasizes, listening gains in reciprocity when alterity, what Glissant has designated as the right to opacity, perseveres.[72] It also gains in incommensurability: Indigenous and settler cultures are ultimately incomparable, unmergeable, never fully bridgeable; I would also add that speakers and listeners in general are ultimately unmergeable. Let us recall Caduff: "What care reveals, here, is a dimension of alterity at the heart of intimacy. . . . To care is to endure the noise of the other. It's a response to and a symptom of the difficulty of being in relation."[73] But that difficulty—caring, listening—is what makes these practices less hungry, less assimilative, more reciprocal, and, hence, greater occasions for light and solidarity.

Isuma's reinvented storytell/ing public sphere privileges listening between members of Inuit communities as well as between Inuit communities and those south of the Nunavut mainland. But Robinson's critical questioning of hungry listening asks that we complicate our understanding of listening. The off-screen publics listen, but are they not more specifically invited to listen differently from hungry listening? Isn't listening troubled by the question "How to listen?" I maintain that it is and that this troubling is constitutive of a unique form of public sphere. Let us not forget that Isuma is a great supporter of the Inuit Qaujimajatuqangit principles; IQ's privileging of listening is mobilized by the ideals of mutual respect, commonality, collaboration, consensus-oriented discussion, the acquisition of knowledge, and care for humans and nonhumans (the land, animals, and the environment). Isuma's work does not guarantee that these principles will be respected, but the video and the webcasts certainly attempt to promote them in their respective public spheres. In her study of Indigenous storytelling, the Stó:lō scholar Jo-ann Archibald defines Native storytelling as a form of education and transmission of knowledge and community values; it is structured, she maintains, by the following Elders' principles (recalling but not identified as the IQ principles): "respect, responsibility, reciprocity, reverence, holism, interrelatedness, and synergy."[74] Reciprocal yet differentiated listening holds a pivotal role in that tradition: it is the activity that keeps the stories alive—the aural receiver is responsible for passing the stories on to other generations; the new storytellers contribute to the communal, collaborative principle of storytelling as they add their perspective to the story; listening is therefore understood as a demanding form of multisensory and affective engagement.[75] Research on Indigenous pedagogies by the Māori scholar of education Linda Tuhiwai Smith has likewise shown that storytelling and oral-tradition conventions, including "structured silences," are devised to develop trust and to share information, perspectives, and strategies; they help to establish contact in meetings and networking between Indigenous peoples.[76] Isuma's webcast public sphere sustains these principles. But let us be more explicit about the aesthetic strategies that work to actualize these principles while preserving the incommensurability of Inuit and non-Inuit cultures. Three major storytell/ing strategies stand out: the decentering of the Venice Biennale's public, mistranslation, and the effective yet never fully achieved reconnection between story and land.

First, note how the video-and-webcasts intervention brings about a major decentering of the Venice Biennale's usual modus operandi—an international event that people go to in order to visit art exhibitions: the video and webcasts were made in Igloolik; they featured people who have lived there and are living there; they were available online on IsumaTV not only to the Igloolik community but also to visitors of the Venice Biennale and worldwide during and after the event. This decentering is pivotal to Isuma's public sphere: it temporarily reverses colonialism's core–periphery dynamic to propose a storytelling practice in which the periphery provisionally becomes the center. This shift articulates the changeability of positions between tellers and listeners; it destabilizes and debunks their standardization; the tellers and the listeners unexpectedly become unknown to one another in order to make room for the incommensurability of Inuit and non-Inuit publics.

Second, the translations—the Inuk interpreter's translation from Inuktitut to English and from English to Inuktitut (to which must be added the English and French subtitles) in *One Day in the Life of Noah Piugattuk* and the off-screen translations from Inuktitut to English in the *Silakut Live from the Floe Edge* webcasts—are systematically hesitant and interrupted by moments of silence; they regularly activate or imply misinterpretations. This specific exploration of (mis)translation entails that although we, the off-screen public, are invited to listen, part of what we are listening to escapes us; it is often impossible to know for sure if the interpreter is in fact misinterpreting or not. As the work of the anthropologist Murielle Nagy has shown, non-Inuit researchers doing fieldwork in the Arctic rely on recorded translations of oral narratives and their own interpretations of these translations to study Inuit communities—a practice that makes misinterpretations unavoidable: "Translations are not perfect duplicates of the original narratives; they are only equivalents. . . . Although translators do their best to transfer into another language what the narrators have said, there are times when the original meaning of words and expressions is distorted, if not lost, during the translation process. Furthermore, once anthropologists interpret translated narratives, there is another level of translation going on, and if the translations do not represent the

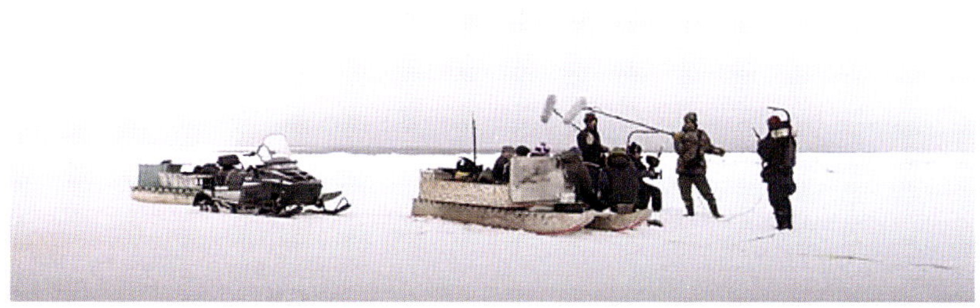

intention of the narrator, elements of the narratives may be misinterpreted."[77] That situation sustains the teller–translator–listener relationship mobilized in Isuma's video-and-webcasts intervention. At the premiere of *One Day in the Life of Noah Piugattuk* held at the Toronto International Film Festival in September 2019, Kunuk confirmed his exploration of mistranslation as key to the history of misunderstanding between Inuit and non-Inuit communities: "That's part of the story. All the misunderstanding that goes through in this film, is the story."[78] But Nagy has also insightfully suggested that the recurrence of and the anthropologist's dependency on mistranslation do not necessarily constitute an impasse for the study of Inuit life insofar as (mis)translations themselves can become a source of information on Inuit language and culture. It might well be the case that the translator chose to mistranslate the narrator's words specifically "to get the closest equivalent in the language of the translation and thus make the translation more fluid" or because

FIGURE 9.5

Isuma, "Stories and Bannok," episode 4 of the Silakut documentary *Silakut Live from the Floe Edge*, webcast live on May 11, 2019 (still). Inuktitut-English. Courtesy of Isuma Distribution International.

the translator "could not find similar concepts in the language of the translation."[79] In Isuma's video and webcasts, mistranslation can similarly be productively understood as the incapacity to fully translate words from one language to another. Mistranslation becomes a tool of resistance—a way *not* to make Inuit stories fully digestible by the listening settlers: a right to opacity à la Glissant. Mistranslation may well have caused misunderstanding between Inuit and non-Inuit communities, but it is also a strategy to preserve their incommensurability, to keep hungry listening and hungry coexistence at bay, to encourage reciprocal yet differentiated listening, deep listening.

Third, the video-and-webcasts intervention keeps connecting storytelling and the land—storytell/ing is about, from, and of the land (figure 9.5). Can it not be posited that the intervention's land situatedness is an aesthetic strategy elaborated not only to reclaim the land but also to let the land—the floe edge, the melting ice, an offshore island—listen to its own environment? As listeners, we (the publics) are continually asked to listen to the ice as it responds to its human and nonhuman surroundings. Land itself is a sensor; glaciers listen, to paraphrase the title of the Canadian anthropologist Julie Cruikshank's book *Do Glaciers Listen? Local Knowledge, Colonial Encounters, and Social Imagination* (2005). Listening is both a human and nonhuman activity; nonhuman listening is a component of the public sphere. The discussion of Forensic Oceanography's work in chapter 4 showed how *Liquid Traces—the Left-to-Die Boat Case* explored the Mediterranean Sea as a sensor: water was described as prehending the shipwrecks. But to be read as a sensor and to make sense of the sea prehensions, the sea had to be captured by other analog or digital sensors (FO's repurposed technologies of surveillance). In Isuma's work, the disclosure of land as a sensor of its surroundings relies not only on analog storytelling but also on digital video and webcasting. This decentering of the human listener must likewise be seen as a powerful aesthetic strategy that disables hungry listening: it sustains the incommensurability of listeners tout court. Storytell/ing's reconnection of story, land, and technology, of human and nonhuman tellers and listeners, is a vital decolonial practice that disrupts the colonial disconnection of land, culture, and community, but the reconnection remains slightly out of joint insofar as it never discloses or matches, once and for all, what and how each component prehends.

WEIRD STORIES ABOUT HOSPITALITY

In 2017, a 16.3-meter-high concrete obelisk by the Nigerian American artist Olu Oguibe (b. 1964, Aba, Federal Republic of Nigeria) was commissioned for documenta 14 and installed in Kassel's Königsplatz square (figure 10.1). Entitled *Das Fremdlinge und Flüchtlinge Monument* (Monument for Strangers and Refugees), it bears a gold inscription on each of its four sides: "I was a stranger and you took me in" (from the Book of Matthew 25:35) in four different languages—Arabic, English, German, and Turkish. The monument rapidly became controversial, especially in the aftermath of the exhibition when the city of Kassel initiated a fund-raising campaign to purchase the work. Transmitting a pro-refugee message in Kassel's central public square, it "struck a chord in a country deeply divided over its refugee policy."[1] Seen as an endorsement of Chancellor Angela Merkel's open-door policy, which welcomed more than one million refugees to Germany in 2015, its acquisition was contested mainly by local right-wing politicians. The obelisk was vandalized in January 2018; it was purchased by the city in June 2018 but dismantled for relocation in October 2018 initially without Oguibe's knowledge or consent. The dispute was resolved with the reinstallation of the work in 2019 on Treppenstraße, a staircase pedestrian street between the Hauptbahnhof station and Friedrichsplatz, close to Königsplatz.[2]

The polemic over *Das Fremdlinge und Flüchtlinge Monument* was not simply an overreaction expressed by a group of worried xenophobes. Rather, it obliquely disclosed the obelisk's countermonumentality, which is still effective today and will

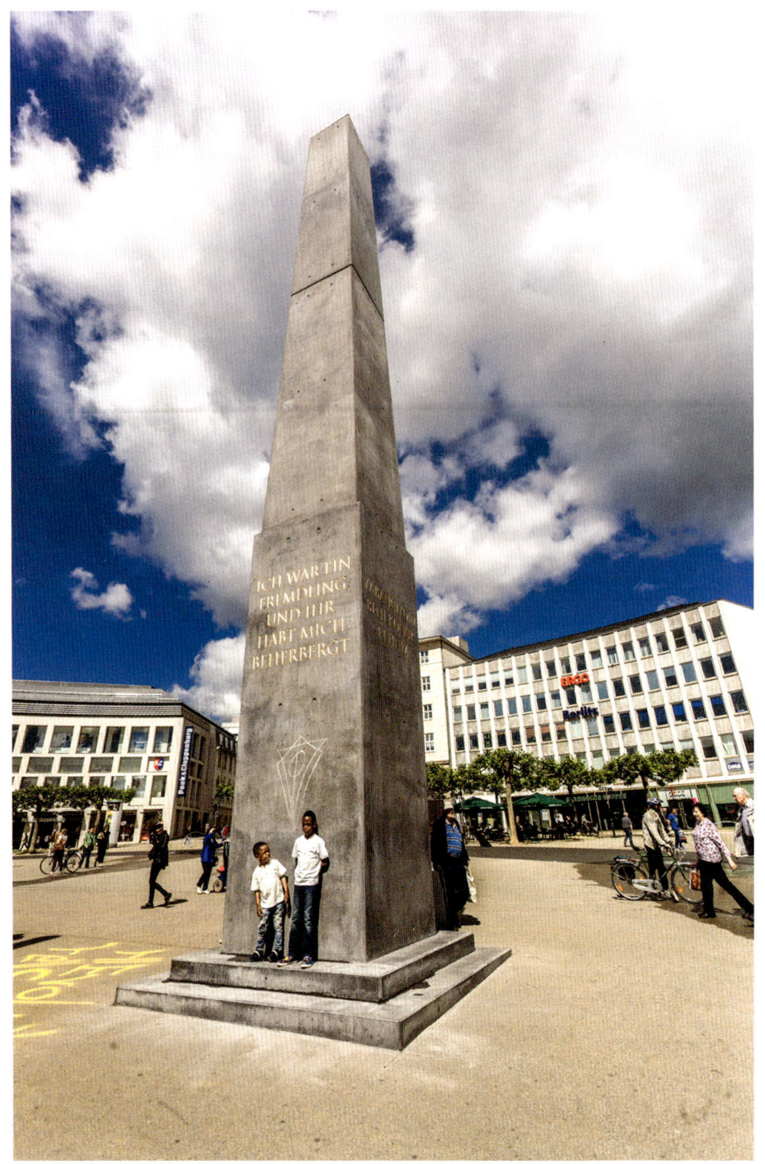

FIGURE 10.1

Olu Oguibe, *Das Fremdlinge und Flüchtlinge
Monument* (Monument for Strangers
and Refugees), 2017. Permanent public
sculpture. Concrete, stainless steel, and
gold leaf. 9¾ × 9¾ × 58½ ft. (3 × 3 × 16.3 m).
Installation view: documenta 14, Königsplatz,
Kassel, Germany. Photo: © Cum Okolo/Alamy
Stock Photo. Courtesy of the artist.

be for many years to come, and which brought to the fore the unresolved tensions between refugeehood and hosting. That countermonumentality lies first and foremost in the obelisk's disruption of the standard temporal codes of monuments: it is less a commemoration of a past historical event than a designation of the ongoing historical present—Europe's self-professed refugee crisis (twenty-first-century migration, tout court) in which "strangers" primarily from Africa and central and western Asia leave their country and seek refuge in the EU to escape living conditions made unbearable by war, structural violence, persecution, and chronic poverty. That historical present remains unsettled, and these "strangers" are not absolute foreigners insofar as many of them come from Europe's former colonies. The installation itself became a displaced object searching for a new home, materializing the wandering fate of migrating beings. Its countermonumentality also unfolds semiotically and semantically: the inscription doesn't refer to anyone in particular; its use of personal pronouns (*I*, *you*, and *me*) is open-ended and unstable. The pronouns are "shifters" in the linguistic, Jakobsonian sense of that notion: their referent is determined in relation to the situational context of their use—the actual addresser and addressee as well as the time and place they are uttered, read, and interpreted. When apprehended in 2017, the inscription was an acknowledgment of European hosting in a period when hospitality had recently expanded but then quickly started to close down again, failing and fading. In 2021 and 2022, the inscription confirms itself as a continuous meditation on the waning of hospitality in a period when the European migration and border regime has become highly restrictive and when refugee status is only exceptionally granted to asylum seekers (as explained in chapter 2). The claim "I was a stranger and you took me in" suddenly loops and reverses; the gratitude twists into a series of questions. Worryingly, it asks the viewer: What and when is hosting? Who is hosting? Why and how to host? There are, after all, many ways to take a stranger in; hosts, after all, are rarely absolute hosts; and the stranger, after all, might well be me or you.

This chapter examines artistic practices that explore loops when responding to necropolitical migration as a constellation of typically unrecognized and undervalued (im)migration crises. They explore what the object-oriented philosopher Timothy Morton has called "weird knowing"—a form of knowledge that comes about when "two levels that appear utterly separate flip into one another" or when a line is twisted to form a curve within itself to allow another curved line to pass through, as in a loop.[3] In Oguibe's *Das Fremdlinge und Flüchtlinge Monument*, what at first appeared to be a confirmation of generosity and gratitude flips into an anxious meditation on hospitality—the indebtedness and the anxiety were in fact always connected, but it is only when the flip occurs that we become aware of their connectedness, of their possible reversibility within the evolving distressing context of migration. The three artworks discussed in this chapter—Stan Douglas's *Doppelgänger* (2019), Decolonizing Architecture Art Research's *Al-Madhafah/The Living Room* (2016–2021), and Kent Monkman's *mistikôsiwak (Wooden Boat People)* (2019)—produce these loops to rethink the hospitality that sustains and mostly fails to sustain present-day migration. Storytell/ing becomes a flipping device that uncovers Europe's and North America's limited and shrinking view of hospitality, but it also invents new hosting practices articulated from the perspective of the ill-named stranger.

The hospitality of countries of destination is an imperative for any citizen-on-the-move seeking asylum or refuge. The artworks considered here fully support yet raise substantial questions about that imperative: Who gets to host? Who has the power to host and unhost? Why, when, and how is hospitality? They raise these questions—and this is the chapter's main claim—by looping storytelling, by elaborating a storytell/ing that takes its "/" from weird knowing in which "two levels that appear utterly separate flip into one another." The flip that operates the weirdness affirms hospitality as a coexistence between countries of origin and countries of destination, between on the one hand citizens migrating not only from some of the poorest but also (surprisingly!) from some of the richest economies worldwide *and* on the other hand not only hosting citizens but also citizens-on-the-move (surprisingly yet again!) of some of the wealthiest economies worldwide. The standard dualisms of twenty-first-century migration are themselves becoming slippery. The flip shows hospitality as an interdependence shaped by unexpected reversals: gratitude becomes angst; welcoming transmutes into detaining; guests turn into hosts and hosts into guests. To substantiate my claim, I start with a brief clarification of Morton's notion of weird knowing; I then mobilize that notion as an analytical tool in my examination of the three works. This analysis is followed by a larger discussion on the challenge of hospitality in matters of migration, where I confront the writings of two major thinkers of that concept—Étienne Balibar and Jacques Derrida—to tease out art's original contribution to that debate. The chapter's overall call is for storytell/ing as a weird flipping procedure: it defines that interpellation from the perspective of the artworks to reconsider the problematic hospitalities sustaining migration today.

Timothy Morton's notion of weird looping or weird knowledge has been formulated not in relation to issues of migration but in relation to environmental degradation. My general understanding of coexistence is nevertheless based on Morton's book where the notion is conceptualized: *Dark Ecology: For a Logic of Future Coexistence* (2016). Suffice it to say that weird looping is as applicable to understanding the necropolitics of migration as it is to studying the Anthropocene—the period in which human activities are said to have become the primary cause of global warming. For each, it pertains to a similar mode of knowledge. Morton contends that although the Anthropocene has scientifically been defined as our current geological period, human-derived environmental degradation is more deeply rooted in a mode of thinking and living that precedes this period, namely the Holocene or even earlier. He designates that mode of knowledge as "agrilogistical," inherent to the logistics of agriculture: it rests on the construction of rigid boundaries between nature and culture (more precisely, the "severance" between human and nonhuman worlds); it also rests on the belief in consistency, noncontradiction, and the metaphysics of presence. Ecologically driven, Morton's work proposes to replace that logic with "ecognosis," a mode of knowledge production that pertains to "coexisting" in that it accepts and prospers on contradictions, inconsistency, and strangeness: a "knowing in a loop—a *weird* knowing" in which "two levels that appear utterly separate flip into one another." Ecognosis is a philosophy and politics of coexistence that involves weirdness insofar as the interdependences it reveals appear uncanny and uncannily. It becomes especially tangible with the Anthropocenic gesture and the ecological interpretation of that gesture: for example, the simple starting of one's car (the act of ignition). When I turn the key, my personal intention is not to destroy lifeforms or, more generally, to destroy the Earth—it is a blind action; it is also the case that my action is "statistically meaningless," but when that action is "scaled up to Earth magnitude so that there are billions of hands that are turning billions of ignitions in billions of starting engines every minute," the sixth mass extinction event is specifically what starting the ignition is both instigating and sustaining.[4] As I become unexpectedly aware of that connection, I discover that I am causally responsible for the event; "I am the criminal"; the change of scale makes me realize that what seemed to be distinct—ignition and the sixth mass extinction event, the human species and I, humanity and geophysics—are in fact deeply related.

Morton's main assertion is that today, the growing planetary awareness of the climate crisis is forcing a transformation in human thought: humans can no longer continue to try to transcend their reliance on other humans and, more deeply, on nonhuman beings and things.

Particularly relevant to artistic practices that investigate looping devices to expose and change the coexistence of migrating and hosting beings in matters of hospitality is Morton's claim that ecognosis—a logic of coexistence that alleviates the Anthropocene's repression of the relatedness of humans and nonhumans—relies on loosening our commitment to the axioms of agrilogistics, in particular the axiom of noncontradiction but also the axiom of presence according to which "existing means being constantly present"—the myth that a thing is real insofar as it is consistently "there" and in full adequacy with itself, the metaphysics that makes it easier for humans to resolve an inconsistency by inventing an action or a tool that will purportedly put an end to it.[5] Seeking alternatives to these axioms, Morton draws on the work of the French feminist philosopher Luce Irigaray to propose a weird essentialism in which all things have an essence (a form, an identity, a substance without which it would not be that thing) even while that essence remains indeterminate. Let us recall this passage from Irigaray's *This Sex Which Is Not One* (*Ce sexe qui n'en est pas un*, 1977): "Woman 'touches herself' all the time, . . . for her genitals are formed of two lips in continuous contact. Thus, within herself, she is already two—but not divisible into one(s)—that caress each other."[6] Weird essentialism is one in which an essence (here, woman) is never resolvable as a separate entity (it is never simply one). Morton also draws on object-oriented ontology to temporalize this claim: if things are not constantly present, it is because they continue to exist even when they have ceased to be concepts or visible phenomena. In other words, beings do not "coincide with their phenomena."[7] To account for the fundamental relatedness of humans and nonhumans—a relatedness that agrilogistics works to suppress in order to rid itself of the inherent inconsistency of things but that ecognosis anxiously welcomes—Morton wants to think knowledge weirdly, to be able to account for existing things and existing coexistences even though they are not discrete, even if they are not phenomenally present, even if they are contradictory, even if they are not consistent.

In his subsequent book, *Humankind: Solidarity with Nonhuman People* (2017), Morton expands his investigation of ecology to include humankind. That expansion is particularly useful to this chapter, which mostly (though not exclusively) addresses the deep relatedness between humans in practices of hospitality. He further defines ecognosis as the necessary weird knowledge mode of the twenty-first century because of the mode's emphasis on two crucial properties of "humankind" (as opposed to "humanity," which rests on the severance of humans and nonhumans). First, humankind is an ecological being: in contrast to humanity, humankind is a symbiotic real in which seemingly opposite components (the chief example here is the parasite and its host) uncannily rely on one another, following affiliations that never simply stabilize. Second, humans and nonhumans coexist in a relation of solidarity: this is the phenomenology or manifestation of the symbiotic real as such.[8]

These features, principles, and procedures are inherent to ecognosis as weird knowing. Ecognosis is a looping activity that uncannily discloses the unsuspected coexistence of levels of reality from which more reciprocal coexistences can be thought out. As a mode of knowledge that privileges contradiction, nonphenomenal presence, discrepancy, weirdness, and looping, ecognosis replaces agrilogistics to establish the interdependence between humans, between humans and nonhumans; it is a plea for humankind as a counterpart to humanity and humanism. Knowing in a loop—weird knowing—can also be understood as potentially productive for the perception and understanding of what Ann Laura Stoler has named the indiscernible "tenacious presence" of colonial subjugation or, more precisely, the "*strange* continuity" between colonial past and present.[9] Weirdness, analogous to John Akomfrah's montage aesthetics of coexistence discussed in chapter 2, is a storytell/ing strategy that "train[s] our senses beyond the more easily identifiable forms" of resilient colonialities.[10] These features will help us tease out the productivity of the three artworks examined in this chapter. As demonstrated in the subsequent sections, these artworks loop storytelling to rethink the hospitality that sustains today's migration; they are looking for hospitality as a humankind coexistence.

DOPPELGÄNGER

Doppelgänger (2019) by the Canadian artist Stan Douglas (b. 1960, Vancouver, Canada), an approximatively 26-minute-long two-channel video installation shown in a loop, was initially presented in Ralph Rugoff's *May You Live in Interesting Times*, the 58th International Art Exhibition held in 2019 in the context of the Biennale di Venezia. The work proposes a distinctive ecognostic understanding and extrapolation of the imperiling reception of citizens-on-the-move in North America (although the geopolitical context is never specifically named; it could involve Europe), here targeted against a Black citizen. The installation is a call for storytell/ing—a storytelling that unfolds as an invitation to unlearn (im)migration, to become aware of how its heroes can easily become its victims, whose fate lies mostly in the hands of state authorities who have the power to host and unhost. *Doppelgänger* is a fiction, and Douglas is the storyteller, but he explores storytell/ing in a video installation that includes us, the viewers in the gallery space, confronted as we are by the continual looping of what we see, of what we hear.

As its title, the installation uses the word *doppelgänger* (from the German *doppel-*, "double," and *-gänger*, "goer"), referring in German folklore to the "apparition of a living person," in contrast to a ghost, or more precisely to a spiritual double, which, should one meet it, is a sign of one's approaching death.[11] In literature, the concept appears in E. T. A. Hoffmann's early novel *Die Elixiere des Teufels* (*The Devil's Elixirs*, 1815–1816), about a man who finds and liberates his double, sentenced to death for the crimes the man himself has committed—the murders of the brother and stepmother of the woman he loves; this release, however, eventually allows the doppelgänger to murder the man's loved one. It also appears in Fyodor Dostoyevsky's *The Double* (1846)—the story of a clerk, Golyadkin, whose character failings are exploited by his double, who takes over his life by flourishing in everything at which the clerk has failed. The figure of the doppelgänger is also central, though less explicitly, to Hoffmann's short story "Der Sandmann" (1816), which was the basis of Douglas's two-channel video installation of the same title in 1995 and the basis of Sigmund Freud's essay *The Uncanny* (1919). In his essay, the psychoanalyst describes the uncanny as the disturbing experience of a place, person, or event lived as both strangely familiar and threatening, an experience conditioned by the release of unconscious (forbidden and therefore repressed) desires. Thematically closer to Douglas's installation, the British science-fiction film *Doppelgänger* (1969) directed by Robert Parrish tells the story of a joint European-NASA mission in 2019 to explore a newly discovered planet on the far side of the sun; the operation ends when an astronaut is killed and his fellow astronaut realizes that the planet is a counter-Earth, a mirror image of Earth.

In all of these literary, filmic, and psychoanalytical versions, the doppelgänger is a disturbing double who both reveals the strangeness of the main protagonist and announces the likelihood of a deadly event, often but not necessarily perpetrated by the doppelgänger while always affecting the life of the main protagonist. And this is largely how it is investigated by Douglas, except for the perpetrator's identity and role. The leading character, a Black spacewoman, and her doppelgänger coexist on a double screen; their lives mirror one another but also reverse and loop each other, leading to the decisive moment in the story when the Mission Control host team starts to cast doubt on the woman's real identity, endangering her in that very process. Here, it is Mission Control and not the doppelgänger that is the perpetrating actor.

Doppelgänger takes on Parrish's science-fiction drama to tell the story of an astronaut and her twin, both named Alice, separated by light-years and living in parallel worlds. The story unfolds across two adjacent square-format translucent screens suspended from the ceiling—whose images are visible on both sides, although reversed. The story is continuously split in two by the double structure, exposing the parallel timelines of the astronaut and her doppelgänger (figures 10.2 and 10.3). The two stories unfold as mirror images of each other, inverted from front to back, setting into play the ecognostic deployment of storytelling. The two Alices are teleported from their respective Earths to a spaceship light-years away, bound for a far-away planet. But each spaceship inexplicably returns to its respective Earth. In each timeline, the Mission Control's crew authorizes the landing of the spaceship and asks Alice "If you measure your life by the tick of the clock," for the purpose of identification. This is *the* determining moment of the story: in both cases, the answer, "[you] live reified time," is sent written as a palindrome, "emit deifier evil," but in one scenario the host crew will simply proceed to read it inversely, while in the other scenario the host crew reads the reversed password as a threat. From that moment on, one of the two scenarios unfolds on the two screens, emphasizing—with the double structure—either the friendly (scenario 1) or unfriendly (scenario 2) divide between the landed but hospitalized Alice on one screen and the hosting team (astronomers and a military agent as well as what strangely appears to be the original Alice) observing her through a glass on the other screen (figure 10.4). In one scenario, Alice is received with compassion, whereas in the second she is treated as a stranger, an intruder, a potential terrorist. The initial teleporting and spaceship sequence then reappears, but the images have been switched from one screen to the other. Shown in a loop, the scenarios keep reemerging, one after the other.

Commenting on these two different outcomes, Douglas states: "Alice is treated like a returning citizen who needs comfort, B12 injections, and bed rest. The other one is treated like a dangerous alien who gets quarantined, interrogated, and shot up with sodium Pentothal."[12] Douglas conceptualizes these alternative outcomes following the phenomenon of quantum entanglement, when two entangled

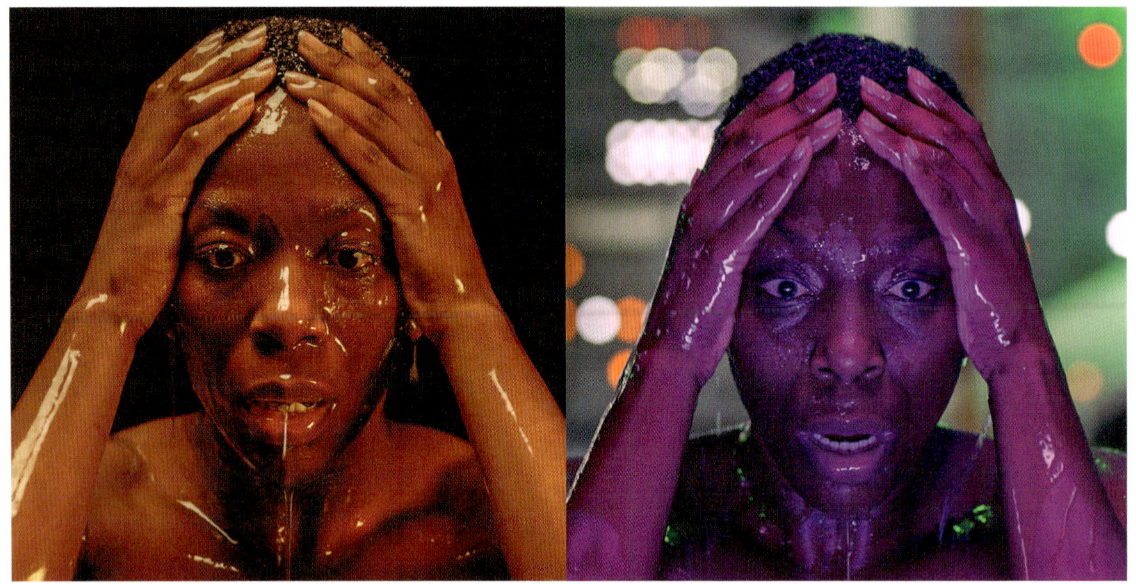

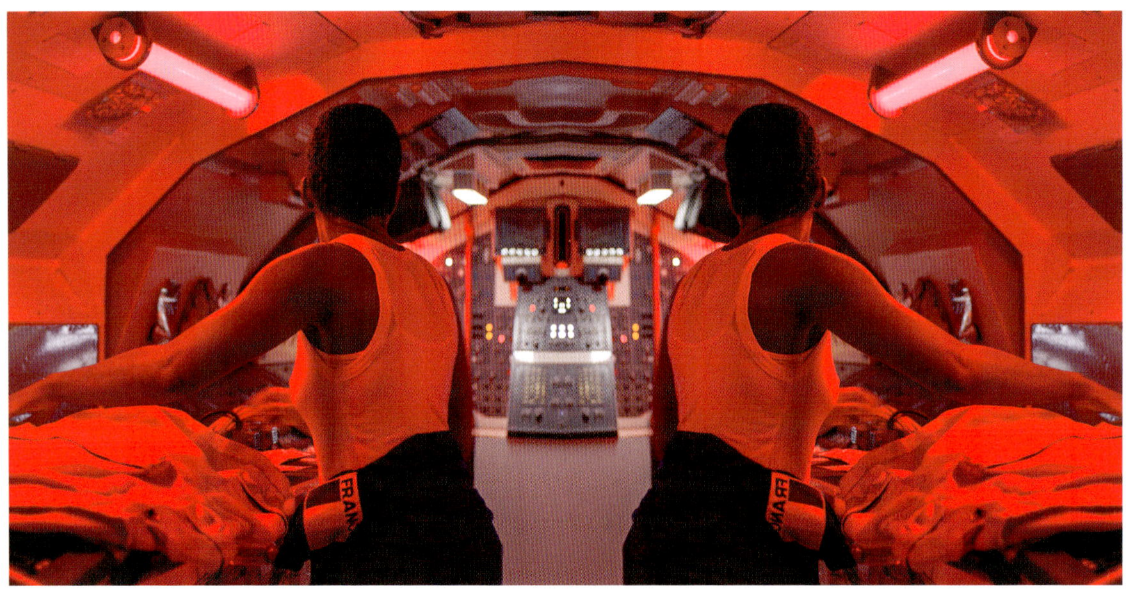

FIGURES 10.2 AND 10.3

Stan Douglas, *Doppelgänger*, 2019 (stills).
Two-channel color video installation,
duration variable. Photos: © Stan Douglas.
Courtesy of the artist, David Zwirner, and
Victoria Miro.

particles are generated and then separated: in these occurrences, the quantum state of one particle cannot be described independently of the state of the other particle, leading to correlations, as the physicist Erwin Schrödinger stated in his letter to Einstein, between observable physical properties of particles.[13] Douglas expands on that theory not only to propose an allegory of (im)migration but also to expose his own understanding of history as made of dissimilar possibilities. Speaking about Alice, he sees her as an immigrant—a figure he wants to celebrate:

It's more her intrepidness. She is going to do this thing. There is a very slight chance that everything will be okay. We don't really know what the planet is like. So when she gets there, either she'll be able to land and things will be okay, or it will be uninhabitable and she's alone and will die when her food runs out. In a way, this is sort of this experience of immigration too, because in immigration, you'll take the risk of going to an unknown place, and just make a new life for yourself. Immigrants are heroes because they get there and they will do everything, every skill they have, every bit of energy they have to make that new life and to make the place they live a better place to be. That's why immigration is such an important thing. Especially in a new world where we're all—except for one group of people, the indigenous people—we're all based on that history.

Alice is the kind of person who would be going there in the hopes that things will work out. So she will teleport there, and if things don't work out, okay, things didn't work out. But if they do, great, she can actually discover or explore a brand new world.[14]

Douglas's praise of immigrants, citizens who autonomously decide to leave their home for a new life, echoes the central tension sustaining *Doppelgänger*'s double-screen story. Alice accepts the adventure of teleportation, as does her double. But a substantial part of the story shows that immigration can go and has gone wrong: Alice is not able to reach the exoplanet, and her trajectory takes her back to Earth; moreover, one of the scenarios leads her to an unwelcoming Earth, where she is treated as a foreigner, an irregular or illegal migrant. Alice is a female hero; she is also the only Black person in the story. Her fate resonates both with today's racist antimigration measures and with what the legal scholar Dimitry Kochenov designates as citizenship's intrinsic racism, sexism, and class discrimination—"its deep and chronic exclusion" of specific categories of being that upholds and reinforces divisions "between the haves and haves-not."[15]

But *Doppelgänger*'s double-channel video installation is not historically deterministic. To appreciate its complexity, it is crucial to relate the work to Douglas's previous projects. Since the early 1990s, the uniqueness of his video installations has stemmed from their engagement with historical narratives. His stories have been and still are critical accounts of modernity—its modernisms, its diverse utopias of emancipation, its colonial thrust, its reliance on the forgetting or exclusion of subjects and events that do not fit its progress-oriented teleology. These critical accounts have materialized in videos and films that perform the crisis and near exhaustion of the narratives. The stories take form on the screen(s) but are deformed through a complex exploration of looping structures, split screens, repetitions, permutation devices, as well as techniques of randomness. The looped projections (the continual reappearance of sequences or of the video itself) reenacts the Nietzschean postulate of eternal recurrence—the eternal play of repetition that structures the universe. They repeat, interrupt, and reactivate the story or put off the resolution of the story indefinitely. In so doing, they elaborate the quasi-collapse of the modern belief in progress while leaving open the possibility of reinventing that belief.[16]

Doppelgänger extends this exploration of nonlinear storytell/ing, of historical narratives tout court, to complicate Alice's story as an (im)migrant. It does so at least at two levels: by inviting us to cognize the historical present ecognosisticly and by implicitly positioning us as potential problematic hosts.

First, the stories are difficult to follow. As Douglas states himself, "*Doppelgänger* . . . has both spatial and temporal aspects. It consists of side-by-side images that appear to be panels of similar parallel action but happen on different planets, light-years apart."[17] The simultaneous counterintuitive perception of the two Alices' as "light-years apart" is never easily experienced by any given viewer. There are too many reversals, mirror inversions, switching of images between the two screens, and doublings to fully understand what is happening, when it is happening, and to whom. Even the twinness of the two Alices' remains unclear: Is the twin a biological twin, a clone, or the same person living the same journey differently in a parallel universe? Despite Douglas's appropriation of early television color codes devised to help the viewer figure out if they are looking at Alice's story or her double's story ("When we're on the original Earth, we're with the original Alice, everything is like a terrestrial house, everything is blue and yellow. And when we're with the duplicate Alice, things are magenta and green"[18]), it is endlessly challenging to follow the stories while attending to their respective color coding. Who is the original, who is the copy? The answer to that question is never utterly evident; it is in fact *the* turning-point question raised by the host team—the answer to which will affect their reception of the astronaut and the astronaut's fate. Could it not be argued that this is the whole point of the work? *Doppelgänger* makes us privileged viewers as it invites us to shift from an agrilogistical mode of knowledge to an ecognostic form of knowledge production based on contradiction, copresence, and the need to weaken the severance between humans, between humans and nonhumans. To better understand the historical present (and one of its significant predicaments, necropolitical migration), we are invited to know in a loop; we are confronted with "a *weird* knowing" in which two scenarios "that appear utterly separate flip into one another." The beings and space–times seem separate, but they in fact coexist; they prosper on copresence, reversals, and mirroring.

Second, once we are ecognostically immersed in the story, its flipping mechanism unfolds dramatically, turning us into welcoming *and/or* unwelcoming hosts. We might be one or the other or both. Alice—like Lewis Carroll's Alice in *Through the Looking-Glass, and What Alice Found* (1871)—attempts to leave the Looking Glass Home. She is a Black female hero. She leaves home to discover another world. But, like Carroll's Alice, she returns to where she came from, caught in a loop.[19] This return initiates the possibility of different outcomes over which Alice doesn't have much control. These outcomes are never determined in advance. There lies *Doppelgänger*'s invitation to think about historical possibilities: Which scenario is the most promising one for a better future and for whose future? What can be done to favor one outcome over another? What would it be—and here I paraphrase a comment made by one member of the Mission Control crew—*not* to presume that Indigenous "aliens" accept their colonization? Which scenario constitutes history in this very moment? These questions can be raised only when we, as viewers, experience the flip of one version of hosting into the opposite version, a host team that we are an implicit part of. It is this experience that makes us realize that the two Alices' fates are primarily in the hands of hosts—the scientists, the military agents, and us, the viewers on the other side of the double screen (figure 10.4).

In his account of necropolitics as a politics of *enemyzation*, injury, and death of the "other," Achille Mbembe states that the world is becoming a "world without strangers" that notably dissolves "the classic distinction between executioner and victim"—a distinction that is itself a looped flip in which victims are perceived as potential killers.[20] *Doppelgänger* brings that outcome forward—Mission Control's xenophobic flipping of an (im)migrant into a latent executioner—as a real possible outcome. But the double structure of the installation allows it (and us) to never

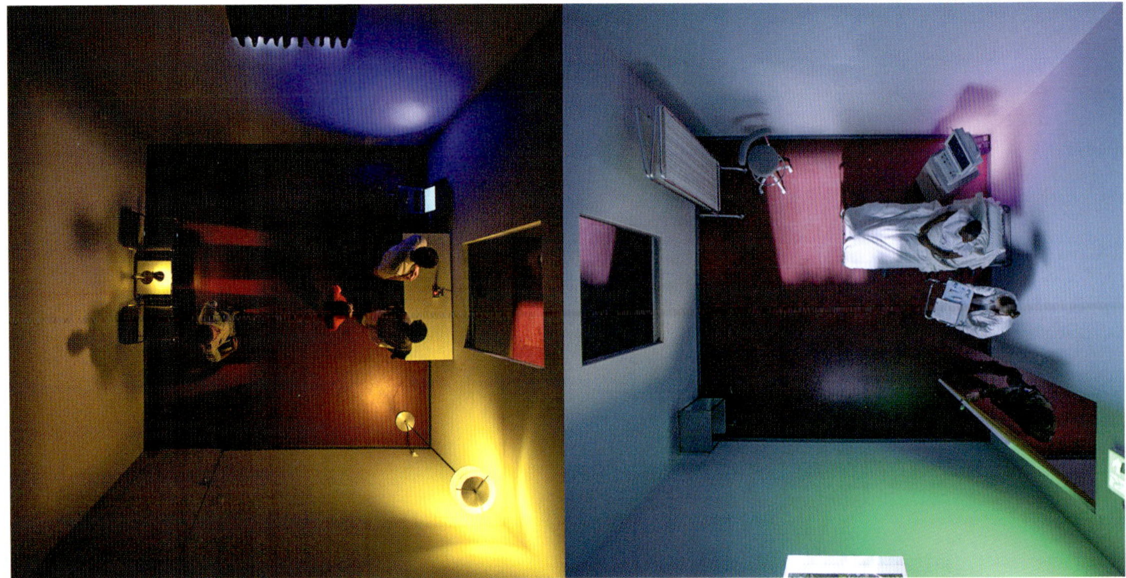

abandon the scenario in which the "stranger" is welcomed. This means that the coexistence the installation keeps staging and complicating is a form of knowledge production that also has the merit of opening up history. Alice can be seen as occupying the enriched position of any other who has learned to think from a majority's and a minority's perspective "at once"—a double perspective that Douglas sees as intrinsic to his own identity as a person of color living in Vancouver.[21] That position leaves us, as though rereading Oguibe's *Das Fremdlinge und Flüchtlinge Monument*, with a crucial responsibility, which is to address the vital question of migratory hospitality: How to host?

FIGURE 10.4

Stan Douglas, *Doppelgänger*, 2019 (still). Two-channel color video installation, duration variable. Photo: © Stan Douglas. Courtesy of the artist, David Zwirner, and Victoria Miro.

One strong answer to that question took the form of a claim formulated to European hosts by Decolonizing Architecture Art Research (DAAR)—a Stockholm-based architectural collective codirected by Sandi Hilal (b. 1973, Beit Sahour, Palestine) and Alessandro Petti (b. 1973, Pescara, Italy), which they cofounded with Eyal Weizman in 2017 in Beit Sahour, Palestine. That claim was *Al-Madhafah/The Living Room* (2016–2021), a complex of different living rooms DAAR made in collaboration with Yasmeen Mahmoud, Ibrahim Muhammad Haj Abdulla, and Ayat Al-Turshan. The project was initiated at a moment when Hilal was preparing herself and her family "to leave Palestine and become a stranger in Sweden."[22] It was performed in various locations, including Mahmoud and Abdulla's house in Boden, Sweden; the ArkDes Museum in Stockholm, where Hilal "amplif[ied]" her own living room in a public space;[23] the Yellow House (Gula Huset) funded by Public Art Agency Sweden—an apartment in an asylum accommodation center in Boden, which was transformed into a public meeting place for refugees as well as a place for them to cook, to learn how to cook, and to eat together (figure 10.5);[24] the retrospective exhibition *Permanent Temporariness* at the NYUAD Art Gallery in Abu Dhabi (2018); the Fawwar Refugee Camp's Women's Centre in the West Bank—a *madhafah* (living room, in Arabic) organized by Ayat Al-Turshan; Hilal and Petti's living room in Stockholm, with the support of the Arab Fund for Art and Culture (AFAC); and the Van Abbemuseum for the exhibition *Position 4* (2018–2019).[25] *Al-Madhafah/The Living Room* architecturalizes a simple yet subversive and brilliant gesture: the activation of living rooms by hosting "strangers" who welcome local guests—an opening that reverses the roles of the guest and the host typical of European migration while still acknowledging the importance of upholding European hospitality.

This undertaking must be seen as an extension of DAAR's previous projects, which have focused predominantly on the architectural requirement to provide a social space for refugees. Hilal headed the West Bank Camp Improvement Program of the United Nations Relief and Works Agency for Palestine Refugees in the Near East between 2008 and 2014. This was followed by Campus in Camps (2015–), a DAAR educational program initiated in the Dheisheh Refugee Camp in Bethlehem to create a space for critical thought and "grounded knowledge production" on democratization. One of the most innovative upshots of that program was uncontestably the construction of tents made out of concrete—tents that solidify, permanentize, symbolize, and immobilize what is typically soft, temporary, degradable,

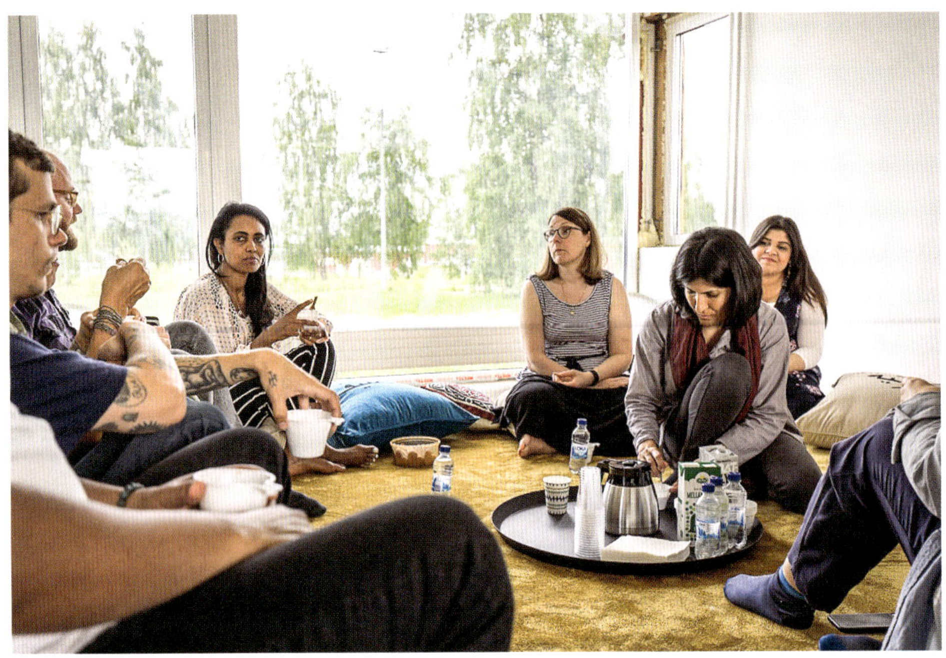

and transportable. Conceived as a place for social events, informal meetings, and conflict resolution, the *Concrete Tent* (2015–2018) in the Dheisheh Refugee Camp was mobilized by the Campus in Camps participants' desire to give an architectural form to the temporality of their experience of refugee camps—places where residents are expected to stay only temporarily as they wait for the processing of their applications, but where they end up living for months and years (figure 10.6). A second *Concrete Tent* was built in 2018 on the Abu Dhabi Campus to facilitate the deployment of a public sphere for students and teachers. The concrete tents

FIGURE 10.5

DAAR—Sandi Hilal and Alessandro Petti, in collaboration with Yasmeen Mahmoud, Ibrahim Muhammad Haj Abdulla, and Ayat Al-Turshan, *Al Madhafah/The Living Room* (2016–2021). Performance. The Yellow House (Gula Huset), Prästholmen, Boden, Sweden. Photo: Ana Naomi de Sousa. Courtesy of DAAR.

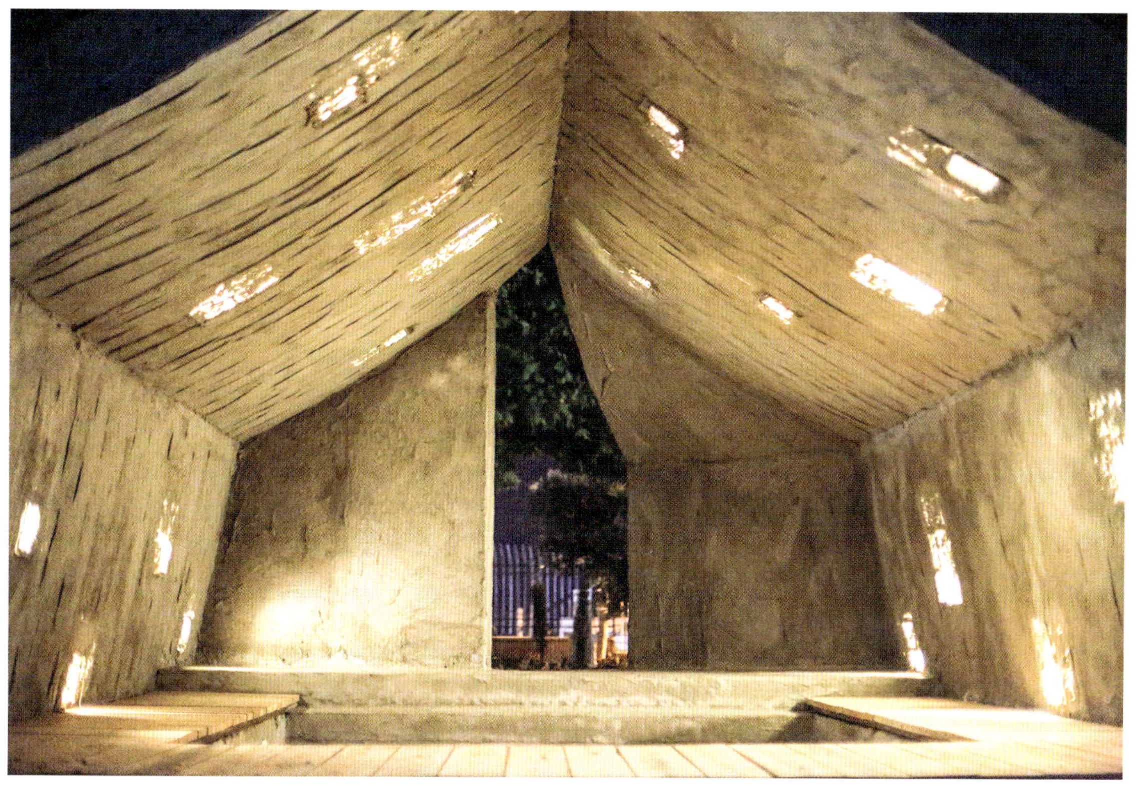

FIGURE 10.6

DAAR—Alessandro Petti and Sandi Hilal, *The Concrete Tent*, 2015. Concrete and canvas. Pavilion, approximately 30 m². Al Feniq Cultural Center, Dheisheh Refugee Camp, Bethlehem, West Bank. Photo: Anna Sara for Campus in Camps. Courtesy of DAAR.

were motivated by two fundamental questions: "Trapped between dreaming of permanency, of becoming full citizens (an illusion for the majority of newcomers), and the disempowered condition of migration and exile, is it possible to imagine a full political life despite the regime of permanent temporariness that limits every decision? Beyond the deprivation of temporariness, or the illusion of permanency, how to aspire to meaningful political action in the present moment?"[26] As these questions suggest, the main aspiration has been to provide a space that enables political thought and action. More importantly, in relation to Boden's *Al-Madhafah* interventions I want to examine here, the significant raison d'être of the tents is to critically rethink hospitality insofar as the permanent temporariness of camps is, as Hilal and Petti define it, "a condition forcing people to live as eternal guests."[27] The guest is underscored as a stagnant, waiting, and disempowering position. It is that position that the project *Al-Madhafah/The Living Room* seeks to undo.

This is Hilal's statement about the living-room project:

Located between the domestic and the public sphere, *Al-Madhafah*, in Arabic, is the living room dedicated to hospitality. It has the potential to subvert the role of guest and host and give a different socio-political meaning to the act of hospitality. It seeks to mobilize the condition of permanent temporariness as an architectural and political concept capable of challenging the binaries of inclusion and exclusion, public and private, guest and host. It activates the rights of temporary people to host and not to eternally be a guest; the right to claim life in their new destination without feeling obliged to revoke the desire of belonging to life back home.[28]

The series was initiated in the town of Boden in 2016 when Hilal was doing fieldwork there for Public Art Agency Sweden. It responded to the historical evolution of the city. Established at the end of the nineteenth century, Boden is a former military town located in the far north of Sweden, just beneath the Arctic Circle; its identity is tightly related to the Boden Fortress, which was built in the first decade of the twentieth century to defend Sweden from possible attacks from the East, mainly Russian attacks launched from Finland—a threat that never materialized. Today, following the decline of the military presence, Boden has become a major reception center for refugees, the Swedish Migration Agency having based its northerly office there. The living-room series was influenced by the Syrian refugee couple Yasmeen Mahmoud and Ibrahim Muhammad Haj Abdulla, who had recently arrived in Boden and resumed their tradition of hospitality as they adapted to their new home.

Most of the information about the initial stages of the project has been captured in the 11-minute, 22-second documentary film *Boden Living Room (Swe Subs)* (2018) by the British filmmaker and journalist Ana Naomi de Sousa.[29] Commissioned by ArkDesk, Stockholm, with the support of Public Art Agency Sweden, the film is a straightforward documentary that shows images of Boden in the winter—emphasizing its unforgivable northern climate. We hear and see Hilal talking about Boden and the elaboration of *Al-Madhafah/The Living Room*. Three stages of the project described in the film are particularly relevant to the unfolding of what I have been calling here, following Morton, "[k]nowing in a loop—a *weird* knowing," in which "two levels that appear utterly separate flip into one another." The film tells us a story that reverses the positions of the guest and the host typical of present-day migration.

First, as Hilal explains, *Al-Madhafah/The Living Room* was conceived as a reply to an architectural structure, more specifically the Yellow House, where refugees are sent to live when they arrive in Boden—a edifice that problematically isolates them from the rest of the town, depriving them of a social life and temporalizing their experience as a waiting (non)activity: "They seem to be waiting for that moment when they will be leaving that place. I think the depression comes out of the fact that they had a dream of arriving to Sweden and by arriving to Boden they were shocked that this was not the dream they were looking for." Not knowing exactly what to do with this situation, she inquired about refugees living elsewhere in Boden. This was the second stage of the project: her meeting with Yasmeen Mahmoud and Ibrahim Muhammad Haj Abdullah. That encounter allowed her to rethink, with Yasmeen and Ibrahim, the predominant host–guest relationship involving migrants living in Europe. This is the moment when weird knowing comes to the fore. Hilal words that flip—the uncanny (unexpected, unannounced) turning over of the guest position into a hosting position—in the following terms: "When someone arrives to a new place, he is obviously a guest. I have no problem to be a guest. . . . But I still want to exercise my right to be a host. And I think that what refugees lose the moment they cross the borders to Europe is their right to host. . . . I think that what refugees miss the most is finally somebody without expecting it coming and knocking [at] their door." The conceptualization of that weird twist from guest to host articulates the flip as a procedure of awareness: exposed to the flip, the viewer, listener, and storyteller (Hilal herself) become aware of the mutability of hospitality: welcoming

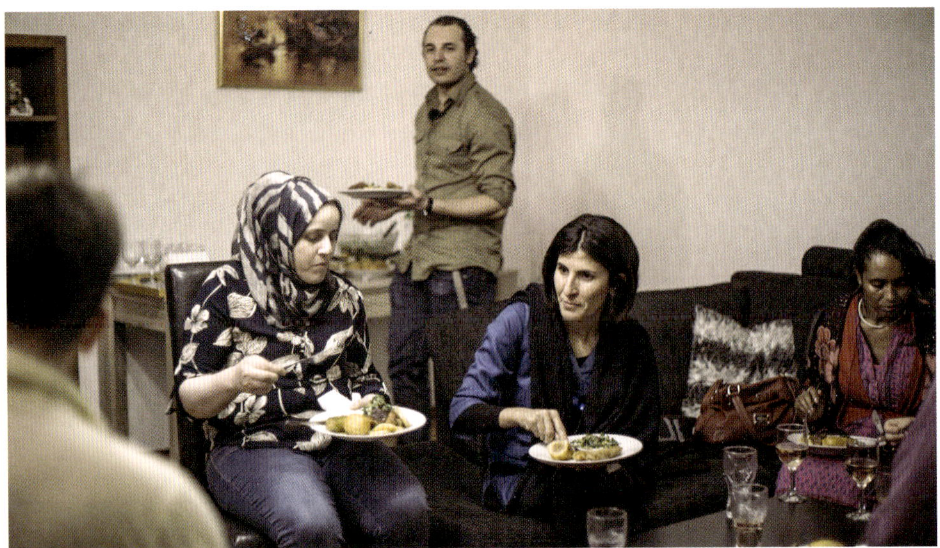

is a reversable and reorientable coexistence in which "strangers" (to borrow Ogu-ibe's countermonument terminology) can be both guests and hosts; as hosts, they have the right to open their space to Swedes and any other guests. The hosting activity is even more than a right: it supports mental health and integration. This conceptualization is followed by the project's third stage, when a reception of locals takes place in Yasmeen and Ibrahim's house in Boden (figure 10.7). The reception is filmed in that very host-shifting moment. To host is to open one's living room to

FIGURE 10.7

DAAR (Sandi Hilal and Alessandro Petti in collaboration with Yasmeen Mahmoud, Ibrahim Muhammad Haj Abdulla, and Ayat Al-Turshan), *Al Madhafah/The Living Room*, 2016–2021. Performance, duration variable, and video stills. Inside Yasmeen Mahmoud and Ibrahim Muhammad Haj Abdulla's house, Boden, Sweden. Photo: Ana Naomi de Sousa. Image courtesy of DAAR.

friends and strangers. When hosting is undertaken by refugees, strangers recover their agency, their autonomy.

To fully appreciate the importance and subversiveness of the *Al-Madhafah/Living Room* project, it is crucial to emphasize that it was initiated in 2016, just after the peak of the "European refugee crisis" in 2015, when an estimated 10,000 migrating citizens were coming to Sweden every week seeking asylum. A total 160,000 finally made their way into Sweden in 2015—corresponding to about 2 percent of the country's population, 9.5 million, double the per capita figure projected by Germany. They were coming mainly from Afghanistan, Syria, Iraq, Somalia, Iran, and Eritrea. This welcoming policy was instituted in continuation with Sweden's World War II and post–World War II commitment to refugees. In the early 2010s, for example, Sweden took in about 80,000 migrants a year. But its open-migration policy started to change dramatically at the end of 2015, becoming steadily restrictive on the grounds that the country could not by itself absorb the massive flow of migrating people and that integration had become logistically and economically difficult. The latest measures include the impossibility of acquiring permanent asylum and, for failed asylum seekers or migrants who have received an expulsion order, the noneligibility for social benefits, such as the free housing and daily allowance that come with asylum. If approved, refugees receive a renewable three-year temporary residency permit.[30] This new policy has been contested by mental health experts who have established that "temporary residence permits create human suffering. That people with subsidiary protection status aren't guaranteed continued safety, that they don't know if they will be deported to the existence from whence they fled, may lead to an increased risk of depression and PTSD."[31] New policies also include the limitation of immigration to family reunification and the denial of entry to those without proper identity documents, even in migratory circumstances where countless people arrive without such documents—a policy that violates the Schengen Agreement. As the journalist James Traub stated in 2016, "Cross-border immigration has, in fact, come to an almost complete stop. Sweden now accepts only those refugees arriving directly from Turkey, Lebanon, and Jordan, and cleared by the U.N. refugee agency."[32]

Al-Madhafah/The Living Room's flip from guest to host is an uncanny reversal precisely because it disobediently troubles the presumption that hospitality, in matters of migration and immigration, is the exclusive privilege of hosting countries and countries of destination. That reversal shows the benefits of weird

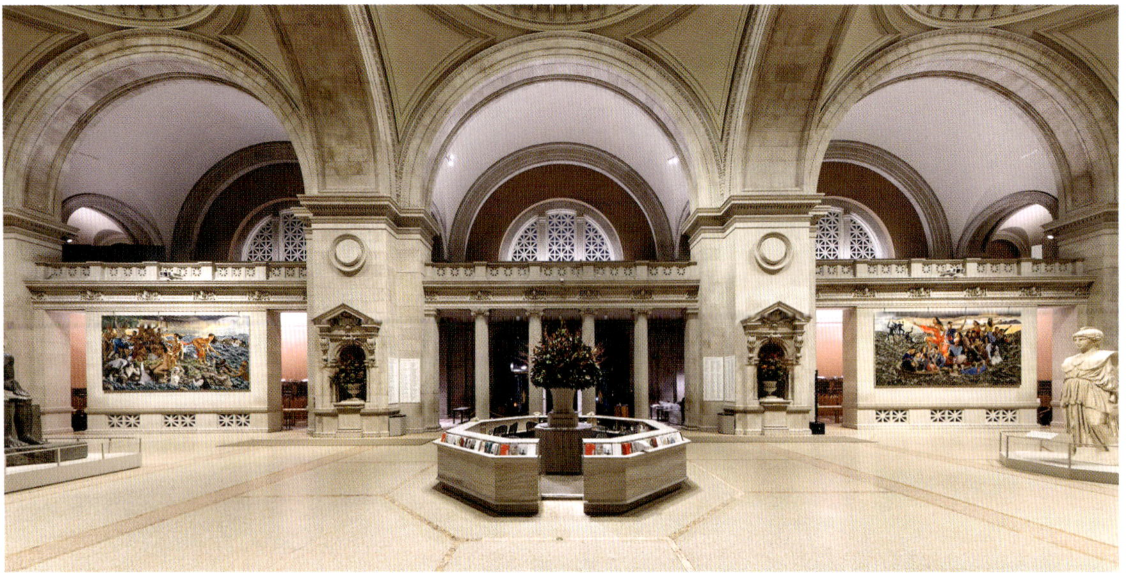

storytell/ing: migrating beings' inscription in social and political life, their appropriation of a fading practice whose decline has contributed to their exclusion.

MISTIKÔSIWAK (WOODEN BOAT PEOPLE)

The storytell/ing flip made its way into the Metropolitan Museum of Art in 2019 for the Met's inaugural Great Hall Commission titled *mistikôsiwak* (*Wooden Boat People*)—a diptych by the Cree artist Kent Monkman (b. 1965, Saint Marys, Canada). The diptych is composed of two large-format acrylic paintings, each measuring 335.28 × 670.6 centimeters and entitled *Welcoming the Newcomers* (2019) and *Resurgence of the People* (2019) (figure 10.8).[33]

FIGURE 10.8

Kent Monkman, *mistikôsiwak (Wooden Boat People)*, 2019. Diptych. Installation view: Metropolitan Museum of Art, New York. Photo: Anna-Marie Kellen. Courtesy of the artist.

The commission is a strong instantiation of Monkman's multimedia practice—a practice that includes painting, installation, film, photography, and performance and is known for its complex investigation of modern settler colonialism (the extensive European colonization of the Americas initiated by Christopher Columbus's Spanish expedition of 1492) as a fierce system of replacement (what Patrick Wolfe has designated a structure of invasion and elimination[34]) of Indigenous peoples from the fifteenth century well into the twenty-first century. Characteristically supported by an imperial authority, settler colonialism was implemented by European colonial powers, including Spain, England, France, and Portugal, to assert sovereignty, territorial expansion, and control over Indigenous lands so as to enable permanent settlement and resource development for settlers.[35] It was carried out by a combination of means, including the depopulation of Indigenous communities, various forms of biocultural assimilations, religious conversion, child abduction, and the resocialization of the Indigenous peoples in colonial institutions (e.g., residential schools and missions).[36] These histories of settler colonialism persist in the present albeit in a transformed way—let us follow Ann Laura Stoler here—and are so deeply "threaded through the fabric of contemporary life forms" that they are never straightforwardly identifiable; they generate new damages and disparities; they likewise persist in the non-Indigenous inhabitation of Indigenous land taken by force or never ceded.[37] Monkman's diptych reassesses these histories and recursions by disrupting the post-Renaissance tradition of Western art (especially history painting)—its representation of European domination, its misrepresentation of North American Indigenous identities and cultures, and its depiction of Indigenous subjects as a "vanishing race" doomed to inevitable extinction.[38] These critical reconsiderations follow, as the art historian Susan Phillips and the historian Mark Salber Phillips stipulate, "a decolonizing agenda."[39] Monkman's gender-fluid alter ego, Miss Chief Eagle Testickle (originally called Miss Chief Share Eagle Testickle), regularly emerges in his work as an agent of disturbance, a glamorous time-traveling Cree trickster enacting a two-spirit, third-gender, and supernatural being who reverses the colonial gaze by challenging pernicious perceptions of Indigenous peoples and histories.[40] Exercising what Nicholas Mirzoeff has called the right to look,[41] she proceeds to undo colonial history, imagining what history might have been and what it can be following this unlearning.

For the Metropolitan Museum of Art commission, Monkman explores *mistikôsiwak* as its main theme. The word, meaning "wooden boat people," initially referred to French settlers, but it is expanded here to refer to European settlers arriving on the shores of the Americas. The diptych's troubling of settler colonialism unfolds by undermining, exacerbating, transfiguring, reversing, and inverting figures and representations appropriated from the Met's collections of European and North American paintings and sculptures, including Peter Paul Rubens's *Venus and Adonis* (probably mid-1630s), Titian's *Venus and Adonis* (1560s), Augustus Saint Gaudens's *Hiawatha* (1871–1872, carved 1874), Eugène Delacroix's *The Natchez* (1823–1824, 1835), Gustave Courbet's *The Woman in the Waves* (1868), Thomas Crawford's *Mexican Girl Dying* (1846, carved 1848), and Emanuel Leutze's *Washington Crossing the Delaware* (1851). As stipulated by the art historian Sasha Suda, the diptych liberates some figures from one painting to the next—for instance, the African slave represented in shackles in *Welcoming the Newcomers* reappears as a physician in *Resurgence of the People*.[42] In a conversation with the curator Jami C. Powell, Monkman describes the critical dialogue he wanted to establish with European and North American art history and, more specifically, with the Met's collection:

I'm looking at Western art history as an outsider. I'm a Cree person studying a tradition of painting that began hundreds of years ago and reached its zenith in the nineteenth century. I thought, here's this grand tradition, which was so capable of storytelling, of presenting narratives, of demonstrating authoritative ideas and themes. It has been discarded by Western art in favor of this individual thinking. I wanted to reclaim it, resurrect it, and find a way to embrace the potential of the language of painting. . . . As I sift through the collection, I look for works that can trigger conversations between colonial or settler works—works made by the settlers about Indigenous people—but I also [think about] how different those points of view are, how foreign those worldviews are from Indigenous worldviews. When I insert Miss Chief into these works, it's about challenging the subjectivity of settler artists who often had no idea or very little knowledge about the cultures that they were representing. What we're looking at is actually a projection of the artists themselves, not real Indigeneity. They were just fantasies; they were romantic ideas that came from books. . . . As I choose the artworks that I riff on, I stitch together conversations about where those artworks are misleading the public, and this is an opportunity in a mainstream museum to confront representations [of Indigenous people] that are often flawed.[43]

Monkman's statement identifies the two main artistic motivations behind the commission, both of them elaborated from a disobedient Cree perspective: his desire to resurrect European art's storytelling tradition and his questioning of artworks created by settlers about Indigenous people. Miss Chief, as a pivotal time-traveling guide, is called upon to uncover and overturn that visual regime. In my examination of the paintings and in light of this chapter's overall objective, I want to emphasize the determining role played by the storytell/ing strategy of weird looping (reversal, inversion, twisting, by which "two levels that appear utterly separate flip into one another") in the diptych's overturning and queering of settler visuality. The diptych represents the settlers' invasion of the so-called New World, but the story is upturned by Miss Chief's presence to describe not only what could have happened without the forceful procedures of invasion and erasure emblematic of settler colonialism but also what has happened on a lesser scale or what might happen despite the tenaciousness of the histories of settler colonialism in the present. Isuma's video-and-webcasts intervention in 2019 about resilience and environmental concern is not far here, even more so when we consider *Resurgence of the People*'s disclosure of environmental degradation, which is central to the *Silakut Live from the Floe Edge* webcasts. The stories depicted in Monkman's two paintings are, moreover, made with twenty-first-century migration in mind: they broaden the reality of Indigenous people to include the forced displacement of other populations worldwide, while upholding Indigenous protagonists as hosts.[44] The flip occurs unexpectedly when the viewer realizes that hospitality has changed hands, when hospitality is seen as what might have been, was, or could be.

Especially passionate in its twisting of hosting, *Welcoming the Newcomers* recreates the arrival of European settlers through the Atlantic. The settlers bring with them militarism, religion, and slavery to secure their objectives of permanent settlement and resource development; but in the artwork they have lost their position of power and domination: themselves victims of a shipwreck, they are just about drowning at sea and seek help from the Indigenous group located on firm ground (on what appears to be a rock island or peninsula) (figure 10.9). The Native inhabitants respond to their distress in various ways: some of them hold out their hands to help settlers out of the sea, while others prevent them from setting foot on the land by attacking them with arrows or simply leaving them to save themselves. Miss Chief Eagle Testickle looks at the viewer as her outstretched hand grasps the hand of a Black man in shackles, drawing him ashore while her other hand reaches out to undoubtedly help an East Indian man wearing an orientalized turban. As she looks back at the viewer, her extended hand introduces and discloses the drowning scene. She invites us within the scene and asks that we position ourselves in relation to that scene. As we perceptually respond to her, we start to notice her tears and mascara-stained cheek.

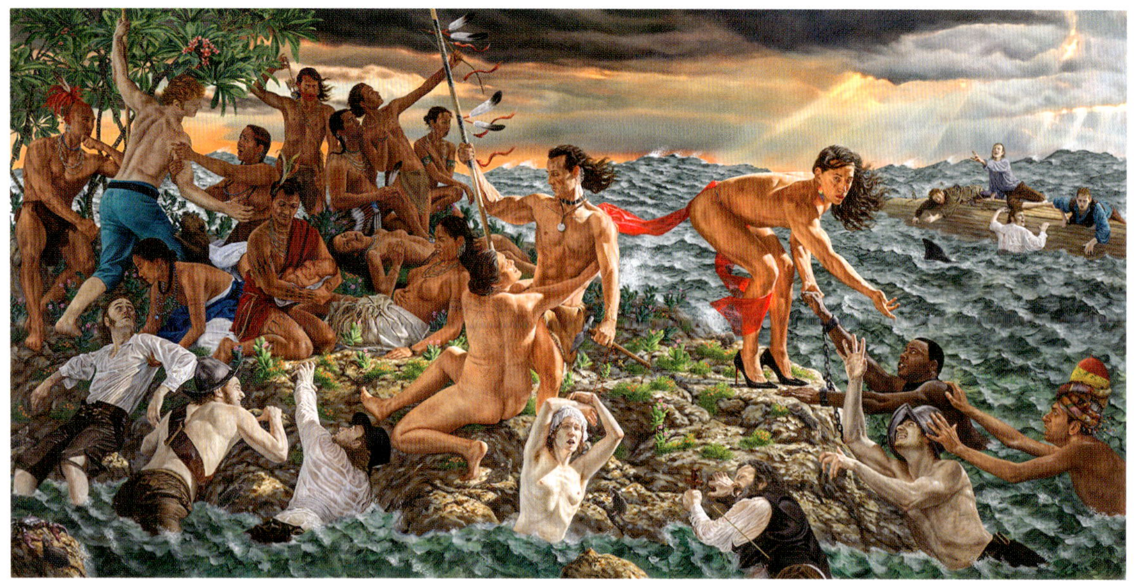

As Nick Estes, an American studies scholar and citizen of the Lower Brule Sioux Tribe, has observed, *Welcoming the Newcomers* subverts the Western art canon through the very act of appropriating it. The work undermines European art's orientalism as well as European and North American art's romanticization of the "New World" and its celebration of invasion; this undermining is enabled mainly by the depiction of Indigenous inhabitants who "maintain their kinship and make new relations—even as some try to ward off colonizers with weapons."[45] But that undermining is also set off by a brilliant flip of the guest–host relation of migration. Miss Chief's power to travel in time elaborates that flip—as the title literally indicates, she welcomes the newcomers—in a setting that is not only historical but also contemporary, in solidarity with today's migrating beings in danger at sea, a

Kent Monkman, *Welcoming the Newcomers*, 2019. Acrylic on canvas. 132 × 264 in. (335.28 × 670.6 cm). Collection of Metropolitan Museum of Art, New York. Courtesy of the artist.

contemporaneity, as I will soon show, that is more explicitly represented in *Resurgence of the People*. Monkman has stated that he was thinking about "migrating populations all over the world" when making the painting.[46] That guest–host flip is not a simple binary reversal. It is in fact rather complex: Indigenous hosts are taking back the role they might have played if the newcomers had not been motivated by their colonial logic of elimination of the "other"; the hosts' responses, however, are rather varied. Miss Chief does not welcome settlers per se but rather other subalterns of colonialism—she distinguishes migrating populations from settlers (as Lorenzo Veracini maintains, "settlers are *founders* of political orders and carry their sovereignty with them[, whereas] migrants can be seen as *appellants* facing a political order that is already constituted"[47]); some settlers are saved but others are killed. This messy response is a substantial dimension of the painting's strength: it dehomogenizes the group of Indigenous actors. Even more relevant to this study is how the Indigenous men and women rescue without hesitation the beings whose colonial fate they share. They disclose their agency in the very act of hosting qua solidarity.

The looping of hospitality is reinforced by *Resurgence of the People*'s depiction of Indigenous men, women, and children traveling in a boat in contemporary times (figure 10.10). Some of the Indigenous models who posed for *Welcoming the Newcomers* resurface in the second painting dressed in present-day clothes. The painting can therefore be seen as *Welcoming the Newcomers*'s future, yet it is a future that is already at play in *Welcoming*'s reimagining of settler colonialism. The boat also includes migrating beings wearing orange life vests, Black and Brown people (a Black doctor, the slave depicted in *Welcoming the Newcomers*, has just delivered a Native child and is now holding an unconscious white body half submerged in the water), as well as two bodies clinging to the vessel. As Indigenous protagonists decisively paddle the boat through the water, they disregard an island occupied by armed soldiers, Royal Canadian Mounted Police, and a white supremacist exhibiting their weapons—figures revealing the obstinacy of settler forcefulness. Miss Chief Eagle Testickle is shown standing on the bow commanding the boat, dressed as she appears in *Welcoming the Newcomers*, her hair and long red scarf blowing in the wind. Based on the figure of George Washington in Emanuel Leutze's painting *Washington Crossing the Delaware* (1851), she is the new hero crossing the river, leading the group, as Estes suggests, "towards a more sustainable and just future . . . guiding the people towards an Indigenous future."[48] And yet, as Estes also observes, the water is troubled by floating plastic bottles, and Miss Chief's face is still marked by

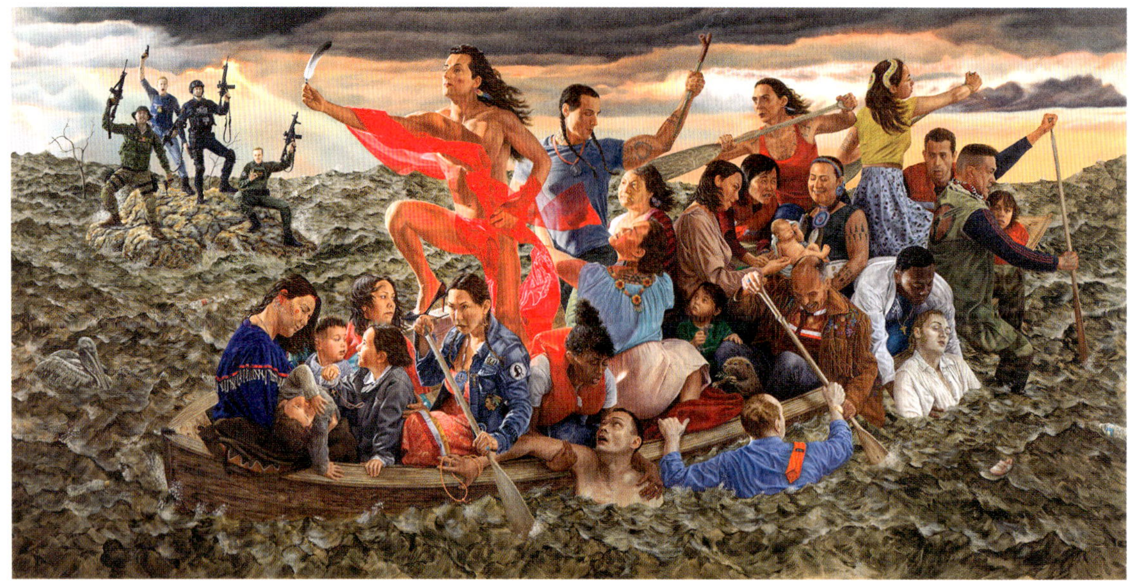

running mascara, showing the history of violence as ongoing. Which is to say that whereas the storytell/ing device of weird looping acts to uncover and reverse the power positions of colonial settlers, its twisting of hospitality remains messy. Let us recall the Haitian anthropologist Michel-Rolph Trouillot: "History is messy for the people who must live it."[49] *Resurgence of the People* reverses the resurgence heroes, showing the Indigenous as the liberators and the settlers as the overpowered, but the reversal of settler colonialism is incomplete (as is the case with *Welcome to Newcomers*). Indigenous peoples are displaced anew—though forced to leave, they are shown as having decided to leave—and armed individuals persist in the background: violence endures. Settler colonialism never simply vanishes: the presence of colonial histories endures, albeit transformed, to paraphrase Stoler, shaping the coexistence of settlers and Indigenous people.

FIGURE 10.10

Kent Monkman, *Resurgence of the People*, 2019. Acrylic on canvas. 132 × 264 in. (335.28 × 670.6 cm). Collection of Metropolitan Museum of Art. Courtesy of the artist.

That tenacity became particularly manifest when the diptych was shown at the Met in the winter of 2020. The museum had failed to address that very section of the painting—the island occupied by armed actors—in its discussion of the diptych. Responding to that omission, the Mississippi Choctaw/Ki'Che Maya art historian, curator, and educator Regan de Loggans specified that "on the didactics and exhibition texts and in the programming associated with *mistikôsiwak (Wooden Boat People)*, the Met has neglectfully chosen not to explain this part of the painting. Considering the very visible police violence against the Wet'suwet'en people during the span of this exhibition, the Met missed an opportunity to discuss the ongoing police violence perpetrated against Indigenous peoples under settler colonial occupation."[50] That is, the Met failed to truly engage with the colonial present. On February 7, 2020, "in solidarity with the Wet'suwet'en people and land defenders," the Indigenous Kinship Collective held a sit-in action at the museum in front of *mistikôsiwak (Wooden Boat People)*, specifically underneath *Resurgence of the People*, to denounce the institution's omission of ongoing police brutality.[51] The main concern behind the Canadian pipeline and railway protests in 2020—which took the form of a series of civil disobedience demonstrations, sit-ins, and blockades by the Wet'suwet'en people and its supporters—was the construction of the Coastal GasLink Pipeline through 190 kilometers of Wet'suwet'en unceded land in Northern British Columbia, on top of ongoing concerns about Indigenous land rights, land ownership, police violence, and the environmental impact of energy projects.[52] Similar environmental concerns are likewise central to *Resurgence of the People*.

Crucial here is how Monkman's diptych expands the notion of the wooden boat people to include a variety of settlers from different periods, "pilgrims, a conquistador, people clamouring onto the shore," as well as—and therein lies the effectiveness of weird reversals—the viewers. This transhistoricity also exposes water (the sea, a river), like John Akomfrah's multichannel *Vertigo Sea* (2015) examined in chapter 2, as the main elemental media of displacement: not only the sailing that enabled the forced displacement of African slaves to Europe and the Americas but also—as Monkman specifies—the "rising waters" of climate change "that continue to displace people" worldwide.[53] As the diptych articulates the flip of Indigenous men and women into hosts and the flip of settlers into fragilized or weakened guests, it also reverses—when understood in the context of today's criminalization of solidarity—the fate of endangered migrating beings. Defying criminalization, it rescues them; it turns their imminent death and elimination into life. But let us insist on the following two points: *mistikôsiwak (Wooden Boat People)* explores flipping as a mode of historical awareness not of what is but of what might have been, of what has been (albeit at a microlevel), and of what could be; and its storytell/ing flips fluctuate, partial and unfinished. I perceive these features as a strength: they recall the stories of migration told by the former squatters in Tuan Andrew Nguyen's *Crimes of Solidarity* (2020)—stories that are retold ventriloquistically to disclose their fractures, unresolvedness, and incompleteness; the plea of Kader Attia's *La Mer Morte* (2015) to heal traumatic wounds without obliterating the injuries; the request of Teresa Margolles's *La promesa* (2012) to unendingly care for injured bodies; and John Akomfrah's open histories. As Morton contends, "The loop form of beings means we live in a universe of finitude and fragility, a world in which objects are suffused with and surrounded by mysterious hermeneutical clouds of unknowing. It means that the politics of coexistence are always contingent, brittle, and flawed, so that in the thinking of interdependence at least one being must be missing. Ecognostic jigsaws are never complete."[54] In Monkland's diptych, there is a sense that the host–guest coexistence can reverse again. The question "How to host?" is productively kept alive.

HOSPITALITY

In an article published in *Le Monde* on August 16, 2018, Étienne Balibar responded to the so-called European refugee crisis—more specifically to what has become, for migrating populations, one of the deadliest border environments in the world (the Mediterranean Sea)—with the requirement that international law be revised to include and protect hospitality as a fundamental right.[55] That requirement articulates a flip from the right *to* hospitality to hospitality *as* a right. Migrant rights, Balibar argues, should be secured by a series of specific injunctions: (1) the outlawing of refoulement (i.e., the illegalization of compulsory returns to countries where refugees are likely to be persecuted); (2) the banning of brutal practices against migrating travelers (including the reinforcement of "hostile environments" for strangers, as promoted by the former British prime minister Theresa May, and materialized in any type of borderzones, including camps); (3) the illegalization of lists inventorying countries of origin, as is current practice in the EU to block the admission of migrants on the basis of specific racial, cultural, religious, and geopolitical criteria; (4) the banning of military operations that target rescue operations and smugglers' networks, which only end up endangering the lives of migrants; and (5) the illegalization of externalization (the practice of externalizing the management of migrant flows to unsafe countries). Distinguishing the *right to hospitality*—a collective, shared responsibility—from the *right of hospitality*, Balibar supports the latter as a "civic activity" that legally forbids the treatment of strangers as "enemies": migrating wanderers, he maintains, "are not a class. They are not a race. . . . I would say that they are a mobile part of humanity, suspended between the violence of a displacement and the violence of a repression."[56]

Balibar's plea is an unequivocal claim for hospitality as a right, as much as Gayatri Chakravorty Spivak's plea is a claim for responsibility as a right: it is a plea addressed to European countries shirking their responsibilities of assistance and protection of migrating populations; it fundamentally counters the criminalization of solidarity. Every single work examined in this chapter is likewise a claim for hospitality in matters of migration and immigration; they articulate hospitality as a response to the necropolitical weakening of that right. But the strange flips they operate complicate Balibar's own inventive flip. They turn hospitality over again, preventing it from being the exclusive responsibility of European states. The migrating being's right to host could easily become the first of Balibar's injunctions, one that could play a major role in preserving the dignity and security of wanderers "suspended between the violence of a displacement and the violence of a repression."

But what is hospitality? How is the concept fundamentally challenged through the storytell/ing device of weird looping? To conclude our discussion, let us consider one of the main European philosophical meditations on hospitality: Jacques Derrida's *Of Hospitality*, initially published in French in 1997. In that book (which originally took the form of a seminar), Derrida first identifies the imposition from which "the question of hospitality begins": the foreigner asking for hospitality must do so in a foreign language, a language "imposed on him by the master of the house, the host, the king, the lord, the authorities, the nation, the State, the father, etc."[57] Foreigners must know the host's language in order to be hosted: this process can only but confirm them as strangers. What makes standard hospitality possible therefore is also what limits it—it requires something from the guest: the guest's own enactment as a foreigner, as Oguibe's *Das Fremdlinge und Flüchtlinge Monument*'s inscription likewise suggests ("I was a stranger and you took me in"), even in cases when the stranger is a "reminder" (let us follow Sara Ahmed here) "of the differences we must celebrate."[58] The question for Derrida then becomes:

How can an absolute hospitality—a hospitality that ceases to be conditional—take place? His answer is formulated as a renewed requirement; hospitality becomes the requirement to welcome the other unconditionally, which he specifies as follows:

> To put it in different terms, absolute hospitality requires that I open up my home and that I give not only to the foreigner (provided with a family name, with the social status of being a foreigner, etc.), but to the absolute, unknown, anonymous other, and that I *give place* to them, that I let them come, that I let them arrive, and take place in the place I offer them, without asking of them either reciprocity (entering into a pact) or even their names. The law of absolute hospitality commands a break with hospitality by right, with law or justice as rights. Just hospitality breaks with hospitality by right; not that it condemns or is opposed to it, and it can on the contrary set and maintain it in a perpetual progressive movement; but it is as strangely heterogeneous to it as justice is heterogeneous to the law to which it is yet so close, from which in truth it is indissociable.[59]

In this passage, Derrida articulates the fundamental antinomy between conditional (lawful) hospitality and unconditional (unlimited, hyperethical) hospitality, two orientations that are set out to transgress each other.[60] Wanting to weaken that antinomy but also wanting to set out the conditions of possibility for absolute hospitality, he maintains that unconditional hospitality must be a law, but for it to be absolute it must be a "law without a law"—"without an imperative, without order and without duty."[61] To be unconditionally hospitable is to "say yes *to who or what turns up*, before any determination, before any anticipation, before any *identification*, whether or not it has to do with a foreigner, an immigrant, an invited guest, or an unexpected visitor, whether or not the new arrival is the citizen of another country, a human, animal, or divine creature, a living or dead thing, male or female."[62] In other words, hospitality is beyond any practice of ownership: it does not belong to anyone; it lies "in the gesture with which one welcomes the other."[63] Ultimately, absolute hospitality is an event: the arrival of a foreigner or a stranger is never programmed in advance; as this unknown person arrives, the host "actively intervenes"[64] by welcoming the other without knowing anything about this arriving being. Such openness entails that foreigners may destroy the house that welcomes them, and this is what makes hospitality a potentially dangerous endeavor; but for Derrida, there is no hospitality without that risk.

Derrida's definition has the merit of leaving open the question of who gets to be a host insofar as hospitality cannot be owned by any actor. That understanding is fully assumed in DAAR's *Al-Madhafah/Living Room* and Monkman's *mistikôsiwak (Wooden Boat People)*—two projects that bring to the fore, respectively, refugees' and Indigenous people's right and desire to host. However, as reviewers of the Derridean concept of hospitality have convincingly pointed out, Derrida's definition is surely asking a lot from the foreigner. As argued by the philosopher Audran Aulanier, when Derridean hosts open themselves unconditionally to the other, they paradoxically expect to be transformed by the event, bringing in a benefit that ends up undermining the notion of absolute hospitality.[65] Moreover, Derrida's philosophical investigation ends with his conceptualization of the event as an opening toward the arriving guest; he says nothing about the ways in which the "foreigner" will be welcomed *after* the event. In short, he doesn't address the challenge of hospitality as an action that unfolds *over time*; he fails to see that hospitality is not simply an opening but also one's ability to actually receive and live with the foreigner's differences.[66] As pointed out in the examination of empathy in chapters 6 and 7, it might well be that the anticipation of relational frictions will discourage the hospitable gesture of opening one's home "to the absolute, unknown, anonymous other."[67] Engaged in absolute hospitality over time, the host will also have to address the newcomer's needs, identity, and culture.

This is where Balibar's call for legislation and where the storytell/ing explored in the artworks investigated in this chapter fully enter the scene of hospitality. The flips elaborated in Olu Oguibe's *Das Fremdlinge und Flüchtlinge Monument*, Stan Douglas's *Doppelgänger*, DAAR's *Al-Madhafah/Living Room*, and Kent Monkman's *mistikôsiwak (Wooden Boat People)* twist European and North American hospitality not only to claim it but also to worry it. What makes them uncannily work as a major reassessment of hospitality is their inclusion of the viewer in the very process of storytell/ing. Without disturbed viewers, weird loops would not be strange at all, and strangeness would simply be a stylistic device or, even worse, a reconfirmation of what is. In these loops, victims unexpectedly become heroes, and heroes become sometimes the victims, sometimes the criminals. Ultimately, what viewers are exposed to and invited to reflect upon is their own role in the depreciation of hospitality. Hospitality is purportedly what some of the richest and most democratic countries in the world do when they respond to incoming strangers and when they welcome back their own citizens. That definition has been substantially complicated in this chapter. On the one hand, when forcibly displaced people grasp their own right to host, hospitality becomes more luminous. On the other hand, hospitality darkens when hosting enables the arbitrary exclusion of an [im]mi-grating citizen by the citizen's own country of origin. This chapter has also shown that hospitality, even when the guests gain the right to host, is an unstable activity. Hosting is always incomplete; it is always susceptible to change over time; hosting easily turns into unhosting and is easily lost as a right; it is as ambivalent (remedy + poison) as care and empathy have turned out to be. Hospitality is a pharmakon coexistence.

CONCLUSION

Between November 21, 2020, and March 14, 2021, the 12th Taipei Biennial presented an exhibition cocurated by Bruno Latour, Martin Guinard, and Eva Lin and entitled *You and I Don't Live on the Same Planet*, which sought to uncover a fundamental disagreement "on how to keep the world inhabitable." That disagreement, the curators maintained, is not so much a political as an ecological divergence pertaining to "what the earth is made of."[1] In the Taipei Fine Arts Museum, the exhibition took the form of a fictional planetarium divided into five distinct planets: planet GLOBAL-IZATION (for people who keep modernizing the planet despite its limits); planet SECURITY (for the antiglobalists who build walls to ensure privacy and shelter); planet ESCAPE (for people planning to settle on Mars before the apocalypse); planet ALTERNATIVE GRAVITY (for people who seek refuge metaphysically); and planet TERRESTRIAL (for people attempting to reconcile prosperity and ecology). In the exhibition catalog's main essay, Latour and Guinard specify that the divergence between planets is not simply a question of inhabitants having dissimilar worldviews or visions about the earth we live on. Rather and more fundamentally, it revolves around earth materialities: the planets clash over "what the earth is really made of." To make their point, they contrast former US president Donald Trump's climate-change-skeptic inhabitation of the world and Swedish climate activist Greta Thunberg's planet. The two authors do not address the interdependence of these different earth materialities. However, and this is what makes their project relevant to what this book aims in part to achieve, they state that the main objective of the exhibition was to articulate new diplomatic encounters between the planet's inhabitants to invite them to reassess both what is dividing us and what we could "have in common nonetheless." This is how they formulate their search for a "weak" and "wicked" (one might add "weird") form of universality. The passage is rather lengthy but worth quoting in full:

By framing the question in such a geopolitical way, we hope to trigger what we call "new diplomatic encounters." Diplomacy defines a set of skills, procedures, and habits of thought which occur either before or after a situation of conflict. The key feature of a diplomatic encounter is that there is no arbiter, referee, or judge who would sit above the situation to decide who is right or wrong about an issue. It is precisely because there is no such a judge that diplomacy is necessary. In the fictional space of the exhibition, we wish to multiply those encounters to mimic what would be needed in the real world, at scale one, and thus to prepare the visitors for the tasks that lie ahead. If diplomacy is needed right now, it is because the dreams of a generally accepted common ground have disappeared with the emergence of this new climatic regime. To be sure, universality had been under attack for many years and from many quarters. It has been shown to be a cover for the land grab by certain nation states of the territories of others in the name of values which we now realize are no longer generally accepted. But such a critique of universality happens just at the time when the ecological crisis obliges all peoples to reassess what is dividing them to the core but also what they might have in common nonetheless. So it seems that one way to search for a "weak" and "wicked" form of universality is to devise diplomatic exercises. . . . It is this milieu that we wish to benefit from by working with artists, scientists and architects to try providing a texture and a representation of those lands that one wants to inhabit. "You and I" indicates a form of confrontation and division, but hopefully a productive one, which we want to examine in particular during our workshop program through the simulation of those diplomatic encounters.[2]

The tensions between planets that Latour and Guinard wanted to explore diplomatically were represented in the exhibition's poster as curved dotted lines—Mortonian loops—circling outside, inside, and between the planets: divergence *and* twisted rapprochement. In their statement, the two authors explained that the main imperative today is to search for commonality anew—a search that must take into account both the generalized disbelief in universalism and the reality of climate change that concerns all of us. Following a Latourian perspective, diplomatic encounters are a set of procedures that can facilitate that search. But it problematically leaves unaddressed the question of who gets to define the diplomatic procedures. That last point helps me to conclude.

You and I Don't Live on the Same Planet was primarily an ecological project, but its framework strongly resonates with contemporary art's response to necropolitical migration—another major predicament of the twenty-first century; the exhibition's different segments (globalization, security, escape, alternative gravity, and terrestriality) echo the main stakes and processes sustaining present-day migration. In contrast, the artworks examined in this book do not so much produce diplomatic encounters as articulate calls—calls to historicize, to become responsible, to empathize, and to story-tell; these calls both disclose the dark coexistences structuring migration and attempt to transform them into more reciprocal forms of coexistence. More importantly, and this is where the Taipei Biennial's exhibition no longer resonates with the contents of this book, these artworks' shared basic assumption is significantly different from the Latourian premise, for, indeed, this study has argued, you and I *do* live on the same planet even if we don't live together, insofar as *you and I live interdependently but might well find ways to live more reciprocally with one another*. The calls are guidelines on how to become aware of interdependence and how to reach mutuality. No one gets to define diplomatic procedures; the plea is to follow the calls.

Writing this book, however, has made me realize that following the calls and carrying through on reciprocity are far from being unilinear endeavors! Coexistences, be they dark or luminous, are necessarily and will always be ambivalent; the imperative therefore is not to repress parerga but to learn from them and see how they can be alleviated. Moreover, all of the artworks examined in this book affirm, albeit differently, the Glissantian right to—even the imperative of—opacity. Without the capacity *not* to reveal who one is, the capacity to move away from fixed categories (such as the other, the refugee, the asylum seeker, the illegal or irregular migrant, the citizen), and the capacity to accept the other's opacity, there is no acknowledgment of the autonomy of migration and, hence, no possible premise of equality and no possible end to necropolitical migration. In the book's introduction, I spoke of calls as vital and vibrant interpellations that ask viewers to meditate and rethink their beliefs, to perceive and transform coexistences. Calls may best be understood, ultimately, as what art uniquely does: by not shying away from ambivalence and opacity as a right, it shows that there are no straightforward answers to necropolitical migration. The calls are calls to be troubled, to ponder, to unlearn—therein lies the luminous dimension of coexistence.

ACKNOWLEDGMENTS

This research was funded by an Insight Grant from the Canadian Social Sciences and Humanities Research Council (SSHRC). Without this generous funding, it would have been impossible to see and resee, experience and reexperience the artworks examined in this book. The grant was also invaluable for the archival research, the documentation of the artworks, and the dissemination of my research. This undertaking was at least four years in the making. My utmost thanks are therefore owed to the MIT Press editor Victoria Hindley for welcoming the project. Her thoughtful guidance, judicious critical feedback, and challenging questions helped me improve the book substantially: it was such a privilege to work with her. I also want to thank Assistant Acquisitions Editor Gabriela Bueno Gibbs for her infallible capacity to address the queries that kept emerging when I was completing the book, as well as the MIT Press editor Virginia Crossman and the copy editor Annie Barva for their remarkably perceptive reading of the manuscript. I extend my indebtedness to the artists, image librarians (notably Charlotte Parmley from Lisson Gallery because of the complexities of my request), archivists, photographers, and gallerists for giving their time and attentiveness during interviews and for granting me permission to reprint the works that finally made their way in the book's final version. My warmest thanks also go to my research assistant, Evgeniya Makarova, who accompanied me in the final stages of the manuscript—I cannot overstate the intelligence, accuracy, sharpness, reliability, proactivity, and vigilance (I could go on and on) of her research interventions. In addition, I want to acknowledge the sensitivity, patience, and responsiveness of the graduate students who followed my seminars related to this book: their participation was key to its evolution and completion. Special thanks as well to Suzanne Paquet and Alexandrine Théorêt (editors of *Art, publics et cultures numériques. Flux d'images et vie des oeuvres* [Montréal: Les Presses de l'Université de Montréal, 2022]); Carolina Rito and Bill Balaskas (editors of *Fabricating Publics: Dissemination of Culture in the Post-truth Era* [London: Open Humanities Press, 2021]); Gabriele Genge, Ludger Schwarte, and Angela Stercken (editors of *Aesthetic Temporalities Today: Present, Presentness, Re-presentation* [Bielefeld, Germany: Verlag, 2020]); Santiago Zabala and Michael Lewis (editors of the *Journal of Italian Philosophy*, vol. 4); and the publishers for allowing me to reprint sections of articles published in these collections. Last but not least, I want to express my deepest gratitude to John, my first reader, for his imperturbable intellectual support throughout this project—his generous feedback has meant a great deal to me.

NOTES

PREFACE

1. Ramaya Tegegne, "A Structure: When the Same Things Keep Coming Up," *Notes from Quarantine* (blog), *Texte zur Kunst*, May 6, 2020, https://www.textezurkunst.de/articles /structure-when-same-things-keep-coming/. The Quebec-based Fédération nationale des communications et de la culture provided a portrayal of the increased vulnerability of the mental health of artists during the COVID-19 pandemic in the report *Pour que les arts demeurent vivants*, published in March 2021. The report can be accessed at https://www.fncom.org/wp-content/uploads/2021/03/Rapport-Plaidoyer-pour-que-les -arts-demeurent-vivants-Mars-2021.pdf. Another report was released on April 13, 2021, by the American Alliance of Museums (AAM): it revealed that 43 percent of museum workers—especially independent curators and consultants—had experienced an income decline during the pandemic. See "Survey Paints Stark Portrait of Museum Workers' Financial Situation," *Artforum*, April 14, 2021, https://www.artforum.com/news/sur vey-paints-stark-portrait-of-museum-workers-financial-situation-85461.

2. "Migrant Boat Sinks off Tunisia Leaving at Least 20 Dead," *BBC News*, December 24, 2020, https://www.bbc.com/news/world-africa-55442746.

3. Patrick Kingsley and Karam Shoumali, "Taking Hard Line, Greece Turns Back Migrants by Abandoning Them at Sea," *New York Times*, August 15, 2020, https://www.nytimes.com /2020/08/14/world/europe/greece-migrants-abandoning-sea.html; Oona Hathaway, Mark Stevens, and Preston Lim, "Law: Refugee Law—the Principle of Non-refoulement," *Just Security*, November 30, 2020, https://www.justsecurity.org/73593/covid-19-and-international-law -refugee-law-the-principle-of-non-refoulement/.

4. Daniel Trilling, "Greece Has a Deadly New Migration Policy—and All of Europe Is to Blame," *Guardian*, August 27, 2020, https://www.theguardian.com/commentisfree/2020/aug /27/greece-migration-europe-athens-refugees.

5. "Bodies of 22 Migrants and Refugees Retrieved off Libya's Coast," al Jazeera, August 24, 2020, https://www.aljazeera.com/news/2020/8/24/bodies-of-22-migrants-and-refugees-retrieved -off-libyas-coast.

6. Emma Reynolds, "Europe's Migrant Crisis Is Worsening during the Pandemic. The Reaction Has Been Brutal," CNN, September 1, 2020, https://www.cnn.com/2020/08/28/europe /europe-migrants-coronavirus-intl/index.html.

7. "Moria Migrants: Fire Destroys Greek Camp Leaving 13,000 without Shelter," *BBC News*, September 2020, https://www.bbc.com/news/world-europe-54082201; Marina Rafenberg, "À Lesbos, le gouvernement grec veut fermer presque toutes les structures d'accueil des réfugiés," *Le Monde*, October 9–10, 2020, https://www.lemonde.fr/international/arti cle/2020/10/09/a-lesbos-le-gouvernement-grec-veut-fermer-presque-toutes-les-struc tures-d-accueil-des-refugies_6055337_3210.html.

8. "At Least 16 Migrants Feared Dead in Shipwreck off Libya: IOM," al Jazeera, September 25, 2020, https://www.aljazeera.com/news/2020/9/25/at-least-16-people-died-in-a-shipwreck-un -migration-agency.

9. Julia Pascual, "Migrants: Dans l'impasse de Calais, des campements succèdent aux campements," *Le Monde*, October 5, 2020, https://www.lemonde.fr/societe/article/2020/10/05/mig rants-dans-l-impasse-de-calais-des-campements-succedent-aux-campements_6054750 _3224.html.

10. Shaun Tandon and Fracesco Fontemaggis, "Sous l'ère Trump, l'accueil des réfugiés au plus bas," *La Presse*, October 1, 2020, https://www.lapresse.ca/international/etats-unis/2020-10-01 /etats-unis/sous-l-ere-trump-l-accueil-des-refugies-au-plus-bas.php.

11. Agence France-Presse, "3000 migrants Honduriens en route vers les États-Unis," *La Presse*, October 1, 2020, https://www.lapresse.ca/videos/international/202010/01/46-1-3000-migrants -honduriens-en-route-vers-les-etats-unis.php/2c66aac5bdb24f35a47ee83984639fb4.

12. "Guatemala Sends Back Some 3,500 Migrants amid COVID-19 Concerns," al Jazeera, October 5, 2020, https://www.aljazeera.com/news/2020/10/5/guatemala-sends-back-almost -3500-migrants-amid-covid-19-concerns.

13. "Des milliers de migrants honduriens bloqués au Guatemala après avoir réussi à passer la frontière," *Le Monde*, January 17, 2021, https://www.lemonde.fr/international/article/2021 /01/17/au-moins-9-000-migrants-honduriens-bloques-par-la-police-du-guatemala-apres -avoir-reussi-a-passer-la-frontiere_6066599_3210.html.

14. Agence France-Presse, "Naufrage de migrants en Tunisie: Le bilan grimpe à 13 morts et 9 disparus," *Le Monde*, October 13, 2020, https://www.lemonde.fr/afrique/article/2020/10/13 /naufrage-de-migrants-en-tunisie-le-bilan-grimpe-a-13-morts-et-9-disparus_6055818_3212 .html.

15. "At Least 74 Migrants Dead in 'Devastating' Shipwreck off Libya," al Jazeera, November 12, 2020, https://www.aljazeera.com/news/2020/11/12/at-least-74-migrants-dead-in-devastat ing-shipwreck-off-libya.

16. Agence France-Presse, "Plus de 370 migrants secourus par l'*Ocean Viking* amenés en Italie," *La Presse*, January 24, 2021, https://www.lapresse.ca/international/europe/2021-01-24/plus -de-370-migrants-secourus-par-l-ocean-viking-amenes-en-italie.php.

17. Katy Fallon, "'We Were Left in the Sea': Asylum Seekers Forced off Lesbos," *Guardian*, March 19, 2021, https://www.theguardian.com/global-development/2021/mar/19/asylum-seekers -forced-off-lesbos-pushback-crisis-europe-borders.

18. "A Mayday Call, a Dash across the Mediterranean . . . and 130 Souls Lost at Sea," *Guardian*, April 25, 2021, https://www.theguardian.com/global-development/2021/apr/25/a-mayday-call -a-dash-across-the-ocean-and-130-souls-lost-at-sea; "Dix-sept migrants retrouvés morts sur un bateau au large des Canaries," *Le Monde*, April 27, 2021, https://www.lemonde.fr/inter national/article/2021/04/27/dix-sept-migrants-retrouves-morts-sur-un-bateau-au-large-des -canaries_6078174_3210.html.

19. "What Is Biden Doing Differently at US Border?," *BBC News*, May 14, 2021, https://www.bbc .com/news/world-us-canada-56255613.

20. "17 Migrants Found Dead off Spain's Canary Islands," *CGTN Africa*, April 27, 2021, https:// africa.cgtn.com/2021/04/27/17-migrants-found-dead-off-spains-canary-islands/.

21. "Plus de 1400 migrants sont arrivés ce weekend sur l'île italienne de Lampedusa," *Le Monde*, May 10, 2021, https://www.lemonde.fr/international/article/2021/05/10/plus-de-1-400-migrants-sont-arrives-ce-week-end-sur-l-ile-italienne-de-lampedusa_6079676_3210.html.

22. "Photos: Death and Despair as African Migrants Arrive in Spain," al Jazeera, May 24, 2021, https://www.aljazeera.com/gallery/2021/5/24/in-pictures-death-and-despair-on-europes-african-frontier.

23. "Calais: Au moins vingt-sept morts dans le naufrage d'une embarcation," *Le Monde*, November 24, 2021, https://www.lemonde.fr/international/article/2021/11/24/calais-au-moins-vingt-migrants-morts-dans-le-naufrage-d-une-embarcation-dans-la-manche_6103452_3210.html; Rajeev Syal, Angelique Chrisafis, and Diane Taylor, "Tragedy at Sea Claims Dozens of Lives in Deadliest Day of Channel Crisis," *Guardian,* November 24, 2021, https://www.theguardian.com/world/2021/nov/24/several-people-dead-migrant-boat-capsizes-channel; "Morts de migrants dans la Manche: Les corps de seize victimes rapatriés au Kurdistan d'Irak," *Le Monde*, December 26, 2021, https://www.lemonde.fr/international/article/2021/12/26/naufrage-de-migrants-dans-la-manche-les-corps-de-seize-victimes-rapatries-au-kurdistan-d-irak_6107316_3210.html?xtor=EPR-32280629-[a-la-une]-20211226-[zone_edito_1_titre_4]&M_BT=58172710913771.

24. "Belarus Border Crisis: How Are Migrants Getting There?," *BBC News*, November 26, 2021, https://www.bbc.com/news/59233244.

25. "More than 160 Migrants Drown in Shipwrecks off Libya, UN Says," al Jazeera, December 21, 2021, https://www.aljazeera.com/news/2021/12/21/un-over-160-migrants-drown-in-shipwrecks-off-libya; Agence France-Presse, "Les corps de 28 migrants retrouvés sur la côte libyenne," *La Presse*, December 26, 2021, https://www.lapresse.ca/international/afrique/2021-12-26/les-corps-de-28-migrants-retrouves-sur-la-cote-libyenne.php.

26. Artemis Moshtaghian, "Trial for Former Officer Charged in Connection with Breonna Taylor's Shooting Pushed to 2022," CNN, April 25, 2021, https://www.cnn.com/2021/04/25/us/breonna-taylor-shooting-brett-hankison-trial-pushed-back/index.html.

27. Ray Sanchez and Eric Levenson, "Derek Chauvin Sentenced to 22.5 Years in Death of George Floyd," CNN, June 25, 2021, https://www.cnn.com/2021/06/25/us/derek-chauvin-sentencing-george-floyd/index.html.

28. Lindsay Richardson, "Thousands Gather to Mark End of Inquest into Death of Joyce Echaquan," *APTNNews*, June 2, 2021, https://www.aptnnews.ca/national-news/thousands-gather-to-mark-end-of-inquest-into-death-of-joyce-echaquan/.

29. Achille Mbembe, *Brutalisme* (Paris: La Découverte, 2020), 23.

30. Nicolas Truong, "Claire Marin: 'Face à la catastrophe, on se rassure en la considérant comme une parenthèse plutôt qu'un avertissement,'" *Le Monde*, March 24, 2020, author's translation, https://www.lemonde.fr/idees/article/2020/03/24/claire-marin-penser-les-maladies-sur-le-modele-de-la-guerre-c-est-se-meprendre-sur-l-essence-du-vivant_6034170_3232.html.

31. Nicolas Truong, "Giorgio Agamben: 'L'épidémie montre clairement que l'état d'exception est devenu la condition normale,'" *Le Monde*, March 24, 2020, author's translation, https://www.lemonde.fr/idees/article/2020/03/24/giorgio-agamben-l-epidemie-montre-clairement-que-l-etat-d-exception-est-devenu-la-condition-normale_6034245_3232.html.

32. George Yancy, "Judith Butler: Mourning Is a Political Act amid the Pandemic and Its Disparities," *Truthout*, April 30, 2020, https://truthout.org/articles/judith-butler-mourning-is-a-political-act-amid-the-pandemic-and-its-disparities/?utm_campaign=Truthout+Share+Buttons&fbclid=IwAR1JeUrLC4E-pcwo0gjkoGDn0AJ2Wkx81-os2W1ixfmWbv6iCCmr-ynz9bM&dm_i=56G9,7F82,31G0UB,SW4W,1.

33. Nicolas Truong, "Didier Fassin: 'Avec le coronavirus, notre vision du monde s'est rétrécie comme jamais,'" *Le Monde*, May 24, 2020, https://www.lemonde.fr/idees/article/2020/05/24/didier-fassin-avec-le-coronavirus-notre-vision-du-monde-s-est-retrecie-comme-jamais_6040578_3232.html.

INTRODUCTION

1. M. NourbeSe Philip, "Covidian Catastrophes: Resonances of Suffering," *Coronavirus Tales* (blog), *Humanities Watch*, April 4, 2020, https://humanitieswatch.org/2020/04/covidian-catastrophes-m-nourbese-philip/?dm_i=56G9,6REU,31G0UB,PZ1S,1.

2. Peter Schjeldahl, "The Art of War in 'Theatre of Operations,'" *New Yorker*, December 2, 2019, https://www.newyorker.com/magazine/2019/12/02/the-art-of-war-in-theater-of-operations.

3. Hannah Ellis-Petersen, "Banksy Uses Steve Jobs Artwork to Highlight Refugee Crisis," *Guardian*, December 11, 2015, https://www.theguardian.com/artanddesign/2015/dec/11/banksy-uses-steve-jobs-artwork-to-highlight-refugee-crisis; also see Carol Diehl, *Banksy: Completed* (Cambridge, MA: MIT Press, 2021).

4. Christine Riding, "The Raft of the *Medusa* in Britain," in *Crossing the Channel: British and French Painting in the Age of Romanticism*, ed. Patrick Noon and Stephen Bann (London: Tate, 2003), 66–94; Karen Wilkin, "Romanticism at the Met," *New Criterion* 22, no. 4 (December 2003): 37–42.

5. Lorenzo Tondo and Maurice Stierl, "Banksy Funds Refugee Rescue Boat Operating in Mediterranean," *Guardian*, August 27, 2020, https://www.theguardian.com/world/2020/aug/27/banksy-funds-refugee-rescue-boat-operating-in-mediterranean.

6. Tondo and Stierl, "Banksy Funds Refugee Rescue Boat."

7. "This Is the MV Louise Michel," Louise Michel, accessed July 13, 2021, https://mvlouisemichel.org; "Le nombre de migrants morts en mer en tentant de rejoindre l'Europe a doublé en un an," *Le Monde*, July 14, 2021, https://www.lemonde.fr/international/article/2021/07/14/le-nombre-de-migrants-morts-en-mer-en-tentant-de-rejoindre-l-europe-a-double-en-un-an_6088196_3210.html?xtor&&M_BT=58172710913771#x3D;EPR-32280629-[a-la-une]-20210714-[zone_edito_1_titre_3].

8. Santiago Zabala, *Why Only Art Can Save Us: Aesthetics and the Absence of Emergency* (New York: Columbia University Press, 2019), author's emphasis.

9. Bouchra Khalili, "Questionnaire: Bouchra Khalili," *Frieze* 199 (November–December 2018), http://www.bouchrakhalili.com/wp-content/uploads/2015/05/Questionnaire_-Bouchra-Khalili-_-Frieze.pdf.

10. Daniel Boffey and Lorenzo Tondo, "Captain of Migrant Rescue Ship Says Italy 'Criminalising Solidarity,'" *Guardian*, June 15, 2019, https://www.theguardian.com/world/2019/jun/15/captain-of-migrant-rescue-ship-says-italy-criminalising-solidarity.

11. UN High Commissioner for Refugees (UNHCR), "Global Trends: Forced Displacements in 2015," June 20, 2016, https://www.unhcr.org/576408cd7.pdf; UNHCR, "Figures at a Glance," June 18, 2020, https://www.unhcr.org/figures-at-a-glance.html.

12. Nicholas De Genova, Glenda Garelli, and Martina Tazzioli, "Autonomy of Asylum? The Autonomy of Migration. Undoing the Refugee Crisis Script," *South Atlantic Quarterly* 117, no. 2 (April 2018): 254.

13. UNHCR, "Figures at a Glance."

14. Emanuela Campanella, "The U.S.-Mexico Migrant Crisis: What Is Really Happening at the Border?," *Global News*, August 22, 2019, https://globalnews.ca/news/5776325/us-mexico -wall-migrants-children-detained/; Zack Stanton, "There's an Immigration Crisis, but It's Not the One You Think," *Politico Magazine*, March 25, 2020, https://www.politico.com/news /magazine/2021/03/25/border-crisis-immigration-explained-biden-trump-mexico-478049.

15. De Genova, Garelli, and Tazzioli, "Autonomy of Asylum?," 254; Campanella, "The U.S.-Mexico Migrant Crisis."

16. Walter D. Mignolo, "DELINKING: The Rhetoric of Modernity, the Logic of Coloniality, and the Grammar of De-coloniality," *Cultural Studies* 21, nos. 2–3 (2007): 453.

17. Mira L. Siegelberg, *Statelessness: A Modern History* (Cambridge, MA: Harvard University Press, 2020), 1.

18. Étienne Balibar, "Pour un droit international de l'hospitalité," *Le Monde*, August 16, 2018, https://www.lemonde.fr/idees/article/2018/08/16/etienne-balibar-pour-un-droit-interna tional-de-l-hospitalite_5342881_3232.html. On the eradication of the other in contemporary migration, also see Daniel Trilling, "Five Myths about the Refugee Crisis," *Guardian*, June 5, 2018, https://www.theguardian.com/news/2018/jun/05/five-myths-about-the-refugee-crisis; and Achille Mbembe, *Necropolitics*, trans. Steven Corcoran (Durham, NC: Duke University Press, 2019), 10–12, 34, 98, 102. For statistics, see UNHCR, "1 Per Cent of Humanity Displaced: UNHCR Global Trends Report," June 18, 2020, https://www.unhcr.org/news /press/2020/6/5ee9db2e4/1-cent-humanity-displaced-unhcr-global-trends-report.html.

19. Daniel Trilling, "Uncomfortable Facts: The Migrant Crisis in the European Media," in *Lost in Media: Migrant Perspectives and the Public Sphere*, ed. Ismail Einashe and Thomas Roueché (Amsterdam: Valiz, 2019), 24.

20. Dimitry Kochenov, *Citizenship* (Cambridge, MA: MIT Press, 2020), xv

21. W. B. Gallie, "Essentially Contested Concepts," *Proceedings of the Aristotelian Society*, no. 56 (1955–1956): 167 198.

22. Michel Agier, *Managing the Undesirables: Refugee Camps and Humanitarian Government*, trans. David Fernbach (Cambridge: Polity Press, 2001), 4; UNHCR, "The 1951 Convention Relating to the Status of Refugees and Its 1967 Protocol," September 2011, https://www.unhcr .org/about-us/background/4ec262df9/1951-convention-relating-status-refugees-its-1967 -protocol.html.

23. Michel Agier, *Définir les réfugiés* (Paris: Presses universitaires de France, 2018), 5, author's translation.

24. On this specific point, which requires Foucauldian "mobile thought" in defining terms, see Ann Laura Stoler, *Duress: Imperial Durabilities in Our Times* (Durham, NC: Duke University Press, 2016), 18–19.

25. Daniel Trilling, "How the Media Contributed to the Migrant Crisis," *Guardian*, August 1, 2019, https://www.theguardian.com/news/2019/aug/01/media-framed-migrant-crisis-disaster-reporting.

26. Fred Moten, *Stolen Life (consent not to be a single being)* (Durham, NC: Duke University Press, 2018), 131.

27. Nicholas De Genova, "The Incorrigible Subject: The Autonomy of Migration and the US Immigration Stalemate," in *Subjectivation in Political Theory and Contemporary Practices*, ed. Andreas Oberprantacher and Andrei Siclodi (London: Palgrave Mcmillan, 2016), 267.

28. Anna Lowenhaupt Tsing, *Friction: An Ethnography of Global Connection* (Princeton, NJ: Princeton University Press, 2011), 6.

29. Aurélien Gamboni, "In the Thickness of the Crossing: Challenging the Liquid Violence of Borders in the Mediterranean—an Interview with Charles Heller," trans. Maya Dalinsky, *Texte zur Kunst* 29, no. 114 (June 2019): 88.

30. Anna Wójcik, "The Politics of Art: An Interview with Jacques Rancière," *Verso* (blog), November 9, 2015, https://www.versobooks.com/blogs/2320-the-politics-of-art-an-interview-with-jacques-ranciere; Jacques Rancière, *The Politics of Aesthetics*, trans. Gabriel Rockhill (London: Continuum, 2014), 13.

31. Mieke Bal, "Lost in Space, Lost in the Library," in *Essays in Migration Aesthetics: Cultural Practices between Migration and Art-Making*, ed. Sam Durrant and Catherine M. Lord (Amsterdam: Rodopi, 2007), 23–26.

32. Tania Bruguera, "Notes on Political Timing Specificity," *Artforum International* 57, no. 9 (May 2019): 205; emphasis is in the original unless otherwise indicated in the notes, https://www.artforum.com/print/201905/notes-on-political-timing-specificity-79513.

33. "Introduction by Paolo Baratta," La Biennale di Venezia—Biennale Architettura, 2021, https://www.labiennale.org/en/architecture/2021/introduction-paolo-baratta.

34. Ariella Aïsha Azoulay, *Potential History: Unlearning Imperialism* (London: Verso, 2019), 2.

35. Azoulay, *Potential History*, 1.

36. Greg Afinogenov, "Blurred Borders: Museum Exhibitions Present Narratives of Migration's Trauma while Obscuring Its Causes," *Art in America*, February 3, 2020, https://www.artnews.com/art-in-america/features/migration-exhibitions-obscure-reality-militarized-borders-1202676742/.

37. Afinogenov, "Blurred Borders."

CHAPTER 1

1. UNHCR, "Global Trends: Forced Displacement in 2018," June 20, 2019, https://www.unhcr.org/5d08d7ee7.pdf; Ashley Westerman, "Nearly 71 Million People Forcibly Displaced Worldwide as of 2018, U.N. Report Says," NPR, June 19, 2019, https://www.npr.org/2019/06/19/733945696/nearly-71-million-people-forcibly-displaced-worldwide-in-2018-says-u-n-report.

2. Nick Cumming-Bruce, "Number of People Fleeing Conflict Is Highest since World War II, U.N. Says," *New York Times*, June 19, 2019, https://www.nytimes.com/2019/06/19/world/refugees-record-un.html.

3. Nicholas De Genova, "The 'Migrant Crisis' as Racial Crisis: Do *Black Lives Matter* in Europe?," *Ethnic and Racial Studies* 41, no. 10 (2017): 1768.

4. De Genova, "The 'Migrant Crisis' as Racial Crisis," 1766.

5. International Organization for Migration (IOM), "Map Tracking Migrant Deaths and Disappearances," Missing Migrants Project, last modified April 2, 2021, https://gmdac.iom.int /map-tracking-migrant-deaths-and-disappearances; and "Le nombre de migrants morts en mer en tentant de rejoindre l'Europe a doublé en un an," *Le Monde*, July 14, 2021, https://www.lemonde.fr/international/article/2021/07/14/le-nombre-de-migrants-morts -en-mer-en-tentant-de-rejoindre-l-europe-a-double-en-un-an_6088196_3210.html? xtor&&M_BT=58172710913771#x3D;EPR-32280629-[a-la-une]-20210714-[zone_edito_1_titre_3].

6. "Migrant Deaths and Disappearances," Migration Data Portal, last modified March 17, 2020, https://migrationdataportal.org/themes/migrant-deaths-and-disappearances.

7. "New Kings of the Wild Frontier," *Economist*, March 6, 2021, 47.

8. Daniel Loick, "We Refugees," trans. Keith Tribe, *Public Seminar*, May 23, 2016, https://pub licseminar.org/2016/05/we-refugees/.

9. William Spindler, "2015: The Year of Europe's Refugee Crisis," UNHCR, December 8, 2015, https://www.unhcr.org/news/stories/2015/12/56ec1ebde/2015-year-europes-refugee-crisis .html.

10. UNHCR, "Europe Refugees & Migrants Emergency Response: Nationality of Arrivals to Greece, Italy, and Spain," March 31, 2016, https://reliefweb.int/sites/reliefweb.int/files/re sources/MonthlyTrendsofNationalities-ArrivalstoGreeceItalyandSpain-31December2015 .pdf.

11. ETIAS Europe, "What Exactly Is ETIAS?," 2016–2019, https://www.etiaseurope.eu.

12. Jean-Baptiste Chastand and Jean-Pierre Stroobants, "L'agence européenne Frontex fragilisée par les accusations d'expulsions illégales," *Le Monde*, January 29, 2021, https:// www.lemonde.fr/international/article/2021/01/29/l-agence-europeenne-frontex-fragilisee -par-les-accusations-d-expulsions-illegales_6067995_3210.html; "New Kings of the Wild Frontier," 48.

13. Charles Heller and Lorenzo Pezzani, "The Perils of Migration: Countervailing Mediations of Risk at the EU's Maritime Frontier," in *The Routledge Companion to Media and Risk*, ed. Bishnupriya Ghosh and Bhaskar Sarkar (New York: Routledge, 2020), 130.

14. "Migrant Deaths and Disappearances."

15. Reece Jones, *Violent Borders: Refugees and the Right to Move* (London: Verso, 2017), 5, 46.

16. Jason De León, *The Land of Open Graves* (Oakland: University of California Press, 2015), 4–5.

17. "Hostile Terrain 94," Undocumented Migration Project, accessed June 7, 2021, https://www .undocumentedmigrationproject.org/hostileterrain94.

18. The visual studies scholar Jill H. Casid has spoken of "the necropolitical conditions of 'migrant crisis,'" focusing on the Mediterranean Sea as a maritime cemetery for refugees attempting to cross it on their way to Europe ("Necropolitics at Sea," in *Migration and the Contemporary Mediterranean: Shifting Cultures in Twenty-First-Century Italy and Beyond*, ed. Claudia Gualtieri [Oxford: Peter Lang, 2018], 193–194). My book is an attempt to further substantiate that claim and expand it beyond the Mediterranean Sea.

19. Achille Mbembe, "Necropolitics," trans. Libby Meintjes, *Public Culture* 15, no. 1 (2003): 12, 21, 39–40, https://voidnetwork.gr/wp-content/uploads/2016/09/Necropolitics-Achille-Mbembe .pdf.

20. Michel Foucault, "Il faut défendre la société," in *Cours au Collège de France, 1976* (Paris: Hautes études, EHESS, Gallimard, and Seuil, 1997), 214; Michel Foucault, *The History of Sexuality*, vol. 1: *An Introduction*, trans. Robert Hurley (New York: Random House, 1990), 139. Also see Didier Fassin, "Another Politics of Life Is Possible," *Theory, Culture, & Society* 26, no. 5 (2009): 44–60; Matthew Sparke, "Health," in *The Sage Handbook of Human Geography*, ed. Roger Lee et al. (London: Sage, 2014), 684–708, see esp. 690.

21. Mbembe, "Necropolitics," 39.

22. Thomas Lemke, "Critique and Experience in Foucault," *Theory, Culture, & Society* 26, no. 6 (July 2011): 26–48, https://www.researchgate.net/publication/258192305_Critique_and_Ex perience_in_Foucault.

23. Mbembe, "Necropolitics," 23.

24. Mbembe, "Necropolitics," 16, 40.

25. Thom Davies, Arshad Isakjee, and Surindar Dhesi, "Violent Inaction: The Necropolitical Experience of Refugees in Europe," *Antipode* 49, no. 5 (2017): 1263–1284, https://onlinelibrary .wiley.com/doi/full/10.1111/anti.12325. Also see Thom Davies and Arshad Isakjee, "Ruins of Empire: Refugees, Race, and the Postcolonial Geographies of European Migrant Camps," *Geoforum* 102 (June 2019): 214–217.

26. Christina Sharpe, *In the Wake: On Blackness and Being* (Durham, NC: Duke University Press, 2016), 30.

27. On the Cold War, especially the American context of migration, see especially Susan Bibler Coutin, "Falling Outside: Excavating the History of Central American Asylum Seekers," *Law & Social Inquiry* 36, no. 3 (Summer 2011): 569–596; and Rebecca Hamlin, "International Law and Administrative Insulation: A Comparison of Refugee Status Determination Regimes in the United States, Canada, and Australia," *Law & Social Inquiry* 37, no. 4 (Fall 2012): 933–968.

28. Derek Gregory, *The Colonial Present: Afghanistan, Palestine, and Iraq* (Malden, MA: Wiley-Blackwell, 2004), 11–12.

29. Lucy Mayblin, *Asylum after Empire: Colonial Legacies in the Politics of Asylum Seeking* (London: Rowman & Littlefield, 2017), 1; Napuli Langa, "About the Refugee Movement in Kreuzberg/ Berlin," *Movements* 1, no. 2 (2015): 1–10, https://movements-journal.org/issues/02.kaempfe/08 .langa--refugee-movement-kreuzberg-berlin.html; Vaughan Robinson and Jeremy Sergott, *Understanding the Decision-Making of Asylum Seekers* (London: Home Office Research, 2002), http://citeseerx.ist.psu.edu/viewdoc/download?doi=10.1.1.473.3461&rep=rep1&type=pdf; Madjiguène Cissé, *The Sans-Papiers: The New Movement of Asylum Seekers and Immigrants without Papers in France: A Woman Draws the First Lessons* (London: Crossroads Books, 1997).

30. Sylvia Wynter and Katherine McKittrick, "Unparalleled Catastrophe for Our Species," in *Sylvia Wynter: On Being as Praxis*, ed. Katherine McKittrick (Durham, NC: Duke University Press, 2015), 22–24, 35–37.

31. Jürgen Osterhammel, *Colonialism: A Theoretical Overview*, trans. Shelley L. Frisch (Princeton, NJ: Markus Wiener, 2010), 16.

32. Margaret Kohn, "Colonialism," in *Stanford Encyclopedia of Philosophy*, online ed. (Stanford, CA: Stanford University, 1997–), entry published May 9, 2006, last modified August 29, 2017, https://plato.stanford.edu/entries/colonialism/.

33. Osterhammel, *Colonialism*, 22.

34. Lorenzo Veracini, *Settler Colonialism: A Theoretical Overview* (London: Palgrave Mcmillan, 2010), 4.

35. Linda Tuhiwai Smith, *Decolonizing Methodologies: Research and Indigenous Peoples* (London: Zed Books, 2012), 64.

36. Kohn, "Colonialism."

37. Tiffany Lethabo King, *The Black Shoals: Offshore Formations of Black and Native Studies* (Durham, NC: Duke University Press, 2019), 16.

38. Gregory, *The Colonial Present*, xv.

39. Daniel Trilling, "Five Myths about the Refugee Crisis," *Guardian*, June 5, 2018, https://www.theguardian.com/news/2018/jun/05/five-myths-about-the-refugee-crisis; Pascale Baligand, "Migration Crisis and Social Trauma," in *The Oxford Handbook of Migration Crises*, ed. Cecilia Menjívar, Marie Ruiz, and Immanuel Ness (New York: Oxford University Press, 2019), 833–848; Heaven Crawley and Dimitris Skleparis, "Refugees, Migrants, Neither, Both: Categorical Fetishism and the Politics of Bounding in Europe's 'Migration Crisis,'" *Journal of Ethnic and Migration Studies* 44, no. 1 (2018): 48, https://www.tandfonline.com/doi/full/10.1080/1369183X.2017.1348224?src=recsys.

40. Shada Islam, "Europe's Migration 'Crisis' Isn't about Numbers. It's about Prejudice," *Guardian*, October 8, 2020, https://www.theguardian.com/world/2020/oct/08/europe-migration-crisis-prejudice-eu-refugee-orban-christian.

41. David Harvey, "Neoliberalism as Creative Destruction," *Annals of the American Academy of Political and Social Science* 610 (March 2007): 29.

42. David Harvey, "Afterthoughts on Piketty's Capital," *David Harvey's Anti-Capitalist Chronicles* (blog), May 17, 2014, http://davidharvey.org/2014/05/afterthoughts-pikettys-capital/.

43. Jörg Matthes and Desirée Schmuck, "The Effects of Anti-immigrant Right-Wing Populist Ads on Implicit and Explicit Attitudes: A Moderated Mediation Model," *Communication Research* 44, no. 4 (March 2015): 1–26, https://www.researchgate.net/publication/277622400_The_Effects_of_Anti-Immigrant_Right-Wing_Populist_Ads_on_Implicit_and_Explicit_Attitudes_A_Moderated_Mediation_Model.

44. Anne Hammerstad, "The Securitization of Forced Migration," in *The Oxford Handbook of Refugee and Forced Migration Studies*, ed. Elena Fiddian-Qasmiyeh et al. (Oxford: Oxford University Press, 2014), 265–277.

45. Office of the High Commissioner for Human Rights (OHCHR), "The Principle of *Non-refoulement* under International Human Rights Law," accessed February 11, 2021, https://www.ohchr.org/Documents/Issues/Migration/GlobalCompactMigration/ThePrincipleNon-RefoulementUnderInternationalHumanRightsLaw.pdf. On campization, see René Kreichauf, "From Forced Migration to Forced Arrival: The Campization of Refugee Accommodation in European Cities," *Comparative Migration Studies* 6, no. 7 (2018): 1–22, https://link.springer.com/content/pdf/10.1186%2Fs40878-017-0069-8.pdf.

46. Lorenzo Tondo, "'Black Book' of Thousands of Illegal Migrant Pushbacks Presented to EU," *Guardian*, December 23, 2020, https://www.theguardian.com/global-development/2020/dec/23/black-book-of-thousands-of-migrant-pushbacks-presented-to-eu.

47. Janie Gosselin, "Les personnes fuient l'enfer libyen," *La Presse*, July 17, 2021, https://www.lapresse.ca/international/afrique/2021-07-17/les-personnes-fuient-l-enfer-libyen.php.

48. Idil Atak and James C. Simeon, "Introduction. The Criminalization of Migration: Context and Consequences," in *The Criminalization of Migration: Context and Consequences*, ed. Idil Atak and James C. Simeon (Montréal: McGill-Queen's University Press, 2018), 4–5.

49. Alison Mountz, *The Death of Asylum: Hidden Geographies of the Enforcement Archipelago* (Minneapolis: University of Minnesota Press, 2020). See also De Genova, "The 'Migrant Crisis' as Racial Crisis," 1766.

50. Sarah R. Champagne, "Forte hausse des rejets de demandes d'immigration humanitaire au Canada en 2020," *Le Devoir*, July 14, 2021, https://www.ledevoir.com/politique/canada/617751/immigration-le-canada-a-refuse-presque-deux-fois-plus-de-demandes-pour-motifs-hu manitaires.

51. Jamie Grierson, "UK to Block Visas for Countries Refusing to Take Back Asylum Seekers," *Guardian*, July 6, 2021, https://www.theguardian.com/politics/2021/jul/06/uk-to-block-visas-from-countries-refusing-to-take-back-undocumented-migrants.

52. Emily Fishbein, with Wael Qarssifi, "Refugees Cling to Hope of Resettlement, Even as World Slams Doors," al Jazeera, October 16, 2020, https://www.aljazeera.com/news/2020/10/16/refugees-cling-to-hope-of-resettlement-even-as-doors-close.

53. Fishbein, "Refugees Cling to Hope of Resettlement."

54. See especially Gerhard Hoffstaedter and Sara Riva, "There Are 70 Million Refugees in the World. Here Are 5 Solutions to the Problem," *Conversation*, June 20, 2019, https://theconversation.com/there-are-70-million-refugees-in-the-world-here-are-5-solutions-to-the-problem-118920; UNHCR, *Refugee Protection and Mixed Migration: The 10-Point Plan in Action* (Geneva: UNHCR, February 2007), chap. 7, https://www.unhcr.org/en-us/50a4c17f9.pdf; and Patrick Kingsley, "10 Ways to Manage the Migration Crisis," *Guardian*, September 4, 2015, https://www.theguardian.com/world/2015/sep/04/10-ways-to-manage-the-migration-crisis.

55. Mbembe, "Necropolitics," 40.

56. Jennifer A. González, "Sea Dreams: Isaac Julien's *Western Union: Small Boats*," in *The Migrant's Time: Rethinking Art History and Diaspora*, ed. Saloni Mathur (Williamstown, MA: Sterling and Francine Clark Institute, 2011), 115.

57. Julia Choe, "African Migration to Europe," *Foreign Affairs*, July 9, 2007, https://www.cfr.org/backgrounder/african-migration-europe.

58. Sara Hamood, *African Transit Migration through Libya to Europe: The Human Cost* (Cairo: American University of Cairo, 2006), http://www.migreurop.org/IMG/pdf/hamood-libya.pdf.

59. Sabine Hess and Bernd Kasparek, "Under Control? Or Border (as) Conflict: Reflections on the European Border Regime," *Social Inclusion* 5, no. 3 (2017): 62, https://www.researchgate.net/publication/319915817_Under_Control_Or_Border_as_Conflict_Reflections_on_the_European_Border_Regime.

60. Anne Ring Petersen, "Migratory Aesthetics and the Politics of Irregular Migration: A Case Study of Isaac Julien's *Western Union: small boats*," in *The Culture of Migration: Politics, Aesthetics, and Histories*, ed. Sten Pultz Moslund, Anne Ring Petersen, and Moritz Schramm (London: I. B. Tauris, 2015), 208.

61. Kobena Mercer, "Avid Iconographies," in *Isaac Julien: With Essays by Kobena Mercer and Chris Darke*, ed. Kobena Mercer, Chris Darke, and Isaac Julien (London: Ellipsis, 2001), 8.

62. González, "Sea Dreams," 126.

63. Sharpe, *In the Wake*, 4.

64. Hannah Arendt, "We Refugees" (1943), in *The Jewish Writings*, ed. Jerome Kohn and Ron H. Feldman (New York: Schocken Books, 2007), 264.

65. Arendt, "We Refugees," 274.

66. Arendt, "We Refugees," 274.

67. Giorgio Agamben, "We Refugees," *Symposium* 49, no. 2 (1995): 114, 116, https://thehubedu-production.s3.amazonaws.com/uploads/1836/1e788430-c11e-4036-8251-5406847cd504/AgambenWeRefugees.pdf.

68. Agamben, "We Regugees," 116.

69. Liliana Riga, Johannes Langer, and Arek Dakessian, "Theorizing Refugeedom: Becoming Young Political Subjects in Beirut," *Theory and Society* 49 (2020): 713, 736–737, https://www.researchgate.net/publication/341168147_Theorizing_refugeedom_becoming_young_political_subjects_in_Beirut.

70. Jacques Rancière, "Who Is the Subject of the Rights of Man?," *South Atlantic Quarterly* 103, nos. 2–3 (Spring–Summer 2004): 304, http://cscs.res.in/dataarchive/textfiles/textfile.2010-11-27.9388690495/file.

71. Michel-Rolph Trouillot, *Silencing the Past: Power and the Production of History* (Boston: Beacon Press, 2015), 23.

72. Zygmunt Bauman, *Strangers at Our Door* (Cambridge: Polity Press, 2016), 15–16.

73. Didier Fassin, *Life: A Critical User's Manual* (Cambridge: Polity Press, 2019), 176.

CHAPTER 2

1. Gayle Clemans, "John Akomfrah's Video Art Lures the Senses While Exploring Ideas about Afrofuturism, Migration, the Environment," *Seattle Times*, March 13, 2020, https://www.seattletimes.com/entertainment/visual-arts/seattle-art-museum-presents-a-rare-west-coast-opportunity-to-see-acclaimed-artist-john-akomfrahs-work-on-big-screens/.

2. Pamela Reynolds, "At the ICA Watershed, John Akomfrah's 'Purple' Mourns a Planet Lost," *ARTery*, May 23, 2019, https://www.wbur.org/artery/2019/05/23/ica-watershed-john-akomfrah-purple.

3. "John Akomfrah: Future History," Seattle Museum of Art, 2020, http://akomfrah.site.seatleartmuseum.org.

4. Anthony Downey, "Vital Materialism: Filming the Anthropocene: John Akomfrah in Conversation with Anthony Downey," *Third Text*, March 2018, http://thirdtext.org/akomfrah-downey.

5. Hannah Ellis-Petersen, "John Akomfrah: 'I Haven't Destroyed This Country. There's No Reason Other Immigrants Would,'" *Guardian*, January 7, 2016, https://www.theguardian.com/artanddesign/2016/jan/07/john-akomfrah-vertical-sea-arnolfini-bristol-lisson-gallery-london-migration.

6. T. J. Demos, "On Terror and Beauty: John Akomfrah's *Vertigo Sea*," *Atlántica* 56 (2015), http://www.revistaatlantica.com/en/contribution/on-terror-and-beauty-john-akomfrahs-vertigo-sea/; Anuradha Vikram, "Underneath the Black Atlantic: Race and Capital in John Akomfrah's *Vertigo Sea*," *X-TRA* 21, no. 3 (Spring 2019): 20–22, https://www.x-traonline.org/article/underneath-the-black-atlantic-race-and-capital-in-john-akomfrahs-vertigo-sea#footnote-4.

7. Adrian Searle, "John Akomfrah's *Vertigo Sea*: Human and Natural History Meet at the Abyss," *Guardian*, January 25, 2016, https://www.theguardian.com/artanddesign/2016/jan/25/john-akomfrah-vertigo-sea-bristol-arnolfini-london-lisson-gallery-auto-de-fe-the-airport-tropikos.

8. Umberto Eco, *The Open Work*, trans. Anna Cancogni (Cambridge, MA: Harvard University Press, 1989), 9, 14.

9. T. J. Demos, "Unspeakable Moments: An Interview with John Akomfrah," *Atlántica* 54 (2014): 59.

10. "John Akomfrah 'London,'" *Art21: Art in the Twenty-First Century*, season 10, September 18, 2020, video, 16:05, https://art21.org/watch/art-in-the-twenty-first-century/s10/john-akomfrah-in-london-segment/.

11. Erik Morse, "The Oceanic Ecologies of John Akomfrah," *ArtReview*, January–February 2016, https://artreview.com/jan-feb-2016-feature-john-akomfrah/.

12. Sean O'Hagan, "John Akomfrah: Progress Can Cause Profound Suffering," *Guardian*, October 1, 2017, https://www.theguardian.com/artanddesign/2017/oct/01/john-akomfrah-purple-climate-change.

13. "John Akomfrah Presents 'Four Nocturnes' Video Installation at Venice Biennale," Lisson Gallery, May 17, 2019, https://www.lissongallery.com/news/john-akomfrah-presents-four-nocturnes-video-installation-at-venice-biennale.

14. "John Akomfrah's New SAF Co-commission Premieres at 58th Venice Biennale," Sharjah Art Foundation, accessed December 8, 2020, http://sharjahart.org/sharjah-art-foundation/news/john-akomfrahs-new-saf-co-commission-premiers-at-58th-venice-biennale.

15. International Union for Conservation of Nature (IUCN), "African Elephant Species Now Endangered and Critically Endangered—IUCN Red List," March 25, 2021, https://www.iucn.org/news/species/202103/african-elephant-species-now-endangered-and-critically-endangered-iucn-red-list; World Wildlife Fund, "Elephant," accessed December 8, 2020, https://www.worldwildlife.org/species/elephant; Laurence Caramel, "En Afrique centrale, le réchauffement climatique affame les éléphants de forêts," *Le Monde*, October 1, 2020, https://www.lemonde.fr/afrique/article/2020/10/01/en-afrique-centrale-le-rechauffement-climatique-affame-les-elephants-de-forets_6054415_3212.html; Emma R. Bush et al., "Long-Term Collapse in Fruit Availability Threatens Central African Forest Megafauna," *Science*,

September 24, 2020, www.sciencemag.org; and Pierre Le Hir, "La protection des éléphants d'Afrique en suspens," *Le Monde*, August 16, 2019, https://www.lemonde.fr/planete/article/2019/08/16/la-protection-des-elephants-d-afrique-en-suspens_5499954_3244.html.

16. Étienne Balibar, "Pour un droit international de l'hospitalité," *Le Monde*, August 16, 2018, https://www.lemonde.fr/idees/article/2018/08/16/etienne-balibar-pour-un-droit-international-de-l-hospitalite_5342881_3232.html. The "acting" component of *Four Nocturnes* was confirmed by John Akomfrah's Studio (Lisson Gallery's image librarian to the author, email, July 2, 2021).

17. Édouard Glissant, *Poetics of Relation*, trans. Betsy Wing (Ann Arbor: University of Michigan Press, 1997), 191.

18. "John Akomfrah: *The Unfinished Conversation* 2012," MoMA, 2019, https://www.moma.org/collection/works/202991.

19. Paul Gilroy, *The Black Atlantic: Modernity and Double-Consciousness* (Cambridge, MA: Harvard University Press, 1993), 104.

20. Demos, "Unspeakable Moments." Also see "John Akomfrah: *The Unfinished Conversation* 2012."

21. *John Akomfrah—Why History Matters*, TateShots, July 2, 2015, video, 7:33, YouTube, https://www.youtube.com/watch?v=jDJYyG7jKVo&lc=UghObzESIzKxYngCoAEC.

22. Roland Barthes, "The Third Meaning: Research Notes on Some Eisenstein Stills" (1970), in *Image Music Text*, trans. Stephen Heath (London: Fontana Press, 1977), 64.

23. Barthes, "The Third Meaning," 53.

24. *John Akomfrah*, Artes Mundi 7, September 17, 2015, video, 5:18, http://www.artesmundi.org/artists/john-akomfrah.

25. João Costa Vargas and Joy James, "Refusing Blackness-as-Victimization: Trayvon Martin and the Black Cyborgs," in *Pursuing Trayvon: Historical Contexts and Contemporary Manifestations of Racial Dynamics*, ed. George Yancy and Janine Jones (Latham, MD: Lexington Books, 2012), 193.

26. *John Akomfrah*, Artes Mundi 7.

27. Juan Canela, "Orchestrated Dialogues: John Akomfrah," *Mousse Magazine*, January 31, 2018, https://juancanela.com/writing/John-Akomfrah-Purple.

28. Downey, "Vital Materialism."

29. Downey, "Vital Materialism."

30. Jane Bennett, *Vibrant Matter: A Political Ecology of Things* (Durham, NC: Duke University Press, 2010), viii; also see Jane Bennett, "Systems and Things: A Response to Graham Harman and Timothy Morton," *New Literary History* 43, no. 2 (Spring 2012): 226.

31. Rebekah Sheldon, "Form/Matter/Chora: Object-Oriented Ontology and Feminist New Materialism," in *The Nonhuman Turn*, ed. Richard Grusin (Minneapolis: University of Minnesota Press, 2015), 196.

32. Bennett, *Vibrant Matter*, viii, 11.

33. Bennett, *Vibrant Matter*, 13, 17.

34. Leela Gandhi, *Postcolonial Theory: A Critical Introduction* (London: Routledge, 1998), 170.

35. N. Katherine Hayles, *Unthought: The Power of the Cognitive Nonconscious* (Chicago: University of Chicago Press, 2017), 32.

36. *John Akomfrah—Why History Matters.*

37. "Border/Talks: A Conversation with John Akomfrah on Sea-Migration, Borders, and Art," interview by Maurice Stierl, *Border/Talks*, September 19, 2016, video, 21:27, YouTube, https://www.youtube.com/watch?v=YJjkNl-tvzs.

38. Achille Mbembe, *Necropolitics*, trans. Steven Corcoran (Durham, NC: Duke University Press, 2019), 2.

39. "Artist Salon with John Akomfrah," interview by Rudolf Frieling, San Francisco Museum of Modern Art, accessed December 10, 2020, video, 37:03, https://www.sfmoma.org/watch/artist-salon-john-akomfrah/.

40. Ellis-Petersen, "John Akomfrah."

41. Derek Gregory, *The Colonial Present: Afghanistan, Palestine, and Iraq* (Malden, MA: Wiley-Blackwell, 2004), xv.

42. Margaret Kohn, "Colonialism," in *Stanford Encyclopedia of Philosophy* , online ed. (Stanford, CA: Stanford University, 1997–), article published May 9, 2006, last modified August 29, 2017, https://plato.stanford.edu/entries/colonialism/.

43. Tiffany Lethabo King, *The Black Shoals: Offshore Formations of Black and Native Studies* (Durham, NC: Duke University Press, 2019), 19.

44. Ann Laura Stoler, "Introduction. 'The Rot Remains': From Ruins to Ruination," in *Imperial Debris: On Ruins and Ruination*, ed. Ann Laura Stoler (Durham, NC: Duke University Press, 2013), 7; Ann Laura Stoler, *Duress: Imperial Durabilities in Our Times* (Durham, NC: Duke University Press, 2016), 4.

45. Stoler, *Duress*, 4–5.

46. Stoler, *Duress*, 7.

47. Stoler, *Duress*, 6.

48. Downey, "Vital Materialism."

49. Clemans, "John Akomfrah's Video Art Lures the Senses."

50. Christina Sharpe, *In the Wake: On Blackness and Being* (Durham, NC: Duke University Press, 2016), 15, 18.

51. M. NourbeSe Philip, as told by Setaey Adamu Boateng, *Zong!* (Middletown, CT: Wesleyan University Press, 2008), 24.

52. Claire Hoffmann, Chus Martínez, and Gioia Dal Molin, assisted by María Montero Sierra, "The Sea. Sounds & Storytelling. Part II," Istituto Svizzero, October 2020, https://www.istitutosvizzero.it/it/arte/the-sea-sounds-storytelling-part-ii/.

53. King, *The Black Shoals*, 16.

54. John Akomfrah and the Otolith Group, "Blackness and Post-cinema: John Akomfrah and the Otolith Group in Conversation," *Frieze* 214 (September 23, 2020), https://www.frieze.com/article/blackness-and-post-cinema-john-akomfrah-and-otolith-group-conversation.

55. *CNRTL, Centre national de ressources textuelles et lexicales du CNRS*, s.v. "Environnement," 2012, author's translation, https://www.cnrtl.fr/definition/environnement; *Techno-science*

.net, s.v. "Environnement," accessed January 5, 2021, author's translation, https://www
.techno-science.net/definition/3469.html.

56. Bruno Latour, *Facing Gaia: Eight Lectures on the New Climatic Regime* (London: Polity, 2017),
    98–100.

57. Georges Canguilhem, *La connaissance de la vie* (Paris: Vrin, 2015), 181.

58. John Durham Peters, *The Marvelous Clouds: Toward a Philosophy of Elemental Media* (Chi-
    cago: University of Chicago Press, 2015), 2, 4.

PART II

1. Inka Stock, Ayşen Üstübici, and Susanne U. Schultz, "Externalization at Work: Responses
   to Migration Policies from the Global South," *Comparative Migration Studies* 7, no. 48 (December 2019): 1, https://comparativemigrationstudies.springeropen.com/track/pdf/10.1186
   /s40878-019-0157-z.

2. Özgün E. Topak, "The Biopolitical Border in Practice: Surveillance and Death at the Greece–
   Turkey Borderzones," *Environment and Planning D: Society and Space* 32, no. 5 (2014): 815,
   https://borderlandscapes.law.ox.ac.uk/sites/default/files/2019-11/The%20biopolitical%20
   border%20in%20practice.pdf. Also see Aramide Odutayo, "Human Security and the International Refugee Crisis," *Journal of Global Ethics* 12, no. 3 (2016): 369.

3. James Baldwin, "The Moral (Social) Responsibility of the Artist" (speech), University of
   Chicago, May 21, 1963, video, 1:03:17, YouTube, https://www.youtube.com/watch?v=PlnDbq
   LNv-M.

CHAPTER 3

1. James Baldwin, "The Moral (Social) Responsibility of the Artist" (speech), University of Chicago, May 21, 1963, video, 1:03:17, author's emphasis, YouTube, https://www.youtube.com
   /watch?v=PlnDbqLNv-M.

2. *Richard Mosse*, National Gallery of Victoria (NGV) Triennial, April 17, 2018, video, 5:18, You-
   Tube, https://www.youtube.com/watch?v=6QOyFAqs_rM.

3. Bernard Stiegler, "Questions de pharmacologie générale: Il n'y a pas de simple pharmakon,"
   Psychotropes 13, no. 3 (2007): 34, author's translation, https://www.cairn.info/revue-psycho
   tropes-2007-3-page-27.htm.

4. Sabine Hess and Bernd Kasparek, "Under Control? Or Border (as) Conflict: Reflections on
   the European Border Regime," *Social Inclusion* 5, no. 3 (2017): 59, https://www.researchgate
   .net/publication/319915817_Under_Control_Or_Border_as_Conflict_Reflections_on_the
   _European_Border_Regime; Sabine Hess and Bernd Kasparek, "The Post-2015 European
   Border Regime: New Approaches in a Shifting Field," *Archivio antropologico mediterraneo*,
   Anno XXII, 21, no. 2 (2019): 1, http://journals.openedition.org/aam/1812. For insightful
   studies on the twenty-first-century EU border crisis, also see Nick Vaughan-Williams, *Europe's Border Crisis: Biopolitical Security and Beyond* (Oxford: Oxford University Press, 2015),

chapters 1, 2, 3; as well as Michel Agier, "Introduction: The Migrant, the Border and the World," in *Borderlands*, trans. David Fernbach (Cambridge: Polity Press, 2017), 1–12.

5. Hess and Kasparek, "The Post-2015 European Border Regime," 3.

6. Étienne Balibar, "What Is a Border?," in *Politics and the Other Scene*, trans. Christine Jones, James Swenson, and Chris Turner (London: Verso, 2002), 84.

7. Bernd Kasparek, "Routes, Corridors, and Spaces of Exception: Governing Migration and Europe," in *Europe at a Crossroads [Managed Inhospitality]*, ed. Michel Feher et al., New Futures Online no. 1 (Brooklyn, NY: Zone Books, 2016), https://www.academia.edu /23091749/_Europe_At_a_Crossroads_Near_Futures_Online.

8. Kasparek, "Routes, Corridors, and Spaces of Exception."

9. Kasparek, "Routes, Corridors, and Spaces of Exception."

10. Hess and Kasparek, "The Post-2015 European Border Regime."

11. Hess and Kasparek, "The Post-2015 European Border Regime."

12. Lucy Mayblin, *Asylum after Empire: Colonial Legacies in the Politics of Asylum Seeking* (London: Rowman & Littlefield, 2017), 24.

13. Duncan Wooldridge, "Richard Mosse *Incoming*," *1000 Words*, 2017, https://www.1000words mag.com/richard-mosse/.

14. Richard Mosse, "Transformation of the Souls," in *Incoming* (London: MACK, 2017), paragraphs 22 and 23.

15. Eugenio Cusumano, "The Sea as Humanitarian Space: Non-governmental Search and Rescue Dilemmas on the Central Mediterranean Migratory Route," *Mediterranean Politics* 23, no. 3 (2018): 387–394, https://www.tandfonline.com/doi/full/10.1080/13629395.2017 .1302223?src=recsys.

16. Giorgio Agamben, *Homo Sacer: Sovereign Power and Bare Life*, trans. Daniel Heller-Roazen (Stanford, CA: Stanford University Press, 1998), 88, 13.

17. René Kreichauf, "From Forced Migration to Forced Arrival: The Campization of Refugee Accommodation in European Cities," *Comparative Migration Studies* 6, no. 7 (2018): 1–22, https://link.springer.com/content/pdf/10.1186%2Fs40878-017-0069-8.pdf.

18. Jürgen Osterhammel, *Colonialism: A Theoretical Overview*, trans. Shelley L. Frisch (Princeton, NJ: Markus Wiener, 2010), 16.

19. El-moutasam Aziz, Laila Manasfi, and Ghassan Salah, "A Bio-political Construction: The Representation of Refugees and Migrants. From the 'Reel' to the 'Real,'" in *Proceedings of POM Beirut 2019* (Swindon, UK: BCS Learning and Development, June 2019), 122, https:// www.researchgate.net/publication/337897171_A_Bio-Political_Construction_The_Rep resentation_of_Refugees_and_Migrants_From_the_%27Reel%27_to_the_%27Real%27; Mosse, "Transformation of the Souls," paragraphs 12 and 13.

20. Mosse, "Transformation of the Souls," paragraph 1.

21. Mosse, "Transformation of the Souls," paragraphs 1, 8, and 22.

22. Aziz, Manasfi, and Salah, "A Bio-political Construction," 123.

23. Louise Wolthers, "Imagining Migration in Europe: Surveillance and Other Visibilities," in *Photographic Powers—Helsinki Photomedia 2014*, ed. Mika Elo and Marko Karo (Helsinki, Finland: Aalto University, 2015), 114–115.

24. Mosse, "Transformation of the Souls," paragraphs 9 and 17.

25. Karen Fog Olwig et al., *The Biometric Border World: Technologies, Bodies, and Identities on the Move* (London: Routledge, 2020), 100.

26. Lilie Chouliaraki and Tijana Stolic, "Rethinking Media Responsibility in the Refugee 'Crisis': A Visual Typology of European News," *Media, Culture, & Society* 39, no. 8 (2017): 1167.

27. Luc Boltanski, *Distant Suffering: Morality, Media, and Politics*, trans. Graham Burchell (Cambridge: Cambridge University Press, 1999), 13.

28. Ben Eastham, "Richard Mosse: *Incoming*," *ArtReview*, May 10, 2017, https://artreview.com /may-2017-review-richard-mosse/.

29. Wes Hill, "Sublime Plight: Richard Mosse, Ai Weiwei, and the Social Turn," *Artlink* 38, no. 3 (September 1, 2018): 10–17, https://www.artlink.com.au/articles/4698/sublime-plight-richard -mosse-ai-weiwei-and-the-soc/; Diego Ramirez, "Racial Phantasmagoria: The Demonisation of the Other in Richard Mosse's 'Incoming,'" *NECSUS* 7, no. 2 (Autumn 2018): 301–307, https://necsus-ejms.org/racial-phantasmagoria-the-demonisation-of-the-other-in-richard -mosses-incoming/; Daniel C. Blight, "*Incoming*: Photography, Contemporary Art, Whiteness," *Americansuburb X*, March 23, 2017, https://americansuburbx.com/2017/03/incoming -photography-contemporary-art-whiteness.html; *Richard Mosse*, NGV Triennial.

30. Blight, "*Incoming*"; Linda Martín Alcoff, "The Problem of Speaking for Others," *Cultural Critique* 20 (Winter 1991–1992): 26.

31. Sean O'Hagan, "Richard Mosse: *Incoming* Review—Shows the White-Hot Misery of the Migrant Crisis," *Guardian*, February 15, 2017, https://www.theguardian.com/artanddesign/2017 /feb/15/richard-mosse-incoming-review-barbican-curve-migrant-crisis.

32. Hess and Kasparek, "Under Control?," 59.

33. Hess and Kasparek, "Under Control?," 59–60.

34. Agamben, *Homo Sacer*, 88, 13.

35. Agamben, *Homo Sacer*, 39. Also see Marie Goupy, "Le temps de la crise et de l'urgence est devenu peu à peu notre horizon politique," *Le Monde*, October 24, 2020, https://www .lemonde.fr/idees/article/2020/10/24/marie-goupy-le-temps-de-la-crise-et-de-l-urgence-est -devenu-peu-a-peu-notre-horizon-politique_6057190_3232.html.

36. Jacques Rancière, "Who Is the Subject of the Rights of Man?," *South Atlantic Quarterly* 103, nos. 2–3 (Spring–Summer 2004): 304, http://cscs.res.in/dataarchive/textfiles/textfile .2010-11-27.9388690495/file.

37. Didier Fassin, *Life: A Critical User's Manual* (Cambridge: Polity Press, 2019), 176.

38. Hess and Kasparek, "The Post-2015 European Border Regime"; also see Liliana Riga, Johannes Langer, and Arek Dakessian, "Theorizing Refugeedom: Becoming Young Political Subjects in Beirut," *Theory and Society* 49 (2020): 713, 736–737, https://www.researchgate.net/ publication/341168147_Theorizing_refugeedom_becoming_young_political_subjects_in_ Beirut.

39. Gloria Anzaldúa, *Borderlands/La Frontera: The New Mestiza* (San Francisco: Spinster/Aunt Lute Press, 1987), 78.

40. Georges Didi-Huberman, *Survival of the Fireflies*, trans. Lia Swope Mitchell (Minneapolis: University of Minnesota Press, 2018), 84.

41. Didi-Huberman, *Survival of the Fireflies*, 85.

42. Renwick McLean, "5 Killed in Mass Attempt to Cross from Morocco to Spanish Enclave," *New York Times*, September 30, 2005, https://www.nytimes.com/2005/09/30/world/europe /5-killed-in-mass-attempt-to-cross-from-morocco-to-spanish.html; Gilles Tremlett, "African Migrants Die in Quest for New Life," *Guardian*, September 30, 2005, https://www.theguard ian.com/world/2005/sep/30/spain.gilestremlett; Florian Schneider, "The Scandal—Notes on the Autonomy of the Image," in *Uncorporate Identity*, ed. Metahaven, with Marina Vishmidt (Baden, Germany: Lars Müller, 2010), 387, http://fls.kein.org/sites/fls.kein.org/files/Scandal .PDF and http://fls.kein.org/view/32.

43. Schneider, "The Scandal," 389–390.

44. Schneider, "The Scandal," 389.

45. Schneider, "The Scandal," 390–391.

46. Schneider, "The Scandal," 388. Also see Florian Schneider, "Enclaves, Exception, and the Camp as a Counter-Laboratory" (lecture), December 20, 2005, New Media Center_kuda .org, video, 2:24:30, https://kuda.org/en/enclaves-exception-and-camp-counter-laboratory -florian-schneider.

47. *Richard Mosse*, NGV Triennial.

48. Roger Silverstone, "Complicity and Collusion in the Mediation of Everyday Life," *New Literary History* 33, no. 4 (Autumn 2002): 762.

49. Gayatri Chakravorty Spivak, "Imperative to Re-imagine the Planet," in *An Aesthetic Education in the Era of Globalization* (Cambridge, MA: Harvard University Press, 2009), 338–339.

50. Spivak, "Imperative to Re-imagine the Planet," 348, 350.

51. Iris Marion Young, *Responsibility for Justice* (New York: Oxford University Press, 2011), 28.

52. Young, *Responsibility for Justice*, 104.

53. Young, *Responsibility for Justice*, 105.

CHAPTER 4

1. Eyal Weizman, "Open Architecture," *e-flux architecture*, June 18, 2019, https://www.e-flux .com/architecture/becoming-digital/248062/open-verification/; and Eyal Weizman, *Forensic Architecture: Violence at the Threshold of Detectability* (Brooklyn, NY: Zone Books, 2018), 2–3.

2. "The *Solid Sea* Installation in Milan," *Domus*, October 24, 2003, https://www.domusweb.it /en/art/2003/10/24/the-solid-sea-installation-in-milan.html; "Multiplicity," ArtLinkArt, accessed February 12, 2021, http://www.artlinkart.com/en/artist/wrk_sr/a4eeswtn.

3. Charles Heller, "De-confining Borders: Towards Freedom of Movement," *e-flux architecture*, July 21, 2020, https://www.e-flux.com/architecture/at-the-border/340426/de-confining -borders-towards-freedom-of-movement/.

4. Charles Heller and Lorenzo Pezzani, "The Perils of Migration: Conflictual Mediations of Risk at the Maritime Frontiers of the European Union," *Critique internationale* 83, no. 2 (2019): 131.

5. John Durham Peters, *The Marvelous Clouds: Toward a Philosophy of Elemental Media* (Chicago: University of Chicago Press, 2015), 2, 4.

6. Alfred North Whitehead, *Process and Reality: An Essay in Cosmology* (New York: Free Press, 1978), 19–23.

7. Weizman, *Forensic Architecture*, 96.

8. Charles Heller and Lorenzo Pezzani, "*Liquid Traces*: Investigating the Deaths of Migrants at the EU's Maritime Frontier," in *The Borders of "Europe": Autonomy of Migration, Tactics of Bordering*, ed. Nicholas De Genova (Durham, NC: Duke University Press, 2017), 109.

9. This information is provided in the video by Charles Heller, but a more detailed account can be found in Forensic Oceanography, "Left-to-Die Boat," Forensic Architecture, accessed July 18, 2020, https://forensic-architecture.org/investigation/the-left-to-die-boat. Also see Heller and Pezzani, "*Liquid Traces*," 110–111.

10. Heller and Pezzani, "*Liquid Traces*," 111.

11. Heller and Pezzani "*Liquid Traces*," 112.

12. The political theorist James Chamberlain has also established the relevance of Iris Young's social connection model of responsibility to the migrant condition, although his analysis of citizens' political responsibility in relation to that injustice does not address the sphere of art. His article is nevertheless important insofar as it succeeds in showing the relevance of Young's model: "I argue," he writes, "that there are two main forms of social connection that ground such a responsibility with respect to migrants—the participation of citizens of prospective receiving states in the structural processes that generate the injustices from which migrants are leaving, and the participation of citizens in the border regimes of their own states." See James A. Chamberlain, "Responsibility for Migrants: From Hospitality to Solidarity," *Political Theory* 48, no. 1 (2020): 77.

13. Iris Marion Young, *Responsibility for Justice* (New York: Oxford University Press, 2011), 28.

14. Young, *Responsibility for Justice*, 92.

15. Young, *Responsibility for Justice*, 92.

16. Young, *Responsibility for Justice*, 96.

17. Young, *Responsibility for Justice*, 95.

18. Young, *Responsibility for Justice*, 97.

19. Maeve Catherine McKeown, "Responsibility without Guilt: A Youngian Approach to Responsibility for Global Injustice," PhD diss., University College London, School of Public Policy, 2014, 23, 42, https://discovery.ucl.ac.uk/id/eprint/1463742/3/McKeown%20Thesis%20(FINAL%2016.03.15).pdf.

20. Weizman, "Open Architecture."

21. Aurélien Gamboni, "In the Thickness of the Crossing: Challenging the Liquid Violence of Borders in the Mediterranean—an Interview with Charles Heller," trans. Maya Dalinsky, *Texte zur Kunst* 29, no. 114 (June 2019): 88.

22. Gamboni, "In the Thickness of the Crossing," 88.

23. Nicholas Mirzoeff, *The Right to Look: A Counterhistory of Visuality* (Durham, NC: Duke University Press, 2011), 1–2.

24. Mirzoeff, *The Right to Look*, 1–2; Weizman, *Forensic Architecture*, 2–3.

25. Heller and Pezzani, "*Liquid Traces*," 107.

26. Heller and Pezzani, "The Perils of Migration: Countervailing Mediations," 136.

27. Eugenio Cusumano, "The Sea as Humanitarian Space: Non-governmental Search and Rescue Dilemmas on the Central Mediterranean Migratory Route," *Mediterranean Politics* 23, no. 3 (2018): 387, https://www.tandfonline.com/doi/full/10.1080/13629395.2017.1302223?src=recsys.

28. Heller and Pezzani, "The Perils of Migration: Countervailing Mediations," 136.

29. Forensic Oceanography, "Death by Rescue—the Lethal Effects of the EU's Policies of Non-assistance," Forensic Architecture, accessed August 2, 2020, https://forensic-architecture.org/investigation/death-by-rescue-the-lethal-effects-of-non-assistance-at-sea; Cusumano, "The Sea as Humanitarian Space," 390–392.

30. Heller and Pezzani, "The Perils of Migration: Countervailing Mediations," 139.

31. "Boats4People's First Campaign Is a Success, the Maritime Borders of the EU Remain Are [*sic*] as Deadly as Ever," migreurop, July 20, 2012, http://migreurop.org/article2197.html.

32. "About WTM," WatchTheMed, May 12, 2013, https://watchthemed.net/index.php/page/index/3.

33. Heller and Pezzani, "The Perils of Migration: Countervailing Mediations," 141.

34. "Mapping Safe Passages: Real-Time Interventions at the Maritime Borders of Europe," *This Is Not an Atlas*, accessed June 10, 2021, https://notanatlas.org/maps/mapping-safe-passages/.

35. Heller and Pezzani, "The Perils of Migration: Countervailing Mediations," 142.

36. Heller and Pezzani, "The Perils of Migration: Countervailing Mediations," 142.

37. Weizman, "Open Architecture."

38. Janie Gosselin, "Les personnes fuient l'enfer libyen," *La Presse*, July 17, 2021, https://www.lapresse.ca/international/afrique/2021-07-17/les-personnes-fuient-l-enfer-libyen.php.

39. Heller, "De-confining Borders."

40. Valeria Graziano, Marcell Mars, and Tomislav Medak, "The Pirate Care Project," pirate.care, 2019, https://pirate.care/pages/concept/.

41. Lorenzo Pezzani, "Hostile Environments," *e-flux architecture*, May 15, 2020, https://www.e-flux.com/architecture/at-the-border/325761/hostile-environments/.

42. Carlo Berti, "Right-Wing Populism and the Criminalization of Sea-Rescue NGOs: The 'Sea-Watch 3' Case in Italy, and Matteo Salvini's Communication on Facebook," *Media, Culture, & Society* 43, no. 3 (2021): 532–550.

CHAPTER 5

1. Gloria Anzaldúa, *Borderlands/La Frontera: The New Mestiza* (San Francisco: Spinster/Aunt Lute Press, 1987), 3.

2. Nicholas Casey, "Cartel Wars Gut Juárez, a Onetime Boom Town," *Wall Street Journal*, March 20, 2010, https://www.wsj.com/articles/SB1000142405274870358090457513200426533354 6; Rory Carroll, "Mexico Drug War: The New Killing Fields," *Guardian*, September 3, 2010, https://www.theguardian.com/world/2010/sep/03/mexico-drug-war-killing-fields.

3. *Entrevista: La promesa, Teresa Margolles*, Museo Universitario Arte Contemporáneo (MUAC), January 13, 2015, video, 4:16, YouTube, https://www.youtube.com/watch?v=KRUOPcPJKuM; "Transcription Audio," Musée d'art contemporain de Montréal, accessed September 14, 2020, author's translation, https://macm.org/expositions/teresa-margolles-mundos/.

4. *Teresa Margolles: La promesa 2012*, conversation between John Zeppetelli and Kim Thúy, Musée d'art contemporain de Montréal, accessed May 4, 2020, video, 1:37, https://macm .org/en/exhibitions/teresa-margolles-mundos/.

5. Most of the information on the Musée d'art contemporain de Montréal was confirmed in Emeren Garcia to the author, email, March 10, 2017.

6. *Entrevista*, author's translation.

7. Judith Butler, *Frames of War: When Is Life Grievable?* (London: Verso, 2009), 38.

8. Mary Martin, "A Tale of Two Cities: Ciudad Juárez, El Paso, and Insecurity at the U.S.-Mexico Border," in *Cities at War: Global Insecurity and Urban Resistance*, ed. Mary Kaldor and Saskia Sassen (New York: Columbia University Press, 2020), 103.

9. Sophie Eastaugh, "The Future of the US-Mexican Border: Inside the 'Split City' of El Paso–Juárez," *Guardian*, January 25, 2017, https://www.theguardian.com/cities/2017/jan/25 /el-paso-juarez-us-mexican-border-life-binational-city; Alice Driver, *More or Less Dead: Feminicide, Haunting, and the Ethics of Representation in Mexico* (Tucson: University of Arizona Press, 2015), xii.

10. Martin, "A Tale of Two Cities," 104.

11. See Chris Bowden, "Mexico's Red Day," *GQ*, July 1, 2008, https://www.gq.com/story/juarez -mexico-border-murder-drug-war; Nick Valencia and Arturo Chacon, "Juarez Shedding Violent Image, Statistics Show," CNN, January 5, 2013, https://www.cnn.com/2013/01/05/world /americas/mexico-juarez-killings-drop/index.html; and William Booth, "In Mexico's Murder City, the War Appears Over," *Washington Post*, August 20, 2012, https://www.washington post.com/world/the_americas/in-mexicos-murder-city-the-war-appears-over/2012/08/19/ aacab85e-e0a0-11e1-8d48-2b1243f34c85_story.html.

12. Corrie Boudreaux, "Public Memorialization and the Grievability of Victims in Ciudad Juárez," *Social Research* 83, no. 2 (Summer 2016): 392.

13. Boudreaux, "Public Memorialization," 393.

14. Boudreaux, "Public Memorialization," 393.

15. See especially Elva Fabiola Orozco, "Mapping the Trail of Violence: The Memorialization of Public Space as a Counter-Geography of Violence in Ciudad Juárez," *Journal of Latin American Geography* 18, no. 3 (October 2019): 141.

16. Sayak Valencia, "NAFTA: Capitalismo Gore and the Femicide Machine," *Scapegoat* 6 (2014): 132.

17. Orozco, "Mapping the Trail of Violence," 141.

18. Driver, *More or Less Dead*, 18–19.

19. Denisa Krásná and Sagar Deva, "Neoliberalism, NAFTA, and Dehumanization: The Case of Femicides in Ciudad Juárez," *Fast Capitalism* 16, no. 1 (2019): 34–35.

20. "Ciudad Juárez, Mexico Population," Population Stat, accessed February 13, 2021, https://populationstat.com/mexico/ciudad-juarez.

21. Martin, "A Tale of Two Cities," 109.

22. Krásná and Deva, "Neoliberalism, NAFTA, and Dehumanization," 33–34. For an early (and excellent) study on feminicides in Ciudad Juárez, see Kathleen Staudt, *Violence and Activism at the Border: Gender, Fear, and Everyday Life in Ciudad Juárez* (Austin: University of Texas Press, 2008).

23. Boudreaux, "Public Memorialization," 394.

24. Butler, *Frames of War*, 41.

25. Verónica Zebadúa-Yañez, "Killing as Performance: Violence and the Shaping of Community," *e-misférica* 2, no. 2 (2005): 1–22, https://hemisphericinstitute.org/en/emisferica-2-2/2-2-essays/killing-as-performance-violence-and-the-shaping-of-community.html.

26. Krásná and Deva, "Neoliberalism, NAFTA, and Dehumanization," 33; Alicia de Alba Gaspar, ed., with Georgina Guzmán, *Making a Killing: Femicide, Free Trade, and la Frontera* (Austin: University of Texas Press, 2010), 1–2; Driver, *More or Less Dead*, 3.

27. Martin, "A Tale of Two Cities," 104.

28. Mary Kaldor, *Global Security Cultures* (Cambridge: Polity, 2018), 38.

29. Martin, "A Tale of Two Cities," 107.

30. Martin, "A Tale of Two Cities," 110, 115.

31. Martin, "A Tale of Two Cities," 126.

32. Martin, "A Tale of Two Cities," 108.

33. Martin, "A Tale of Two Cities," 105.

34. "IDP Definition," in *UNHCR Emergency Handbook*, accessed July 9, 2021, https://emergency.unhcr.org/entry/44826/idp-definition. Also see "Forced Migration or Displacement," Migration Data Portal, last modified July 8, 2020, https://migrationdataportal.org/themes/forced-migration-or-displacement.

35. Anzaldúa, *Borderlands/La Frontera*, 3.

36. Julia Banwell, "Agency and Otherness in Teresa Margolles' Aesthetic of Death," *Altre modernità/Otras modernidades/Autres modernités/Other Modernities* 4 (October 2010): 45–54, https://riviste.unimi.it/index.php/AMonline/article/view/688/909; Julia Banwell, *Teresa Margolles and the Aesthetics of Death* (Cardiff: University of Wales Press, 2015), 5–24.

37. Michael Silverstein, "Shifters, Linguistic Categories, and Cultural Description," in *Meaning in Anthropology*, ed. Keith H. Basso and Henry A. Selby (Albuquerque: University of New Mexico Press, 1976), 27.

38. Banwell, *Teresa Margolles and the Aesthetics of Death*, 38.

39. *Entrevista*, author's translation.

40. Orozco, "Mapping the Trail of Violence," 141.

41. *Teresa Margolles: La promesa 2012.*

42. The art historian Georges Didi-Huberman saw this disquieting aesthetics already at play in Tony Smith's Minimalist *Die* (1962/1968) and the other black cubes Smith made during that same period: "Facing it, our *look* worries. But how can a simple cube come to worry our *look*? . . . Painted in black . . . , Tony Smith's sculptures . . . appear as monuments endowed with a very dark lucidity in which volumes constantly raise the question—and build the dialectic—of their own condemnation to emptiness" (Georges Didi-Huberman, *Ce que nous voyons, ce qui nous regarde* [Paris: Éditions de Minuit, 1992], 67, 77, author's translation).

43. "Carol Gilligan," EthicsofCare.org, July 16, 2011, https://ethicsofcare.org/carol-gilligan/. For an introduction to Gilligan's work, see especially Carol Gilligan, *In a Different Voice: Psychological Theory and Women's Development* (Cambridge, MA: Harvard University Press, 2016).

44. On the difficulty of securing an ethics of care, see, for example, Daniel Engster, "Rethinking Care Theory: The Practice of Caring and the Obligation to Care," *Hypatia* 20, no. 3 (Summer 2005): 50.

45. Carlo Caduff, "Hot Chocolate," *Critical Inquiry* 45 (Spring 2019): 788.

46. Caduff, "Hot Chocolate," 789.

47. Joan C. Tronto, *Moral Boundaries: A Political Argument for an Ethic of Care* (New York: Routledge, 1993), 103.

48. María Puig de la Bellacasa, *Matters of Care: Speculative Ethics in More Than Human Worlds* (Minneapolis: University of Minnesota Press, 2017), 2–4.

49. Puig de la Bellacasa, *Matters of Care*, 7.

50. Puig de la Bellacasa, *Matters of Care*, 9.

51. Caduff, "Hot Chocolate," 794.

52. Puig de la Bellacasa, *Matters of Care*, 20, 99.

53. Puig de la Bellacasa, *Matters of Care*, 1, 19.

54. Caduff, "Hot Chocolate," 803.

55. *Collins Dictionary*, s.v. "carer," accessed January 25, 2022, https://www.collinsdictionary.com/dictionary/english/carer, and *Online Etymology Dictionary*, s.v. "care (*v.*)," accessed January 25, 2022, https://www.etymonline.com/word/care.

56. *Entrevista*, author's translation.

57. Sara Ahmed, *The Cultural Politics of Emotions* (New York: Routledge, 2004), 32.

58. Orozco, "Mapping the Trail of Violence," 148; Boudreaux, "Public Memorialization," 405; Staudt, *Violence and Activism at the Border*, 19. Orozco refers specifically to this "funeralization of the city's landscape" as an antifeminicide attempt "to expose the deadly effects of an inherited colonial gender structure that naturalized extreme gender violence" (134).

59. Butler, *Frames of War*, 38.

60. Alexander Ortega, "Songs of the Cross: Guillermo Galindo's Border-Healing Ritual," *Slug Mag*, September 29, 2016, https://www.slugmag.com/arts/art/interviews-features/guillermo-galindo/.

61. Gabriele Sassone, "Injury and Repair: Kader Attia," *Mousse Magazine*, October 5, 2018, http://moussemagazine.it/injury-and-repair-kader-attia-2018/.

62. Iris Marion Young, *Responsibility for Justice* (New York: Oxford University Press, 2011), 105.

63. Young, *Responsibility for Justice*, 105.

PART III

1. *Merriam-Webster*, s.v. "empathy (*n.*)," accessed February 13, 2021, https://www.merriam-webster.com/dictionary/empathy.
2. Nancy Eisenberg, "Empathy and Sympathy: A Brief Review of the Concepts and Empirical Literature," *Anthrozoös* 2, no. 1 (1988): 16.

CHAPTER 6

1. Amy Coplan and Peter Goldie, introduction to *Empathy: Philosophical and Psychological Perspectives*, ed. Amy Coplan and Peter Goldie (Oxford: Oxford University Press, 2011), ix.
2. Jean Decety and Jason M. Cowell, "Friends or Foes: Is Empathy Necessary for Moral Behavior?," *Perspectives on Psychological Science* 9, no. 5 (2014): 534, https://www.ncbi.nlm.nih.gov/pmc/articles/PMC4241340/.
3. Tania Singer and Olga M. Klimecki, "Empathy and Compassion," *Current Biology* 24, no. 18 (September 22, 2014): R875, https://www.researchgate.net/publication/265909916_Empathy_and_Compassion; Stephen Morris, "Empathy on Trial: A Response to Its Critics," *Philosophical Psychology* 32, no. 4 (2019): 509.
4. Tania Singer and Claus Lamm, "The Social Neuroscience of Empathy," *Annals of the New York Academy of Sciences* 1156 (2009): 82, https://www.researchgate.net/profile/Claus-Lamm/publication/281218239_The_Social_Neuroscience_of_Empathy/links/5696360708ae4b80df38ffb1/The-Social-Neuroscience-of-Empathy.pdf.
5. Frédérique de Vignemont and Tania Singer, "The Empathic Brain: How, When, and Why?," *Trends in Cognitive Sciences* 10, no. 10 (November 2006): 435, author's emphasis, https://www.researchgate.net/publication/6841239_The_empathic_brain_How_when_and_why.
6. Fritz Breithaupt, *The Dark Sides of Empathy*, trans. Andrew B. B. Hamilton (Ithaca, NY: Cornell University Press, 2019), 10.
7. Heidi L. Maibom, "Introduction to the Philosophy of Empathy," in *The Routledge Handbook of Philosophy of Empathy*, ed. Heidi L. Maibom (London: Routledge, 2017), 2.
8. Jean Decety and Philip L. Jackson, "The Functional Architecture of Human Empathy," *Behavioral and Cognitive Neuroscience Reviews* 3, no. 2 (June 2004): 73, https://www.researchgate.net/publication/51369194_The_Functional_Architecture_of_Human_Empathy.
9. Decety and Cowell, "Friends or Foes," 529–530.
10. Coplan and Goldie, introduction to *Empathy*, xii.
11. Coplan and Goldie, introduction to *Empathy*, xiii.
12. Dominic McIver Lopes, "An Empathic Eye," in Coplan and Goldie, *Empathy*, 118–119.
13. Jane Sadler, "Empathy in Film," in Maibom, *The Routledge Handbook of Philosophy of Empathy*, 317–326.

14. Decety and Cowell, "Friends or Foes," 534.

15. E. Ann Kaplan, "Empathy and Trauma Culture: Imaging Catastrophe," in Coplan and Goldie, *Empathy*, 257.

16. Rudolf A. Makkreel, "How Is Empathy Related to Understanding?," in *Issues in Husserl's Ideas II*, ed. Thomas Nenon and Lester Embree (Dordrecht, Netherlands: Springer, 1996), 200. For a similar view, see Karsten Stueber, *Rediscovering Empathy: Agency, Folk Psychology, and the Human Sciences* (Cambridge, MA: MIT Press, 2006).

17. See, for example, Amy Coplan, "Understanding Empathy: Its Features and Effects," in Coplan and Goldie, *Empathy*, 5; Michael Stocker and Elizabeth Hegeman, *Valuing Emotions* (Cambridge: Cambridge University Press, 1996), 116; and Martin L. Hoffman, *Empathy and Moral Development* (Cambridge: Cambridge University Press, 2000), 63.

18. Singer and Klimecki, "Empathy and Compassion," R875.

19. Nancy Eisenberg and Paul A. Miller, "The Relation of Empathy to Prosocial and Related Behaviors," *Psychological Bulletin* 101, no. 1 (February 1987): 91–119, https://www.researchgate.net/publication/19598630_The_Relation_of_Empathy_to_Prosocial_and_Related_Behaviors.

20. Coplan and Goldie, introduction to *Empathy*, xxiv.

21. Douglas Watt, "Toward a Neuroscience of Empathy: Integrating Affective and Cognitive Perspectives," *Neuropsychoanalysis* 9, no. 2 (2007): 122.

22. Watt, "Toward a Neuroscience of Empathy," 122. See also Nancy Eisenberg, "Empathy and Sympathy: A Brief Review of the Concepts and Empirical Literature," *Anthrozoös* 2, no. 1 (1988): 15–17; Nancy Eisenberg, "Emotion, Regulation, and Moral Development," *Annual Review of Psychology* 51 (2000): 665–697; Bill Underwood and Bert Moore, "Perspective-Taking and Altruism," *Psychological Bulletin* 91, no. 1 (1982): 143–173; and Martin L. Hoffman, "A Comprehensive Theory of Prosocial Moral Development," in *Constructive and Destructive Behavior*, ed. Arthur C. Bohart and Deborah J. Stipek (Washington, DC: American Psychological Association, 2001), 61–86.

23. C. Daniel Batson, *The Altruism Question: Toward a Social Psychological Answer* (New York: Psychology Press, 1991), 6.

24. Nel Noddings, *Caring: A Feminine Approach to Ethics and Moral Education* (Berkeley: University of California Press, 1984), 30.

25. Decety and Jackson, "The Functional Architecture of Human Empathy," 72.

26. Decety and Jackson, "The Functional Architecture of Human Empathy," 73.

27. Decety and Jackson, "The Functional Architecture of Human Empathy," 80–81, 83.

28. Decety and Jackson, "The Functional Architecture of Human Empathy," 73.

29. Giacomo Rizzolatti and Laila Craighero, "The Mirror-Neuron System," *Annual Review of Neuroscience* 27, no. 1 (2004): 172, https://www.researchgate.net/publication/8491604_The_Mirror-Neuron_System.

30. Valeria Gazzola, Lisa Aziz-Zadeh, and Christian Keysers, "Empathy and the Somatotopic Auditory Mirror System in Humans," *Current Biology* 16, no. 18 (September 19, 2006): 1824–1829, https://www.sciencedirect.com/science/article/pii/S0960982206021178.

31. Singer and Lamm, "The Social Neuroscience of Empathy," 83.

32. Singer and Klimecki, "Empathy and Compassion," R875.

33. Singer and Klimecki, "Empathy and Compassion," R875.

34. Jesse Prinz, "Against Empathy," *Southern Journal of Philosophy* 49 (2011): 214–233; Jesse Prinz, "Is Empathy Necessary for Morality?," in Coplan and Goldie, *Empathy*, 211–229; Jean Decety, "Empathy in Medicine," *Annales médico-psychologiques* 178 (2020): 197–206.

35. Singer and Lamm, "The Social Neuroscience of Empathy," 83. Also see Decety and Jackson, "The Functional Architecture of Human Empathy"; and Jean Decety and Claus Lamm, "Human Empathy Through the Lens of Social Neuroscience," *Scientific World Journal* 6 (February 2006): 1146–1163, https://www.researchgate.net/publication/6795222_Human_Empathy_Through_the_Lens_of_Social_Neuroscience.

36. C. Daryl Cameron et al., "Empathy Is Hard Work: People Choose to Avoid Empathy Because of Its Cognitive Costs," *Journal of Experimental Psychology: General* 148, no. 6 (2019): 963, https://www.apa.org/pubs/journals/releases/xge-xge0000595.pdf.

37. Coplan, "Understanding Empathy," 13.

38. Paul Bloom, *Against Empathy: The Case for Rational Compassion* (New York: Ecco, 2016), 3, 9.

39. Bloom, *Against Empathy*, 3.

40. Bloom, *Against Empathy*, 9.

41. Prinz, "Against Empathy"; also see Prinz, "Is Empathy Necessary for Morality?"

42. Bloom, *Against Empathy*, 9.

43. Xiaojing Xu et al., "Do You Feel My Pain? Racial Group Membership Modulates Empathic Neural Responses," *Journal of Neuroscience* 29, no. 26 (July 2009): 8525–8529, https://www.jneurosci.org/content/29/26/8525; Yawei Cheng et al., "Love Hurts: An fMRI Study," *NeuroImage* 51 (2010): 923–929; Decety and Cowell, "Friends or Foes," 526.

44. Nils Bubandt and Rane Willerslev, "The Dark Side of Empathy: Mimesis, Deception, and the Magic of Alterity," *Comparative Studies in Society and History* 57, no. 1 (2015): 7, 29.

45. Fritz Breithaupt, "The Bad Things We Do Because of Empathy," *Interdisciplinary Science Reviews* 43, no. 2 (2018): 166.

46. Breithaupt, *The Dark Sides of Empathy*, 6–7.

47. Breithaupt, *The Dark Sides of Empathy*, 8–9.

48. Breithaupt, "The Bad Things We Do Because of Empathy," 166.

49. Breithaupt, *The Dark Sides of Empathy*, 12.

50. Breithaupt, "The Bad Things We Do Because of Empathy," 166.

51. Breithaupt, *The Dark Sides of Empathy*, 1, author's emphasis.

52. Breithaupt, *The Dark Sides of Empathy*, 17.

53. Breithaupt, "The Bad Things We Do Because of Empathy," 170; Breithaupt, *The Dark Sides of Empathy*, 18.

54. Jill Bennett, "Lived Experience and the Limits (and Possibilities) of Empathy," *Cultural Studies Review* 25, no. 2 (2019): 84, 87, author's emphasis, https://epress.lib.uts.edu.au/journals/index.php/csrj/issue/view/470.

55. Breithaupt, *The Dark Sides of Empathy*, 9.

56. Morris, "Empathy on Trial," 514.

57. Bloom, *Against Empathy*, 8.

58. See Antonio Damasio, *Descartes' Error: Emotion, Reason, and the Human Brain* (London: Penguin, 2005); and Antonio Damasio, *Looking for Spinoza: Joy, Sorrow, and the Feeling Brain* (New York: Harcourt, 2003).

59. Philemon Eva, review of *Against Empathy: The Case for Rational Compassion*, by Paul Bloom, *Psychotherapy and Politics International* 15, no. 2 (June 2017): 1418–1419, https://doi.org/10.1002/ppi.1418.

60. Decety and Cowell, "Friends or Foes," 534.

61. Breithaupt, *The Dark Sides of Empathy*, 18. For a more detailed definition of perspective taking, see Decety and Cowell, "Friends or Foes," 530.

CHAPTER 7

1. Achille Mbembe, *Necropolitics*, trans. Steven Corcoran (Durham, NC: Duke University Press, 2019), 1–2.

2. E. Ann Kaplan, "Empathy and Trauma Culture: Imaging Catastrophe," in *Empathy: Philosophical and Psychological Perspectives*, ed. Amy Coplan and Peter Goldie (Oxford: Oxford University Press, 2011), 255. In her argument, Kaplan refers to the work of Sara Ahmed and Teresa Brennan. See Sara Ahmed, *The Cultural Politics of Emotions* (New York: Routledge, 2004); and Teresa Brennan, *The Transmission of Affect* (Ithaca, NY: Cornell University Press, 2004).

3. Kaplan, "Empathy and Trauma Culture," 256.

4. Kaplan, "Empathy and Trauma Culture," 256.

5. Kaplan, "Empathy and Trauma Culture," 257.

6. Kaplan, "Empathy and Trauma Culture," 275.

7. Roger Silverstone, "Complicity and Collusion in the Mediation of Everyday Life," *New Literary History* 33, no. 4 (Autumn 2002): 762, 774.

8. Silverstone, "Complicity and Collusion in the Mediation of Everyday Life," 776–777.

9. Ismail Einashe and Thomas Roueché, "Introduction: The Power of the Story," in *Lost in Media: Migrant Perspectives and the Public Sphere*, ed. Ismail Einashe and Thomas Roueché (Amsterdam: Valiz, 2019), 13; Daniel Trilling, "Uncomfortable Facts: The Migrant Crisis and the European Media," in Einashe and Roueché, *Lost in Media*, 27.

10. "Candice Breitz: *Love Story*," Tate, accessed December 14, 2020, https://www.tate.org.uk/whats-on/tate-liverpool/exhibition/candice-breitz-love-story.

11. "Migrant Crisis: Migration to Europe Explained in Seven Charts," *BBC News*, March 4, 2016, https://www.bbc.com/news/world-europe-34131911. A note on terminology: "The BBC uses the term *migrant* to refer to all people on the move who have yet to complete the legal process of claiming asylum. This group includes people fleeing war-torn countries such as Syria, who are likely to be granted refugee status, as well as people who are seeking jobs and better lives, who governments are likely to rule are economic migrants."

12. Sabine Hess and Bernd Kasparek, "Under Control? Or Border (as) Conflict: Reflections on the European Border Regime," *Social Inclusion* 5, no. 3 (2017): 59, https://www.researchgate.net/publication/319915817_Under_Control_Or_Border_as_Conflict_Reflections_on_the_European_Border_Regime; Sabine Hess and Bernd Kasparek, "The Post-2015 European Border Regime: New Approaches in a Shifting Field," *Archivio antropologico mediterraneo*, Anno XXII, 21, no. 2 (2019): 1–2, http://journals.openedition.org/aam/1812.

13. Ai Weiwei, "The Refugee Crisis Isn't about Refugees. It's about Us," *Guardian*, February 2, 2018, https://www.theguardian.com/commentisfree/2018/feb/02/refugee-crisis-human-flow-ai-weiwei-china.

14. "Ai Weiwei," Tate, accessed July 23, 2021, https://www.tate.org.uk/art/artists/ai-weiwei-8208; "Ai Weiwei Cites Change in German Attitudes as Reason for Move to UK," *Guardian*, August 22, 2019, https://www.theguardian.com/artanddesign/2019/aug/22/ai-weiwei-cites-change-in-german-attitudes-as-reason-for-move-to-uk.

15. Ai, "The Refugee Crisis Isn't about Refugees."

16. Luísa Santos, "Ai Weiwei: Grafting as a Documentary Tactic in Art," in *Critical Distance in Documentary Media*, ed. Gerda Cammaer, Blake Fitzpatrick, and Bruno Lessard (Cham, Switzerland: Palgrave Macmillan, 2018), 102.

17. Kaplan, "Empathy and Trauma Culture," 256.

18. Peter Bradshaw, "*Human Flow* Review—Ai Weiwei Surveys Shocking Plight of Migrants on the Move," *Guardian*, December 7, 2017, https://www.theguardian.com/film/2017/dec/07/human-flow-review-ai-weiwei-migration-documentary.

19. T. J. Demos, "Migrant World: On Ai Weiwei's *Human Flow*," *BOMB*, July 27, 2018, author's emphasis, https://bombmagazine.org/articles/migrant-world-on-ai-weiweis-human-flow/.

20. Hanna Schenkel, "Obstructed Progress: Ai Weiwei's 'Human Flow' and the Global Refugee Crisis," *Metro Magazine: Media & Education Magazine* 197 (August 2018): 76, https://www.humanflow.com.

21. Georges Didi-Huberman, "From a High Vantage Point," trans. Laura Garmeson, *Esprit* 7–8 (July 2018): 15, https://www.cairn-int.info/journal-esprit-2018-7-page-65.htm.

22. Didi-Huberman, "From a High Vantage Point," 52.

23. Fritz Breithaupt, "The Bad Things We Do Because of Empathy," *Interdisciplinary Science Reviews* 43, no. 2 (2018): 170.

24. Kaja Silverman, *The Threshold of the Visible World* (New York: Routledge, 1996), 73.

25. Saidiya V. Hartman, *Scenes of Subjection: Terror, Slavery, and Self-Making in Nineteenth-Century America* (New York: Oxford University Press, 1997), 18–19.

26. Ai, "The Refugee Crisis Isn't about Refugees."

27. Xan Brooks, "Ai Weiwei: 'Without the Prison, the Beatings, What Would I Be?,'" *Guardian*, September 17, 2017, https://www.theguardian.com/film/2017/sep/17/ai-weiwei-without-the-prison-the-beatings-what-would-i-be.

28. Jean Decety and Jason M. Cowell, "Friends or Foes: Is Empathy Necessary for Moral Behavior?," *Perspectives on Psychological Science* 9, no. 5 (2014): 534, https://www.ncbi.nlm.nih.gov/pmc/articles/PMC4241340/.

29. Jennifer Alsever, "Is Virtual Reality the Ultimate Empathy Machine?," *Wired*, November 2015, https://www.wired.com/brandlab/2015/11/is-virtual-reality-the-ultimate-empathy-machine/.

30. *CARNE y ARENA: Art and Technology*, conversation between Jenna Pirog and Alejandro G. Iñárritu, June 4, 2018, Phillips Collection, video, 1:01:08, YouTube, https://www.youtube.com/watch?v=-XcvJ6lUTwI.

31. *CARNE y ARENA: Art and Technology*.

32. Peter Bradshaw, "*Carne y Arena* Review—Dazzling Virtual Reality Exhibit Offers a Fresh Look at the Refugee Crisis," *Guardian*, May 22, 2017, https://www.theguardian.com/film/2017/may/22/carne-y-arena-review-inarritu-virtual-reality-refugee-cannes-2017.

33. Olivia Gauthier, "A Border Crossing Simulation Probes Virtual Reality's Ethical Limitations," *Hyperallergic*, September 14, 2017, https://hyperallergic.com/399290/a-border-crossing-simulation-probes-virtual-realitys-ethical-limitations/.

34. Fondazione Prada, "Alejandro G. Iñárritu: CARNE y ARENA," August 8, 2018, http://www.fondazioneprada.org/project/carne-y-arena/?lang=en.

35. Christian Stiegler, *The 360° Gaze: Immersions in Media, Society, and Culture* (Cambridge, MA: MIT Press, 2021), 8.

36. Jaron Lanier, *Dawn of the New Everything: Encounters with Reality and Virtual Reality* (New York: Holt, 2017), 47, 52, 235.

37. Lanier, *Dawn of the New Everything*, 48.

38. Jeremy Bailenson, *Experience on Demand: What Virtual Reality Is, How It Works, and What It Can Do* (New York: Norton, 2018), 83–84.

39. "Syrian Refugee Crisis," United Nations Virtual Reality (UNVR), accessed July 20, 2020, http://unvr.sdgactioncampaign.org/cloudsoversidra/#.XzAH6i17R24.

40. Chris Milk, "How Virtual Reality Can Create the Ultimate Empathy Machine," *TED Talks*, March 2015, TED2015, video, 10:18, https://www.ted.com/talks/chris_milk_how_virtual_reality_can_create_the_ultimate_empathy_machine. Also see Beckett Mufson, "Can Virtual Reality Make Us More Human?," *Vice*, April 22, 2015, https://www.vice.com/en_us/article/jpvgy8/can-virtual-reality-make-us-more-human.

41. Paul Bloom, "It's Ridiculous to Use Virtual Reality to Empathize with Refugees," *Atlantic*, February 3, 2017, https://www.theatlantic.com/technology/archive/2017/02/virtual-reality-wont-make-you-more-empathetic/515511/.

42. Steve F. Anderson, *Technologies of Vision: The War between Data and Images* (Cambridge, MA: MIT Press, 2017), 200.

43. Anderson, *Technologies of Vision*, 201–202, 209.

44. Fritz Breithaupt, *The Dark Sides of Empathy*, trans. Andrew B. B. Hamilton (Ithaca, NY: Cornell University Press, 2019), 12.

45. *CARNE y ARENA: Art and Technology*.

46. Kaplan, "Empathy and Trauma Culture," 257.

47. Dominic McIver Lopes, "An Empathic Eye," in Coplan and Goldie, *Empathy*, 118–119.

48. Reece Jones, *Violent Borders: Refugees and the Right to Move* (London: Verso, 2017), 31–32.

49. Jones, *Violent Borders*, 44–45.

50. Geoffrey Alan Boyce, Samuel N. Chambers, and Sarah Launius, "Bodily Inertia and the Weaponization of the Sonoran Desert in US Boundary Enforcement: A GIS Modeling of Migration Routes through Arizona's Altar Valley," *Journal on Migration and Human Security* 7, no. 1 (March 2019): 24, https://journals.sagepub.com/doi/full/10.1177/2331502419825610. Also see Peter Andreas, "The Transformation of Migrant Smuggling across the US-Mexican Border," in *Global Human Smuggling: Comparative Perspectives*, ed. David Kyle and Rey Koslowski (Baltimore: Johns Hopkins University Press, 2001), 107–125; Wayne A. Cornelius, "Death at the Border: Efficacy and Unintended Consequences of US Immigration Control Policy," *Population and Development Review* 27, no. 4 (2001): 661–685; Raquel Rubio-Goldsmith et al., *The "Funnel Effect" & Recovered Bodies of Unauthorized Migrants Processed by the Pima County Office of the Medical Examiner, 1990–2005* (Tucson, AZ: Binational Migration Institute, 2006); Daniel E. Martínez et al., "Structural Violence and Migrant Deaths in Southern Arizona: Data from the Pima County Office of the Medical Examiner, 1990–2013," *Journal on Migration and Human Security* 2, no. 4 (2014): 257–286; Jason De León, *The Land of Open Graves* (Oakland: University of California Press, 2015); Jeremy Slack et al., "The Geography of Border Militarization: Violence, Death, and Health in Mexico and the United States," *Journal of Latin American Geography* 15, no. 1 (2016): 7–32.

51. Boyce, Chambers, and Launius, "Bodily Inertia and the Weaponization of the Sonoran Desert," 25.

52. Boyce, Chambers, and Launius, "Bodily Inertia and the Weaponization of the Sonoran Desert," 32.

53. De León, *The Land of Open Graves*, 3.

54. Immigrant Movement International, "Migrant Manifesto," Tania Bruguera (website), November 2011, https://www.taniabruguera.com/cms/682-0-International+Migrant+Manifesto.htm.

55. Susie Kantor, "The Projects," in *Tania Bruguera: Talking to Power = Hablándole al poder*, ed. Lucía Sanromán and Susie Kantor (San Francisco: Yerba Buena Center for the Arts, 2018), 141–153. Also see *Tania Bruguera: "Immigrant Movement International*," Art21, June 19, 2015, video, 6:32, YouTube, https://www.youtube.com/watch?v=9puLh5MCIqk.

56. Paul O'Neill, "Tania Bruguera," *BOMB* 128 (Summer 2014): 132–133, https://bombmagazine.org/articles/tania-bruguera/; Claire Bishop and Tania Bruguera, *Tania Bruguera in Conversation/En conversación con Claire Bishop* (New York: Fundación Cisneros/Colección Patricia Phelps de Cisneros, 2020), 78.

57. Bishop and Bruguera, *Tania Bruguera in Conversation*, 15.

58. "Tania Bruguera Creates Hyundai Commission Inspired by Shifting Migration," *Artlyst*, October 1, 2018, https://www.artlyst.com/news/tania-bruguera-creates-hyundai-commission-inspired-by-shifting-migration/.

59. Yoli Terziyska, "Tania Bruguera: *10,145,915*: Tate Modern," *Afterimage* 46, no. 1 (March 2019): 57.

60. Catherine Wood, introduction to *Tania Bruguera*, ed. Catherine Wood (London: Tate, 2019), 22.

61. Terziyska, "Tania Bruguera," 59.

62. Terziyska, "Tania Bruguera," 59.

63. Wood, introduction to Wood, *Tania Bruguera*, 22.

64. Wood, introduction to Wood, *Tania Bruguera*, 22.

65. Tania Singer and Claus Lamm, "The Social Neuroscience of Empathy," *Annals of the New York Academy of Sciences* 1156 (2009): 83, https://www.researchgate.net/profile/Claus-Lamm/publication/281218239_The_Social_Neuroscience_of_Empathy/links/5696360708ae4b80df38ffb1/The-Social-Neuroscience-of-Empathy.pdf.

66. Tania Singer and Olga M. Klimecki, "Empathy and Compassion," *Current Biology* 24, no. 18 (September 22, 2014): R875, https://www.researchgate.net/publication/265909916_Empathy_and_Compassion.

67. Terziyska, "Tania Bruguera," 61.

68. Johannes Birringer, "*Art in America (The Dream)*: A Conversation with Tania Bruguera," *Performance Research* 3, no. 1 (1998): 24–31, https://www.taniabruguera.com/cms/files/pdf_art_in_america_the_dream.pdf.

69. Amandas Ong, "Tania Bruguera on Transforming Tate Modern's Turbine Hall," *Apollo*, October 2, 2018, https://www.apollo-magazine.com/tania-bruguera-on-transforming-tate-moderns-turbine-hall/.

70. Christa Noel Robbins, "Tania Bruguera: The Structure of Address after the Participatory Turn," *Minnesota Review*, no. 85 (2015): 170, https://www.academia.edu/19204982/_Tania_Bruguera_The_Structure_of_Address_after_the_Participatory_Turn_Minnesota_Review_A_Journal_of_Creative_and_Critical_Writing_Number_85_2015_. See also Nicolas Bourriaud, *Relational Aesthetics*, trans. Simon Pleasance and Fronza Woods, with Mathieu Copeland (Dijon, France: Les presses du réel, 1998); Claire Bishop, *Artificial Hells: Participation Art and the Politics of Spectatorship* (London: Verso, 2012); Nato Thompson, *Living as Form: Socially Engaged Art from 1991–2011* (New York: Creative Time, 2012); and Grant H. Kester, *The One and the Many: Contemporary Collaborative Art in a Global Context* (Durham, NC: Duke University Press, 2011).

71. Robbins, "Tania Bruguera," 172.

72. Lauren Berlant, *Cruel Optimism* (Durham, NC: Duke University Press, 2011).

73. Judith Butler, *Precarious Life: The Powers of Mourning and Violence* (London: Verso, 2006), 139.

74. Robbins, "Tania Bruguera," 177.

75. Ong, "Tania Bruguera on Transforming Tate Modern's Turbine Hall," author's emphasis.

76. *Tania Bruguera and Tate Neighbours—the Art of Social Change*, Tate Exchange, December 21, 2018, video, 6:42, YouTube, https://www.youtube.com/watch?v=9TI9QSAs9gs.

77. Tania Bruguera, "Tania Bruguera in Conversation with Afua Hirsch and Saskia Sassen," in Wood, *Tania Bruguera*, 83.

78. Antonio Donini, "Humanitarianism in the 21st Century," *Humanitaire*, June 25, 2010, https://journals.openedition.org/humanitaire/771.

79. Miriam Ticktin, "Thinking beyond Humanitarian Borders," *Social Research* 83, no. 2 (Summer 2016): 255, https://www.researchgate.net/publication/309514428_Thinking_beyond_humanitarian_borders.

80. Hess and Kasparek, "The Post-2015 European Border Regime."

81. Didier Fassin, *Humanitarian Reason: A Moral History of the Present*, trans. Rachel Gomme (Berkeley: University of California Press, 2011), 8. On the questioning of humanitarianism, also see Michael Barnett and Thomas G. Weiss, eds., *Humanitarianism in Question: Politics, Power, Ethics* (Ithaca, NY: Cornell University Press, 2008).

82. Michel Foucault, *Résumé des Cours au Collège de France 1972–1980* (Paris: Julliard, 1989), 154; Jeremy Carrette, *Religion and Culture: Michel Foucault* (New York: Routledge, 1999), 34.

83. Fassin, *Humanitarian Reason*, 1–2.

84. Charles Heller and Lorenzo Pezzani, "The Perils of Migration: Countervailing Mediations of Risk at the EU's Maritime Frontier," in *The Routledge Companion to Media and Risk*, ed. Bishnupriya Ghosh and Bhaskar Sarkar (New York: Routledge, 2020), 136.

85. Heller and Pezzani, "The Perils of Migration," 136.

86. Lilie Chouliaraki and Pierluigi Musarò, "The Mediatized Border: Technologies and Affects of Migrant Reception in the Greek and Italian Borders," *Feminist Media Studies* 17, no. 4 (2017): 546, https://core.ac.uk/download/pdf/84339901.pdf.

87. Ticktin, "Thinking beyond Humanitarian Borders," 256, 261–262.

88. Ticktin, "Thinking beyond Humanitarian Borders," 259–261.

89. Craig Calhoun, "The Idea of Emergency: Humanitarian Action and Global (Dis)Order," in *Contemporary States of Emergency: The Politics of Military and Humanitarian Interventions*, ed. Didier Fassin and Mariella Pandolfi (Brooklyn, NY: Zone Books, 2010), 30, 33. Also see Craig Calhoun, "A World of Emergencies: Fear, Intervention, and the Limits of Cosmopolitan Order," *Canadian Review of Sociology* 41, no. 4 (2004): 373–395, https://www.researchgate.net/publication/227723245_A_World_of_Emergencies_Fear_Intervention_and_the_Limits_of_Cosmopolitan_Order.

90. Calhoun, "The Idea of Emergency," 55.

91. Ticktin, "Thinking beyond Humanitarian Borders," 265.

92. Sofie Bäärnhielm et al., "Mental Health for Refugees, Asylum Seekers, and Displaced Persons: A Call for a Humanitarian Agenda," *Transcultural Psychiatry* 54, nos. 5–6 (2017): 565, https://journals.sagepub.com/doi/full/10.1177/1363461517747095.

93. Abby Stoddard et al., *Aid Worker Security Report 2020: Contending with Threats to Humanitarian Health Workers in the Age of Epidemics*, Humanitarian Outcomes, report, August 2020, last modified January 2021, https://www.humanitarianoutcomes.org/AWSR2020.

94. Heller and Pezzani, "The Perils of Migration," 139.

95. No More Deaths and La Coalición de Derechos Humanos, *Disappeared: How US Border Enforcement Agencies Are Fueling a Missing Persons Crisis*, Part 2: Interference with Humanitarian Aid: Death and Disappearance on the US-Mexico Border, 2018, http://www.thedisappearedreport.org/uploads/8/3/5/1/83515082/disappeared_report_part_2.pdf.

96. Valeria Graziano, Marcell Mars, and Tomislav Medak, "The Pirate Care Project," pirate.care, 2019, https://pirate.care/pages/concept/.

97. Lorenzo Pezzani, "Hostile Environments," *e-flux architecture*, May 15, 2020, https://www.e-flux.com/architecture/at-the-border/325761/hostile-environments/.

PART IV

1. Ismail Einashe and Thomas Roueché, "Introduction: The Power of the Story," in *Lost in Media: Migrant Perspectives and the Public Sphere*, ed. Ismail Einashe and Thomas Roueché (Amsterdam: Valiz, 2019), 14–15.

2. Gayatri Chakravorty Spivak, "Imperative to Re-imagine the Planet," in *An Aesthetic Education in the Era of Globalization* (Cambridge, MA: Harvard University Press, 2009), 338–339.

3. Gayatri Chakravorty Spivak, "Can the Subaltern Speak?," in *Marxism and the Interpretation of Culture*, ed. Cary Nelson and Lawrence Grossberg (Urbana: University of Illinois Press, 1988), 308.

CHAPTER 8

1. Édouard Glissant, *Poetics of Relation*, trans. Betsy Wing (Ann Arbor: University of Michigan Press, 1997), 191.

2. Jack Radley, "Decolonial Reality: An Interview with Bouchra Khalili," *Berlin Art Link*, December 17, 2019, http://www.bouchrakhalili.com/wp-content/uploads/2020/06/An-Interview-with-Bouchra-Khalili-Berlin-Art-Link.pdf.

3. *Bouchra Khalili: The Tempest Society/Twenty-Two Hours—Museum Folkwang*, Institut für Kunstdokumentation, 2018, video, 3:00, https://vimeo.com/287973251.

4. Dorothea Schoene, "Absorbing Displacement: Bouchra Khalili in Conversation with Dorothea Schoene," Ibraaz, September 27, 2012, https://www.ibraaz.org/usr/library/documents/main/absorbing_displacement_bouchra_khalili_in_conversation_with_dorothea_schoene.pdf. Also see "Bouchra Khalili: The Mapping Journey Project," MoMA, accessed September 20, 2020, https://www.moma.org/calendar/exhibitions/1627.

5. Radley, "Decolonial Reality."

6. Hendrik Folkerts, "Twenty-Two Hours," *Mousse Magazine*, Summer 2018, http://www.bouchrakhalili.com/wp-content/uploads/2015/05/Mousse_Mag_Bouchra_Khalili.pdf; Radley, "Decolonial Reality."

7. "Q & A: Bouchra Khalili," *ArtReview*, November 15, 2018, https://artreview.com/artco-mundi-8-bouchra-khalili/.

8. Michel Giraud, "La créolisation: Le muscle ou la graisse," *L'homme: Revue française d'anthropologie* 207–208 (2013): 333–347, https://journals.openedition.org/lhomme/24699.

9. Holly Fraser, "Bouchra Khalili," *Hunger*, no. 12 (Spring 2017): 83, http://www.bouchrakhalili.com/wp-content/uploads/2015/05/201703_Hunger_KHAL_Interview.pdf.

10. Louise Steiwer, "The Spleen of the Periphery," interview with Angela Melitopoulos, *Kunstkritikk*, November 21, 2018, https://kunstkritikk.com/the-spleen-of-the-periphery/.

11. "*Crossings* (2017)," Angela Olga Anderson (website), accessed November 9, 2020, https://www.angelaolgaanderson.net.

12. Steiwer, "The Spleen of the Periphery"; Angela Melitopoulos and Maurizio Lazzarato, "Assemblages: Félix Guattari and Machinic Animism," *e-flux* 36 (July 2012), https://www.e-flux.com/journal/36/61259/assemblages-flix-guattari-and-machinic-animism/.

13. Melitopoulos, in Steiwer, "The Spleen of the Periphery."

14. Melitopoulos, in Steiwer, "The Spleen of the Periphery."

15. "'Moria Is Hell': Asylum Seekers Protest Conditions at Greek Camp," *Reuters*, October 1, 2019, https://www.reuters.com/article/us-europe-migrants-greece-lesbos-protest-idUSKBN1 WG3W7; Marina Rafenberg, "En Grèce, le cri de colère des réfugiés et des ONG contre l'accord UE-Turquie," *Le Monde*, March 20, 2017, https://www.lemonde.fr/europe/article /2017/03/20/en-grece-le-cri-de-colere-des-refugies-et-des-ong-contre-l-accord-ue-turquie _5097450_3214.html.

16. Pascale Criton, "*Chaosmose*, une lecture collective," *Chimères* 2, no. 77 (2012): 9, https:// www.cairn.info/revue-chimeres-2012-2.htm. Also see Anne Querrien and Éric Alliez, eds., "The Guattari Effect," special issue of *Multitudes* 34, no. 3 (Fall 2008), https://www.cairn-int .info/journal-multitudes-2008-3.htm.

17. Félix Guattari, *Chaosmosis: An Ethico-aesthetic Paradigm*, trans. Paul Bains and Julian Pefanis (Sydney, Australia: Power Publications, 2006), 20.

18. Lauren Berlant, "Intuitionists: History and the Affective Event," *American Literary History* 20, no. 4 (Winter 2008): 846; Lauren Berlant, *Cruel Optimism* (Durham, NC: Duke University Press, 2011), 52–54.

19. Melitopoulos, in Steiwer, "The Spleen of the Periphery." Confirmed by Angela Melitopoulos in a meeting in Edinburgh with the author (in the context of the artist's talk, "Cine(so) matic Cartographies," at the Edinburgh International Science Festival), April 17, 2019.

20. Vic Kolenc, "*Border Tuner*'s Night Lights Gone; Leaves Legacy of Archived, Binational Voices, Art Fund," *El Paso Times*, November 14, 2019, http://www.lozano-hemmer.com/texts /bibliography/articles_border_tuner/ElPasoTimes_14Nov2019.pdf.

21. Angela Kocherga, "Interactive Public Art Exhibit Spotlights Border Voices," *Albuquerque Journal*, November 17, 2019, http://www.lozano-hemmer.com/texts/bibliography/articles _border_tuner/Albuquerque_17Nov2019.pdf.

22. Cynthia Bejarano and Ma. Eugenia Hernández Sánchez, "The Mantling and Dismantling of a Tent City in the U.S.-Mexico Border," in *Handbook on Human Security, Borders, and Migration*, ed. Natalia Ribas-Mateos and Timothy J. Dunn (Cheltenham, UK: Edward Elgar, 2021), 83; Sarah M. Vasquez, "An Installation Traverses Texas and Mexico to Promote Cross-Border Communication," *Hyperallergic*, November 12, 2020, http://www.lozano-hemmer .com/texts/bibliography/articles_border_tuner/Hyperallergic_22Nov2019.pdf.

23. Rafael Lozano-Hemmer, conversation with the author, Zoom, June 17, 2021.

24. Wendy Brown, *Walled States, Waning Sovereignty* (Brooklyn, NY: Zone Books, 2010), 37–38.

25. Will Weissert, "El Paso Has a Wall, but That Doesn't Mean Trump's Wall Will Fix Things at the Border, El Paso Residents Say," *Business Insider*, February 11, 2019, https://www.busi nessinsider.com/el-paso-wall-doesnt-mean-walls-are-the-answer-locals-say-2019-2. Also see Julián Aguilar and Darla Cameron, "As Trump Arrives for Rally, El Pasoans Say History Shows He Was Wrong about Their City," *Texas Tribune*, February 11, 2019, https://www.texas tribune.org/2019/02/11/donald-trump-arrives-el-paso-rally-locals-say-he-got-history-wrong/.

26. Weissert, "El Paso Has a Wall."

27. Gloria Anzaldúa, *Borderlands/La Frontera: The New Mestiza* (San Francisco: Spinster/Aunt Lute Press, 1987), 78.

28. *Border Tuner*, bordertuner.net, accessed February 8, 2020, video, 6:12, https://www.border tuner.net/videos.

29. Mary Martin, "A Tale of Two Cities: Ciudad Juárez, El Paso, and Insecurity at the U.S.-Mexico Border," in *Cities at War: Global Insecurity and Urban Resistance*, ed. Mary Kaldor and Saskia Sassen (New York: Columbia University Press, 2020), 106.

30. Rafael Lozano-Hemmer, conversation with the author, Zoom, June 17, 2021.

31. Leah Sandals, "Montreal Artist Tunes In to Connections at Mexico-US Border," *Canadian Art*, November 28, 2019, http://www.lozano-hemmer.com/texts/bibliography/articles _border_tuner/CanadianArt_28Nov2019.pdf.

32. Élisabeth Vallet, "L'immigration spectacle," *Le Devoir*, March 27 and 28, 2021.

33. Zack Hatfield, "Tuan Andrew Nguyen," *Artforum*, October 19, 2020, https://www.artforum .com/interviews/tuan-andrew-nguyen-on-crimes-of-solidarity-84243.

34. Rahel Aima, "At the Edge Of: Tuan Andrew Nguyen," *Mousse Magazine*, October 13, 2020, http://moussemagazine.it/tuan-andrew-nguyen-rahel-aima-2020/.

35. Hatfield, "Tuan Andrew Nguyen."

36. *"Crimes of Solidarity/Crimes de solidarité*," Tuan Andrew Nguyen (website), accessed November 3, 2020, https://www.tuanandrewnguyen.com/crimesofsolidarity.

37. "France: Court Decision Is a Triumph for Solidarity," European Council on Refugees and Exiles (ECRE), July 13, 2018, https://www.ecre.org/france-court-decision-is-a-triumph-for -solidarity/.

CHAPTER 9

1. Sheila Watt-Cloutier, *The Right to Be Cold: One Woman's Story of Protecting Her Culture, the Arctic, and the Whole Planet* (Toronto: Penguin Random House Canada, 2015), xvii–xviii.

2. See especially one of the first articles written on cyberbalkanization: Marshall Van Alstyne and Erik Brynjolfsson, "Could the Internet Balkanize Science?," *Science* 274, no. 5292 (November 1996): 1479–1480, https://www.researchgate.net/publication/228558486_Could_the _Internet_Balkanize_Science.

3. Gayatri Chakravorty Spivak, *An Aesthetic Education in the Era of Globalization* (Cambridge, MA: Harvard University Press, 2009), 339, 348.

4. "IDP Definition," in *UNHCR Emergency Handbook*, accessed July 9, 2021, https://emergency .unhcr.org/entry/44826/idp-definition.

5. Jo-ann Archibald, *Indigenous Storywork: Educating the Heart, Mind, Body, and Spirit* (Vancouver: University of British Columbia Press, 2008), 7.

6. *"Silakut Live from the Floe Edge*," Art Gallery of Alberta, accessed October 12, 2019, https://www .youraga.ca/whats-happening/calendar/silakut-live-floe-edge; and Isuma, "Isuma Making Independent Inuit Video for 30 Years," IsumaTV, accessed November 3, 2019, http://www .isuma.tv/isuma.

7. Katarina Soukup, "Report: Travelling through Layers: Inuit Artists Appropriate New Technologies," *Canadian Journal of Communication* 31, no. 1 (2006), https://www.cjc-online.ca/index.php/journal/article/view/1769/1889.

8. asinnajaq, "Isuma Is a Cumulative Effort," *Canadian Art*, Spring 2019, https://canadianart.ca/features/isuma-is-a-cumulative-effort/.

9. Leah Sandals, "Zacharias Kunuk Speaks on Isuma's Venice Biennale Project," *Canadian Art*, May 8, 2019, https://canadianart.ca/news/zacharias-kunuk-speaks-on-isumas-venice-biennale-project/.

10. D. L. Johnson et al., "Meanings of Environmental Terms," *Journal of Environmental Quality* 26 (May–June 1997): 584; John P. Rafferty, "Biodiversity Loss," in *Encyclopædia Britannica*, online ed., June 14, 2019, https://www.britannica.com/science/biodiversity-loss; Henrik Selin and Michael E. Mann, "Global Warming," in *Encyclopædia Britannica*, online ed., April 27, 2020, https://www.britannica.com/science/global-warming. For a less human-centered and more complex definition of environmental degradation, see Kia Hamid Yeganeh, "A Typology of Sources, Manifestations, and Implications of Environmental Degradation," *Management of Environmental Quality* 31, no. 3 (2020): 765, 778.

11. In *One Day in the Life of Noah Piugattuk* (2019), Noah Piugattuk is played by actor Apayata Kotierk; Isumataq (the boss) is played by Kim Bodnia.

12. Sandals, "Zacharias Kunuk Speaks on Isuma's Venice Biennale Project."

13. "Floe Edge ᓯᓈᖅᑎᒪᓂᖅ," *Travel Nunavut*, accessed June 17, 2021, https://tn.alphabetcreative.com/things-to-see-do/floe-edge/.

14. Watt-Cloutier, *The Right to Be Cold*. Also see Sébastien Jodoin, Arielle Corobow, and Shannon Snow, "Realizing the Right to Be Cold? Framing Processes and Outcomes Associated with the Inuit Petition on Human Rights and Global Warming," *Law & Society Review* 54, no. 1 (2020): 168–200.

15. Sandals, "Zacharias Kunuk Speaks on Isuma's Venice Biennale Project."

16. Alberto Acosta, "Extractivism and Neoextractivism: Two Sides of the Same Curse," in *Beyond Development: Alternative Visions from Latin America*, ed. Miriam Lang and Dunia Mokrani (Quito, Ecuador: Transnational Institute, Fundación Rosa Luxemburg, 2013), 62. Also see Ulrich Brand, Kristina Dietz, and Miriam Lang, "Neo-extractivism in Latin America: One Side of a New Phase of Global Capitalist Dynamic," *Ciencia política* 11, no. 21 (2016): 127, https://www.researchgate.net/publication/309285525_Neo-Extractivism_in_Latin_America_One_Side_of_a_New_Phase_of_Global_Capitalist_Dynamics.

17. "Stolen Lives: The Indigenous Peoples of Canada and the Indian Residential Schools / Historical Background," Facing History and Ourselves, accessed October 11, 2020, https://www.facinghistory.org/stolen-lives-indigenous-peoples-canada-and-indian-residential-schools/historical-background/inuit; "Census Profile, 2016 Census: Igloolik, Hamlet [Census Subdivision], Nunavut, and Yukon [Territory]," Statistics Canada, accessed June 17, 2021, https://www12.statcan.gc.ca/census-recensement/2016/dp-pd/prof/details/page.cfm?Lang=E&Geo1=CSD&Code1=6204012&Geo2=PR&Code2=60&Data=Count&SearchText=Nunavut&SearchType=Begins&SearchPR=01&B1=All.

18. "Stolen Lives."

19. Minnie Aodla Freeman, "Inuit," in *The Canadian Encyclopedia*, online ed. (Toronto: Historica Canada, n.d.), entry published June 8, 2010, last modified September 24, 2020, https://www.thecanadianencyclopedia.ca/en/article/inuit.

20. Willem Rasing, *Too Many People: Contact, Disorder, Change in an Inuit Society, 1822–2015* (Iqaluit, Canada: Nunavut Arctic College Media, 2017), 224.

21. Truth and Reconciliation Commission of Canada, *Honouring the Truth, Reconciling for the Future* (2015), http://trc.ca/assets/pdf/Honouring_the_Truth_Reconciling_for_the_Future_July_23_2015.pdf.

22. Rasing, *Too Many People*, 244.

23. Michael J. Kral, *The Return of the Sun: Suicide and Reclamation among Inuit of Arctic Canada* (New York: Oxford University Press, 2019), 10.

24. Robert Paine, introduction to *Patrons and Brokers in the East Arctic* (St. John's, Canada: Institute of Social and Economic Research, Memorial University of Newfoundland, 1971), 1–7.

25. Rasing, *Too Many People*, 239.

26. Kral, *The Return of the Sun*, 10.

27. Kral, *The Return of the Sun*, 23.

28. Kral, *The Return of the Sun*, 11–14.

29. Rasing, *Too Many People*, 206.

30. Melanie McGraph, *The Long Exile: A Tale of Inuit Betrayal and Survival in the High Arctic* (London: HarperCollins, 2006).

31. Margaret Kohn, "Colonialism," in *Stanford Encyclopedia of Philosophy*, online ed. (Stanford, CA: Stanford University, 1997–), article published May 9, 2006, last modified August 29, 2017, https://plato.stanford.edu/entries/colonialism/.

32. Patrick Wolfe, *Traces of History: Elementary Structures of Racism* (London: Verso, 2013), 2.

33. Kral, *The Return of the Sun*, 44.

34. Peter Kulchyski and Warren Bernauer, "Modern Treaties, Extraction, and Imperialism in Canada's Indigenous North: Two Case Studies," *Studies in Political Economy* 93, no. 1 (March 2014): 3–24; Glen Sean Coulthard, *Red Skin, White Masks: Rejecting the Colonial Politics of Recognition* (Minneapolis: University of Minnesota Press, 2014); Arn Keeling and John Sandlos, eds., *Mining and Communities in Northern Canada: History, Politics, and Memory* (Calgary, Canada: University of Calgary Press, 2015); Dawn Hoogeveen, "Sub-surface Property, Free-Entry Mineral Staking, and Settler Colonialism in Canada," *Antipode* 47, no. 1 (2015): 121–138, http://blogs.ubc.ca/gcog328/files/2015/09/Hoogeveen-2015-Property-Free-entry-Mineral-Staking-Settler-Colonialism.pdf.

35. Warren Bernauer, "The Limits to Extraction: Mining and Colonialism in Nunavut," *Canadian Journal of Development Studies/Revue canadienne d'études du développement* 40, no. 3 (2019): 405.

36. Hugh Brody, *The Other Side of Eden: Hunters, Farmers, and the Shaping of the World* (New York: North Point Press, 2000); Colin G. Calloway, *One Vast Winter Count: The Native American West before Lewis and Clark* (Lincoln: University of Nebraska Press, 2003).

37. Nunavut Department of Education, *Inuit Qaujimajatuqangit: Education Framework for Nunavut Curriculum* (Iqaluit, Nunavut: Nunavut Department of Education, 2007), 22, https://www.gov.nu.ca/sites/default/files/files/Inuit%20Qaujimajatuqangit%20ENG.pdf.

38. Mark Kalluak, "About Inuit Qaujimajatuqangit," in *Inuit Qaujimajatuqangit: What Inuit Have Always Known to Be True*, ed. Joe Karetak, Frank Tester, and Shirley Tagalik (Black Point, Canada: Fernwood, 2017), 41.

39. Nunavut Department of Education, *Inuit Qaujimajatuqangit*, 32–34; "Glossary," in Karetak, Tester, and Tagalik, *Inuit Qaujimajatuqangit*, 225–230.

40. Norman Cohn to the author, email, January 16, 2020.

41. Nicole M. Herman-Mercer et al., "Vulnerability of Subsistence Systems due to Social and Environmental Change: A Case Study in the Yukon-Kuskokwim Delta, Alaska," *Arctic* 72, no. 3 (September 2019): 258–272, https://www.researchgate.net/publication/335767843_Vulnerability_of_Subsistence_Systems_Due_to_Social_and_Environmental_Change_A_Case_Study_in_the_Yukon-Kuskokwim_Delta_Alaska.

42. Macarena Gómez-Barris, *The Extractive Zone: Social Ecologies and Decolonial Perspectives* (Durham, NC: Duke University Press, 2017), 5.

43. Jingzhong Ye et al., "The Incursions of Extractivism: Moving from Dispersed Places to Global Capitalism," *Journal of Peasant Studies* 47, no. 1 (February 2020): 155. On extractivism in its plural understanding, see Eduardo Gudynas, "Extractivisms: Tendencies and Consequences," in *Reframing Latin American Development*, ed. Ronaldo Munck and Raúl Delgado Wise (London: Routledge, 2018), 61–62.

44. Sandals, "Zacharias Kunuk Speaks on Isuma's Venice Biennale Project."

45. "Baffin Island Residents Resist Proposed Iron Mine Plans," *CBC News*, April 7, 2008, https://www.cbc.ca/news/canada/north/baffin-island-residents-resist-proposed-iron-mine-plans-1.751291.

46. "WWF Canada's Final Written Submission for the Nunavut Impact Review Board's Reconsideration of the Mary River Project Certificate for Baffinland's Mary River 'Phase 2' Proposal," WWF-Canada, accessed December 4, 2019, https://wwf.ca/wp-content/uploads/2020/03/wwf_final_written_submission_for_mary_river_phase_2_September-2019.pdf; "Mary River Mine," Baffinland, accessed December 9, 2019, https://www.baffinland.com/mary-river-mine/mary-river-mine/; "Mary River Project," Qikiqtani Inuit Association, accessed December 9, 2019, https://www.qia.ca/about-us/departments/major-projects/what-is-the-mary-river-project/; Beth Brown, "Baffinland Cuts Contracts, Leaves 96 Inuit without Work," *CBC News*, November 15, 2019, https://www.cbc.ca/news/canada/north/baffinland-contracts-cut-mary-river-inuit-jobs-1.5361604; Meagan Deuling, "Baffinland Must Clarify Effects on Narwhal before Expansion of Nunavut Iron Ore Mine," *CBC News*, April 26, 2019, https://www.cbc.ca/news/canada/north/second-technical-meeting-for-baffinland-1.5111345; Sara Frizzell, "Environmental Group Asks to Suspend Baffinland Mine's Approval Process," *CBC News*, November 2, 2019, https://www.cbc.ca/news/canada/north/baffinland-phase-2-hearings-oceans-north-1.5345336.

47. "Pond Inlet Review Committee Submission to the Nunavut Planning Commission," *NunatsiaqNews*, November 2017, https://fr.scribd.com/document/368673433/Pond-Inlet-Review-Committee-Submission-to-the-Nunavut-Planning-Commission.

48. Sandals, "Zacharias Kunuk Speaks on Isuma's Venice Biennale Project."

49. Norman Cohn to the author, email, January 16, 2020.

50. Norman Cohn to the author, email, May 28, 2021.

51. Isabelle Brideau, *The Duty to Consult Indigenous Peoples*, Research Publication 2019-17-E (Ottawa, Canada: Library of Parliament, 2019), 1, https://lop.parl.ca/sites/PublicWebsite /default/en_CA/ResearchPublications/201917E.

52. Brideau, *The Duty to Consult Indigenous Peoples*.

53. Jillian Kestler-D'Amours, "Understanding the Wet'suwet'en Struggle in Canada," al Jazeera, March 1, 2020, https://www.aljazeera.com/news/2020/3/1/understanding-the-wetsuweten -struggle-in-canada.

54. For a larger discussion on such claims in Canada, Australia, New Zealand, and the United States, see Robert Nichols, *Theft Is Property! Dispossession and Critical Theory* (Durham, NC: Duke University Press, 2020), 4.

55. Sandals, "Zacharias Kunuk Speaks on Isuma's Venice Biennale Project."

56. "What Is the Floe Edge?," Arctic Kingdom, February 1, 2019, https://arctickingdom.com /what-is-the-floe-edge/.

57. Andrew Baldwin, "On the Politics of Climate Change, Migration, and Human Rights," in *Climate Change, Migration, and Human Rights Law and Policy Perspectives*, ed. Dimitra Manou et al. (London: Routledge, 2017), 223.

58. Norman Cohn, phone conversation with the author, January 15, 2020.

59. Jürgen Habermas, *The Structural Transformation of the Public Sphere: An Inquiry into a Category of Bourgeois Society*, trans. Thomas Burger and Frederick Lawrence (Cambridge, MA: MIT Press, 1991), 27.

60. Jürgen Habermas, *Between Fact and Norms: Contributions to a Discourse Theory of Law and Democracy*, trans. William Rehg (Cambridge, MA: MIT Press, 1996), 361.

61. Nancy Fraser, "Rethinking the Public Sphere: A Contribution to the Critique of Actually Existing Democracy," in *Habermas and the Public Sphere*, ed. Craig Calhoun (Cambridge, MA: MIT Press, 1992), 109–142.

62. Oskar Negt and Alexander Kluge, *Public Sphere and Experience: Toward an Analysis of the Bourgeois and Proletarian Public Sphere*, trans. Peter Labanyi, Jamie Owen Daniel, and Assenka Oksiloff (Minneapolis: University of Minnesota Press, 1993).

63. Chantal Mouffe, *Agonistics: Thinking the World Politically* (London: Verso, 2013).

64. John B. Thompson, *The Media and Modernity: A Social Theory of the Media* (Stanford, CA: Stanford University Press, 1995); Manuel Castells, "The New Public Sphere: Global Civil Society, Communication Networks, and Global Governance," *Annals of the American Academy of Political and Social Science* 616, no. 1 (March 2008): 78–93.

65. Eve Tuck and K. Wayne Yang, "Decolonization Is Not a Metaphor," *Decolonization: Indigeneity, Education, & Society* 1, no. 1 (2012): 7; Andrea Smith, "Sovereignty as Deferred Genocide," in *Otherwise Worlds: Against Settler Colonialism and Anti-Blackness*, ed. Tiffany Lethabo King, Jenell Navarro, and Andrea Smith (Durham, NC: Duke University Press, 2020), 122.

66. Jean-Luc Nancy, *Listening*, trans. Charlotte Mandell (New York: Fordham University Press, 2007).

67. Dylan Robinson, *Hungry Listening: Resonant Theory for Indigenous Sound Studies* (Minneapolis: University of Minnesota Press, 2020), 2.

68. Robinson, *Hungry Listening*, 3.

69. Robinson, *Hungry Listening*, 14.

70. Robinson, *Hungry Listening*, 50–51.

71. Robinson, *Hungry Listening*, 9, 53. On the ethics of incommensurability, also see Tuck and Yang, "Decolonization Is Not a Metaphor," 8–9, 28–29.

72. Robinson, *Hungry Listening*, 64.

73. Carlo Caduff, "Hot Chocolate," *Critical Inquiry* 45 (Spring 2019): 803.

74. Archibald, *Indigenous Storywork*, ix.

75. Archibald, *Indigenous Storywork*, 7, 27, 8.

76. Linda Tuhiwai Smith, *Decolonizing Methodologies: Research and Indigenous Peoples* (London: Zed Books, 2012), 51.

77. Murielle Nagy, "Time, Space, and Memory," in *Critical Inuit Studies: An Anthology of Contemporary Arctic Ethnography*, ed. Pamela Stern and Lisa Stevenson (Lincoln: University of Nebraska Press, 2006), 71.

78. "One Day in the Life of Noah Piugattuk Cast and Crew Q&A," *TIFF Talks*, September 14, 2019, video, 23:46, YouTube, https://www.youtube.com/watch?v=Mbmrx3ROgJ8.

79. Nagy, "Time, Space, and Memory," 71–72.

CHAPTER 10

1. Kate Brown, "The City of Kassel Is Buying the Controversial Monument to Refugees That Was the Heart of documenta," *artnet*, June 20, 2018, https://news.artnet.com/art-world/documenta-refugee-monument-1306169.

2. "Vandals Deface Olu Oguibe's documenta Monument," *Artforum*, January 31, 2018, https://www.artforum.com/news/vandals-deface-olu-oguibe-s-documenta-monument-73940; Dorian Batycka, "After Dispute with documenta Artist, City of Kassel Demands Removal of Monument for Refugees," *Hyperallergic*, October 1, 2018, https://hyperallergic.com/463306/after-dispute-with-documenta-artist-city-of-kassel-removes-monument-for-refugees/; "Olu Oguibe's Monument to Refugees Re-installed in Kassel," *ArtReview*, April 24, 2019, https://artreview.com/news-24-april-2019-olu-oguibe-obelisk-returns-to-kassel/.

3. Timothy Morton, *Dark Ecology: For a Logic of Future Coexistence* (New York: Columbia University Press, 2016), 5, 7.

4. Morton, *Dark Ecology*, 35, also see 66.

5. Morton, *Dark Ecology*, 47, 10.

6. Luce Irigaray, *This Sex Which Is Not One*, trans. Catherine Porter, with Carolyn Burke (Ithaca, NY: Cornell University Press, 1985), 24.

7. Morton, *Dark Ecology*, 74.

8. Timothy Morton, *Humankind: Solidarity with Nonhuman People* (London: Verso, 2017), 2–3.

9. Ann Laura Stoler, *Duress: Imperial Durabilities in Our Times* (Durham, NC: Duke University Press, 2016), 4, 28.

10. Stoler, *Duress*, 6.

11. *Encyclopaedia Britannica Online*, s.v. "Doppelgänger," August 6, 2019, https://www.britannica.com/art/doppelganger.

12. Ella Huzenis, "Artist Stan Douglas Wants to Take You to Another Earth," *Interview Magazine*, January 31, 2020, https://www.interviewmagazine.com/art/artist-stan-douglas-doppelganger-david-zwirner.

13. "Biennale Arte 2019—Stan Douglas," Biennale Channel, May 28, 2019, video, 2:58, YouTube, https://www.youtube.com/watch?v=2hIr1M6smJE.

14. Huzenis, "Artist Stan Douglas Wants to Take You to Another Earth."

15. Dimitry Kochenov, *Citizenship* (Cambridge, MA: MIT Press, 2020), xv.

16. Christine Ross, *The Past Is the Present; It's the Future Too: The Temporal Turn in Contemporary Art* (New York: Continuum, 2012), chap. 7.

17. Efi Michalarou, "Art-Presentation: Stan Douglas–Doppelgänger," *dreamideamachine Art View*, 2020, http://www.dreamideamachine.com/en/?p=54030.

18. Huzenis, "Artist Stan Douglas Wants to Take You to Another Earth."

19. It is important here to specify that Timothy Morton refers to Lewis Carroll's *Through the Looking-Glass, and What Alice Found There* (1871) in his explanation of the strange loops of weird knowing. See Morton, *Dark Ecology*, 7.

20. Achille Mbembe, *Necropolitics*, trans. Steven Corcoran (Durham, NC: Duke University Press, 2019), 34, 39.

21. Gilles Godmer, *Stan Douglas* (Montréal: Musée d'art contemporain de Montréal, 1996), 20: "Cultural appropriation is how one learns a foreign language, and it's maybe even how one learns one's own language. This is especially true of people who are not of a given majority culture, because the dominant languages and customs will constantly imply that the outsider's presence is either irrelevant or dangerous. So someone, like myself, who is born into a culture as the majority's 'minority,' will often learn to think and act from two positions at once because, even though it might be the only culture you know, you can come to understand how you are constantly objectified or excluded."

22. Sandi Hilal, "Al Madhafah: The Living Room," Shared History, accessed January 3, 2021, https://sharedhistory.eu/11-archive/44-al-madhafah.

23. Sandi Hilal, "المضافة / *The Living Room*: The Right to Host," *Obieg* 11 (2019), https://obieg.u-jazdowski.pl/en/numery/goscinnosc/the-living-room-the-right-to-host.

24. "The Yellow House, Boden," Decolonizing Architecture Art Research (DAAR), accessed October 17, 2020, http://www.decolonizing.ps/site/boden/; "Prästholmen," Public Art Agency Sweden, May 31, 2018, https://publicartagencysweden.com/konstnaren-har-ordet-sandi-hilal-om-prastholmen/.

25. Public Art Agency, "Public Art Agency Sweden: Inauguration of *Al-Madafah* by Sandi Hilal," *e-flux architecture*, August 31, 2018, https://www.e-flux.com/announcements/212290/inauguration-of-al-madafah-by-sandi-hilal/.

26. DAAR, "About," accessed October 17, 2020, http://www.decolonizing.ps/site/about/; also see Sandi Hilal and Alessandro Petti, "The Concrete Tent," in *Permanent Temporariness* (Stockholm: Art & Theory, 2018), 241.

27. DAAR, "About."

28. Public Art Agency, "Public Art Agency Sweden." Also see "Introduction: *Living Room*," DAAR, accessed October 17, 2020, http://www.decolonizing.ps/site/introduction-living-room/.

29. Ana Naomi de Sousa's video *Boden Living Room (Swe Subs)* can be seen on at least two websites: Hilal, "المضافة / *The Living Room*"; and "Introduction: *Living Room*," DAAR.

30. Admir Skodo, "Sweden: By Turns Welcoming and Restrictive in Its Immigration Policy," *Migration Information Source*, December 6, 2018, https://www.migrationpolicy.org/article/sweden-turns-welcoming-and-restrictive-its-immigration-policy.

31. Swedish Federation for Lesbian, Gay, Bisexual, Transgender, Queer, and Intersex Rights, "Inhumane Consequences of Suggestions to Alter Asylum Rights," September 15, 2020, https://www.rfsl.se/en/organisation/asylum-and-migration/omanskliga-foljder-av-forslag-till-andringar-i-asylratten/.

32. James Traub, "The Death of the Most Generous Nation on Earth," *Foreign Policy*, February 10, 2016, https://foreignpolicy.com/2016/02/10/the-death-of-the-most-generous-nation-on-earth-sweden-syria-refugee-europe/.

33. I thank PhD candidate Chris Gismondi from McGill University for bringing these works to my attention.

34. Patrick Wolfe, "Settler Colonialism and the Elimination of the Native," *Journal of Genocide Research* 8, no. 4 (2006): 388, https://www.tandfonline.com/doi/full/10.1080/14623520601056240.

35. Carole Blackburn, "The Treaty Relationship and Settler Colonialism in Canada," in *Shifting Forms of Continental Colonialism: Unfinished Struggles and Tensions*, ed. Dittmar Schorkowitz, John R. Chávez, and Ingo W. Schröder (Singapore: Palgrave MacMillan, 2019), 415.

36. Wolfe, "Settler Colonialism and the Elimination of the Native," 388.

37. Stoler, *Duress*, 5; Andrew Herscher and Ana María León, "The Settler Colonial Present," *e-flux architecture*, October 12, 2020, https://www.e-flux.com/architecture/the-settler-colonial-present/353516/editorial/.

38. Valentina Di Liscia, "Kent Monkman Introduces Candid Indigenous Narratives to the Metropolitan Museum's Great Hall," *Hyperallergic*, December 24, 2019, https://hyperallergic.com/534039/kent-monkman-introduces-candid-indigenous-narratives-to-the-met ropolitan-museums-great-hall/; also see Randall Griffey, "Kent Monkman Reverses Art History's Colonial Gaze," Metropolitan Museum of Art, December 17, 2019, https://www.metmuseum.org/blogs/now-at-the-met/2019/kent-monkman-mistikosiwak-wooden-boat-people-colonial-gaze.

39. Susan Phillips and Mark Salber Phillips, "Welcoming the Newcomers: Decolonizing History Painting, Revisioning History," in *Revision and Resistance:* mistikôsiwak (Wooden Boat People) *at the Metropolitan Museum of Art: Kent Monkman*, ed. Sara Angel, with others (Toronto: Art Canada Institute, 2020), 69.

40. Shirley Madill, "Introducing Miss Chief Eagle Testickle," in Angel, *Revision and Resistance*, 19.

41. Nicholas Mirzoeff, *The Right to Look: A Counterhistory of Visuality* (Durham, NC: Duke University Press, 2011).

42. Sasha Suda, "A Practice of Recovery: *mistikôsiwak (Wooden Boat People)*," in Angel, *Revision and Resistance*, 93.

43. Jami C. Powell, "Inside Kent Monkman's Studio," in Angel, *Revision and Resistance*, 35.

44. Jarrett Earnest, "The Canadian Cree Artist Remixing History in the Met's Great Hall," *Vulture*, September 11, 2019, https://www.vulture.com/2019/09/the-mets-great-hall-commission-kent-monkmans-mistiksiwak.html.

45. Nick Estes, "Waves of History," in Angel, *Revision and Resistance*, 107.

46. Powell, "Inside Kent Monkman's Studio," 38.

47. Lorenzo Veracini, *Settler Colonialism: A Theoretical Overview* (London: Palgrave Mcmillan, 2010), 3.

48. Estes, "Waves of History," 108.

49. Michel-Rolph Trouillot, *Silencing the Past: Power and the Production of History* (Boston: Beacon: 2015), 110.

50. Regan de Loggans, "*Mistikôsiwak*: Monkman at the Met," *Canadian Art*, April 29, 2020, https://canadianart.ca/essays/mistikosiwak-kent-monkman-at-the-met/.

51. De Loggans, "*Mistikôsiwak*."

52. Jillian Kestler-D'Amours, "Understanding the Wet'suwet'en Struggle in Canada," al Jazeera, March 1, 2020, https://www.aljazeera.com/news/2020/3/1/understanding-the-wetsuweten-struggle-in-canada.

53. Powell, "Inside Kent Monkman's Studio," 38.

54. Morton, *Dark Ecology*, 6.

55. Étienne Balibar, "Pour un droit international de l'hospitalité," *Le Monde*, August 16, 2018, https://www.lemonde.fr/idees/article/2018/08/16/etienne-balibar-pour-un-droit-international-de-l-hospitalite_5342881_3232.html.

56. Balibar, "Pour un droit international de l'hospitalité," author's translation.

57. Jacques Derrida, *Of Hospitality: Anne Dufourmantelle Invites Jacques Derrida to Respond*, trans. Rachel Bowlby (Stanford, CA: Stanford University Press, 2000), 15.

58. Derrida, *Of Hospitality*, 24–25; Sara Ahmed, *Strange Encounters: Embodied Others in Postcoloniality* (London: Routledge, 2000), 4.

59. Derrida, *Of Hospitality*, 25–26.

60. Derrida, *Of Hospitality*, 75–76.

61. Derrida, *Of Hospitality*, 83.

62. Derrida, *Of Hospitality*, 76.

63. Anne Dufourmantelle, "L'hospitalité, une valeur universelle?," *Insistance* 2, no. 8 (2012): 57–62, https://www.cairn.info/revue-insistance-2012-2-page-57.htm.

64. Jacques Derrida and Elisabeth Roudinesco, *De quoi demain: Dialogue* (Paris: Flammarion, 2003), 16, author's translation.

65. Audran Aulanier, "Derrida et Waldenfels: Sur l'hospitalité, quelques réflexions," CIELAM, June 18, 2020, https://cielam.univ-amu.fr/node/3149.

66. Joan Stavo-Debauge, "L'oubli de ce dont c'est le cas," *Sociologies*, in "L'urgence politique et l'appauvrissement des concepts," ed. Joan Stavo-Debauge, Martin Deleixhe, and Louise Carlier, special issue of *HospitalitéS*, March 2018, http://journals.openedition.org /sociologies/6796.

67. Derrida, *Of Hospitality*, 25.

CONCLUSION

1. "12th Taipei Biennial: *You and I Don't Live on the Same Planet*," Taipei Biennial, accessed December 16, 2020, https://universes.art/en/taipei-biennial/2020#c71841.

2. Bruno Latour and Martin Guinard, "'You and I Don't Live on the Same Planet'—New Diplomatic Encounters," Taipei Biennial, accessed December 16, 2020, https://universes.art/en /taipei-biennial/2020/curatorial-concept.

BIBLIOGRAPHY

Acosta, Alberto. "Extractivism and Neoextractivism: Two Sides of the Same Curse." In *Beyond Development: Alternative Visions from Latin America*, edited by Miriam Lang and Dunia Mokrani, 61–86. Quito, Ecuador: Transnational Institute, Fundación Rosa Luxemburg, 2013.

Afinogenov, Greg. "Blurred Borders: Museum Exhibitions Present Narratives of Migration's Trauma while Obscuring Its Causes." *Art in America*, February 3, 2020. https://www.artnews.com /art-in-america/features/migration-exhibitions-obscure-reality-militarized-borders-1202676742/.

Agamben, Giorgio. *Homo Sacer: Sovereign Power and Bare Life*. Translated by Daniel Heller-Roazen. Stanford, CA: Stanford University Press, 1998.

Agamben, Giorgio. "We Refugees." *Symposium* 49, no. 2 (1995): 114–119. https://thehubedu-pro duction.s3.amazonaws.com/uploads/1836/1e788430-c11e-4036-8251-5406847cd504/AgambenWeRef ugees.pdf.

Agier, Michel. "Introduction: The Migrant, the Border and the World." In *Borderlands*. Translated by David Fernbach. Cambridge: Polity Press, 2017.

Agier, Michel. *Définir les réfugiés*. Paris: Presses universitaires de France, 2018.

Agier, Michel. *Managing the Undesirables: Refugee Camps and Humanitarian Government*. Translated by David Fernbach. Cambridge: Polity Press, 2001.

Ahmed, Sara. *The Cultural Politics of Emotions*. New York: Routledge, 2004.

Ahmed, Sara. *Strange Encounters: Embodied Others in Post-coloniality*. London: Routledge, 2000.

Ai Weiwei. "The Refugee Crisis Isn't about Refugees. It's about Us." *Guardian*, February 2, 2018. https://www.theguardian.com/commentisfree/2018/feb/02/refugee-crisis-human-flow-ai-weiwei -china.

Aima, Rahel. "At the Edge Of: Tuan Andrew Nguyen." *Mousse Magazine*, October 13, 2020. http:// moussemagazine.it/tuan-andrew-nguyen-rahel-aima-2020/.

Akomfrah, John, and the Otolith Group. "Blackness and Post-cinema: John Akomfrah and the Otolith Group in Conversation." *Frieze* 214 (September 23, 2020). https://www.frieze.com/article /blackness-and-post-cinema-john-akomfrah-and-otolith-group-conversation.

Anderson, Steve F. *Technologies of Vision: The War between Data and Images*. Cambridge, MA: MIT Press, 2017.

Andreas, Peter. "The Transformation of Migrant Smuggling across the US-Mexican Border." In *Global Human Smuggling: Comparative Perspectives*, edited by David Kyle and Rey Koslowski, 107–125. Baltimore: Johns Hopkins University Press, 2001.

Angel, Sara, ed., with David Balzer, Stephanie Burdzy, Michael Rattray, Dianna Symonds, Patricia Treble, and Simone Wharton. *Revision and Resistance:* mistikôsiwak (Wooden Boat People) *at the Metropolitan Museum of Art: Kent Monkman.* Toronto: Art Canada Institute, 2020.

Anzaldúa, Gloria. *Borderlands/La Frontera: The New Mestiza.* San Francisco: Spinster/Aunt Lute Press, 1987.

Archibald, Jo-ann. *Indigenous Storywork: Educating the Heart, Mind, Body, and Spirit.* Vancouver: University of British Columbia Press, 2008.

Arendt, Hannah. "We Refugees." In *The Jewish Writings*, edited by Jerome Kohn and Ron H. Feldman, 264–274. New York: Schocken Books, 2007.

Artforum. "Vandals Deface Olu Oguibe's documenta Monument." January 31, 2018. https://www .artforum.com/news/vandals-deface-olu-oguibe-s-documenta-monument-73940.

ArtReview. "Olu Oguibe's Monument to Refugees Re-installed in Kassel." April 24, 2019. https:// artreview.com/news-24-april-2019-olu-oguibe-obelisk-returns-to-kassel/.

ArtReview. "Q & A: Bouchra Khalili." November 15, 2018. https://artreview.com/artes-mundi-8 -bouchra-khalili/.

asinnajaq. "Isuma Is a Cumulative Effort." *Canadian Art*, Spring 2019. https://canadianart.ca /features/isuma-is-a-cumulative-effort/.

Atak, Idil, and James C. Simeon. "Introduction. The Criminalization of Migration: Context and Consequences." In *The Criminalization of Migration: Context and Consequences*, edited by Idil Atak and James C. Simeon, 3–33. Montréal: McGill-Queen's University Press, 2018.

Aulanier, Audran. "Derrida et Waldenfels: Sur l'hospitalité, quelques réflexions." CIELAM, June 18, 2020. https://cielam.univ-amu.fr/node/3149.

Aziz, El-moutasam, Laila Manasfi, and Ghassan Salah. "A Bio-political Construction: The Representation of Refugees and Migrants. From the 'Reel' to the 'Real.'" In *Proceedings of POM Beirut 2019*, 118–125. Swindon, UK: BCS Learning and Development, June 2019. https://www.research gate.net/publication/337897171_A_Bio-Political_Construction_The_Representation_of_Refugees _and_Migrants_From_the_%27Reel%27_to_the_%27Real%27.

Azoulay, Ariella Aïsha. *Potential History: Unlearning Imperialism.* London: Verso, 2019.

Bäärnhielm, Sofie, Kees Laban, Meryam Schouler-Ocak, Cécile Rousseau, and Laurence J. Kirmayer. "Mental Health for Refugees, Asylum Seekers, and Displaced Persons: A Call for a Humanitarian Agenda." *Transcultural Psychiatry* 54, nos. 5–6 (2017): 565–574. https://journals.sagepub .com/doi/full/10.1177/1363461517747095.

Bailenson, Jeremy. *Experience on Demand: What Virtual Reality Is, How It Works, and What It Can Do.* New York: Norton, 2018.

Bal, Mieke. "Lost in Space, Lost in the Library." In *Essays in Migration Aesthetics: Cultural Practices between Migration and Art-Making*, edited by Sam Durrant and Catherine M. Lord, 21–35. Amsterdam: Rodopi, 2007.

Baldwin, Andrew. "On the Politics of Climate Change, Migration, and Human Rights." In *Climate Change, Migration, and Human Rights Law and Policy Perspectives*, edited by Dimitra Manou, Andrew Baldwin, Dug Cubie, Anja Mihr, and Teresa Thorp, 119–225. London: Routledge, 2017.

Baldwin, James. "The Moral (Social) Responsibility of the Artist" (speech). University of Chicago, May 21, 1963. YouTube video, 1:03:17. https://www.youtube.com/watch?v=PlnDbqLNv-M.

Balibar, Étienne. *Politics and the Other Scene*. Translated by Christine Jones, James Swenson, and Chris Turner. London: Verso, 2002.

Balibar, Étienne. "Pour un droit international de l'hospitalité." *Le Monde*, August 16, 2018. https://www.lemonde.fr/idees/article/2018/08/16/etienne-balibar-pour-un-droit-international-de-l-hospitalite_5342881_3232.html.

Baligand, Pascale. "Migration Crisis and Social Trauma." In *The Oxford Handbook of Migration Crises*, edited by Cecilia Menjívar, Marie Ruiz, and Immanuel Ness, 833–848. New York: Oxford University Press, 2019.

Banwell, Julia. "Agency and Otherness in Teresa Margolles' Aesthetic of Death." *Altre modernità/Otras modernidades/Autres modernités/Other Modernities* 4 (October 2010): 45–54. https://riviste.unimi.it/index.php/AMonline/article/view/688/909.

Banwell, Julia. *Teresa Margolles and the Aesthetics of Death*. Cardiff: University of Wales Press, 2015.

Barnett, Michael, and Thomas G. Weiss, eds. *Humanitarianism in Question: Politics, Power, Ethics*. Ithaca, NY: Cornell University Press, 2008.

Barthes, Roland. *Image Music Text*. Translated by Stephen Heath. London: Fontana Press, 1977.

Batson, C. Daniel. *The Altruism Question: Toward a Social Psychological Answer*. New York: Psychology Press, 1991.

Batycka, Dorian. "After Dispute with documenta Artist, City of Kassel Demands Removal of Monument for Refugees." *Hyperallergic*, October 1, 2018. https://hyperallergic.com/463306/after-dispute-with-documenta-artist-city-of-kassel-removes-monument-for-refugees/.

Bauman, Zygmunt. *Strangers at Our Door*. Cambridge: Polity Press, 2016.

Bejarano, Cynthia, and Ma. Eugenia Hernández Sánchez. "The Mantling and Dismantling of a Tent City in the U.S.-Mexico Border." In *Handbook on Human Security, Borders, and Migration*, edited by Natalia Ribas-Mateos and Timothy J. Dunn, 71–89. Cheltenham, UK: Edward Elgar, 2021.

Bennett, Jane. "Systems and Things: A Response to Graham Harman and Timothy Morton." *New Literary History* 43, no. 2 (Spring 2012): 225–233.

Bennett, Jane. *Vibrant Matter: A Political Ecology of Things*. Durham, NC: Duke University Press, 2010.

Bennett, Jill. "Lived Experience and the Limits (and Possibilities) of Empathy." *Cultural Studies Review* 25, no. 2 (2019): 84–88. https://epress.lib.uts.edu.au/journals/index.php/csrj/issue/view/470.

Berlant, Lauren. *Cruel Optimism*. Durham, NC: Duke University Press, 2011.

Berlant, Lauren. "Intuitionists: History and the Affective Event." *American Literary History* 20, no. 4 (Winter 2008): 845–860.

Bernauer, Warren. "The Limits to Extraction: Mining and Colonialism in Nunavut." *Canadian Journal of Development Studies/Revue canadienne d'études du développement* 40, no. 3 (2019): 404–422.

Berti, Carlo. "Right-Wing Populism and the Criminalization of Sea-Rescue NGOs: The 'Sea-Watch 3' Case in Italy, and Matteo Salvini's Communication on Facebook." *Media, Culture, & Society* 43, no. 3 (2021): 532–550.

Birringer, Johannes. "*Art in America (The Dream)*: A Conversation with Tania Bruguera." *Performance Research* 3, no. 1 (1998): 24–31. https://www.taniabruguera.com/cms/files/pdf_art_in_amer ica_the_dream.pdf.

Bishop, Claire. *Artificial Hells: Participation Art and the Politics of Spectatorship*. London: Verso, 2012.

Bishop, Claire, and Tania Bruguera. *Tania Bruguera in Conversation/En conversación con Claire Bishop*. New York: Fundación Cisneros/Colección Patricia Phelps de Cisneros, 2020.

Blackburn, Carole. "The Treaty Relationship and Settler Colonialism in Canada." In *Shifting Forms of Continental Colonialism: Unfinished Struggles and Tensions*, edited by Dittmar Schorkowitz, John R. Chávez, and Ingo W. Schröder, 415–435. Singapore: Palgrave MacMillan, 2019.

Blight, Daniel C. "*Incoming*: Photography, Contemporary Art, Whiteness." *Americansuburb X*, March 23, 2017. https://americansuburbx.com/2017/03/incoming-photography-contemporary-art -whiteness.html.

Bloom, Paul. *Against Empathy: The Case for Rational Compassion*. New York: Ecco, 2016.

Bloom, Paul. "It's Ridiculous to Use Virtual Reality to Empathize with Refugees." *Atlantic*, February 3, 2017. https://www.theatlantic.com/technology/archive/2017/02/virtual-reality-wont-make -you-more-empathetic/515511/.

Boltanski, Luc. *Distant Suffering: Morality, Media, and Politics*. Translated by Graham Burchell. Cambridge: Cambridge University Press, 1999.

Boudreaux, Corrie. "Public Memorialization and the Grievability of Victims in Ciudad Juárez." *Social Research* 83, no. 2 (Summer 2016): 391–417.

Bourriaud, Nicolas. *Relational Aesthetics*. Translated by Simon Pleasance and Fronza Woods, with Mathieu Copeland. Dijon, France: Les presses du réel, 1998.

Boyce, Geoffrey Alan, Samuel N. Chambers, and Sarah Launius. "Bodily Inertia and the Weaponization of the Sonoran Desert in US Boundary Enforcement: A GIS Modeling of Migration Routes through Arizona's Altar Valley." *Journal on Migration and Human Security* 7, no. 1 (March 2019): 23–35. https://journals.sagepub.com/doi/full/10.1177/2331502419825610.

Brand, Ulrich, Kristina Dietz, and Miriam Lang. "Neo-extractivism in Latin America: One Side of a New Phase of Global Capitalist Dynamic." *Ciencia política* 11, no. 21 (2016): 125–159. https://www .researchgate.net/publication/309285525_Neo-Extractivism_in_Latin_America_One_Side_of_a _New_Phase_of_Global_Capitalist_Dynamics.

Breithaupt, Fritz. "The Bad Things We Do Because of Empathy." *Interdisciplinary Science Reviews* 43, no. 2 (2018): 166–174.

Breithaupt, Fritz. *The Dark Sides of Empathy*. Translated by Andrew B. B. Hamilton. Ithaca, NY: Cornell University Press, 2019.

Brennan, Teresa. *The Transmission of Affect*. Ithaca, NY: Cornell University Press, 2004.

Brideau, Isabelle. *The Duty to Consult Indigenous Peoples*. Research Publication 2019-17-E. Ottawa, Canada: Library of Parliament, 2019. https://lop.parl.ca/sites/PublicWebsite/default/en_CA/ResearchPublications/201917E.

Brody, Hugh. *The Other Side of Eden: Hunters, Farmers, and the Shaping of the World*. New York: North Point Press, 2000.

Brody, Hugh. *The People's Land: Inuit, Whites and the Eastern Arctic*. Vancouver: Douglas and McIntyre, 1975.

Brown, Kate. "The City of Kassel Is Buying the Controversial Monument to Refugees That Was the Heart of documenta." *artnet*, June 20, 2018. https://news.artnet.com/art-world/documenta-refugee-monument-1306169.

Brown, Wendy. *Walled States, Waning Sovereignty*. Brooklyn, NY: Zone Books, 2010.

Bruguera, Tania. "Notes on Political Timing Specificity." *Artforum International* 57, no. 9 (May 2019): 205. https://www.artforum.com/print/201905/notes-on-political-timing-specificity-79513.

Bruguera, Tania. "Tania Bruguera in Conversation with Afua Hirsch and Saskia Sassen." In Wood, *Tania Bruguera*, 80–111.

Bubandt, Nils, and Rane Willerslev. "The Dark Side of Empathy: Mimesis, Deception, and the Magic of Alterity." *Comparative Studies in Society and History* 57, no. 1 (2015): 5–34.

Butler, Judith. *Frames of War: When Is Life Grievable?* London: Verso, 2009.

Butler, Judith. *Precarious Life: The Powers of Mourning and Violence.* London: Verso, 2006.

Caduff, Carlo. "Hot Chocolate." *Critical Inquiry* 45 (Spring 2019): 787–803.

Calhoun, Craig. "The Idea of Emergency: Humanitarian Action and Global (Dis)Order." In *Contemporary States of Emergency: The Politics of Military and Humanitarian Interventions*, edited by Didier Fassin and Mariella Pandolfi, 29–58. Brooklyn, NY: Zone Books, 2010.

Calhoun, Craig. "A World of Emergencies: Fear, Intervention, and the Limits of Cosmopolitan Order." *Canadian Review of Sociology* 41, no. 4 (2004): 373–395. https://www.researchgate.net/publication/227723245_A_World_of_Emergencies_Fear_Intervention_and_the_Limits_of_Cosmopolitan_Order.

Calloway, Colin G. *One Vast Winter Count: The Native American West before Lewis and Clark*. Lincoln: University of Nebraska Press, 2003.

Cameron, C. Daryl, Cendri A. Hutcherson, Amanda M. Ferguson, Julian A. Scheffer, Eliana Hadjiandreou, and Michael Inzlicht. "Empathy Is Hard Work: People Choose to Avoid Empathy

Because of Its Cognitive Costs." *Journal of Experimental Psychology: General* 148, no. 6 (2019): 962–976. https://www.apa.org/pubs/journals/releases/xge-xge0000595.pdf.

Canela, Juan. "Orchestrated Dialogues: John Akomfrah." *Mousse Magazine*, January 31, 2018. https://juancanela.com/writing/John-Akomfrah-Purple.

Canguilhem, Georges. *La connaissance de la vie*. Paris: Vrin, 2015.

Carrette, Jeremy. *Religion and Culture: Michel Foucault*. New York: Routledge, 1999.

Casid, Jill H. "Necropolitics at Sea." In *Migration and the Contemporary Mediterranean: Shifting Cultures in Twenty-First-Century Italy and Beyond*, edited by Claudia Gualtieri, 193–214. Oxford: Peter Lang, 2018.

Castells, Manuel. "The New Public Sphere: Global Civil Society, Communication Networks, and Global Governance." *Annals of the American Academy of Political and Social Science* 616, no. 1 (March 2008): 78–93.

Chamberlain, James A. "Responsibility for Migrants: From Hospitality to Solidarity." *Political Theory* 48, no. 1 (2020): 57–83.

Cheng, Yawei, Chenyi Chen, Ching-Po Lin, Kun-Hsien Chou, and Jean Decety. "Love Hurts: An fMRI Study." *NeuroImage* 51 (2010): 923–929.

Chouliaraki, Lilie, and Pierluigi Musarò. "The Mediatized Border: Technologies and Affects of Migrant Reception in the Greek and Italian Borders." *Feminist Media Studies* 17, no. 4 (2017): 535–549. https://core.ac.uk/download/pdf/84339901.pdf.

Chouliaraki, Lilie, and Tijana Stolic. "Rethinking Media Responsibility in the Refugee 'Crisis': A Visual Typology of European News." *Media, Culture, & Society* 39, no. 8 (2017): 1162–1177.

Cissé, Madjiguène. *The Sans-Papiers: The New Movement of Asylum Seekers and Immigrants without Papers in France: A Woman Draws the First Lessons*. London: Crossroads Books, 1997.

Coates, Kenneth, and Judith Powell. *The Modern North: People, Politics, and the Rejection of Colonialism*. Toronto: Lorimer, 1989.

Coplan, Amy. "Understanding Empathy: Its Features and Effects." In Coplan and Goldie, *Empathy*, 2–18.

Coplan, Amy, and Peter Goldie, eds. *Empathy: Philosophical and Psychological Perspectives*. Oxford: Oxford University Press, 2011.

Coplan, Amy, and Peter Goldie. Introduction to Coplan and Goldie, *Empathy*, ix–xlviii.

Cornelius, Wayne A. "Death at the Border: Efficacy and Unintended Consequences of US Immigration Control Policy." *Population and Development Review* 27, no. 4 (2001): 661–685.

Coulthard, Glen Sean. *Red Skin, White Masks: Rejecting the Colonial Politics of Recognition*. Minneapolis: University of Minnesota Press, 2014.

Coutin, Susan Bibler. "Falling Outside: Excavating the History of Central American Asylum Seekers." *Law & Social Inquiry* 36, no. 3 (Summer 2011): 569–596.

Crawley, Heaven, and Dimitris Skleparis. "Refugees, Migrants, Neither, Both: Categorical Fetishism and the Politics of Bounding in Europe's 'Migration Crisis.'" *Journal of Ethnic and Migration Studies* 44, no. 1 (2018): 48–64. https://www.tandfonline.com/doi/full/10.1080/1369183X.2017.1348224?src=recsys.

Criton, Pascale. "*Chaosmose*, une lecture collective." *Chimères* 2, no. 77 (2012): 7–10. https://www.cairn.info/revue-chimeres-2012-2.htm.

Cruikshank, Julie. *Do Glaciers Listen? Local Knowledge, Colonial Encounters, and Social Imagination*. Vancouver: UBC Press, 2005.

Cusumano, Eugenio. "The Sea as Humanitarian Space: Non-governmental Search and Rescue Dilemmas on the Central Mediterranean Migratory Route." *Mediterranean Politics* 23, no. 3 (2018): 387–394. https://www.tandfonline.com/doi/full/10.1080/13629395.2017.1302223?src=recsys.

Damasio, Antonio. *Descartes' Error: Emotion, Reason, and the Human Brain*. London: Penguin, 2005.

Damasio, Antonio. *Looking for Spinoza: Joy, Sorrow, and the Feeling Brain*. New York: Harcourt, 2003.

Davies, Thom, and Arshad Isakjee. "Ruins of Empire: Refugees, Race, and the Postcolonial Geographies of European Migrant Camps." *Geoforum* 102 (June 2019): 214–217.

Davies, Thom, Arshad Isakjee, and Surindar Dhesi. "Violent Inaction: The Necropolitical Experience of Refugees in Europe." *Antipode* 49, no. 5 (2017): 1263–1284. https://onlinelibrary.wiley.com/doi/full/10.1111/anti.12325.

De Alba Gaspar, Alicia, ed., with Georgina Guzmán. *Making a Killing: Femicide, Free Trade, and la Frontera*. Austin: University of Texas Press, 2010.

Decety, Jean. "Empathy in Medicine." *Annales médico-psychologiques* 178 (2020): 197–206.

Decety, Jean, and Jason M. Cowell. "Friends or Foes: Is Empathy Necessary for Moral Behavior?" *Perspectives on Psychological Science* 9, no. 5 (2014): 525–537. https://www.ncbi.nlm.nih.gov/pmc/articles/PMC4241340/.

Decety, Jean, and Philip L. Jackson. "The Functional Architecture of Human Empathy." *Behavioral and Cognitive Neuroscience Reviews* 3, no. 2 (June 2004): 71–100. https://www.researchgate.net/publication/51369194_The_Functional_Architecture_of_Human_Empathy.

Decety, Jean, and Claus Lamm. "Human Empathy Through the Lens of Social Neuroscience." *Scientific World Journal* 6 (February 2006): 1146–1163. https://www.researchgate.net/publication/6795222_Human_Empathy_Through_the_Lens_of_Social_Neuroscience.

Decolonizing Architecture Art Research (DAAR). "About." DAAR website. Accessed October 17, 2020. http://www.decolonizing.ps/site/about/.

De Genova, Nicholas, ed. *The Borders of "Europe": Autonomy of Migration, Tactics of Bordering*. Durham, NC: Duke University Press, 2017.

De Genova, Nicholas. "The Incorrigible Subject: The Autonomy of Migration and the US Immigration Stalemate." In *Subjectivation in Political Theory and Contemporary Practices*, edited by Andreas Oberprantacher and Andrei Siclodi, 267–285. London: Palgrave Mcmillan, 2016.

De Genova, Nicholas. "The 'Migrant Crisis' as Racial Crisis: Do *Black Lives Matter* in Europe?" *Ethnic and Racial Studies* 41, no. 10 (2017): 1765–1782.

De Genova, Nicholas, Glenda Garelli, and Martina Tazzioli. "Autonomy of Asylum? The Autonomy of Migration. Undoing the Refugee Crisis Script." *South Atlantic Quarterly* 117, no. 2 (April 2018): 239–265.

De León, Jason. *The Land of Open Graves*. Oakland: University of California Press, 2015.

De Loggans, Regan. "*Mistikôsiwak*: Monkman at the Met." *Canadian Art*, April 29, 2020. https://canadianart.ca/essays/mistikosiwak-kent-monkman-at-the-met/.

Demos, T. J. "Migrant World: On Ai Weiwei's *Human Flow*." *BOMB*, July 27, 2018. https://bombmagazine.org/articles/migrant-world-on-ai-weiweis human flow/.

Demos, T. J. "On Terror and Beauty: John Akomfrah's *Vertigo Sea*." *Atlántica* 56 (2015). http://www.revistaatlantica.com/en/contribution/on-terror-and-beauty-john-akomfrahs-vertigo-sea/.

Demos, T. J. "Unspeakable Moments: An Interview with John Akomfrah." *Atlántica* 54 (2014): 59.

Derrida, Jacques. *Of Hospitality: Anne Dufourmantelle Invites Jacques Derrida to Respond*. Translated by Rachel Bowlby. Stanford, CA: Stanford University Press, 2000.

Derrida, Jacques, and Elisabeth Roudinesco. *De quoi demain: Dialogue*. Paris: Flammarion, 2003.

De Vignemont, Frédérique, and Tania Singer. "The Empathic Brain: How, When, and Why?" *Trends in Cognitive Sciences* 10, no. 10 (November 2006): 435–441. https://www.researchgate.net/publication/6841239_The_empathic_brain_How_when_and_why.

Didi-Huberman, Georges. *Ce que nous voyons, ce qui nous regarde*. Paris: Éditions de minuit, 1992.

Didi-Huberman, Georges. "From a High Vantage Point." Translated by Laura Garmeson. *Esprit* 7–8 (July 2018): 1–52. https://www.cairn-int.info/journal-esprit-2018-7-page-65.htm.

Didi-Huberman, Georges. *Survival of the Fireflies*. Translated by Lia Swope Mitchell. Minneapolis: University of Minnesota Press, 2018.

Diehl, Carol. *Banksy: Completed*. Cambridge, MA: MIT Press, 2021.

Di Liscia, Valentina. "Kent Monkman Introduces Candid Indigenous Narratives to the Metropolitan Museum's Great Hall." *Hyperallergic*, December 24, 2019. https://hyperallergic.com/534039/kent-monkman-introduces-candid-indigenous-narratives-to-the-metropolitan-museums-great-hall/.

Donini, Antonio. "Humanitarianism in the 21st Century." *Humanitaire*, June 25, 2010. https://journals.openedition.org/humanitaire/771.

Downey, Anthony. "Vital Materialism: Filming the Anthropocene: John Akomfrah in Conversation with Anthony Downey." *Third Text*, March 2018. http://thirdtext.org/akomfrah-downey.

Driver, Alice. *More or Less Dead: Feminicide, Haunting, and the Ethics of Representation in Mexico*. Tucson: University of Arizona Press, 2015.

Dufourmantelle, Anne. "L'hospitalité, une valeur universelle?" *Insistance* 2, no. 8 (2012): 57–62. https://www.cairn.info/revue-insistance-2012-2-page-57.htm.

Earnest, Jarrett. "The Canadian Cree Artist Remixing History in the Met's Great Hall." *Vulture*, September 11, 2019. https://www.vulture.com/2019/09/the-mets-great-hall-commission-kent-monkmans-mistiksiwak.html.

Eastham, Ben. "Richard Mosse: *Incoming*." *ArtReview*, May 10, 2017. https://artreview.com/may-2017-review-richard-mosse/.

Eco, Umberto. *The Open Work*. Translated by Anna Cancogni. Cambridge, MA: Harvard University Press, 1989.

Einashe, Ismail, and Thomas Roueché. "Introduction: The Power of the Story." In Einashe and Roueché, *Lost in Media*, 11–16.

Einashe, Ismail, and Thomas Roueché, eds. *Lost in Media: Migrant Perspectives and the Public Sphere*. Amsterdam: Valiz, 2019.

Eisenberg, Nancy. "Emotion, Regulation, and Moral Development." *Annual Review of Psychology* 51 (2000): 665–697.

Eisenberg, Nancy. "Empathy and Sympathy: A Brief Review of the Concepts and Empirical Literature." *Anthrozoös* 2, no. 1 (1988): 15–17.

Eisenberg, Nancy, and Paul A. Miller. "The Relation of Empathy to Prosocial and Related Behaviors." *Psychological Bulletin* 101, no. 1 (February 1987): 91–119. https://www.researchgate.net/publication/19598630_The_Relation_of_Empathy_to_Prosocial_and_Related_Behaviors.

Engster, Daniel. "Rethinking Care Theory: The Practice of Caring and the Obligation to Care." *Hypatia* 20, no. 3 (Summer 2005): 50–74.

Estes, Nick. "Waves of History." In Angel, *Revision and Resistance*, 104–111.

Eva, Philemon. Review of *Against Empathy: The Case for Rational Compassion*, by Paul Bloom. *Psychotherapy and Politics International* 15, no. 2 (June 2017): 1418–1419. https://doi.org/10.1002/ppi.1418.

Fassin, Didier. "Another Politics of Life Is Possible." *Theory, Culture, & Society* 26, no. 5 (2009): 44–60.

Fassin, Didier. *Humanitarian Reason: A Moral History of the Present*. Translated by Rachel Gomme. Berkeley: University of California Press, 2011.

Fassin, Didier. *Life: A Critical User's Manual*. Cambridge: Polity Press, 2019.

Folkerts, Hendrik. "Twenty-Two Hours." *Mousse Magazine*, Summer 2018. http://www.bouchrakhalili.com/wp-content/uploads/2015/05/Mousse_Mag_Bouchra_Khalili.pdf.

Foucault, Michel. *Cours au Collège de France, 1976*. Paris: Hautes études, EHESS, Gallimard, and Seuil, 1997.

Foucault, Michel. *Résumé des Cours au Collège de France 1972–1980*. Paris: Julliard, 1989.

Foucault, Michel. *The History of Sexuality*. Vol. 1: *An Introduction*. Translated by Robert Hurley. New York: Random House, 1990.

Fraser, Holly. "Bouchra Khalili." *Hunger*, no. 12 (Spring 2017): 80–85. http://www.bouchrakhalili.com/wp-content/uploads/2015/05/201703_Hunger_KHAL_Interview.pdf.

Fraser, Nancy. "Rethinking the Public Sphere: A Contribution to the Critique of Actually Existing Democracy." In *Habermas and the Public Sphere*, edited by Craig Calhoun, 109–142. Cambridge, MA: MIT Press, 1992.

Freeman, Minnie Aodla. "Inuit." In *The Canadian Encyclopedia*, online ed. Toronto: Historica Canada, n.d. Entry published June 8, 2010; last modified September 24, 2020. https://www.thecanadi anencyclopedia.ca/en/article/inuit.

Gallie, W. B. "Essentially Contested Concepts." *Proceedings of the Aristotelian Society*, no. 56 (1955–1956): 167–198.

Gamboni, Aurélien. "In the Thickness of the Crossing: Challenging the Liquid Violence of Borders in the Mediterranean—an Interview with Charles Heller." Translated by Maya Dalinsky. *Texte zur Kunst* 29, no. 114 (June 2019): 82–95.

Gandhi, Leela. *Postcolonial Theory: A Critical Introduction*. London: Routledge, 1998.

Gauthier, Olivia. "A Border Crossing Simulation Probes Virtual Reality's Ethical Limitations." *Hyperallergic*, September 14, 2017. https://hyperallergic.com/399290/a-border-crossing-simulation -probes-virtual-realitys-ethical-limitations/.

Gazzola, Valeria, Lisa Aziz-Zadeh, and Christian Keysers. "Empathy and the Somatotopic Auditory Mirror System in Humans." *Current Biology* 16, no. 18 (September 19, 2006): 1824–1829. https:// www.sciencedirect.com/science/article/pii/S0960982206021178.

Gilligan, Carol. *In a Different Voice: Psychological Theory and Women's Development*. Cambridge, MA: Harvard University Press, 2016.

Gilroy, Paul. *The Black Atlantic: Modernity and Double-Consciousness*. Cambridge, MA: Harvard University Press, 1993.

Giraud, Michel. "La créolisation: Le muscle ou la graisse." *L'homme: Revue française d'anthropologie* 207–208 (2013): 333–347. https://journals.openedition.org/lhomme/24699.

Glissant, Édouard. *Poetics of Relation*. Translated by Betsy Wing. Ann Arbor: University of Michigan Press, 1997.

Godmer, Gilles. *Stan Douglas*. Montréal: Musée d'art contemporain de Montréal, 1996.

Gómez-Barris, Macarena. *The Extractive Zone: Social Ecologies and Decolonial Perspectives*. Durham, NC: Duke University Press, 2017.

González, Jennifer A. "Sea Dreams: Isaac Julien's *Western Union: Small Boats*." In *The Migrant's Time: Rethinking Art History and Diaspora*, edited by Saloni Mathur, 115–129. Williamstown, MA: Sterling and Francine Clark Institute, 2011.

Gregory, Derek. *The Colonial Present: Afghanistan, Palestine, and Iraq*. Malden, MA: Wiley-Blackwell, 2004.

Griffey, Randall. "Kent Monkman Reverses Art History's Colonial Gaze." Metropolitan Museum of Art, December 17, 2019. https://www.metmuseum.org/blogs/now-at-the-met/2019/kent -monkman-mistikosiwak-wooden-boat-people-colonial-gaze.

Guattari, Félix. *Chaosmosis: An Ethico-aesthetic Paradigm*. Translated by Paul Bains and Julian Pefanis. Sydney, Australia: Power Publications, 2006.

Gudynas, Eduardo. "Extractivisms: Tendencies and Consequences." In *Reframing Latin American Development*, edited by Ronaldo Munck and Raúl Delgado Wise, 61–76. London: Routledge, 2018.

Habermas, Jürgen. *Between Fact and Norms: Contributions to a Discourse Theory of Law and Democracy*. Translated by William Rehg. Cambridge, MA: MIT Press, 1996.

Habermas, Jürgen. *The Structural Transformation of the Public Sphere: An Inquiry into a Category of Bourgeois Society*. Translated by Thomas Burger and Frederick Lawrence. Cambridge, MA: MIT Press, 1991.

Hamlin, Rebecca. "International Law and Administrative Insulation: A Comparison of Refugee Status Determination Regimes in the United States, Canada, and Australia." *Law & Social Inquiry* 37, no. 4 (Fall 2012): 933–968.

Hammerstad, Anne. "The Securitization of Forced Migration." In *The Oxford Handbook of Refugee and Forced Migration Studies*, edited by Elena Fiddian-Qasmiyeh, Gil Loescher, Katy Long, and Nando Sigona, 265–277. Oxford: Oxford University Press, 2014.

Hamood, Sara. *African Transit Migration through Libya to Europe: The Human Cost*. Cairo: American University of Cairo, 2006. http://www.migreurop.org/IMG/pdf/hamood-libya.pdf.

Hartman, Saidiya V. *Scenes of Subjection: Terror, Slavery, and Self-Making in Nineteenth-Century America*. New York: Oxford University Press, 1997.

Harvey, David. "Neoliberalism as Creative Destruction." *Annals of the American Academy of Political and Social Science* 610 (March 2007): 22–44.

Hatfield, Zack. "Tuan Andrew Nguyen." *Artforum*, October 19, 2020. https://www.artforum.com/interviews/tuan-andrew-nguyen-on-crimes-of-solidarity-84243.

Hayles, N. Katherine. *Unthought: The Power of the Cognitive Nonconscious*. Chicago: University of Chicago Press, 2017.

Heller, Charles. "De-confining Borders: Towards Freedom of Movement." *e-flux architecture*, July 21, 2020. https://www.e-flux.com/architecture/at-the-border/340426/de-confining-borders-towards-freedom-of-movement/

Heller, Charles, and Lorenzo Pezzani. "*Liquid Traces*: Investigating the Deaths of Migrants at the EU's Maritime Frontier." In *The Borders of "Europe": Autonomy of Migration, Tactics of Bordering*, edited by Nicholas De Genova, 95–119. Durham, NC: Duke University Press, 2017.

Heller, Charles, and Lorenzo Pezzani. "The Perils of Migration: Conflictual Mediations of Risk at the Maritime Frontiers of the European Union." *Critique internationale* 83, no. 2 (2019): 101–123.

Heller, Charles, and Lorenzo Pezzani. "The Perils of Migration: Countervailing Mediations of Risk at the EU's Maritime Frontier." In *The Routledge Companion to Media and Risk*, edited by Bishnupriya Ghosh and Bhaskar Sarkar, 130–147. New York: Routledge, 2020.

Herman-Mercer, Nicole M., Melinda Laituri, Maggie Massey, Ellie Matkin, Ryan C. Toohey, Kelly Elder, Paul F. Schuster, Edda Mutter, and Nicole Giguère. "Vulnerability of Subsistence Systems due to Social and Environmental Change: A Case Study in the Yukon-Kuskokwim Delta, Alaska." *Arctic* 72, no. 3 (September 2019): 258–272. https://www.researchgate.net/publication/335767843 _Vulnerability_of_Subsistence_Systems_Due_to_Social_and_Environmental_Change_A_Case _Study_in_the_Yukon-Kuskokwim_Delta_Alaska.

Herscher, Andrew, and Ana María León. "The Settler Colonial Present." *e-flux architecture*, October 12, 2020. https://www.e-flux.com/architecture/the-settler-colonial-present/353516/editorial/.

Hess, Sabine, and Bernd Kasparek. "The Post-2015 European Border Regime: New Approaches in a Shifting Field." *Archivio antropologico mediterraneo*, Anno XXII, 21, no. 2 (2019): 1–16. http:// journals.openedition.org/aam/1812.

Hess, Sabine, and Bernd Kasparek. "Under Control? Or Border (as) Conflict: Reflections on the European Border Regime." *Social Inclusion* 5, no. 3 (2017): 58–68. https://www.researchgate.net /publication/319915817_Under_Control_Or_Border_as_Conflict_Reflections_on_the_European _Border_Regime.

Hilal, Sandi. "المضافة / *The Living Room*: The Right to Host." *Obieg* 11 (2019). https://obieg.u-jaz dowski.pl/en/numery/goscinnosc/the-living-room-the-right-to-host.

Hilal, Sandi, and Alessandro Petti. "The Concrete Tent." In *Permanent Temporariness*. Stockholm: Art & Theory, 2018.

Hill, Wes. "Sublime Plight: Richard Mosse, Ai Weiwei, and the Social Turn." *Artlink* 38, no. 3 (September 1, 2018): 10–17. https://www.artlink.com.au/articles/4698/sublime-plight-richard-mosse-ai -weiwei-and-the-soc/.

Hoffman, Martin L. "A Comprehensive Theory of Prosocial Moral Development." In *Constructive and Destructive Behavior*, edited by Arthur C. Bohart and Deborah J. Stipek, 61–86. Washington, DC: American Psychological Association, 2001.

Hoffman, Martin L. *Empathy and Moral Development*. Cambridge: Cambridge University Press, 2000.

Hoffmann, Claire, Chus Martínez, and Gioia Dal Molin, assisted by María Montero Sierra. "The Sea. Sounds & Storytelling. Part II." Istituto Svizzero, October 2020. https://www.istitutosvizzero .it/it/arte/the-sea-sounds-storytelling-part-ii/.

Hoogeveen, Dawn. "Sub-surface Property, Free-Entry Mineral Staking, and Settler Colonialism in Canada." *Antipode* 47, no. 1 (2015): 121–138. http://blogs.ubc.ca/geog328/files/2015/09/Hoo geveen-2015-Property-Free-entry-Mineral-Staking-Settler-Colonialism.pdf.

Huzenis, Ella. "Artist Stan Douglas Wants to Take You to Another Earth." *Interview Magazine*, January 31, 2020. https://www.interviewmagazine.com/art/artist-stan-douglas-doppelganger-david -zwirner.

Irigaray, Luce. *This Sex Which Is Not One*. Translated by Catherine Porter, with Carolyn Burke. Ithaca, NY: Cornell University Press, 1985.

Jodoin, Sébastien, Arielle Corobow, and Shannon Snow. "Realizing the Right to Be Cold? Framing Processes and Outcomes Associated with the Inuit Petition on Human Rights and Global Warming." *Law & Society Review* 54, no. 1 (2020): 168–200.

Johnson, D. L., S. H. Ambrose, T. J. Bassett, M. L. Bowen, D. E. Crummey, J. S. Isaacson, D. N. Johnson, P. Lamb, M. Saul, and A. E. Winter-Nelson. "Meanings of Environmental Terms." *Journal of Environmental Quality* 26 (May–June 1997): 581–589.

Jones, Reece. *Violent Borders: Refugees and the Right to Move*. London: Verso, 2017.

Kaldor, Mary. *Global Security Cultures*. Cambridge: Polity Press, 2018.

Kalluak, Mark. "About Inuit Qaujimajatuqangit." In Karetak, Tester, and Tagalik, *Inuit Qaujimajatuqangit*, 41–60.

Kantor, Susie. "The Projects." In *Tania Bruguera: Talking to Power = Hablándole al poder*, edited by Lucía Sanromán and Susie Kantor, 97–172. San Francisco: Yerba Buena Center for the Arts, 2018.

Kaplan, E. Ann. "Empathy and Trauma Culture: Imaging Catastrophe." In Coplan and Goldie, *Empathy*, 255–276.

Karetak, Joe, Frank Tester, and Shirley Tagalik, eds. *Inuit Qaujimajatuqangit: What Inuit Have Always Known to Be True*. Black Point, Canada: Fernwood, 2017.

Kasparek, Bernd. "Routes, Corridors, and Spaces of Exception: Governing Migration and Europe." In *Europe at a Crossroads [Managed Inhospitality]*, edited by Michel Feher, William Callison, Milad Odabaei, and Aurélie Windels. New Futures Online no. 1. Brooklyn, NY: Zone Books, 2016. https://www.academia.edu/23091749/_Europe_At_a_Crossroads_Near_Futures_Online.

Keeling, Ann, and John Sandlos, eds. *Mining and Communities in Northern Canada: History, Politics, and Memory*. Calgary, Canada: University of Calgary Press, 2015.

Kester, Grant H. *The One and the Many: Contemporary Collaborative Art in a Global Context*. Durham, NC: Duke University Press, 2011.

Khalili, Bouchra. "Questionnaire: Bouchra Khalili." *Frieze*, no. 199 (November–December 2018). http://www.bouchrakhalili.com/wp-content/uploads/2015/05/Questionnaire_-Bouchra-Khalili-_-Frieze.pdf.

King, Tiffany Lethabo. *The Black Shoals: Offshore Formations of Black and Native Studies*. Durham, NC: Duke University Press, 2019.

Kochenov, Dimitry. *Citizenship*. Cambridge, MA: MIT Press, 2020.

Kohn, Margaret. "Colonialism." In *Stanford Encyclopedia of Philosophy*, online ed. Stanford, CA: Stanford University, 1997–. Entry published May 9, 2006; last modified August 29, 2017. https://plato.stanford.edu/entries/colonialism/.

Kral, Michael J. *The Return of the Sun: Suicide and Reclamation among Inuit of Arctic Canada*. New York: Oxford University Press, 2019.

Krásná, Denisa, and Sagar Deva. "Neoliberalism, NAFTA, and Dehumanization: The Case of Femicides in Ciudad Juárez." *Fast Capitalism* 16, no. 1 (2019): 31–40.

Kreichauf, René. "From Forced Migration to Forced Arrival: The Campization of Refugee Accommodation in European Cities." *Comparative Migration Studies* 6, no. 7 (2018): 1–22. https://link.springer.com/content/pdf/10.1186%2Fs40878-017-0069-8.pdf.

Kulchyski, Peter, and Warren Bernauer. "Modern Treaties, Extraction, and Imperialism in Canada's Indigenous North: Two Case Studies." *Studies in Political Economy* 93, no. 1 (March 2014): 3–24.

Langa, Napuli. "About the Refugee Movement in Kreuzberg/Berlin." *Movements* 1, no. 2 (2015): 1–10. https://movements-journal.org/issues/02.kaempfe/08.langa--refugee-movement-kreuzberg-berlin.html.

Lanier, Jaron. *Dawn of the New Everything: Encounters with Reality and Virtual Reality*. New York: Holt, 2017.

Latour, Bruno. *Facing Gaia: Eight Lectures on the New Climatic Regime*. London: Polity, 2017.

Latour, Bruno, and Martin Guinard. "'You and I Don't Live on the Same Planet'—New Diplomatic Encounters." 12th Taipei Biennial, November 21, 2020–March 14, 2021. Accessed December 16, 2020. https://universes.art/en/taipei-biennial/2020/curatorial-concept.

Lemke, Thomas. "Critique and Experience in Foucault." *Theory, Culture, & Society* 26, no. 6 (July 2011): 26–48. https://www.researchgate.net/publication/258192305_Critique_and_Experience_in_Foucault.

Loick, Daniel. "We Refugees." Translated by Keith Tribe. *Public Seminar*, May 23, 2016. https://publicseminar.org/2016/05/we-refugees/.

Lopes, Dominic McIver. "An Empathic Eye." In Coplan and Goldie, *Empathy*, 118–133.

Madill, Shirley. "Introducing Miss Chief Eagle Testickle." In Angel, *Revision and Resistance*, 18–27.

Maibom, Heidi L. "Introduction to the Philosophy of Empathy." In Maibom, *The Routledge Handbook of Philosophy of Empathy*, 1–9.

Maibom, Heidi L., ed. *The Routledge Handbook of Philosophy of Empathy*. London: Routledge, 2017.

Makkreel, Rudolf A. "How Is Empathy Related to Understanding?" In *Issues in Husserl's Ideas II*, edited by Thomas Nenon and Lester Embree, 199–212. Dordrecht, Netherlands: Springer, 1996.

Martin, Mary. "A Tale of Two Cities: Ciudad Juárez, El Paso, and Insecurity at the U.S.-Mexico Border." In *Cities at War: Global Insecurity and Urban Resistance*, edited by Mary Kaldor and Saskia Sassen, 103–132. New York: Columbia University Press, 2020.

Martín Alcoff, Linda. "The Problem of Speaking for Others." *Cultural Critique* 20 (Winter 1991–1992): 5–32.

Martínez, Daniel E., Robin C. Reineke, Raquel Rubio-Goldsmith, and Bruce O. Parks. "Structural Violence and Migrant Deaths in Southern Arizona: Data from the Pima County Office of the Medical Examiner, 1990–2013." *Journal on Migration and Human Security* 2, no. 4 (2014): 257–286.

Matthes, Jörg, and Desirée Schmuck. "The Effects of Anti-immigrant Right-Wing Populist Ads on Implicit and Explicit Attitudes: A Moderated Mediation Model." *Communication Research* 44, no. 4 (March 2015): 1–26. https://www.researchgate.net/publication/277622400_The_Effects_of_Anti-Immigrant_Right-Wing_Populist_Ads_on_Implicit_and_Explicit_Attitudes_A_Moderated_Mediation_Model.

Mayblin, Lucy. *Asylum after Empire: Colonial Legacies in the Politics of Asylum Seeking*. London: Rowman & Littlefield, 2017.

Mbembe, Achille. *Brutalisme*. Paris: La Découverte, 2020.

Mbembe, Achille. "Necropolitics." Translated by Libby Meintjes. *Public Culture* 15, no. 1 (2003): 11–40. https://voidnetwork.gr/wp-content/uploads/2016/09/Necropolitics-Achille-Mbembe.pdf.

Mbembe, Achille. *Necropolitics*. Translated by Steven Corcoran. Durham, NC: Duke University Press, 2019.

McGraph, Melanie. *The Long Exile: A Tale of Inuit Betrayal and Survival in the High Arctic*. London: HarperCollins, 2006.

McKeown, Maeve Catherine. "Responsibility without Guilt: A Youngian Approach to Responsibility for Global Injustice." PhD diss., University College London, School of Public Policy, 2014. https://discovery.ucl.ac.uk/id/eprint/1463742/3/McKeown%20Thesis%20(FINAL%2016.03.15).pdf.

Melitopoulos, Angela, and Maurizio Lazzarato. "Assemblages: Félix Guattari and Machinic Animism." *e-flux* 36 (July 2012). https://www.e-flux.com/journal/36/61259/assemblages-flix-guattari-and-machinic-animism/.

Mercer, Kobena. "Avid Iconographies." In *Isaac Julien: With Essays by Kobena Mercer and Chris Darke*, edited by Kobena Mercer, Chris Darke, and Isaac Julien, 7–21. London: Ellipsis, 2001.

Michalarou, Efi. "Art-Presentation: Stan Douglas–*Doppelgänger*." *dreamideamachine Art View*, 2020. http://www.dreamideamachine.com/en/?p=54030.

Mignolo, Walter D. "DELINKING: The Rhetoric of Modernity, the Logic of Coloniality, and the Grammar of De-coloniality." *Cultural Studies* 21, nos. 2–3 (2007): 449–514. https://docs.ufpr.br/~clarissa/pdfs/DeLinking_Mignolo2007.pdf.

Mirzoeff, Nicholas. *The Right to Look: A Counterhistory of Visuality*. Durham, NC: Duke University Press, 2011.

Morris, Stephen. "Empathy on Trial: A Response to Its Critics." *Philosophical Psychology* 32, no. 4 (2019): 508–531.

Morse, Erik. "The Oceanic Ecologies of John Akomfrah." *ArtReview*, January–February 2016. https://artreview.com/jan-feb-2016-feature-john-akomfrah/.

Morton, Timothy. *Dark Ecology: For a Logic of Future Coexistence*. New York: Columbia University Press, 2016.

Morton, Timothy. *Humankind: Solidarity with Nonhuman People*. London: Verso, 2017.

Mosse, Richard. *Incoming*. London: MACK, 2017.

Moten, Fred. *Stolen Life (consent not to be a single being)*. Durham, NC: Duke University Press, 2018.

Mouffe, Chantal. *Agonistics: Thinking the World Politically*. London: Verso, 2013.

Mountz, Alison. *The Death of Asylum: Hidden Geographies of the Enforcement Archipelago*. Minneapolis: University of Minnesota Press, 2020.

Nagy, Murielle. "Time, Space, and Memory." In *Critical Inuit Studies: An Anthology of Contemporary Arctic Ethnography*, edited by Pamela Stern and Lisa Stevenson, 71–88. Lincoln: University of Nebraska Press, 2006.

Nancy, Jean-Luc. *Listening*. Translated by Charlotte Mandell. New York: Fordham University Press, 2007.

Negt, Oskar, and Alexander Kluge. *Public Sphere and Experience: Toward an Analysis of the Bourgeois and Proletarian Public Sphere*. Translated by Peter Labanyi, Jamie Owen Daniel, and Assenka Oksiloff. Minneapolis: University of Minnesota Press, 1993.

Nichols, Robert. *Theft Is Property! Dispossession and Critical Theory*. Durham, NC: Duke University Press, 2020.

Noddings, Nel. *Caring: A Feminine Approach to Ethics and Moral Education*. Berkeley: University of California Press, 1984.

Nunavut Department of Education. *Inuit Qaujimajatuqangit: Education Framework for Nunavut Curriculum*. Iqaluit, Nunavut: Nunavut Department of Education, 2007. https://www.gov.nu.ca/sites/default/files/files/Inuit%20Qaujimajatuqangit%20ENG.pdf.

Odutayo, Aramide. "Human Security and the International Refugee Crisis." *Journal of Global Ethics* 12, no. 3 (2016): 365–379.

Olwig, Karen Fog, Kristina Grünenberg, Perle Møhl, and Anja Simonsen. *The Biometric Border World: Technologies, Bodies, and Identities on the Move*. London: Routledge, 2020.

O'Neill, Paul. "Tania Bruguera." *BOMB* 128 (Summer 2014): 124–133. https://bombmagazine.org/articles/tania-bruguera/.

Ong, Amandas. "Tania Bruguera on Transforming Tate Modern's Turbine Hall." *Apollo*, October 2, 2018. https://www.apollo-magazine.com/tania-bruguera-on-transforming-tate-moderns-turbine-hall/.

Orozco, Elva Fabiola. "Mapping the Trail of Violence: The Memorialization of Public Space as a Counter-Geography of Violence in Ciudad Juárez." *Journal of Latin American Geography* 18, no. 3 (October 2019): 132–157.

Osterhammel, Jürgen. *Colonialism: A Theoretical Overview*. Translated by Shelley L. Frisch. Princeton, NJ: Markus Wiener, 2010.

Paine, Robert. Introduction to *Patrons and Brokers in the East Arctic*, 1–7. St. John's, Canada: Institute of Social and Economic Research, Memorial University of Newfoundland, 1971.

Paine, Robert. *The White Arctic: Anthropological Essays on Tutelage and Ethnicity*. St. John's, Canada: Institute of Social and Economic Research, Memorial University of Newfoundland, 1977.

Peters, John Durham. *The Marvelous Clouds: Toward a Philosophy of Elemental Media*. Chicago: University of Chicago Press, 2015.

Petersen, Anne Ring. "Migratory Aesthetics and the Politics of Irregular Migration: A Case Study of Isaac Julien's *Western Union: Small Boats*." In *The Culture of Migration: Politics, Aesthetics, and Histories*, edited by Sten Pultz Moslund, Anne Ring Petersen, and Moritz Schramm, 205–222. London: I. B. Tauris, 2015.

Pezzani, Lorenzo. "Hostile Environments." *e-flux architecture*, May 15, 2020. https://www.e-flux.com/architecture/at-the-border/325761/hostile-environments/.

Philip, M. NourbeSe, as told by Setaey Adamu Boateng. *Zong!* Middletown, CT: Wesleyan University Press, 2008.

Phillips, Susan, and Mark Salber Phillips. "Welcoming the Newcomers: Decolonizing History Painting, Revisioning History." In Angel, *Revision and Resistance*, 68–77.

Powell, Jami C. "Inside Kent Monkman's Studio." In Angel, *Revision and Resistance*, 30–47.

Prinz, Jesse. "Against Empathy." *Southern Journal of Philosophy* 49 (2011): 214–233.

Prinz, Jesse. "Is Empathy Necessary for Morality?" In Coplan and Goldie, *Empathy*, 211–229.

Public Art Agency. "Public Art Agency Sweden: Inauguration of *Al-Madafah* by Sandi Hilal." *e-flux architecture*, August 31, 2018. https://www.e-flux.com/announcements/212290/inauguration -of-al-madafah-by-sandi-hilal/.

Puig de la Bellacasa, María. *Matters of Care: Speculative Ethics in More Than Human Worlds*. Minneapolis: University of Minnesota Press, 2017.

Querrien, Anne, and Éric Alliez, eds. "The Guattari Effect." Special issue of *Multitudes* 34, no. 3 (Fall 2008). https://www.cairn-int.info/journal-multitudes-2008-3.htm.

Radley, Jack. "Decolonial Reality: An Interview with Bouchra Khalili." *Berlin Art Link*, December 17, 2019. http://www.bouchrakhalili.com/wp-content/uploads/2020/06/An-Interview-with-Bouchra -Khalili-Berlin-Art-Link.pdf.

Ramirez, Diego. "Racial Phantasmagoria: The Demonisation of the Other in Richard Mosse's 'Incoming.'" *NECSUS* 7, no. 2 (Autumn 2018): 301–307. https://necsus-ejms.org/racial-phantasma goria-the-demonisation-of-the-other-in-richard-mosses-incoming/.

Rancière, Jacques. *The Politics of Aesthetics*. Translated by Gabriel Rockhill. London: Continuum, 2014.

Rancière, Jacques. "Who Is the Subject of the Rights of Man?" *South Atlantic Quarterly* 103, nos. 2–3 (Spring–Summer 2004): 297–310. http://cscs.res.in/dataarchive/textfiles/textfile.2010-11-27 .9388690495/file.

Rasing, Willem. *Too Many People: Contact, Disorder, Change in an Inuit Society, 1822–2015*. Iqaluit, Nunavut: Nunavut Arctic College Media, 2017.

Riding, Christine. "The Raft of the *Medusa* in Britain." In *Crossing the Channel: British and French Painting in the Age of Romanticism*, edited by Patrick Noon and Stephen Bann, 66–94. London: Tate, 2003.

Riga, Liliana, Johannes Langer, and Arek Dakessian. "Theorizing Refugeedom: Becoming Young Political Subjects in Beirut." *Theory and Society* 49 (2020): 709–744. https://www.researchgate.net /publication/341168147_Theorizing_refugeedom_becoming_young_political_subjects_in_Beirut.

Rizzolatti, Giacomo, and Laila Craighero. "The Mirror-Neuron System." *Annual Review of Neuroscience* 27, no. 1 (2004): 169–192. https://www.researchgate.net/publication/8491604_The_Mirror -Neuron_System.

Robbins, Christa Noel. "Tania Bruguera: The Structure of Address after the Participatory Turn." *Minnesota Review*, no. 85 (2015): 170–179. https://www.academia.edu/19204982/_Tania_Bruguera

_The_Structure_of_Address_after_the_Participatory_Turn_Minnesota_Review_A_Journal_of _Creative_and_Critical_Writing_Number_85_2015_.

Robinson, Dylan. *Hungry Listening: Resonant Theory for Indigenous Sound Studies*. Minneapolis: University of Minnesota Press, 2020.

Robinson, Vaughan, and Jeremy Sergott. *Understanding the Decision-Making of Asylum Seekers*. London: Home Office Research, 2002. http://citeseerx.ist.psu.edu/viewdoc/download?doi =10.1.1.473.3461&rep=rep1&type=pdf.

Ross, Christine. *The Past Is the Present; It's the Future Too: The Temporal Turn in Contemporary Art*. New York: Continuum, 2012.

Rubio-Goldsmith, Raquel, Melissa McCormick, Daniel Martínez, and Inez Duarte. *The "Funnel Effect" & Recovered Bodies of Unauthorized Migrants Processed by the Pima County Office of the Medical Examiner, 1990–2005*. Tucson, AZ: Binational Migration Institute, 2006.

Sadler, Jane. "Empathy in Film." In Maibom, *The Routledge Handbook of Philosophy of Empathy*, 317–326.

Sandals, Leah. "Montreal Artist Tunes In to Connections at Mexico-US Border." *Canadian Art*, November 28, 2019. https://www.lozano-hemmer.com/texts/bibliography/articles_border_tuner /CanadianArt_28Nov2019.pdf.

Sandals, Leah. "Zacharias Kunuk Speaks on Isuma's Venice Biennale Project." *Canadian Art*, May 8, 2019. https://canadianart.ca/news/zacharias-kunuk-speaks-on-isumas-venice-biennale-project/.

Santos, Luísa. "Ai Weiwei: Grafting as a Documentary Tactic in Art." In *Critical Distance in Documentary Media*, edited by Gerda Cammaer, Blake Fitzpatrick, and Bruno Lessard, 91–107. Cham, Switzerland: Palgrave Macmillan, 2018.

Sassone, Gabriele. "Injury and Repair: Kader Attia." *Mousse Magazine*, October 5, 2018. http:// moussemagazine.it/injury-and-repair-kader-attia-2018/.

Schenkel, Hanna. "Obstructed Progress: Ai Weiwei's 'Human Flow' and the Global Refugee Crisis." *Metro Magazine* 197 (August 2018): 72–77.

Schjeldahl, Peter. "The Art of War in 'Theatre of Operations.'" *New Yorker*, December 2, 2019. https://www.newyorker.com/magazine/2019/12/02/the-art-of-war-in-theater-of-operations.

Schneider, Florian. "The Scandal—Notes on the Autonomy of the Image." In *Uncorporate Identity*, edited by Metahaven, with Marina Vishmidt, 384–391. Baden, Germany: Lars Müller, 2010. http:// fls.kein.org/sites/fls.kein.org/files/Scandal.PDF and http://fls.kein.org/view/32.

Schoene, Dorothea. "Absorbing Displacement: Bouchra Khalili in Conversation with Dorothea Schoene." *Ibraaz*, September 27, 2012. https://www.ibraaz.org/usr/library/documents/main/ab sorbing_displacement_bouchra_khalili_in_conversation_with_dorothea_schoene.pdf.

Searle, Adrian. "John Akomfrah's *Vertigo Sea*: Human and Natural History Meet at the Abyss." *Guardian*, January 25, 2016. https://www.theguardian.com/artanddesign/2016/jan/25/john-akom frah-vertigo-sea-bristol-arnolfini-london-lisson-gallery-auto-de-fe-the-airport-tropikos.

Sharpe, Christina. *In the Wake: On Blackness and Being*. Durham, NC: Duke University Press, 2016.

Sheldon, Rebekah. "Form/Matter/Chora: Object-Oriented Ontology and Feminist New Materialism." In *The Nonhuman Turn*, edited by Richard Grusin, 193–222. Minneapolis: University of Minnesota Press, 2015.

Siegelberg, Mira L. *Statelessness: A Modern History*. Cambridge, MA: Harvard University Press, 2020.

Silverman, Kaja. *The Threshold of the Visible World*. New York: Routledge, 1996.

Silverstein, Michael. "Shifters, Linguistic Categories, and Cultural Description." In *Meaning in Anthropology*, edited by Keith H. Basso and Henry A. Selby, 11–55. Albuquerque: University of New Mexico Press, 1976.

Silverstone, Roger. "Complicity and Collusion in the Mediation of Everyday Life." *New Literary History* 33, no. 4 (Autumn 2002): 761–780.

Singer, Tania, and Olga M. Klimecki. "Empathy and Compassion." *Current Biology* 24, no. 18 (September 22, 2014): R875–R878. https://www.researchgate.net/publication/265909916_Empathy_and_Compassion.

Singer, Tania, and Claus Lamm. "The Social Neuroscience of Empathy." *Annals of the New York Academy of Sciences* 1156 (2009): 81–96. https://www.researchgate.net/profile/Claus-Lamm/publication/281218239_The_Social_Neuroscience_of_Empathy/links/5696360708ae4b80df38ffb1/The-Social-Neuroscience-of-Empathy.pdf.

Skodo, Admir. "Sweden: By Turns Welcoming and Restrictive in Its Immigration Policy." *Migration Information Source*, December 6, 2018. https://www.migrationpolicy.org/article/sweden-turns-welcoming-and-restrictive-its-immigration-policy.

Slack, Jeremy, Daniel E. Martínez, Alison E. Lee, and Scott Whiteford. "The Geography of Border Militarization: Violence, Death, and Health in Mexico and the United States." *Journal of Latin American Geography* 15, no. 1 (2016): 7–32.

Smith, Andrea. "Sovereignty as Deferred Genocide." In *Otherwise Worlds: Against Settler Colonialism and Anti-Blackness*, edited by Tiffany Lethabo King, Jenell Navarro, and Andrea Smith, 118–132. Durham, NC: Duke University Press, 2020.

Smith, Linda Tuhiwai. *Decolonizing Methodologies: Research and Indigenous Peoples*. London: Zed Books, 2012.

Soukup, Katarina. "Report: Travelling through Layers: Inuit Artists Appropriate New Technologies." *Canadian Journal of Communication* 31, no. 1 (2006). https://www.cjc-online.ca/index.php/journal/article/view/1769/1889.

Sparke, Matthew. "Health." In *The Sage Handbook of Human Geography*, edited by Roger Lee, Noel Castree, Rob Kitchin, Victoria Lawson, Anssi Paasi, Christopher Philo, Sarah Radcliffe, Susan M. Roberts, and Charles W. J. Withers, 684–708. London: Sage, 2014.

Spivak, Gayatri Chakravorty. *An Aesthetic Education in the Era of Globalization*. Cambridge, MA: Harvard University Press, 2009.

Spivak, Gayatri Chakravorty. "Can the Subaltern Speak?" In *Marxism and the Interpretation of Culture*, edited by Cary Nelson and Lawrence Grossberg, 271–313. Urbana: University of Illinois Press, 1988.

Staudt, Kathleen. *Violence and Activism at the Border: Gender, Fear, and Everyday Life in Ciudad Juárez*. Austin: University of Texas Press, 2008.

Stavo-Debauge, Joan. "L'oubli de ce dont c'est le cas." In "L'urgence politique et l'appauvrissement des concepts," edited by Joan Stavo-Debauge, Martin Deleixhe, and Louise Carlier. Special issue of *HospitalitéS*, March 2018. http://journals.openedition.org/sociologies/6796.

Steiwer, Louise. "The Spleen of the Periphery." Interview with Angela Melitopoulos. *Kunstkritikk*, November 21, 2018. https://kunstkritikk.com/the-spleen-of-the-periphery/.

Stiegler, Bernard. "Questions de pharmacologie générale: Il n'y a pas de simple pharmakon." *Psychotropes* 13, no. 3 (2007): 27–54. https://www.cairn.info/revue-psychotropes-2007-3-page-27.htm.

Stiegler, Christian. *The 360° Gaze: Immersions in Media, Society, and Culture*. Cambridge, MA: MIT Press, 2021.

Stock, Inka, Ayşen Üstübici, and Susanne U. Schultz. "Externalization at Work: Responses to Migration Policies from the Global South." *Comparative Migration Studies* 7, no. 48 (December 2019): 1–9. https://comparativemigrationstudies.springeropen.com/track/pdf/10.1186/s40878-019-0157-z.

Stocker, Michael, and Elizabeth Hegeman. *Valuing Emotions*. Cambridge: Cambridge University Press, 1996.

Stoddard, Abby, Paul Harvey, Monica Czwarno, and Meriah-Jo Breckenridge. *Aid Worker Security Report 2020: Contending with Threats to Humanitarian Health Workers in the Age of Epidemics*. Humanitarian Outcomes report, August 2020, last modified January 2021. https://www.humanitarianoutcomes.org/AWSR2020.

Stoler, Ann Laura. *Duress: Imperial Durabilities in Our Times*. Durham, NC: Duke University Press, 2016.

Stoler, Ann Laura. "Introduction: 'The Rot Remains': From Ruins to Ruination." In *Imperial Debris: On Ruins and Ruination*, ed. Ann Laura Stoler, 1–36. Durham, NC: Duke University Press, 2013.

Stueber, Karsten. *Rediscovering Empathy: Agency, Folk Psychology, and the Human Sciences*. Cambridge, MA: MIT Press. 2006.

Suda, Sasha. "A Practice of Recovery: *mistikôsiwak (Wooden Boat People)*." In Angel, *Revision and Resistance*, 92–101.

Terziyska, Yoli. "Tania Bruguera: 10,145,915: Tate Modern." *Afterimage* 46, no. 1 (March 2019): 57–64.

Thompson, John B. *The Media and Modernity: A Social Theory of the Media*. Stanford, CA: Stanford University Press, 1995.

Thompson, Nato. *Living as Form: Socially Engaged Art from 1991–2011*. New York: Creative Time, 2012.

Ticktin, Miriam. "Thinking beyond Humanitarian Borders." *Social Research* 83, no. 2 (Summer 2016): 255–271. https://www.researchgate.net/publication/309514428_Thinking_beyond_humanitarian_borders.

Topak, Özgün E. "The Biopolitical Border in Practice: Surveillance and Death at the Greece–Turkey Borderzones." *Environment and Planning D: Society and Space* 32, no. 5 (2014): 815–853. https://borderlandscapes.law.ox.ac.uk/sites/default/files/2019-11/The%20biopolitical%20border%20in%20practice.pdf.

Trilling, Daniel. "Five Myths about the Refugee Crisis." *Guardian*, June 5, 2018. https://www.theguardian.com/news/2018/jun/05/five-myths-about-the-refugee-crisis.

Trilling, Daniel. "How the Media Contributed to the Migrant Crisis." *Guardian*, August 1, 2019. https://www.theguardian.com/news/2019/aug/01/media-framed-migrant-crisis-disaster-reporting.

Trilling, Daniel. "Uncomfortable Facts: The Migrant Crisis in the European Media." In Einashe and Roueché, *Lost in Media*, 21–28.

Tronto, Joan C. *Moral Boundaries: A Political Argument for an Ethic of Care*. New York: Routledge, 1993.

Trouillot, Michel-Rolph. *Silencing the Past: Power and the Production of History*. Boston: Beacon Press, 2015.

Tsing, Anna Lowenhaupt. *Friction: An Ethnography of Global Connection*. Princeton, NJ: Princeton University Press, 2011.

Tuck, Eve, and K. Wayne Yang. "Decolonization Is Not a Metaphor." *Decolonization: Indigeneity, Education, & Society* 1, no. 1 (2012): 1–40.

Underwood, Bill, and Bert Moore. "Perspective-Taking and Altruism." *Psychological Bulletin* 91, no. 1 (1982): 143–173.

Valencia, Sayak. "NAFTA: Capitalismo Gore and the Femicide Machine." *Scapegoat* 6 (2014): 131–136.

Van Alstyne, Marshall, and Erik Brynjolfsson. "Could the Internet Balkanize Science?" *Science* 274, no. 5292 (November 1996): 1479–1480. https://www.researchgate.net/publication/228558486_Could_the_Internet_Balkanize_Science.

Vargas, João Costa, and Joy James. "Refusing Blackness-as-Victimization: Trayvon Martin and the Black Cyborgs." In *Pursuing Trayvon: Historical Contexts and Contemporary Manifestations of Racial Dynamics*, edited by George Yancy and Janine Jones, 193–205. Latham, MD: Lexington Books, 2012.

Vasquez, Sarah M. "An Installation Traverses Texas and Mexico to Promote Cross-Border Communication." *Hyperallergic*, November 12, 2020. http://www.lozano-hemmer.com/texts/bibliography/articles_border_tuner/Hyperallergic_22Nov2019.pdf.

Vaughan-Williams, Nick. *Europe's Border Crisis: Biopolitical Security and Beyond*. Oxford: Oxford University Press, 2015.

Veracini, Lorenzo. *Settler Colonialism: A Theoretical Overview*. London: Palgrave Mcmillan, 2010.

Vikram, Anuradha. "Underneath the Black Atlantic: Race and Capital in John Akomfrah's *Vertigo Sea*." *X-TRA* 21, no. 3 (Spring 2019): 18–33. https://www.x-traonline.org/article/underneath-the-black-atlantic-race-and-capital-in-john-akomfrahs-vertigo-sea#footnote-4.

Watkins, Mel, ed. *Dene Nation: The Colony Within*. Toronto: University of Toronto Press, 1977.

Watt, Douglas. "Toward a Neuroscience of Empathy: Integrating Affective and Cognitive Perspectives." *Neuropsychoanalysis* 9, no. 2 (2007): 119–140.

Watt-Cloutier, Sheila. *The Right to Be Cold: One Woman's Story of Protecting Her Culture, the Arctic, and the Whole Planet*. Toronto: Penguin Random House Canada, 2015.

Weizman, Eyal. *Forensic Architecture: Violence at the Threshold of Detectability*. Brooklyn, NY: Zone Books, 2018.

Weizman, Eyal. "Open Architecture." *e-flux architecture*, June 18, 2019. https://www.e-flux.com /architecture/becoming-digital/248062/open-verification/.

Whitehead, Alfred North. *Process and Reality: An Essay in Cosmology*. New York: Free Press, 1978.

Wilkin, Karen. "Romanticism at the Met." *New Criterion* 22, no. 4 (December 2003): 37–42.

Wolfe, Patrick. "Settler Colonialism and the Elimination of the Native." *Journal of Genocide Research* 8, no. 4 (2006): 387–409. https://www.tandfonline.com/doi/full/10.1080/14623520601056240.

Wolfe, Patrick. *Traces of History: Elementary Structures of Racism*. London: Verso, 2013.

Wolthers, Louise. "Imagining Migration in Europe: Surveillance and Other Visibilities." In *Photographic Powers—Helsinki Photomedia 2014*, edited by Mika Elo and Marko Karo, 110–131. Helsinki, Finland: Aalto University, 2015.

Wood, Catherine. Introduction to Wood, *Tania Bruguera*, 16–31.

Wood, Catherine, ed. *Tania Bruguera*. London: Tate, 2019.

Wynter, Sylvia, and Katherine McKittrick. "Unparalleled Catastrophe for Our Species." In *Sylvia Wynter: On Being as Praxis*, edited by Katherine McKittrick, 10–89. Durham, NC: Duke University Press, 2015.

Xu, Xiaojing, Xiangyu Zuo, Xiaoying Wang, and Shihui Han. "Do You Feel My Pain? Racial Group Membership Modulates Empathic Neural Responses." *Journal of Neuroscience* 29, no. 26 (July 2009): 8525–8529. https://www.jneurosci.org/content/29/26/8525.

Ye, Jingzhong, Jan Douwe van der Ploeg, Sergio Schneider, and Teodor Shanin. "The Incursions of Extractivism: Moving from Dispersed Places to Global Capitalism." *Journal of Peasant Studies* 47, no. 1 (February 2020): 155–183.

Yeganeh, Kia Hamid. "A Typology of Sources, Manifestations, and Implications of Environmental Degradation." *Management of Environmental Quality* 31, no. 3 (2020): 765–783.

Young, Iris Marion. *Responsibility for Justice*. New York: Oxford University Press, 2011.

Zabala, Santiago. *Why Only Art Can Save Us: Aesthetics and the Absence of Emergency*. New York: Columbia University Press, 2019.

Zebadúa-Yañez, Verónica. "Killing as Performance: Violence and the Shaping of Community." *e-misférica* 2, no. 2 (2005): 1–22. https://hemisphericinstitute.org/en/emisferica-2-2/2-2-essays/killing-as-performance-violence-and-the-shaping-of-community.html.

INDEX

Note: Page numbers in italics indicate figures.

Anderson, Steve, 205–206, 207
Angilirq, Paul Apak, 258
Anthropocene, 285–286
Anti-immigration orientation, 34, 35–36
Anzaldúa, Gloria, 99–100, 127, 138, 250
Arab Fund for Art and Culture (AFAC), 295
Arab Spring, 82, 109, 113, 114
Archibald, Jo-ann, 277
Arctic, 12, 14, 53, 233, 255, 257–258, 268, 269, 278, 298
    Indigenous communities of, 269
Arctic Archipelago, 266
Arctic Circle, 264, 275
Arctic climate, 265
Arendt, Hannah, 29, 43–44, 82, 108
Argentina military dictatorship, victims of, 53
Aristoteles, 244
Arizona, 25–26, 209–210
ArkDes Museum, Stockholm, Sweden, 295, 299
Arnait Video Productions, 258
Arora, Gabo, *Clouds over Sidra*, 203–205, *204*
Art, 15, 21, 304
    calls as a response to twenty-first-century migration, 8, 9, 15, 16–17
    as care, 126, 127–131, 142–146, 149–156, 227
    coexistence in (definition), 6–9, 38–46, 285–287
    materiality and, 149–156
    as possible redistribution of the sensible, 16, 67, 254
    redefinition as counterforensic practice, 110
    as a responsible practice, 77
    why and how it matters, 67–73, 165
Arte de conducta, 211
Arte útil interventions, 211
Artforum, 251
Artifacts, forced migration of, 17
Artists, responsibility of, 77, 79
Asinnajaq, 258
Assassination, 53
Assimilationism, 43
Associazione per gli Studi Giuridici sull'Immigrazione, 117
Associazione Ricreativa e Culturale Italiana, 117
Asylum, 7, 8, 35, 36, 84, 173, 196, 209, 223, 227, 249, 254, 295

Asylum seekers, 12, 24, 25, 31, 37, 226, 244, 284, 301, 317
Atak, Idil, 35–36
Athens, 88, 240, 243
Atlantic Middle Passage, 38, 45, 55
Atlas Performing Arts Center, 196
Attenborough, David, *The Blue Planet*, 50
Attia, Kader, 9
    La Mer Morte, 19, 53, 153, *155*, 310
Attica, 240
Aulanier, Audran, 313
Automatic Identification Systems (AIS), 109–110, 114, 115
Autonomy, of migration, 8, 10, 14, 29, 38, 46, 70, 82, 97–99, 100, 103, 105–106, 111, 124, 159, 194, 195, 198, 208, 210, 226, 229, 238, 246, 317
Ayim, Nana Oforiatta, 58
Azoulay, Ariella Aïsha, 17–18

Baffin Island, Nunavut, 260, 264
Baffinland, 262
Baffinland Iron Mines Corporation, 258, 260, 269, 270, 271, 272
Baffinland Phase 2 Review Committee of the Hamlet of Mittimitalik, 271
Bailenson, Jeremy, 203
Bakhtin, Mikhaïl, 106
Bal, Mieke, 16
Baldwin, Alec, 182
Baldwin, Andrew, 273
Baldwin, James, 77, 79
Balibar, Étienne, 58, 83, 223, 284, 310, 311, 313
Bangladesh, 25, 185, 236
Bank of Greece, 240
Banksy, 2, 9, 126
    art as a search-and-rescue endeavor by, 5
    Raft of the Medusa, The, 2–3, *3*, 5
    rescue boat funded by, 4–6, *4*, 126
Banwell, Julia, 141
Baratta, Paolo, 16
Barbican's Curve Gallery, 85, 97
Bare life
    Agamben's formulation of, 44, 92, 98
    of migrating beings, 89, 91, 92, 93, 98, 99
Barthes, Roland, 61–62

Maibom, Heidi L., 163
Makkreel, Rudolf, 165
Malaysia, 25, 37
Malta, 114, 115
Manifesta 7 (European Biennial of
    Contemporary Art), 105
Manifesta 13 (European Biennial of
    Contemporary Art), 251
Maquiladoras, 129–130, 134–137
Mardini, Sarah Ezzat, 182
Margolles, Teresa, 9, 77, 108, 135, 136, 138, 143
    call for responsibility as care, 131, 143, 146,
        149
    En el aire, 141
    Karla, Hilario Reyes Gallegos, 138
    La Gran América, 138, *140*
    La promesa, 75, 127, *128*, 129–131, 134–135, 138,
        140–141, 143–146, *145*, 149–156, *151*, 152, 222,
        251, 310
    Muro Ciudad Juárez, 138, *139*
    Pesquisas, 138
    Pista de baile, 138
    Sillón tapizado frente a línea fronteriza, 138,
        140
    Vaporización, 141, *142*
Martin, Mary, 132, 136, 137
Mary River Phase 2 Review Committee, 271
Mary River Project, 258, 260, 262, 269–270,
    272–273
Materialism
    base, 149
    new, 64, 65, 149
    vital, 48, 63, 68
May, Theresa, 310
Mbembe, Achille, 26, 28, 38, 65, 177, 293
McGraph, Melanie, 266
McKeown, Maeve Catherine, 119
Media
    cyberbalkanization and, 255–256
    elemental, 114–115, 121, 309
    empty empathy and, 179–184, 221–222
    regimes of visibility, 96
    representation of migrating beings as
        voiceless, 181, 231, 252
    representations of catastrophes, 179–185
Mediation, dissolution of frames of, 203

Mediterranean Sea, 5, 6, 8, 10, 24–25, 38, 53, 69,
    76, 87–88, 92, 103, 109, 110–117, 122, 124, 153,
    185, 207, 223, 236, 280, 310
Melitopoulos, Angela, 9, 243, 244
    call for storytell/ing, 240–246
    Crossings, 49, 233, 235, 240–246, *241*, *242*, 251–
        252, 256
Melville, Herman, 50
    Moby-Dick, 50, 55
Memento mori, 153
Mental health care, 226
Mercer, Kobena, 40
Merkel, Angela, 171, 281
Met Breuer, 18
Métis histories, 267
Metropole colonialism, 32
Metropolitan Museum of Art, 302–310
Mexican migrants, embodied experience of,
    99
Mexico, 129, 134–136. *See also* US-Mexico
    border
Mexico City (DF), Mexico, 129
Middle Passage, 38, 45, 55
Migrancy. *See also* Migrating beings
    gender and, 131
    imperiled, 131
    necropolitical evolution of, 29–38, 179
    sexuality and, 131
Migrant
    as a contested concept, 12
    etymology of, 14
    as a political subject, 29, 38, 42–46, 58, 73, 99,
        106, 195, 222, 233, 244, 269
Migrant management, 35, 79
Migrant/refugee "crisis," critique and
    redefinition of the notion, 6–8
Migrants. *See* Migrating beings
Migrant studies, 224
Migrating beings, 11, 13, 92. *See also* Migration
    agency of, 31, 45, 58, 65, 97–98, 216, 301, 307
    autonomy of, 8, 14, 38, 92, 97, 99, 105, 148,
        154, 198, 210, 238, 301
    bare life of, 89, 91, 92, 93, 98, 99
    criminalization of, 35–36, 92, 224
    elimination of, 8, 76, 121
    necropolitical management of, 93

Schenkel, Hanna, 193
Schjeldahl, Peter, 1
Schneider, Florian, 9, 82
    Ceuta, 103–105, *104*
    Museum of the Stealing of Souls, The, 105
Schrödinger, Erwin, 291
Sea-Eye, 122
Searle, Adrian, 50–51
Securitization, 25, 34, 79, 97–99, 122, 249
    humanitarian–securitization shift, 82–85, 92,
        223, 224
    proliferation of conflicting security
        cultures, 136–138
Security cultures, proliferation of conflicting,
    136–138
Sedentarization, 266
Segregation, of migrants, 44, 92
Self-determination, 273
Self–other differentiation, 162, 164–167, 169,
    172, 194, 195, 205
Senegalese refugees, 87–88
Senses, training of the, 67, 287
Sensible, redistribution of the, 16, 45, 67, 233,
    254
Sensing technologies, 114, 115, 116
Sensorium, 16
September 11, 2001, 34, 137, 208
Serbia, 6, 83
Servicio Médico Forense Organization
    (SEMEFO), 140–141
Settler colonialism, 32, 33, 267, 276, 303–310
Sharpe, Christina, 29, 43, 49, 70
    In the Wake, 69
Shihui Han, 170
Shipwrecks, 38–40, 88, 110, 115, 121–122, 124,
    280, 305. *See also* Left-to-Die Boat
Sicily Channel, 115
Siegelberg, Mira, 8
SILA, 258
Silverman, Kaja, 194
Silverstone, Roger, 82, 105–106, 181, 182
Simeon, James C., 35–36
Singer, Peter, 170
Singer, Tania, 162, 166, 168–169, 218–219
SITU Research, 109, 111
Skouries, Greece, 240, 243, 244, 245, 256

Slavery, 2, 3–4, 17, 21, 30, 33, 42, 45, 48, 53, 54, 56,
    65–66, 69, 70, 73, 207, 243, 305
Smith, Adam, 161
Smith, Linda Tuhiwai, 32, 277
Social justice, struggle for, 108, 117–119, 156, 180
Social justice organizations, 196
Social media, overempathizing and, 221
Somalia, 2, 6, 23, 87, 182, 236, 301
Sonoran Desert, 8, 25–26, 76, 158, 196, 200, 207,
    209
Sontag, Susan, 147
Sony, 135
South Sudan, 23
Soviet Union, 266
Spain, 5, 25, 103, 105, 117, 303
Spectacle, 97, 192
Spectators, responsibilization of, 76–77, 80
Spivak, Gayatri Chakravorty, 82, 100, 106–107,
    195–196, 232, 256, 311
Squat Saint-Just, 251
Staatliche Kunsthalle Baden-Baden, 130
Stadler, Jane, 165
Stage of being, inviting actors and agents back
    onto the, 63–68
State actors, accountability of, 141, 226
States of exception, 44, 45, 98, 99
Stein, Edith, 164–166, 169
Stiegler, Bernard, 81–82, 107, 147
Stiegler, Christian, 203
Stierl, Maurice, 5
Stockholm, Sweden, 295, 299
Stoler, Ann Laura, 66–67, 68, 269, 287, 303, 308
Stolic, Tijana, 96
Storytell/ing, 15, 17, 232–233, 235, 280, 292, 302,
    308, 311, 313
    call to, 233, 235, 288
    as collective endeavor, 233, 239, 244, 245–
        246, 250, 252, 275 (*see also specific group
        projects*)
    to counter media representation, 252, 257
    as a form of education and transmission of
        knowledge, 277–278
    Indigenous, 277
    the land and, 280
    looping structures, 283, 284, 285–287
    as a movement, 238, 239, 245–246, 251